THE

WORKS

OF THE

REV. ROBERT HALL, A.M.

WITH

A MEMOIR OF HIS LIFE, BY DR. GREGORY; REMINISCENCES, BY JOHN GREENE, ESQ.; AND HIS CHARACTER AS A PREACHER, BY THE REV. JOHN FOSTER.

PUBLISHED UNDER THE SUPERINTENDENCE OF

OLINTHUS GREGORY, LL.D., F.R.A.S.,

PROFESSOR OF MATHEMATICS IN THE ROYAL MILITARY ACADEMY

AND

JOSEPH BELCHER, D.D

IN FOUR VOLUMES.

VOL. II.

NEW YORK:
HARPER & BROTHERS, PUBLISHERS
329 & 331 PEARL STREET,
FRANKLIN SQUARE
1858.

ADVERTISEMENT

In this Volume, Mr. Hall's Political Tracts are arranged in the order of their publication. To them succeeds various Tracts, which, though not strictly political, bear an obvious relation to the subjects of politics and political economy; employing the latter term, not in its restricted sense, which regards merely the *wealth* of nations, but in the more extended acceptation, which embraces the momentous topics of general security, freedom, comfort, and happiness. Some of these pieces, though very extensively circulated to promote the purposes for which they were respectively written, were never issued by sale, and it is now exceedingly difficult to procure a single copy of them. Others, which were regularly published, have been long out of print.

The origin of the Fragments on Village Preaching and general Toleration I have briefly described in a prefatory note, p. 171.

The Summary of the arguments on Christian Communion could not be included in the first volume without unduly augmenting its bulk; it is, therefore, inserted in this.

The Miscellaneous Pieces appeared originally in *Felix Farley's Bristol Journal*, and have not since been *published* with their author's permission. They serve, however, to show with what taste and elegance he could, in early life, indulge in the lighter species of composition; and what eminence he might have attained in that department of literature, had not his inclinations as well as his profession led him to devote his rich endowments to infinitely higher purposes.

OLINTHUS GREGORY.

CONTENTS OF VOL. II.

TRACTS, POLITICAL AND MISCELLANEOUS.

ARTICLES FROM THE ECLECTIC REVIEW.

MISCELLANEOUS PIECES.

CHRISTIANITY CONSISTENT WITH A LOVE OF FREEDOM:

BEING

AN ANSWER

TO

A SERMON,

LATELY PUBLISHED, BY THE REV. ——.

[PUBLISHED IN 1791.]

PREFACE.

It may be proper just to remark, that the animadversions I have made on Mr. ———'s sermon did not arise from my conviction of there being any thing even of plausibility in his reasonings, but from an apprehension that certain accidental and occasional prejudices might give some degree of weight to one of the weakest defences of a bad cause that was ever undertaken. I have taken up more time in showing that there is no *proper connexion* between the Unitarian doctrine and the principles of liberty than the subject may seem to require; but this will not be thought superfluous by those who recollect that that idea seems to be the great hinge of Mr. ———'s discourse, and that it appears among the orthodox part of the dissenters to have been productive already of unhappy effects. I shall only add, that these remarks would have appeared much sooner but for severe indisposition, and that I was induced to write them chiefly from a persuasion that they might perhaps, in the present instance, have somewhat of additional weight as coming from one who is *not* a Unitarian.

Cambridge, *Sept.* 17, 1791.

NOTE BY THE EDITOR.

"CHRISTIANITY consistent with a Love of Freedom," was written when Mr. Hall was twenty-seven years of age: and he never would consent to its republication. He continued to think the main principles correct and important; but he regarded the tone of animadversion as severe, sarcastic, and unbecoming. Two or three editions have, how ever, been printed surreptitiously; and one of them, which now lies before me, is so complete an imitation of the original edition of 1791 as usually to escape detection. It is printed with an old-fashioned type and on dingy-coloured paper, to suit its assumed age. But on comparing it closely with the genuine edition, I find that three of the capital letters, on different pages, have too modern and broad a face; and on holding up the paper on which it is printed to a strong light, I perceive a water-mark which gives the date 1818 to the *paper* of a pamphlet which purports to be *printed* in 1791! If the lower class of booksellers will have recourse to such contemptible forgeries as this, an author is evidently no longer master of his intellectual property, nor can he when he pleases withdraw it from the public eye.

This, though one of the earliest productions laid by Mr. Hall before the public, is, with the exception already adverted to, by no means calculated to deteriorate his reputation. It contains some splendid passages, and the concluding four or five pages exhibit a fine specimen of that union of severe taste, and lofty genius, and noble sentiment, which is evinced, I think, more frequently in his compositions than in those of any other modern author.

I have no fear of incurring blame for having cancelled throughout the name of the individual against whom Mr. Hall's strictures were levelled. Venerable for his age, and esteemed for his piety, who would now voluntarily cause him, or those who love him, a pang?

ROYAL MILITARY ACADEMY, *June* 1, 1831.

CHRISTIANITY

CONSISTENT WITH A LOVE OF FREEDOM, &c.

THIS is a period distinguished for extraordinary occurrences, whether we contemplate the world under its larger divisions, or in respect to those smaller communities and parties into which it is broken and divided. We have lately witnessed with astonishment and regret the attempts of a celebrated orator to overthrow the principles of freedom, which he had rendered himself illustrious by defending; as well as to cover with reproach the characters of those by whom, in the earlier part of life, he was most caressed and distinguished. The success of these efforts is pretty generally known, and is such as it might have been expected would have been sufficient to deter from similar attempts. But we now behold a dissenting minister coming forth to the public under the character of a flatterer of power and an *accuser of his brethren.* If the splendid eloquence that adorns every part of Mr. BURKE's celebrated book cannot shelter the author from confutation, and his system from contempt, Mr. ———, with talents far inferior, has but little to expect in the same cause. It is not easy to conceive the motives which could impel him to publish his sermon. From his own account it should seem he was anxious to disabuse the legislature, and to convince them there are many among the dissenters who highly disapprove the sentiments and conduct of the more patriotic part of their brethren. How far he may be qualified from his talents or connexions, as a mouth, to declare the sentiments of any considerable portion of the dissenters I shall not pretend to decide, but shall candidly confess, there are not wanting among us persons who are ready upon all occasions to oppose those principles on which the very existence of our dissent is founded. Every party will have its apostates of this kind; it is our consolation, however, that their numbers are comparatively small, that they are generally considered as our reproach, and that their conduct is in a great measure the effect of necessity, as they consist almost entirely of persons who can only make themselves heard by confusion and discord. If our author wishes to persuade the legislature the friends of arbitrary power are conspicuous for their number or their rank in the dissenting interest, he has most effectually defeated his own intentions, as scarce any thing could give them a meaner opinion of that party, in both these respects, than this publica tion of its champion. The sermon he has obtruded upon the public is filled with paradoxes of so singular a complexion, and so feebly supported, that I find it difficult to lay hold of any thing in the form of argument with sufficient steadiness for the purpose of discussion.

I shall endeavour, however, with as much distinctness as I am able, to select the fundamental principles on which the discourse rests, and shall attempt, as I proceed, to demonstrate their falsehood and danger.

Our author's favourite maxim is the inconsistency of the Christian profession with political science, and the certain injury its spirit and temper must sustain from every kind of interference with the affairs of government. Political subjects he considers as falling within the *peculiar* province of the irreligious; ministers in particular, he maintains, should ever observe, amid the concussions of party, an entire neutrality; or if at any time they depart from their natural line of conduct, it should only be in defence of the measures of government, in allaying dissensions, and in convincing the people they are incompetent judges of their rights. These are the servile maxims that run through the whole of this extraordinary discourse; and that I may give a kind of method to the following observations upon them, I shall show, in the first place, the relation Christianity bears to civil government, and its consistency with political discussion, as conducted either by ordinary Christians or ministers; in the next place, I shall examine some of the pretences on which the author founds his principles.

SECTION I.

On the Duty of common Christians in Relation to Civil Polity.

THE momentous errors Mr. ——— has committed appear to me to have arisen from an inattention to the proper design of Christianity, and the place and station it was intended to occupy. On this subject I beg the reader's attention to the following remarks:—

1st. Christianity was subsequent to the existence and creation of man. It is an institution intended to improve and ennoble our nature, not by subverting its constitution or its powers, but by giving us a more enlarged view of the designs of Providence, and opening a prospect into eternity. As the existence of man is not to be *dated* from the publication of Christianity, so neither is that order of things that flows from his relation to the present world altered or impaired by that divine system of religion. Man under the Christian dispensation is not a new structure erected on the ruin of the former; he may rather be compared to an ancient fabric restored, when it had fallen into decay, and beautified afresh by the hand of its original founder. Since Christianity has made its appearance in the world, he has continued the same kind of being he was before, fills the same scale in the order of existence, and is distinguished by the same propensities and powers.

In short, Christianity is not a reorganization of the principles of man, but an institution for his improvement. Hence it follows, that whatever rights are founded on the constitution of human nature cannot be diminished or impaired by the introduction of revealed religion, which occupies itself entirely on the interests of a future world, and takes no share in the concerns of the present in any other light than as it is a state of preparation and trial. Christianity is a discovery of a future life, and acquaints us with the means by which its happiness may be secured; civil government is altogether an affair of the present state, and is no more than a provision of human skill, designed to ensure freedom and tranquillity during our continuance on this temporary stage of existence. Between institutions so different in their nature and their object it is plain no real opposition can subsist; and if ever they are represented in this light, or held inconsistent with each other, it must proceed from an ignorance of their respective genius and functions. Our relation to this world demands the existence of civil government; our relation to a future renders us dependent on the aid of the Christian institution; so that in reality there is no kind of contrariety between them, but each may continue without interference in its full operation. Mr. ———, however, in support of his absurd and pernicious tenets, always takes care to place civil government and Christianity in opposition, while he represents the former as carrying in it somewhat antichristian and profane. Thus he informs us, *that civil government is a stage erected on which man acts out his character, and shows great depravity of heart.* All interference in political parties he styles *an alliance with the world, a neglecting to maintain our separation, and to stand upon our own hallowed ground. There is one way*, says he, by which he means to insinuate there is only one, *in which you may all interfere in the government of your country, and that is by prayer to God, by whom kings reign.* These passages imply that the principles of civil polity and religion must be at perpetual variance, as without this supposition, unsupported as it is in fact, they can have no force or meaning.

2d. Mr. ——— misleads his reader by not distinguishing the innocent entertainments or social duties of our nature from those acts of piety which fall within the *immediate province* of Christianity.

The employments of our particular calling, the social ties and endearments of life, the improvement of the mind by liberal inquiry, and the cultivation of science and of art, form, it is true, no part of the Christian system, for they flourished before it was known; but they are intimately connected with the happiness and dignity of the human race. A Christian should act ever consistent with his profession, but he need not always be attending to the peculiar duties of it. The profession of religion does not oblige us to relinquish any undertaking on account of its being *worldly*, for we must then go out of the world; it is sufficient that every thing in which we engage is of such a nature as will not violate the principles of virtue, or occupy so much of our time or attention as may interfere with more sacred and important duties.

Mr. ——— observes, *Jesus Christ uniformly waived interesting himself in temporal affairs, especially in the concerns of the then existing government;* and hence he draws a precedent to regulate the conduct of his followers. That our Saviour did not intermeddle with the policy of nations I am as willing as our author to admit; for the improvement of this, any more than any other science which might be extremely short and defective, formed no part of his mission, and was besides rendered quite unnecessary, by that energy of mind which, prompted by curiosity, by our passions and our wants, will ever be abundantly sufficient to perpetuate and refine every civil or human institution He never intended that his followers, on becoming Christians, should forget they were men, or consider themselves as idle or uninterested spectators on the great theatre of life. The author's selection of proofs is almost always unhappy, but in no instance more than the present, when he attempts to establish his doctrine of the unlawfulness of a Christian interfering in the administration of government on our Saviour's silence respecting it,—a circumstance of itself sufficient to support a quite contrary conclusion; for if it had been his intention to discountenance the study of political subjects, he would have furnished us without doubt with some general regulations, some stated form of policy, which should for ever preclude the necessity of such discussion; or, if that were impracticable, have let us into the great secret of living without government; or, lastly, have supplied its place by a theocracy similar to that of the Jews. Nothing of this has he accomplished, and we may therefore rest assured the political affairs of nations are suffered to remain in their ancient channels, and to be conducted as occasions may arise by Christians or by others, without distinction.

3d. The principles of freedom ought, in a more peculiar manner, to be cherished by Christians, because they alone can secure that liberty of conscience and freedom of inquiry which is essential to the proper discharge of the duties of their profession. A full toleration of religious opinions, and the protection of all parties in their respective modes of worship, are the natural operations of a free government; and every thing that tends to check or restrain them materially affects the interests of religion. Aware of the force of religious belief over the mind of man, of the generous independence it inspires, and of the eagerness with which it is cherished and maintained, it is towards this quarter the arm of despotism first directs its attacks, while through every period the imaginary right of ruling the conscience has been the earliest assumed, and the latest relinquished. Under this conviction, an enlightened Christian, when he turns his attention to political occurrences, will rejoice in beholding every advance towards freedom in the government of nations, as it forms, not only a barrier to the encroachments of tyranny, but a security to the diffusion and establishment of truth. A considerable portion of personal freedom may be enjoyed, it is true, under a despotic government, or, in other words, a great part of human actions may be left uncontrolled; but with this an enlightened mind will never rest satisfied, because it is at best but an indulgence flowing from motives of policy, or the lenity of the prince, which may be at any time withdrawn the hand that bestowed it. Upon the same principles, religious toleration may have an accidental and precarious existence, in states whose policy is the most arbitrary; but, in such a situation, it seldom lasts long, and can never rest upon a secure and permanent basis, disappearing for the most part along with those temporary views of interest or policy on which it was founded. The history of every age will attest the truth of this observation.

Mr. ———, in order to prepare us to digest his principles, tells us, in the first page of his discourse, *that the gospel dispensation is spiritual, the worship it enjoins simple and easy, and if liberty of conscience be granted, all its exterior order may be regarded under every kind of human government.* This is very true, but it is saying no more than that the Christian worship may be always carried on if it is not interrupted, a point, I presume, no one will contend with him. The question is, can every form of government furnish a *security* for liberty of conscience; or, which is the same thing, can the rights of private judgment be safe under a government whose professed principle is, that the subject has no *rights at all*, but is a vassal dependent upon his superior lord? Nor is this a futile or chimerical question; it is founded upon fact. The state to which it alludes is the condition at present of more than half the nations of Europe; and if there were no better patriots than this author, it would soon be the condition of them all The blessings which we estimate highly we are naturally eager to perpetuate, and whoever is acquainted with the value of religious freedom will not be content to suspend it on the clemency of a prince, the indulgence of ministers, or the liberality of bishops, if ever such a thing existed; he will never think it secure, till it has a constitutional basis; nor even then, till by the general spread of its principles every individual becomes its guarantee, and every arm ready to be lifted up in its defence. Forms of policy may change, or they may survive the spirit that produced them; but when the seeds of knowledge have been once sown, and have taken root in the human mind, they will advance with a steady growth, and even flourish in those alarming scenes of anarchy and confusion in which the settled order and regular machinery of government are wrecked and disappear.

Christianity, we see then, instead of weakening our attachment to the principles of freedom, or withdrawing them from our attention, renders them doubly dear to us, by giving us an interest in them, proportioned to the value of those religious privileges they secure and protect.

Our author endeavours to cast reproach on the advocates for liberty by attempting to discredit their piety, for which purpose he assures us, to be active in this cause is disreputable, and brings the reality of our religion into just suspicion. "*Who are the persons*," he asks, "*that embark? Are they the spiritual, humble, and useful teachers, who travel in birth, till Christ be formed in the hearts of their hearers? No. They are philosophical opposers of the grand peculiarities of Christianity.*" It is of little consequence of what descriptions of persons the friends of freedom consist, provided their principles are just, and their arguments well founded; but here, as in other places, the author displays an utter ignorance of facts. Men who know no age but their own must draw their precedents from it; or, if Mr. ——— had glanced only towards the history of England, he must have remembered, that in the reigns of Charles the First and Second, the chief friends of freedom were the puritans, of whom many were republicans, and the remainder zealously attached to a *limited* monarchy. It is to the distinguished exertions of this party we are in a great measure indebted for the preservation of our free and happy constitution. In those distracted and turbulent times which preceded the restoration of Charles the Second, the puritans, who to a devotion the most fervent united an eager attachment to the doctrines of grace, as they are commonly called, displayed on every occasion a love of freedom, pushed almost to excess; while the cavaliers, their opponents, who ridiculed all that was serious, and, if they had any religion at all, held sentiments directly repugnant to the tenets of Calvin, were the firm supporters of arbitrary power. If the Unitarians then are at present distinguished for their zeal in the cause of freedom, it cannot be imputed to any alliance between their religious and political opinions, but to the conduct natural to a minority, who, attempting bold innovations, and maintaining sentiments very different from those which are generally held, are sensible they can only shelter themselves from persecution and reproach, and gain an impartial hearing from the public, by throwing down the barriers of prejudice, and claiming an unlimited freedom of thought.

4th. Though Christianity does not assume any immediate direction in the affairs of government, it inculcates those duties and recommends that spirit which will ever prompt us to cherish the principles of freedom. It teaches us to check every selfish passion, to consider ourselves as parts of a great community, and to abound in all the fruits of an active benevolence. The particular operation of this principle will be regulated by circumstances as they arise, but our obligation to cultivate it is clear and indubitable. As this author does not pretend that the nature of a government has no connexion with the felicity of those who are the subjects of it, he cannot without the utmost inconsistency deny, that to watch over the interests of our fellow-creatures in this respect is a branch of the great duty of social benevolence. If we are bound to protect a neighbour, or even an enemy, from violence, to give him raiment when he is naked, or food when he is hungry, much more ought we to do our part towards the preservation of a free government; the only basis on which the enjoyment of these blessings can securely rest. He who breaks the fetters of slavery, and delivers a nation from thraldom, forms, in my opinion, the noblest comment on the great law of love, while he distributes the greatest blessing which man can receive from man; but next to that is the merit of him who, in times like the present, watches over the edifice of public liberty, repairs its foundations, and strengthens its cement, when he beholds it hastening to decay.

It is not in the power of every one, it is true, to benefit his age or country in this distinguished manner, and accordingly it is nowhere expressly commanded; but where this ability exists it is not diminished by our embracing Christianity, which consecrates every talent to the public good. On whomsoever distinguished endowments are bestowed, as Christians we ought to rejoice when, instead of being wasted in vain or frivolous pursuits, we behold them employed on objects of the greatest general concern; among which those principles of freedom will ever be reckoned which determine the destiny of nations and the collective felicity of the human race.

5th. Our author expresses an ardent desire for the approach of that period when all men will be Christians. I have no doubt that this event will take place, and rejoice in the prospect of it; but whenever it arrives it will be fatal to Mr. ———'s favourite principles; for the professors of Christianity must then become politicians, as the wicked, on whom he at present very politely devolves the business of government, will be no more: or perhaps he indulges a hope that even then there will be a sufficient number of sinners left to conduct political affairs, especially as wars will then cease, and social life be less frequently disturbed by rapine and injustice. It will still, however, be a great hardship that a handful of the wicked should rule innumerable multitudes of the just, and cannot fail, according to our present conceptions, to operate as a kind of check on piety and virtue. How Mr. ——— will settle this point I cannot pretend to say, except he imagines men will be able to subsist without any laws or civil regulations, or intends to revive the long-exploded tradition of Papias, respecting the personal reign.

Had Christianity been intended only for the benefit of a few, or as the distinction of a small fraternity, there might have been some pretence for setting its profession in opposition to human policy, since it might then have been conducted without their interference; but a religion which is formed for the whole world, and will finally be embraced by all its inhabitants, can never be clogged with any such impediment as would render it repugnant to the social existence of mankind.

SECTION II.

On the Duty of Ministers in Respect to Civil Polity.

Mr. ——— is extremely severe upon those of his brethren who, forsaking the quiet duties of their profession, as he styles them, have dared to interfere in public affairs. This he considers a most flagrant offence, an alarming departure from their proper province; and in the fulness of his rage, he heaps upon them every epithet which contempt or indignation can suggest; calls them meddling, convivial, political ministers, devoid of all seriousness and dignity. It is rather extraordinary this severe correction should be administered by a man who is at that moment guilty of the offence he is chastising; reproaches political preachers in a political sermon; ridicules theories of government, and at the same time advances one of his own, a most wretched one indeed, but delivered in a tone the most arrogant and decisive. It is not political discussion then, it seems, that has ruffled the gentle serenity of our author's temper; for he too, we see, can bend, when it pleases him, from his spiritual elevation, and let fall his oracular responses on the duty of subjects and of kings. But the persons on whom he denounces his anathemas have presumed to adopt a system of politics inconsistent with his own, and it is less his piety than his pride that is shocked and offended. Instead of submitting to be moulded by any adept in cringes and posture-master of servility, they have dared to assume the bold and natural port of freemen.

It will be unnecessary to say much on the duty of ministers in respect to political affairs, as many of the reflections which this subject would suggest have been already advanced under a former head. A few considerations, however, present themselves here, to which I shall beg the reader's attention.

The duties of the ministerial character, it will on all hands be confessed, are of a nature the most sacred and important. To them should be directed the first and chief attention of every person who sustains it, and whatever is found to interfere with these momentous engagements should be relinquished as criminal and improper. But there is no profession which occupies the mind so fully as not to leave many intervals of leisure, in which objects that lie out of its immediate province will have a share of our attention; and I see not why these periods of recess may not be employed with as much dignity and advantage in acquiring an acquaintance with the principle of government, as wasted in frivolous amusements or an inactive indolence. Mr. ———, with his usual confidence, lays it down as a maxim, that the science of politics cannot be cultivated without a neglect of ministerial duties; and one would almost be tempted to suppose he had published his sermon as a confirmation of this remark, as a more striking example of political ignorance in a teacher of religion has scarcely ever been exhibited. As far, therefore, as the preacher himself is concerned, the observation will be admitted in its full force; but he has surely no right to make his own weakness the standard of another's strength.

Political science, as far as it falls under our present contemplation, may be considered in two points of view. It may either intend a discussion of the great objects for which governments are formed, or it may intend a consideration of the means which may be employed, and the particular contrivances that may be fallen upon to accomplish those objects. For example, in vindicating the revolution in France, two distinct methods may be pursued with equal propriety and success It may be defended upon its *principles* against the friends of arbitrary power, by displaying the value of freedom, the equal rights of mankind, the folly and injustice of those regal or aristocratic pretensions by which those rights were invaded; accordingly, in this light it has been justified with the utmost success. Or it may be defended upon its *expedients*, by exhibiting the elements of government which it has composed, the laws it has enacted, and the tendency of both to extend and per petuate that liberty which is its ultimate object. But though each of these modes of discussion falls within the province of politics, it is obvious the degree of inquiry, of knowledge, and of labour they require differs widely. The first is a path which has been often and successfully trod, turns upon principles which are common to all times and places, and which demand little else to enforce conviction than calm and dispassionate attention. The latter method, involving a question of expediency, not of right, would lead into a vast field of detail, would require a thorough acquaintance with the situation of persons and of things, as well as long and intimate acquaintance with human affairs. There are but few ministers who have capacity or leisure to become great practical politicians. To explore the intricacies of commercial science, to penetrate the refinements of negotiation, to determine with certainty and precision the balance of power, are undertakings, it will be confessed, which lie very remote from the ministerial department; but the *principles* of government, as it is a contrivance for securing the freedom and happiness of men, may be acquired with great ease.

These principles our ancestors understood well, and it would be no small shame if, in an age which boasts so much light and improvement as the present, they were less familiar to us. There is no class of men to whom this species of knowledge is so requisite, on several accounts, as dissenting ministers. The jealous policy of the establishment forbids our youth admission into the celebrated seats of learning; our own seminaries, at least till lately, were almost entirely confined to candidates for the ministry; and as on both these accounts, among us the intellectual improvement of our religious teachers rises superior to that of private Christians, in a greater degree than in the national church, the influence of their opinions is wider in proportion. Disclaiming, as they do, all pretensions to dominion, their public character, their professional leisure, the habits of study and composition which they acquire, concur to point them out as the natural guardians, in some measure, of our liberties and rights. Besides, as they are appointed to teach the whole compass of social duty, the mutual obligations of rulers and subjects will of necessity fall under their notice, and they cannot explain or enforce the *reasons* of submission without displaying the *proper end* of government and the *expectations* we may naturally form from it; which, when accurately done, will lead into the very depths of political science.

There is another reason, however, distinct from any I have yet mentioned, flowing from the nature of an established religion, why dissenting ministers, above all men, should be well skilled in the principles of freedom. Wherever, as in England, religion is established by law, with splendid emoluments and dignities annexed to its profession, the clergy, who are candidates for these distinctions, will ever be prone to exalt the prerogative, not only in order to strengthen the arm on which they lean, but that they may the more successfully ingratiate themselves in the favour of the prince, by flattering those ambitious views and passions which are too readily entertained by persons possessed of supreme power. The boasted alliance between church and state, on which so many encomiums have been lavished, seems to have been little more than a compact between the priest and the magistrate to betray the liberties of mankind, both civil and religious. To this the clergy on their part at least have continued steady, shunning inquiry, fearful of change, blind to the corruptions of government, skilful to *discern the signs of the times*, and eager to improve every opportunity, and to employ all their art and eloquence to extend the prerogative and smooth the approaches of arbitrary power. Individuals are illustrious exceptions to this censure; it however applies to the body, to none more than to those whose exalted rank and extensive influence determine its complexion and spirit. In this situation, the leaders of that church, in their fatal attempt to recommend and embellish a slavish system of principles, will, I trust, be ever carefully watched and opposed by those who hold a similar station among the dissenters; that at all events there may remain one asylum to which insulted freedom may retire unmolested. These considerations are sufficient to justify every dissenting minister in well-timed exertions for the public cause, and from them we may learn what opinion to entertain of Mr. ———'s weak and malignant invectives.

From the general strain of his discourse, it would be natural to conclude he was an enemy to every interference of ministers on political occasions; but this is not the case. *Ministers*, says he, *may interfere as peace-makers, and by proper methods should counteract the spirit of faction raised by persons who seem born to vex the state.* After having taught them to remain in a quiet neutrality, he invests them all at once with the high character of arbiters between the contending parties, without considering that an office of so much delicacy would demand a most intimate acquaintance with the pretensions of both. Ministers, it should seem, instead of declining political interference, are to become such adepts in the science of government, as to distinguish with precision the complaints of an oppressed party from the clamours of a faction, to hold the balance between the ruler and the subject with a steady hand, *and to point out, on every occasion, and counteract the persons who are born to vex the state.* If any should demand by what means they are to furnish themselves for such extraordinary undertakings, he will learn it is not by political investigation or inquiry this profound skill is to be attained, but by a studied inattention and neglect, of which this author, it must be confessed, has given his disciples a most edifying example in his first essay. There is something miraculous in these endowments. This battle is not to the strong, nor these riches to men of understanding. Our author goes a step further, for when he is in the humour for concessions no man can be more liberal. *So far as revolutions*, says he, *are parts of God's plan of government, a Christian is not to hinder such changes in states as promise an increase of happiness to mankind. But nowhere in the New Testament can a Christian find countenance in becoming a forward active man in regenerating the civil constitutions of nations.* A Christian is not to oppose revolutions, as far as they are parts of God's plan of government. The direction which oracles afford has ever been complained of for its obscurity; and this of Mr. ———, though no doubt it is fraught with the profoundest wisdom, would have been more useful had it furnished some criterion to distinguish those transactions which *are* parts of God's plan of government. We have hitherto imagined the elements of nature and the whole agency of man are comprehended within the system of Divine Providence; but as in this sense every thing becomes a part of the divine plan, it cannot be his meaning. Perhaps he means to confine the phrase *of God's plan of government* to that portion of human agency which is consistent with the divine will and promises, as he says, an increase of happiness to mankind. If this should be his intention, the sentiment is just, but utterly subversive of the purpose for which it is introduced, as it concurs with the principle of all reformers in leaving us no other direction in these cases than reason and experience, determined in their exertions by a regard to the general happiness of mankind. On this basis the wildest projectors profess to erect their improvements. On this principle too do the dissenters proceed, when they call for a repeal of the Test Act, when they lament the unequal representation of parliament, when they wish to see a period to ministerial corruption, and to the encroachments of a hierarchy equally servile and oppressive; and thus by one unlucky concession this author has admitted the groundwork of reform in its fullest extent, and has demolished the whole fabric he was so eager to rear. He must not be offended if principles thus corrupt and thus feebly supported should meet with the contempt they deserve, but must seek his consolation in his own adage, as the correction of folly is certainly *a part of God's plan of government.* The reader can be at no loss to determine whom the author intends by a *busy active man in regenerating the civil constitutions of nations.* The occasion of the sermon and complexion of its sentiments concur in directing us to Dr. Priestley,—a person whom the author seems to regard with a more than *odium theologicum*, with a rancour exceeding the measure even of his profession. The religious tenets of Dr. Priestley appear to me erroneous in the extreme; but I should be sorry to suffer any difference of sentiment to diminish my sensibility to virtue or my admiration of genius. From him the poisoned arrow will fall pointless. His enlightened and active mind, his unwearied assiduity, the extent of his researches, the light he has poured into almost every department of science, will be the admiration of that period when the greater part of those who have favoured, or those who have opposed him, will be alike forgotten. Distinguished merit will ever rise superior to oppression, and will draw lustre from reproach. The vapours which gather round the rising sun, and follow it in its course, seldom fail at the close of it to form a magnificent theatre for its reception, and to invest with variegated tints, and with a softened effulgence, the luminary which they cannot hide.*

* Whether or not the beautiful passage in the text was suggested by a floating vague recollection of the following lines of Pope, or were an avowed imitation of them, cannot now be determined. But

It is a pity, however, our author in reproaching characters so illustrious was not a little more attentive to facts; for unfortunately for him Dr. Priestley has not in any instance displayed that disaffection to government with which he has been charged so wantonly. In his Lectures on History and his Essay on Civil Government, which of all his publications fall most properly within the sphere of politics, he has delineated the British constitution with great accuracy, and has expressed his warm admiration of it as the best system of policy the sagacity of man has been able to contrive. In his Familiar Letters to the Inhabitants of Birmingham, a much later work, where the seeds of that implacable dislike were scattered which produced the late riots, he has renewed that declaration, and has informed us that he has been pleasantly ridiculed by his friends as being a unitarian in religion and a trinitarian in politics. He has lamented, indeed, in common with every enlightened citizen, the existence of certain corruptions, which, being gradually introduced into the constitution, have greatly impaired its vigour; but in this he has had the honour of being followed by the prime minister himself, who began his career by proposing a reform in parliament—merely to court popularity it is true, at a time when it would not have been so safe for him to insult the friends of freedom after having betrayed their interest, as he has since found it.

Dr. Priestley has, moreover, defended with great ability and success the principles of our dissent, exposing, as the very nature of the undertaking demands, the folly and injustice of all clerical usurpations; and on this account, if on no other, he is entitled to the gratitude of his brethren. In addition to this catalogue of crimes, he has ventured to express his satisfaction on the liberation of France; an event which, promising a firmer establishment to liberty than any recorded in the annals of the world, is contemplated by the friends of arbitrary power throughout every kingdom of Europe with the utmost concern. These are the demerits of Dr. Priestley, for which this political astrologist and sacred calculator of nativities pronounces upon him that he is *born to vex the state.* The best apology candour can suggest will be to hope Mr. ——— has never read Dr. Priestley's political works; a conjecture somewhat confirmed from his disclaiming all attention to political theories, and from the extreme ignorance he displays through the whole of his discourse on political topics. Still it is to be wished he would have condescended to understand what he means to confute, if it had been only to save himself the trouble and disgrace of this publication.

be this as it may, I think it will be readily admitted, that the rhythm and harmony of the passage in prose are decidedly superior to those in the lines of the poet:—

"Envy will merit, as its shade, pursue,
But, like a shadow, prove the substance true:
For envied wit, like Sol eclips'd, makes known
Th' opposing body's grossness, not its own.
When first that sun too powerful beams displays,
It draws up vapours which obscure its rays;
But e'en those clouds at last adorn its way,
Reflect new glories and augment the day."—Ed

The manner in which he speaks of the Birmingham riots, and the cause to which he traces them, are too remarkable to pass unnoticed.

When led, says he, speaking of the sufferers, *by officious zeal, from the quiet duties of their profession into the senator's province: unhallowed boisterous passions in others; like their own, God may permit to chastise them.* For my own part I was some time before I could develop this extraordinary passage; but I now find the darkness in which it is veiled is no more than that mystic sublimity which has always tinctured the language of those who are appointed to interpret the counsels of Heaven.

I would not have Mr. ——— deal too freely in these visions, lest the fire and illumination of the prophet should put out the reason of the man; a caution the more necessary in the present instance, as it glimmers so feebly already in several parts of his discourse that its extinction would not be at all extraordinary. We are, no doubt, much obliged to him for letting us into a secret we could never have learned any other way. We thank him heartily for informing us that the Birmingham riots were a judgment, and as we would wish to be grateful for such an important communication, we would whisper in his ear in return, that he should be particularly careful not to suffer this itch of prophesying to grow upon him, men being extremely apt in this degenerate age to mistake a prophet for a madman, and to lodge them in the same place of confinement. The best use he could make of his mantle would be to bequeath it to the use of posterity, as for the want of it I am afraid they will be in danger of falling into some very unhappy mistakes. To their unenlightened eyes it will appear a reproach, that in the eighteenth century, an age that boasts its science and improvement, the first philosopher in Europe, of a character unblemished, and of manners the most mild and gentle, should be torn from his family, and obliged to flee an outcast and a fugitive from the murderous hands of a frantic rabble; but when they learn that there were not wanting teachers of religion who secretly triumphed in these barbarities, they will pause for a moment, and imagine they are reading the history of Goths or of Vandals. Erroneous as such a judgment must appear in the eyes of Mr. ———, nothing but a ray of his supernatural light could enable us to form a juster decision. Dr. Priestley and his friends are not the first that have suffered in a public cause; and when we recollect that those who have sustained similar disasters have been generally conspicuous for a superior sanctity of character, what but an acquaintance with the counsels of Heaven can enable us to distinguish between these two classes of sufferers, and while one are the favourites of God, to discern in the other the objects of his vengeance. When we contemplate this extraordinary endowment, we are no longer surprised at the superiority he assumes through the whole of his discourse, nor at that air of confusion and disorder which appears in it, both of which we impute to his dwelling so much in the insufferable light, and amid the coruscations and flashes of the divine glory; a sublime but perilous situation, described with great force and beauty by Mr. Gray:—

> "He passed the flaming bounds of place and time,
> The living throne, the sapphire blaze,
> Where angels tremble while they gaze,
> He saw; but blasted with excess of light,
> Closed his eyes in endless night."

SECTION III.

On the Pretences Mr. —— advances in Favour of his Principles.

Having endeavoured to justify the well-timed exertions of Christians and of ministers in the cause of freedom, it may not be improper to examine a little more particularly under what pretences Mr. —— presumes to condemn this conduct.

1st. The first that naturally presents itself is drawn from those passages of Scripture, in which the design of civil government is explained, and the duty of submission to civil authority is enforced. That on which the greatest stress is laid is found in the thirteenth chapter of the Epistle to the Romans. "Let every soul be subject to the higher powers; for there is no power but of God: the powers which be are ordained of God. Whoever therefore resisteth the power, resisteth the ordinance of God; and they that resist shall receive unto themselves damnation. The ruler is the minister of God to thee for good. But if thou doest that which is evil, be afraid, for he beareth not the sword in vain. Wherefore ye must be subject, not only for wrath, but conscience' sake." This passage, which, from the time of Sir Robert Filmer to the present day, has been the stronghold of the doctrine of passive obedience and non-resistance, will admit of an easy solution, by attending to the nature of Christianity, and the circumstances of its professors during the period it was written. The extraordinary privileges and dignity conferred by the gospel on believers, must have affected the minds of the first Christians, just emerging from the shades of ignorance, and awakened to new hopes, with singular force. Feeling an elevation to which they were strangers before, and looking down upon the world around them as the vassals of sin and Satan, they might be easily tempted to imagine the restraint of laws could not extend to persons so highly privileged, and that it was ignominious in the free men of Jesus Christ to submit to the yoke of idolatrous rulers. Natural to their situation as these sentiments might be, none could be conceived of more detrimental to the credit and propagation of a rising religion, or more likely to draw down upon its professors the whole weight of the Roman Empire, with which they were in no condition to contend. In this situation, it was proper for the apostle to remind Christians their religion did not interfere with the rights of princes, or diminish their obligation to attend to those salutary regulations which are established for the protection of innocence and the punishment of the guilty. That this only was the intention of the writer may be inferred from the considerations he adduces to strengthen his advice. He does not draw his arguments for submission from any thing *peculiar* to the *Christian system*, as he must have done had he intended to oppose that religion to the natural rights of mankind, but from the utility and necessity of civil restraints. "The ruler is the minister of God to thee for good," is the reason he urges for submission. Civil government, as if he had said, is a salutary institution, appointed to restrain and punish outrage and injustice, but exhibiting to the quiet and inoffensive nothing of which they need to be afraid. "If thou doest that which is evil, be afraid, for he beareth not the sword in vain." He is an avenger to execute wrath upon him that doeth evil. Christians were not to consider themselves privileged above their fellow-citizens, as their religion conferred upon them no civil immunities, but left them subject to all the ties and restraints, whatever they were, which could be justly imposed by the civil power on any other part of mankind.

The limits of every duty must be determined by its *reasons*, and the only ones assigned *here*, or that *can* be assigned for submission to civil authority, are its *tendency to do good;* wherever, therefore, this shall cease to be the case, submission becomes absurd, having no longer any *rational view*. But at what time this evil shall be judged to have arrived, or what remedy it may be proper to apply, Christianity does not decide, but leaves to be determined by an appeal to natural reason and right. By one of the strongest misconceptions in the world, when we are taught that Christianity does not bestow upon us any *new* rights, it has been thought to strip us of our *old;* which is just the same as it would be to conclude, because it did not first furnish us with hands or feet, it obliges us to cut them off.

Under every form of government, that civil order which affords protection to property and tranquillity to individuals must be obeyed; and I have no doubt that before the revolution in France, they who are now its warmest admirers, had they lived there, would have yielded a quiet submission to its laws, as being conscious the social compact can only be considered as dissolved by an expression of the general will. In the mean time, they would have continued firm in avowing the principles of freedom, and by the spread of political knowledge have endeavoured to train and prepare the minds of their fellow-citizens for accomplishing a change so desirable.

It is not necessary to enter into a particular examination of the other texts adduced by Mr. ——— in support of his sentiments, as this in Romans is by much the most to his purpose, and the remarks that have been made upon it may, with very little alteration, be applied to the rest. He refers us to the second chapter of the first Epistle of Peter. "Submit yourselves to every ordinance of man for the Lord's sake; whether it be to the king as supreme, or unto governors as unto them that are sent by him, for the punishment of evil-doers, and for the praise of them that do well." Here it is sufficient to remark, all that can be inferred from this passage is, that Christians are not to hold themselves exempt from the obligation of obedience on account of their religion, but are to respect legislation as far as it is found productive of benefit in social life.

With still less propriety he urges the first of Timothy, "where in the second chapter we are exhorted to supplications, prayers, intercessions, and giving of thanks for all men, for kings, and for all that are in authority, that we may lead a quiet and peaceable life, in all godliness and honesty." I am unacquainted with any who refuse a compliance with this apostolical admonition, except the nonjurors may be reckoned of this class, whose political sentiments are of a piece with our author's.

While he pleads with so much eagerness for the duty of passive obedience, we are not, however, to suppose he wishes to extend it to all mankind. He admits, "*that society, under the wisest regulations, will degenerate, and there will be periods when associated bodies must be resolved again into its first principles.*" All resistance to authority, every revolution, is not in his own opinion criminal; it is Christians only who are never to have a share in these transactions, never to assert their rights. With what different sentiments did the apostle of the gentiles contemplate his character, when disdaining to accept a clandestine dismission from an unjust imprisonment, he felt a glow of indignant pride burn upon his cheek, and exclaimed, with a Roman energy, "I was free born!"

2d. Another reason which this author assigns for a blind deference to civil authority is, that Christianity is "*distinct from, and independent of human legislation.*" This principle no Protestant Dissenter will be inclined to question, but instead of lending any support to the system of passive obedience, it will overturn it from its foundation; for if religion be really distinct from and independent of human legislation, it cannot afford any standard to ascertain its limits; as the moment it is applied to this purpose it ceases to be a thing distinct and independent. For example, it is not doubted that a Christian may lawfully engage in trade or commerce; but if it be asked why his profession does not interfere with such an undertaking, the proper reply will be, religion is a thing distinct and independent. Should it be again inquired, why a Christian may become a trader, yet must not commit a theft, we should answer, that this latter action is not a thing distinct, or independent of religion, but falls immediately under its cognizance, as a violation of its laws. Thus it appears, that whatever portion of human conduct is really *independent* of religion is lawful for that *very reason*, and can then only become criminal or improper, when it is suffered to intrench upon more sacred or important duties. The truth is, between two institutions, such as civil government and religion, which have a separate origin and end, no opposition can subsist but in the brain of a distempered enthusiast.

The author's text confutes his doctrine, for had our Saviour annihilated our rights, he would have become a *judge* and *divider* over us, in the worst sense, if that could be said to be divided which is taken away. When any two institutions are affirmed to be distinct and independent, it can only mean they do not *interfere*; but that must be a genius of no common size who can infer from religion not *interfering* with the rights of mankind, that they cease to be, or that the patrimony over which our Lord declined to exercise *any authority* he has scattered and destroyed.

3d. Similar to the last I have considered is that pretence for excluding Christians from any concern in political affairs, taken from the conduct of our Saviour. Mr. ——— tells us, that Christ uniformly waived interesting himself in the concerns of the then existing government; and to the same purpose he afterward remarks, he always declined the functions of a civil magistrate.

The most careless reader will remark, the whole weight of this argument rests upon a supposition that it is unlawful for a Christian to sustain any other character in civil life than that in which our Saviour literally appeared; a notion as extravagant as was ever nourished in the brain of the wildest fanatic. Upon this principle he must have gone through such a succession of offices, and engaged in such an endless variety of undertakings, that in place of thirty-three years, he needed to have lived thirty-three centuries. On this ground the profession of physic is unlawful for a Christian, because our Lord never set up a dispensary; and that of law, because he never pleaded at the bar. Next to the weakness of advancing such absurdity is that of confuting it.

4th. The author, in proof of his political tenets, appeals to the devotional feelings of his hearers. "I ask you," says he, "who make conscience of entering into your closets, and shutting your doors, and praying to your Father which seeth in secret; what subjects interest you most then? Are not factious passions hushed; the undue heat you felt in political disputation remembered with sorrow?" He must be at a great loss for argument who will have recourse to such loose and flimsy declamation. When engaged in devout admiration of the Supreme Being, every other object will be lost in the comparison; but this, though the noblest employment of the mind, was never intended to shut out all other concerns. The affections which unite us to the world have a large demand upon us, and must succeed in their turn. If every thing is to be deemed criminal that does not interest the attention in the very moment of worship, political concerns are not the only ones to be abandoned, but every undertaking of a temporal nature, all labour and ingenuity must cease. Science herself must shroud her light. These are notions rather to be laughed at than confuted, for their extravagance will correct itself. Every attempt that has been made to rear religion on the ruins of nature, or to render it subversive of the economy of life, has hitherto proved unsuccessful, while the institutions that have flowed from it are now scarcely regarded in any other light than as humiliating monuments of human weakness and folly. The natural vigour of the mind, when it has once been opened by knowledge, and turned towards great and interesting objects, will always overpower the illusions of fanaticism; or, could Mr. ———'s principles be carried into effect, we should soon behold men returning again to the state of a savage, and a more than monkish barbarity and ignorance would overspread the earth. That abstraction from the world it is his purpose to recommend is in truth as inconsistent with the nature of religion as with the state and condition of man; for Christianity does not propose to take us *out* of the world, but to preserve us from the pollutions which are *in* it.

It is easy to brand a passion for liberty with the odious epithet of faction; no two things, however, can be more opposite. Faction is a combination of a few to oppress the liberties of many; the love of freedom is the impulse of an enlightened and presiding spirit, ever intent upon the welfare of the community or body to which it belongs, and ready to give the alarm when it beholds any unlawful conspiracy formed, whether it be of rulers or of subjects, with a design to oppress it. Every tory upholds a faction; every whig, as far as he is sincere and well-informed, is a friend to the equal liberties of mankind. Absurd as the preacher's appeal must appear on such an occasion to the devout feelings of his hearers, we have no need to decline it. In those solemn moments factious passions cannot indeed be too much hushed, but that warmth which animates the patriot, which glowed in the breast of a Sidney or a Hampden, was never chilled or diminished, we may venture to affirm, in its nearest approaches to the uncreated splendour; and if it mingled with their devotion at all, could not fail to infuse into it a fresh force and vigour by drawing them into a closer assimilation to that great Being who appears under the character of the avenger of the oppressed and the friend and protector of the human race.

5th. Lastly, the author endeavours to discredit the principles of freedom by holding them up as intimately connected with the Unitarian heresy. "We are not to be surprised," he says, "if men who vacate the rule of faith in Jesus Christ should be defective in deference and in obedient regards to men who are raised to offices of superior influence for the purposes of civil order and public good." The persons he has in view are the Unitarians, and that my reader may be in full possession of this most curious argument, it may be proper to inform him that a Unitarian is a person who believes Jesus Christ had no existence till he appeared on our earth, while a trinitarian maintains that he existed with the Father from all eternity. What possible connexion can he discern between these opinions and the subject of government?

In order to determine whether the supreme power should be vested in king, lords, and commons as in England, in an assembly of nobles as in Venice, or in a house of representatives as in America or France, must we first decide upon the person of Christ? I should imagine we might as well apply to astronomy first, to learn whether the earth flattens at the poles. He explains what he means by *vacating* the rule of faith in Christ when he charges the Unitarians with a partial denial at least of the inspiration of the Scripture, particularly the epistles of St. Paul. But, however clear the inspiration of the Scriptures may be, as no one pleads for the inspiration of civil governors, the deference which is due to the first, as coming from God, can be no reason for an unlimited submission to the latter. Yet this is Mr. ———'s argument, and it runs thus: Every opposition to Scripture is criminal, because it is inspired, and therefore every resistance to temporal rulers is criminal, though they are *not* inspired.

The number of passages in Paul's epistles which treat of civil government is small, the principal of them have been examined, and whether they are inspired or not has not the remotest relation to the question before us. The inspiration of an author adds weight to his sentiments, but makes no alteration in his meaning, and unless Mr. ——— can show that Paul inculcates unlimited submission, the belief of his inspiration can yield no advantage to his cause. Among those parties of Christians who have maintained the inspiration of the Scriptures in its utmost extent, the number of such as have inferred from them the doctrine of passive obedience has been extremely small; it is therefore ridiculous to impute the rejection of this tenet by Unitarians to a disbelief of plenary inspiration. It behooves Mr. ——— to point out, if he is able, any one of the Unitarians who ever imagined that Paul means to recommend unlimited obedience; for till that is the case it is plain their political opinions cannot have arisen from any contempt of that apostle's authority.

As there is no foundation in the nature of things for imagining any alliance between heretical tenets and the principles of freedom, this notion is equally void of support from fact or history. Were the socinian sentiments, in particular, productive of any *peculiar impatience under* the restraints of government, this effect could not fail of having made its appearance on their first rise in Poland, while their influence was fresh and vigorous; but nothing of this nature occurred, nor was any such reproach cast upon them. That sect in England which has been always most conspicuous for the love of freedom have for the most part held sentiments at the greatest remove from socinianism that can be imagined. The seeds of those political principles which broke out with such vigour in the reign of Charles the First, and have since given rise to the denomination of whigs, were sown in the latter end of the reign of Queen Elizabeth by the hand of the puritans, among whom the unitarian doctrine was then utterly unknown. The dissenters, descended from those illustrious ancestors, and inheriting their spirit, have been foremost in defence of liberty, not only or chiefly of late, since the spread of the socinian doctrine, but before that system had gained any footing among us.

The knowledge and study of the Scriptures, far from favouring the pretensions of despotism, have almost ever diminished it, and been attended with a proportional increase of freedom. The union of Protestant princes preserved the liberties of the Germanic body, when they were in danger of being overwhelmed by the victorious arm of Charles the Fifth; yet a veneration for the Scriptures, at a time when they had almost fallen into oblivion, and an appeal to their decisions in all points, was the grand characteristic of the new religion. If we look into Turkey we shall find the least of that impatience under restraints which Mr. ——— laments of any place in the world, though Paul and his epistles are not much studied there.

There are not wanting reasons which at first view might induce us to conclude unitarianism was less favourable to the love of freedom than almost any other system of religious belief. If any party of Christians were ever free from the least tincture of enthusiasm, it is the Unitarian: yet that passion has by every philosopher been judged friendly to liberty; and to its influence, though perhaps improperly, some of its most distinguished exertions have been ascribed. Hume and Bolingbroke, who were atheists, leaned towards arbitrary power. Owen, Howe, Milton, Baxter, some of the most devout and venerable characters that ever appeared, were warmly attached to liberty, and held sentiments on the subject of government as free and unfettered as Dr. Priestley. Thus every pretence for confounding the attachment to freedom with the sentiments of a religious party is most abundantly confuted both from reason and from fact. The zeal Unitarians have displayed in defence of civil and religious liberty is the spirit natural to a minority who are well aware they are viewed by the ecclesiastical powers with an unparalleled malignity and rancour. Let the dissenters at large remember they too are a minority, a great minority, and that they must look for their security from the same quarter, not from the compliments of bishops or presents from maids of honour.*

To abandon principles which the best and most enlightened men have in all ages held sacred, which the dissenters in particular have rendered themselves illustrious by defending, which have been sealed and consecrated by the blood of our ancestors, for no other reason than that the Unitarians chance to maintain them, would be a weakness of which a child might be ashamed! Whoever may think fit to take up the gauntlet in the socinian controversy will have my warmest good wishes; but let us not employ those arms against each other which were given us for our common defence.

SECTION IV.

On the Test Act.

AMID all the wild eccentricities which, abounding in every part of this extraordinary publication, naturally diminish our wonder at any thing such a writer may advance, I confess I am surprised at his declaring his wish for the continuance of the Test Act. This law, enacted in the latter end of the reign of Charles the Second to secure the nation from popery when it stood upon the brink of that precipice, is continued, now that the danger no longer exists which first occasioned it, for the express purpose of preserving the church from the inroads of dissenters. That church, it must be remembered, existed for ages before it received any such protection; yet it is now the vogue to mag-

* Some of my readers perhaps need to be informed that I here allude to Mr. Martin, who, for similar services to those Mr. ——— is now performing, has been considerably caressed by certain bishops, who have condescended to notice and to visit him. I think we do not read that Judas had any acquaintance with the high-priests till he came to transact business with them.

nify its importance to that degree that one would imagine it was its sole prop, whose removal would draw the whole fabric after it, or at least make it totter to its base. Whether these apprehensions were really entertained by the clergy who gave the signal for the commencement of hostilities on a late occasion, or whether they were only impelled by that illiberal tincture and fixed antipathy to all who differ from them which hath ever marked their character, may be doubted; but to behold a dissenting minister joining with them in an unnatural warfare against his brethren is a phenomenon so curious that it prompts us to inquire into its cause. Let us hear his reasons. He and many others were convinced, he tells us, "that some of the persons who applied for the repeal were influenced by enmity against the doctrinal articles of the established church, and they could not sacrifice their pious regard to truth, though in a church they had separated from, to the policy of men who with respect to God our Saviour only consult how they may cast him down from his excellency." When we hear the clergy exclaim that their church is in danger, we pretty well understand what they mean; they speak broad, as Mr. Burke says, and intend no more than that its emoluments are endangered; but when a serious dissenter expresses his pious regard to the doctrines of the church, it is the *truth* of those articles he must be supposed to have in view. Let us consider for a moment what advantage the Test Act is capable of yielding them. All those who qualify for civil offices by a submission to this law consist of two classes of people: they are either persons who are attached to the articles of the church, from whom therefore no danger could accrue, or they are persons who have signified their assent to doctrines which they inwardly disapprove, and who have qualified themselves for trust by a solemn act of religious deception. It is this latter class alone, it should be remembered, whom the Test Act can at all influence, and thus the only security this celebrated law can afford the articles of the church is founded in a flagrant violation of truth in the persons who become their guarantees. Every attempt that has been made to uphold religion by the civil arm has reflected disgrace upon its authors; but of all that are recorded in the history of the world, perhaps this is the most absurd in its principle and the least effectual in its operation. For the truth of sacred mysteries in religion, it appeals to the corruptest principles of the human heart, and to those *only;* for no one can be tempted by the Test Act to profess an attachment to the doctrines of the church till he has been already allured by the dignity or emolument of a civil office. By compelling all who exercise any function in the state, from the person who aspires to its highest distinctions to those who fill the meanest offices in it, to profess that concurrence in religious opinions which is known never to exist, it is adapted beyond any other human invention to spread among all orders of men a contempt for sacred institutions, to enthrone hypocrisy, and reduce deception to a system! The truth of any set of opinions can only be perceived by *evidence;* but what evidence can any one derive from the mere mechanical action of receiving bread and wine at the hands of a parish priest? He who believes them already needs not to be initiated by any such ceremony; and by what magic touch those simple elements are to convert the unbeliever, our author, who is master of so many secrets, has not condescended to explain. He will not pretend to impute the first spread of these doctrines in the infancy of the Christian religion or their revival at the Reformation to any such means, since he imagines he can trace them in the New Testament. It is strange if that evidence which was powerful enough to introduce them where they were unknown is not sufficient to uphold them where they are already professed and believed. At least, the Test Act, it must be confessed, has yielded them no advantage, for they have been controverted with more acrimony and admitted by a smaller number of persons since that law was enacted, than in any period preceding.

Were the removal of this test to overthrow the establishment itself, a consequence at the same time in the highest degree improbable, the articles of the church, if they are true, would remain unendangered, their evidence would continue unimpaired, an appeal to the inspired writings from which they profess to be derived would be open, the liberty of discussion would be admitted in as great an extent as at present; this difference only would occur, that an attachment to them would no longer be suspected of flowing from corrupt and sinister motives. They would cease to be with the clergy the ladder of promotion, the cant of the pulpit, the ridicule of the schools. The futility of this or any other law, as a security to religious doctrines, may be discerned from this single reflection, that in the national church its own articles have, for a length of time, been either treated with contempt, or maintained with little sincerity and no zeal; while among the dissenters, where they have had no such aids, they have found a congenial soil, and continue to flourish with vigour.

On the political complexion of this test, as it does not fall so properly within my present view, I shall content myself with remarking, that harmless as it may appear at first sight, it carries in it the seeds of all the persecutions and calamities which have ever been sustained on a religious account. It proscribes, not an individual who has been convicted of a crime, but a whole party, as unfit to be trusted by the community to which they belong; and if this stigma can be justly fixed on any set of men, it ought not to stop *here, or anywhere,* short of the actual excision of those who are thus considered as rotten and incurable members of the political body. In annexing to religious speculation the idea of political default, the principle of this law would justify every excess of severity and rigour. If we are the persons it supposes, its indulgence is weak and contemptible; if we are of a different description, the nature of its pretensions is so extraordinary as to occasion serious alarm, and call aloud for its repeal. Mr. ———, indeed, calls this and similar laws a restraint very prudently imposed upon those who dissent from the established religion.*

This restraint, however, is no less than a political annihilation, debarring them, though their talents were ever so splendid, from mingling

* Page 6

in the counsels, or possessing any share in the administration of their country. With that natural relish for absurdity which characterizes this author, he imagines they have justly incurred this evil for dissenting from an *erroneous* religion.

He tells us in the course of his sermon,* that the grand "principle of separation from the church lies in the unworldly nature of our Saviour's kingdom." This reason for separation implies, that any attempt to blend worldly interests or policy with the constitution of a church is improper; but how could this be done more effectually than by rendering the profession of its articles a preliminary step to every kind of civil pre-eminence? Yet this abuse, which in his own estimation is so enormous as to form the great basis of separation, he wishes to perpetuate; and, all things considered, hopes "that which is at rest will not be disturbed." In another part of his discourse,† he asks what temporalities has the church of Christ to expect? It is the mother of harlots which says, "I sit a queen, and shall see no sorrow." Would any one imagine this was the language of a man who, in pleading for a Test Act, has rested the support of his creed on those very temporalities he affects so much to disdain, and has committed his religion to the arms of that mother of harlots to be reared and nourished! When speaking of the Test Act in the seventh page of his discourse, he thus expresses himself: "Surely the cross of Christ ought not to be insulted by persons eager to press into the temple of Mammon." Who could treat it with more poignant severity than is couched in this declaration? yet this is the language of a person who desires its continuance. In truth, his representations on this subject are pregnant with such contradictions, and rise above each other in so singular a gradation of absurdity, as will not be easily conceived, and perhaps hath scarce ever been equalled. At the very outset of his sermon he declares, "Whenever the gospel is secularized it is debased and misrepresented, and in proportion to the quantity of foreign infusions is the efficacy of this saving health diminished." But human ingenuity would be at a loss to contrive a method of secularizing the gospel more completely than by rendering it the common passport of all who aspire to civil distinctions. I am really weary of exposing the wild and extravagant incoherence of such a reasoner. From a man who, professing to be the apologist of his party, betrays its interests, and exhibits its most illustrious members to reproach; who, himself a dissenter, applauds the penalties which the hierarchy has inflicted a "*prudent restraint;*" who with the utmost poignance censures a law which he solemnly invokes the legislature to perpetuate; and proposes to secure the truths of religion by the "profanation of its sacraments,"‡ by "debasing the gospel," and "insulting the cross;" any thing may be expected but consistence and decency. When such an author assures us he was not impelled by vanity to publish,§ we may easily give him credit; but he should remember, though it may be a virtue to subdue vanity, it is base to extinguish shame. The tear which he tells us started from the eyes of his audience, we will

* Page 35. † Page 26. ‡ Page 8. § Page 6.

hope, for their honour, was an effusion of regret natural to his friends on hearing him deliver sentiments which they considered as a disgrace to himself, and a calumny on his brethren. His affecting to pour contempt upon Dr. Price, whose talents and character were revered by all parties, and to hold him up as the *corrupter* of the dissenters, will not fail to awaken the indignation of every generous mind. Whether *they* were greater friends to their country whose pride and oppression scattered the flames of discord across the Atlantic, poured desolation into the colonies, dismembered the empire, and involved us in millions of debt, or the man who with a warning voice endeavoured to avert those calamities, posterity will decide.

He gives us a pompous enumeration* of the piety, learning, and talents of a large body of his brethren who concur with him in a disapprobation of the theological and political tenets of the Unitarians. The weakness of mingling them together has been shown already; but if these great and eminent men, whom the world never heard of before, possess that zeal for their religion they pretend, let them meet their opponents on the open field of controversy, where they may display their talents and prowess to somewhat more advantage than in *skulking* behind a *consecrated altar.*

There are many particulars in the address and sermon of an extraordinary complexion which I have not noticed at all, as it was not my intention to follow the author step by step, but rather to collect his scattered representations into some leading points of view. For the same reason I make no remarks on his barbarous imagery or his style, everywhere incoherent and incorrect, sometimes indecent, which cannot fail of disgusting every reader of taste. In a rude daubing peculiar to himself, where in ridicule of Dr. Priestley he has grouped together a *foreigner*, a *ship*, and *cargo* of *drugs*, he has unfortunately sketched his own likeness, except in the circumstance of the *ship*, with tolerable accuracy; for, without the apology of having been *shipped* into England, he is certainly a *foreigner* in his native tongue, and his publication will be allowed to be a *drug.*

Had he known to apply the remark with which his address commences, on the utility of accommodating instruction to the exigence of times, he would have been aware that this is not a season for drawing off the eyes of mankind from political objects. They were in fact never turned towards them with equal ardour, and we may venture to affirm they will long continue to take that direction. An attention to the political aspect of the world is not now the fruit of an idle curiosity, or the amusement of a dissipated and frivolous mind, but is awakened and kept alive by occurrences as various as they are extraordinary. There are times when the moral world seems to stand still; there are others when it seems impelled towards its goal with an accelerated force. The present is a period more interesting perhaps than any which has been known in the whole flight of time. The scenes of Providence thicken upon us so fast, and are shifted with so strange a rapidity, as if the great drama of the world were drawing to a

* Page 6.

close.* Events have taken place of late, and revolutions have been effected, which, had they been foretold a very few years ago, would have been viewed as visionary and extravagant; and their influence is yet far from being spent. Europe never presented such a spectacle before, and it is worthy of being contemplated with the profoundest attention by all its inhabitants. The empire of darkness and of despotism has been smitten with a stroke which has sounded through the universe. When we see whole kingdoms, after reposing for centuries on the lap of their rulers, start from their slumber, the dignity of man rising up from depression, and tyrants trembling on their thrones, who can remain entirely indifferent, or fail to turn his eye towards a theatre so august and extraordinary! These are a kind of throes and struggles of nature to which it would be a sullenness to refuse our sympathy. Old foundations are breaking up; new edifices are rearing. Institutions which have been long held in veneration as the most sublime refinements of human wisdom and policy, which age hath cemented and confirmed, which power hath supported, which eloquence hath conspired to embellish and opulence to enrich, are falling fast into decay. New prospects are opening on every side, of such amazing variety and extent as to stretch farther than the eye of the most enlightened observer can reach.

Some beneficial effects appear to have taken place already, sufficient to nourish our most sanguine hope of benefits much more extensive. The mischief and folly of wars begin to be understood, and that mild and liberal system of policy adopted which has ever indeed been the object of prayer to the humane and the devout, but has hitherto remained utterly unknown in the cabinets of princes. As the mind naturally yields to the impression of objects which it contemplates often, we need not wonder if, amid events so extraordinary, the human character itself should appear to be altering and improving apace. That fond attachment to ancient institutions, and blind submission to opinions already received, which has ever checked the growth of improvement, and drawn on the greatest benefactors of mankind danger or neglect, is giving way to a spirit of bold and fearless investigation. Man seems to be becoming more erect and independent. He leans more on himself, less on his fellow-creatures. He begins to feel a consciousness in a higher degree of personal dignity, and is less enamoured of artificial distinctions. There is some hope of our beholding that simplicity and energy of character which marks his natural state, blended with the humanity, the elegance, and improvement of polished society.

The events which have already taken place, and the further changes they forbode, will open to the contemplative of every character innumerable sources of reflection. To the philosopher they present many new and extraordinary facts, where his penetration will find ample scope in attempting to discover their cause, and to predict their effects.

* This glowing picture, as accurately descriptive of recent events as of those it was intended to portray, might tempt us almost to fancy that, after the revolution of a cycle of forty years, time had brought us back to the same state of things.—Ed.

He will have an opportunity of viewing mankind in an interesting situation, and of tracing the progress of opinion through channels it has rarely flowed in before. The politician will feel his attention powerfully awakened, on seeing new maxims of policy introduced, new institutions established, and such a total alteration in the ideas of a great part of the world, as will oblige him to study the art of government, as it were, afresh. The devout mind will behold in these momentous changes the finger of God, and discerning in them the dawn of that glorious period in which wars will cease and antichristian tyranny shall fall, will adore that unerring wisdom whose secret operation never fails to conduct all human affairs to their proper issue, and impels the great actors on that troubled theatre to fulfil, when they least intend it, the counsels of Heaven, and the predictions of its prophets.

AN APOLOGY

FOR THE

FREEDOM OF THE PRESS,

AND FOR

GENERAL LIBERTY:

TO WHICH ARE PREFIXED,

REMARKS ON BISHOP HORSLEY'S SERMON,

Preached on the 30th January, 1793.

[PUBLISHED IN 1793.]

ADVERTISEMENT TO THE THIRD EDITION.

Since this pamphlet was first published, the principles it aims to support have received confirmation from such a train of disastrous events, that it might have been hoped we should have learned those lessons from misfortunes which reason had failed to impress. Uninstructed by our calamities, we still persist in an impious attack on the liberties of France, and are eager to take our part in the great drama of crimes which is acting on the continent of Europe. Meantime the violence and injustice of the internal administration keeps pace with our iniquities abroad. Liberty and truth are silenced. An unrelenting system of prosecution prevails. The cruel and humiliating sentence passed upon Mr. Muir and Mr. Palmer, men of unblemished morals and of the purest patriotism, the outrages committed on Dr. Priestley, and his intended removal to America, are events which will mark the latter end of the eighteenth century with indelible reproach. But what has liberty to expect from a minister who has the audacity to assert the king's right to land as many foreign troops as he pleases without the previous consent of parliament? If this doctrine be true, the boasted equilibrium of the constitution, all the barriers which the wisdom of our ancestors have opposed to the encroachments of arbitrary power, are idle, ineffectual precautions. For we have only to suppose for a moment an inclination in the royal breast to overturn our liberties, and of what avail is the nicest internal arrangement against a foreign force? Our constitution, on this principle, is the absurdest system that was ever conceived; pretending liberty for its object, yet providing no security against the great antagonist and destroyer of liberty,—the employment of military power by the chief magistrate. Let a foreign army be introduced into this or any other country, and quartered upon the subject without his consent, and what is there wanting, if such were the design of the prince, to complete the subjection of that country? Will armed foreigners be overawed by written laws or unwritten customs, by the legal limitations of power, the paper lines of demarkation? But Mr. Pitt contends, that though the sovereign may land foreign troops at his pleasure, he cannot subsist them without the aid of parliament. He may overrun his dominions with a mercenary army, it seems, but after he has subdued his subjects, he is compelled to have recourse to them for supplies. What a happy contrivance! Unfortunately, however, it is found that princes with the unlimited command of armies, have hit upon a nearer and more efficacious method of raising supplies than by an act of parliament. But it is needless any further to expose the effrontery, or detect the sophistry of this shameless apostate. The character of Pitt is written in sunbeams. A veteran in frauds while in the bloom of youth, betraying first, and then persecuting his earliest friends and connexions, falsifying every promise, and violating every political engagement, ever making the fairest professions a prelude to the darkest actions, punishing with the utmost rigour the publisher of the identical paper he himself had circulated,* are traits in the conduct of Pitt which entitle him to a fatal pre-eminence in guilt. The qualities of this man balance in an extraordinary manner, and sustain each other: the influence of his station, the extent of his enormities, invest him with a kind of splendour, and the contempt we feel for his meanness and duplicity is lost in the dread of his machinations, and the abhorrence of his crimes. Too long has he insulted the patience of his countrymen; nor ought we, when we observe the indifference with which the iniquities of Pitt's administration are viewed, to reproach the Romans for tamely submitting to the tyranny of Caligula or Domitian.

We had fondly hoped a mild philosophy was about to diffuse over the globe the triumph of liberty and peace. But alas! these hopes are fled. The continent presents little but one wide picture of desolation, misery, and crimes: *on the earth distress of nations and perplexity, men's hearts failing them for fear, and for looking after those things which are coming on the earth.*

That the seeds of public convulsions are sown in every country of Europe (our own not excepted) it were vain to deny, seeds which, without the wisest precautions and the most conciliating councils, will break out, it is to be feared, in the overthrow of all governments. How this catastrophe may be averted, or how, should that be impossible, its evils may be mitigated and diminished, demands the deepest consideration of every European statesman. The ordinary routine of ministerial chicanery is quite unequal to the task. A philosophic comprehension of mind, which, leaving the beaten road of politics, shall adapt itself to new situations and profit by the vicissitudes of opinion, equally removed from an attachment to antiquated forms and useless innovations, capable of rising above the emergency of the moment to the most remote consequences of a transaction; combining the past, the present, and the future, and knowing how to defend with firmness, or concede with dignity; these are the qualities which the situation of Europe renders indispensable. It would be a mockery of our present ministry to ask whether *they* possess those qualities.

With respect to the following Apology for the Freedom of the Press, the author begs leave to claim the reader's indulgence to its numerous imperfections, and hopes he will recollect, as an excuse for the warmth of his expressions, it is an eulogium on a *dead friend.*

*Mr. Holt, a printer, at Newark, is now imprisoned in Newgate for two years, for reprinting verbatim, An Address to the People on Reform, which was sanctioned for certain, and probably written, by the Duke of Richmond and Mr. Pitt.

ORIGINAL PREFACE.

The accidental detention of the following pamphlet in the press longer than was expected gave me an opportunity before it was published of seeing Bishop Horsley's Sermon, preached before the House of Lords, on the 30th of January; and as its contents are relevant to my subject, a few remarks upon it may not be improper. His lordship sets out with a severe censure of that "*freedom of dispute*" on matters of "*such high importance as the origin of government, and the authority of sovereigns*," in which he laments it has been the "*folly of this country for several years past*" to indulge. If his lordship has not inquired into those subjects himself, he can with little propriety pretend to decide in so imperious and peremptory a manner; unless it be a privilege of his office to dogmatize without examination, or he has discovered some nearer road to truth than that of reasoning and argument. It seems a favourite point with a certain description of men to stop the progress of inquiry, and throw mankind back into the darkness of the middle ages, from a persuasion that ignorance will augment their power, as objects look largest in a mist. There is in reality no other foundation for that alarm which the bishop expresses. Whatever is not comprehended under revelation falls under the inspection of reason; and since from the whole course of Providence, it is evident that all political events and all the revolutions of government are effected by the instrumentality of men, there is no room for supposing them too sacred to be submitted to the human faculties. The more minds there are employed in tracing their principles and effects, the greater probability will there be of the science of civil policy, as well as every other, attaining to perfection.

Bishop Horsley, determined to preserve the character of an original, presents us with a new set of political principles, and endeavours to place the exploded doctrine of passive obedience and non-resistance upon a new foundation. By a curious distinction between the *ground* of authority and of obedience, he rests the former on human compact. the latter on divine obligation. "*It is easy to understand*," he says, "*that the principle of the private citizen's submission must be quite a distinct thing from the principle of the sovereign's public title. And for this plain reason: The principle of submission to bind the conscience of every individual must be something universally known.*" He then proceeds to inform us, that the kingly title in England is founded on the act of settlement; but that as thousands and tens of thousands of the people have never heard of that act, the principle which compels their allegiance must be something distinct from it, with which they may all be acquainted. In this reasoning, he evidently confounds the obligation of an *individual* to submit to the existing authority with that of the community collectively considered. For *any particular number* of persons to set themselves by force to oppose the established practice of a state is a plain violation of the laws of morality, as it would be productive of the utmost disorder; and no government could stand were it permitted to individuals to counteract the general will, of which, in ordinary cases, legal usages are the interpreter. In the worst state of political society, if a people have not sufficient wisdom or courage to correct its evils and assert their liberty, the attempt of individuals to *force* improvements upon them is a presumption which merits the severest punishment. Social order would be inevitably dissolved, if every man declined a practical acquiescence in that political regulation which he did not personally approve. The duty of submission is, in this light, founded on principles which hold under every government, and are plain and obvious. But the principle which attaches a people to their allegiance, collectively considered, must exactly coincide with the title to authority; as must be evident from the very meaning of the term authority, which, as distinguished from force, signifies a right to demand obedience. Authority and obedience are correlative terms, and consequently in all respects correspond, and are commensurate with each other.

"*The divine right*," his lordship says, "*of the first magistrate in every polity to the citizen's obedience is not of that sort which it were high-treason to claim for the sovereign of this country. It is a right which in no country can be denied, without the highest of all treasons. The denial of it were treason against the paramount authority of God.*" To invest any human power with these high epithets is ridiculous at least, if not impious. The right of a prince to the obedience of his subjects, wherever it exists, may be called divine, because we know the Divine Being is the patron of justice and order; but in that sense, the authority of a petty constable is equally divine; nor can the term be applied with any greater propriety to supreme than to subordinate magistrates. As to "*submission being among the general rules which proceed from the will of God, and have been impressed upon the conscience of every man by the original constitution of the world*," nothing more is comprehended under this pomp of words than that submission is, for the most part, a duty—a sublime and interesting discovery! The minds of princes are seldom of the firmest texture; and they who fill their heads with the magnificent chimera of divine right prepare a victim, where they intend a god. Some species of government is essential to the well-being of mankind; submission to some species of government is consequently a duty; but what kind of government shall be appointed, and to what limits submission shall extend, are mere human questions, to be adjusted by mere human reason and contrivance.

As the natural consequence of divine right, his lordship proceeds to inculcate the doctrine of passive obedience and non-resistance, in the most unqualified terms; assuming it as a principle to be acted upon under governments the most oppressive, in which he endeavours to shelter himself under the authority of Paul. The apostolic exhortation, as addressed to a few individuals, and adapted to the local circumstances of Christians at that period, admits an easy solution; but to imagine it prescribes the duty of the Roman Empire, and is intended to subject millions to the capricious tyranny of one man, is a reflection as well on the character of Paul as on Christianity itself.

On principles of reason, the only way to determine the agreement of any thing with the will of God is to consider its influence on the happiness of society; so that in this view, the question of passive obedience is reduced to a simple issue: Is it best for the human race that every tyrant and usurper be submitted to without check or control? It ought likewise to be remembered, that if the doctrine of passive obedience be true, princes should be taught it, and instructed, that to whatever excesses of cruelty and caprice they proceed, they may expect no resistance on the part of the people. If this maxim appear to be conducive to general good, we may fairly presume it concurs with the will of the Deity; but if it appear pregnant with the most mischievous consequences, it must disclaim such support. From the known perfection of God, we conclude he wills the happiness of mankind; and that though he condescends not to interpose miraculously, that kind of civil polity is most pleasing in his eye which is productive of the greatest felicity.

On a comparison of free with arbitrary governments, we perceive the former are distinguished from the latter by imparting a much greater share of happiness to those who live under them; and this in a manner too uniform to be imputed to chance or secret causes. He who wills the end must will the means which ascertain it. His lordship endeavours to diminish the dread of despotic government, by observing, that in its worst state it is attended with more good than ill, and that the "*end of government under all its abuses is generally answered by it.*" Admitting this to be true, it is at best but a consolation proper to be applied where there is no remedy, and affords no reason why we should not mitigate political as well as other evils, when it lies in our power. We endeavour to correct the diseases of the eye, or of any other organ, though the malady be not such as renders it useless.

The doctrine of passive obedience is so repugnant to the genuine feelings of human nature, that it can never be completely acted on; a secret dread that popular vengeance will awake, and nature assert her rights, imposes a restraint which the most determined despotism is not able to shake off. The rude reason of the multitude may be perplexed, but the sentiments of the heart are not easily perverted.

In adjusting the different parts of his theory, the learned bishop appears a good deal embarrassed. "*It will be readily admitted,*" he says (p. 9), "*that of all sovereigns, none reign by so fair and just a title as those who derive their claim from some such public act* (*as the act of settlement*) *of the nation which they govern.*" That there are different degrees in *justice*, and even in *divine right* (which his lordship declares all sovereigns possess), is a very singular idea. Common minds would be ready to imagine, however various the modes of *injustice* may be, *justice* were a thing absolute and invariable, nor would they conceive how "*a divine right, a right the denial of which is high-treason against the authority of God*," can be increased by the act of a nation. But this is not all. It is no just inference (he tells us) that the obligation upon the private citizen to submit himself to the authority thus raised arises wholly from the act of the people conferring it, or from their compact with the person on whom it is conferred. But if the sovereign derives his claim from this act of the nation, how comes it that the obligation of the people to submit to his claim does not spring from the same act? Because "*in all these cases*," he affirms, "*the act of the people is only the means which Providence employs to advance the new sovereign to his station.*" In the hand of the Supreme Being, the whole agency of men may be considered as an *instrument;* but to make it appear that the right of dominion is independent of the people, men must be shown to be instruments in political affairs in a more absolute sense than ordinary. A divine interposition of a more immediate kind must be shown, or the mere consideration of God's being the original source of all power will be a weak reason for absolute submission. Anarchy may have *power* as well as despotism, and is equally a link in the great chain of causes and effects.

It is not a little extraordinary that Bishop Horsley, the apologist of tyranny, the patron of passive obedience, should affect to admire the British constitution, whose freedom was attained by a palpable violation of the principles for which he contends. He will not say the barons at Runnemede acted on his maxims in extorting the Magna Charta from King John, or in demanding its confirmation from Henry the Third. If he approves of their conduct he gives up his cause, and is compelled at least to confess the principles of passive obedience were not true at that time; if he disapproves of their conduct, he must, to be consistent, reprobate the restraints which it imposed on kingly power. The limitations of monarchy, which his lordship pretends to applaud, were effected by resistance; the freedom of the British constitution flowed from a departure from passive obedience, and was therefore stained with high-treason "*against the authority of God.*" To these conclusions he must inevitably come, unless he can point out something peculiar to the spot of Runnemede or to the reign of King John, which confines the exception to the general doctrine of submission to that particular time and place. With whatever colours the advocates of passive obedience may varnish their theories, they must of necessity be enemies to the British constitution. Its spirit they detest; its corruptions they cherish; and if at present they affect a zeal for its preservation, it is only because they despair of any form of government being erected in its stead which will give equal permanence to abuses. Afraid to destroy it at once, they take a malignant pleasure in seeing it waste by degrees under the pressure of internal malady.

Whatever bears the semblance of *reasoning* in Bishop Horsley's discourse will be found, I trust, to have received a satisfactory answer; but to animadvert with a becoming severity on the temper it displays is a less easy task. To render him the justice he deserves in that respect would demand all the fierceness of his character.

We owe him an acknowledgment for the frankness with which he avows his decided preference of the clergy of France to dissenters in England,—a sentiment we have often suspected, but have seldom had the satisfaction of seeing openly professed before.

"*None*," he asserts, "*at this season, are more entitled to our offices of love than those with whom the difference is wide in points of doctrine, discipline, and external rites; those venerable exiles, the prelates and clergy of the fallen church of France.* Far be it from me to intercept the compassion of the humane from the unhappy of any nation, tongue, or people; but the extreme tenderness he professes for the fallen church of France is well contrasted by his malignity towards dissenters. Bishop Horsley is a man of sense: and though doctrine, discipline, and external rites comprehend the whole of Christianity, his tender, sympathetic heart is superior to prejudice, and never fails to recognise in a persecutor a friend and a brother. Admirable consistency in a Protestant bishop, to lament over the fall of that antichrist whose overthrow is represented by unerring inspiration as an event the most splendid and happy! It is a shrewd presumption against the utility of religious establishments that they too often become seats of intolerance, instigators to persecution, nurseries of Bonners and of Horsleys.

His lordship closes his invective against dissenters, and Dr. Priestley in particular, by presenting a prayer in the spirit of an indictment. We are happy to hear of his lordship's prayers, and are obliged to him for remembering us in them; but should be more sanguine in our expectation of benefit if we were not informed the prayers of the *righteous* only avail much. "*Miserable men*," he tells us, we "*are in the gall of bitterness, and in the bond of iniquity.*" With respect to the first, we must have plenty of that article, since he has distilled his own; and if the bonds of iniquity are not added, it is only because they are not within the reach of his mighty malice.

It is time to turn from this disgusting picture of sanctimonious hypocrisy and priestly insolence to address a word to the reader on the following pamphlet. The political sentiments of Dr. Horsley are in truth of too little consequence in themselves to engage a moment's curiosity, and deserve attention only as they indicate the spirit of the times. The freedom with which I have pointed out the abuses of government will be little relished by the pusillanimous and the interested, but is, I am certain, of that nature which it is the duty of the people of England never to relinquish, or suffer to be impaired by any human force or contrivance. In the present crisis of things, the danger to liberty is extreme, and it is requisite to address a warning voice to the nation, that may disturb its slumbers, if it cannot heal its lethargy. When we look at the distraction and misery of a neighbouring country, we behold a scene that is enough to make the most hardy republican tremble at the idea of a revolution. Nothing but an obstinate adherence to abuses can ever push the people of England to that fatal extremity. But if the state of things continues to grow worse and worse, if the friends of reform, the true friends of their country, continue to be overwhelmed by calumny and persecution, the confusion will probably be dreadful, the misery extreme, and the calamities that await us too great for human calculation.

What must be the guilt of those men who can calmly contemplate the approach of anarchy or despotism, and rather choose to behold the ruin of their country than resign the smallest pittance of private emolument and advantage? To reconcile the disaffected, to remove discontents, to allay animosities, and open a prospect of increasing happiness and freedom, is yet in our power. But if a contrary course be taken, the sun of Great Britain is set for ever, her glory departed, and her history added to the catalogue of the mighty empires which exhibit the instability of all human grandeur, of empires which, after they rose by virtue to be the admiration of the world, sunk by corruption into obscurity and contempt. If any thing shall then remain of her boasted constitution, it will display magnificence in disorder, majestic desolation, Babylon in ruins, where, in the midst of broken arches and fallen columns, posterity will trace the *monuments* only of our ancient freedom!

ADVERTISEMENT TO THE NEW EDITION

As the following pamphlet has been long out of print, the reader will naturally expect some reason should be assigned for its republication. I might satisfy myself with safely affirming that I have no alternative left but either to publish it myself, or to permit it to be done by others, since the copyright has long since transpired; and I have been under the necessity of claiming as a favour what I could not insist upon as a right.

In addition to this, a most erroneous inference has been drawn from my suffering it to fall into neglect. It has been often insinuated that my political principles have undergone a revolution, and that I have renounced the opinions which it was the object of this pamphlet to establish. I must beg leave, however, to assert, that fashionable as such changes have been, and sanctioned by many conspicuous examples, I am not ambitious of the honour attached to this species of conversion, from a conviction that he who has once been the advocate of freedom and of reform, will find it much easier to change his conduct than his principles—to worship the golden image than to believe in the divinity of the idol. A reluctance to appear as a political writer, an opinion, whether well or ill founded, that the Christian ministry is in danger of losing something of its energy and sanctity by embarking on the stormy element of political debate, were the motives that determined me, and which, had I not already engaged, would probably have effectually deterred me from writing upon politics These scruples have given way to feelings still stronger, to my extreme aversion to be classed with political apostates, and to the suspicion of being deterred from the honest avowal of my sentiments on subjects of great moment by hopes and fears to which, through every period of my life, I have been a total stranger. The effect of increasing years has been to augment, if possible, my attachment to the principles of civil and religious liberty, and to the cause of reform as inseparably combined with their preservation; and few things would give me more uneasiness than to have it supposed I could ever become hostile or indifferent to these objects.

The alterations in the present edition are nearly all of minor importance; they chiefly consist of slight literary corrections, which very rarely affect the sense. It was not my wish or intention to impair the *identity* of the performance. There is in several parts an acrimony and vehemence in the language, which the candid reader will put to the account of juvenile ardour, and which, should it be deemed excessive, he will perceive could not be corrected without producing a new composition. One passage in the preface, delineating the character of the late Bishop Horsley, is omitted. On mature reflection, it appeared to the writer not quite consistent either with the spirit of Christianity or with the reverence due to departed genius. For the severity with which he has treated the political character of Mr. Pitt he is not disposed to apologize, because he feels the fullest conviction that the policy, foreign and domestic, of that celebrated statesman, has inflicted a more incurable wound on the constitution, and entailed more permanent and irreparable calamities on the nation, than that of any other minister in the annals of British history. A simple reflection will be sufficient to evince the unparalleled magnitude of his apostacy, which is, that the memory of the *son* of Lord Chatham, the vehement opposer of the American war, the champion of reform, and the idol of the people, has become the rallying point of toryism, the type and symbol of whatever is most illiberal in principle and intolerant in practice.

1821

AN APOLOGY.

SECTION I.

On the Right of Public Discussion.

SOLON, the celebrated legislator of Athens, we are told, enacted a law for the capital punishment of every citizen who should continue neuter when parties ran high in that republic. He considered, it should seem, the declining to take a decided part on great and critical occasions an indication of such a culpable indifference to the interests of the commonwealth as could be expiated only by death. While we blame the rigour of this law, we must confess the principle on which it was founded is just and solid. In a political contest relating to particular men or measures, a well-wisher to his country may be permitted to remain silent; but when the great interests of a nation are at stake, it becomes every man to act with firmness and vigour. I consider the present as a season of this nature, and shall therefore make no apology for laying before the public the reflections it has suggested.

The most capital advantage an enlightened people can enjoy is the liberty of discussing every subject which can fall within the compass of the human mind: while this remains, freedom will flourish; but should it be lost or impaired, its principles will neither be well understood nor long retained. To render the magistrate a judge of truth, and engage his authority in the suppression of opinions, shows an inattention to the nature and design of political society. When a nation forms a government, it is not wisdom but *power* which they place in the hand of the magistrate; from whence it follows, his concern is only with those objects which *power* can operate upon. On this account the administration of justice, the protection of property, and the defence of every member of the community from violence and outrage fall naturally within the province of the civil ruler, for these may all be accomplished by *power;* but an attempt to distinguish truth from error, and to countenance one set of opinions to the prejudice of another, is to apply power in a manner mischievous and absurd. To comprehend the reasons on which the right of public discussion is founded, it is requisite to remark the difference between *sentiment* and *conduct.* The *behaviour* of men in society will be influenced by motives drawn from the prospect of good and evil: here then is the proper department of government, as it is capable of applying that good and evil by which actions are determined. Truth, on the contrary, is quite of a different nature, being supported only by *evidence*, and as when this is represented we cannot withhold our assent, so where this is wanting no power or authority can command it.

However some may affect to dread controversy, it can never be of ultimate disadvantage to the interests of truth or the happiness of mankind. Where it is indulged in its full extent, a multitude of ridiculous opinions will no doubt be obtruded upon the public; but any ill influence they may produce cannot continue long, as they are sure to be opposed with at least equal ability and that superior advantage which is ever attendant on truth. The colours with which wit or eloquence may have adorned a false system will gradually die away, sophistry be detected, and every thing estimated at length according to its true value. Publications, besides, like every thing else that is human, are of a mixed nature, where truth is often blended with falsehood, and important hints suggested in the midst of much impertinent or pernicious matter; nor is there any way of separating the precious from the vile but by tolerating the whole. Where the right of unlimited inquiry is exerted, the human faculties will be upon the advance; where it is relinquished, they will be of necessity at a stand, and will probably decline.

If we have recourse to experience, that kind of enlarged experience in particular which history furnishes, we shall not be apt to entertain any violent alarm at the greatest liberty of discussion: we shall there see that to this we are indebted for those improvements in arts and sciences which have meliorated in so great a degree the condition of mankind. The middle ages, as they are called, the darkest period of which we have any particular accounts, were remarkable for two things,—the extreme ignorance that prevailed, and an excessive veneration for received opinions; circumstances which, having been always united, operate on each other, it is plain, as cause and effect. The whole compass of science was in those times subject to restraint; every new opinion was looked upon as dangerous. To affirm the globe we inhabit to be round was deemed heresy, and for asserting its motion the immortal Galileo was confined in the prisons of the inquisition. Yet it is remarkable, so little are the human faculties fitted for restraint, that its utmost rigour was never able to effect a thorough unanimity, or to preclude the most alarming discussions and contro versies. For no sooner was one point settled than another was started; and as the articles on which men professed to differ were always extremely few and subtle, they came the more easily into contact, and their animosities were the more violent and concentrated. The shape of the tonsure, or manner in which a monk should shave his head, would then throw a whole kingdom into convulsions. In proportion as the world has become more enlightened, this unnatural policy of restraint has retired, the sciences it has entirely abandoned, and has taken its last stand on religion and politics. The first of these was long con idered of a nature so peculiarly sacred, that every attempt to alter it, or to impair the reverence for its received institutions, was regarded under the name of heresy as a crime of the first magnitude. Yet dangerous as free inquiry may have been looked upon when extended to the principles of religion, there is no department where it was more necessary, or its interference more decidedly beneficial. By nobly daring to exert it when all the powers on earth were combined in its suppression, did Luther accomplish that reformation which drew forth primitive Christianity, long hidden and concealed under a load of abuses, to the view of an awakened and astonished world. So great is the force of truth when it has once gained the attention, that all the arts and policy of the court of Rome, aided throughout every part of Europe by a veneration for antiquity, the prejudices of the vulgar, and the cruelty of despots, were fairly baffled and confounded by the opposition of a solitary monk. And had this principle of free inquiry been permitted in succeeding times to have full scope, Christianity would at this period have been much better understood, and the animosity of sects considerably abated. Religious toleration has never been complete even in England; but having prevailed more here than perhaps in any other country, there is no place where the doctrines of religion have been set in so clear a light or its truth so ably defended. The writings of Deists have contributed much to this end. Whoever will compare the late defences of Christianity by Locke, Butler, or Clark with those of the ancient apologists, will discern in the former far more precision and an abler method of reasoning than in the latter; which must be attributed chiefly to the superior spirit of inquiry by which modern times are distinguished. Whatever alarm then may have been taken at the liberty of discussion, religion it is plain hath been a gainer by it; its abuses corrected, and its divine authority settled on a firmer basis than ever.

Though I have taken the liberty of making these preliminary remarks on the influence of free inquiry in general, what I have more immediately in view is to defend its exercise in relation to government. This being an institution purely human, one would imagine it were the proper province for freedom of discussion in its utmost extent. It is surely just that every one should have a right to examine those measures by which the happiness of all may be affected. The control of the public mind over the conduct of ministers, exerted through the medium of the press, has been regarded by the best writers both in our country and on the continent as the main support of our liberties. While this remains we cannot be enslaved; when it is impaired or diminished we shall soon cease to be free.

Under pretence of its being seditious to express any disapprobation of the *form* of our government, the most alarming attempts are made to wrest the liberty of the press out of our hands. It is far from being my intention to set up a defence of republican principles, as I am persuaded whatever imperfections may attend the British constitution, it is competent to all the ends of government, and the best adapted of any to the *actual* situation of this kingdom. Yet I am convinced there is no crime in being a republican, and that while he obeys the laws every man has a right to entertain what sentiments he pleases on our form of government, and to discuss this with the same freedom as any other topic. In proof of this I shall beg the reader's attention to the following arguments.

1. We may apply to this point in particular the observation that has been made on the influence of free inquiry in general, that it will issue in the firmer establishment of truth and the overthrow of error. Every thing that is really excellent will bear examination, it will even invite it; and the more narrowly it is surveyed, to the more advantage it will appear. Is our constitution a good one? it will gain in our esteem by the severest inquiry. Is it bad? then its imperfections should be laid open and exposed. Is it, as is generally confessed, of a mixed nature, excellent in theory, but defective in its practice? freedom of discussion will be still requisite to point out the nature and source of its corruptions, and apply suitable remedies. If our constitution be that perfect model of excellence it is represented, it may boldly appeal to the *reason* of an enlightened age, and need not rest on the support of an implicit faith.

2. Government is the creature of the people, and that which they have created they surely have a right to examine. The great Author of nature, having placed the right of dominion in no particular hands, hath left every point relating to it to be settled by the consent and approbation of mankind. In spite of the attempts of sophistry to conceal the origin of political right, it must inevitably rest at length on the acquiescence of the people. In the case of individuals it is extremely plain. If one man should overwhelm another with superior force, and after completely subduing him under the name of government, transmit him in this condition to his heirs, every one would exclaim against such an act of injustice. But whether the object of his oppression be one or a million can make no difference in its nature, the idea of equity having no relation to that of numbers. Mr. Burke, with some other authors, are aware that an original right of dominion can only be explained by resolving it into the will of the people, yet contend that it becomes inalienable and independent by length of time and prescription. This fatal mistake appears to me to have arisen from confounding the right of dominion with that of private property. Possession for a certain time, it is true, vests in the latter a complete right, or there would be no end to vexatious claims; not to mention that it is of no consequence to society where property lies, provided its regulations be clear and its possession undisturbed. For the same reason it is of the essence of private property to be held for the sole use of the owner, with liberty to employ it in what way he pleases consistent with the safety of the community. But the right of dominion has none of the qualities that distinguish private possession. It is never indifferent to the community in whose hands it is lodged, nor is it intended in any degree for the benefit of those who conduct it. Being derived from the will of the people, explicit or implied, and existing solely for their use, it can no more become independent of that will than water can rise above its source. But if we allow the people are the true origin of political power, it is absurd to require them to resign the right of discussing

any question that can arise either upon its form or its measures. as this would put it for ever out of their power to revoke the trust which they have placed in the hands of their rulers.

3. If it be a crime for a subject of Great Britain to express his disapprobation of that form of government under which he lives, the same conduct must be condemned in the inhabitant of any other country. Perhaps it will be said a distinction ought to be made on account of the superior excellence of the British constitution. This superiority I am not disposed to contest, yet cannot allow it to be a proper reply, as it takes for granted that which is supposed to be a matter of debate and inquiry. Let a government be ever so despotic, it is a chance if those who share in the administration are not loud in proclaiming its excellence. Go into Turkey, and the pachas of the provinces will probably tell you that the Turkish government is the most perfect in the world. If the excellence of a constitution, then, is assigned as the reason that none should be permitted to censure it, who, I ask, is to determine on this its excellence? If you reply, every man's own reason will determine, you concede the very point I am endeavouring to establish, the liberty of free inquiry: if you reply, our rulers, you admit a principle that equally applies to every government in the world, and will lend no more support to the British constitution than to that of Turkey or Algiers.

4. An inquiry respecting the comparative excellence of civil constitutions can be forbidden on no other pretence than that of its tending to sedition and anarchy. This plea, however, will have little weight with those who reflect to how many ill purposes it has been already applied; and that when the example has been once introduced of suppressing opinions on account of their imagined ill tendency, it has seldom been confined within any safe or reasonable bounds. The doctrine of tendencies is extremely subtle and complicated. Whatever would diminish our veneration for the Christian religion, or shake our belief in the being of a God, will be allowed to be of a very evil tendency; yet few, I imagine, who are acquainted with history, would wish to see the writings of skeptics or Deists suppressed by law; being persuaded it would be lodging a very dangerous power in the hands of the magistrate, and that truth is best supported by its own evidence. This dread of certain opinions on account of their tendency has been the copious spring of all those religious wars and persecutions which are the disgrace and calamity of modern times.

Whatever danger may result from the freedom of political debate in some countries, no apprehension from that quarter need be entertained in our own. Free inquiry will never endanger the existence of a good government; scarcely will it be able to work the overthrow of a bad one. So uncertain is the issue of all revolutions, so turbulent and bloody the scenes that too often usher them in, the prejudice on the side of an ancient establishment so great, and the interests involved in its support so powerful, that while it provides in any tolerable measure for the happiness of the people, it may defy all the efforts of its enemies.

The real danger to every free government is less from its enemies than from itself. Should it resist the most temperate reforms, and maintain its abuses with obstinacy, imputing complaint to faction, calumniating its friends, and smiling only on its flatterers; should it encourage informers and hold out rewards to treachery, turning every man into a spy, and every neighbourhood into the seat of an inquisition, let it not hope it can long conceal its tyranny under the mask of freedom. These are the avenues through which despotism must enter; these are the arts at which integrity sickens, and freedom turns pale.

SECTION II.

On Associations.

THE associations that have been formed in various parts of the kingdom appear to me to have trodden very nearly in the steps I have been describing. Nothing could have justified this extraordinary mode of combination but the actual existence of those insurrections and plots, of which no traces have appeared, except in a speech from the throne. They merit a patent for insurrections who have discovered the art of conducting them with so much silence and secrecy, that in the very places where they are affirmed to have happened they have been heard of only by rebound from the cabinet. Happy had it been for the repose of unoffending multitudes if the associators had been able to put their mobs in possession of this important discovery before they set them in motion.

No sooner had the ministry spread an alarm through the kingdom against republicans and levellers, than an assembly of court-sycophants, with a placeman at their head, entered into what they termed an association at the Crown and Anchor tavern, whence they issued accounts of their proceedings. This was the primitive, the metropolitan association, which, with few exceptions, gave the tone to the succeeding, who did little more than copy its language and its spirit. As the popular ferment has, it may be hoped, by this time in some measure subsided, it may not be improper to endeavour to estimate the utility and develop the principles of these societies.

1. The first particular that engages the attention is their *singular* and *unprecedented* nature. The object is altogether new. The political societies that have been hitherto formed never thought of interfering with the operations of law, but were content with giving, by their union, greater force and publicity to their sentiments. The diffusion of principles was their object, not the suppression; and, confiding in the justness of their cause, they challenged their enemies into the field of controversy. These societies, on the other hand, are combined with an express view to extinguish opinions, and to overwhelm freedom of inquiry by the terrors of criminal prosecution. They pretend not to enlighten the people by the spread of political

knowledge, or to confute the errors of the system they wish to discountenance: they breathe only the language of menace; their element is indictment and prosecution, and their criminal justice formed on the model of Rhadamanthus, the poetic judge of Hell.

Castigatque, auditque, dolos subigitque fateri.

2. They are not only new in their nature and complexion, but are unsupported by any just pretence of expedience or necessity. The British constitution hath provided ample securities for its stability and permanence. The prerogatives of the crown in all matters touching its dignity are of a nature so high and weighty as may rather occasion alarm than need corroboration. The office of attorney-general is created for the very purpose of prosecuting sedition; and he has the peculiar privilege of filing a bill against offenders in the king's name, without the intervention of a grand jury. If the public tranquillity be threatened, the king can imbody the militia as well as station the military in the suspected places; and when to this is added the immense patronage and influence which flows from the disposal of seventeen millions a year, it must be evident the stability of the British government can never be shaken by the efforts of any minority whatever. It comprehends within itself all the resources of defence which the best civil polity ought to possess. The permanence of every government must depend, however, after all, upon opinion, a general persuasion of its excellence, which can never be increased by its assuming a vindictive and sanguinary aspect. While it is the object of the people's approbation it will be continued, and to support it much beyond that period by mere force and terror would be impossible were it just, and unjust were it possible. The law hath amply provided against *overt acts* of sedition and disorder, and to suppress *mere opinions* by any other method than reason and argument is the height of tyranny. Freedom of thought, being intimately connected with the happiness and dignity of man in every stage of his being, is of so much more importance than the preservation of any constitution, that to infringe the former under pretence of supporting the latter is to sacrifice the means to the end.

3. In attempting to define the boundary which separates the liberty of the press from its licentiousness, these societies have undertaken a task which they are utterly unable to execute. The line that divides them is too nice and delicate to be perceived by every eye, or to be drawn by every rude and unskilful hand. When a public outrage against the laws is committed, the crime is felt in a moment; but to ascertain the qualities which compose a libel, and to apply with exactness the general idea to every instance and example which may occur, demand an effort of thought and reflection little likely to be exerted by the great mass of mankind. Bewildered in a pursuit which they are incapable of conducting with propriety, taught to suspect treason and sedition in every page they read and in every conversation they hear, the necessary effect of such an employment must be to perplex the understanding and degrade the heart. An admirable

expedient for transforming a great and generous people into a contemptible race of spies and informers!

For private individuals to combine together at all with a view to quicken the vigour of criminal prosecution is suspicious at least, if not illegal; in a case where the liberty of the press is concerned, all such combinations are utterly improper. The faults and the excellences of a book are often so blended, the motives of a writer so difficult to ascertain, and the mischiefs of servile restraint so alarming, that the criminality of a book should always be left to be determined by the particular circumstances of the case. As one would rather see many criminals escape than the punishment of one innocent person, so it is infinitely better a multitude of errors should be propagated than one truth be suppressed.

If the suppression of Mr. Paine's pamphlet be the object of these societies, they are ridiculous in the extreme; for the circulation of his works ceased the moment they were declared a libel: if any other publication be intended, they are premature and impertinent, in presuming to anticipate the decision of the courts.

4. Admitting, however, the principle on which they are founded to be ever so just and proper, they are highly impolitic. All violence exerted towards opinions which falls short of *extermination* serves no other purpose than to render them more known, and ultimately to increase the zeal and number of their abetters. Opinions that are false may be dissipated by the force of argument; when they are true their punishment draws towards them infallibly more of the public attention, and enables them to dwell with more lasting weight and pressure on the mind. The progress of reason is aided, in this case, by the passions, and finds in curiosity, compassion, and resentment powerful auxiliaries.

When public discontents are allowed to vent themselves in reasoning and discourse, they subside into a calm; but their confinement in the bosom is apt to give them a fierce and deadly tincture. The reason of this is obvious: as men are seldom disposed to complain till they at least imagine themselves injured, so there is no injury which they will remember so long, or resent so deeply, as that of being threatened into silence. This seems like adding triumph to oppression, and insult to injury. The apparent tranquillity which may ensue is delusive and ominous; it is that awful stillness which nature feels while she is awaiting the discharge of the gathered tempest.

The professed object of these associations is to strengthen the hands of government: but there is one way in which it may strengthen its own hands most effectually; recommended by a very venerable authority, though one from which it hath taken but few lessons. "He that hath *clean hands*," saith a sage adviser, "shall grow stronger and stronger." If the government wishes to become more vigorous, let it first become more pure, lest an addition to its strength should only increase its capacity for mischief.

There is a characteristic feature attending these associations, which is sufficient to acquaint us with their real origin and spirit, that is the silence, almost total, which they maintain respecting political abuses. Had they been intended, as their title imports, merely to furnish an antidote to the spread of republican schemes and doctrines, they would have loudly asserted the necessity of reform, as a conciliatory principle, a centre of union, in which the virtuous of all descriptions might have concurred. But this, however conducive to the good of the people, would have defeated their whole project, which consisted in availing themselves of an alarm which they had artfully prepared, in order to withdraw the public attention from real grievances to imaginary dangers The Hercules of reform had penetrated the Augean stable of abuses; the fabric of corruption, hitherto deemed sacred, began to totter, and its upholders were apprehensive their iniquity was almost full. In this perplexity they embraced an occasion afforded them by the spread of certain bold speculations (speculations which owed their success to the corruptions of government) to diffuse a panic, and to drown the justest complaints in unmeaning clamour. The plan of associating, thus commencing in corruption, and propagated by imitation and by fear, had for its *pretext* the fear of republicanism; for its *object* the perpetuity of abuses. Associations in this light may be considered as mirrors placed to advantage for reflecting the finesses and tricks of the ministry. At present they are playing into each other's hands, and no doubt find great entertainment in deceiving the nation. But let them be aware lest it should be found, after all, none are so much duped as themselves. Wisdom and truth, the offspring of the sky, are immortal; but cunning and deception, the meteors of the earth, after glittering for a moment, must pass away.

The candour and sincerity of these associators is of a piece with their other virtues: for while they profess to be combined in order to prevent riots and insurrections, attempted to be raised by republicans and levellers, they can neither point out the persons to whom that description applies, nor mention a single riot that was not fomented by their principles, and engaged on their side. There have been three riots in England of late on a political account; one at Birmingham, one at Manchester, and one at Cambridge; each of which has been levelled against dissenters and friends of reform.*

The Crown and Anchor association, as it was first in order of time, seems also determined, by pushing to a greater length the maxims of arbitrary power, to maintain its pre-eminence in every other respect. The divine right of monarchy, the sacred anointing of kings, passive obedience and non-resistance, are the hemlock and night shade which these physicians have prescribed for the health of the nation; and are yet but a specimen of a more fertile crop which they have promised out of the hotbed of their depravity. The opinions which they have

* The conduct of an honourable member of the House of Commons, respecting the last of these, was extremely illiberal. He informed the house, that the riot at Cambridge was nothing more than that the mob compelled Mr. Musgrave, one of his constituents, who had been heard to speak seditious words, to sing God save the King—a statement in which he was utterly mistaken. Mr. Musgrave, with whom I have the pleasure of being well acquainted, was neither guilty of uttering seditious discourse, nor did he, I am certain, comply with the requisition His whole crime consists in the love of his country, and a zeal for parliamentary reform It would be happy for this nation, if a portion only of the integrity and disinterested virtue which adorn his character could be infused into our great men.

associated to suppress are contained, they tell us, in the terms liberty and equality; after which they proceed to a dull harangue on the mischiefs that must flow from equalizing property. All mankind, they gravely tell us, are not equal in virtue, as if that were not sufficiently evident from the existence of their society. The notion of equality in property was never seriously cherished in the mind of any man, unless for the purpose of calumny: and the *term* transplanted from a neighbouring country never intended *there* any thing more than *equality of rights*— as opposed to feudal oppression and hereditary distinctions. An equality of rights may consist with the greatest inequality between the thing to which those rights extend. It belongs to the very nature of *property* for the owner to have a full and complete right to that which he possesses, and consequently for all properties to have *equal* rights; but who is so ridiculous as to infer from thence that the *possessions* themselves are equal? A more alarming idea cannot be spread among the people, than that there is a large party ready to abet them in any enterprise of depredation and plunder. As all men do not know that the element of the associators is calumny, they are really in danger for a while of being believed, and must thank themselves if they should realize the plan of equality their own malice has invented.

I am happy to find that Mr. Law, a very respectable gentleman, who had joined the Crown and Anchor society, has publicly withdrawn his name, disgusted with their conduct; by whom we are informed they receive anonymous letters, vilifying the characters of persons of the first eminence, and that they are in avowed alliance with the ministry for prosecutions, whom they entreat to order the *solicitor-general to proceed on their suggestions.* When such a society declares "*itself to be unconnected with any political party,*" our respect for human nature impels us to believe it, and to hope their appearance may be considered as an era in the annals of corruption which will transmit their names to posterity with the encomiums they deserve. With sycophants so base and venal, no argument or remonstrance can be expected to have any success. It is in vain to apply to reason when it is perverted and abused, to shame when it is extinguished, to a conscience which has ceased to admonish: I shall therefore leave them in the undisturbed possession of that true philosophical indifference which steels them against the reproaches of their own hearts and the contempt of all honest men.

All the associations, it is true, do not breathe the spirit which disgraces that of the Crown and Anchor. But they all concur in establishing a political test, on the first appearance of which the friends of liberty should make a stand. The opinions proposed may be innocent; but the precedent is fatal, and the moment subscription becomes the price of security, the Rubicon is passed. Emboldened by the success of this expedient, its authors will venture on more vigorous measures; test will steal upon test, and the bounds of tolerated opinion will be continually narrowed, till we awake under the fangs of a relentless despotism.

SECTION III.

On a Reform of Parliament.

WHATEVER difference of opinion may take place in points of less importance, there is one in which the friends of freedom are entirely agreed, that is, the necessity of reform in the representation. The theory of the English constitution presents three independent powers: the king, as executive head, with a negative in the legislature, an hereditary House of Peers, and an assembly of Commons, who are appointed to represent the nation at large. From this enumeration it is plain that the people of England can have no liberty, that is, no share in forming the laws but what they exert through the medium of the last of those bodies; nor then, but in proportion to its independence of the other. The independence, therefore, of the House of Commons is the column on which the whole fabric of our liberty rests. Representation may be considered as complete when it collects to a sufficient extent and transmits with perfect fidelity the real sentiments of the people; but this it may fail of accomplishing through various causes. If its electors are but a handful of people, and of a peculiar order and description; if its duration is sufficient to enable it to imbibe the spirit of a corporation; if its integrity be corrupted by treasury influence, or warped by the prospect of places and pensions; it may by these means not only fail of the end of its appointment, but fall into such an entire dependence on the executive branch as to become a most dangerous instrument of arbitrary power. The usurpation of the emperors at Rome would not have been safe unless it had concealed itself behind the formalities of a senate.

The confused and inadequate state of our representation at present is too obvious to escape the attention of the most careless observer. While, through the fluctuation of human affairs, many towns of ancient note have fallen into decay, and the increase of commerce has raised obscure hamlets to splendour and distinction, the state of representation standing still amid these vast changes, points back to an order of things which no longer subsists. The opulent towns of Birmingham, Manchester, and Leeds send no members to parliament; the decayed boroughs of Cornwall appoint a multitude of representatives. Old Sarum sends two members, though there are not more than one or two families that reside in it. The disproportion between those who vote for representatives and the people at large is so great, that the majority of our House of Commons is chosen by less than eight thousand in a kingdom consisting of as many millions. Mr. Burgh, in his excellent political disquisitions, has made a very laborious calculation on this head, from which it appears that the affairs of this great empire are decided by the suffrages of between five and six thousand electors; so that our representation, instead of being co-extended with the people, fails of this in a proportion that is truly enormous. The qualifications, moreover, that confer the right of election are capricious and irregular. In some places it belongs to the corporation, or to those whom they think proper to make free; in some to every housekeeper; in others it is attached to a particular estate, whose proprietor is absolute lord of the borough, of which he makes his advantage by representing it himself or disposing of it to the best bidder. In counties the right of election is annexed only to one kind of property, that of freehold; the proprietor of copyhold land being entirely deprived of it, though his political situation is precisely the same.

The consequence of this perplexity in the qualifications of electors is often a tedious scrutiny and examination before a committee of the House of Commons, prolonged to such a length that there is no time when there are not some boroughs entirely unrepresented. These gross defects in our representation have struck all sensible men very forcibly; even Mr. Paley, a courtly writer in the main, declares the bulk of the inhabitants of this country have little more concern in the appointment of parliament than the subjects of the grand seignior at Constantinople.

On the propriety of the several plans which have been proposed to remedy these evils it is not for me to decide; I shall choose rather to point out two general principles which ought, in my opinion, to pervade every plan of parliamentary reform; the first of which respects the mode of election, the second the independence of the elected. In order to give the people a true representation, let its basis be enlarged and the duration of parliaments shortened. The first of these improvements would diminish bribery and corruption, lessen the violence and tumult of elections, and secure to the people a real and unequivocal organ for the expression of their sentiments.

Were every householder in town and country permitted to vote, the number of electors would be so great, that as no art or industry would be able to bias their minds, so no sums of money would be sufficient to win their suffrages. The plan which the Duke of Richmond recommended was, if I mistake not, still more comprehensive, including all that were of age, except menial servants. By this means, the different passions and prejudices of men would check each other, the predominance of any particular or local interest be kept down, and from the whole there would result that *general impression*, which would convey with precision the unbiassed sense of the people.

But besides this, another great improvement, in my opinion, would be, to shorten the duration of parliament, by bringing it back to one year. The *Michel Gemote*, or great council of the kingdom, was appointed to meet under Alfred twice a year, and by divers ancient statutes after the conquest, the king was bound to summon a parliament every year or oftener, if need be; when, to remedy the looseness of this latter phrase, by the 16th of Charles the Second it was enacted, the holding of parliaments should not be intermitted above three years at most; and in the 1st of King William, it is declared as one of the rights of the people, that for redress of all grievances, and preserving the laws, parliaments ought to be held frequently; which was again reduced to a certainty by another statute, which enacts that a new parliament shall be called within three years after the termination of the former. To this term did they continue limited till the reign of George the First; when, after the rebellion of 1715, the septennial act was passed, under the pretence of diminishing the expense of elections, and preserving the kingdom against the designs of the pretender. A noble lord* observed, on that occasion, he was at an utter loss to describe the nature of this prolonged parliament, unless he were allowed to borrow a phrase from the Athanasian Creed; for it was, "neither created, nor begotten, but proceeding." Without disputing the upright intentions of the authors of this act, it is plain they might on the same principle have voted themselves perpetual, and their conduct will ever remain a monument of that short-sightedness in politics which in providing for the pressure of the moment puts to hazard the liberty and happiness of future times. It is intolerable, that in so large a space of a man's life as seven years he should never be able to correct the error he may have committed in the choice of a representative, but be compelled to see him every year dipping deeper into corruption; a helpless spectator of the contempt of his interests and the ruin of his country. During the present period of parliaments a nation may sustain the greatest possible changes; may descend by a succession of ill counsels from the highest pinnacle of its fortunes to the lowest point of depression; its treasure exhausted, its credit sunk, and its weight almost completely annihilated in the scale of empire. Ruin and felicity are seldom dispensed by the same hand, nor is it likely any succour in calamity should flow from the wisdom and virtue of those by whose folly and wickedness it was inflicted.

The union between a representative and his constituents ought to be strict and entire; but the septennial act has rendered it little more than nominal. The duration of parliament sets its members at a distance from the people, begets a notion of independence, and gives the minister so much leisure to insinuate himself into their graces, that before the period is expired they become very mild and complying. Sir Robert Walpole used to say, that "every man had his price:" a maxim on which he relied with so much security, that he declared he seldom troubled himself with the election of members, but rather chose to stay and buy them up when they came to market. A very interesting work, lately published, entitled, "Anecdotes of Lord Chatham," unfolds some parts of this mystery of iniquity, which the reader will probably think equally new and surprising, There is a regular office, it seems,—that of manager of the House of Commons,—which generally devolves on one of the secretaries of state, and consists in securing, at all events, a majority in parliament by a judicious application of promises and bribes. The sums disbursed by this honourable office are involved under the head of Secret Service Money; and so delicate is this employment of manager of the House of Commons considered, that we have an account in the above-mentioned

* The Earl of Peterborough.

treatise of a new arrangement of ministry, which failed for no other reason than that the different parties could not agree on the proper person to fill it.*

This secret influence which prevails must be allowed to be extremely disgraceful; nor can it ever be effectually remedied but by contracting the duration of parliaments.

If it be objected to annual parliaments that by this means the tumult and riot attendant on elections will be oftener repeated, it ought to be remembered that their duration is the chief source of these disorders. Render a seat in the House of Commons of less value, and you diminish at once the violence of the struggle. In America, the election of representatives takes place throughout that vast continent in one day, with the greatest tranquillity.

In a mixed constitution like ours it is impossible to estimate the importance of an independent parliament; for as it is here our freedom consists, if this barrier to the encroachments of arbitrary power once fails, we can oppose no other. Should the king attempt to govern without a parliament, or should the upper house pretend to legislate independently of the lower, we should immediately take the alarm; but if the House of Commons falls insensibly under the control of the other two branches of the legislature, our danger is greater, because our apprehensions are less. The forms of a free constitution surviving when its spirit is extinct would perpetuate slavery by rendering it more concealed and secure. On this account, I apprehend, did Montesquieu predict the loss of our freedom, from the legislative power becoming more corrupt than the executive; a crisis to which, if it has not arrived already, it is hastening apace. The immortal Locke, far from looking with the indifference too common on the abuses in our representation, considered all improper influence exerted in that quarter as threatening the very dissolution of government. "*Thus*," says he, "*to regulate candidates and electors, and new-model the ways of election, what is it but to cut up the government by the roots, and poison the very fountain of public security?*"

No enormity can subsist long without meeting with advocates; on which account we need not wonder that the corruption of parliament has been justified under the mild denomination of influence, though it must pain every virtuous mind to see the enlightened Paley engaged in its defence. If a member votes consistently with his convictions, his conduct in that instance has not been determined by influence; but if he votes otherwise, give it what gentle name you please, he forfeits his integrity; nor is it possible to mark the boundaries which should limit his compliance; for if he may deviate a little to attain

* As I have taken my information on this head entirely on the authority of the work called "Anecdotes of Lord Chatham," the reader may not be displeased with the following extract, vol. ii. page 121:—"The management of the House of Commons, as it is called, is a confidential department unknown to the constitution. In the public accounts it is immersed under the head of Secret Service Money. It is usually given to the secretary of state when that post is filled by a commoner. The business of the department is to distribute with *art* and *policy* among the members who have no ostensible places sums of money for their support during the session; besides contracts, lottery-tickets, and other douceurs. It is no uncommon circumstance, at the end of a session, for a gentleman to receive five hundred or a thousand pounds for *his services*."

the see of Winchester, he may certainly step a little farther to reach the dignity of primate. How familiar must the practice of corruption have become when a philosophical moralist, a minister of religion, of great talents and virtue, in the calm retirement of his study, does not hesitate to become its public apologist!

The necessity of a reform in the constitution of parliament is in nothing more obvious than in the ascendency of the aristocracy. This colossus bestrides both houses of parliament; legislates in one, and exerts a domineering influence over the other. It is humiliating, at the approach of an election, to see a whole county send a deputation to an earl or duke, and beg a representative as you would beg an alms. A multitude of laws have been framed, it is true, to prevent all interference of peers in elections; but they neither are nor can be effectual while the House of Commons opens its doors to their sons and brothers. If our liberty depends on the balance and control of the respective orders in the state, it must be extremely absurd to blend them together by placing the father in one department of the legislature and his family in the other.

Freedom is supposed by some to derive great security from the existence of a regular opposition; an expedient which is in my opinion both the offspring and the cherisher of faction. That a minister should be opposed when his measures are destructive to his country can admit of no doubt; that a systematic opposition should be maintained against any man merely as a minister, without regard to the principles he may profess, or the measures he may propose, which is intended by a regular opposition, appears to me a most corrupt and unprincipled maxim. When a legislative assembly is thus thrown into parties, distinguished by no leading principle, however warm and animated their debates, it is plain they display only a struggle for the emoluments of office. This the people discern, and in consequence listen with very little attention to the representations of the minister on the one hand, or the minority on the other; being persuaded the only real difference between them is, that the one is anxious to gain what the other is anxious to keep. If a measure be good, it is of no importance to the nation from whom it proceeds; yet will it be esteemed by the opposition a point of honour not to let it pass without throwing every obstruction in its way. If we listen to the minister for the time being, the nation is always flourishing and happy; if we hearken to the opposition, it is a chance if it be not on the brink of destruction. In an assembly convened to deliberate on the affairs of a nation, how disgusting to hear the members perpetually talk of their connexions, and their resolution to act with a particular set of men, when, if they have happened by chance to vote according to their convictions rather than their party, half their speeches are made up of apologies for a conduct so new and unexpected! When they see men united who agree in nothing but their hostility to the minister, the people fall at first into amazement and irresolution; till perceiving political debate is a mere scramble for profit and power, they endeavour to become as corrupt as their betters. It is not in that roar of faction which deafens the ear and sickens the heart the still voice of Liberty is heard. She turns from the disgusting scene, and regards these struggles as the pangs and convulsions in which she is doomed to expire.

The era of parties, flowing from the animation of freedom, is ever followed by an era of faction, which marks its feebleness and decay. Parties are founded on *principle*, factions on *men;* under the first, the people are contending respecting the system that shall be pursued; under the second, they are candidates for servitude, and are only debating *whose livery* they shall wear. The purest times of the Roman republic were distinguished by violent dissensions; but they consisted in the jealousy of the several *orders* of the state among each other; on the ascendence of the patricians on the one side and the plebeians on the other; a useful struggle, which maintained the balance and equipoise of the constitution. In the progress of corruption things took a turn; the permanent parties which sprang from the fixed principles of government were lost, and the citizens arranged themselves under the standard of particular leaders, being bandied into factions, under Marius or Sylla, Cæsar or Pompey; while the republic stood by without any interest in the dispute, a passive and helpless victim. The crisis of the fall of freedom in different nations, with respect to the causes that produce it, is extremely uniform. After the manner of the ancient factions, we hear much in England of the Bedford party, the Rockingham party, the Portland party,—when it would puzzle the wisest man to point out their political distinction. The useful jealousy of the separate orders is extinct, being all melted down and blended into one mass of corruption. The House of Commons looks with no jealousy on the House of Lords, nor the House of Lords on the House of Commons; the struggle in both is maintained by the ambition of powerful individuals and families, between whom the kingdom is thrown as the prize, and the moment they unite they perpetuate its subjection and divide its spoils.

From a late instance we see they quarrel only about the partition of the prey, but are unanimous in defending it. To the honour of Mr. Fox and the band of illustrious patriots of which he is the leader, it will however be remembered that they stood firm against a host of opponents when, assailed by every species of calumny and invective, they had nothing to expect but the reproaches of the present and the admiration of all future times. If any thing can rekindle the sparks of freedom, it will be the flame of their eloquence; if any thing can re animate her faded form, it will be the vigour of such minds.

The disordered state of our representation, it is acknowledged on all hands, must be remedied some time or other; but it is contended that it would be improper at present, on account of the political ferment that occupies the minds of men and the progress of republican principles; a plausible objection, if delay can restore public tranquillity: but unless I am greatly mistaken, it will have just a contrary effect. It is hard to conceive how the discontent that flows from the abuses of government can be allayed by their being perpetuated. If they are of such a nature that they can neither be palliated nor denied, and are made the ground of invective against the whole of our constitution, are not they its best friends who wish to cut off this occasion of scandal and complaint? The *theory* of our constitution, we say, and justly, has been the admiration of the world; the cavils of its enemies, then, derive their force entirely from the disagreement between that theory and its practice: nothing therefore remains but to bring them as near as human affairs will admit to a perfect correspondence. This will cut up faction by the roots, and immediately distinguish those who wish to reform the constitution from those who wish its subversion. Since the abuses are real, the longer they are continued the more they will be known; the discontented will be always gaining ground, and, though repulsed, will return to the charge with redoubled vigour and advantage. Let reform be considered as a chirurgical operation, if you please; but since the constitution must undergo it or die, it is best to submit before the remedy becomes as dangerous as the disease. The example drawn from a neighbouring kingdom as an argument for delay ought to teach us a contrary lesson. Had the encroachments of arbitrary power been steadily resisted, and remedies been applied as evils appeared, instead of piling them up as precedents, the disorders of government could never have arisen to that enormous height, nor would the people have been impelled to the dire necessity of building the whole fabric of political society afresh. It seems an infatuation in governments that in tranquil times they treat the people with contempt, and turn a deaf ear to their complaints; till, public resentment kindling, they find when it is too late that in their eagerness to retain every thing they have lost all.

The pretences of Mr. Pitt and his friends for delaying this great business are so utterly inconsistent that it is too plain they are averse in reality to its ever taking place. When Mr. Pitt is reminded that he himself at the beginning of his ministry recommended parliamentary reform, he replies, It was necessary then on account of the calamitous state of the nation, just emerged from an unsuccessful war and filled with gloom and disquiet. But, unless the people are libelled, they now are still more discontented,—with this difference, that their uneasiness formerly arose from events but remotely connected with unequal representation, but that this is now the chief ground of complaint. It is absurd, however, to rest the propriety of reform on any turn of public affairs. If it be not requisite to secure our freedom, it is vain and useless; but if it be a proper means of preserving that blessing, the nation will need it as much in peace as in war. When we wish to retain those habits which we know it were best to relinquish, we are extremely ready to be soothed with momentary pretences for delay, though they appear on reflection to be drawn from quite opposite topics, and therefore to be equally applicable to all times and seasons.

A similar delusion is practised in the conduct of public affairs. If the people be tranquil and composed, and have not caught the passion of reform, it is impolitic, say the ministry, to disturb their minds by agitating a question that lies at rest; if they are awakened, and touched with a conviction of the abuse, we must wait, say they, till the ferment subsides, and not lessen our dignity by seeming to yield to popular clamour: if we are at peace, and commerce flourishes, it is concluded we cannot need any improvement in circumstances so prosperous and happy; if, on the other hand, we are at war, and our affairs unfortunate, an amendment in the representation is dreaded, as it would seem an acknowledgment that our calamities flowed from the ill conduct of parliament. Now, as the nation must always be in one or other of these situations, the conclusion is, the period of reform can never arrive at all.

This pretence for delay will appear the more extraordinary in the British ministry from a comparison of the exploits they have performed with the task they decline. They have found time for involving us in millions of debt—for cementing a system of corruption that reaches from the cabinet to the cottage—for carrying havoc and devastation to the remotest extremities of the globe—for accumulating taxes which famish the peasant and reward the parasite—for bandying the whole kingdom into factions, to the ruin of all virtue and public spirit—for the completion of these achievements they have suffered no opportunity to escape them. Elementary treatises on time mention various arrangements and divisions, but none have ever touched on the chronology of statesmen. These are a generation who measure their time not so much by the revolutions of the sun as by the revolutions of power. There are two eras particularly marked in their calendar,—the one the period they are in the ministry, and the other when they are out,—which have a very different effect on their sentiments and reasoning. Their course commences in the character of friends to the people, whose grievances they display in all the colours of variegated diction. But the moment they step over the threshold of St. James's, they behold every thing in a new light; the taxes seem lessened, the people rise from their depression, the nation flourishes in peace and plenty, and every attempt at improvement is like heightening the beauties of Paradise or mending the air of Elysium.

SECTION IV.

On Theories, and the Rights of Man.

AMONG the many alarming symptoms of the present time, it is not the least that there is a prevailing disposition to hold in contempt the *theory* of liberty as false and visionary. For my own part, it is my determination never to be deterred by an obnoxious name from an open avowal of any principles that appear useful and important. Were the ridicule now cast on the Rights of Man confined to a mere phrase, as the title of a book, it were of little consequence; but when *that* is made the pretence for deriding the doctrine itself, it is matter of serious alarm.

To place the rights of man as the basis of lawful government is not peculiar to Mr. Paine; but was done more than a century ago by men of no less eminence than Sidney and Locke. It is therefore extremely disingenuous to impute the system to Mr. Paine as its author. His structure may be false and erroneous, but the foundation was laid by other hands. That there are *natural rights*, or, in other words, a certain liberty which men may exercise, independent of permission from society, can scarcely be doubted by those who comprehend the meaning of the terms. Every man must have a natural right to use his limbs in what manner he pleases that is not injurious to another. In like manner he must have a right to worship God after the mode he thinks acceptable; or, in other words, he ought not to be compelled to consult any thing but his own conscience. These are a specimen of those rights which may properly be termed *natural;* for, as philosophers speak of the primary qualities of matter, they cannot be increased or diminished. We cannot conceive the right of using our limbs to be created by society, or to be rendered more complete by any human agreement or compact.

But there still remains a question whether this natural liberty must not be considered as entirely relinquished when we become members of society. It is pretended that the moment we quit a state of *nature*, as we have given up the control of our actions in return for the superior advantages of law and government, we can never appeal again to any original principles, but must rest content with the advantages that are secured by the terms of the society. These are the views which distinguish the political writings of Mr. Burke, an author whose splendid and unequalled powers have given a vogue and fashion to certain tenets which, from any other pen, would have appeared abject and contemptible. In the field of reason the encounter would not be difficult, but who can withstand the fascination and magic of his eloquence? The excursions of his genius are immense. His imperial fancy has laid all nature under tribute, and has collected riches from every scene of the creation and every walk of art. His eulogium on the Queen of France is a masterpiece of pathetic composition; so select are its images, so fraught with tenderness, and so rich with colours "dipped in heaven," that he who can read it without rapture may have merit as a reasoner, but must resign all pretensions to taste and sensibility. His imagination is, in truth, only too prolific: a world of itself, where he dwells in the midst of chimerical alarms, is the dupe of his own enchantments, and starts, like Prospero, at the spectres of his own creation.

His intellectual views in general, however, are wide and variegated, ather than distinct; and the light he has let in on the British constitution in particular resembles the coloured effulgence of a painted medium, a kind of mimic twilight, solemn and soothing to the senses, but better fitted for ornament than use.

A book has lately been published under the title of "Happiness and Rights," written by Mr. Hey, a respectable member of the university of Cambridge, whose professed object is, with Mr. Burke, to overturn the doctrine of natural rights. The few remarks I may make upon it are less on account of any merit in the work itself than on account of its author, who, being a member of considerable standing in the most liberal of our universities, may be presumed to speak the sentiments of that learned body. The chief difference between his theory and Mr Burke's seems to be the denial of the existence of any rights that can be denominated natural, which Mr. Burke only supposes *resigned* on the formation of political society. "*The rights*," says Mr. Hey, "*I can conjecture (for it is but a conjecture) to belong to me as a mere man are so uncertain and comparatively so unimportant, while the rights I feel myself possessed of in civil society are so great, so numerous, and many of them so well defined, that I am strongly inclined to consider society as creating or giving my rights, rather than recognising and securing what I could have claimed if I had lived in an unconnected state.*"—(p. 137.)

As government implies restraint, it is plain a portion of our freedom is given up by entering into it; the only question can then be, how far this resignation extends, whether to a part, or to the whole? This point may perhaps be determined by the following reflections:—

1. The advantages that civil power can procure to a community are *partial.* A small part in comparison with the condition of man can fall within its influence. Allowing it to be a rational institution, it must have that end in view which a reasonable man would propose by appointing it; nor can it imply any greater sacrifice than is strictly necessary to its attainment. But on what account is it requisite to unite in political society? Plainly to guard against the injury of others; for were there no injustice among mankind no protection would be needed, no *public force* necessary: every man might be left without restraint or control. The attainment of all possible good, then, is *not* the purpose of laws, but to secure us from external injury and violence; and as the means must be proportioned to the end, it is absurd to suppose that by submitting to civil power, with a view to some *particular* benefits, we should be understood to hold all our advantages dependent upon that authority. Civil restraints imply nothing more than a surrender of our liberty in some points in order to maintain it undisturbed in others of more importance. Thus we give up the liberty by repelling force by force, in return for a more equal administration of justice than private resentment would permit. But there are some rights which cannot with any propriety be yielded up to human authority, because they are perfectly consistent with every benefit its appointment can procure. The free use of our faculties in distinguishing truth from falsehood, the exertion of corporeal powers without injury to others, the choice of a religion and worship, are branches of natural freedom which no government can justly alter or diminish, because their restraint cannot conduce to that security which is its proper object. Government, like every other contrivance, has a *specific* end; it implies the resignation of just as much liberty as is needful to attain it; whatever is demanded more is superfluous, a species of tyranny, which ought to be corrected by withdrawing it. The relation of master and servant, of pupil and instructer, of the respective members of a family to their head, all include some restraint, some abridgment of natural liberty. But in these cases it is not pretended that

the surrender is total; and why should this be supposed to take place in political society, which is *one* of the relations of human life? this would be to render the foundation infinitely broader than the superstructure.

2. From the notion that political society precludes an appeal to natural rights, the greatest absurdities must ensue. If that idea be just, it is improper to say of any administration that it is despotic or oppressive unless it has receded from its first form and model. Civil power can never exceed its limits until it deviates into a new track. For if every portion of natural freedom be given up by yielding to civil authority, we can never claim any other liberties than those precise ones which were ascertained in its first formation. The vassals of despotism may complain perhaps of the hardships which they suffer; but unless it appear they are of *a new kind* no injury is done them, for no right is violated. Rights are either natural or artificial; the first cannot be pleaded after they are relinquished, and the second cannot be impaired but by a departure from ancient precedents. If a man should be unfortunate enough to live under the dominion of a prince who, like the monarchs of Persia, could murder his subjects at will, he may be unhappy, but cannot complain; for on Mr. Hey's theory he never had any rights but what were created by society, and on Mr. Burke's he has for ever relinquished them. The claims of *nature* being set aside, and the constitution of the government despotic from the beginning, his misery involves no injustice and admits of no remedy. It requires little discernment to see that this theory rivets the chains of despotism, and shuts out from the political world the smallest glimpse of emancipation or improvement. Its language is, he that is a slave let him be a slave still.

3. It is incumbent on Mr. Burke and his followers to ascertain the *time* when natural rights are relinquished. Mr. Hey is content with tracing their existence to society, while Mr. Burke, the more moderate of the two, admitting their foundation in nature, only contends that regular government absorbs and swallows them up, bestowing artificial advantages in exchange. But at what period, it may be inquired, shall we date this wonderful revolution in the social condition of man? If we say it was as early as the first dawn of society, natural liberty had never any existence at all, since there are no traces even in tradition of a period when men were utterly unconnected with each other. If we say this complete surrender took place with the first rudiments of law and government in every particular community, on what principle were subsequent improvements introduced? Mr. Burke is fond of resting our liberties on Magna Charta and the Bill of Rights; but he ought to remember, that as they do not carry us to the commencement of our government, which was established ages before, our forefathers had long ago resigned their natural liberty. If those famous stipulations only recognised such privileges as were in force before, they have no claim to be considered as the foundations of our constitution; but if they formed an *era* in the annals of freedom, they must have been erected on the basis of those natural rights which Mr. Burke

ridicules and explodes. When our ancestors made those demands, it is evident they did not suppose an appeal to the rights of nature precluded. Every step a civilized nation can take towards a more equal administration is either an assertion of its natural liberty or a criminal encroachment on just authority. The influence of government on the stock of natural rights may be compared to that of a manufactory on the rude produce; it adds nothing to its quantity, but only qualifies and fits it for use. Political arrangement is more or less perfect in proportion as it enables us to exert our natural liberty to the greatest advantage; if it is diverted to any other purpose, it is made the instrument of gratifying the passions of a few, or imposes greater restraint than its object prescribes; it degenerates into tyranny and oppression.

The greatest objection to these principles is their perspicuity, which makes them ill relished by those whose interest it is to hide the nature of government from vulgar eyes, and induce a persuasion that it is a secret which can only be unfolded to the *initiated* under the conduct of Mr. Burke, the great *hierophant* and revealer of the mysteries. A mystery and a trick are generally two sides of the same object according as it is turned to the view of the beholder.

The doctrine of Mr. Locke and his followers is founded on the natural equality of mankind; for as no man can have any natural or inherent right to rule any more than another, it necessarily follows that a claim to dominion, wherever it is lodged, must be ultimately referred back to the explicit or implied consent of the people. Whatever source of civil authority is assigned different from this will be found to resolve itself into *mere force*. But as the natural equality of one generation is the same with that of another, the people have always the same right to new-model their government, and set aside their rulers. This right, like every other, may be exerted capriciously and absurdly; but no human power can have any pretensions to intercept its exercise. For civil rulers cannot be considered as having any claims that are coextended with those of the people, nor as forming a party separate from the nation. They are appointed by the community to *execute* its will, not to *oppose* it; to manage the *public*, not to pursue any *private* or *particular* interests. Are all the existing authorities in state to lie then, it may be said, at the mercy of the populace, liable to be dissipated by the first breath of public discontent? By no means; they are to be respected and obeyed as interpreters of the public will. Till they are set aside by the unequivocal voice of the people, they are a law to every member of the community. To resist them is rebellion; and for any particular set of men to attempt their subversion by force is a heinous crime, as they represent and imbody the collective majesty of the state. They are the exponents, to use the language of algebra, of the precise quantity of liberty the people have thought fit to legalize and secure. But though they are a law to every member of the society separately considered, they cannot bind the society itself, or prevent it, when it shall think proper, from forming an entire new arrangement; a right that no compact can alienate or diminish, and which has been exerted as often as a free government has been formed. On this account, in resolving the right of dominion into compact, Mr. Locke appears to me somewhat inconsistent, or he has expressed himself with less clearness and accuracy than was usual with that great philosopher. There must have been a previous right to insist on stipulations in those who formed them; nor is there any reason why one race of men is not as competent to that purpose as another.

With the enemies of freedom it is a usual artifice to represent the sovereignty of the people as a license to anarchy and disorder. But the tracing up civil power to that source will not diminish our obligation to obey; it only explains its reasons, and settles it on clear determinate principles. It turns blind submission into rational obedience, tempers the passion for liberty with the love of order, and places mankind in a happy medium between the extremes of anarchy on the one side and oppression on the other. It is the polar star that will conduct us safe over the ocean of political debate and speculation, the law of laws, the legislator of legislators.

To reply to all the objections that have been advanced against this doctrine would be a useless task, and exhaust the patience of the reader; but there is one drawn from the idea of a majority much insisted on by Mr. Burke and Mr. Hey, of which the latter gentleman is so enamoured that he has spread it out into a multitude of pages. They assert that the theory of natural rights can never be realized, because every member of the community cannot concur in the choice of a government, and the minority, being compelled to yield to the decisions of the majority, are under tyrannical restraint. To this reasoning it is a sufficient answer, that if a number of men act together at all, the necessity of being determined by the sense of the majority in the last resort is so obvious that it is always implied. An exact concurrence of many particular wills is impossible; and therefore when each taken separately has precisely the same influence, there can be no hardship in suffering the result to remain at issue till it is determined by the coincidence of the greater number. The idea of *natural liberty*, at least, is so little violated by this method of proceeding, that it is no more than what takes place every day in the smallest society, where the necessity of being determined by the voice of the majority is so plain that it is scarcely ever reflected upon. The defenders of the rights of man mean not to contend for impossibilities. We never hear of a right to fly, or to make two and two five. If the majority of a nation approve its government, it is in this respect as free as the smallest association or club; any thing beyond which must be visionary and romantic.

The next objection Mr. Hey insists upon is, if possible, still more frivolous, turning on the case of young persons during minority. He contends, that as some of these have more sense than may be found among common mechanics and the lowest of the people, *natural right* demands their inclinations to be consulted in political arrangements. Were there any method of ascertaining exactly the degree of understanding possessed by young persons during their minority, so as to distinguish early intellects from the less mature, there would be some force in the objection; in the present case, the whole supposition is no more than one of those chimeras which this gentleman is ever fond of combating, with the same gravity and to as little purpose as Don Quixote his windmill.

The period of minority, it is true, varies in different countries, and is perhaps best determined everywhere by ancient custom and habit. An early maturity may confer on sixteen more sagacity than is sometimes found at sixty; but what then? A wise government, having for its object human nature at large, will be adapted, not to its accidental deviations, but to its usual aspects and appearances. For an answer to his argument against natural rights, drawn from the exclusion of women from political power, I beg leave to refer the author to the ingenious Miss Wolstonecraft, the eloquent patroness of female claims; unless, perhaps, every other empire may appear mean in the estimation of those who possess with an uncontrolled authority the empire of the heart.

"The situation" says Mr. Hey (p. 137), "in which any man finds himself placed when he arrives at the power of reflecting appears to be the consequence of a vast train of events, extending backwards hundreds or thousands of years for aught he can tell, and totally baffling all the attempts at comprehension by human faculties."

From hence he concludes all inquiry into the rights of man should be forborne. "What rights this being (God) may have possibly intended that I might claim from beings like myself, if he had thought proper that I had lived among them in an *unconnected* state, that is to say, what are the rights of a mere *man*, appears a question involved in such obscurity that I cannot trace even any indication of that Being having intended me to inquire into it."

If any thing be intended by these observations, it is that we ought never to attempt to ameliorate our condition till we are perfectly acquainted with its causes. But as the subjects of the worst government are probably as ignorant of the train of events for some thousands of years back as those who enjoy the best, they are to rest contented, it seems, until they can clear up that obscurity, and inquire no farther.

It would seem strange to presume an inference good from not knowing how we arrived at it. Yet this seems as reasonable as to suppose the political circumstances of a people fit and proper on account of our inability to trace the causes that produced them. To know the source of an evil is only of consequence as it may chance to conduct us to the remedy. But the whole paragraph I have quoted betrays the utmost perplexity of thought; confounding the *civil condition* of individuals with the political institution of a society. The former will be infinitely various in the same community, arising from the different character, temper, and success of its members; the latter unites and pervades the whole, nor can any abuses attach to it but what may be displayed and remedied.

It is perfectly disingenuous in this author to represent his adver saries as desirous of committing the business of legislation indiscriminately to the meanest of mankind.* He well knows the wildest democratical writer contends for nothing more than popular government by *representation.* If the labouring part of the people are not competent to *choose* legislators, the English constitution is essentially wrong; especially in its present state, where the importance of each vote is enhanced by the paucity of the electors.

After the many examples of misrepresentation which this author has furnished, his declamations on the levelling system cannot be matter of surprise. An equality of rights is perfectly consistent with the utmost disproportion between the objects to which they extend. A peasant may have the same right to the exertion of his faculties with a Newton; but this will not fill up the vast chasm that separates them.

The ministry will feel great obligations to Mr. Hey for putting off the evil day of reform to a far distant period,—a period so remote, that they may hope before it is completed their names and their actions will be buried in friendly oblivion. He indulges a faint expectation, he tells us, that the practice of governments may be improved *in two or three thousand years.*

A smaller edition of this work has lately been published, considerably abridged, for the use of the poor, who, it may be feared, will be very little benefited by its perusal. Genius may dazzle, eloquence may persuade, reason may convince; but to render popular cold and comfortless sophistry, unaided by those powers, is a hopeless attempt.

I have trespassed, I am afraid, too far on the patience of my readers, in attempting to expose the fallacies by which the followers of Mr. Burke perplex the understanding, and endeavour to hide in obscurity the true sources of political power. Were there indeed any impropriety in laying them open, the blame would not fall on the friends of freedom, but on the provocation afforded by the extravagance and absurdity of its enemies. If princely power had never been raised to a level with the attributes of the Divinity by Filmer, it had probably never been sunk as low as popular acquiescence by Locke. The confused mixture of liberty and oppression which ran through the feudal system prevented the theory of government from being closely inspected; particular rights were secured, but the relation of the people to their rulers was never explained on its just principles till the transfer of superstition to civil power shocked the common sense of mankind, and awakened their inquiries. They drew aside the veil, and where they were taught to expect a mystery they discerned a fraud. There is however no room to apprehend any evil from political investigation that will not be greatly overbalanced by its advantages. For besides that truth is always beneficial, tame submission to usurped power has

* "A man whose hands and ideas have been usefully confined for thirty or forty years to the labour and management of a farm, or the construction of a wall or piece of cloth, does indeed, in one respect, appear superior to an infant three months old. The man could make a law of some sort or other; the infant could not. The man could, in any particular circumstances of a nation, say these words, We will go to war, or we will not go to war; the infant could not. But the difference between them is more in appearance than in any useful reality. The man is totally unqualified to judge what ought to be enacted for laws."—*Hey*, p 31

hitherto been the malady of human nature. The dispersed situation of mankind, their indolence and inattention, and the opposition of their passions and interests are circumstances which render it extremely difficult for them to combine in resisting tyranny with success. In the field of government, as in that of the world, *the tares of despotism were sown while men slept!* The necessity of regular government, under some form or other, is so pressing, that the evil of anarchy is of short duration. Rapid, violent, destructive in its course, it is an inundation which, fed by no constant spring, soon dries up and disappears. The misfortune on these occasions is, that the people, for want of understanding the principles of liberty, seldom reach the true source of their misery; but after committing a thousand barbarities, onlv change their masters, when they should change their system

SECTION V.

On Dissenters.

Of that foul torrent of insult and abuse which it has lately been the lot of the friends of liberty to sustain, a larger portion hath fallen to the share of dissenters than any other description of men. Their sentiments have been misrepresented, their loyalty suspected, and their most illustrious characters held up to derision and contempt. The ashes of the dead have been as little spared as the merit of the living; and the same breath that has attempted to depreciate the talents and virtues of a Priestley is employed to blacken the memory of a Price. The effusions of a distempered loyalty are mingled with execrations on that unfortunate sect; as if the attachment to the king were to be measured by the hatred to dissenters. Without any shadow of criminality, they are doomed to sustain perpetual insult and reproach; their repose disturbed, and their lives threatened and endangered. If dissent be in truth a crime of such magnitude that it must not be tolerated, let there be at least a punishment prescribed by law, that they may know what they have to expect, and not lie at the mercy of an enraged and deluded populace. It is natural to inquire into the cause of this extreme virulence against a particular class of the community, who are distinguished from others only by embracing a different form and system of worship.

In the practice of the moral virtues it will hardly be denied that they are at least as exemplary as their neighbours; while in the more immediate duties of religion, if there be any distinction, it lies in their carrying to a greater height sentiments of seriousness and devotion. The nature of their *public conduct* will best appear from a rapid survey of some of those great political events in which it has had room to display itself; where, though our history has been ransacked to supply invective, it will be seen their merits more than compensate for any errors they may have committed. Their zeal in opposing Charles I. has been an eternal theme of reproach; but it should be remembered that when that resistance first took place the parliament consistsd for the most part of churchmen, and was fully justified in its opposition by the arbitrary measures of the court. Had the pretensions of Charles been patiently acquiesced in, our government had long ago been despotic.

What medium might have been found between tame submission and open hostility, and whether matters were not afterward pushed to an extremity against the unfortunate monarch, it is not for me to determine, nor does it concern the vindication of dissenters. For, long before the final catastrophe which issued in the king's death, the favourable intentions of parliament were overruled by the ascendency of Cromwell, the parliament itself oppressed by his arms, and the influence both of churchmen and dissenters bent under military usurpation. The execution of Charles was the deed of a faction, condemned by the great body of the puritans as a criminal severity. But whatever blame they may be supposed to have incurred on account of their conduct to Charles, the merit of restoring monarchy in his son was all their own. The entire force of the empire was in their hands; Monk himself of their party; the parliament, the army, all puritans; yet were they disinterested enough to call the heir to the throne, and yield the reins into his hands, with no other stipulation than that of liberty of conscience, which he violated with a baseness and ingratitude peculiar to his character. All the return he made them for the recovery of his power consisted in depriving two thousand of their ministers, and involving the whole body in a persecution by which not less than ten thousand are supposed to have perished in imprisonment and want. But their patriotism was not to be shaken by these injuries. When, towards the latter end of Charles the Second's reign, the character of his successor inspired a dread of the establishment of popery, to avert that evil they cheerfully acquiesced in an exclusion from all places of emolument and trust,—an extraordinary instance of magnanimity. When James the Second began to display arbitrary views, dissenters were among the first to take the alarm, regarding with jealousy even an indulgence when it flowed from a dispensing power. The zeal with which they co-operated in bringing about the revolution, the ardour with which they have always espoused its principles, are too well known to need any proof, and can only be rendered more striking by a contrast with the conduct of the high church party. The latter maintained in its utmost extent the doctrine of passive obedience and non-resistance; were incessantly engaged in intrigues to overturn the revolution, and affirmed the doctrine of divine right to be an ancient and indisputable tenet of the English church. Whoever wishes to ascertain the existence of those arts by which they embroiled the reign of King William may see them displayed at large in Burnet's History of his own Times.

The attachment of dissenters to the house of Hanover was signalized in a manner too remarkable to be soon forgotten. In the rebellions of 15 and '45 they ventured on a breach of the law by raising and officering regiments out of their own body, for which the parliament were reduced to the awkward expedient of passing an act of indemnity This short sketch of their political conduct, as it is sufficient to establish their loyalty beyond suspicion, so may it well augment our surprise at the extreme obloquy and reproach with which they are treated. Mr. Hume, a competent judge, if ever there was one, of political principles, and who was far from being partial to dissenters, candidly confesses that to them we are indebted for the preservation of liberty.

The religious opinions of dissenters are so various, that there is perhaps no point in which they are agreed, except in asserting the rights of conscience against all human control and authority. From the time of Queen Elizabeth, under whom they began to make their appearance, their views of religious liberty have gradually extended, commencing at first with a disapprobation of certain rites and ceremonies, the remains of papal superstition. Their total separation from the church did not take place for more than a century after; till despairing of seeing it erected on a comprehensive plan, and being moreover persecuted for their difference of sentiment, they were compelled at last reluctantly to withdraw. Having been thus directed by a train of events into the right path, they pushed their principles to their legitimate consequences, and began to discern the impropriety of all religious establishments whatever,—a sentiment in which they are now nearly united. On this very account, however, of all men they are least likely to disturb the peace of society; for they claim no other liberty than what they wish the whole human race to possess, that of deciding on every question where conscience is concerned. It is sufferance they plead for, not establishment; protection, not splendour. A disposition to impose their religion on others cannot be suspected in men whose distinguishing religious tenet is the disavowal of all human authority.

Their opinion respecting establishments is founded upon reasons which appear to them weighty and solid. They have remarked, that in the three first and purest ages of religion, the church was a stranger to any alliance with temporal powers; that far from needing their aid, Christianity never flourished so much as while they were combined to suppress it; and that the protection of Constantine, though well intended, diminished its purity more than it added to its splendour.

The only pretence for uniting Christianity with civil government is the support it yields to the peace and good order of society. But this benefit will be derived from it, at least in as great a degree, without an establishment as with it. Religion, if it has any power, operates on the *conscience* of men. Resting solely on the belief of invisible realities, and having for its object the good and evil of eternity, it can derive no additional weight or solemnity from human sanctions; but will appear to the most advantage upon hallowed ground, remote from the noise and tumults of worldly policy. Can it be imagined that a dissenter, who believes in divine revelation, does not feel the same moral restraints as if he had received his religion from the hands of parliament? Human laws may debase Christianity, but can never improve it; and being able to add nothing to its evidence, they can add nothing to its force.

Happy had it been, however, had civil establishments of religion been *useless* only, instead of being productive of the greatest evils. But when Christianity is established by law, it is requisite to give the preference to some particular system; and as the magistrate is no better judge of religion than others, the chances are as great of his lending his sanction to the false as to the true. Splendour and emolument must likewise be in some degree attached to the national church; which are a strong inducement to its ministers to defend it, be it ever so remote from the truth. Thus error becomes permanent, and that set of opinions which happens to prevail when the establishment is formed continues, in spite of superior light and improvement, to be handed down without alteration from age to age. Hence the disagreement between the public creed of the church and the private sentiments of its ministers; an evil growing out of the very nature of a hierarchy, and not likely to be remedied before it brings the clerical character into the utmost contempt. Hence the rapid spread of infidelity in various parts of Europe; a natural and never-failing consequence of the corrupt alliance between church and state. Wherever we turn our eyes, we shall perceive the depression of religion is in proportion to the elevation of the hierarchy. In France, where the establishment had attained the utmost splendour, piety had utterly decayed; in England, where the hierarchy is less splendid, more remains of the latter; and in Scotland, whose national church is one of the poorest in the world, a greater sense of religion appears among the inhabitants than in either of the former. It must likewise be plain to every observer that piety flourishes much more among dissenters than among the members of any establishment whatever. This progress of things is so natural, that nothing seems wanting in any country to render the thinking part of the people infidels but a splendid establishment. It will always ultimately debase the clerical character, and perpetuate, both in discipline and doctrine, every error and abuse.

Turn a Christian society into an established church, and it is no longer a voluntary assembly for the worship of God; it is a powerful corporation, full of such sentiments and passions as usually distinguish those bodies; a dread of innovation, an attachment to abuses, a propensity to tyranny and oppression. Hence the convulsions that accompany religious reform, where the truth of the opinions in question is little regarded amid the alarm that is felt for the splendour, opulence, and power which they are the means of supporting. To this alliance of Christianity with civil power it is owing that ecclesiastical history presents a chaos of crimes; and that the progress of religious opinions, which, left to itself, had been calm and silent, may be traced in blood.

Among the evils attending the alliance of church and state, it is not the least that it begets a notion of their interests having some kind of inseparable, though mysterious connexion; so that they who are dissatisfied with the one, must be enemies to the other. Our very language is tinctured with this delusion, in which church and king are blended together with an arrogance that seems copied from Cardinal Wolsey's *Ego et rex meus*, I and my king; as if the establishment were of more consequence than the sovereign who represents the collective majesty of the state. Let the interference of civil power be withdrawn, and the animosity of sects will subside for want of materials to inflame it; nor will any man suspect his neighbour for being of a different religion more than for being of a different complexion from himself. The practice of toleration, it is true, has much abated the violence of those convulsions which, for more than a century from the beginning of the Reformation, shook Europe to its base; but the source and spring of intolerance is by no means exhausted. The steam from that infernal pit will issue through the crevices until they are filled up with the *ruins* of all human establishments.

The alliance between church and state is, in a *political point of view*, extremely suspicious, and much better fitted to the genius of an arbitrary than a free government. To the former it may yield a powerful support; to the latter it must ever prove dangerous. The spiritual submission it exacts is unfavourable to mental vigour, and prepares the way for a servile acquiescence in the encroachments of civil authority. This is so correspondent with *facts*, that the epithet high church, when applied to politics, is familiarly used in our language to convey the notion of arbitrary maxims of government.

As far as submission to civil magistrates is a branch of moral virtue, Christianity will, under every form, be sure to enforce it; for among the various sects and parties into which its profession is divided, there subsists an entire agreement respecting the moral duties it prescribes. To select, therefore, and endow a *particular order* of clergy to teach the duties of submission is useless as a means to secure the peace of a society, though well fitted to produce a slavish subjection. Ministers of that description, considering themselves as allies of the state, yet having no civil department, will be disposed, on all occasions, to strike in with the current of the court; nor are they likely to confine the obligation to obedience within any just and reasonable bounds. They will insensibly become an army of spiritual janizaries. Depending, as they everywhere must, upon the sovereign, his prerogative can never be exalted too high for their emolument, nor can any better instruments be contrived for the accomplishment of arbitrary designs. Their compact and united form, composing a chain of various links which hangs suspended from the throne, admirably fits them for conveying the impression that may sooth, inflame, or mislead the people.

These are the evils which, in my opinion, attach to civil establishments of Christianity. They are, indeed, often mitigated by the virtue of their members; and among the English clergy in particular, as splendid examples of virtue and talents might be produced as any which the annals of human nature can afford; but in all our reasonings concerning *men*, we must lay it down as a maxim that the greater part are moulded by circumstances. If we wish to see the *true spirit* of a hierarchy, we have only to attend to the conduct of what is usually termed the high church party.

While they had sufficient influence with the legislature, they impelled it to persecute; and now that a more enlightened spirit has brought that expedient into disgrace, they turn to the people and endeavour to inflame their minds by the arts of calumny and detraction. When the dissenters applied for the repeal of the corporation and test acts, an alarm was spread of the church being in danger, and their claim was defeated. From the late opposition of the bishops to the repeal of the penal statutes, we learn that they have lost the power rather than the inclination to persecute, or they would be happy to abolish the monuments of a spirit they ceased to approve. The nonsense and absurdity comprised in that part of our laws would move laughter in a company of peasants; but nothing is thought mean or contemptible which is capable of being forged into a weapon of hostility against dissenters. To perpetuate laws which there is no intention to execute is certainly the way to bring law into contempt; but the truth is, that, unwilling to relinquish the right of persecution, though they have no immediate opportunity of exerting it, they retain these statutes as a body in reserve, ready to be brought into the field on the first occasion that shall offer.*

The prejudice entertained against us is not the work of a day, but the accumulation of ages, flowing from the fixed antipathy of a numerous and powerful order of men, distributed through all the classes of society; nor is it easy to conceive to what a pitch popular resentment may be inflamed by artful management and contrivance. Our situation in this respect bears a near resemblance to that of the primitive Christians, against whom, though in themselves the most inoffensive of mankind, the malice of the populace was directed to a still greater degree by similar arts, and upon similar principles. The clamour of the fanatic rabble, the devout execration of dissenters, will remind the reader of ecclesiastical history of the excesses of pagan ferocity, when the people, instigated by their priests, were wont to exclaim, *Christianos ad leones*. There is the less hope of this animosity being allayed from its having arisen from *permanent causes.* That Christianity is a simple institution, unallied to worldly power; that a church is a voluntary society, invested with a right to choose its own officers, and acknowledging no head but Jesus Christ; that ministers are brethren whose emolument should be confined to the voluntary contributions of the people, are maxims drawn from so high an authority, that it may well be apprehended that the church is doomed to vanish before them. Under these circumstances, whatever portion of talents or of worth dissenters may possess serves only to render them more hated, because more formidable. Had they merely revelled with the wanton, and drunk with the drunken,—had they been clothed with curses, they might have been honoured and esteemed notwith-

* This disgrace to the legislation of a great and free country has, at length, but not till more than a third part of a century had elapsed after the above reproach was penned, been finally removed by an enactment for which the dissenters are especially indebted to the able and zealous exertions of that noble example and advocate of all liberal principles, Lord John Russell.—Ed

standing, as true sons of the church; but their dissent is a crime too indelible in the eyes of their enemies for any virtue to alleviate, or any merit to efface.

Till the test business was agitated, however, we were not aware of our labouring under such a weight of prejudice. Confiding in the mildness of the times, and conscious that every trace of resentment was vanished from our own breasts, we fondly imagined that those of churchmen were equally replete with sentiments of generosity and candour. We accordingly ventured on a renewal of our claim as men and as citizens; but had not proceeded far before we were assailed with the bitterest reproaches. The innocent design of relieving ourselves from a disgraceful proscription was construed by our enemies into an attack on the church and state. Their opposition was both more violent and more formidable than was expected. They let us see, that however languidly the flame of their devotion may burn, that of resentment and party spirit, like vestal fire, must never be extinguished in their temples. Calumnies continued to be propagated, till they produced the riots at Birmingham, that ever memorable era in the annals of bigotry and fanaticism, when Europe beheld with astonishment and regret the outrage sustained by philosophy in the most enlightened of countries, and in the first of her sons! When we hear such excesses as these justified and applauded, we seem to be falling back apace into the darkness of the middle ages.

The connexion between civil and religious liberty is too intimate to make it surprising that they who are attached to the one should be friendly to the other. The dissenters have accordingly seldom failed to lend their support to men who seemed likely to restore the vigour of a sinking constitution. Parliamentary reform has been cherished by them with an ardour equal to its importance. This part of their character inflames opposition still further; and affords a pretext to their enemies for overwhelming the cause of liberty under an obnoxious name. The reproach on this head, however, is felt as an honour when it appears by their conduct that they despair of attacking liberty with success while the reputation of dissenters remains undiminished The enmity of the vicious is the test of virtue.

Dissenters are reproached with the appellation of republicans, but the truth of the charge has neither appeared from facts nor been supported by any reasonable evidence. Among them, as among other classes (and in no greater proportion), there are persons to be found, no doubt, who, without any hostility to the present government, prefer in theory a republican to a monarchical form; a point on which the most enlightened men in all ages have entertained very different opinions. In a government like ours, consisting of three simple elements, as this variety of sentiment may naturally be expected to take place, so if any predilection be felt towards one more than another, that partiality seems most commendable which inclines to the republican part. At most it is only the love of liberty to excess. The mixture of monarchy and nobility is chiefly of use as it gives regularity, order, and stability to popular freedom. Were we, however, without any proof, to admit that dissenters are more tinctured with republican principles than others, it might be considered as the natural effect of the absurd conduct of the legislature. Exposed to pains and penalties, excluded from all offices of trust, proscribed by the spirit of the present reign, menaced and insulted wherever they appear, they must be more than men if they felt no resentment, or were passionately devoted to the ruling powers. To expect affection in return for injury is to gather where they have not scattered, and reap where they have not sown. The superstition of dissenters is not so abject as to prompt them to worship the constitution through fear. Yet as they have not forgotten the benefits it imparted, and the protection it afforded till of late, they are too much its friends to flatter its defects or defend its abuses. Their only wish is to see it reformed, and reduced to its original principles.

In recent displays of loyalty they must acknowledge themselves extremely defective. They have never plundered their neighbours to show their attachment to their king; nor has their zeal for religion ever broke out into oaths and execrations. They have not proclaimed their respect for regular government by a breach of the laws; or attempted to maintain tranquillity by riots. These beautiful specimens of loyalty belong to the virtue and moderation of the high church party alone, with whose character they perfectly correspond.

In a scurrilous paper which has been lately circulated with malignant industry, the dissenters at large, and Dr. Price in particular, are accused, with strange effrontery, of having involved us in the American war; when it is well known they ever stood aloof from that scene of guilt and blood.

Had their remonstrances been regarded, the calamities of that war had never been incurred; but, what is of more consequence in the estimation of anonymous scribblers, there would have remained one lie less to swell the catalogue of their falsehoods.

From the joy which dissenters have expressed at the French revolution, it has been most absurdly inferred that they wish for a similar event in England; without considering that such a conclusion is a libel on the British constitution, as it must proceed on a supposition that our government is as despotic as the ancient monarchy of France. To imagine the feelings must be the same when the objects are so different shows a most lamentable degree of malignity and folly.

Encompassed as dissenters are by calumny and reproach, they have still the satisfaction to reflect, that these have usually been the lot of distinguished virtue; and that in the corrupt state of men's interests and passions, the unpopularity of a cause is rather a presumption of its excellence.

They will be still more happy if the frowns of the world should be the means of reviving that spirit of evangelical piety which once distinguished them so highly. Content if they can gain protection, without being so romantic as to aspire to praise, they will continue firm, I doubt not, in those principles which they have hitherto acted on, unseduced by rewards, and unshaken by dangers. From the passions o their enemies, they will appeal to the judgment of posterity;—a more impartial tribunal. Above all, they will calmly await the decision of the Great Judge, before whom both they and their enemies must appear, and the springs and sources of their mutual animosity be laid open; when the clouds of misrepresentation being scattered, it will be seen they are a virtuous and oppressed people, who are treading, though with unequal steps, in the path of those illustrious prophets, apostles, and martyrs of whom the world was not worthy. In the mean time they are far from envying the popularity and applause which may be acquired in a contrary course; esteeming the reproaches of freedom above the splendours of servitude.

SECTION VI.

On the Causes of the Present Discontents.

We have arrived, it is a melancholy truth which can no longer be concealed,—we have at length arrived at that crisis when nothing but speedy and effectual reform can save us from ruin. An amendment in the representation is wanted, as well to secure the liberty we already possess as to open the way for the removal of those abuses which pervade every branch of the administration. The accumulation of debt and taxes to a degree unexampled in any other age or country, has so augmented the influence of the crown as to destroy the equipoise and balance of the constitution. The original design of the funding system, which commenced in the reign of King William, was to give stability to the revolution by engaging the moneyed interest to embark on its bottom. It immediately advanced the influence of the crown, which the whigs then exalted as much as possible as a countervail to the interests of the pretender.

The mischief of this short-sighted policy cannot be better described than in the language of Bolingbroke. "Few men," says he, "at that time looked forward enough to foresee the consequences of the new constitution of the revenue that was soon afterward formed, nor of the method of the funding system that immediately took place; which, absurd as they are, have continued since, till it has become scarce possible to alter them. Few people, I say, foresaw how the multiplication of taxes and the creation of funds would increase yearly the power of the crown, and bring our liberties, by a natural and necessary progression, into a more real though less apparent danger than they were in before the revolution; a due reflection on the experience of other ages and countries would have pointed out national corruption as the natural and necessary consequence of investing the crown with the management of so vast a revenue; and also the loss of liberty as the natural and necessary consequence of national corruption."*

If there be any truth in these reflections, how much must our apprehensions be heightened by the prodigious augmentation of revenue and

* Letter II. on the Study of History.

debt since the time of George the First! What a harvest has been reaped from the seeds of corruption then sown!—The revenue is now upwards of seventeen millions, and though nine are employed to pay the interest of the national debt, this is small consolation when we reflect that that debt is the remnant of wasteful, destructive wars, and that till there is a change in the system we are continually liable to similar calamities. The multiplied channels through which seventeen millions of money must flow into the treasury, the legion of officers it creates, the patronage its expenditure on the several branches of the administration supplies, have rendered the influence of the crown nearly absolute and decisive. The control of parliament sinks under this pressure into formality: the balance of the different orders becomes a mere theory, which serves to impose upon ignorance and varnish corruption. There is no power in the state that can act as a sufficient antagonist to the silent irresistible force of royal patronage.

The influence of the crown, by means of its revenue, is more dangerous than prerogative, in proportion as corruption operates after a more concealed manner than force. A violent act of prerogative is sensibly felt and creates an alarm; but it is the nature of corruption to lay apprehension asleep, and to effect its purposes while the forms of liberty remain undisturbed. The first employs force to enslave the people; the second employs the people to enslave themselves. The most determined enemy to freedom can wish for nothing more than the continuance of present abuses. While the semblance of representation can be maintained, while popular delusion can be kept up, he will spare the *extremities* of liberty. He aims at a higher object, that of *striking at the heart.*

A fatal lethargy has long been spreading among us, attended, as is natural, with a prevailing disposition both in and out of parliament to treat plans of reform with contempt. After the accession, place and pension bills were frequently passed by the commons though rejected by the lords; nothing of that nature is now ever attempted. A standing army in time of peace was a subject of frequent complaint, and is expressly provided against by the Bill of Rights: it is now become a part of the constitution; for though the nominal direction be placed in parliament, the mutiny bill passes as a matter of course, the forces are never disbanded; the more completely to detach them from the community, barracks are erected; and martial law is established in its utmost severity. If freedom can survive this expedient, copied from the practice of foreign despots, it will be an instance of unexampled good fortune. Mr. Hume terms it a mortal distemper in the British constitution, of which it must *inevitably* perish.

To whatever cause it be owing, it is certain the measures of administration have, during the present reign, leaned strongly towards arbitrary power. The decision on the Middlesex election was a blow aimed at the vitals of the constitution. Before the people had time to recover from their panic they were plunged into the American war—a war of pride and ambition, and ending in humiliation and disgrace. The spirit of the government is so well understood, that the most violent even of the clergy are content to drop their animosity, to turn their affections into a new channel, and to devote to the house of Hanover the flattery and the zeal by which they ruined the race of Stuart. There cannot be a clearer symptom of the decay of liberty than the dread of speculative opinions, which is at present carried to a length in this nation that can scarcely be exceeded. Englishmen were accustomed till of late to make political speculation the amusement of leisure and the employment of genius;—they are now taught to fear it more than death. Under the torpid touch of despotism the patriotic spirit has shrunk into a narrow compass; confined to gaze with admiration on the proceedings of parliament, and listen to the oracles of the minister with silent acquiescence and pious awe. Abuses are sacred, and the pool of corruption must putrify in peace. Persons who a few years back were clamorous for reform are making atonement for having been betrayed into any appearance of virtue by a quick return to their natural character. Is not the kingdom peopled with spies and informers? Are not inquisitorial tribunals erected in every corner of the land? A stranger who, beholding a whole nation filled with alarm, should inquire the cause of the commotion, would be a little surprised on being informed, that instead of any appearance of insurrection or plots, a pamphlet had only been published. In a government upheld by so immense a revenue, and boasting a constitution declared to be the envy of the world, this abject distrust of its own power is more than a million lectures on corruptions and abuses. The wisdom of ages, the masterpiece of human policy, complete in all its parts, and that needs no reformation, can hardly support itself against a sixpenny pamphlet, devoid, it is said, of truth or ability! To require sycophants to blush is exacting too great a departure from the decorum of their character but common sense might be expected to remain after shame is extinguished.

Whoever seriously contemplates the present infatuation of the people and the character of the leaders will be tempted to predict the speedy downfall of liberty. They cherish the forms while they repress the spirit of the constitution; they persecute freedom and adorn its sepulchre. When corruption has struck its roots so deep, it may be doubted whether even the liberty of the press be not of more detriment than advantage. The prints which are the common sources of information are replete with falsehood; virtue is calumniated; and scarcely are any characters safe from their blast, except the advocates of corruption. The greater part no doubt are in the pay of ministry or their adherents. Thus delusion spreads, and the people are instructed to confound anarchy with reform, their friends with their oppressors.

Who can hear without indignant contempt the ministers' annual eulogium on the English constitution! Is the parliament so ignorant, then, that it needs to go to school every session to learn those elements of political knowledge which every Briton understands? Or is the nature of the British constitution a secret in the breast of the ministry, to be opened with the budget? Indisputable excellence wants no encomium; but this flattery is intended to bury in an admiration of its merit all remembrance of its defects. Whatever remains of beauty or vigour it possesses are held in no estimation but as they produce an acquiescence in abuses. It is its imperfections only ministers admire, its corruptions that solace them. The topics of their encomium are as absurd as the purpose is infamous. The flourishing state of trade and manufactures is displayed in proof of the unequalled excellence of the British constitution, without reflecting that a temporary decay will support with equal force an opposite conclusion. For if we owe our present prosperity to the nature of the government, our recent calamities must be traced to the same source, and that constitution which is now affirmed to be the best, must be allowed during the American war to have been the worst. That there is a connexion between commercial prosperity and the nature of a government must be admitted; but its operation is gradual and slow, not felt from year to year, but to be traced by the comparison of one age and country with another. But allowing that our wealth may increase along with the increase of abuses, the nation we hope is not so sordid as to look upon wealth as the supreme good; however well that idea may correspond with the views of a ministry who seem determined to leave us no other. Freedom, as it animates industry by securing its rewards, opens a path to wealth; but if that wealth be suffered to debase a people and render them venal and dependent, it will silently conduct them back again to misery and depression. Rome was never more opulent than on the eve of departing liberty. Her vast wealth was a sediment that remained on the reflux of the tide. It is quite unnecessary to remind the reader how all this at present is reversed, and that the unbounded prodigality of Mr. Pitt and his successors in the conduct of the war, which the corruption of parliament enabled them to maintain, has plunged the nation into the deepest abyss of poverty and distress.

It is singular enough, but I hope not ominous, that the flattery bestowed by the poets of antiquity on the ruling powers resembles, in every thing but its elegance, the adulation of modern sycophants. The extent of empire, the improvement of arts, the diffusion of opulence and splendour, are the topics with which Horace adorned the praises of Augustus: but the penetration of Tacitus developes, amid these flattering appearances, the seeds of ruin. The florid bloom but ill concealed that fatal malady which preyed upon the vitals.

Between the period of national honour and complete degeneracy there is usually an interval of national vanity, during which examples of virtue are recounted and admired without being imitated. The Romans were never more proud of their ancestors than when they ceased to resemble them. From being the freest and most high-spirited people in the world, they suddenly fell into the tamest and most abject submission. Let not the name of Britons, my countrymen, too much elate you; nor ever think yourselves safe while you abate one jot of that holy jealousy by which your liberties have been hitherto secured. The richer the inheritance bequeathed you, the more it merits your care for its preservation. The possession must be continued by that spirit with which it was at first acquired; and as it was gained by vigilance, it will be lost by supineness. A degenerate race repose on the merit of their forefathers; the virtuous create a fund of their own. The former look back upon their ancestors to hide their shame; the latter look forward to posterity to levy a tribute of admiration. In vain will you confide in the forms of a free constitution. Unless you reanimate those forms with fresh vigour, they will be melancholy memorials of what you once were, and haunt you with the shade of departed liberty. A silent stream of corruption poured over the whole land has tainted every branch of the administration with decay. On your temperate but manly exertions depend the happiness and freedom of the latest posterity. That assembly which sits by right of representation will be little inclined to oppose your will expressed in a firm decisive manner. You may be deafened by clamour, misled by sophistry, or weakened by division, but you cannot be despised with impunity. A vindictive ministry may hang the terrors of criminal prosecution over the heads of a few with success; but at their peril will they attempt to intimidate a nation. The trick of associations, of pretended plots, and silent insurrections, will oppose a feeble barrier to the impression of the popular mind.

The theory of the constitution in the most important particulars is a satire on the practice. The theory provides the responsibility of ministers as a check to the execution of ill designs; but in reality we behold the basest of the tribe retreat from the ruin of their country, loaded with honours and with spoils. Theory tells us the parliament is free and independent; experience will correct the mistake by showing its subservience to the crown. We learn from the first that the legislature is chosen by the unbiased voice of all who can be supposed to have a will of their own; we learn from the last the pretended electors are but a handful of the people, who are never less at their own disposal than in the business of election. The theory holds out equal benefits to all, and equal liberty, without any other discrimination than that of a good and bad subject: its practice brands with proscription and disgrace a numerous class of inhabitants on account of their religion. In theory the several orders of the state are a check on each other; but corruption has oiled the wheels of that machinery, harmonized its motions, and enabled it to bear, with united pressure, on the happiness of the people.

The principal remedy for the diseases of the state is undoubtedly a reform in parliament; from which, as a central point, inferior improvements may issue; but as I have already treated on that subject at large, I shall not insist on it here. I cannot close this pamphlet, however, without adverting for a moment to a few of the principal objects which well merit the attention of the legislature.

On the abuses in the church it is to little purpose to expatiate, as they are too numerous to be detailed, and too inveterate to be corrected. Unless it be a maxim that honesty will endanger her existence, her creeds ought in all reason to correspond with the sentiments of her members. The world, it is to be feared, will be little edified by the example of a church which, in compelling its ministers to subscribe opinions that few of them believe, is a discipline of fraud. Nor is the collection of tithes calculated to soften the odium. As a mode of union with the parishioners, they are fruitful of contention; as a restraint on the improvement of land, impolitic and oppressive; as a remnant of the Jewish law, superstitious and absurd. True magnanimity would instruct the clergy to recede from a claim which they will probably be compelled shortly to relinquish. But no reform, it seems, must take place in the church any more than in the state, that its corruptions may keep pace with the progress of its ally.

The condition of the poor in this country calls for compassion and redress. Many of them, through the want of mental improvement, are sunk almost beneath the level of humanity;* and their hard-earned pittance is so diminished by taxes, that it is with the utmost difficulty they can nourish their children, and utterly impossible to afford them education. The poor laws enacted for their relief, by confining their industry to a particular spot, and denying them the privilege of residing where they may exert it to the greatest advantage, are an accumulated oppression. Were industry allowed to find its level, were the poor-laws abolished, and a small portion of that expense which swells the tide of corruption, the splendours of the great, and the miseries of war, bestowed on the instruction of the common people, the happy effects would descend to the remotest posterity, and open a prospect which humanity might delight to anticipate. In England, we have been adding wheel to wheel, and spring to spring, till we have rendered the machine of government far too complicated; forgetting, in the midst of wars, negotiations, and factious disputes, that the true end of civil polity is the happiness of the people. We have listened to every breeze that moves along the surface of Europe, and descried danger from afar; while, deaf to the complaints of the poor, we have beheld ignorance, wretchedness, and barbarity multiply at home, without the smallest regard. Is it possible to behold with patience the numberless tribe of placemen, pensioners, and sycophants who are enriched at the public expense; a noxious spawn engendered by the corruptions of government, and nourished by its diseases. Were our immense revenue conducive to the maintenance of royal dignity, or proportioned to the exigences of the state, it would be borne with pleasure; but at present it bids fair to be the purchase of our servitude.

Our laws, in order to become a proper rule of civil life, much want revision and amendment. They are moreover never promulgated. For this omission Judge Blackstone assigns a very curious reason: "That being enacted by our representatives, every man is supposed, in the eye of the law, to be present in the legislature." It would be an improvement on this delegated knowledge of the law, if the penalty were also delegated, and criminals punished by representation. The

* The change in this respect since the first publication of the "Apology" is of the most gratifying kind. All ranks of society, and all persuasions of Christians, have vied with each other in their efforts to give religious and other useful instruction to the children of the poor. Still there remains much to be done, and we are in this point of the general education of the lower classes *very* far behind the Americans, especially those in the state of New-York.—Ed.

laws in their present state are so piled into volumes, encumbered with precedents, and perplexed with intricacies, that they are often rather a snare than a guide, and are a fruitful source of the injustice they are intended to prevent. The expense is as formidable as the penalty; nor is it to any purpose to say they are the same to the poor as to the rich, while by their delay, expense, and perplexity they are placed on an eminence which opulence only can ascend. The commendation bestowed so liberally by foreigners on English jurisprudence was never meant to be extended to our municipal code, which is confused, perplexed, and sanguinary in the extreme; but to the trial by jury, and the dignified impartiality which marks the conduct of judges. For want of gradual improvements, to enable it to keep pace with the progress of society, the most useful operations of law are clouded by fictions.*

These are a few only of the maladies which indicate a bad habit of the political body: nor can a true estimate be made of our situation so much by adverting to *particular evils* as by an attention to the general aspect of affairs. The present crisis is, in my apprehension, the fullest of terror and of danger we have ever experienced. In the extension of excise laws, in the erection of barracks, in the determined adherence to abuses displayed by parliament, in the desertion of pretended patriots, the spread of arbitrary principles, the tame subdued spirit of the nation, we behold the seeds of political ruin quickening into life. The *securities* of liberty, as was long since remarked by Dr. Price, have given way; and what remains is little more than an *indulgence*, which cannot continue long when it ceases to be cherished in the affections of the people. The little of public virtue that still subsists is no match for disciplined armies of corruption. The people are perishing for lack of knowledge. Disquieted by imaginary alarms, insensible to real danger that awaits them, they are taught to court that servitude which will be a source of misery to themselves and to posterity.

Deplorable as the prospect is, a precarious hope may be founded, perhaps, on the magnitude of abuses. There is, it has often been remarked, an ultimate point both of elevation and depression in the affairs of kingdoms, to which when they arrive they begin to turn of their own accord and to fall back into their ancient channels. We are certainly entitled to all the comfort that consideration is capable of affording. Taxation can hardly be more oppressive, representation more venal and inadequate, the influence of the people more extinguished, or falsehood and deception more triumphant than they are at present.

There is also another circumstance attending the present crisis which, if we are wise enough to improve it, may be of the utmost advantage. Of the numberless political parties which have hitherto distracted our attention and divided our attachment there now remain but two,—the patrons of corruption and the friends of liberty; they who are waiting for the disorders of government to ripen into arbitrary power, and they who are anxious to bring back the constitution to its original

* See an excellent publication on this subject, entitled "Juridical Essays," by Mr. Randall.

principles. The colours by which they are distinguished are too bold and strong to be ever confounded; or if there could be any possible embarrassment in the choice, the ministry have condescended to remove that obscurity, by pursuing an interest, not only distinct from, but directly opposed to, that of the people. The clamour of whigs and tories hath happily subsided; and pretended patriots are at length so kind as to unmask before the people, and stand forth in their native character, the objects of just detestation. We cannot wish for better lessons of public virtue than is furnished by the contrast of their vices.

On the present war, until the views of the ministry are more unfolded, it behooves me to speak with tenderness and reserve. If nothing more be intended than the maintenance of national honour and the faith of treaties, it will merit the warmest support of every well-wisher to his country. But if the re-establishment of the ancient government of France be any part of the object; if it be a war with freedom, a confederacy of kings against the rights of man; it will be the last humiliation and disgrace that can be inflicted on Great Britain; and were there any truth in tales of incantation, to behold us engaged in such a cause were enough to disturb the repose of our ancestors and move the ashes of the dead! The steps preparatory to the war, the inflamed passions and the character of our allies, afford an ill omen of the temper with which it will be conducted. The pretence respecting the Netherlands certainly entitles the ministry to the praise of consistence. It is quite of a piece with the candour and sincerity which affirmed the balance of Europe to be destroyed by the seizure of Oczakow, but denied it was endangered by the conquest of Poland and the invasion of France.

The French revolution, we cannot but remember, was from the first an object of jealousy to ministers. There needed not the late unhappy excesses, the massacres of September, and the execution of Louis, to excite or display their hostility. It appeared in the insult and derision of their retainers, from the highest to the lowest. If they meant fairly to the interests of general liberty, why that uneasiness at the fall of despotism in a neighbouring country? Why render parliament a theatre of abuse on a revolution whose commencement was distinguished by unexampled mildness and tranquillity? But this part of their conduct was likewise consistent. Intent on the destruction of liberty in one country, they were disconcerted at seeing it revive in another; and before they ventured to extinguish the dying taper, waited for the surrounding scene to be shut up in darkness. I am perfectly aware that to speak in terms of decency and respect of the French revolution is to incur, in the prevailing disposition of the times, the last of infamies. If we dare to rejoice at the emancipation of a great people from thraldom, it must be at the peril of the foulest imputations that imagination can invent or malignity apply. In contempt, however, of these calumnies, I am free to confess the French revolution has always appeared to me, and does still appear, the most splendid event recorded in the annals of history. The friends of liberty contemplate the crimes and disorders with which it has been stained* with the deepest regret, but they still hope that they will in the result be more than compensated by the grandeur of its principles and the beneficence of its effects. Instead of wishing for a similar event in England, they are intent on reform chiefly to avoid that necessity. Under every *form* of government they know how to recognise the divine aspect of freedom, and without it can be satisfied with none. The evils of anarchy and of despotism are two extremes which they equally dread; and between which no middle path can be found but that of effectual reform. To avert the calamities that await us on either side, the streams of corruption must be drained off, the independence of parliament restored, the ambition of aristocracy repressed, and the majesty of the people lift itself up. It is possible to retreat from the brink of a precipice, but wo to that nation which sleeps upon it!

* The execution of the king was certainly a most cruel and unjustifiable transaction, alike repugnant to law, order, and humanity. Without being conducive to any views of policy whatever, it seems to have been merely a gratification of the most detestable passions. The treatment of the beautiful and unfortunate queen and of the royal family is barbarous and unmanly in the extreme When we look at their sufferings, humanity weeps, and pity forgets their crimes.

REVIEW

OF THE

APOLOGY FOR THE FREEDOM OF THE PRESS,

PUBLISHED IN

THE CHRISTIAN GUARDIAN:

AND

MR. HALL'S REPLY.

[PUBLISHED IN 1822.]

REVIEW

OF

MR. HALL'S FREEDOM OF THE PRESS.*

Extracted from the Christian Guardian for Jan. 1822.

"THE political principles of the Bible are simple, distinct, and plain. The sacred writers enter into no niceties, draw no lines of exact demarkation, meet no involved cases of civil casuistry; but, speaking of mankind generally as alike depraved and unruly, and of governments as the creations of God's providence, they inculcate, without qualification, reservation, or restriction, the obvious and indispensable duties of submission, honour, and obedience.

"It has been, however, very much the fashion of late to get rid of these unpleasant and '*degrading*' injunctions by pleading the change of time and circumstances, and the difference between the laws and system of government under which we are privileged to live and those of the apostolic days. Now, as to the general duty of obedience, it is obvious that it must apply rather *more* than *less* strongly to those who live under a paternal government than to those who live under a tyrannical one. At the same time we are ready to allow, that the system of freedom which, in this country, gives to the people a share in the legislature and an influence over the government, renders the submission due from them less *implicit* and *uninquiring*, at the same time that it increases the obligation to its cheerful payment.

"But although it be conceded that under a constitution which renders the people a party to their own government, it is lawful and proper for laymen to interest themselves intimately in political concerns, and even to a certain extent to participate in political contests, there is one body of men whom we could ever wish to see taking no other part in these matters than as moderators, instructers, and peacemakers.

"The ministers of the gospel must, in the discharge of their duty,—they must, if they will '*declare the whole counsel* of God,' sometimes touch upon those passages of Scripture which inculcate the *duties of subjects*. While St. Paul, in the days of Nero himself, was led by the Holy Spirit to write, 'Submit to every ordinance of man for the Lord's sake;' and to pronounce, without hesitation, 'He that resisteth the power,' tyrannical as it was in the extreme, 'resisteth the ordinance of God;' and while similar passages abound in the inspired volume, it cannot be thought consistent with the character of a preacher of the gospel to maintain an absolute *silence* on these topics. But there is one rule which, in our opinion, ministers would do well to follow, and that is, to go no further than the Bible will carry them. The war of parties and factions, the continual struggle of political leaders, the various questions of constitutional casuistry, are subjects which lie beyond this boundary, and with which they would do well not to embroil themselves. The servant of the Lord is exhorted 'not to strive,' but 'to cut off occasion

* In order that the propriety of Mr. Hall's reply may be fairly estimated, it has been thought right to reprint the original article that called it forth.—ED.

from them which desire occasion:' and, assuredly, he will find that the bare discharge of his plain duty in these things will expose him to sufficient obloquy and reproach.

"Entertaining this view of the subject, it is with sorrow that we observe the republication, under his own immediate sanction, of Mr. Hall's 'Apology for the Freedom of the Press.' This work was first given to the world about thirty years ago, and has been long since forgotten, or remembered only as one of the sins of its author's youth. Since its disappearance Mr. H. has so much better employed his time and his great talents, that he may now be considered as standing in the very first rank among the non-conformists of the present day. And is it not a lamentable thing to see such a man stepping forward, in the ripeness of his years and at the height of his well-earned reputation, to obtrude himself on the public in the degraded character of a violent party-scribe:—and yet, in what other light can we consider the man who, in so uncalled-for and gratuitous a manner, and at so comparatively peaceful a period, sends into the world, with the sanction of his name, and of his latest corrections, a new edition of such a pamphlet as this?

"He indeed states, as an excuse for the republication, that the term of copyright being expired, it was no longer in his power to prevent the reprinting of this work. The law, however, is not so; the power of perpetuating its oblivion lay still in his hands. But had he even been correct on this point, where was the necessity for his being an active agent in this reappearance?

"To characterize the tract before us appropriately we need only observe, that the principal topics discussed by this '*minister of the gospel*' are, the right of public discussion, the propriety of political associations, *parliamentary reform*, the rights of men, the character of dissenters, the present discontents. The work is extremely personal, and great bitterness is shown towards the late Bishop Horsley, Mr. Burke, and Mr. Pitt. We shall not imitate Mr. Hall's example by entering into a discussion on the subject of Mr. Pitt's political character; but we should have hoped that the reflection of his undoubted integrity and of that perfect devotion to his country which led him to sacrifice even life itself, in its service, might have spared him, at the distance of sixteen years from his death, a new volley of bitter reproach from one whose vocation is '*the gospel of peace*.'

"As to the character of Bishop Horsley, it is now placed far beyond the reach of his adversaries; and the Christian world will know how to appreciate invectives against such a man from one who is at the same time the eulogist of Priestley and Price, the Socinians, and of Mary Wolstonecraft, the female libertine and Deist.

"Looking, then, upon this work as one of which a critical analysis would be ill placed in the pages of the Christian Guardian, we shall conclude with a specimen or two of the political creed of Mr. Hall, and of the manner in which he supports it.

"He is, then, as far as professed doctrine can make him, plainly and clearly a radical reformer. He pleads for 'annual parliaments,' for universal suffrage, for the unfettered publication of every kind of blasphemy, for the *exclusion* of the relatives of noblemen from the House of Commons, for the overthrow of all ecclesiastical establishments, and for 'the sovereignty of the people.' In what part of the sacred volume he has discovered the least sanction for any one of these notions we are at a loss to imagine.

"In fact, the whole pamphlet is an argument in favour of the supremacy and infallibility of the people, and of the necessity of paying the most implicit obedience to the least expression of their will. Now, could these notions have been carried into practice at the time they were written (soon after the Birmingham riots), and could a legislature have been formed upon Mr. H.'s universal suffrage plan, the necessary and inevitable consequence would have been, that as the feeling of the multitude ran violently against all the friends of the French revolution, Mr. H. and most of his fellow-labourers and admirers would have been silenced, banished, or hanged. So much for the *effects* which might be expected to follow Mr. Hall's plan. And as for the *principles* upon which that plan is founded, we find him broadly stating in the latter end of this work, with admirable consistency, that 'calumny and reproach are usually the lot of distinguished virtue,' and that '*the unpopularity of a cause is rather a presumption of its excellence*.' Now, if the fact be so, it cannot be for the good of the people that this perpetually erroneous criterion should govern the affairs of the state.

"Mr. Hall concludes his prefixed advertisement with the hope 'that the reader will recollect, as an excuse for the warmth of his expression, that the work is an *eulogium on a dead friend;*' which is asserting, in other words, that the press is enslaved and its liberty departed. And, having written this some years since, he now coolly republishes it, after witnessing the acquittals of Hone and Wooller, and while the wretched Carlile is braving every effort that can be made to stop the torrent of blasphemy which has so long issued from his warehouse.

"Again, Mr. H. assured us, thirty years since, that we had then '*at length arrived* at that crisis when nothing but speedy and effectual reform could save us from ruin.' Now, since the first publication of this prediction we have maintained a contest of long duration with the greatest conqueror of modern times, and have fairly subdued him. We have immensely augmented the extent of our empire, and increased its ratio of population. We have tripled our commerce and our revenue. We have improved, it is to be hoped, the state of our internal population by the establishment of schools and the increase of places of worship; and we have made some progress in the commencement at least of the great work of evangelizing the whole world.

"And after all this, Mr. Hall comes forward with much admirable simplicity to tell us of this wonderful prophecy of his, delivered only the third part of a century since, that without *immediate reform in parliament*, *ruin* was then *inevitable.* Now, it is certain that this same *immediate reform* has not yet taken place, although one whole generation has passed away since the promulgation of this prediction. Has the dreadful alternative then fallen upon us? Have we been crushed by this *inevitable ruin?*

"The present comparatively prosperous and improving circumstances of the kingdom answers No! to this question. The general state of the country, the average condition of the great mass of the people, is *better*, and not *worse*, than at the time when Mr. Hall first published this direful presage.

"If there be any exception to this state of general improvement, it is to be found in the depression of the agricultural interest of the country. But we are told by those who ought to be judges that the evils which threaten these classes have arisen from the want of sufficient legislative protection. And do we not know from the conduct of the mobs of 1815 that a reformed parliament, a universal suffrage parliament, according to Mr. Hall's plan, would have withheld even the partial protection which has hitherto been granted, and would have thereby made what is now distress and perplexity, absolute ruin and destruction? So much for the necessity and the effects of reform.

"It is with the most painful feelings that we are thus compelled to animadvert on this uncalled-for and altogether unnecessary republication. We repeat, that the general principle upon which we disapprove of it is, that a minister of the gospel will always best consult the interests of his flock and the dignity of his own character by abstaining from any political discussion which transgresses the bounds prescribed in the Holy Scriptures. Mr. Hall has overstepped these limits, and has plunged into the thickest of the war of party politics. He has also chosen, we apprehend, the side which is generally found in most direct opposition to the Scripture injunctions of peace, quietness, and obedience. And as the weight of his character and the authority of his name render error from his pen trebly dangerous, we have felt only the more imperatively called upon to enter our protest against the principles which he has endeavoured to lay down, and to unmask the sophistry of the arguments by which he has attempted to support them."

MR. HALL'S REPLY.

To the Editor of the Leicester Journal.

SIR,

A VIOLENT attack on my character having appeared in your paper a few weeks since, contained in an extract from a periodical work entitled the *Christian Guardian*, I rely on your impartiality for permitting me to repel the accusation through the same medium. If the misrepresentations which I have to complain of had been confined within the bounds of decency, I should have consulted my ease by remaining silent: but the writer, whoever he is, has availed himself of the impunity attached to anonymous communications so unsparingly that I might be justly charged, not only with a criminal indifference to character, but with being accessary to the delusion of the public, were I to make no reply.

The amount of my offence consists in uttering a new edition of political pamphlet, which made its first appearance many years since and passed through several editions. This writer says I might have suppressed it; but the contrary is the fact. The term of copyright is well known to extend to fourteen years, after which any one is at liberty to republish a work without the consent of the author. More than that time had elapsed since the last edition, and as it was at the option of any bookseller to reprint it, so I was assured from various quarters that whether I consented or not it would certainly be republished. The only alternative that remained was, either to suffer it to come forth in a form perhaps most incorrect and mingled with foreign infusions, or to publish it under my own eye, and with such alterations and corrections as the author might deem proper. The latter was preferred, and for this a torrent of invective has issued from the *Christian Guardian.*

It certainly is very unusual for a writer to suppress his own publications, unless he has recanted the principles they contain. To persevere in doing so naturally exposes him to the suspicion either that he has renounced his former opinions or that he is afraid to avow them: but neither of these situations is mine. I have changed no principle and I feel no fear. Why then should I act in such a manner as must render me perpetually liable to either of these imputations? For a considerable time, indeed, after loud and repeated importunities, I declined a compliance with the wishes expressed for republication, from a sincere reluctance to engage in political controversy. By one party, in the mean while, it was my fortune to be so unequivocally claimed as a convert, and by the other so assailed with reproaches as an apostate, that I was convinced by experience there was no other way of putting an end to the misrepresentations of both but to republish the original pamphlet. Had I never written it, the same motives which made me reluctant to reprint might probably have prevented my writing it; but since there is not a principle in it which I can conscientiously retract, and my silence has occasioned numerous misrepresentations and mistakes, the fair and manly part was doubtless to republish it. An ingenuous mind is not less ashamed of receiving praises it is conscious it has not deserved, than indignant at reproaches which are not merited.

But a minister of the gospel, it seems, is on no occasion to meddle with party politics. How exactly this maxim was adhered to at the commencement of the late war, when military banners were consecrated, and the people everywhere summoned to arms

> "By pulpit, drum ecclesiastic,
> Beat with fist instead of a stick,"

must be fresh in the recollection of my readers.

The men who in the garb of clergymen bustle at electioneering meetings, forsooth, are not really such, but merely assume the disguise of that holy order, since it would be uncandid to suppose they can so universally lose sight of what is befitting ministers of the gospel. The venerable bench of bishops who sit in the House of Lords either attend in silent pomp without taking any part in the deliberations, or they violate the character of ministers of the gospel. We must have been grossly imposed upon by the public prints, which informed us of the clergy of a whole archdeaconry, or diocess, meeting to petition parliament against the Catholic claims, since they could never, with one consent, depart so far from the decorum of ministers of the gospel!

The plain state of the case is, not that the writer is offended at my meddling with politics, but that I have meddled on the wrong side. Had the same mediocrity of talent been exerted in eulogizing the measures of ministers, his greetings would have been as loud as his invective is bitter. But it was exerted to expose public abuses, to urge the necessity of reform, and lay open the tergiversation of the heaven-born minister and Sunday duellist, who, after devoting the day of rest to deeds of blood, has by a strange fatality obtained a sort of political beatification. *Hinc illæ lachrymæ!*

Another head of accusation is, that I have censured the character of Bishop Horsley, whose character, the reviewer tells us, "is far removed beyond my attack, while I have eulogized Dr. Price and Dr. Priestley, Socinians." To this it is sufficient to reply that Dr. Price was *not* a Socinian, but an Arian; he wrote professedly in confutation of socinianism; and though I disapprove of his religious principles, I feel no hesitation in affirming, in spite of the frantic and unprincipled abuse of Burke, that a more ardent and enlightened friend of his country never lived than that venerable patriarch of freedom. Such were the sentiments of the worshipful corporation of London, who in token of their esteem presented him with the freedom of the city in a golden box; such was the judgment of Mr. Pitt, who long professed himself his admirer, and condescended to seek his advice on questions of finance. Dr. Priestley, it is acknowledged, was a Socinian; but it was not under the character that he was eulogized. It was as the friend of liberty, the victim of intolerance, and the author of some of the most brilliant philosophical discoveries of modern times, for which he was celebrated throughout Europe, and his name enrolled as a member of the most illustrious institutions; so that my eulogy was but a mere feeble echo of the applause which resounded from every civilized portion of the globe. And are we suddenly fallen back into the darkness and ignorance of the middle ages, during which the spell of a stupid and unfeeling uniformity bound the nations in iron slumbers, that it has become a crime to praise a man for talents which the whole world admired, and for virtues which his enemies confessed, merely because his religious creed was erroneous? If any thing could sink orthodoxy into contempt, it would be its association with such gothic barbarity of sentiment, such reptile meanness. What renders the wretched bigotry of the reviewer the more conspicuous is, that the eulogy in question was written almost immediately after the Birmingham riots, that disgraceful ebullition of popular phrensy, during which a ferocious mob tracked his steps like bloodhounds, demolished his house, destroyed his library and apparatus, and advancing from thence to the destruction of private and public buildings, filled the whole town and vicinity with terror and dismay. What sort of a *Christian Guardian* the reviewer would have proved on that occasion may be easily inferred from his passing over these atrocities in silence, while he discharges his malice on their unoffending victim.

The maxim *De mortuis nil nisi bonum* admits of exceptions; and as I am vilified for censuring Bishop Horsley, whose character, it is affirmed, "is far removed beyond my attack," while I praised Priestley, the Socinian, justice compels me to remark (what the reviewer probably knows well enough), that in the virtues of private life Dr. Priestley was as much superior to his antagonist as he was inferior in the correctness of his speculative theology.

From the principles avowed in the *Apology*, this writer asserts that it is evident I am to be classed to all intents and purposes with *radical reformers.* This charge is grounded on my recommendation of annual parliaments and universal suffrage. Now he either knows that Mr. Pitt, in conjunction with the Duke of Richmond, presided at public meetings in which annual parliaments and the extension of the right of suffrage to all householders were recommended, or he does not. If he pleads ignorance of the fact, what presumption is it for a man so uninformed to write upon the subject! If he knows it, let me ask, was Mr. Pitt a *radical reformer* at the time he recommended those measures? If he was, I plead guilty to the charge; but if he was *not*, the recommendation of a similar plan is no evidence of my being a *radical*. For my own part, I feel the utmost contempt of the charge of radicalism. A radical reformer, if we attend to the import of words, is one that goes to the *root* of the evil, that proposes not merely to palliate, but to extirpate it. And what is that reform worth that proposes less? He who labours under an inveterate malady wishes for *radical* cure: he would put little value on a remedy that should mitigate the pain without reaching the source of the disorder. If the appellation of *radical reformer* is intended to denote a revolutionist, it is most absurdly applied to the advocate of annual parliaments and universal suffrage, because the first of these measures is merely a revival of the ancient practice, and the latter most consonant to the genius of a free constitution, which presupposes the extension of the elective franchise to all who can be presumed to have a will of their own: the exercise of this right, coupled with the practice of voting by ballot, would in my humble opinion be the best expedient for securing the freedom and tranquillity of elections. Be this as it may, a sincere proposal of *reform* must differ essentially from the proposal of a revolution. If by styling me a *radical* reformer this writer intends to impute revolutionary views, I say it is a calumny and a falsehood; and I challenge him to produce a single sentence in my publications which sustains such a charge, or which convicts me of hostility to the existing order of things, as consisting of king, lords, and commons. But if he means that I am for such a reform as will cut up corruption by the roots, I feel no inclination to disavow it. He wishes, it is evident, to fix the impression that I am hostile to the regal branch of the constitution, but shrinks from making the assertion, and endeavours to convey the venom of his accusations through the subtle vehicle of a dark and ambiguous phraseology.

For what purpose but that of exciting hatred and horror he has thought fit to couple my name with the mention of Hone and Carlile it is not easy to conjecture. The blasphemy of their publications is quite as disgusting to me as to himself; but I am at a loss to conceive the justness of that reasoning which would infer that no political corruption however enormous, no maladministration however flagrant, must be exposed to animadversion until these men have ceased to exhale their impieties. Let this principle once be admitted, and we shall never want Hones and Carliles in abundance; to remove a shield so easily purchased and so effectual in the protection of every abuse might be deemed an infatuation.

"He (the author of the Apology) pleads," says the reviewer, "for annual parliaments, for universal suffrage, for the unfettered publication of every kind of blasphemy, for the exclusion of the relatives of noblemen from the House of Commons, for the overthrow of all ecclesiastical establishments, and for the sovereignty of the people. In what part of the sacred volume," he adds, "he has discovered the least sanction for any one of these notions we are at a loss to imagine." The fatuity of this remark baffles all description. For why may I not retort his own language, and say, This author pleads for septennial parliaments, for limited suffrage, for the admission of the relatives of noblemen in the House of Commons, and for the support of ecclesiastical establishments; but in what part of the sacred volume he finds the least sanction for them I am at a loss to imagine? But when did I plead for the publication of blasphemy, fettered or unfettered? To plead for the liberty of divulging speculative opinions is one thing, and to assert the right of uttering blasphemy is another. For blasphemy, which is the speaking contumeliously of God, is not a speculative error; it is an overt act; a crime which no state should tolerate. In relation to the question of ecclesiastical establishments, since I am challenged to produce any passage from Scripture which sanctions my opposition to them, I beg leave to refer him to our Lord's declaration, *Every plant which my heavenly Father has not planted shall be rooted up.* That *national* churches, or exclusive establishments of religion by the civil magistrate, are one of these plants will not be denied; since nothing of that kind, it is universally allowed, existed during the three first and purest ages of Christianity, and not being authorized by the *great* Head of the church, it must, if we believe him, be rooted up. I have used the term *great* Head of the church, by way of distinction from that *little* head* which the Church of England has invented, and on which, whether it be a beauty or a deformity in the body of Christ, the Scriptures are certainly as silent as on universal suffrage and annual parliaments.

It may not be improper in this place to notice a curious argument which the reviewer adduces in support of his darling tenet of passive obedience and non-resistance, from the prevailing and inherent depravity of human nature. He reminds us that mankind are represented in Scripture as "alike depraved and unruly," and from these premises, attempts to enforce that interpretation of Scripture which would annihilate the liberties of mankind, and reduce them, without "restriction or reservation," to a passive submission to their political superiors. On another occasion I have sufficiently rescued the sentiments of the inspired writers from such a detestable imputation, by showing that their design is merely to inculcate the general duty of obedience to government, as the ordinance of God, while they leave the just bounds of authority, and the limits of obedience, to the regulation and adjustment of reason and experience; a task to which they are perfectly adequate. But how does the depravity of human nature evince the necessity of passive obedience and non-resistance, unless it is contended that the ruling part of mankind are *not* depraved? That mankind are naturally "depraved and unruly" affords a good argument for the existence of *government itself;* but since they are "*alike* depraved and unruly," since governors partake of the same corruption as the people, aggravated too often by the possession of power, which inflames the passions and corrupts the heart, to allege the depravity of human nature as a reason for submission to arbitrary power, involves the absurdity of supposing that the cure of one degree of wickedness is to be obtained

* I know of no passage in the works of our author which presents, in my judgment, so gross a violation of good taste as is here exhibited.—ED.

by affording unlimited license to a greater Retrace the annals of all times and nations, and you will find in the triumph of despotism the triumph of wickedness; you will find that men have been virtuous, noble, and disinterested, just in proportion as they have been free.

The reviewer affects to triumph over me, on account of the supposed failure of the prediction, that ruin would speedily ensue unless prevented by reform. "Has this dreadful alternative," he asks, "fallen upon us? The present comparatively prosperous and improving circumstances of the kingdom, answers No. The general state of the country, the average condition of the great mass of the people, is *better* and not *worse* than at the time when Mr. Hall first published this direful presage."

I am at a loss to reply in suitable terms to a writer who seems to glory in setting truth at defiance. Let me ask the reader, whether he thinks there is a single person to be found in the nation who really believes our condition as a people is improved within the last thirty years? Where is this improvement to be found? Is it in the augmentation of the national debt to three times its former amount: in the accumulated weight of taxes; in the increase of the poor-rates; in the depression of land to less than one-half of its former value; in the ruin of the agricultural interest; in the thousands and tens of thousands of farmers who are distrained for rent, and they and their families reduced to beggary? Has this writer already forgotten the recent distress of the manufacturing class, who, from failure of employment and the depression of wages, were plunged into despair, while numbers of them quitted their homes, and sought a precarious and scanty relief, by dragging through the country loaded wagons and carts, like beasts of burden? Is it in the rapid and portentous multiplication of crimes, by which our prisons are glutted with malefactors? If these are indications of increasing prosperity, we may justly adopt the language of the liturgy, from such prosperity, "Good Lord, deliver us."

To do the writer justice, he has the grace to admit something like an exception respecting the agricultural interest, though he expresses himself with the diffidence becoming the solution of so difficult a problem. "If any exception," he says, "can be found, it is in the agricultural interest;" but he adds, "If those are to be believed *who ought to be judges*, this is to be ascribed to the want of legal protection." Now, two corn-bills have been passed of late years for the express protection of the agriculturist; the last of these in open contempt of the sentiments and wishes of the people. Previously to the passing of these bills, agriculture was in a comparatively flourishing state; since these laws were enacted it has experienced a depression beyond all example; and in the face of these facts, this writer has the assurance to inform us, that in the opinion of those *who ought to be judges*, the evil is wholly to be ascribed to the *want* of legal protection. But who are these highly-privileged mortals, who are to be implicitly believed because "they ought to be judges?" If there is any class of persons whose opinion on these questions is entitled to deference and respect, they are undoubtedly political economists, men who have made the sources of national wealth the principal subject of their inquiry: and where will he find one, from Adam Smith to the present time, who has not reprobated the interference of legislature with the price of corn? To say nothing of the reasoning of that great philosopher, which is unanswerable, common sense will teach us, that laws to raise the price of produce are unjust and oppressive taxes upon the whole community, for the exclusive benefit of a part. There is a description of men who are accustomed systematically to yield up their understandings to others, who in their view "ought to be judges:" it is needless to add, that the present writer is evidently of this *servum pecus*, this tame and passive herd; and that his knowledge of the subject is just what might be expected from one who thinks by proxy. These men, forgetting, or affecting to forget, that the exercise of power, in whatever hands it is placed, will infallibly degenerate into tyranny unless it is carefully watched, make it their whole business to screen its abuses; to suppress inquiry, stifle complaint, and inculcate on the people as their duty a quiet and implicit submission to the direction of those who, to speak in the vocabulary of slaves, "ought to be judges." These are the men by whom the constitution is endangered; these the maxims by which free states are enslaved. If that freedom which is the birthright of Britons is destined to go down to succeeding generations, it must result from the prevalence of an opposite spirit; a lofty enthusiasm, an ardent attachment to liberty, and an incessant jealousy of the tendency of power to enlarge its pretensions and extend its encroachments.

The reviewer asserts, that "my whole pamphlet is an argument in favour of the supremacy and infallibility of the people, and of the necessity of paying an implicit obedience to the least expression of their will."

This, I must assure the reader, is a gross and wilful misrepresentation. In no part of the pamphlet have I pleaded for any such doctrine. All that I have asserted is, that in proportion as the *House of Commons* is in unison with the people, animated by the same sympathies, and affected by the same interests, in the same proportion will it accomplish the design of its functions as a *representative* assembly; and that a reform is absolutely necessary, in order to restore it to that conjunction of interests and of feelings on which its utility, as the popular branch of the legislature, depends. The necessity of such a union between the people and their representatives is manifest from the very meaning of the terms, for it were quite needless for them to be at the pains of choosing men who, in consequence of a foreign bias, are prepared to contradict their sentiments and neglect their interests. A House of Commons which should chiefly consist of court sycophants and tyrants would exhibit nothing more than the mockery of representation. By artfully transferring what I have said of *one* branch of the legislature to the *whole*, and presenting even that in an exaggerated form, he has represented me as reducing the government to such an immediate and incessant dependence on the popular will as never entered my thoughts, and would be utterly incompatible with the genius of a limited monarchy.

Having already trespassed on the patience of my readers, I shall close with one remark on the eulogium pronounced by the reviewer on the character of the late Mr. Pitt. He appears to be extremely shocked with the freedom and severity of my strictures on his conduct, as implying a forgetfulness of his singular disinterestedness, and his "perfect devotion to his country." As this has become a favourite topic with the admirers of that celebrated minister, it is necessary to remind them that there are other vices besides the love of money, and other virtues besides that of dying poor. It may be easily admitted, that the ambition which grasps at the direction of an empire, and the pitiful passion for accumulation, were not the inmates of the same bosom. In minds of a superior order, ambition, like Aaron's rod, is quite sufficient to swallow up the whole fry of petty propensities. Far be it from me to wish to withhold an atom of the praise justly due to him. That he devoted much time and a considerable portion of talent to the affairs of his country is undeniable. The evils which he has brought upon us were not the production of an ordinary mind, nor the work of a day, nor done in sport; but what I contend for is, that, to say nothing of his unparalleled apostacy, his devotion to his country, and, what was worse, its devotion to him, have been the source of more calamity to this nation than any other event that has befallen it; and that the memory of Pitt will be identified in the recollection of posterity with accumulated taxes, augmented debt, extended pauperism, a debasement and prostration of the public mind, and a system of policy, not only hostile to the cause of liberty at home, but prompt and eager to detect and tread out every spark of liberty in Europe; in a word, with all those images of terror and destruction which the name imports. The enthusiasm with which his character is regarded by a numerous class of his countrymen will be ascribed, by a distant age, to that mysterious infatuation which, in the inscrutable counsels of Heaven, is the usual, the destined precursor of the fall of states.

I am, Sir,

Your humble servant,

ROBERT HALL.

LEICESTER, *Feb.* 5, 1822.

NOTE BY THE EDITOR.

Some excellent persons who did not know Mr. Hall often express great concern that so good a man should have suffered his thoughts to be so much engrossed in politics as they suppose must have been the case. The truth, however, is, that few men gave themselves less to political matters than Mr. Hall. At the deeply-interesting period in which he wrote his political tracts, the whole world was absorbed in the contemplation of political events and the discussion of political principles. Among the disputants of the two great parties into which this country was divided, clergymen and other ministers took a most active part, and the class denominated evangelical were by no means the least active. Some of the most eminent of them, indeed, engaged in that sad and then frequent profanation of holy places and things, the consecration of the colours of a volunteer corps in a parish church; and one even put on a military cockade in order to incite his parishioners to come forward in the public cause. The genuine principles of our admirable constitution were thought by many to be in imminent peril; yet all who wrote in their defence were exposed to obloquy. A learned prelate asserted in the House of Lords that "the people had nothing to do with the laws but to obey them," and his sentiment was loudly applauded. In a kindred spirit, during the trials of Muir and Palmer for "leasing-making," or sedition, in Scotland, one of the lords of justiciary declared that "*no man had a right to speak of the constitution unless he possessed landed property*;" and another affirmed, that "*since the abolition of* TORTURE *there was no adequate punishment for sedition*." In such a season of violent excitement, when upright men of every shade of opinion thought the most valuable principles at stake, no wonder that heats and animosities prevailed, and that all expressed themselves with vehemence,—often with acerbity. Mr. Hall, then under thirty years of age, was of too ardent and generous a spirit to be quiescent in that signal crisis of public affairs. He discharged what, in the exigency, appeared to him an imperious duty, and then remained silent, until after an interval of many years, at the entreaty of his friends, he broke the silence in a brief effort of self-defence against anonymous misrepresentation. For some years, indeed, so great was his indifference to political concerns that he scarcely ever read a newspaper, or did more in conversation than advert for a moment, if at all, to public measures. His political principles, however, remained the same through life, with those simple modifications which the lapse of time and the occurrence of new events were calculated to produce in the breast of a considerate man. Though he thought them important, he uniformly regarded them as subordinate to others. He cherished with delight the anticipations of a new and better order of things among mankind; but he looked mainly for the realizing of his hopes to the operation of a higher class of principles than the politics of this world can supply,—principles of heavenly origin, which, flowing from religious truth, and acting at once upon the spiritual part of our nature, change and improve the mass of society by transforming the characters of the men who compose it.

Some of the following pieces yield ample proofs of the prevalence of these sentiments.

That there are occasions on which pious men not only may, but must, if they act fully on scriptural principles, censure public men and public measures, has been clearly shown by one of the gentlest as well as most excellent of men—Granville Sharp—in his essay on "*The Law of Passive Obedience.*"

AN ADDRESS

TO THE PUBLIC,

ON AN IMPORTANT SUBJECT, CONNECTED WITH

THE RENEWAL OF THE CHARTER

OF THE

EAST INDIA COMPANY.

[PUBLISHED IN 1813.]

AN ADDRESS.

As the subject of the renewal of the charter of the East India Company is shortly to come before parliament with a view to a final decision, it is presumed that it will not be deemed impertinent to invite the attention of the legislature to a particular connected with that subject which is judged of high importance. The point to which we refer respects the propriety of inserting a clause in the new charter authorizing the peaceable dissemination of Christian principles in India.* For want of such a provision, the missionaries who have lately visited that country have been under the necessity of going there by the circuitous route of America, besides meeting with considerable obstructions in their attempts to settle, and being exposed to much vexation and interruption in their quiet efforts to plant the Christian faith. It must surely be considered as an extraordinary fact, that in a country under the government of a people professing Christianity, *that* religion should be the only one that is discountenanced and suppressed.

That the most complete toleration should be extended to the various modes of belief prevailing in those remote dependencies of our empire, and that none of the inhabitants should be subjected to the slightest inconvenience on account of their adherence to the religious system of their forefathers, is readily admitted; nor would any event give more serious concern to the writer of this address, than an interference with that right of private judgment which he deems an inalienable prerogative of human nature. But for a Christian nation to give a

* The object for which Mr. Hall and many other pious men so earnestly pleaded, was accomplished, at least as to its practical results; though there is still room to interpose obstructions if men in power should be inclined to present them. The act which passed in 1813, "for continuing in the East India Company for a farther term the possession of the British territories in India," contains four clauses (viz. 33, 34, 35, 36) which relate to "persons desirous of going to India for the purpose of promoting the religious and moral improvement of the natives." The nature of this part of the enactment will be understood from the subjoined brief official abstract:—

"If the court of directors think fit to refuse the applications for permission made in behalf of such persons, they are to transmit the applications to the board of commissioners, who, if they see no valid objection to granting the permission, may authorize the said persons to proceed to any of the company's principal settlements, provided with a certificate of sanction from the directors. The court of directors, however, may make representations concerning such persons to the board of commissioners: and those persons on arriving in the East Indies are to be subject to the regulations of the local governments. Further, the governments in India may declare the certificates and licenses of such persons to be void, if they shall appear by their conduct to have forfeited their claims to protection."

Besides these clauses there are others, from 49 to 54 inclusive, which relate to a "church establishment in India. A bishop and three archdeacons to be appointed; their salaries are specified: the episcopal jurisdiction is to be limited by letters-patent from the king; pensions to be allowed after fifteen years' service." Of the bishops who have been appointed since the passing of this act, three, viz. *Middleton*, *Heber*, and *James*, have been already brought by the climate of India to a premature grave.—Ed.

decided preference to polytheism and idolatry by prohibiting the dissemination of a purer faith, and thus employ its powers in suppressing the truth, and prolonging the existence of the most degrading and deplorable superstitions, is a line of conduct equally repugnant to the dictates of religion and the maxims of sound policy. To oppose by force the propagation of revealed truth from any worldly considerations whatever is such a sacrifice of right to expediency as can be justified on no principles but what will lead to the subversion of all morality and religion.

If Christianity be a communication from heaven, to oppose its extension is *to fight against God;* an impiety which, under every possible combination of circumstances, must expect a severe rebuke; but the guilt of which is inconceivably aggravated when the opposition proceeds from the professors of that very religion. We have no example in the history of the world of such a conduct; we have no precedent of a people prohibiting the propagation of their own faith; a species of intolerance exposed, not only to the objections which lie in common against all restraints upon conscience, but to a train of absurdities peculiar to itself, at the same time that it imposes a character of meanness on the ruling powers, by the virtual confession it includes that they have either no religion or a religion of which they are ashamed. As the equality of all religions, the distinguishing tenet of deism, is alike repugnant to the dictates of reason and the oracles of truth, so it is ill calculated to conciliate the esteem of eastern nations, on whom it can have no other effect than to desecrate the British name by depriving it of the veneration which nature, unsophisticated by impiety, has inseparably connected with sentiments of religious belief. Powerfully impressed as they are with religious principles and prejudices, however erroneous, we can scarcely adopt a more effectual expedient for securing their contempt and abhorrence than an avowed indifference to whatever concerns that momentous subject.

It is an undeniable fact that no persons have been so popular in India as the men who have exerted themselves with the most steady and persevering zeal in the dissemination of Christian principles; of which we have a striking example in the excellent Schwartz, for many years a missionary on the coast of Coromandel, who by his wise and benevolent conduct rendered on various occasions the most essential service to the British interests, and became the object of the enthusiastic attachment of the natives.*

The attempt to propagate Christianity in India is not a new experiment; it has been now tried for more than a century: it received the warmest support of George the First, of illustrious memory, as well as of the then archbishop of Canterbury; and in the hands of Ziegenbalgius and his successors was crowned with distinguished success.† Similar attempts have been more recently made in Bengal and the

* See the Reports of the Society at Bartlett's Buildings, for promoting Christian Knowledge.

† See the excellent letters from his majesty and the archbishop, addressed to Ziegenbalgius, in Buchanan's Ecclesiastical Researches

adjacent provinces; and several Christian societies have been planted by the labours of missionaries in those parts of India. It deserves particular attention, that no inconvenience, not even the slightest, has arisen from these enterprises; and that whatever agitation has been witnessed among the natives at different times, the propagation of Christianity has never been the cause or even the pretext. When intelligence of the insurrection of Vallore reached England, there were not wanting persons who endeavoured to ascribe it to the jealousy and uneasiness excited by the efforts of missionaries; but no attempt could be more unsuccessful, since, in the course of a most accurate investigation of the circumstances connected with that event, we have it on the authority of Lord Teignmouth that not even the name of a missionary was mentioned. It arose from causes totally distinct. Thus have we the experience of more than a century to justify the conclusion that nothing is to be feared for the tranquillity of India from the operations of missionaries, subject as they must ever be to the control of the constituted authorities.

The number of natives who profess Christianity is not small nor inconsiderable. The disciples of Schwartz and his successors on the eastern side of the peninsula amount to fifty thousand, and the Syrian Christians on the coast of Malabar to several hundred thousands; the greater part of them converted from the Brahmins and the higher classes. They have subsisted there from the fifth century, are in possession of one hundred and nineteen churches, some of them sumptuous and splendid edifices; and their superior elevation of character and purity of manners are attested on the most respectable authority to be such as the possession of the Christian faith might be expected to inspire.* In addition to this, translations of the New Testament in almost all the vernacular dialects of India have been recently circulated, and a considerable number of the natives are assiduously and constantly employed in preaching the gospel; so that it is too late to think of checking its career: the possession it has taken of the public mind will necessarily render all such attempts impracticable. The only question which remains to be decided is, whether its further propagation shall be left solely in the hands of natives, or whether intelligent and respectable Europeans, who come more immediately into contact with the British government, and in whose prudence and experience greater confidence may be reposed, shall be allowed to superintend its movements. The good seed having struck its root too deep ever to be extirpated, the only alternative is either to leave it to its spontaneous growth, aided by the labour of Hindoos, or to place it under a more skilful and enlightened cultivation.

Though strangers to the theory, the inhabitants of Hindostan have been long familiarized to the practice of toleration. In no part of the world is there a greater variety of sects, or more contrariety in the modes of religious belief, subsisting without the slightest disturbance;

* See the interesting narrative of Dr. Buchanan's visit to the Syrian Christians, in his Ecclesiastical Researches.

even the grand division of the natives into Hindoos and Mahometans was continued for ages, without interruption to the public harmony.

But if nothing is to be feared from the dissemination of Christian principles in India, the advantages resulting from it, whether we consult the interest of the natives or our own, are too obvious to require to be enumerated, and too important to be overlooked. With respect to its aspect on the natives, will it be contended that a more powerful instrument can be devised for meliorating and raising their character, than grafting upon it the principles of our holy religion, which, wherever it prevails, never fails to perfect whatever is good, and to correct whatever is evil, in the human constitution, and to which Europe is chiefly indebted for those enlightened views and that high sense of probity and honour which distinguish it so advantageously in a comparison with Asiatic nations? The prevalence of Christianity everywhere marks the boundary which separates the civilized from the barbarous or semi-barbarous parts of the world; let but this boundary be extended, and the country included within its limits may be considered as redeemed from the waste, and prepared to receive the precious seeds of civilization and improvement. Independently of eternal prospects, it may be safely affirmed that polytheism and idolatry draw after them such a train of absurd and dismal consequences as to be quite incompatible with the due expansion of the human intellect, and necessarily to prevent the operations of reason from reaching their maturity and perfection. Wherever Christianity prevails mankind are uniformly progressive; it communicates that just manner of thinking upon the most important subjects which, extending its influence thence to every department of speculative and moral truth, inspires a freedom of inquiry and an elevation of sentiment which raise the disciples of revelation immeasurably above the level of unassisted nature.

The Hindoo superstition is characterized by a puerile extravagance of conception, as hostile to the cultivation of reason as the enormity of its practices is revolting to humanity. It oppresses the former by its gigantic absurdities; it extinguishes the latter by the cruelty of its rites. The annual destruction of female infants in Guzerat and Kutch is estimated at fifteen or twenty thousand.* Till lately, it had been the custom, from time immemorial, to immolate, at the island of Saugor, and at other places esteemed holy, on the banks of the Ganges, human victims, or to destroy them by sharks. From a late investigation, it appears that the number of women who sacrifice themselves on the funeral pile of their husbands, within thirty miles of Calcutta, is on an average upwards of two hundred annually.† A multitude of courtesans are uniformly attached to the principal temples, and the most obscene symbols exhibited to inflame the passions of their votaries.‡

While the history of all times and nations evinces the inseparable alliance of impurity and cruelty with the worship of idols, is it consistent with the dictates of humanity, not merely to witness these enor-

* See Moore's Hindoo Infanticide.

† See Buchanan's Memoir, p. 96, Appendix. In a letter lately received from Dr. Carey, he estimates the whole number of women annually sacrificed throughout India at ten thousand.

‡ See Sonnerat's Voyage aux Indes et à la Chine, p. 219.

mities without attempting to correct them, but to oppose the communication of the only remedy which is capable of effecting a cure?

The base venality, together with the spirit of artifice and intrigue, which distinguish the natives of Hindostan, have rendered it the theatre of perpetual revolutions, robbed its native governments of every principle of stability, and rendered poisonings, assassinations, and treachery expedients so constantly resorted to by the parties in conflict, that it is impossible to peruse its history without shuddering. To affirm that there is nothing in their superstitions calculated to correct these vices is saying little, when in fact they derive a powerful sanction from the maxims of their religion, and from the character of their gods. There is not one of their deities portrayed in their Shasters whose moral character is tolerably correct. How much Christianity is wanted to exalt the sentiments and purify the principles of this corrupt and effeminate race is too obvious to need to be insisted on.

That their conversion is practicable is ascertained beyond controversy by the success which has already attended the experiment; that no apprehensions are to be entertained for the permanence of British power in consequence of the attempt is manifest from experience; that to consult the welfare of the subject is the first duty of the sovereign, and the chief distinction between the exercise of legitimate authority and the operation of lawless tyranny, will not be disputed in an enlightened age; and that the Christian religion is the greatest blessing we have received, the most precious boon we can bestow, none but infidels will deny. It surely will not be asserted that we are under less obligation to communicate a good because that good may be traced to the immediate interposition of Heaven, or because it contains the seed and germ of eternal felicity. He who believes the Bible must know that the heathen are to be given to Christ for his inheritance, the uttermost parts of the earth for his possession, and that therefore to *forbid his being preached to the gentiles that they may be saved* is an attempt to contravene the purposes of the Most High, equally impotent and presumptuous. *Let the potsherds strive against the potsherds of the earth, but wo unto him who striveth against his Maker.* Such conduct, persevered in, must infallibly draw down the judgments of God on the people to whose infatuated counsels it is to be ascribed. Whoever considers the aspect of the times must be invincibly prejudiced not to discern the symptoms of a peculiar crisis, the distinguishing features of which are, the rapid subversion of human institutions and the advancement of the kingdom of God. *The stone cut out without hands has already fallen upon the image, and made it like the chaff of the summer threshing-floor:* the next event we are to look for in the order of Providence is its enlarging itself, *till it becomes a great mountain, and fills the whole earth.* If there ever was a period when the propagation of the true religion might be resisted with impunity, that period is past; and the Master of the universe is now addressing the greatest potentates in the language of an ancient oracle:—*Be wise now, ye kings; be instructed, ye judges of the earth.* Encompassed as we are with the awful tokens of a pre siding and avenging Providence, dissolving the fabrics of human wisdom, extinguishing the most ancient dynasties, and tearing up kingdoms by their roots, it would be the height of infatuation any longer to oppose the reign of God, whose purposes will pursue their career in spite of the efforts of human policy, which must either yield their co-operation, or be broken by its force.

All that is desired on this occasion is simply that the word of God may be permitted to have free course. Whether it be consistent with sound policy for the British government to employ any part of its resources in aid of the cause of Christianity in India is a question which it is not necessary to discuss, while its friends confine their views to a simple toleration, and request merely that its teachers may not be harassed or impeded in their attempts to communicate instruction to the natives. Before such a liberty can be withheld, the principles of toleration must be abandoned; nor will it be practicable to withhold it without exciting a sanguinary persecution, where men are to be found who will eagerly embrace the crown of martyrdom rather than relinquish the performance of what appears to them a high and awful duty. And what a spectacle will it exhibit, for a Christian government to employ force in the *support* of idolatry and the *suppression* of truth!

Instead of dwelling on the necessary effects of such a measure, let us consider for a moment the beneficial consequences likely to result from an opposite mode of conduct. On that improvement of character which the cordial reception of revealed truth cannot fail to operate, it will be easy to graft some of the best habits and institutions of European nations, advancing gradually through an interminable series of social order and happiness. Under the fostering hand of religion, reason will develop her resources, and philosophy mature her fruits. Nor will the advantages accruing to the British interests from a change so salutary be less certain or less important. The possession of the same faith will occasion such an approximation of the habits and sentiments of the natives to our own, as will render the union firm, by rendering it cordial. While a total opposition in their views on the most important points subsists between the sovereign and the subjects,—while objects adored by the one are held in contempt and abhorrence by the other, they may be artificially connected, but it is impossible they should be united: it is rather a juxtaposition of inanimate parts, than a union of minds. In such a situation the social tie wants that cementing principle which is requisite to give it strength and stability; it is a strained and unnatural position, in which things are held contrary to their native bent; in which authority is upheld merely by force, without deriving support from that sympathy of congenial sentiment which forms its truest basis. Hence the precarious tenure by which European states have successively held dominion in India, where all has been submitted to the arbitration of the sword; where the moment force has been withdrawn or relaxed authority has ceased, and each in its turn has gained a transient ascendency, none a firm and tranquil possession.

In order to obviate the mischiefs arising from such a state of things, it is extremely desirable, providing it be practicable, to impart to our subjects in the East some principle which shall draw them into closer contact with the ruling power; and what principle equally operative and efficient with the possession of a common religion? Though the universal diffusion of Christianity over India will probably be a work of time, its influence in strengthening the social compact, by augmenting the attachment of the natives, will be uniformly progressive; and while external tranquillity is secured by the superiority of our policy and our arms, we shall every year be making our way into their hearts: we shall be establishing an interior dominion, and may confidently reckon on the unshaken fidelity of every Christian convert. This is not mere conjecture: for in all the trying vicissitudes experienced by the British interests in India, the Hindoo Christians have invariably approved themselves our firmest friends and abetters.

Though the writer of this address is afraid of being tedious, there is another consideration connected with the present subject which he deems of too much importance not to be mentioned. The possession of India, it is well known, is an object to which our enemies are looking with eager desire, accompanied with jealousy at that splendour which the vastness of our oriental empire confers on the British name and character. No efforts will they deem too great, no sacrifices too expensive, to rob us of so bright a jewel. What events may arise hereafter to facilitate the accomplishment of their wishes it is beyond the power of human sagacity to conjecture: one thing is certain, that nothing will oppose a more formidable obstacle to their designs than the diffusion of Christianity. They who have received that inestimable blessing will infallibly cling with ardour to the people to whom they are indebted for it. They will feel more than a natural affection to the country which has opened to them the prospect of immortality, and nourished them with the bread of life. In all the struggles to retain or to acquire dominion in the East, the Christian portion of the population will, to a man, be the zealous partisans of Great Britain; a firm and immoveable band, whose devoted attachment will in some measure compensate for their inferiority of number. In this species of policy too, in this most unexceptionable mode of conciliating esteem, we shall have nothing to apprehend from the intrigues of our rivals, who are equally indisposed and disqualified to engage in such an enterprise.

If we consider what may be the probable intention of Providence in opening so extensive a communication between Europe and the most ancient seats of idolatry, and more especially of subjecting such immense territories in the East to the British arms, we can conceive no end more worthy of the Deity in these momentous changes than to facilitate the propagation of true religion.

Our acquisition of power there has been so rapid, so extensive, and so disproportioned to the limits of our native empire, that there are few events in which the interposition of Providence may be more distinctly traced. From the possession of a few forts in different parts of the coast, which we were permitted to erect for the protection of our commerce, we have risen, in the course of less than half a century, to a summit of power whence we exert a direct dominion over fifty millions, and a paramount influence over a hundred millions of men. By an astonishing train of events, a large portion of the population of the oriental world has been subjected to the control of an island placed in the extremities of the west of Europe. Kingdoms have fallen after kingdoms, and provinces after provinces, with a rapidity which resembles the incidents of a romance, rather than the accustomed order of political events. It is remarkable, too, that this career of conquest has uniformly directed its steps towards those parts of the earth, and to those only, which are the primeval seats of pagan idolatry; forming an intimate connexion between the most enlightened of Christian nations and the victims of the most inveterate and deplorable system of superstition mankind have ever witnessed. As we must be blind not to discern the finger of God in these transactions, it behooves us to consider for what purposes we are lifted to so high a pre-eminence.

It is certainly not to be ascribed to a blind predilection, which aims at no other object than to gratify ambition, by extending the power and augmenting the grandeur of Great Britain; a motive too puerile to satisfy the requisitions of human reason, much more to limit the views of an eternal mind.

The possession of sovereignty over extensive kingdoms is a sacred trust, for which nations are not less responsible than individuals, a delegation from the supreme Fountain of power; and as the unalterable laws of nature forbid us to confound men with things, or to forget the reciprocal obligations subsisting between the sovereign and the subject, we can scarcely be guilty of a greater crime than to consider the latter as merely subservient to the interests of the former. Every individual of the immense population subjected to our sway has claims on our justice and benevolence which we cannot with impunity neglect: the wants and sufferings of every individual utter a voice which goes to the heart of humanity. In return for their allegiance we owe them protection and instruction, together with every effort to meliorate their condition and improve their character. It is but fair to acknowledge that we have not been wholly insensible to these claims, and that the extension of our power has been hitherto highly beneficial. But why, in the series of improvements, has Christianity been neglected? Why has the communication of the greatest good we have to bestow been hitherto fettered and restrained; and while every modification of idolatry, not excepting the bloody and obscene orgies of Juggernaut, has received support, has every attempt to instruct the natives in the things which belong to their peace been suppressed? It will surely appear surprising to posterity, that a nation, glorying in the purity of its faith as its highest distinction, should suffer its transactions in the East to be characterized by a spirit of infidelity, as though it were imagined the foundations of empire could be laid only in apostacy and impiety; at a moment, too, when Europe, convulsed to its centre, beholds these frantic erections swept with the besom of destruction. Their astonishment will be the more excited when they compare our conduct in this instance with the unprecedented exertions we are making for the diffusion of religious knowledge in other directions; with the operations of the Bible Society, which, formed for the sole purpose of conveying the oracles of God to all quarters, has risen to an importance that entitles it to be regarded as a national concern; in which statesmen, nobles, and prelates have enrolled their names, emulous of the honour of advancing to the utmost the noble design of the institution; with the Bartlett's Buildings Society, employed for upwards of a century in attempts to convert the natives of Hindostan, which includes in the list of its members every bishop and every dignified ecclesiastic in the realm; with the numerous translations going on in all the dialects of the East, to which the learned, both in Europe and in Asia, are looking with eager expectation. When posterity shall compare the conduct we are reprobating with these facts, how great their astonishment to find the piety of the nation has suffered itself to lie prostrate at the feet of a few individuals, the open or disguised enemies of the faith of Jesus!

It is impossible, in connexion with the circumstances to which we have adverted, to mistake the real sentiments of the British people, or not to perceive that the illustrious associations already mentioned are entitled, on a question of this nature, to be considered as its genuine and legitimate organ.

It ought never to be forgotten, in the consideration of this subject, that it is inseparably connected with liberty of conscience. Religious toleration implies not merely the freedom of thought, which no human power can restrain, and which equally subsists under the most tyrannical and the most enlightened governments; it comprehends also the freedom of communication and the right of discussion, within the limits of sober and dispassionate argument. He who is impressed with a conviction of the importance of the Christian verities, it is reasonable to suppose, will be anxious to communicate them: he will probably feel as St. Paul did in a similar situation, whose spirit was stirred within him when he beheld Athens wholly given up to idolatry: he may be touched with so strong a commiseration for the victims of religious imposture, and so powerful a sense of the duty of attempting to correct it, as to be ready to adopt the language employed on another occasion—"We *cannot* but speak the things which we have seen and heard."

None but the determined enemy of truth and decency will deny that such a state of mind is possible, or that it is more allied to virtue than to vice. If at this juncture a superior power interposes, and says, You shall not impart your conviction, however strong; you shall not attempt to dispel delusions the most gross, or correct enormities the most flagrant, though no other means are thought of but calm expostulation and argument; in what, I would ask, does such an interference differ from persecution? Here is conscience on one side, an enlightened conscience, as all Christians must confess, and force on the other ; which is precisely the position in which things are placed by every instance of persecution. If Christianity was ever persecuted, if the martyrologies of all times and nations are not to be exploded as mere fiction and romance, this is persecution, and persecution of a most portentous character, being directed, in support of a system we detest, against the religion by which we expect to be saved. Here are a people, indignant posterity will exclaim, who profess subjection to the Saviour of the world, and hold in their hands the oracles which foretell the universal extension of his dominion, who yet make it a crime to breathe his name in pagan lands, and employ their power to fence out the scene of his future triumphs, and render it, as far as possible, inaccessible to his religion. With what efficacious sincerity and edifying fervour must this people have prayed, "Thy kingdom come!" Admirable successors of the Constantines and the Charlemagnes of a former age! Faithful stewards of the manifold gifts of God!

When the parallel between the conduct of modern missionaries and the first preachers of the gospel is insisted on, it is usual to attempt to annul the conclusion deduced from the comparison, by remarking that the latter were possessed of miraculous powers, to which the former make no pretensions. That this circumstance occasions a real disparity in the means of ensuring success will be readily acknowledged; but that it makes any difference whatever in the right of imparting instruction will not hastily be conceded. Had such supernatural interpositions never accompanied the publication of the gospel, it had wanted its credentials, and been essentially defective in the proof of its divine origination. It was necessary for a new dispensation, when first ushered into the world, to be accompanied with a direct appeal to the senses, with the visible signatures of a Divine hand; and it is the glory of our holy religion to have possessed them in a variety and splendour that astonished mankind, and laid a foundation for the faith and obedience of all succeeding ages. At its *entrance*, such an economy was requisite to prepare the way. But when these miraculous occurrences, after enduring the severest scrutiny, under circumstances the most favourable to investigation, were committed to writing, and formed a compact body of external evidences,—when the supernatural origin of the Christian faith had taken its place among the most indubitable of recorded facts, it was no longer necessary to be continually repeating the same proofs, nor consistent with the majesty of Heaven to be ever laying the foundation afresh. It was time to assume the truth of religion as a thing proved.

As we were none of us eyewitnesses of the miracles wrought in the primitive ages, but rest our belief on historical documents, it is not impossible, as far as the truth of Christianity is concerned, to lay open to pagans the sources of our conviction, and by that means to place them in nearly the same situation with ourselves; to say nothing of that internal evidence which *commends itself to every man's conscience in the sight of God.* This is actually the mode in which the light of Revelation has been chiefly diffused since the cessation of miraculous gifts; which in the opinion of some terminated with the apostles, in the judgment of others were continued through the first three centuries, but are universally allowed to have ceased long before the conversion of the northern and western parts of Europe. Did the disciples of St. Columba, who spread Christianity through the German provinces on the Baltic, through the kingdoms of Sweden, Norway, and Denmark, owe their success to miraculous powers? Did St. Aüstin and his associates, who laid the foundations of the religious establishments in England, make such pretensions?

To demand miracles in order to justify the propagation of Christianity in pagan countries is to attribute to it a state of perpetual weakness and pupilage: it is to cancel all that is past, to accuse the most illustrious missionaries of enthusiasm, and the faith of our forefathers of folly and credulity. The principle we are attempting to expose, not content with inflicting a stigma on a particular sect or party, involves the whole Christian community established in these realms in the foul reproach of being the illegitimate offspring of fanaticism or imposture. It is only necessary for us to place ourselves in imagination at that period when the foundation of the church was laid in this and in other European countries, to perceive that the same objections which are made to the present efforts of missionaries apply with equal force to those that are past. They who first exhibited the mystery of the Cross to the view of our rude ancestors were equally destitute of miraculous powers with ourselves. But they felt the power of the world to come: they were deeply impressed with the dignity and excellence of the Christian dispensation, and touched with a passionate regard for the honour of God and the salvation of souls. These were the motives which impelled them forward; these the weapons of their warfare. The ridicule attempted to be poured on men of the same principles and character, engaged in the same object, is, in fact, reflected on these their predecessors, and is precisely a repetition of the conduct of the impenitent Jews, who honoured the memory and built the sepulchres of departed, while they were imbuing their hands in the blood of living, prophets. We collect, with eager veneration, the names and achievements of the first heralds of the gospel; we dwell with exultation on the heroic fortitude they displayed in encountering the opposition of fierce barbarians, amid their efforts to reclaim them from a sanguinary superstition, and to imbue their minds with the principles of an enlightened piety. We look up to them as to a superior order of beings, and in the character of the instructers of mankind in the sublimest lessons, entitled to a distinction above all Greek, above all Roman fame; yet, with ineffable absurdity, and a most contemptible littleness of mind, if it please Providence at distant intervals to raise up a few congenial spirits, we are prepared to treat them with levity and scorn. It is the misfortune of some men to labour under an incapacity of discerning living worth;—a sort of moral virtuosi, who form their estimate of characters, as the antiquarian of coins, by the rust of antiquity.

"Urit enim fulgore suo, qui prægravat artes
Infra se positas: extinctus amabitur idem."—*Horace.*

I would not be understood, in the remarks made on this part of the subject, to explode the expectation of the renewal of miraculous agency; which some of the most able divines have unquestionably formed, from a perusal of the prophetic oracles. The inference I would wish to establish is simply this, that we are not justified in neglecting the means of propagating the truth we already possess by the absence of higher succour; and that it would ill become the Christian world to abandon the attempts to convert the inhabitants of pagan countries, in deference ro the clamours of men, who demand miracles merely becanse they believe they will not be vouchsafed, and decry the ordinary methods of procedure, because they are within our reach, and have already been crowned with success. To such the language of the prophet Amos may be addressed with propriety:—*Wo unto you that desire the day of the Lord! to what end is it for you? The day of the Lord is darkness, and not light.* Chap. v. 18.

AN

APPEAL TO THE PUBLIC,

ON THE SUBJECT OF

THE FRAMEWORK KNITTERS' FUND

[PUBLISHED IN 1819.]

ADVERTISEMENT.

IMPRESSED as the writer of these pages has long been with the critical state of the stocking manufactory, and the intolerable evils resulting from a progressive depression of wages, he could not refrain from communicating his sentiments on this most interesting subject. He is aware of his inability to discuss it with that precision and force which superior talents might command. His only apology is, that he has *done what he could.* His reason for suppressing his name is simply, that while it might possibly create prejudice in some quarters he is not aware that it would bestow additional weight in any

AN APPEAL.

It is with the highest satisfaction I perceive that the wretched state of the labouring mechanics in Leicestershire has at length arrested the attention and drawn forth the liberality of a discerning public. But while we rejoice to see such a feeling awakened, we must be permitted to express our surprise and concern at the very scanty and penurious contribution it has hitherto produced. After witnessing such an unexampled depression in the remuneration of labour as to place the means of subsistence totally out of the reach of the industrious poor, when the only alternative presented is that of effective aid afforded by the more opulent or the total ruin and extinction of the labouring classes, it was natural to expect that the extent and magnitude of the exertion would bear some proportion to the greatness of the object and the exigence of the case. That this expectation is as yet far from being realized requires no proof, nor will it be possible to prevent the recurrence of that intolerable state of suffering which we have recently witnessed, without more extensive and vigorous efforts.

It is frequently asserted, we are aware, that the rate of wages, like every other article, should be left to find its own level, and that all attempts at artificial regulation, either by voluntary association or legal enactment, is repugnant to the true principles of political economy That commerce ought to be left to its native operation to a much greater extent than it is, we have learned from the highest authority; nor is it proposed to implore the interference of legislature in aid of our present object. But there is a peculiarity in the case of manual labour to which we suspect the persons who urge this objection have not attended.

When the price of a particular commodity sinks so low as not to produce the ordinary profits of stock, a part or the whole of the capital is withdrawn; a less quantity is produced in proportion to the diminu tion of the demand, in consequence of which the price rises to its former level. Thus the irregularity corrects itself, and little or no permanent mischief ensues. But the situation of the labourer is widely different; he has no other article to dispose of besides his personal industry and skill, on which he depends for his subsistence from day to day, nor can he, without being reduced to immediate distress, withhold them from the market, or even diminish their exertion to any considerable degree. The only commodity he has to part with is of such a nature that it will not permit him to adjust the supply to the demand. He must instantly offer it to sale at whatever price it will fetch, or suffer all the agonies of want. Hence this is the kind of property of all others the most defenceless and which most needs protection. That the rate of wages has a tendency to keep pace with the price of the necessaries of life is undeniable, but, from the cause we have now mentioned, it is long before that tendency becomes effective; the labourer and the mechanic are the *last* who experience the beneficial effect of an elevation in prices.

But admitting the objection to which we have adverted to be more weighty than it is, where is the equity of urging it in opposition to the claims of the labouring classes, while it is treated with the utmost neglect on other occasions? What is the object, let me ask, of the laws for the regulation of trade, which form so large a part of our acts of parliament, but to secure to certain descriptions of the community a higher price for the respective commodities which they produce, and thus to direct the application of capital to a specific object? What is the design, the avowed object at least, of the corn bill but to encourage agriculture by securing a higher price for its productions than they could command were they exposed to the effects of foreign competition? What is the design of the additional duty lately imposed on foreign wool but to bestow an artificial elevation on the price of that article as a means of promoting its domestic growth? and why so extensive a list of prohibitory statutes, except they are intended to encourage our home manufactures by securing to them a higher price? Not to multiply words on so plain a subject, suffice it to remark, that all laws and regulations of the legislature respecting trade and agriculture, with the exception of such as immediately relate to revenue, have for their immediate object the modification of price; it is by that means, and that alone, that they furnish encouragement to that species of productive industry which it is deemed expedient to favour. Hence it is evident that the vaunted maxim of leaving every kind of production and labour to find its own level is not adhered to; that it has always been violated in this country from the remotest times. An adherence to it would create a total revolution in our mercantile system, and while it is trampled under foot every day, it just commands a sufficient degree of theoretic assent to render it, in the hands of the artful and designing, a *bugbear* to deter the humane from rendering effectual assistance to the distressed and laborious part of the community. But what, let me once more ask, what reason can be assigned for leaving this class unprotected, the most helpless in society, from the cause already specified; while the agricultural, the manufacturing, and the mercantile interests are shielded with jealous attention by a multitude of legal provisions?

Why a philosophical theory, which is violated with impunity every moment, should then only be deemed sacred when it stands opposed to the claims of a starving and industrious population, we are at a loss to conjecture. Let it be remembered, however, that an application to the legislature forms no part of the present plan: although, if every other expedient should fail, we see no reason why its aid should not be exerted in favour of the Leicestershire framework knitters as well as of the Spitalfields weavers, who were a few years ago effectually relieved by the establishment of a *minimum*,* with the entire approbation of the principal manufacturers. The excellent Mr. Wilberforce had a principal share in procuring that regulation; nor is it to be doubted that, in conjunction with other humane and enlightened senators, he would be ready to exert, if necessary, the same efforts for the mitigation of similar distress.

The measure now intended is of a less bold and hazardous character. It is proposed simply by means of voluntary contribution to afford a subsistence, scanty it will probably be at the best, to that portion of the labouring class who are destitute of employment, that they may not be compelled to offer their labour for next to nothing, and thus reduce the general rate of wages to that scale of depression which has been already productive of such calamitous effects. On the present system, those who are thrown out of employment are tempted to offer their service for a remuneration totally inadequate to their wants. But a material inequality of wages for the same quantity of work is unnatural, and therefore cannot be permanent; the consequence is, that the wages of all the workmen are soon reduced to the rate at which the first hands are engaged. Thus a small surplus of labour beyond what the state of the demand requires becomes an engine for effecting a deep and universal depression; and the misery of a few, instead of exciting an effort for their relief, becomes the signal for a more extended infliction of the same calamity. To this evil no conceivable remedy short of legislative interference can be applied, except the creation of a fund capable of supplying the more pressing necessities of those whom the vicissitudes of trade may deprive of employment. This is the only expedient that furnishes the faintest prospect of giving permanence and stability to the statement to which the principal manufacturers have agreed; and on the vigour with which it is carried into effect depends our only chance of obviating the recurrence, with fresh aggravations, of the distress we have lately witnessed.

The benefits resulting from the successful operation of the measure we are recommending will not be confined to its immediate objects, it will extend its influence to every class of the community; and the alleviation which it will afford to the almost insupportable burthen of the poor-rates will be of eminent advantages to the parishes. Suppose in a particular parish a hundred frames at work, and each of the framework knitters earns, clear of all deductions, ten shillings a week instead of six, that parish is benefited to the amount of a thousand pounds; and considering the utter inadequacy of the former wages to procure the necessaries of life, the alteration will be nearly equivalent to an *annual* donation of a thousand pounds to the parochial treasure. That it is the interest of the manufacturing villages to exert themselves to the utmost in perpetuating the present statement is an inference which must force itself on the attention of the most careless observer; and nothing but the most infatuated preference of the present to the future

* The *lowest* rate at which labour should be paid for.

can prevent them from giving to the fund a liberal support Trades men of every description are deeply interested in the success of the present measure, since the permanent rise of wages will increase the power of purchase, and give a new impulse to every species of trade. Supposing the number engaged in all the various departments of the stocking manufactory to amount to thirty thousand, no extravagant computation, and little less than three hundred thousand pounds, in addition to the present sum, will annually find its way into the market; the agriculturist will find his account in the increased demand for raw produce, the manufacturer and the dealer, both wholesale and retail, in a more extended purchase of wrought goods. The landed proprietor will also be essentially benefited; for who does not know that the value of land must always bear a certain proportion to the demand for manufactures, and to the general diffusion of prosperity? Thus all orders will reap the advantage of a change of system.

On a subject so immediately connected with the claims of humanity it is surely not too much to expect, that nothing more will be necessary to inspire an aversion to the system recently adopted than a recollection of its actual effect in the ruin and prostration of the industrious mechanic. That man is little to be envied whose enjoyments are not essentially imbittered by the prospect of surrounding misery, who daily beholds with untroubled composure innumerable countenances clouded with dejection and despair. Were the state of suffering with which we have long been familiar removed from immediate observation, we could scarcely hear of it without agitation;—how much more afflicting to be placed in the midst of it, to feel it pressing on our senses in all directions, without the power of contributing any thing to its mitigation and relief, beyond a barren and impotent commiseration! Is there no hazard of contracting a fatal induration by a daily familiarity with indigence which we cannot alleviate, with scenes of wo we can neither remove nor diminish? To *go* into the house of mourning is good, since it is adapted to impress salutary lessons; but to *dwell* in a situation where every house is become such is a state to which nothing but utter insensibility can be reconciled.

There are, however, higher if not more affecting considerations connected with the present subject. If the evil which we have now the means of escaping should return, it will be in vain for us to flatter our selves with a long duration of tranquillity; a starving must not be expected to be a contented population, nor will any change be deprecated by those to whom existence itself has become a burthen. The instinctive feelings of nature will urge to some desperate effort, and they will cease to be restrained by legal coercion who already suffer more than the utmost rigour of the law can inflict. The heart that is withered with despair obtains an awful emancipation from the ordinary restraints of human action; and when a considerable portion of the people is reduced to that extremity, what is to be expected but that the physical energies which are found inadequate to the subsistence of their possessors by the exercise of honest industry will take an unnatural and destructive direction?

The manufacture of this county is so fortunately circumstanced in being exempted from foreign interference and competition, that nothing can materially injure it except its internal mismanagement. In the article of hosiery we possess a monopoly. While cotton thread is allowed to be exported, and to give birth to numerous foreign establishments, the kinds of wool necessary for our manufacture are prohibited from going abroad. We have the exclusive command of the market, and are under no necessity of having recourse to a reduction of price in order to defeat the competition of foreign manufacturers. All is in our own power; and if a spirit of miserable and short-sighted rivalry is suffered to depress the hire and extinguish the comforts of the labouring mechanic, it is the odious spectacle of a family quarrelling among themselves. Secured from external injury, and less affected by the vicissitudes of war and peace than perhaps any other branch of commerce, because it is concerned in an article of the first necessity, those who are employed in it have only to remain true to themselves, and they may bid defiance to every effort of hostility. "If ye bite and devour," says holy writ, "see that ye are not consumed one of another." What can be more detestable than to see a system pursued which can have no other possible termination or object than the sacrifice of the happiness of the many to a few, an inconceivable few, whose prosperity is cemented by the tears of a distressed and ruined population!

In order to give employment to those who are thrown out of work, and to lighten the poor-rates, some parishes have established manufactories of their own. While the system of depression continued, it was natural to have recourse to an expedient which accomplished its immediate object. But if it is proposed to give perpetuity to the present statement, that practice must be abandoned. The parishes can afford to dispose of their goods at little or no profit; but the regular manufacturers, it is natural to expect, will not submit to be undersold by a class of persons whom they cannot but regard as intruders: hence arises a new source of competition, and a consequent depression of wages. It is in vain to expect that the manufacturer will adhere to a liberal statement of wages while he is exposed to a rivalry conducted upon unequal terms.

It is surely not too much to hope, that the good sense of parishes will prompt them to put a speedy end to this practice, and that no selfish calculation of local or immediate advantage will tempt them to support a system pregnant with extensive mischief.

It gives the writer sincere concern to hear that there are even some framework knitters themselves so blind to their own interest as to refuse to contribute to the general fund. With men who are resolved to shut their eyes on consequences, and are unwilling to sacrifice the smallest immediate to the greatest future advantage, it is in vain to reason, since they have renounced the prerogative of thinking beings. As the framework knitters are the description of persons immediately interested, it is they who must give the first impulse. It is in vain for those to look for help who are unwilling to help themselves; and when so small a portion of their earnings is sufficient, with the assistance of a generous public, to secure them from the recurrence of recent sufferings, it is not in the power of words to express the folly which hesitates to make the necessary sacrifice. The whole system of life is a series of compromises with unavoidable evil, in which material inconveniences are endured for the acquisition of future good; and he who aspires to enjoyments unaccompanied by the necessity of self-denial and sacrifice will not retain them long. Such, also, is the power of combination, that small as is the sum which each individual is called to disburse, the amount of numerous contributions will lay a solid foundation for future prosperity, by protecting them from the encroachments of unfeeling rapacity.

It is asserted there are some manufacturers who have absolutely prohibited their workmen from contributing their quota to the fund. For the honour of human nature, we hope the report is unfounded. We are reluctant to suppose there can be found in a Christian country men so callous to the sentiments of humanity as to interdict the means of self-preservation, or of temper so despotic as to attempt to infringe on the essential right of every reasonable being to consult his interest by providing for future contingencies. Let it suffice to have refused their aid to their fellow-creatures while struggling in the waves, without driving them back when they have gained the shore. We earnestly recommend the periodical publication of a correct list of the contributors and the non-contributors, together with the reasons assigned for the conduct of the latter, that blame may be imputed only where it is due, and the patrons of oppression (if such there be) may be made amenable to the tribunal of public opinion.

From a partial view of the magnitude of the object before us, and of the extent of the mischief which requires to be remedied, those districts which are not the seat of manufacture have manifested a reluctance to contribute; a narrow and mistaken policy, which deserves the severest reprobation. Whether the workmen in the principal manufacture of a populous county sink into wretchedness and beggary, or are maintained in a state of comfort, can never be an uninteresting circumstance to any part of its inhabitants. Humanity apart, it requires but little attention to perceive that as the ability to purchase, and consequently the extent of purchases, is regulated, not by the wants, but by the pecuniary resources of the buyer, to those who have any thing to dispose of, the poverty of their customers must necessarily be injurious. But the framework knitters and their families constitute the most numerous class of consumers in the county, and the quantity of their consumption must be proportioned to the extent of their earnings. The circulation of money depends as much on the wages of labour as on the profits of stock; and if thirty thousand persons rise from abject poverty to a capacity of commanding a larger share of the necessaries and many of the comforts of life, the money which procures them will flow into every channel, so as to benefit alike the tradesman, the agriculturist, and the landed proprietor. The infusion of a new *pabulum* of life into the extremities will strengthen and invigorate the whole body.

Let not the inhabitants of those towns and villages where no manufacture is carried on suffer themselves to be deluded into false security, and because they hear not the sound of the knitting-frame, nor behold its productions spread before their eyes, flatter themselves with the hope of impunity in the midst of surrounding distress. The ties of civil society are too close and intricate, the reciprocal action of its respective parts too great, to admit of a local circumscription of calamity. The natural effect of a remarkable depression in the staple manufacture of a county is to spread commercial embarrassment and distress throughout the whole, of which we have already had sufficient experience in the difficulties under which trade of every description has laboured, in consequence of the paucity of money and the diminution of demand. The tradesman, it is true, feels the effect in its first stage of operation, the agriculturist in the next, in a diminished consumption of his raw produce.

In the moral system, it is a part of the wise arrangements of Providence that no member shall suffer alone; that if the lower classes are involved in wretchedness and beggary, the more elevated shall not enjoy their prosperity unimpaired. That constitution of society is radically unsound of which the inferior order is vicious and miserable: a wretched and degraded populace is a rent in the foundation; or, if we may be allowed to change the figure, a taint of rottenness at the root of society, which will infallibly wither and decay its remotest branches. Alarming as the present aspect of affairs unquestionably is, the most appalling feature of the times is the prevailing discontent of the lower orders; discontent, arising not so much from the infusion of speculative principles as from the impression of actual distress. Alleviate their distress, convince them at least of your solicitude to do it, and you extirpate the seeds of disaffection far more effectually than by all the arts of intimidation. But if an insensibility to their sufferings in the higher ranks goads them to despair, nourishes an appetite for change, and prepares them to lend themselves to the sophistry of artful demagogues and unprincipled empirics, what will be the consequence but a divided and distracted empire, where instead of uniting to consolidate the resources of general prosperity, the necessity of employing one part of the nation in the coercion or punishment of the other dissipates its efforts, and cripples its energy? We have the highest authority for asserting that a "kingdom divided against itself cannot stand;" and surely no schism in the body politic can be more fatal than that which alienates the hands from the head,—the physical strength of society from its presiding intellect.

It may be objected to these observations, that, however just, they are irrelevant to the subject in hand, which relates, not to a national, but to a provincial object. To which the reply is obvious, that every manufacturing county constitutes an important part of the nation, and that there is no absurdity in supposing that the arrangement which is adapted to the situation of one may be applied with equal advantage to another. Be this as it may, if the tranquillity of a central department of the empire can be maintained by a measure which, while it rescues a numerous description of persons from the deepest misery, is beneficial to all and burthensome to none, much is contributed to the fund of national prosperity, composed, as it is, of separate portions of individual enjoyment and security.

Waiving, for the present, the consideration of the tendency of the measure in question to promote the welfare of the nation, the writer of these lines must be permitted to avow his attachment to his *natale solum*, to the soil that gave him birth, which recalls the image of his youth, with those affecting recollections which nature longest retains, and reluctantly quits. The philanthropy which affects to feel alike for every part of mankind is false and spurious; that alone is genuine which glows with a warmth proportioned to the nearness of its objects. But who that is not utterly devoid of such sentiments, can compare the present condition of this county with the past without deep emotion? The writer well remembers it when it was the abode of health and competence; a temperate and unstrained industry diffused plenty through its towns and villages; the harsh and dissonant sound of the loom was not unpleasant to the ear, mingled with the evidence of the activity which it indicated, and the comfort it produced; the advance of summer invited the peasant to a grateful change of labour, while the village poured forth its cheerful population to assist in preparing the tedded grass, and reap the golden harvest; content resided in its valleys, joy echoed from its hills; the distresses of poverty were almost unknown, except by the idle and the profligate, its natural victims; and even the transition from peace was rather heard at a distance than felt as a positive calamity. Some provinces, it is confessed, abounded with more splendid objects, with more curious specimens of art, and grander scenes of nature; but it was surpassed by none in the general diffusion of prosperity. But what a contrast is now presented, in the languid and emaciated forms and dejected looks of our industrious mechanics, who with difficulty drag their trembling limbs over scenes where their fathers gazed with rapture, "pleased with each rural sight, each rural sound!" A rapid depression of wages, like a gangrene, preys upon their vitals, and exhausts their strength. The crisis is arrived which is to decide the destiny of this part of the kingdom; its fate for the present generation, to say the least, depends, under Providence, entirely on the success of the measure now in agitation; and how, let me ask, can its hereditary nobility exert themselves more laudably than by stretching forth the hand to save from ruin the county which gave them birth, and includes the fund of their wealth, the scene of their magnificence, and the sepulchre of their fathers!

Though this appeal is, with the utmost propriety, made to them in the first instance, it is not confined to that elevated order; there is not a description of persons within the limits of the county who ought to contemplate the crisis with indifference; and so essential is the success of the present expedient to every hope of deliverance, that, whatever be his station, he who withholds his quota from the general contribution may justly consider himself as accessary to its ruin.

If there be any motive wanting, in addition to those which have been already urged, to excite us to exertion, it is found in the exemplary conduct of the principal sufferers. Never were privations so distressing endured with more manly fortitude; and, for my own part, I cannot look back on the patience and the constancy displayed through such a protracted scene of suffering, without ascribing it to a calm confidence in that Providence which, sooner or later, never fails to interpose in behalf of such as trust in it, and which, at length, has inspired wisdom to discover, and resolution to apply, the only remedy. They have deplored their misery, they have exhibited their grievances to the view of the public, in the language of nature and of truth, but rarely, if ever, have they forgotten their duties. Far from shrinking from the necessity of making the first sacrifice, they have cheerfully come forward to establish the present fund, to which they have engaged to contribute sixpence a week out of their scanty earnings. We will not suppose for a moment a reluctance on the part of the public to assist and encourage a description of persons whose welfare is inseparably combined with their own, and who, to the praise of patient endurance under the severest of trials, have added that of united and manly exertion to prevent their recurrence

A REPLY

TO THE PRINCIPAL OBJECTIONS ADVANCED BY

COBBETT AND OTHERS

AGAINST THE

FRAMEWORK KNITTERS' FRIENDLY RELIEF SOCIETY.

[PUBLISHED IN 1821.]

A REPLY.

THE virulent opposition made to the *Framework Knitters' Friendly Relief Society*—a protective policy to secure themselves from the pressure of poverty and the pains of hunger—may well excite the surprise of the reflecting and humane part of the public. This violence with which it is assailed forms, indeed, the most remarkable feature of the business, and is alone sufficient to awaken suspicion of a design not distinctly avowed. Its opponents are loud in proclaiming their conviction that it cannot possibly endure, that it must shortly come to an end. Why then not leave it to its fate? Why display this anxiety to accelerate its overthrow, these violent and persevering efforts to crush the feeble and precipitate the falling? If, as they contend, it contains within itself the seeds of speedy dissolution, no evil can result from abandoning it to the operation of its native tendencies, and suffering it to die a natural death. Is it not apparent that all this commotion and effort indicate a suspicion that it is not so fraught with the elements of self-destruction as they pretend, and that it *requires* to be powerfully assailed.

Its opponents confidently assert that it has no tendency to keep up the rate of wages, that these are regulated by causes over which it has no control, and that, in defiance of every possible arrangement, they will infallibly find their level. If such is really their conviction, their zeal is still more preposterous. For where is the policy or the prudence of exposing themselves to the suspicion of insensibility to the distresses of the working classes by opposing a scheme which can have no effects, produce no consequences while it continues, and the futility of which will be shortly apparent to all? The list of prices agreed upon between the employers and their men, they assert, is higher than the state of the trade will allow; and that, could it be maintained, it would be detrimental to the manufacturing interest by preventing the sale of the article. Admitting this, it would afford a sufficient reason for opposing a measure which had a tendency to produce that effect, namely, the continuance of the statement. But as it is loudly affirmed that the Framework Knitters' Union has no such tendency, but will leave the rate of wages just as it was, why this superfluity of zeal in opposing what can produce no mischief? If such is their real opinion, they are fighting with a shadow—combating a phantom. This, however, will hardly be supposed. Men are not accustomed to exert themselves with vehemence against an object of which they entertain no apprehension: they usually proportion their efforts to their alarms.

It is impossible not to discern, in the wanton and virulent attack of Cobbett and others on the *Framework Knitters' Society*, that more is meant than meets the ear—that a purpose is aimed which is not yet ripe for disclosure. Of this we may be assured, that there lurks at the bottom of this opposition a secret persuasion that the permanence of the Union will effect a permanent elevation of wages, above that extreme point of depression to which they had before subsided.

Here the first question which arises is, whether the recompense of labour previous to the establishment of a fund was such on an average as to enable a workman to procure for himself and his family the ordinary necessaries of life. For the answer to this we might refer the reader to our opponents, who, with some variation in their statements, unanimously acknowledge they were not sufficient for that purpose. The anonymous writer who styles himself "An Observer" feebly attempts, it is true, to palliate the wretched condition of the workmen by referring us to the price of provisions, not in Leicestershire, be it remembered, but in Taunton,* and by informing us that a man working a frame of *thirty-two or finer gauge* twelve hours a day can earn eight shillings a week.† As in this very passage he is declaiming against "extreme statements as suspicious," who would suspect that the very passage which censures contains an example of it? But so it is; for the writer is informed by the most experienced manufacturers that the kind of work adduced is of a superior order, on which very few, in comparison, are employed; and that the average earnings previous to the Union were from five shillings and sixpence to six shillings a week, not a moiety of the sum adequate to the decent support of an industrious family. The enormous pressure on the parishes which are the principal seats of manufacture place the matter of fact for which we are contending beyond all controversy. But that the "labourer is worthy of his hire" is as much the dictate of reason as of Scripture: and if there be any spectacle which shocks the natural feeling of justice, it is the sight of industry rewarded with famine—of a life devoted to severe and incessant toil, without the power of procuring the means of its own support. This is a state of things from which humanity recoils, but such was the condition of the greater part of the workmen previous to the *Union.*

The next question is, whether the sufferers have not a natural right to attempt the melioration of their condition, and by any means consistent with the peace of society, and the inviolable security of property, endeavour to rescue themselves from a state in which death is preferable to life. For what purpose, let me ask, is reason bestowed, if not to assist its possessor in contriving the means of alleviating his calamities and of improving his situation? The skill and labour of the poor man constitute his whole possession, and he has a right to place it to the best advantage, for precisely the same reason that the rich capitalist is entitled to make the most advantageous disposal of his

* Observer, p. 5. † Ibid p. 6.

wealth. He has consequently, if he pleases, a right to set aside a portion of his earnings towards securing the means of a just and natural remuneration of his industry. I call that a just and natural remuneration which enables him to procure the necessaries of life for himself and his family. If, by the exercise of foresight and self-denial, he can evade the fatal necessity of lying entirely at the mercy of his master, where is the impropriety of his conduct, or of what have the public to complain? But such is precisely the principle of the *Framework Knitters' Union.* It is merely the policy of self-defence; an instrument invented by themselves, and supported principally from their own resources, for securing that recompense of labour which their employers with much unanimity affirmed to be reasonable, and which they voluntarily consented to give. It is not to be confounded for a moment with a combination to *raise* wages; it is merely a provision for securing the terms mutually stipulated between their employers and themselves. The necessity of some such measure was demonstrated by experience; a statement had been promised on a former occasion, but it was found that while there was a surplus of labour in the market, however inconsiderable, it was converted into a means of effecting a universal depression, far below the scale to which it would have naturally descended, in consequence of the decreased demand. That wages should decline to a certain extent along with the demand is the natural consequence of the vicissitudes of trade; still it is but equitable that they should bear some proportion to each other. We will suppose out of ten thousand hands engaged in this manufacture that one thousand are out of employ; here, supposing the remainder to labour with only their usual degree of assiduity, there are nine-tenths of the manufacture produced which was made when they were all at work. The probable demand has diminished one-tenth. But if the effect of this is to reduce the wages nearly one-half, so as to place the necessaries of life out of the reach of the workmen, is not this a result to be deplored? and if any means consistent with the peace of society can be contrived to prevent it, ought they not to be adopted? In this case it is in vain to allege that the depression in question is rendered necessary in consequence of the decreased demand, because they bear no proportion one to the other. The demand is by the supposition diminished one-tenth—the wages are reduced nearly one-third. Such was the exact state of things at the late *turn-out* in Leicestershire. A proportion of about one in ten were unemployed, and this surplus of labour was converted, by a process not very creditable to the humanity of its authors, into an instrument of universal depression to the extent already stated. The method by which it was accomplished is extremely simple. Those who were out of employ were driven by the distress of their situation to offer their services on terms the most disadvantageous; the offer was accepted; and this afforded a pretext for gradually lowering the wages of the rest, who had no alternative but to submit to the abatement proposed or quit their employ. Further reductions were imposed, which for the same reason were for the most part submitted to; till, through a few successive stages, the wages of all were brought to the same level. Thus the wretched workmen were reduced to the necessity of acquiescing, not in that abatement of wages which was proportioned to the diminished demand, but in the terms which a small minority were induced to accept; and the destitution and despair of a few became the gauge by which the miseries of all were measured out. If there is a man to be found who is perfectly reconciled to such a procedure, who sees nothing in it inconsistent with the dictates of the most refined and enlightened humanity, his mental structure is such as I shall never envy.

Since in the case before us it is the surplus of labour alone which affords the facility of effecting a depression so destructive by obliging those who are unemployed to engage themselves at a price by which they could not live, the object of the *Union* is simply to take away that necessity, by withdrawing that portion of redundant labour which produced it,—a mode of proceeding perfectly analogous to that which takes place in every branch of trade and manufacture. He who is engaged in these endeavours invariably to adjust the extent of the supply to the demand: if his capital enables him, he withholds his commodities from the market when it is glutted, and reproduces them when they are more eagerly called for. Is there any principle of political economy conceived to be violated by this discretionary power of the manufacturer to adjust his productions to his demand—to withdraw them from the market at his pleasure, when he foresees their sale will fetch no adequate returns? But this, *mutatis mutandis*, or with a slight change of names, is exactly the case under present discussion. The labour and skill of the mechanic or the artist constitute the article *he* has to dispose of; and the Framework Knitters' Fund, against which such a clamour has been raised by interested and designing men, is nothing more or less than a provision for withholding such a portion of that article as he perceives cannot be employed without ruinous consequences. If the principles of political economy are those of justice and common sense, they will authorize no more interference with the labouring mechanic than with the tradesman or manufacturer; and if the manufacturer is not compelled to dispose of his productions on destructive terms, why should the mechanic be obliged thus to dispose of his labour? It will be acknowledged, it is more *difficult* for the mechanic to adjust his labour to the demand, than it is for the manufacturer to regulate his supply by the state of the market; but this is a distinct consideration; the Framework Knitters' Fund is contrived with a view to obviate this difficulty—it has already done it to a great degree, and nothing but a more general co-operation of the workmen, and of parishes, is wanted to enable them to surmount it altogether.

The principles of political economy exclude the exercise of compulsion only, and by consequence all sort of legislative interference in commercial transactions: they were never understood by a single writer to control the exercise of free agency in any class of the community, and consequently not in the *Leicestershire framework knitters.* The science of political economy assumes for its basis that every person best understands his own business; that the desire of improving his condition is inherent in man; and that when every one is left to pursue his individual interest in his own way, without injuring others, the combined successes arising from the unfettered endeavours of each to advance his particular interest will produce a greater aggregate of wealth than it is possible to realize under a pervading system of legislative control. This is the master-principle of that science, and on this principle the makers of stockings must be supposed to understand their own interest best; they have had a long and severe training in the school of adversity; and they are unanimously of opinion that the establishment of a fund out of their own earnings, in aid of such as are out of employ, is the most efficient expedient for maintaining an adequate rate of wages. Having learned from experience that no agreement with their masters will stand unless it is protected by such a provision, they have made it chiefly from their own resources, assisted by those parishes whose interest is deeply implicated in their support.

As far as the fund is supported by the voluntary contributions of the men and of the parishes, both actuated solely by a view to their own interest, the whole proceeding is perfectly consonant to the principles of political economy, correctly interpreted; and for the voluntary contributions of the public, they are to be considered as entirely provisionary, to be continued no longer than is necessary to give stability to an infant institution; in which light they are abundantly justified by the principles of humanity, which are paramount to every other.

The total want of candour or of information in Mr. Cobbett is apparent in his neglecting to advert to the voluntary contributions of the framework knitters. The reader of his coarse invectives would be led to conclude that the men contributed nothing, that it was merely a project of the public to aid the operative class in a particular manufacture; when in fact the whole affair originated with themselves, by whom it has all along been chiefly supported, and on whose exertions, aided by the parishes which are deeply interested in its preservation, its permanence entirely depends. As our opponents, there is little doubt, "hissed for this fly," it is probable he was not put in possession of a circumstance which forms the nerves and sinews of the Union, but supplied with that information only which best suited their purpose. A serious alarm must have been felt to prompt them to have recourse to such an ally.

"Flectere si nequeo superos, Acheronta movebo."

The omission of this fact enables him to invest the whole business with an air of ridicule for which a just statement of the case would have furnished no pretence. An extensive combination of the public to assist the framework knitters may, considered by itself, appear somewhat romantic; but when it is viewed in the light of a temporary support to an institution which has to struggle with difficulties arising from the ignorance of some and the self-interested perverseness and prejudice of others, it assumes a different character. The public have, in my humble opinion, displayed both humanity and wisdom in lending their aid to a plan which has already effected much good, and promises in its fuller development to accomplish much more; but their assistance, however meritorious, must be considered as provisionary, while the permanence of the plan wholly depends on the exertions of the workmen and the parishes. It is on the principle of an appropriation of a part of their earnings to their mutual assistance, and as a means of enabling parishes to alleviate a numerous class at the least possible expense, that its merits must be tried and its advantages estimated.

The "Observer" asserts that it has done little or nothing towards alleviating the general distress. The truth of this assertion, however, may be safely left to the discernment of the public. Let *them* say whether the situation of the workmen has not been materially improved during the two years that the *Union* has subsisted. When its effect has been to raise wages at least one-third, is it possible to doubt whether such an augmentation has been productive of a proportionable increase of comfort; or what but an experience of its advantages could have prompted men not remarkably gifted with self-denying habits, to persist so long in making such a sacrifice?

Cobbett loudly and repeatedly asserts that the manufacturers *cannot afford* to give higher wages, referring to the conduct of those Nottinghamshire and Derbyshire houses which continue to stand out, as a decisive proof of his position. "If the price," he says, "can be afforded, why do not those hosiers in most extensive business give it? If they *aver* that they can afford it, why do they not give it? Mind, it is the hosiers in most extensive business that aver this, and yet they do not give the price."* It is a sufficient reply to these triumphant interrogations, that the most respectable hosiers *do* give it, and that they who do not find by experience that they can procure their work to be done on lower terms; the reason of which is a surplus of labour in the market, whose operation in causing a universal depression has been already described.

It is the opinion of the most judicious manufacturers the writer has had the opportunity of consulting, that the demand for hosiery was little, if at all, diminished at the period immediately preceding the greatest depression of wages, nor was the number out of employ previously to its taking place more than ordinary. The system of depression in this county, it is a matter of public notoriety, did not originate in a decreased demand, nor did it proceed in any assignable proportion to that supposed diminution; it originated entirely in a vicious competition among a few individuals for the monopoly of the London market. It was the eagerness of certain individuals to undersell each other in that market which gave birth to the system, and to all the unspeakable calamities which have resulted from it. The process by which it was effected has been already explained so often that I am afraid to repeat it: it was brought about through the medium of such as were out of employ, who by offering themselves on inferior terms afforded an opportunity eagerly embraced of gradually reducing the rest to the same level. The hosiers must surely be allowed to be the best judges what wages

* Cobbett, p. 70.

they can afford, a great majority of whom have recorded their judg ment on this subject by a voluntary agreement to give the *statement* price signed and attested by their own hand. Ask any one of them who may have departed from it why he did so? and if the reason he assigns is founded on a decreased demand, and the consequent necessity of depressing wages, I would almost consent to yield to our opponents the whole question at issue. No: this is not the answer, the writer of this can aver from his own knowledge it is not: it is always a reference to some other person, who is affirmed (whether truly or not signifies nothing) to get his work performed at a cheaper rate. In answer then to the question urged with so much exultation by Cobbett, "If the manufacturers can afford to give higher wages, why are they not given?" suffice it to say, that men are often little disposed to give what it is in their power to withhold; and that what is abated in wages is either added to profits or goes to enable them to undersell their competitors, and by that means command a more extensive trade. Could it be proved that the *statement* had produced a glut in the market by exceeding the demand, there would be some plausibility in Mr. Cobbett's representation; as it is, nothing can be more futile.

With a rudeness congenial with his habits, he grossly insults the anonymous writer who styles himself "Humanus," for asserting that men of little or no capital have compelled the superior manufacturers to depress the wages of their workmen in order to prevent themselves from being excluded from the market. This he represents as the greatest of all absurdities; telling him that he ought to have styled himself fool or hypocrite for hazarding such a statement. If insolence were the proper corrective of folly, Mr. Cobbett would of all men be best qualified to administer the cure, though on that supposition his interference would be impertinent in the present instance. His confident assertion of the impossibility of a fact which is known to exist by all intelligent men in the county is a specimen of his ignorance of the trade on which he so dogmatically decides. Men of little or no capital are incapable of bearing stock; they must dispose of their article at whatever price they can get, without waiting for a more favourable season. Hence they are the first to make sacrifices, to diminish the extent of which, and to enable them to sell immediately without absolute loss, they are under peculiar temptations to beat down the wages of their workmen, temptations from which the more opulent manufacturer is exempt; and when there is any considerable number out of employ they easily find the means of effecting their object. A system, it is well known to all who reside in this county, is established by which an extensive trade in hosiery is conducted by persons of little or no capital. Their bills, weekly drawn on London, are accepted, which is equivalent to a weekly supply of capital; and the inducement to afford this accommodation is the extremely low price of the goods which are manufactured *under the statement.* Is there a hosier in Leicestershire who will venture to deny the justice of this statement? In fact, this system has been carried to such an extent that the most opulent hosiers have of late succeeded worst, old-established houses have quitted the business in disgust, and the trade has been gradually transferred to those who have profited by the gradual depression of wages.

If the Framework Knitters' Union is dissolved, it is universally allowed they will sink and lower, nor can any limits be assigned to which they may not descend. Before its formation nearly half the subsistence of the workmen was drawn from the parishes, or in other words from the public. But what can be conceived more monstrous than a manufacture carried on at the public expense, but not for the public benefit, where all the profits are appropriated to one description of persons, while the public are taxed to an enormous amount to enable a few individuals to secure to themselves those advantages? Is there an anomaly in the social system more prodigious than this, or more pregnant with the most alarming consequences? Is it a greater enormity, let me ask, to be compelled to support a numerous herd of sinecurists, pensioners, and "eaters of taxes," to use the elegant phraseology of Mr. Cobbett, than to pay half the wages of an extensive manufacture, without deriving from it one farthing of profit, while it swells out a putrid stream of pauperism which overflows the land? Mr. Cobbett perhaps sees nothing in such a state repugnant to his feelings: in the despair of the poor, and the utter incapacity of the parishes to relieve their wants, he seems to exult, as the infallible prognostic of some great convulsion; but there are those, and I hope not a few, who will contemplate such a prospect with horror.

He is anxious to impress the belief that the distress of the framework knitters is to be ascribed to the accumulation of taxes, and to no other cause. This, from beginning to end, is his darling theme. It is far from my intention to deny that the general decay of trade and commerce is intimately connected with the enormous weight of taxation: or that it is in vain to expect a return to national prosperity, unless some efficient means are devised to lighten their pressure. It is equally certain, however, though the exhausting effect of excessive taxation may have prepared a way for the evils we deplore, that a system has been adopted in the hosiery trade which has aggravated the calamity of the working class far beyond the necessary operation of that general cause. The taxes are the same in the west of England as in the midland counties; but the wages in the clothing districts have not been reduced: the manufacture of cloth has been all along adjusted to the demand. The weight of taxes is as heavy in the Staffordshire potteries as here; but the remuneration of labour has remained steady and uniform. Less work is given out in proportion as the demand slackens; and I have it from the best authority, that the earnings of the workmen are at this moment abundantly adequate to their means of subsistence. They are three times as high as those of the stocking-makers were before the formation of the *Union*. By the system pursued in these branches, the evils resulting from a decreased demand are kept within their natural limits; no adventitious ingredient is infused into the cup, no artificial aggravation added to their sufferings. But in the hosiery manufacture it is just the reverse: the calamity indirectly inflicted on the industrious poor by means of such as are out of employ is incalculably greater than that which results from the failure of employment; and the destitution of a part becomes, in skilful hands, a mighty engine for the destruction of the whole.

What is the remedy proposed by our opponents? "The only effectual relief," Humanus says, "for the distresses of the framework knitters, is for a great part of the present hands to leave the trade, and that not for a season, but entirely and for ever." We needed not the information of this sagacious adviser, that the root of the mischief lies in a redundancy of hands, that it is devoutly to be wished that parents would cease as much as possible to train up their children to this calling, that masters would take fewer apprentices, and some method could be discovered to lessen the number engaged in this branch of manufacture. This is all very desirable. But what is to become of the existing generation? To what employ can they turn with advantage who have acquired no other craft, and whose habits totally disqualify them for agricultural labour, were it to be procured? Under these circumstances, to advise them to "retire entirely and for ever," is to recommend suicide and death. Is not the *general* decay of trade and manufacture the topic of universal complaint, and must not the greatest difficulty be encountered where all the ranks of employment are dense with population and crowded to excess, in attempting to open a fresh career for their industry? Unless something more practicable and definite is suggested, to bid them retire because they are not wanted, is not to advise, but to mock them.

The formation of a fund towards the support of such as are incapable of procuring work but upon such terms as are ruinous to every description of their brethren, presents a specific remedy for the existing disorder, and the only one which is equivalent to a cruel mockery of their woes.

The principal sophism which pervades the strictures of Mr. Cobbett and others on this subject, is a vicious generalization, in consequence of which he imagines he has sufficiently accounted for the wretched state of the workmen in a particular manufacture, by referring it to the cause which has produced a declension in the state of trade and manufacture in general; whence he infers that he is entitled to pour ridicule and contempt upon every expedient which is distinct from the removal of that cause. But along with the general source of a decline in commerce there are a number of *particular circumstances* which must be noticed, in order to account for that state of depression in which some branches are found, in comparison with others. As far as our political embarrassments alone are concerned, their operation must be *equally* disadvantageous to every species of productive labour, to every kind of trade and manufacture whatever. But these are not all equally depressed, which they must have been if the political state of the nation was alone sufficient to account for all the phenomena. The fact is, that while every department of manufacture is probably injured by our pecuniary embarrassments, the working classes in some are found to be in a much more favourable situation than in others. The remuneration of labour, for example, in the western clothing districts, in the Staffordshire potteries, I might add in no part of the kingdom, has been depressed as it has been here. The reason of this has been again and again explained; it has arisen from the illiberal advantage which has been taken of a surplus of labour; while in the districts just referred to, that practice has not been adopted, less work is given out when less is demanded, and the earnings are sufficient to procure all the necessaries, and some of the comforts of life. As the distemper is local and specific, the remedy must be of the same description.

The list of prices agreed upon is considerably less than is sufficient to maintain the condition which honest industry ought ever to occupy, decidedly less than might be afforded in a more prosperous state of the country. It is such, however, as the great body of the masters have declared themselves able to give, while they affirm they can do no more. Since their conviction of their ability to do this is a deliberate recorded opinion, let the reader judge of the audacity of Mr. Cobbett in the following assertion: "He, Humanus," says Mr. Cobbett, "affirms that the hosiers in the most extensive business aver they can afford the statement prices. We might treat this as nothing, we might call it a falsehood, because it is against reason, and because the averment is not produced and attested; we have the bare word of an anonymous writer for it; that is all, and that is nothing." "We might call it a falsehood;" Certainly Mr. Cobbett might, who displays throughout such an infinite familiarity with the "father of lies;" but let us hope no other man could be found who would stigmatize as a falsehood the assertion that such is the averment of the manufacturers, after they had signed and attested it with their own hand. This recorded opinion is an unanswerable confutation of the assertion so often repeated by our opponents, that the hosiers cannot afford the *statement* price; for surely they will not be so absurd as to impute to them a formal resolution of giving wages which they were conscious at the time they could not well afford. It may therefore be assumed as a fact, placed beyond all dispute, that the *statement* proposed is such as will leave a reasonable rate of profits to the hosiers,—from whence we adduce two conclusions; first, that the assertion of those who maintain that the *statement*, were it adhered to, would be ruinous to the trade, is a falsehood, because it is formally contradicted by the persons who must be allowed, in what immediately concerns their own interest, to be the best judges: secondly, that besides the operation of taxes in deteriorating wages, other causes, of a more specific nature, have contributed to produce that effect, and that consequently the whole argumentation of Mr. Cobbett, which proceeds upon the denial of this, falls to the ground.

It is repeatedly objected by the "Observer," that the proposed *statement* can never become permanent, because it is impossible to induce the masters to adhere unanimously to their agreement. To this I answer, that such unanimity is not contemplated, nor is it necessary. The principal, perhaps the only benefit of the agreement is, that it stamps a legal character on the proceedings of the men, which might otherwise expose them to the penalties of combination. If they become sufficiently enlightened to their own interests, to afford an adequate support to the fund, the surplus labour will be disposed of, and it will no longer be in the power of those who may be disposed to convert it into an instrument of universal depression. The list of prices agreed upon at Nottingham, in the year 1819, to which the "Observer refers, produced no permanent effect in Nottinghamshire nor in Derby shire, because no fund was established in those counties to support it in Leicestershire the same agreement was followed by the most efficient consequences, because it received that support. And this is the reason, and the only reason, that every thing reverted so soon to its former state; not, as this writer affirms, in consequence of a diminution of demand produced by the *statement;* for had this been the cause, the effect would have been felt in Leicestershire equally, but it was not, solely because the surplus of labour was removed by the provisions of the fund.

The "Observer" further remarks, that "it borders on the ludicrous to talk of men *plunged in the very depths of despair*, from their scanty earnings raising a fund for their unemployed associates; and unless they can do this, their project must fail." This writer forgets that he had before represented these very men in a tolerably comfortable state, referring us for proof to the price of provisions in the Taunton market. It suited the scope of his argument then to elevate their condition, whom he now, for a similar purpose, "*plunges into the very depths of despair.*" The reader will, in a moment, perceive what credit is due to a writer who is entangled in such contradictions, who attributes to the same persons comfort and despair, just as it suits his convenience. But passing these inconsistencies, the reply is obvious, that if the manufacturers in the neighbouring counties imitate the example of this, their men, no longer plunged into the very depths of despair, will be incomparably more able to subscribe sixpence a week to the fund, than to procure subsistence in their present circumstances. The "Observer" must be aware that their competence to contribute their quota is assumed only on the supposition of the *statement* being given; and he must not be permitted to change suppositions backwards and forwards, with the same dexterity that he converts comfort into despair. Since it is allowed by our opponents, that where no fund exists, the workmen are "in the depths of despair," the only question is, what must be done? How is the intolerable load under which they are groaning to be alleviated or removed? Mr. Cobbett's grand panacea is, recourse to the parishes; not that he is so ignorant as to suppose it possible they should afford effectual relief, but that he foresees other effects resulting from it, which he is evidently much more anxious to realize. "But," says he, "are you to have no redress? Are you to starve, in short? No: no man, woman, or child is to starve; the law says so, and rely upon the law A man works constantly; he is sober, he wastes nothing. His master can or will give him no more; and with what he gets he is starving, with his family. Now what says the law? Why, that he shall be relieved, that he shall share out of the common stock, out of that which was originally one man's as well as another's; out of that which God gave for all—out of the *land*."* But is he nc aware that the pressure of parish rates is already almost intolerabl

* Cobbett, p. 97.

that they are levied on thousands who are themselves on the brink of pauperism; and that in many parts of the country, they have reduced the value of land to such a state, that even were they occupied free of rent, the farmer could hardly subsist by the produce? It is true they may not have reached the point which Mr. Cobbett triumphantly contemplates, the utter ruin and extinction of landed proprietors; but they have already attained a portentous magnitude, which no lover of his country can contemplate without dismay.

This seems to be the proper place for noticing a monstrous position advanced by this writer, with a confidence which can only be surpassed by its falsehood. "Viewing the thing in its true light," he says, "what is the nation, and particularly *the landed proprietor*, to gain by an additional sum being given to you in wages? What is he to gain by a million of money paid to stocking weavers *more* than is now paid to them? Is there not a million *less* to be laid out by somebody else? If the labourer pays a crown a year more for stockings, has he not a crown less to lay out in bread and beer? If indeed, the additional million paid to you were to be expended by you, or flung into the sea; or if the additional million were to drop down into your hands from the clouds, in either of these cases there might be some sense in Humanus's argument: as the thing is, it is nonsense."* This is the reasoning, be it remembered, of the man who in the same pamphlet ascribes all our calamities "to so large a portion being taken from those who labour, to be given to those who do not labour."† If the above reasoning is correct, it will follow that the value of land would not be diminished, though the stocking weavers earned nothing at all, but were entirely supported by the parish. On this supposition, it is true they would have no wages, but some other persons possess them, or, which is the same thing, their amount, which if they had *not*, they would be less able to purchase the produce of the soil, in exact proportion to that amount. More error and absurdity, I will venture to assert, were never penned within the same compass than are contained in the paragraph just quoted. It proceeds on the following extraordinary assumptions; First, That all the purchasers of hosiery are also purchasers of the other parts of the produce of the British soil, and that in the same proportion. For if this is not the case; if they either do not purchase the other parts of our produce at all, or not in the same proportion, how will it follow that they must necessarily buy just so much *less* of our corn, and of every other article which the land produces, because they buy *more* of our hosiery! Look at foreign nations: our stockings make their way into a large proportion of the habitable world; but are all the inhabitants of the regions into which they penetrate accustomed to purchase equal proportions of the other branches of our rude produce? The far greater part, it is well known, purchase none of these, and few if any in the same proportion.

Secondly, It assumes for granted that all who purchase hosiery expend to the *utmost extent of their income*, so that if they give five shillings a year *more* for hosiery, they must necessarily lay out five shillings *less* in other articles of consumption. "They have, it seems

* Cobbett, p. 91. † Ibid. p. 117

just *so much* that they can lay out upon stockings."* It must be evident to the intelligent reader that this mode of reasoning presupposes an exact equality of expenditure and of income, and that consequently it is applicable only to such whose circumstances oblige them to practise in every instance the strictest and most rigid economy. But the chief purchases of manufacture are made by consumers of a very different description; by persons whose situation enables them to sustain a much greater advance of price than is here mentioned, without the necessity of abridging themselves in other modes of indulgence. If Mr. Cobbett's reasoning were just, the demand for every article, at distinct periods, would be exactly proportioned to its price; but experience shows the contrary, that the demand is not regulated solely by the price, but by many other concurrent causes, which it is needless at present to specify. He forgets the "eaters of taxes," the nobility, the gentry, the landed proprietors, the opulent merchants, the thriving tradesmen, together with the myriads of others, who are in easy circumstances and live within their income, all of whom wear stockings, and can well afford an advance of a few shillings on that head, without a proportional diminution in every other branch of expenditure. Though this class of the community may not be the most numerous, it cannot be doubted that they are the chief purchasers of manufacture.

Thirdly, His argument goes upon the supposition, that it is of no consequence to the public *where* wealth is deposited, provided it is not "thrown into the sea." Admitting the truth of this, how can the taxes be the cause of our calamities, as he asserts, "by taking from those who labour, and giving to those who do not labour?"† and how unreasonable and absurd his violent outcry against the landholders, pensioners, and sinecurists! To the accumulation of wealth in *their* hands he attributes all our distresses, who yet are as little disposed, we presume, as any men "to throw it into the sea."

May they not retort upon him and say, "You ascribe the ruin of the nation to the transfer of its wealth into the hands of those who do not labour from those who do. But our money is employed either in loans or in consumption. The capital we lend is employed by merchants and manufacturers in maintaining productive labour, while the money we consume tends immediately, by taking off the produce, to keep up the value of land; and it is certain, considered under either mode of operation, that were it transferred to others, we, its present possessors, should have so much *less* to employ or to spend?" I am far from supposing this reasoning would be correct; but I have no hesitation in affirming it is the legitimate consequence of his principle, which is, that the landed proprietor would not be benefited by the improved condition of the working classes, nor injured even by the extinction of wages, unless "they were thrown into the sea." The operative part of the people, those we mean who are immediately employed in productive labour, probably compose much less than a moiety of the whole nation: the remaining part of the population must, as far as the present argument is concerned, be classed with those who

* Cobbett, p. 90.

† Cobbett, p. 92.

do not labour. Suppose the wages of the stocking weavers were universally depressed so as to be totally inadequate to their support, which was actually the case before the late regulations; in consequence of the competition among the manufacturers, a correspondent abatement of the price of the article would be the necessary consequence; hosiery would be just so much the cheaper, and the deduction from the wages being subtracted from the price would be in fact given to the purchasers. A very large proportion of these however, consist of such as *do not labour.* Here then we have an example of the transfer of property from "those who do, to those who do not labour," which Mr. Cobbett represents as the root and origin of all our evils; yet, strange to tell, this same writer affirms that the process by which this is effected is productive of no injury to the public. A portion of the wages withheld would, in consequence of the abatement of price, pass into the hands even of the placemen, pensioners, and sinecurists themselves. Let me ask whether this would not, on his own principles, be a direct transfer of so much money from those "who labour to those who do not?" yet is he guilty of the absurdity of saying that an arrangement which he asserts to be so destructive to the whole nation in every other instance, would in this produce no inconvenience whatever, either to the public or to the landed proprietor.

The reader is probably by this time weary of attending to the palpable contradictions of this arrogant and superficial declaimer: suffice it to remark that it requires little or no penetration to perceive that the extinction of wages, and the consequent absolute pauperism of the working classes, would effect the deepest depression of the value of land in every manufacturing district; and that no remedy would be found in the decreased price of the article, since the saving arising from it would be reaped, not by the landholder, but by the public, in minute and almost invisible portions through all its diversity of ranks, and by foreign nations.

Mr. Cobbett, with much confidence and equal exultation, predicts the destruction of the landed interest as the certain, the inevitable consequence of the present crisis. Whatever probability may attach to these dismal forebodings arises chiefly, if not wholly, from the alarming increase of poor-rates, and this latter from the inadequate remuneration of labour. For what is it else, except in time of sickness, which drives a poor man to have recourse to parish relief? Were the rates of wages sufficient to procure with facility the means of human subsistence, is it possible to doubt that the parochial burdens would be most essentially alleviated, that the farmer and the householder would find it much easier to pay the ordinary rent? The ingenuity of Mr. Cobbett, however, has enabled him to discover that were a million a year added to the wages of labour, the landed proprietor would not derive the advantage of a farthing.

These and such like extravagances will be quite sufficient to satisfy the reader that he is a popular declaimer, not a philosopher; a firebrand not a luminary. He emits fire and smoke in abundance, like a volcano, but the whole effect is to desolate, not to enlighten. His principal artifice consists in the exhibition of a few specious and bold generali ties, which he illustrates and confirms by a few prominent facts culled for his purpose, without the slightest attempt at that patient induction and inquiry which alone lead to solid and useful results. Shrewd, intemperate, presumptuous, careless of the truth of his representations and indifferent to their consequences, provided they make an impression, he is well qualified, it must be confessed, by his faults no less than his talents, by his inflammatory style and incendiary spirit, for the office he assumes, to scatter delusion, to excite insurrection, the Polyphemus of the mob, "the one-eyed monarch of the blind." His strictures, however, on the topic under consideration are pregnant with instruction it was not his design to communicate. Whatever the inhabitants of this county may think of the Framework Knitters' Union, *he* plainly foresees in the consequences of its failure, the materials of ferocious delight; he sees without the aid of inspiration an inundation of miseries to follow, paupers crowding by thousands to the doors of overseers, parishes dismayed and perplexed, the poor clamouring for bread which cannot be given them, and rushing upon the point of the bayonet to avoid a more cruel and lingering death; the commencement of that tempest, in a word, which he boasts having crossed the Atlantic to witness, which is to shake all that is stable, to prostrate all that is great, and to accumulate a pile for the elevation of future demagogues.

Rome trembled when Cataline rejoiced. Let the friends of peace and order then, let the landed proprietor especially, take warning; they stand upon the brink of a precipice, from which, if they suffer themselves to be precipitated, it will be no small aggravation of their calamity to perceive the ease with which it might have been prevented; together with the contemptible agency, and the flimsy sophistry which accelerated their overthrow. If it is some consolation to the fallen to have perished by a noble hand, the indignity of being baffled and deluded by the author of the Political Register must be more humiliating than words can express.

Having extended these strictures beyond my original design, and exhausted, it is to be feared, the patience of my readers, it is my intention to detain them no longer than while I notice an objection to the *Union*, more plausible than any of the preceding, though, for the reasons which follow, entirely destitute of solidity.

It is alleged by its opponents, that the provision of a fund for the support of such as are out of employ affords a direct encouragement to idleness, the most baleful habit a poor man can contract. This objection, could it be sustained, would undoubtedly be weighty; whether it can or not, must depend upon the previous question, Will the number out of employ be *permanently* greater if the *statement* continues, than on the contrary supposition? That it may have that effect for a short time, we are not disposed to deny: the manufacturers having suspended their operations to a considerable degree, some hoping for the dissolution of the society, others from an apprehension of that event, it is probable the moment it were announced, all hands would be set to work. A spirit of vigour and activity would seem for a moment to pervade the trade. But look a step or two further. The number employed in manufacturing, the strained exertions they would be necessitated to make to compensate for the lowness of their wages, and the deteriorated state of the article would combine to produce a glut, which reacting both in the wages and the price, would eventually, and at no great distance neither, produce a greater surplus of labour than exists at present. As my opinion on such a subject may be deemed of little value, I must be allowed to add, that it perfectly coincides with that of the most intelligent men in the trade, and is strongly corroborated by the fact, that there were as many out of work at the time when wages were the most depressed, as at other seasons. Many of them wrought sixteen instead of twelve hours a day; the fabric produced was also of a deteriorated quality, incapable of being vended in foreign markets, insomuch, that I am credibly informed, that in different parts of Europe, in Germany particularly, its being known to be *British* is a sufficient reason for refusing it. The demand for labour then, there is every reason to believe, would not be permanently augmented by returning to the former system, and consequently the number out of employ not diminished. For reasons already specified, it is almost certain the reverse would be the case, and the surplus labour keep pace with the redundant superfluity of manufacture.

The project of raising it by lowering wages has been tried, and found unavailing; and whatever attempts are made to renew it, will resemble the labour of Sisyphus; it will be rolling a stone which will for ever fall back.

The sum proposed to be paid from the fund to such as are out of work, is, at the most, six shillings and sixpence a week, sufficient indeed to preserve them from lying utterly at the mercy of their masters, but certainly not such as to render their situation attractive, nor greater than the parishes would be under the necessity of paying shortly to a much greater number, were the society abolished. While it provides a remedy for the existing evils, it leaves sufficient inducement to seek out other channels for their industry, whenever the state of society shall afford them.

We are far from contending that the system which it is our object to recommend is one of unmingled perfection, productive of good only, without the least alloy; for such is not the condition of human institutions, or of human affairs. The possibility of perversion and abuse inseparably adheres to every conceivable plan for ameliorating the condition of mankind; and he who refuses his approbation to every thing short of perfection, must stand still in hopeless inactivity and despair. If it has been shown that the plan adopted in Leicestershire provides the only remedy for an evil which is progressive and intolerable, that the inconveniences attending it bear no proportion to its advantages, and above all, that the principal objections urged by its opponents will apply with equal force to every other mode of proceeding, and most of all to that which *they* recommend, every reasonable demand is satisfied. Whether this has been accomplished or not, must be left to the decision of an enlightened public; nor let it be deemed presumptuous to say, that if such had not been the firm persuasion of the author, these pages had not appeared.

If he should be thought to have treated Mr. Cobbett with too much severity, he wishes it to be clearly understood that his censure is in no degree founded on the professed attachment of that writer to the cause of reform. Educated in the principles of Mr. Fox, and in those of the earliest and best days of Mr. Pitt, to which advancing years and experience have increased his attachment, it is impossible he should entertain a doubt that an important reform in our representation is essentially connected with the freedom, the glory, and the happiness of the British empire. But he sees in Mr. Cobbett what the intelligent part of the public will at once discern, a design to push the industrious classes of the community to despair, and to aggravate their distresses, in order to accelerate the catastrophe he contemplates; whether it involves the preservation of the constitution, or a total subversion of the existing order of things, must be left to the judgment of the reader. On the most favourable supposition, "to do evil that good may come," to wish to see the industrious part of the population couched under a supernumerary weight, that they may become instrumental in effecting some great and undefined revolution in public affairs, is a policy which he shall ever detest; nor can he sufficiently deprecate the infusion of political venom into the discussions which the present *Union* has produced.

Let those who, from interested motives, or from motives of a still worse description, concur with Mr. Cobbett in vilifying and exploding the present plan, propose something better, unless they are determined to exemplify that malignant potency of evil by which "one sinner destroys much good." It is surely not too much to demand, before they proceed to dilapidate the only asylum offered to the industrious mechanic, that instead of exposing him houseless and shivering to the inclement blast, they should provide some better accommodation in its room. Other expedients have been devised; a large subscription was raised, and many thousands advanced in Nottinghamshire, with a view to employ the indigent framework knitters in public works. But the scheme, as might have been foreseen, proved abortive. The exertion could not be continued, a succession of public works is not easily found; and after alleviating the distress of a single winter, every thing returned back to its former channel. A similar plan, the writer is informed, is in contemplation for this county, and as far as it is adopted to relieve the pressure of the fund, we shall rejoice in its success; but if it is intended to supersede it, or to withdraw that support which the difficulties attending an infant institution may demand, it will, in my humble opinion, be unspeakably injurious. That it will produce no permanent relief to the existing distress, is evident from the example of Nottingham; and however praiseworthy the motives of its projectors, it is but the part of candour to warn the workmen and the parishes, that if their dependence upon it tempts them to relax their present exertions, they will discover, when it is too late, that they have lost the substance by grasping at a shadow. The evil required to be remedied originates in permanent causes, such as will mock the operation of all temporary expedients.

With respect to the apprehension which some have professed to entertain, of the removal of the manufacture to the neighbouring counties.

or to some distant part of the kingdom, little requires to be said. Man is the same in every county, and the energy which has been displayed by the Leicestershire weavers will, there is no doubt, be successfully imitated elsewhere, and produce the same results. In Nottinghamshire we are happy to find, from the latest intelligence, that the most numerous and respectable part of the hosiers have already acceded to the *statement*, and little doubt is entertained of the speedy concurrence of the rest. This apprehension, therefore, if there ever was any ground for it, the event has dispelled. Had it been otherwise, are the operative classes in this department to starve or reduce to ruin every other description, by ineffectual efforts to support them, in the contemplation of a remote contingency, and for the sake of securing a manufacture, which, upon such terms, can only be considered as an epidemic disease, an imposthume, a source of misery to all who are employed in it, and of embarrassment and distress to the whole community? The competition for such a manufacture is a competition for ruin.

Before I conclude, let me be permitted to remind the reader that there is such a sin as oppression; that it consists not in that gross violation of justice which is cognizable by law, and against which the wisdom of all civilized nations has provided; but in taking such an advantage of the weakness and necessity of the poor as converts them into mere instruments of a superior power, the victims of selfish emolument, with no other consideration than how far their physical exertions may be rendered subservient to the gratification of an unfeeling rapacity. He is the oppressor who is not restrained by the dictates of humanity from pushing, to its utmost extent, the natural superiority which riches everywhere possess over poverty; and the stratagems by which this may be effected are too numerous and too subtle to fall within the cognizance of any earthly tribunal. When the Scripture denounces, with such awful severity, the doom of such as "withhold their hire from those who reaped the field,"* we must not suppose it refers so much to a violation of compact, an offence which the laws of no civilized country would permit, as to the *inadequacy* of the recompense itself. In the eye of Heaven, wages may justly be said to be *withheld* from the labourer, when they are totally inadequate to his subsistence, and such as nothing but helpless indigence could induce him to accept. Instead of inquiring how much of this species of guilt may be justly chargeable on a certain class of manufacturers in this town and county, which would only suggest matter for irritating reflection and fruitless recriminations, let us rather rejoice that a new scene has opened, and a plan been adopted, which, we trust, will cut off the opportunity from the bad, and the temptation from the good, of renewing a system which should be consigned to eternal oblivion.† In this view, we have no hesitation in asserting that the perpetuity of the Friendly Society is intimately connected with the interest of both worlds, since it is no less the dictate of humanity and of justice, than of sound policy.

* James v. 4.

† See "Letters to Buxton," published by Longman and Co. which breathe throughout the eloquence of the heart, and in which the cause of humanity is pleaded, and the sufferings of the industrious classes painted with a pathos it is impossible to resist.

PROCEEDINGS

PROCEEDINGS.

At a meeting of persons, inhabitants of the town of Leicester and its vicinity, held the 17th of December, 1823,

THOMAS BABINGTON, Esq. in the Chair;

Resolved,

1. That the individuals composing the present meeting are deeply impressed with the conviction that the state of slavery is repugnant to justice, humanity, and sound policy, to the principles of the British constitution, and to the spirit of the Christian religion; and that they cannot consider the legal perpetuation of slavery, in principle, more defensive than the slave-trade itself.

2. That they call to mind, with sorrow and shame, that there are eight hundred thousand persons in a state of personal slavery in the colonies of Great Britain, deprived of those civil privileges and religious advantages to which, as our fellow-subjects, they are entitled.

3. That although a hope was long indulged that the abolition of the slave-trade would have produced most beneficial consequences to the slave population in the colonies, no effectual steps have been taken, during the sixteen years which have elapsed since that event, for mitigating in any material degree the evils of negro bondage, or for putting an end to a system which outrages every feeling of humanity

4. That the House of Commons having, during the last session of parliament, unanimously passed the following resolutions, viz.

"1. That it is expedient to adopt effectual and decisive measures for melio rating the condition of the slave population in his majesty's colonies;

"2. That, through a determined and persevering, but judicious and temperate enforcement of such measures, this House looks forward to a progressive improvement in the character of the slave population; such as may prepare them for a participation in those civil rights and privileges which are enjoyed by other classes of his majesty's subjects;

"3. That this House is anxious for the accomplishment of this purpose at the earliest period that may be compatible with the well-being of the slaves, the safety of the colonies, and with a fair and equitable con sideration of the state of property therein;"

the individuals present feel themselves called upon to promote these objects to the utmost of their power by all prudent and lawful means.

5. That for this purpose a society be now formed in Leicester and its vicinity, as an auxiliary to the Society for the Mitigation and Gradual Abolition of Slavery throughout the British Dominions.

6. That subscriptions be received by the treasurer, at the bank of Messrs. Mansfield & Co., and by the secretary; and that all persons subscribing annually

to the society be members of it, and be entitled to attend and vote at all general meetings.

7. That all persons subscribing ten shillings or upwards yearly, or five pounds at one time, be governors of the society.

8. That the business of the society be conducted by a president, a treasurer, a secretary, and a committee, consisting of not less than fifteen governors, and that five constitute a quorum; and that the president, treasurer, and secretary be, ex-officio, members of the committee.

9. That the committee meet once every two months, and at such other times as they may fix, and call general meetings of the subscribers when they shall judge it requisite; and that any five members of it be authorized to direct the secretary to summon a special meeting of the committee, giving three days' notice thereof.

ADDRESS.

THAT slavery is the most deplorable condition to which human nature can be reduced is too evident to require the labour of proof. By subjecting one human creature to the absolute control of another, it annihilates the most essential prerogative of a reasonable being, which consists in the power of determining his own actions in every instance in which they are not injurious to others. The right improvement of this prerogative is the source of all the virtue and happiness of which the human race is susceptible. Slavery introduces the most horrible confusion, since it degrades human beings from the denomination of persons to that of things; and by merging the interests of the slave in those of the master, he becomes a mere appendage to the existence of another, instead of preserving the dignity which belongs to a reasonable and accountable nature. Knowledge and virtue are foreign to his state; ignorance the most gross and dispositions the most depraved are requisite to reduce him to a level with his condition.

But degrading as slavery is in its mildest form, that species of it which prevails in our West India colonies* is of the very worst description, far less tolerable than that which subsisted in Greece and Rome during the reign of paganism. It would be difficult to find a parallel to it in any age or nation, with the exception of those unhappy persons who are carried captive by the piratical states of Barbary. Scourged, branded, and sold at the discretion of their masters, the slaves in our West India islands are doomed to a life of incessant toil for the benefit of those from whom they receive no recompense whatever: they are indebted for their principal subsistence to the cultivation of small portions of land allotted them under the name of provision grounds: and the only time ordinarily allowed for that purpose is the day which the laws of all Christian states have devoted to rest. On that day, instead of being assembled to listen to the oracles of God, and to imbibe the consolations of piety, they are necessitated to work for their living, and to dispose of the produce of their labour at the public market; the natural consequence is, that the far greater

* The following authorized summary of the number of slaves in the British colonies, in June, 1830, may be interesting to some readers.

Antigua, 29,839. Bahama Isles, 10,841. Barbadoes, 81,902. Berbice, 21,319. Bermuda, 4,608. Cape of Good Hope, 35,509. Demerara and Essequibo, 69,467. Dominica, 15,392. Grenada, 24,342. Jamaica, 331,119. Mauritius, 76,774. Montserrat, 6,262. Nevis, 9,259. St. Christopher's, 19,310. St. Lucia, 13,661. St. Vincent, 23,589. Tobago, 12,723. Trinidad, 24,452. Virgin Islands 5,436.

Total number of slaves in the British colonies, 825,804.

Free blacks in the British colonies, about 51,000.

The slave population of the United States of America, in 1828, amounted to 1,838,155.—ED part of them are as ignorant of the first principles of Christianity as though they had remained in the land of their forefathers.

They are driven to the field by the cart-whip.* They are followed

* Since this address was written, the persevering efforts of the Anti-Slavery Society, and other associations formed for the attainment of the same admirable object, have led to *some* diminution of the evils under which the slaves in the West Indian isles have so long groaned.

In the year 1823, the House of Commons passed the following resolutions :—

"1. That it is expedient to adopt effectual and decisive measures for meliorating the condition of the slave population in his majesty's colonies.

"2. That, through a determined and persevering, but at the same time judicious and temperate enforcement of such measures, this House looks forward to a progressive improvement in the character of the slave population, such as may prepare them for a participation in those civil rights and privileges which are enjoyed by other classes of his majesty's subjects.

"3. That this House is anxious for the accomplishment of this purpose at the earliest period that shall be *compatible with the well-being of the slaves themselves, with the safety of the colonies, and with a fair and equitable consideration of the interests of private property.*"

In consequence of these resolutions, several of the colonial legislatures have made enactments enforcing a more humane treatment of the slave population. Thus, in Dominica, St. Christopher's, Nevis, and Demerara, the "cart-whip" is absolutely prohibited as an instrument of punishment, and in some of them "as an emblem of authority." In Jamaica, and a few other islands, it is enacted, "that no slave shall receive more than ten lashes, *except in presence of owner or overseer*, &c. ; nor, in such presence, more than *thirty-nine* in any one day, nor until recovered from former punishment, under penalty of 20*l*." It is further enacted, that "no collar or chains shall be put on slaves, but by order of a magistrate, on penalty of 50*l*. Justices of peace to cause such collar, &c. to be removed, under a penalty of 100*l*."

Such, we are told, has been the law ever since the year 1826. But how is it administered? The following narrative, published in the Kingston "Watchman" of the 10th of July, 1830, may suffice as an answer to the question. It exhibits a case of outrageous cruelty, combined with a gross violation of the sanctity of the Sabbath.

"Yesterday morning, William Henry Hall, Esq., a magistrate of this city, preferred a complaint to the sitting magistrates, J. Smith and J. Nethersole, Esqrs., against Mr. W. J. Harvey, a white person, employed on the wharf of Messrs. John Wilson and Co., for cruelty towards two negro men slaves, belonging to the drogging (coasting) schooner *Judith Farmer*, lying along-side that wharf.

"Mr. Hall stated, that about six o'clock on Monday afternoon, he received information that two negroes had been flogged in the workhouse early that morning, by order of Mr. Harvey, their owner, and on their return to the vessel, that they were chained down to the deck by the wrist, where they remained the whole day, with the lacerated parts exposed to the heat of the sun. He then proceeded to the wharf with two constables, and on going on board found the negroes still chained on the deck. They had on only their shirts. He ordered a pair of pantaloons to be given to each of them, and desired the constables to release them from the chain, and to take them to the cage; at the same time warning Mr. Harvey, the owner of the slaves, and Captain Bacon, the commander of the schooner, to appear on the following morning before the sitting magistrates.

"Captain Bacon, the commander of the vessel, stated, that on Sunday morning the two men present, Bush and Bull, left the vessel with two other negroes, named John Uter and William: that they returned on board early on Monday morning, and resumed their work. Shortly after, Mr Harvey came on board, and on demanding their reasons for not loading the vessel on Sunday, they answered that they thought it very hard they were not to be allowed even one Sunday; they were not insolent. Mr. Harvey then seized them, and placed them in a boat, for the purpose of giving them a flogging in the workhouse, to which place he took them. When he returned on board with the negroes (about seven o'clock the same morning), he ordered witness to chain them, which he did. Mr. Harvey came on board several times during the day, and saw where the negroes were lying, and the naked state in which they were, but gave no orders that they should be removed out of the heat of the sun, or that pantaloons be put on them. Bush and Bull remained in that exposed situation from about seven o'clock in the morning till six in the evening, when the magistrate and constables released them. He had no fault to find with the negroes; they certainly were not the very best of negroes; Bush was a little trickified, but generally he had no fault to find with them They were flogged and chained for no other offence than for not loading the vessel on a Sunday.

"[During the examination, Mr. Harvey whispered something twice or thrice to Captain Bacon, who answered, 'I must speak the truth, Mr. Harvey;' for doing which he has since been discharged.]

"There were several other witnesses present, ready to corroborate the statement of Mr. Hall and the captain, as well as to prove Mr. Harvey's general cruel treatment of the negroes under his control, but the magistrates refused to examine them.

"Mr. Smith (one of the magistrates) said, he conceived that Mr. Harvey acted *very properly* in correcting his negroes as he did. He was of opinion that it was highly necessary that they should have been on board on Sunday; and with regard to their being exposed to the sun all day, he knew that they *preferred* being in the *sun* than to be in the *shade*. In fact, he *knew it*, and therefore dismissed the complaint "

The proceeding in this case was vindicated by other newspapers, and particularly by the "Courant" In reply to them the editor of the "Watchman" puts the following questions :—

"1st. By what law was Mr. Harvey authorized to punish, by the infliction of thirty-nine lashes each, two men, merely because they would not work on the Sabbath-day?

"2d Was it necessary to ensure obedience, after they had been flogged, to handcuff them to a chain cable, on the deck of a vessel, from seven o'clock in the morning till half-past six o'clock in the evening?

by a driver, with this dreadful instrument constantly in his hand, with which he is empowered to inflict, at his own discretion, a certain number of lashes on their backs, with no exception whatever in favour of the softer sex. During the four or five months of their harvest they are compelled to protract their labour through half the night, or through the whole of each alternate night. They are every moment liable to be removed, at the will of their masters, to the remotest parts of the island, or to be transported into other islands. The ties of kindred are violently torn asunder, and the mother and children often assigned to different purchasers, and separated to distant parts. The ordinance of marriage is scarcely known among them; while the most unrestrained licentiousness and profligacy of manners, as well in their intercourse with each other as with the whites, is indulged and encouraged.

The practice of emancipation, which has long prevailed to a great extent, and been followed by the happiest effects, in the old Spanish colonies, is discountenanced by the laws of our colonies, and loaded with such heavy fines in some of them as almost to amount to a prohibition. The design of such regulations is unquestionably to confer perpetuity on the present system, and extinguish in the breast of the negroes the faintest hope of the enjoyment of freedom.

Nothing was wanting to complete the misery of such a state, except to attach absolute impunity to the atrocities which the unlimited subjection of the weak to the strong is sure to produce; and this is amply provided for by that regulation universally adopted in our colonies, which excludes the testimony of a negro against a white inhabitant. In consequence of this law, the vilest miscreant may inflict whatever cruelties he pleases on the wretched blacks, provided he takes care that no white person be present. There are laws, it is true, which constitute the murder of a negro a capital offence, and which limit the measure of his punishment; but, as if for the very purpose of rendering them nugatory and ridiculous, conviction is made to depend on a circumstance attending the perpetration of crimes, which it is most easy to exclude. Thus, in opposition to the genius of all enlightened legislation, the greatest facilities are presented to oppression—the greatest impediments thrown in the way of detection—and, in all that relates to the treatment of slaves, the voice of truth is silenced, evidence sup-

---

"3d. Was it, or was it not, cruelty to confine them, in the manner described, during the whole day, in a hot sun, in a state of partial nudity, at the risk of their lives?

"4th. What would have been the consequence, had it come on suddenly to blow (as it is *said* to have done on the day previous) half a gale of wind? And whether such an event might not have been attended with the loss of those unfortunate individuals' lives?

"If Mr. Harvey, or the magistrates, will reply satisfactorily to these questions, we will then acquit the former of the charge of cruelty, and the latter of having outraged common sense, by declaring that he 'acted very properly in correcting his negroes as he did!'

"Mr. Harvey went round, on the *Saturday*, to the different wharfs from which his vessel, the *Judith Farmer*, had to take goods, and requested those goods to be left on the bridge of the wharf, so as to enable him to employ his negroes on Sunday in taking them off, and therewith loading his vessel! In order to avoid what they very properly considered a hardship, namely, loading the vessel on Sunday, the negroes went away, and did not return until six o'clock the following morning. For this *heinous* crime two of these men received thirty-nine lashes each, and were handcuffed to the chain cable of a vessel in Kingston harbour, until liberated by a magistrate; and yet this is the kind of conduct that Mr. James Smith and Mr. John Nethersole attempt to justify, and to examine and decide upon which they, as magistrates, meet and award JUSTICE by dismissing the complaint."—ED

pressed, the claims of justice studiously defeated, and the redress of the most atrocious injuries rendered next to impossible.

There is another particular in the state of the laws respecting negroes too remarkable to be passed over in silence. It is the obvious dictate of justice, and the practice of all civilized states, that, till guilt is proved, innocence shall be presumed; and that the *onus probandi*, the obligation of adducing evidence, shall rest with the accuser in the first instance. In the West India islands the reverse of this is established, and every negro, or man of colour, though free, is *presumed* to be a slave, and liable to be treated as such, unless he can furnish documentary evidence of his freedom. It is enacted that the presumption shall always be taken against him: so that if he loses his certificate of freedom, or it is stolen from him, it is at the option of any person to claim him, and replunge him into the horrors of slavery. By this means many are daily deprived of their freedom; and the danger of incurring that calamity is constantly suspended over the heads of the innocent.

It is no small aggravation of the cruelty of this system that its unhappy victims have not been exposed to it as the punishment of crime, but by the violence of ruffians, who, having traversed the ocean in quest of human prey, forcibly tore them from their native shores and the embraces of their dearest relatives, in order to expose them to sale in a distant quarter of the globe. The forms of judicial inquiry, the examination of witnesses, the proof of guilt, and the sentence of a judge were not the precursors of this most dire calamity; it was the assault of brutal violence on helpless weakness and unsuspecting innocence—it was the grasp of the marauder and the assassin hurrying away his victims amid shrieks of horror and the piercing accents of despair which prepared these scenes of wo. These and the descendants of these are the persons who compose the black population of our islands. Their number is computed at present at 800,000; and if we direct our view to that portion of the British dominions, we behold the shocking spectacle of nearly a million of our fellow-subjects, with no other imputation than that of a darker skin, doomed to a condition which, were it assigned as the punishment of the greatest guilt, would be accused of immoderate severity. We behold these children of nature, for the purpose chiefly of supplying us with the ingredient which sweetens our repasts, compelled by men who call themselves Christians to exhaust to its dregs a more bitter cup than is usually allotted to the greatest adepts in crime.

It is confidently asserted by advocates of slavery that the situation of the negroes in our islands is preferable to that of the labouring classes in England. But the falsehood of this assertion is sufficiently proved by the numerous elopements which take place there: on referring to a very recent Jamaica paper, we observe a list of more than a hundred runaway slaves; so that admitting this to be a fair specimen of what usually occurs, the number of slaves who attempt to escape from their masters in one island only amounts annually to five or six thousand. It appears that the far greater part were branded.

many of them in different parts of the body, and not a few are designated by their wounds and sores, the effects of immoderate punishment. A moment's reflection must convince us that the condition must be intolerable from which such numbers daily attempt their escape at the hazard of tortures and of death.

We are in possession of a religion the communication of which would afford some compensation for the injuries we have inflicted, and let in a ray of hope on the benighted mind. To say that no effectual provision has been made for this purpose is to assert the smallest part of the truth. The religious instruction of the negroes has not only been neglected, but such regulations introduced as renders it nearly impracticable. The attempts of this sort which have been made have not resulted from any legislative enactment, but merely from the zeal of private individuals exposed for the most part to the utmost opposition and obloquy; nor will it admit of a doubt that but for the seasonable interference of the government at home all such proceedings would long since have been suppressed. The colonial legislatures have displayed nearly as much aversion to the religious instruction of the slaves as to the extension of their civil immunities; and, judging from their conduct, we should be tempted to infer they were no less careful to exclude them from the hope of heaven than from happiness on earth.

It would be natural to suppose such a system could have few charms for the spectator, that the presence of such a mass of degradation and misery would be a source of continual annoyance, and that no exertion would be spared by those who have it most in their power to diminish its pressure and lighten its horrors. On the contrary, the West India planters view it with the utmost complacency; in their eyes it seems to be a most finished and exquisite specimen of social order, a masterpiece of policy, the most precious legacy bequeathed them by their ancestors, which they are bound to maintain inviolate in every part, to defend at the greatest risk, and to transmit unimpaired to future generations. They anticipate with the utmost confidence the perpetual duration of the system, and reprobate every measure which has the remotest tendency to endanger its existence as the offspring of indescribable folly and wickedness. To such a degree are their moral perceptions vitiated, that they really believe they have a prescriptive right to be guilty of injustice, to trample on the image of their Maker, to erase his superscription, and to treat that portion of their species which fortune has subjected to their power as mere beasts of burden, divested of the essential characteristics of humanity. In this instance impious speculations have been resorted to in palliation of practical enormities; nor have there been wanting those who avow their persuasion that the negro is more nearly allied to the orang-outang than to the human kind.

Hence it appears that a state of slavery is in its operation as mischievous to the master as to the slave. If its effects on the latter are more visible in his corporeal structure, in his debased physiognomy, his dejected countenance, his lacerated skin, and not unfrequently in his "wounds, and bruises, and putrifying sores," its effects on the mind

L 2

of the former are not less perceivable in the most inveterate prejudice, a pride which spurns the restraints of justice, a violence which is deaf to the dictates of compassion—in a word, in a capricious and uncontrollable self-will, which lays waste all the finer sensibilities of the soul, and renders its possessor too often a rebel to his God, a torment to himself, and a terror to his fellow-creatures.

Sixteen years have now elapsed since the abolition of the slave-trade,* and during this period few or none of those improvements have taken place in the treatment of slaves which were expected to result from that measure. At that time it was generally contended that as the planters would be necessitated thenceforth to keep up the number of their slaves without the aid of fresh importations, this itself would draw after it such an amelioration in the management of them as would ensure the happiest results without legislative interference. The interest of the proprietors, it was supposed, would so obviously coincide with the dictates of humanity as to give these the force of law. It is too manifest, however, from the event, that in forming this conclusion we did not take sufficiently into account the short-sightedness of rapacity, the force of habit, the contagion of example, and the incurable propensity of human nature to abuse absolute power, in whatever hands it is placed. The enormities which formerly characterized the slave system have suffered little or no abatement; all its most odious peculiarities are retained, while by the just retribution of Providence the planters are reduced to the utmost embarrassment and distress.

After witnessing such an obstinate adherence to a system equally injurious to the negroes and to themselves—after every suggestion of improvement has been indignantly rejected, and not a single effort made in behalf of the slave population, if we except a few verbal enactments passed with no other view, it is evident from the event, than to elude inquiry and silence complaint—it would be more than vain, it would be foolish and preposterous, to look for any substantial redress from colonial legislators. *They* are the aggressors, *they* are the authors of the evils we complain of; and how can it be expected they should legislate against themselves? To leave the slaves in *their* hands, what is it less than to recommend the lamb to the protection of the wolf?

Slavery, considered as a perpetual state, is as incapable of vindication as the trade in slaves: they are integral parts of the same system, and in point of moral estimate must stand or fall together. If it be unjust to sell men into slavery who are guilty of no crime, it must be equally so to retain them in that state; the last act of injustice is but the sequel and completion of the first. If the natives of Africa were originally despoiled of their freedom by rapine and violence, no man is entitled to avail himself of the condition to which they are reduced, by compelling them to labour for his benefit; nor is it less evident that they could not possibly transmit the forfeiture to their children of those rights which they never forfeited for themselves. Thus it appears

* The resolution of the House of Commons for the abolition of the slave-trade passed in June 1806.—Ed.

that the claims of the planters to hold their negroes in perpetual bondage is vitiated in its *origin;* and having commenced in an act of injustice, can never acquire the sanction of right.

But here we are most anxious to guard against the misrepresentation of our sentiments. Convinced as we are that negro slavery is most iniquitous in its origin, most mischievous in its effects, and diametrically opposite to the genius of Christianity and of the British constitution, we are yet far from proposing a sudden revolution. Universal experience shows, that in the body politic, no less than in the natural, inveterate diseases admit only of a slow and gradual cure; and we should deprecate an immediate emancipation almost as much as the planters themselves, from a full conviction that the debasing operation of slavery long continued disqualifies its subjects for performing the functions and enjoying the immunities of a free citizen.

Our object is, in the first place, to produce such an amelioration of their treatment as shall soften the rigour of their bondage; and in the next, that provision for their moral and religious instruction, which by developing their faculties and improving their character may ultimately qualify them for the possession of the freedom of which they have been cruelly deprived. With this view we wish to see the competency of negro evidence established as the only efficient check to wanton barbarity; the employment of rewards as well as punishments; the instruction of the slaves in the principles of the Christian religion; the uninterrupted enjoyment of the Sabbath; the institution of marriage and the inviolability of its rights firmly established; the exclusion of the cart-whip from the field of labour; together with the repeal of that abominable law which renders them liable to be sold in execution for the payment of their master's debts. If in addition to these most wholesome regulations facilities were afforded for the purchase of their freedom similar to those which have been adopted in the old Spanish colonies with the happiest effect, freedoms would be gradually obtained in such proportion and in such numbers only as would perfectly consist with the security and tranquillity of the colonies. Thus a race of freemen fitted by their constitution and their habits for the employments of a tropical climate, united with us by civil and religious ties, would rise up in the room of the present wretched victims of oppression,—a race that, having a country to preserve and rights to defend, would be a source of national strength instead of inspiring terror and distrust.

The superiority of free labour, in point of emolument, to the labour of slaves, having been demonstrated by such an ample induction of facts that it may be safely classed with the most established maxims of political economy, the practice of gradual emancipation would be of essential benefit to the planters, and greatly augment the value of our West India possessions. Indeed, there cannot be a more cogent proof of the folly of pertinaciously adhering to the present system, than the acknowledged inability to sustain a competition with the growers of sugar in the East Indies. In order to raise the price of East India produce so as to enable the planter in the west to keep the market, an extra duty is imposed to a large amount, and the people of England are obliged to pay upwards of two millions a year more for that article than would be necessary if a fair competition were allowed; in other words, the inhabitants of Great Britain are assessed to the amount of more than two millions annually, for no other purpose than to maintain the slave system in the West Indies; and in opposition to the dictates of humanity, the precepts of religion, and the principles of political economy and impartial justice, we contribute more to perpetuate our own disgrace, than it would be deemed prudent to bestow in the purchase of the greatest blessing. All our plans of domestic improvement, joined to all the efforts which we make for the diffusion of religion and virtue in foreign nations, our schools, our Bible societies, and our missions, justly considered as the peculiar glory of the age, cost us a mere scantling compared to what is annually devoted to that very pious and benevolent object the perpetuation of slavery in the West Indies; we throw mites into the treasury of the sanctuary, and heap ingots on the altar of Moloch.

And why, it is natural to ask, why is it necessary to load the importation of sugar from the East Indies with such heavy duties, in order to enable the growers of the same article in an opposite quarter of the globe, at not one-third the distance, to sustain a competition? Purely because the East India sugar is produced by the labour of freemen, the West India by the labour of slaves. The industry of the former is animated by hope, that of the latter depressed by despair; one is sustained by the energies of nature, the other extorted by the mechanical operation of the lash; the former labour for themselves, the latter for their masters; and such is the distinction between these two species of industry, that it more than annihilates the local difference between three or four, and twelve thousand miles. Surely the good sense of the nation will at last awake to a perception of this flagrant enormity and express its impatience at the ignominy and injustice of such an assessment, in that firm and constitutional tone which the legislature will not despise.

Let us not be discouraged if in this great enterprise our attempts are not immediately crowned with success. The slave-trade, be it remembered, was long upheld by a combination of private interests, in opposition to the remonstrances of reason, humanity, and religion; but it fell at last. Such unquestionably will be the fate of slavery. It may, like its twin-brother, be supported for a time by that grand obstruction to all enlightened legislation, the opposition of interested individuals, who may obscure truth by sophistry, and intimidate justice by a formidable array of influence; but it is one of the felicities of a free country that nothing can be permanent which will not sustain the ordeal of inquiry and the shock of discussion.

We indulge a hope, though the measures of administration during the last session of parliament fell far short of our wishes, that it was from a want of resolution more than of good intention; that they have formed on the whole a correct view of the subject, and that they are not unwilling to receive that support from the expression of the public mind which a com bination of private interests renders necessary. Be this as it may, as we are always answerable for the evils which it is in our power to prevent, and some of the greatest disorders in society have been corrected by the interference of the public through its constitutional organs, we cannot continue passive spectators of a system which inflicts interminable degradation and misery on eight hundred thousand of our fellow subjects, without deeply partaking of its guilt.

The scene of their suffering is distant indeed, but not so remote as to exempt them from the operation of our laws: they form an integral part of the British dominions, and wo to that nation which extends its power to those from whom it withholds its justice! That distance which did not secure them from spoliation and captivity while in Africa should not be allowed for a moment to intercept our attention to their welfare and commiseration of their sufferings, now that they are transported to the West Indies. Through the aid of the public voice, the government of the day carried triumphantly in 1807 the great question of the abolition of the slave-trade. Let us endeavour by a simultaneous movement to strengthen the hands of the present administration if, as we hope, they are well disposed, to stimulate them if they are sluggish, and to propel them at all events in the right direction, by such a firm and unanimous display of the public sentiment and feeling on this great occasion as no free government will think it proper to neglect; that we may, though late, make some reparation for the accumulated injuries of ages that are past, and signalize our connexion with Africa by other characters than those of rapine, violence, and blood.

We cannot suppose for a moment that government will suffer the extraordinary conduct recently displayed by the local authorities of Jamaica to have any influence in preventing its adoption of such measures for the amelioration of the present system as justice and humanity may dictate. To be bearded and insulted by persons in their situation would be mortifying enough, if the ridicule attached to their proceedings did not interfere with more serious emotions. To say that government has nothing to fear from the West India islands would be scarcely correct, for we have much to fear; but it is not from their strength, but their weakness, which is such, that were we to withdraw our support they would fall like ripe fruit into the lap of the first invader. They are so much accustomed, it seems, to proceed by the method of intimidation, as to forget their absolute dependence on Great Britain for protection, as well from domestic as from foreign dangers; nor could we wish them a more cruel revenge than to leave them to their own resources. If, by adopting such regulations as the humanity and wisdom of parliament shall prescribe, they can make it clearly appear that their pecuniary interests are affected (which in our opinion will be impossible) let them by all means receive a suitable compensation; but let us be permitted at the same time to express our hope that government will not be diverted from its course by the growling of a tiger which refuses to quit its prey.

The interference, then, of an enlightened public to circulate information, to strengthen the hands and second the movements of government in this most just enterprise, is imperiously demanded. We cannot sit still, year after year, silent spectators of the most enormous oppression exercised within the limits of the British dominions, without partaking of its guilt. We cannot remain silent and inactive, without forgetting who we are, and what we have done; that we are the country which, after a tedious struggle with a host of prejudices arrayed in support of opulent oppression, have overthrown the slave-trade, torn it up by the roots, and branded in the eyes of all nations the sale of human flesh, as the most atrocious of social crimes. We must forget that we are the countrymen of Granville Sharp, who, by incredible exertions, succeeded at length in purifying the British soil from this its foulest pollution, and rendered it for ever impossible for a slave to breathe its air. We must sever ourselves from all alliance of spirit with a Wilberforce and a Clarkson, who looked forward to the final emancipation of the negro race as the consummation of their labours, and were sustained in their arduous contest by the joy which that prospect inspired. We must lose sight of still more awful considerations, and forget our great Original, "who hath formed of one blood all nations of men, to dwell on all the face of the earth."

FRAGMENTS.

DEFENCE OF VILLAGE PREACHING
HINTS ON TOLERATION,
THE RIGHT OF WORSHIP, &c.

[WRITTEN IN 1801, 1802, AND 1811.]

NOTE BY THE EDITOR.

The disquisition of which the interesting Fragments now presented to the public are alone preserved was commenced in 1801. About that time the late Bishop Horsley advanced the opinion in various charges and sermons (extracts from one of which are subjoined in a note)* that the dissenters and Methodists, in their attempts to introduce the preaching of the gospel in villages where the evangelical doctrines were not taught in the established church, were actuated by what were then termed "jacobinical" motives, and by a desire to overthrow the episcopalian form of church government. This opinion, repeatedly announced in the oracular tone too often assumed by that learned prelate, obtained an extraordinary

* Extracts from Bishop Horsley's Charge, published in 1800.

After observing that the laity of England have as little relish for socinianism as for atheism, and that they think much alike of him who openly disowns the Son and of him who denies the Father, insomuch that the advocates of this blasphemy have preached themselves out of all credit with the people, he proceeds as follows:—

"Still the operations of the enemy are going on—still going on by stratagem. The stratagem still a pretence of reformation. But the reformation the very reverse of what was before attempted. Instead of divesting religion of its mysteries, and reducing it to a mere philosophy in speculation and a mere morality in practice, the plan is now to affect a great zeal for orthodoxy—to make great pretensions to an extraordinary measure of the Holy Spirit's influence—to alienate the minds of the people from the established clergy by representing them as sordid worldlings, without any concern about the souls of men, indifferent to the religion which they ought to teach, and to which the laity are attached, and destitute of the Spirit of God. In many parts of the kingdom conventicles have been opened in great numbers, and congregations formed of one knows not what denomination. The pastor is often, in appearance at least, an illiterate peasant or mechanic. The congregation is visited occasionally by preachers from a distance. Sunday-schools are opened in connexion with these conventicles. There is much reason to suspect that the expenses of these schools and conventicles are defrayed by associations formed in different places: for the preachers and schoolmasters are observed to engage in expenses for the support and advancement of their institutions to which, if we may judge from appearances, their own means must be altogether inadequate. The poor are even bribed, by small pecuniary gifts from time to time, to send their children to these schools of they know not what, rather than to those connected with the established church, in which they would be bred in the principles of true religion and loyalty. It is very remarkable that these new congregations of nondescripts have been mostly formed since the jacobins have been laid under the restraints of those two most salutary statutes commonly known by the names of the Sedition and Treason bills,—a circumstance which gives much ground for suspicion that sedition and atheism are the real objects of these institutions rather than religion. Indeed, in some places this is known to be the case. In one topic the teachers of all these congregations agree,—abuse of the established clergy, as negligent of their flocks, cold in their preaching, and destitute of the Spirit. In this they are joined by persons of a very different cast, whom a candour of which they on their part set but a poor example is unwilling to suspect of any ill design, though it is difficult to acquit them of the imputation of an indiscretion in their zeal, which in its consequences may be productive of mischief very remote, I believe, from their intention. It is a dreadful aggravation of the dangers of the present crisis in this country, that persons of real piety should, without knowing it, be lending their aid to the common enemy, and making themselves in effect accomplices in a conspiracy against the Lord and against his Christ. The jacobins of this country, I very much fear, are at this moment making a tool of Methodism, just as the illuminées of Bavaria made a tool of freemasonry; while the real Methodist, like the real freemason, is kept in utter ignorance of the wicked enterprise the counterfeit has in hand."—P. 18–20.

In page 25, &c. the bishop corrects a misrepresentation of a speech delivered by him in the House of Lords, and gives the following as a faithful statement of it. "I said," says he, "that schools of jacobinical religion and jacobinical politics, that is to say, schools of atheism and disloyalty, abound in this country—schools in the shape and disguise of charity—schools and Sunday-schools in which the minds of the children of the very lowest orders are enlightened, that is to say, taught to despise religion, and the laws, and all subordination. This I know to be the fact. But the proper antidote for the poison of the jacobinical schools will be schools for children of the same class, under the management of the parochial clergy:—Sunday-schools therefore under your own inspection I would advise you to encourage."—P. 26.

currency; and there was every reason to fear that some strong legislative measures for the prevention of these encroachments (as they were regarded) upon the functions of a parish minister would be adopted. The necessity of such measures was urged again and again with the utmost violence and intolerance in several of the daily and other periodical publications; so that considerable apprehensions were naturally entertained that these exertions of Christian benevolence would be altogether checked or greatly restricted.

In such a state of things Mr. Hall commenced this essay, but the public ebullition subsiding, he relinquished his design of publication, and indeed destroyed a portion of what he had written.

In the years 1810 and 1811 the friends of village preaching by dissenters, and of Sunday-schools under their superintendence, were again alarmed by a fresh attempt to restrain their operations, though not undertaken in a hostile spirit, in an act brought into parliament by Lord *Sidmouth.* His lordship proposed some new restrictions upon persons who wished to qualify as dissenting teachers and others, either by separate license or by some other method thought to be appropriate, on itinerant preaching. He also proposed to deprive lay-preachers of certain exemptions which had hitherto been granted. Against these measures petitions were sent to parliament from all parts of the kingdom; and the bill, being opposed by Lords *Grey*, *Holland*, *Erskine*, *Liverpool*, *Moira*, *Stanhope*, by Dr. Manners Sutton, then *Archbishop of Canterbury*, and by *Lord Chancellor Eldon*, was lost May 21st, 1811, on the motion of Lord *Erskine*, which was agreed to without a division. The minds of those classes of the public that were interested in the diffusion of evangelical knowledge among the poor were, however, agitated by this question for several months. In such a state of things, Mr. Hall determined to revise and complete what he had formerly begun; but the failure of Lord Sidmouth's plan induced him again to lay aside his pen, and again to destroy great part of the manuscript. The portions which escaped destruction have been found since Mr. Hall's death. They want the advantage of entire continuity, as well as of the author's finishing touch; and being composed at distant periods, and in part evidently rewritten to suit the modification of the general purpose occasioned by the later attempts at restriction, they exhibit a slight repetition of sentiment. It has, however, been thought right to preserve the whole of them, as they unfold and place in different lights some valuable principles of general application.

For a full account of the proceedings on Lord Sidmouth's bill, the reader may advantageously consult "A Sketch of the History and Proceedings of the Deputies appointed to protect the Civil Rights of the Protestant Dissenters."

FRAGMENT ON VILLAGE PREACHING.

---

* * * Where they beheld the papal power overturned, they were ready to imagine the season was approaching, so clearly foretold, when true religion should emerge from the clouds of superstition which environed her, and enlighten the world. Who will say that these hopes indicated depravity in the minds of those who cherished them too fondly? It was surely not very criminal to rejoice at the prospect of the extinction of evil, and the universal prevalence of justice, peace, and happiness; or to mistake "the times and seasons which the Father has put into his own power." Good men were, of all others, least likely to suspect that their hopes would be blasted by a wickedness of which the world afforded no example. Whatever of this delusion, however, might have prevailed heretofore, the virtuous part of the public are completely recovered from it; nor has it had the smallest influence in stimulating the exertions which it is the purpose of this publication to defend.

The only shadow of argument on which Bishop Horsley founds his accusation that village preaching has a political object is, that it has been chiefly prevalent since the Pitt and Grenville bills, as they are styled, were passed; which put a stop to political meetings. Hence he infers that it is only a new channel into which the old stream is directed. Here, however, he is entirely mistaken. The true source of this increased activity is to be found in the missions, the first of which was established some years before the Grenville bills were passed. The attention of the religious public was strongly excited on that occasion to the indispensable necessity of "preaching the gospel to every creature," and the result was, a resolution to exert more zealous and extensive efforts to diffuse the knowledge of saving truth at home than had before been employed. Agreeable to this it will be found, on inquiry, that those who most distinguished themselves in political debates have had the least share (if they have had any) in promoting these measures; and that the invariable effect of engaging in these plans has been to diminish the attention bestowed on political objects. This indeed could not fail to be the consequence: for as the mind is too limited to be very deeply impressed with more than one object at a time, a solicitude to promote the interests of piety must insensibly diminish the ardour for every thing that is not necessarily involved in it; not to say, that the spirit of devotion which such designs imply and promote is peculiarly incompatible with the violence and acrimony of political passions. He who is truly intent on promoting the eternal happiness of mankind must look on futurity with so steady an eye, that he is in more danger of falling into indifference to the spectacle that is passing before him than of suffering himself to be too much inflamed by it. He is under more temptation to desert his proper rank in society, to undervalue the importance of worldly activity, and to let opportunities of exertion slide through his hands, than to indulge turbulent and ambitious views.

Hence we find in the first ages of the church, heathens made frequent complaints of the inactivity of Christians, but never accused them of turbulence; and that while many fled into deserts, from austerity and devotion, not one, during the prevalence of paganism, endured the chastisement of the laws for sedition or treason. The pious of every age have been among the quiet of the land.

If our legislators are aware (as I hope they are) of the inconceivable benefits which are derived, in a political view, from the diffusion of pure and undefiled religion, no fascination of great talents or of high rank, no fear of misrepresentation or calumny, will tempt them to be guilty of a legislative suicide, by exerting their authority to suppress it; since nothing can ever give equal efficacy to the laws or stability to the government. The law of itself can only address fears; religion speaks to the conscience, and commands it to respect that justice on which the law is founded. Human law can only arm itself with penalties which may be averted, despised, or endured; religion presents, in the displeasure of our Maker, an evil that can have no bounds. Human laws can only take cognizance of disorders in their last stage, proposing only the punishment of the delinquent, without attempting to prevent the crime: religion establishes a tribunal in our own breast, where that which is concealed from every other eye is arraigned, and the very embryo of crime detected and destroyed.

If we examine the sources of crimes, we shall perceive the chief temptation to violate the principles of justice and humanity arises from a discontent with the allotments of Providence: men are apt to attach an importance to what they see another possesses. But what can be so sovereign a cure for this discontent as religion, which teaches that all things are under the disposal of infinite Wisdom; that life is but a passage to an eternal condition of being; that every thing the world admires is passing away, and that he only who "doeth the will of God abideth for ever?"

Religion must infallibly promote obedience to the laws, by subduing those violent passions which give birth to crimes. As our hopes and fears must all turn on the present scene, or on futurity, it is plain that a principle which throws an infinite weight into the latter scale must greatly diminish the influence of the former. On this account, real piety must ever be an enemy to intemperate enjoyments and to extravagant hopes. In addition to this, Christianity enforces obedience to civil rulers with the utmost clearness and under the most solemn sanction, adopting the duties of a citizen into the family of religion, and commanding its disciples to revere civil government as the ordinance of God; and to be "subject, not chiefly for wrath, but for conscience sake." Who are so likely to be loyal subjects as those who consider lawful princes, in the exercise of their functions, as the representatives of the Supreme Ruler, and judges as the dispensers of the portion confided to them of eternal justice? The public may be assured, that as nothing is more remote from the views of those who are most active in promoting village preaching than an intention to promote political discontent, so nothing is more removed from the practice of the preachers. That there may be an imprudent or an unprincipled individual who profanes the function of a preacher by introducing political remarks (a practice too common with those who are loudest in the condemnation of dissenters) is possible, though it has never been my lot to hear of any among our village preachers; but that such instances are extremely rare, and when they occur never fail to be discountenanced in the strongest manner, both by dissenters and Methodists, may be affirmed with the utmost confidence. There is no maxim more constantly inculcated by all who have any influence in these measures, than that of scrupulously abstaining from every, even the remotest, allusion to politics. They have preached liberty indeed, but it is that liberty which Jesus Christ proclaimed at Nazareth, that holy and divine liberty with which the Son makes his followers free; not that liberty whose thrilling accents awake nations to arms, but that which is enjoyed in the highest perfection in the quiet of the sanctuary, where all is still; as in the temple of Solomon the sound of the lifted hammer was not heard. They propose a revolution, but it is that by which men are translated from the kingdom of Satan to the kingdom of God and his Christ. They propose great innovations, but such as consist in exhorting men to newness of heart.

His lordship expresses his approbation of Sunday-schools, provided they are placed under the inspection and control of the clergy. If the clergy will take the trouble of forming and inspecting Sunday-schools, they may confer a great benefit on the public, and gain much honour to themselves: whether the nation will tamely submit to have the business of education exclusively in the hands of any one set of men remains to be tried. The attempt to support an ecclesiastical establishment, by invading the freedom of education, resembles more the policy of a Julian than the gentleness of Christ. To invade the freedom of charity is a stretch of tyranny still more odious. To control the movements of benevolence, and construe the impulse of compassion into a crime, is such an outrage as can only be paralleled in the darkest ages, and in the most barbarous minds. Of what crimes have the dissenters been convicted we will boldly ask; of such infamy that even the exercise of benevolence in them must wear the aspect of guilt; and that they must be degraded, not only beneath the rights of citizens, but the possibilities of virtue? What have these helots of England done to deserve this more than Spartan cruelty? In the name of eternal justice, I invoke the injured majesty of our common nature to repel an attack so injurious, founded on aspersions so foul and detestable.

It is asserted that these revolutionary designs are carried on under pretences of superior piety. It is matter of accusation that the dissenters make these pretences. If the dissenters, however, profess to have more piety than the members of the established church, it will be shrewdly suspected to arise from a very plain reason, namely, that they have more. Hypocrisy is the vice of individuals, not of numerous bodies of men, who can have no motive sufficiently extensive in its operation to engage them to submit to its restraints. The same conclusion results from another consideration. Nothing but a conscientious preference can, generally speaking, incline a man to a mode of religious profession which in the mildest times is unpopular, and at some seasons not exempt from danger and disgrace. Without contending for any superiority in the principles of dissent, the very circumstance of becoming a dissenter, or of continuing such, at some expense of worldly reputation and advantage, indicates a mind over which religious con siderations have great influence. They who never scarcely think of religion at all, or who abandon themselves to the tide of opinion and fashion, are safely conducted into the haven of the established church. To be content with merely being tolerated, instead of sharing the honours and emoluments of an opulent establishment, to have all the avenues which lead to greatness shut against them, is a sacrifice which nothing but conscientious piety, however mistaken, can prompt them to make In addition to which, it may be remarked, that a religious minority, from a conviction that their conduct will be exposed to a severe scrutiny, and that nothing can sustain them against the contempt of the world but superior correctness of morals, have a motive for cherishing the spirit of their institution which others want.

On these accounts it will not, we hope, be deemed presumptuous if we take it for granted that the dissenters, and especially that class of them who have signalized their zeal for the religious instruction of the poor, have really more piety than falls to the share of the great body of the people of England. But how is it possible for pious men to enter into a conspiracy to overturn the constitution of their country, and to overwhelm every thing in anarchy? For this purpose they must unite themselves intimately with the infidel faction: they must make common cause with those detestable monsters whose pestilential breath has blasted, in other countries, every thing cheering to the eye or refreshing to the heart. They must forget the infinite contrariety of principle which divides them; they must forget the daggers of these assassins, which, after destroying their enemies, they never fail to turn against their associates, impelled by an insatiable eagerness for destruction. They must put their fortune, their character, their life, in the hands of men with whom it would not be safe to trust themselves in a room. There is nothing more opposite than the spirit of piety and the spirit of faction. There enters into the composition of faction a meddlesome and mischievous activity, blended with a callousness of heart. Devotion softens the temper; faction knows no delicacy in the choice of its society. It wants no other qualities in its associates than turbulence and discontent, a conscience which no crimes can startle, and an impudence which no detection can confront. Devotion, alarmed at wickedness, and disgusted with folly, is apt to carry the principle of selection too far. Faction delights in scenes of tumult and noise; devotion in solitude and retirement. Faction busies itself with forming external movements, and values itself only on the change it produces in the situation of external objects; the treasures and conquests of religion are internal. Faction draws its nourishment from an overweening conceit of superior wisdom, accompanied with a proportionable contempt of the understanding and virtue of other men; the solid foundation of piety is laid in humility, or a deep conviction of our sinfulness and fallibility. I will not say that men of real piety have never been betrayed into factious enterprises, or have not on some occasions pushed their opposition to government too far; but it may be safely affirmed, that whenever they have done so it must have arisen from an extraordinary concurrence of circumstances; generally from the oppression which makes a wise man mad· that it is most foreign to their general character, and that nothing is a more effectual antidote to political turbulence than the prevalence of piety.

Before we proceed further, I must be permitted to lament that propensity to credit and propagate the most hideous calumnies which seems to have arisen to an unprecedented height in this age. It may answer a temporary purpose, but it is well if it does not recoil on those who employ it. It resembles the policy of insurrections and riots, which, though they may occasionally punish or crush an obnoxious sect, no wise government will adopt, for fear of a reaction. To fill the minds of the public with hatred, jealousies, and suspicions is to poison the fountains of public security. When this spirit is once awakened among a people, the character and conduct of its rulers seldom fail, in the long run, to be injured by it. Under disasters which the utmost wisdom cannot prevent, under burdens which the strictest economy may impose, government presents a plain, a palpable, and permanent pretext of discontent and suspicion. Misery finds a sort of relief in attributing its sufferings to the conduct of others, and while it soothes its anguish by resentment and clamour, it fastens on the object that first presents itself. This object will naturally be the rulers of the nation. Nor is there any thing with respect to which men are more liable to be mistaken than the share which the imprudence or misconduct of civil government has in the production of public calamities. So various, so subtle, so complicated in their operation are the causes which conduct to prosperity or decline in the affairs of nations, that it is a matter of the utmost delicacy to determine what share is to be assigned to human agency, and what to contingencies and events. This obscurity furnishes infinite scope for the exercise of candour in the well disposed, and for the indulgence of suspicion and discontent in the factious. In scenes so complicated, and when the steps are so numerous and so untraceable between the first movement and the last, it is equally difficult to form a right estimate of events when we are very remote or when we are very near them. If we attempt to survey a remote era, we are lost in naked generalities; when we turn our eyes on the scene before us, our attention is apt to be limited to detached parts; we are apt to confound proximate with remote causes, to mistake casual coincidence for natural connexion, and to give a disproportionate importance to whatever we immediately feel. Let them who have any doubt of the dreadful effects of calumny look at what took place in France, where they will find it was the principal engine employed by the Brissotines to overturn the monarchy, and afterward by Robespierre to deluge that devoted country with blood. By inspiring everlasting jealousies and unbounded fears, he contrived to extirpate every remain of tenderness and pity, and to preserve the minds of the people in constant agitation, like the sea in a storm. It was this that whetted the daggers of assassins. It was the withering blast of this spirit that destroyed every thing amiable and noble in that unhappy kingdom, resigned to the desolating sway of selfishness and revenge. Nothing can be more fatal to public repose; nothing can tend more immediately to quicken the seeds of convulsion. That this malignant leaven should be infused into the public mind by any hands must be matter of deep regret; that it should be mingled and prepared by those hands from which the world is wont to look for benedictions and blessings seems awful and portentous.

Let not this, however, be understood to intimate that there is any room to apprehend the dissenters may be provoked to verify the suspicions and calumnies to which they are incessantly exposed. The writer would be understood to speak merely of the tendency of such infusions on the nation at large; not at all of their influence on the dissenters or Methodists. Their loyalty is of too fine a texture to be affected by the efflux or influx of public opinion. While they enjoyed the countenance of the public their loyalty was sustained by a higher motive than popularity, nor will any discouragement tempt them to forfeit it. In the mean time they place a firm reliance, first on the protection of Heaven, the judge of their innocence, next on the impartial justice and parental kindness of their gracious sovereign, to prevent them from being overwhelmed and swallowed up by the reproaches of their enemies.

Enough has been said on this head, I trust, to satisfy every unprejudiced person that nothing is more remote from the design of these institutions than the promotion of seditious or revolutionary plans.

It is time to proceed to a distinct charge, which is that of hostility to the Church of England. It is confidently asserted by the prelate to whom we have so often had occasion to allude, that it is the constant practice of itinerant preachers to calumniate the clergy, by representing them as a set of hirelings, destitute of the spirit of piety, and utterly indifferent to the welfare of their flocks; by which artifices they alienate the affections of the people from the established pastors, and prepare them for becoming dissenters; or what, in the dialect of the learned prelate, is the same thing, schismatics.

Although it is extremely disagreeable to be obliged to contradict a positive assertion in a manner equally positive, yet truth compels us on this occasion to declare, that the statement here made is without any sort of foundation in truth. The practice of vilifying the established clergy is so far from being commonly adopted in the discourses either of dissenters or Methodists, that it may be safely affirmed, if there are any instances of conduct so highly improper, they are extremely rare, and that where the dissenters offend in this particular once, the established clergy are guilty of it ten times. It is a practice which the late Mr. Wesley discouraged, in his connexion, to the utmost; nor are the dissenters, as a body, less scrupulous and delicate on that head. Still, however, it will be said, a principle of hostility to the established church seems inseparable from these exertions; the tendency of preaching in the parishes of authorized ministers must be to alienate the people from the established mode of worship, and, in the issue, to endanger the existence of the national church.

As this objection wears a more plausible appearance than any other, and has been urged in a great variety of forms, the author must beg the patience of the reader, while he gives it a full and distinct examination.

1. The objection we are considering seems to imply, on the part of those who urge it, an inattention to the true genius and design of a religious establishment. We must distinguish between the design of religion itself and the design of that support which is given to it by human laws. The design of religion itself is to discipline the mind and prepare the heart for the happiness of heaven. The design of supporting a particular form of religion by law is much less extensive; it is to derive from it that security which it never fails to confer on the interests of civil society. This may be termed the indirect benefit of religion; with a view to which the policy of legislation has thought it right to incorporate it with human laws. The establishment of a religion is not to be considered as a final end. In respect to importance it is never to be confounded with religion, or even to be placed on a level with the peace and good order of society, to which it ought ever to be in perfect subordination. It aims at nothing further than to secure such a prevalence of religion as shall make men conscientious and upright. By whatever means this is accomplished, the true design of every religious establishment is answered. From the indisposition of mankind to direct their thoughts to a futurity; from their proneness to immerse themselves in present and sensible objects, and the ignorance which follows of course, it has been thought necessary to set apart a particular order of men to inculcate its truths and to exemplify its duties. Laws will not be obeyed, harmony in society cannot be maintained, without virtue; virtue cannot subsist without religion. The sentiments of religion, it is thought, will be effaced from the mind by the influence of worldly passions and pursuits, unless it is recognised by the sovereign, and public teachers appointed by the state.

Whoever attends to this must perceive that the establishment was intended, not to correct an excess, but to supply a defect; not to prevent men from becoming too devout, but to preserve them from falling into irreligion and vice. It was not because men are too much dis-

M 2

posed to be religious, but because they are too apt to forget it, that our forefathers thought proper to give it a legal establishment. On a similar principle universities were established and colleges endowed, to stimulate literary ardour and facilitate the means of acquiring knowledge; and not that it might be made a crime to receive instruction in any other place. If peculiar privileges and honours were conferred on these seminaries, it was not with a view to limit, confine, and discourage, but to animate the exertions of literary talent. If they seemed to narrow the stream, it was only with a view to deepen the current.

To attempt to restrain the prevalence of religion, to suppress the efforts of good men for the promotion of piety, under pretence of guarding the established church, is to lose sight of the design of all religion, and to counteract the purpose for which the establishment of it in particular was made. It would be to found the security of the church on the ruins of religion.

2. They who urge the objection seem not to have reflected sufficiently on the prodigious advantages which the Church of England possesses for securing its existence and prosperity. The large portion of property it holds gives it a great national weight and importance. The regular gradations of authority and rank cement its several parts closely together, and prepare it on all occasions to act with the utmost promptitude and unanimity. Its ministers, vested with legal authority and character, are the natural objects of a veneration of which nothing but personal misbehaviour can deprive them.

Mankind are apt to be strongly prejudiced in favour of whatever is countenanced by antiquity, enforced by authority, and recommended by custom. The pleasure of acquiescing in the decision of others is by most men so much preferred to the toil and hazard of inquiry, and so few are either able or disposed to examine for themselves, that the voice of law will generally be taken for the dictates of justice.

Nor is it the weakness only of mankind that inclines them to look with a favourable eye on what is established; some of the most amiable propensities of the heart lean the same way,—deference to superior wisdom and to great names; the love of quiet, and the dread of confusion and disorder. These considerations will prevail over minds which are too virtuous to be moved by a gross self-interest. Further, the religion of the state will ever be the religion of the vain and aspiring. A degree of ridicule never fails to be attached to a religious minority. In all the efforts of churchmen, their movements are facilitated by the current of public opinion, while dissenters are on every occasion obstructed by public prejudice. Thus churchmen set out with a partiality on their side which nothing but neglect and misconduct can destroy; dissenters, with a weight of suspicion and dislike which nothing but discreet and exemplary behaviour can remove.

If we contemplate, in connexion with the subject we are upon, the manners and institutions of the British nation, we shall perceive that the established church in these kingdoms possesses such pledges of its safety as are not to be found in any Protestant community besides. A finished English education is, in all its stages, clerical; the public seminaries of instruction, together with the two universities, being almost entirely under the conduct of ecclesiastics; by which means a reverence for the church is imbibed with the first elements of knowledge. Its splendid literary establishments, its magnificent libraries the accumulation of ages, and, above all, the great and illustrious names it has produced in every department of genius and of learning, the glory of the world; who have conferred dignity, not so much on their profession as on their species; gives it, in a literary view, a decided superiority, and in popular opinion an exclusive esteem. The policy of modern times has, in addition to this, confided to its ministers more and more of the administration of laws, in which they are become the immediate organs of justice to the people; and the claims of spiritual authority are hence enforced by the habits of civil submission.

Freed from the fetters of celibacy, which, if they augment its zeal, must narrow its influence in popish countries, it strikes its roots deep into the social soil, and forms numerous alliances, so that there is scarcely a considerable family in the nation which is not immediately interested in its support. A popish clergy, secluded from the enjoyments of domestic life, may be expected indeed to have a more eager ambition for the advancement of their order in consequence of their passions being all directed to one point; but as their manners must be less amiable, so from this insulated condition they are liable to fall without a struggle and without pity. They are a loose appendage of the state, not a part of its growth and substance. With respect to the English clergy it is quite otherwise. As they are continually receiving supplies from the mass of the community, so they are continually restoring to it in the persons of their sons and daughters what it has lost. By these means a continual communication is maintained with the body of the people, manners are assimilated, and the ties of tenderness and attachment extended. The gradations of rank also which are established in it contribute to the same purpose, and exhibit an image of the political constitution planted in every corner of the kingdom and mingled with every order of the state; while its inferior members propagate its influence among the commonalty, it allies itself on the side of its dignitaries with all that is august, basks in the smile of monarchs, and shares in the splendour of courts.

A society which has such numerous pledges for its security, which so many motives concur to favour, so many passions to support, must be guilty of some extraordinary misconduct before it can forfeit the attachment of the people. It is evident it can only fall under the weight of its own abuses.

3. It is possible indeed to conceive a degree of secularity and dissipation which may first greatly impair its influence and finally endanger its existence. In an age not remarkable for credulity or superstition, as the conduct of ecclesiastics will have more weight than their pretensions, nothing can long secure them from popular contempt but exemplary morals and diligence.

To invest idleness and dissipation with the privileges of laborious piety is an impracticable attempt. For by a constitution more ancient than that of any priesthood, superior degrees of sanctity and of exertion will gain superior esteem as their natural reward. We must not wonder to find the public forget the reverence due to the sacred profession when its members forget the spirit and neglect the duties on which that reverence was founded. The natural equity of mankind will not suffer the monopoly of contradictory goods. If the people are expected to reverence an order, it must be from the consciousness of benefits received. If the clergy claim authority, it must be accompanied with a solicitude for the spiritual interest of their flocks, and labour sustained. To enjoy at once both honour and ease never fell to the share of any profession. If the clergy neglect their charge, if they conform to the spirit of the world, and engage with eagerness in the pursuits of ambition or of pleasure, it will be impossible for any human policy to preserve them from sinking in the public esteem.

4. As far as the attachment of the people to their established ministers is diminished in consequence of misconduct on their part, it will not be remedied by excluding other instructers. To deprive them of every other means of information may make them heathens, but will not make them churchmen. The established ministers are either equal to others in zeal and diligence, or inferior. If they are equally laborious and exemplary, what have they to fear, while they have every advantage in their possession which superior learning, a legal character, and the countenance of their superiors can confer? To assert that the same degree of diligence and piety in a clergyman will not produce an equal effect as when they are exerted by a dissenter is to yield the cause of the establishment at once; for it is to affirm that there is a source of weakness in the very nature of an establishment which prevents equal means in other respects from being equally influential; an extraordinary assertion, which the friends of the established church would be, we should suppose, the last to make. The policy of an establishment is founded on a supposition that it is the most effectual mode of inculcating some degree of religion, and of impressing sentiments of piety on the minds of men. But if, on the contrary, it be found that exertions merely equal made in any other form produce more powerful effects, that supposition is invalidated, and the structure raised upon it falls to the ground. To give religion a legal subsistence, it seems by this reasoning, is so far from arming it with superior energy, that it is of all the modes under which it can appear the most disadvantageous, and ignorance and fanaticism gain an easy triumph over it.

If the other supposition be taken, that the established ministers are inferior to others in diligence and exertion, and that on this account their popularity is endangered, to give them the monopoly of religious instruction is to violate every principle of reason and equity. It is punishing the innocent for the faults of the guilty. It is to reward a breach of trust with an enlargement of power. Instead of quickening indolence or correcting abuse it is conferring impunity on both. The natural remedy for whatever inconveniences are experienced or apprehended from established abuses is the institution of discipline and the exercise of wholesome correction by the rulers of the church, who are invested with adequate power for that purpose. To look out and ask for an external force to repel the consequences of an inward disease,—to demand the interposition of the legislature to protect them from the effects of their own abuses while they refuse the proper remedy, is repugnant to every maxim of justice. They ought at least to wait until the abuses they complain of are remedied—until the internal resources of reformation are employed. With little propriety or grace can they complain of impertinent intruders who are inattentive to the duties of their allotted station. In the report of the Lincolnshire clergy* it is frankly acknowledged that much of the decline of religion is to be imputed to the neglect of the clergy; and yet almost in the same breath they express a desire that the legislature would give them power to expel intruders from their parishes. It has usually been expected that superior claims should be founded at least on the pretence of superior merits. But here the order of things is reversed. At the very moment they are asking for an increase of power, they confess themselves unworthy of it, by having abused or neglected to employ the power already intrusted into their hands. Not content to escape without punishment, they ask to be rewarded for a breach of ecclesiastical trust and the want of clerical virtues. Whatever we may think of their delicacy, we cannot but commend their prudence in not putting their names to such a paper.

5. It deserves to be considered what effect the prohibition of other instruction is likely to have on the conduct of the clergy themselves. Is it likely to diminish or increase the frequency of non-residence, or the extent of secular and dissipated habits? Will it tend to augment their professional diligence and zeal, the surest support of an ecclesiastical order? Will the monopoly of religious instruction fail to produce the effect of all other monopolies? While men are accustomed to compare rival pretensions, while emulation continues to be classed among human passions, these questions will admit of but one answer. A generous competition is the animating spirit of every profession, without which it droops and languishes. If we look around us we shall perceive that all the discoveries which have enriched science, and the improvements which have embellished life, are to be ascribed to the competition of nations with nations, of cities with cities, and of men with men. From causes too obvious to need explanation, there is less of this spirit in the clerical profession than in any other, which is the principal reason of the talent of preaching having been so little cultivated.

It is easy to see, then, what will be the consequence of extinguishing the small remains of emulation or jealousy, call it by what name you please, which springs from the complete toleration of a diversity of sects. If the dread of intrusion (as it is called) into their parishes is not sufficient to prevent some from neglecting their pastoral duties, this

* Circulated in 1801 or 1802.—Ed.

neglect will be much more profound when there is nothing to disturb their repose. When the minister fears no rival, and the people despair of any remedy, the inattention of the one and the ignorance of the other will increase in equal proportion.

THE IMPOLICY OF INTOLERANCE.

There is another objection frequently urged against village preaching which will deserve our attention. It is alleged that the gross fanaticism which distinguishes the self-appointed teachers of religion tends to bring Christianity into contempt, and threatens the most serious mischief to the cause of enlightened piety. That fanaticism is an evil, and that a considerable portion of it may frequently be blended with those efforts to revive religion for which we are pleading, will not be denied. A little reflection, however, may convince us that the danger from this quarter is not so alarming as might be apprehended at first sight.

Fanaticism, as far as we are at present concerned with it, may be defined, such an overwhelming impression of the ideas relating to the future world as disqualifies for the duties of life.

1. From the very nature of fanaticism, it is an evil of short duration. As it implies an irregular movement or an inflamed state of the passions, when these return to their natural state it subsides. Nothing that is violent will last long. The vicissitudes of the world and the business of life are admirably adapted to abate the excesses of religious enthusiasm. In a state where there are such incessant calls to activity, where want presses, desire allures, and ambition inflames, there is little room to dread an excessive attention to the objects of an invisible futurity.

A few rare examples of this kind might perhaps be found by diligent inquiry, over which infidelity would triumph and piety drop a tear. It is not uncommon, however, to find those who at the commencement of their religious course have betrayed symptoms of enthusiasm become in the issue the most amiable characters. With the increase of knowledge the intemperate ardour of their zeal has subsided into a steady faith and fervent charity, so as to exemplify the promise of Scripture, that "the path of the just" shall be "as the shining light, which shineth more and more unto the perfect day." As the energy of the religious principle is exerted in overcoming the world, so that variety of action and enlarged experience which the business of life supplies serves to correct its excesses and restrain its aberrations.

There are some who, proscribing the exercise of the affections entirely in religion, would reduce Christianity to a mere rule of life; but as such persons betray an extreme ignorance of human nature as well as of the Scriptures, I shall content myself with remarking, that the apostles, had they lived in the days of these men, would have been as little exempt from their ridicule as any other itinerants. If the supreme love of God, a solicitude to advance his honour, ardent desires after happiness, together with a comparative deadness to the present state, be enthusiasm, it is that enthusiasm which animated the Saviour and breathes throughout the Scriptures.

2. In admitting that a portion of enthusiasm may possibly be blended with the efforts to revive serious religion alluded to, we are far from meaning to insinuate that that is their distinguishing character; or that those who exert themselves in that way can, as a body, be justly classed with fanatics. The far greater part are men of good natural sense united to fervent piety. If not possessed of the advantages of a learned education, they are by no means ignorant. They have living knowledge. Familiarly conversant with the Bible, they are men of devotional habits and of exemplary conduct. The insulting epithets applied to such men might naturally provoke retaliation, and lead to an inquiry how far the learning so ostentatiously displayed is connected with religious knowledge; when it would perhaps be found that some of their revilers are better able to solve a geometrical problem than a theological difficulty, and are better acquainted with the epistles of Horace than those of St. Paul. But as it is my wish strenuously to avoid whatever might awaken angry passions, I forbear to press these inquiries.

Enthusiasm is an evil much less to be dreaded than superstition. The latter is a disease of opinion, which may be transmitted with fresh accumulation of error from age to age. It is the spirit of slumber in which whole nations are immersed. Placing religion, which is most foreign to its nature, in depending for acceptance with God on absurd penances or unmeaning ceremonies, it resigns the understanding to ignorance and the heart to insensibility. No generous sentiments, no active virtues ever issue from superstition.

Superstition is the disease of nations, enthusiasm that of individuals; the former grows more inveterate by time, the latter is cured by it.

We hope the remembrance of popish cruelties is not so far effaced from the minds of our countrymen as to permit them to see the forge of the giant without terror.

* * * * * * * *

* * * * * * * * * *

ON TOLERATION.

We have arrived at the last part of our subject, which relates to the expediency and justice of legal interference in the suppression of these attempts. And here I feel a solicitude lest I should give a wrong touch to the ark of religious liberty, and injure the cause which I wish to promote.

1. Toleration of a diversity of worship has now been legally established and uninterruptedly practised for more than a century; during which we have enjoyed a degree of internal peace and prosperity unexampled in any former age. This, which was the thing most wanted to perfect the constitution, has softened and harmonized the

spirits of men, has mitigated the fierceness of religious factions, and has made them of one heart and mind in the love of their country and attachment to its sovereign. The national wealth has been augmented, commerce extended, arts invented or improved, and society embellished with an additional portion of elegance and humanity. The resources of public strength have been enlarged, and the nation has become more formidable in war and more respected in peace. The struggles of party produce no other effects than clamorous invective and intrigue; and public rumour, instead of being occupied with the horrors of civil commotion, announces the intelligence of the fall of the ministry, or some new arrangement in the cabinet. This toleration has materially advanced the interest of the established church itself, by abating the acrimony of its adversaries, and affording room for the display of talent in other communities, the surest prevention of indolence in its own.

The principles of toleration also harmonize with that refinement of thinking and spirit of research which has distinguished the last century; in consequence of which this important advantage has been reaped, that the opinions of the speculative, which always have ultimately great effect, coincide with the practice of the constitution. Hence it is that England may be considered as the native soil of bold original minds; nor is there any danger of our being reasoned into a dislike of the constitution.

And shall we endanger the loss of all these advantages by adopting a new course of policy? What security will they afford us who invite us to tread in new and perilous paths? What security will they afford us, that the same tranquillity and the same prosperity will accompany us in so great a change; when the very essence of the constitution shall have been altered, and the very words which Englishmen were proud to pronounce expunged from the vocabulary?

A dread of innovation has hitherto prevented the correction of some flagrant abuses; yet it is rather extraordinary that some of those who profess to have most of that dread are among the most clamorous for an innovation in the toleration act.

But is not this a most serious innovation? Must we then understand these men to mean that they are only enemies to such innovations as are on the side of liberty, and that they are prepared to trample on the most fundamental laws, to promote persecution and tyranny? With such men it is to little purpose to expostulate; we leave them to the enjoyment of that calm sunshine which must fill the hearts of men of so much purity and benevolence.

To others it may be proper to suggest, that if innovations are dangerous, they are not equally so, and that there is a great difference between innovations which favour the spirit of a constitution and those that contradict it. The former may be compared to the natural growth of the human body, the latter to the violent dismemberment of its parts. The former completes an imperfect analogy; the latter destroys just proportions. The former is the removal of an obstruction which prevents the equable motion of the machine; the latter occasions the collision of interfering principles. When oppressive laws are ingrafted on a free constitution, the contrast of liberty and tyranny will make the oppression to be doubly felt. In such a situation, the free and undaunted spirit which the constitution has cherished suffers violence. The precedents of past times, the examples of their ancestors, the fundamental principles of the constitution, have taught them to consider themselves as free. By the proposed laws they are instructed to look upon themselves in a new light. They are commanded to unlearn all that they have learned, to descend from the dignity of freemen to the abject condition of a slave. Slavery may exist where freedom is unknown, without endangering the public tranquillity; in some countries perhaps without destruction of public happiness. But the slightest invasion of the liberties of a free country awakens a jealousy and resentment which are not easily appeased. Let those then who are alarmed at the danger of innovation seriously reflect on the possible consequences of an innovation so momentous. A free and a despotic state may both be compatible with liberty; but who ever would voluntarily make the transition from one to the other?

2. The liberty of worshipping God in that manner which the conscience of every individual dictates, provided nothing be introduced into worship incompatible with good morals, may be justly claimed as an inalienable right. The relation which subsists between man and his Maker, and the consequent obligation to worship him, is prior to the civil relation between magistrates and subjects. It is a more important relation, since all the good a creature can enjoy is derived from it, and all his reasonable hopes of happiness on the goodness of the Almighty. It differs, too, from every other in that it is invisible, perpetual, and eternal. A man may or may not be the member of a civil community, but he is always the creature of God. For these reasons, political duties, or those which result from the relation of the subject to the prince, must, in their nature, be subordinate to religious. When the commands of a civil superior interfere with those which we conscientiously believe to be the laws of God, submission to the former must be criminal; for the two obligations are not equipollent, but the former is essential, invariable, and paramount to every other: "Whether it be right," said the apostles, "to obey God or man, judge ye." But if an active obedience in such circumstances be *criminal*, to prescribe it cannot be *innocent*, since it would be absurd to affirm that exercise of authority to be right to which it is wrong to submit. Rights and duties are correlatives. A right to command necessarily implies the enforcing that which is right with respect to those to whom the duty of submission belongs. Nor is it to any purpose to allege that the worship prescribed is rational and scriptural, and far more excellent than that which is prohibited. For if we remember that worship is no other than the outward expression of the love and fear of God, we must perceive, that to become acceptable it is above all things necessary that it be such as approves itself to the mind of the worshipper; such as he sincerely believes will be pleasing to God. It is impossible to please God without a sincere intention to please him We may hope, from him who knows our frame, for a merciful indul

gence to the imperfections which spring from involuntary ignorance or latent prejudice. It agrees with his benignity to suppose he will graciously accept that worship which is not the best in itself, providing it be the best we know how to present. But to worship with those rites and ceremonies which our conscience does not approve, however excellent in themselves, is an insult to the Deity. A Jew, for example, who joined in the worship of a Christian church, while he retained the incredulity which distinguishes his nation, would be guilty of the highest impiety; nor would it be any extenuation of his fault to allege that the worship in which he assisted was founded on Scripture, and commanded by God, while his conviction was contrary. He who is utterly careless of the favour of God, and without any solicitude respecting a future world, will naturally follow the stream of authority or fashion, and adopt any mode of religion which happens to have the ascendency. But the sincere worshipper of God will find it impossible to comply with any religious injunctions which appear to him to interfere with the will of God.

Besides, as is urged with great force by Mr. Locke, if the magistrate of one country has a right to impose his religion under pains and penalties, the magistrates of all other countries must have an equal right. Religious truth will vary with the boundaries of nations; and with equal justice the pope will be revered in Spain, Mahomet in Turkey, and Brahma in India. It is easy to see to what those principles tend which imply that there is nothing determinate, nothing sacred in religion, and that all modes of worship are equally pleasing to God, and equally useful. The principles of persecution, pushed to their just consequence, terminate in Hobbism.*

It is worth while to consider what is likely to be the effect of enacting coercive laws in religion. If the men at whom they are aimed are conscientious, they will still persevere. They will reply to the injunction of silence what the apostles did to the chief priest, "whether it be right to obey God or man, judge ye." They will still persist in their attempts to evangelize the poor. This will necessitate the exercise of greater severities, the failure of which will be considered as a demand for punishments still heavier, until the magistrate has proceeded to banishment, confiscation, and death. For it is the inconvenience attending persecution that it is necessarily progressive. Small punishments only irritate. It commences with an intention of suppressing error; baffled in its first attempt, and stung with disappointment, it soon loses sight of its original design; it soon degenerates into a settled resolution to subdue contumacy, and strike terror. It becomes a fearful struggle between power and fortitude; the power of inflicting suffering, and that of enduring, which shall wear the other out. Let those, then, who are advocates for coercive measures, not content themselves with contemplating those mild expedients which may first present themselves to their minds, but prepare for the consequences,

* It is curious that Mr. Hall and his distinguished friend Sir James Macintosh should, unknown to each other, at different times and by a different course, arrive at a coincident result not likely to occur to ordinary minds. Sir James, in his valuable "Preliminary Dissertation," ENCY. BRITAN. p. 319, says, "A Hobbist is the only consistent persecutor"—ED.

and lay their accounts with being impelled to the exercise of the last severities. Let them expect to see dungeons crammed with prisoners, and scaffolds streaming with blood. Will any thing but the most unremitting vigilance, the most unrelenting system of espionage, prevent every class of dissenters and Methodists from fleeing from such a country, and seeking an asylum in a foreign land?

It is not easy to conceive the wound which this will inflict on the population and prosperity of the empire. That the dissenters are, as a body, an industrious and sober people, their enemies will not deny; and that the commercial prosperity of a country is closely involved in the preservation of such a class of people is equally undeniable The loss sustained by France in the exile of a million of Protestants, by the repeal of the edict of Nantes, has never yet been repaired. Nor was there ever a period when the hazarding such a loss would be more impolitic than the present; when the flourishing state of trade and commerce is essential to the stability of the government, and in a manner to the national existence. For the diminution of revenue, and the disorganization which a considerable failure in the produce of the taxes would occasion, we shall meet with a miserable compensation in a forced and hypocritical uniformity in worship.

> "Non tali auxilio nec defensioribus istis
> Tempus eget"——
>
> *Virgil.*

Will they whose pride and violence have produced this be able to remedy the mischief? Will lofty pretensions to unity, will tragic declamations on the sin of schism, and abandoning dissenters to the uncovenanted mercies of God?

The consequences of such an event deserve also to be considered in another point of view. It surely requires but little candour to acknowledge that the deprivations and discredit to which dissenters are exposed make it probable that, however in the judgment of their opponents they are erroneous, they are at least conscientious. Whatever may be imagined of the caprice, the levity, or obstinacy of individuals, nothing but a sense of duty, it may be fairly presumed, could prevail on numerous bodies of men to place themselves in that situation. In every country, it is no impeachment of the national establishment to suppose that many of those who continue out of its pale, and decline its emoluments, are men of serious piety. If we may form any conjecture of the dissenters of the present day from those of former times, it is obvious that my last remark will apply to them with peculiar force. As the loss of virtue is the greatest loss a nation can sustain, so the expulsion of those who have been distinguished by possessing a superior degree of piety is an ill omen, an alarming advance towards a general corruption of morals. Men of true piety, in whatever communities they are found, "are the salt of the earth." Their example corroborates the sentiments of virtue, and preserves from degradation the standard of morals. Vice, naturally mean and cowardly, is abashed and confounded before the majesty of virtue.

The efficacy of good examples in the formation of public opinion is incalculable. Though men justify their conduct by reasons, and sometimes bring the very rules of virtue to the touchstone of abstraction, yet they principally act from example. Metaphysical reasons have, in reality, had as little to do in the formation of the principles of morals, as rules of grammar in the original structure of language, or those of criticism in the formation of orators and poets.

* * * * * * * * * *

* * * * * * * * * *

But if the influence of example is so extensive, and if it be admitted that the dissenters, as a body, are exemplary for industry, sobriety, and a serious sense of religion, the sacrifice of so large a portion of national virtue must be confessed to be an evil of the first magnitude; to say nothing of the justice of the Divine administration, which is wont to make the departure of the pious from among a people the signal for pouring out its vials upon guilty cities and nations. Though such an event is alarming at all times, yet the peculiar complexion of the present renders it more so than ever. To every impartial observer it must be obvious that the present times are distinguished by an unexampled relaxation of manners; or such levity and indifference to every thing serious as threatens an open revolt from Christianity That rapacity and luxury, a love of pleasure, together with an open disdain for the duties of religion, have rapidly advanced within the last twenty years, can as little be denied.

And is this a season in which we can safely sacrifice a large portion of public virtue and piety? I am aware that the dissenters are considered as a precise and narrow-minded people, whose minds have not expanded with the growing improvements of the age, and that not a little ridicule has attached to them on that account: but may not this unyielding austerity, and these recluse manners, be a useful corrective to the dissipation of the age? While the polished manners of one class of society contribute to its embellishment, may not the severer virtues of another be equally beneficial in affording it stability and strength? Refinement may point the spire, but it is the plain principles of virtue which alone form the basis of the social fabric.

It will not be thought a digression from the present subject to remark the consequences which followed in France from the repeal of the edict of Nantes; to which the measures in question bear a strong resemblance. By that event France deprived herself of a million of her most industrious subjects, who carried their industry, their arts, and their riches into other countries. The loss which her trade and manufactures sustained by this event was no doubt prodigious. But it is not in that view my subject leads me to consider the ill consequences of that step. She lost a people whose simple, frugal manners, and whose conscientious piety, were well adapted to stem the growing corruption of the times, while the zeal and piety of their pastors were a continual stimulus to awaken the exertions of the national clergy.

If France had never had her Saurins, her Claudes, her De Plessis Mornays, her national church had never boasted the genius of Bossuet and the virtues of Fenelon. From that fatal moment she put a period to the toleration of the Protestants, the corruptions of the clergy, the abuses of the church, the impiety of the people, met with no check, till infidelity of the worst sort pervaded and ruined the nation. When the remote as well as immediate effects of that edict which suppressed the Protestants are taken into the account,—when we consider the careless security and growing corruption which hung over the Gallican church in consequence of it, it will not be thought too much to affirm, that to that measure may be traced the destruction of the monarchy and the ruin of the nation.

He who considers what it is that constitutes the force of penal laws will find it is their agreement with the moral feelings which nature has planted in the breast. When the actions they punish are such, and only such, as the tribunal of conscience has already condemned, they are the constant object of respect and reverence. They enforce and corroborate the principles of moral order, by publishing its decisions and executing its sanctions. They present to the view of mankind an august image of a moral administration,—a representation in miniature of the eternal justice which presides in the dispensations of the Almighty. We behold nothing of the passions of men; we forget their agency, and seem to see nothing but justice and order appearing for a moment on the earth, to restore the tranquillity and correct the disorders of society. The sentiments of morality and the sanctions of law maintain, in such a situation, a reciprocal influence over each other. The former derive additional authority from public opinion, and the latter appear sacred and venerable in consequence of their coincidence with the dictates of conscience. When criminal law thus concurs with the maxims of private morality, by corroborating the dictates of conscience and inspiring the love of justice, tranquillity, and order, and the advancement of the public good, every innocent person becomes interested in maintaining their authority and promoting their execution. Every sentiment of the mind, the sense of security, the love of the public, the sentiment of justice, the abhorrence of crime, are leagued on the side of the laws, and are so many securities for their due execution. It has been found by experience, as the result of these principles, that laws become feeble and relaxed, not only when they punish innocent objects, but when the punishments they assign are disproportionate to the offence. The want of harmony between the decision of the public and the private tribunal interposes an invariable obstruction to their observance; for crimes must be detected and punishments inflicted by men who will not lend their aid to enforce what they secretly condemn. Hence laws which are enacted with precipitance and passion, or under the influence of party motives, when they come to be executed will have to encounter a perpetual friction, arising from their repugnance to the manners and sentiments of the public. By these means public opinion, which is nothing but the aggregate of the sentiments of individuals, often limits, happily for mankind, the assumed omnipotence of legislation. They are framed in one element, they are executed in another; they must live in a different atmosphere from that in which they are born.

But admitting that the efforts of zeal and the vigilance of government supply this defect, and secure the punishment of those who transgress these laws, it deserves to be considered in what manner their punishment will impress the public. With what feelings will they contemplate the ruin or imprisonment of virtuous men for the exercise of what they esteem the rights of conscience! Will the condign punishment of their countrymen, not for disturbing the public peace or for the violation of property, but for a well-meant endeavour to diffuse the principles of piety and the blessings of religion, augment their reverence for the laws? or rather will it not produce in some an indignation against such flagrant injustice, in others confuse the distinction of right and wrong? When they see atrocious crimes and eminent virtues pursued and punished with the same severity, it must tend to destroy all respect for legislation. They will be no longer solicitous to manifest their innocence, but to secure their impunity; and to the honour of obeying will succeed that of evading the laws. Nor is this all. In the detection of these artificial crimes the assistance of the profligate and abandoned alone can be expected, which will complete the triumph of wickedness over piety and innocence. To the alliance between church and state we are already familiarized; but an alliance, under pretence of securing the church, between the ministers of religion and a detestable spawn of spies and informers will appear surprising; nor is it difficult to foresee what ideas it will impress of that religion which stands in need of such aid, or of those ministers who stoop to employ it. Until by some strange revolution all the traces of genuine Christianity and all the history of its propagation are effaced from the mind, it will be impossible for men to mistake this for the religion of Jesus,—a religion which grew up in the midst of sufferings, and whose only weapon is love. In such proceedings they will look for the marks and signs of the true church, and instead of the successors of the apostles, they will imagine they behold a Jewish sanhedrim solemnly commanding the illiterate disciples of Jesus to "teach no more in that name."

It is more than probable that a similar reply will be made to that of the apostles on a similar occasion, "Whether it be right to obey God or man, judge ye." Under a full conviction that they are in the path of duty, and promoting the eternal happiness of mankind, it is not easy to see how they can desist. Whatever political superiors may imagine, he who conceives himself implicated in the command to "preach the gospel to every creature" will find it morally impossible to yield active obedience to any contrary command. "We cannot," saith the apostle, but speak the things which we have heard and seen."

To nominal Christians, who may rather be said to comply with the religion of their country than to believe it, on such a subject it is in vain to appeal; but they who are impressed with the importance of eternal things, and know "the gospel to be the power of God unto salvation," will feel no hesitation how to determine in this case.

In perfect consistency with a cheerful submission to the civil authority of their superiors, they will consider it a duty resulting from their allegiance to Jesus Christ to persist in their endeavours to convert mankind.

That coercive measures will tend to ferment a spirit of division in the kingdom can admit of little doubt. Many, it may be reasonably expected, will feel a generous concern for the oppressed, though they may ridicule the cause in which they suffer; while men of enlarged minds, and who are thoroughly imbued with the love of liberty, will perceive in any one act of oppression, however insulated, a precedent most dangerous to freedom. The mischief in itself may appear little, and the merit of the sufferers inconsiderable in their eyes; but they will consider it as an experiment on the public mind, calculated to prepare them for other acts of oppression; they will consider every thing as alarming that impairs the integrity of freedom, from a conviction that a vessel may be sunk by the smallest leak.

Thus two formidable parties will probably be produced in the king dom, inflamed with mutual animosity and suspicion. Of the parliament which assembled in the year 1640, on the eve of those commotions which afterward broke out into a civil war and issued in such fatal extremities, the puritans formed but a small part. The majority of the number consisted of persons attached to the established church, but who felt indignant at the oppression* of the puritans and the cruelties of Laud. Their attachment to liberty taught them to identify themselves with the sufferers, and to discover in the severities of the Star-chamber and the High-commission Court an exertion of an arbitrary power utterly incompatible with the security of a free people.

Although many causes, it must be confessed, contributed to the ruin of the unfortunate Charles, no single one had so much influence as that religious intolerance which was so unhappy a feature in his character; as, on the other hand, nothing contributed so much to support the pre carious authority of Cromwell, and to produce an artificial calm in the midst of so many raging factions, so many stormy elements, as a general liberty of conscience. This, as is remarked by the celebrated Bishop of Meaux, was the great secret of his policy.

The policy of Charles, instead of making him regarded as the common father of his subjects and the guardian of their welfare, providing for the happiness of every part with parental care and impartial solicitude, made him to become the head of a party while he lent himself as the instrument of gratifying its mean and sanguinary passions; by which means he became the idol of a faction, but lost the hearts of his people. The policy of Cromwell mitigated resentment, conciliated prejudice, and made those acquiesce in his pretensions and concur to maintain his authority who agreed in nothing else. How precious must that liberty of conscience be, and how fearful the resentment of its loss, which could prompt a great people to suffer their native prince to wander in exile and subsist on the alms of rival courts; and reconcile them to the yoke of a master whose power was not supported by the smallest shadow of justice! If such effects followed from invading liberty of conscience at a time when its right had never been ascer

* Clarendon, vol. i. p. 184

tained, what may we not apprehend from its violation after an uninter rupted possession of it for a hundred years?—when it has become familiar to our laws, habits, and manners, and the apprehension of its danger has been succeeded by an experience of its advantages. What will be the ultimate issue, should Providence in its infinite wisdom suffer our adversaries to prevail and the cruelties of persecution to be renewed, it belongs not to me to conjecture: but it may be granted me to express my humble hope we shall stand firm in the day of trial,—not forgetting that persecution and sufferings have been the lot of the most eminent of God's servants; that in walking in this path we are encompassed with "a cloud of witnesses;" with apostles, prophets, and evangelists, whose words will teach, whose examples will encourage us to adorn that cause by our sufferings which we are no longer permitted to aid by our exertions.

Having executed to the best of my ability the plan I proposed, my freedom, I trust, will be pardoned if I suggest a few hints of advice to those who are employed in disseminating the knowledge of Christianity in villages.

1. To abstain from political reflection and from censuring either the constitution of the church or the clergy, is a part of prudence on which I ever would hope it is needless to insist.

2. Though I am convinced that those who attempt to evangelize the poor do not fail to inculcate the morality of the gospel, it may yet be doubted whether this is done with sufficient distinctness and detail. A notion prevails among some that to preach the gospel includes nothing more than a recital or recapitulation of the peculiar doctrines of Christianity. If these are firmly believed and zealously embraced, they are ready to suppose the work is done, and that all the virtues of the Christian character will follow by necessary consequence. Hence they satisfy themselves with recommending holiness in general terms, without entering into its particular duties; and this in such a manner as rather to predict it as the result of certain opinions than to enforce it on the ground of moral obligation, which tends to disjoin faith and virtue by turning all the solicitude of men to the former, while the latter is left to provide for itself, and to make them substitute the agitation of the passions and the adoption of a speculative creed in the room of that renovation of heart and life which the Scriptures render necessary.

Some apology, it is true, ought to be made for those who have leaned to this extreme from the circumstances in which they have been placed. Having been called to preach to people who were ignorant of the very first truths of religion, they have supposed it necessary to employ themselves in laying the foundation. On the supposition we were to address an audience that was not acquainted with the primary doctrines, it would be necessary to begin with relating the facts and teaching the doctrines which are the basis of the Christian dispensation. The *credenda*, or things to be believed, must necessarily precede the *facienda*, or things to be done. But though things must proceed in this order no durable separation should be made of the doctrines from the duties of Christianity, lest the people should acquire a corrupt taste, and, satisfied with their first attainments and impressions, neglect to cultivate that "holiness without which no man shall see the Lord." When they have been long detained in the elementary doctrines, they are not unfrequently found to acquire a distaste for the practical parts of Scripture,—an impatience of reproof,—a dislike, in short, of every thing but what flatters them with a favourable opinion of their character and their state. Proud, bigoted, disputatious, careless of virtue, tenacious of subtleties, their religion evaporates in opinion, and their supposed conversion is nothing more than an exchange of the vices of the brute for those of the speculator in theological difficulties.

The best method of preventing this fatal abuse of evangelical doctrine is to inculcate in immediate connexion with it those virtues of the Christian character by which faith must be tried, frequently, distinctly, and fully. Instead of recommending practical religion only in general terms, under the phrase of holiness or any other, let us, in imitation of inspired preachers, explain in what that holiness consists. When John came preaching "repentance because the kingdom of heaven was at hand," he did not satisfy himself with barren and general abstractions: in reply to the inquiries of those who asked him what they must do, he entered into details, he imparted specific advice, and enjoined specific duties corresponding to the different conditions of men and their relation to each other in society. Had he contented himself with merely reiterating the command to repent in general terms, as, it is to be feared, is too often the case, his hearers might have mistaken a transient compunction, a vague sensation of uneasiness, for the duty demanded: but by that particularity of application he adopted, the conscience was informed and the necessity perceived of "bringing forth fruits meet for repentance."

The conscience is not likely to be touched by general declamations on the evil of sin and the beauty of holiness without delineation of character: they may alarm at first, but after a while, if they be often asserted merely as general truths which involve the whole human race, they will supply no materials for self-examination or painful retrospect. They will in process of time be regarded as doctrinal points, and pass from the conscience into the creed. He must know little of human nature who perceives not the callousness of the human heart, and the perfect indifference with which it can contemplate the most alarming truths when they are presented in a general abstract form. It is not in this way that religious instruction can be made permanently interesting. It is when particular vices are displayed as they appear in real life, when the arts of self-deception are detected, and the vain excuses by which the sinner palliates his guilt, evades the conviction of conscience, and secures a delusive tranquillity—in a word, it is when the heart is forced to see in itself the original of what is described by the apostle, and, perceiving that "the secrets of his heart are made manifest, he falls down and confesses that God is among us of a truth." The reproof which awakened David from his guilty slumber, and made him weep and tremble, turned, not on the general evil of sin, but on the peculiar circumstances of aggravation attending that which he had committed. The sermon of Peter on the day of Pentecost, which produced such decisive effects, was not a general declamation on the evil of sin, but it contained a specific charge against his hearers of having rejected and crucified their Messiah. When Paul was called before Felix, being well acquainted with his character he adapted his discourse accordingly, and "reasoned of righteousness, temperance, and judgment to come," until "Felix trembled." The delineations of character and the injunctions of Scripture on practical points are not couched in general terms; they are diversified and particular; nor can it justly be doubted that the more of individuality, if I may be allowed the expression, our pictures of human nature possess, the more impressive will they become. It is in this department of public instruction there is scope for endless variety—for the highest exertions of intellect, and the richest stores of knowledge.

The doctrines of Christianity, though of infinite importance, are yet few and simple, capable of few combinations, and of little variety of illustration; too precise to leave any thing for the understanding to invent; too awful to permit the imagination to embellish. It is not in the statement of Christian doctrines, considered in themselves, that experience, talents, and knowledge find scope for their exertion.

* * * * * * * * * *

* * * * * * * *

ON THE RIGHT OF WORSHIP.*

Worship consists in the performance of all those external acts, and the observance of all those rites and ceremonies, in which men engage with the professed and sole view of honouring God. It is consequently in a pre-eminent manner the concern of conscience; for, as God is the supreme master and legislator, it is impossible for a conscientious man, in compliance with human injunctions, either to omit any part of that worship which he apprehends God to require, or to perform any which he has forbidden. In worship the creature has to do only with his Creator. There are, unquestionably, some regards due to God, some expressions of our reverence to him and our dependence upon him, which it is our duty to render; and the duties which have God immediately for their object must be in their obligation paramount to every other; that is, such that the commands of no human superior can discharge us from it. It remains only to be considered by what criterion these duties are to be ascertained.

Among the different modes of worship which prevail in different countries, and in the same country, to what standard are we to appeal? by what principle is the solution to be made? Either the mere will of the magistrate or the conscience of the individual must decide in

* This appears to have been written in 1811; the preceding twenty-three pages in 1801 and 1802

this case. I say the *mere* will, because if the promulgation of his will be enforced by arguments and reasons, these arguments are necessarily submitted to the judgment of the subject; and consequently, as far as they are concerned, he is still left to his conscience. But if such a power as this be vested in the magistrate, it is highly necessary to examine the consequences to which it will lead. It will legitimate all the persecutions which the heathen emperors inflicted on the primitive Christians, as well as the more recent popish cruelties. For from what principle did those persecutions flow, but that the magistrate possessed a right to determine and prescribe the religion of his subjects, and that a refusal to comply with his authority involved political guilt? The just pretensions of magistracy in this respect are surely equal; nor can any reason be assigned for denying that authority to heathen or popish princes within their dominions which will not equally apply to Protestant princes.

The dominion of God over his creatures is original, inalienable, and supreme; so that men must be contemplated as the subjects of God, before we consider them as members of a civil community. The formation of states and the enaction of laws are operations which regard man in his transient and local situation as the inhabitant of the present world. There is, on the principles of Theism, above and beyond these, an original and fundamental moral law which unites him to his Maker, and obliges him to fear, serve, and obey him as his superior Lord. That this law is more original and comprehensive than any other is evident from this consideration, that it comprehends sovereign as well as subjects; that it regards men in those invariable, essential qualities in which they all agree; and that it can never be suspended by time or change.

As men are the creatures of God originally and essentially, and continually accountable to him, whatever laws are established for the government of particular societies are in the nature of *by-laws*, with relation to the duties which intelligent creatures owe to God; and whenever civil magistrates interfere with these, they are guilty of the same absurdity as a particular corporation would be who formed municipal regulations inconsistent with the law of the land. No particular society has a right to make rules for its regulation which interfere with the general laws of that kingdom of which it is a part; for this would be to introduce an *imperium in imperio*, a multitude of legislatures, and a confusion and uncertainty in the principles of justice.

In like manner, no human power can justly make laws which shall interfere with those duties which are previously due to God. As a necessary consequence of this, it follows, that whatever right men possess to worship God after the dictates of conscience, in a state of nature, is not diminished or impaired by entering into society. If seditious purposes be concealed under the pretext of assembling for religious worship, let the severest laws be enacted for their punishment. Let the claims of liberty of conscience be permitted as a cover for nothing which does not belong to it.

There is less reason, however, for entertaining any alarm on this head in tolerating worshipping assemblies than any other; for they are always public. They invite inspection. Who would be so infatuated as to attempt to connect treasonable or seditious designs with assemblies which are open to every one, and whose time and place of meeting are universally known? Besides, the very business of worship is at the greatest distance possible from every thing tending to inflame political passions. Directed to a spiritual and invisible Being, it withdraws the mind from the world, and turns the thoughts into a channel the most remote from those affections which disturb the repose of society.

It would be strange indeed if those exercises which have the most direct influence in tranquillizing the heart, and reducing all earthly things to comparative insignificance, must be forbidden, from an apprehension of their becoming engines of insurrection and tumult. They cannot be perverted in the smallest degree to this purpose without their danger being perceived; and it will then be soon enough to apply remedies.

This reasoning does not apply against the magistrate selecting some one particular sect, or some one set of religious opinions, and bringing them under his exclusive patronage and encouragement; in other words, the erection of a religious establishment. Whatever the advantages or inconveniences may be which result from religious establishments is foreign to the subject in hand, which regards only the free and full toleration of different sects, as long as they contain themselves within the limits of civil submission.

It will be alleged, that on these principles a multitude of ignorant enthusiasts and wild fanatics will start up, and under the pretence of preaching the gospel, bring religion into contempt, and thence eventually open a door for profaneness and impiety. That this may in some instances be the consequence of unlimited toleration of Christian worship cannot perhaps be denied; as little can it be denied that this is a great evil. It is much to be lamented that any should engage in the functions of a Christian minister who, in addition to an unblemished character, is not possessed of a competent measure of ability. But this inconvenience may be only one instance, among an infinity of others, of a partial evil connected with a principle productive of the greatest good.

Pure and unmixed good is not the portion of earth. We cannot specify a single law in the natural or moral world, which falls within the sphere of our observation, which is not productive (along with permanent good) of occasional evils. This mixture of partial evil with the source of general happiness seems to be an essential part of the imperfections of the present state. If the magistrate is invested with the power of suppressing all whom he thinks incompetent to the office of a preacher, there can be no liberty and no tranquillity. But it is surely of more consequence to a state to preserve the most valuable portion of its liberty, than to preserve a perfect exemption from fanaticism. The care of the former falls within the proper province of a magistrate. The latter is consistent with a high degree of national prosperity. Religious enthusiasm becomes dangerous to a state only when it is the subject of oppression. There is in it an elastic quality which repels rigorous coercion. The vivid impressions of religious objects which it includes rather tend to sink the value of all earthly interests, to annihilate the world and all its concerns, and to produce a conduct which, though it may be wild and incoherent, yet if left to itself will be mild, inoffensive, and benevolent. Besides, enthusiasm, consisting in a preternatural state of exaltation, has a strong tendency to subside in a short time, and with the increase of knowledge to purify itself until it settles into calm enlightened piety. It is not, like superstition, a permanent evil. The enthusiast is impatient of control in his religious concerns, but does not aspire after dominion. In proportion as the passions are strongly possessed by invisible objects, the interests of the present state lose their ascendency, and the enraptured enthusiast is more in danger of becoming indolent than factious. The most effectual way of transporting such characters into political excesses is to inflame them by oppression,—when they naturally learn to consider their enemies as the enemies of God, and throw the whole weight of their religious prejudices and passions into the scale of political opposition; while, on the other hand, a complete toleration is the most effectual remedy for their intemperance; leaving them leisure to reflect, and affording room for the ordinary motives and principles of life to resume their ascendency.

In the history of those sects which have been the most justly branded with enthusiasm, we shall uniformly find that while they were exasperated by persecution they were fierce and wild, and their fanaticism continued unsubdued; but no sooner were they left unmolested than those features in their character which excited alarm gradually wore off, and they ceased to be formidable.

The history of the Baptists who rose, in the sixteenth century, in Germany, and of the Quakers in England, confirm the truth of this remark.

Though the tyrannical measures pursued by Charles the First, at the beginning of his reign, naturally excited alarm and awoke opposition, it seems evident the civil war could never have been kindled but for the intolerable cruelties inflicted by Laud on nonconformists, which cemented the various sects, and made them unite in a vehement opposition to the government of Charles, while their tenets were too discordant to permit them to unite in any thing else. The magnitude of eternal interests and the mighty force of religious passions were superadded to the causes already existing of political contention, and by their union kindled those flames of war which consumed the land. Cromwell, on the other hand, whose usurpation was supported by no law, and who had to contend with the whole weight of virtuous prejudice in favour of the constitution he had overturned, and the family he had expelled, practised an opposite policy, and contrived to retain in subjection three kingdoms, by granting to the rival sects a general toleration, and balancing their power against each other. The importance of this expedient in the preservation of his power has been acknowledged, both in England and on the continent, by the most inveterate enemies of that extraordinary man. The eloquent Bishop of Meaux, in his funeral oration for Henrietta of France, ascribes his success principally to this measure of his administration. Since the revolution, at which a universal religious toleration took place, amid all our calamities and reverses, an unexampled duration of domestic peace has been enjoyed, with two very short interruptions from occasions foreign from the topic under present consideration; and during this protracted period, the mild spirit of legislation has communicated itself to all sects, and in a very eminent degree mitigated the acrimony of religious zeal.

A species of religious fanaticism, it is confessed, made its appearance in the sixteenth century in Germany, and in the next century in England, which was of a highly political complexion, and struck immediately at the root of civil power, the distinctions of rank, and the offices of magistracy; but even the history of the Baptists in Germany, and of the Fifth-monarchy men, supply reasons for toleration, since we see that the obnoxious tenets which distinguished them soon disappeared, and that under milder treatment their successors have retained only some peculiarities of the most harmless kind. The extravagant flights of fanaticism, its visionary spirit, which might tempt its possessors to trample upon the rules of society, can never last long or extend far; for the principles of self-preservation, the physical wants of the lower orders especially, who are most obnoxious to such impressions, the spirit of imitation, the habit of submission to superiors, together with the ordinary occupations of life, are principles of perpetual operation, the influence of which will soon surmount the strongest feelings, which operate only occasionally and by starts, and will consequently force the mind back into its proper element. For the same reasons it can never extend far. Minds only of a peculiar texture will feel its impression. A vast majority of every community will be too wise, too busy, too sensual, or too phlegmatic, to be transported into dangerous excesses by causes which operate on the imagination, and which have no relation to the more ordinary sources of pain and pleasure. No fanaticism of this kind has made its appearance at present, nor is there any room to presume it will. Some degree of enthusiasm, perhaps, generally accompanies religious impressions in uncultivated minds, at their commencement. Enthusiasm may be defined, that religious state of mind in which the imagination is unduly heated, and the passions outrun the understanding. But when persons are first deeply impressed with the infinitely momentous concerns of a future life, and are thereby introduced, as it were, into a new world, it is too much to expect their religious affections shall be perfectly regulated, or their conduct, under circumstances so novel, be consistent with the exactest rules of propriety New situations, whether resulting from a moral and internal change, or from outward circumstances, make it necessary for some time to pass before those who are led into them know perfectly how to adjust their behaviour to them. But if the profession of piety be sincere (and of hypocrisy we are not at present speaking), it will eventually secure, together with the essential moral virtues, a regard to decorum and to all the minuter properties of social intercourse. In the mean time, where the love of God and man predominates, it will ill become the governor of a Christian country, and still less the governor of a Christian church, to suffer himself to be so much offended at the intemperate effusions of honest zeal as to disregard the substance of religion because it may be deficient in some of its more amiable appendages.

If we adopt the maxims of a profane and careless world, we shall be taught to look upon all zealous Christians as enthusiasts or hypocrites; for when have they not, by a majority of mankind, been represented in that light? To men of the world it appears so strange that men should be affected by the consideration of invisible realities in any degree proportioned to the influence of present objects, it is so utterly remote from all their practical estimates, that they have no means of accounting for it without imputing it to a partial insanity or deliberate hypocrisy. But this is only one among numberless glaring inconsistencies of human conduct. For these very persons, it is probable, have never formally renounced the authority of Jesus Christ, who commands us to "seek *first* the kingdom of God," nor the certainty of an eternal state, in comparison of which the interests and prospects of the present are annihilated; and yet they are surprised to find that good and evil should be estimated with regard to their respective magnitude, and that any should be weak enough to credit the declarations and obey the precepts of our common Lord. Such is the fascination of the world, and so complete its triumph in effecting a total divorce of the speculations from the practical belief of professed Christians. If the truths which religion reveals, and the hopes it inspires, respect an infinite good, and the present life be, as we know by experience, short and transitory, it must be the truest wisdom to be deeply solicitous to attain that good, and to be disposed to make any sacrifice of present pleasure and convenience with a view to it; and when this is the habitual state of the mind, it will imprint some traces of itself in the external deportment, which the irreligious part of mankind will be sure to brand with the name of hypocrisy or fanaticism.

The primitive Christians encountered this reproach, and their successors must expect it in proportion as they tread in their steps. That world to which we are hastening will determine who are justly chargeable with folly,—they who treat eternal things according to their true nature, who, making the service of God their supreme concern, pass the time of their sojourning here in fear; or they, the language of whose conduct is, "let us eat and drink, for to-morrow we die."

To suppose that that religious state of mind in which devout affections are highly [raised]* is enthusiastic, is a most pernicious mistake, and would in its consequences utterly extirpate religion, and expunge

* Whenever a word is placed thus between brackets, it is supplied conjecturally, the manuscript being illegible.—Ed.

a great part of the Scriptures. The smallest acquaintance with the New Testament must convince every one that the apostles and primitive Christians were no strangers to the strongest religious emotions.

We read of a "joy unspeakable and full of glory," of a "peace that passeth all understanding," with innumerable other expressions of a similar kind, which indicate strong and vehement emotions of mind. That the great objects of Christianity, called eternity, heaven, and hell, are of sufficient magnitude to justify vivid emotions of joy, fear, and love, is indisputable, if it be allowed we have any relation to them; nor is it less certain that religion could never have any powerful influence if it did not influence through the medium of the affections. All objects which have any permanent influence influence the conduct in this way. We may possibly be first set in motion by their supposed connexion with our interest; but unless they draw to themselves particular affections, the pursuit soon terminates.

The cool calculation of interest operates only at times; we are habitually borne forward in all parts of our career by specific affections and passions; some more simple and original, others complicated and acquired. In men of a vulgar cast, the grosser appetites,—in minds more elevated, the passions of sympathy, taste, ambition, the pleasures of imagination,—are the springs of motion. The world triumphs over its votaries by approaching them on the side of their passions; and it does not so much deceive their reason as captivate their heart.

It is in this way the love of the world must be repelled. As it is not chiefly by imposing on the understanding, or misleading the rational assent, that the world triumphs over its votaries, so the mere inculcation of religious truth on the intellect, without forming deep and lasting impressions on the heart, will never be sufficient to emancipate us from its control. The difficulties which accrue in a religious career, especially at its outset, are so many and formidable, that unless we are deeply *interested* as well as convinced, perseverance is impracticable. In that victory over the world which is promised to faith, it is necessary to oppose feeling to feeling, and pleasure to pleasure. The intemperate attachment to sensual pleasure must be subdued by the fear of punishment; the vain and extravagant hopes which present scenes inspire must be effaced by hopes more solid and more animating; and to wean us from the breasts of earthly, we must be led to the breasts of spiritual consolation.

The world amuses, enchants, transports us; how shall religion teach us to triumph over it, if it present nothing but speculative conclusions, and if the views of a rational self-interest which it displays were not intimately associated with objects adapted to engage and fill the heart? Would the primitive Christians have taken *joyfully* the spoiling of their goods, because they had in heaven a more enduring substance? Would they not only have felt calm and resolute, but accounted "it all joy when they suffered divers persecutions," if the objects of eternity had not occupied a large share of their affections?

The familiar acknowledgment, *Video meliora, proboque deteriora sequor*,—the frequency with which men act contrary to the most mature convictions of reason and conscience, shows how inefficacious is a mere speculative conviction when opposed to inveterate habits and passions. What is the defect here experienced, but a want of the correspondent feelings and impressions from which that state of desire results which impels to virtuous action?

As the objects of religion are infinite and eternal, if the mind is duly affected by them at all, they have a tendency to enlarge and propagate their correspondent affections more and more; and will probably tend ultimately to absorb and extinguish all other hopes and fears.

Though good men are continually approaching nearer and nearer to this state, it is neither possible nor desirable they should reach it in this life. The multitude of pains, difficulties, and perplexities with which they have to encounter are continually drawing their attention to present objects; and the duties of the present state could not be performed in that exalted state of spirituality. An eminent degree and vigour of the religious affections, then, ought not to be denominated fanaticism, unless they arise from wrong views of religion, or are so much indulged as to disqualify for the duties of society. Within these limits, the more elevated devotional sentiments are, the more perfect is the character, and the more suited to the destination of a being, who has, indeed, an important part to act here, but who stands on the confines of eternity. He may justly be styled a fanatic, who, under a pretence of spirituality, neglects the proper business of life, or who, from mistaken views of religion, elevates himself to an imaginary superiority to the rules of virtue and morality. Whatever other kind of fanaticism, real or pretended, [exists,] seems not to fall, in the smallest degree, under the conduct of the civil magistrate; nor is there any danger of immorality being inculcated under any corruption of the Christian doctrine. Many religious systems, considered in their theory, may seem to tend to the encouragement of vice; they may, in their speculative consequences, set aside the obligations of virtue; but the uncorrupted dictates of conscience, the general sentiments of mankind respecting right and wrong, and the close alliance between devotion and virtue will always counteract this tendency, so far that the same persons will be more moral with very erroneous religious opinions than without religion. A practical disregard to piety is the prolific source of vice. We shall find the minds of every sect of Christians who are zealous in religion superior to those who are careless and profane. Whatever tends to draw the attention to God and eternity tends to destroy the dominion of sin. Under the varied forms of religious belief which have prevailed among the different parties of Christians, little variation has taken place in the rule of life. In the first age of Christianity, the church was accused, by the malice of its enemies, of the most shameful and unnatural practices; which it disclaimed, but, at the same time, very injudiciously insinuated that the Gnostics were guilty of the crimes which were alleged: but the result of the more calm and dispassionate investigation of later times has been a growing conviction that these surmises had no foundation in fact. The doctrines of our holy religion may be wofully curtailed and corrupted, and its profession sink into formality; but its moral precepts are so plain and striking, and guarded by such clear and awful sanctions, as to render it impossible it can ever be converted into an active instrument of vice. Let the appeal be made to facts. Look through all the different sects and parties into which professed Christians are unhappily divided. Where is there one to be found who has innovated in the rule of life, by substituting vice in place of virtue? The fears entertained from this quarter must be considered as chimerical and unfounded, until they are confirmed by the evidence of facts. In those districts in which the dissenters and Methodists have been most zealous and successful in village preaching, are the morals of the people more corrupted than in other places? Are they distinguished by a greater degree of profligacy, intemperance, and debauchery than the inhabitants of other parts of the country? The advocates of rigorous measures will scarcely have the temerity to put the question upon this issue; and until they do, all their pretended dread of the growth of licentiousness from village preaching will be considered as nothing but artifice.

To contend for the legal monopoly of religious instruction, under pretence of securing the morals of the people, is a similar kind of policy with that of the papists, who withhold the Scriptures from the common people lest they should be betrayed into heresy. We all perceive, the design of the papist in this restriction is to prevent the diffusion of knowledge, which would be fatal to ghostly dominion. Is it not equally evident that the prohibition to instruct the populace in the principles of Christianity originates in this jealousy of power?

We must at least be permitted to express our surprise at the profound sagacity of those who can discover a design to destroy morality by inculcating religion, and a purpose of making men vicious by making them serious. Plain men must be excused if they are startled by such refined and intricate paradoxes.

It highly becomes those who are the advocates for the interference of government to restrain the efforts of Methodists and dissenters to diffuse the principles of knowledge and piety, to advert to the consequences which must result.

Those who are conscientious will feel it their duty, in opposition to the mandates of authority, to proceed patiently, enduring whatever punishment the legislature may think proper to inflict. The government, irritated at their supposed criminal obstinacy, will be tempted to enact severer laws accompanied with severer penalties, which the truly conscientious will still think it their duty to brave, imitating the example of the primitive teachers of Christianity, who departed from the presence of the council "rejoicing that they were thought worthy to suffer for the name of Christ." Thus will commence a struggle between the ruling powers and the most upright part of the subjects, which shall first wear each other out,—the one by infliction, the other by endurance; prisons will be crowded, cruel punishments will become familiar, and blood probably will be spilt. The nation will be afflicted with the frightful spectacle of innocent and exemplary characters suffering the utmost vengeance of the law for crimes which the sufferers glory in having committed.

It is an inherent and inseparable inconvenience in persecution that it knows not where to stop. It only aims at first to crush the obnoxious sect; it meets with a sturdy resistance; it then punishes the supposed crime of obstinacy, till at length the original magnitude of the error is little thought of in the solicitude to maintain the rights of authority. This is illustrated in the letter of Pliny to Trajan,* treating of the persecution of Christians. *Their obstinacy* in refusing to comply with the mandates of supreme authority [constituted the crime.] In other penal laws a proportion is usually observed between the crime and the punishment, the evil and the remedy; but here the pride of dictating and imposing mingles itself and draws [reasons] for severity even from the insignificance of the error and of the persecuted sect, which should be its protection.

As the power of the community is delegated to the magistrate to enable him to punish such delinquencies and to avenge such injuries as it would be unsafe to leave to the resentment of the individual to punish, the voice of law should ever be in harmony with the voice of conscience and of reason. It should punish only those actions which are previously condemned in the tribunal of every man's own breast. The majesty of law, considered as an authoritative rule of action, can only be maintained by its agreement with the simple and unsophisticated decisions of the mind respecting right and wrong. On these principles law is entitled to profound veneration as a sort of secondary morality, or an application of the principles of virtue and social order to the real situation and actual circumstances of mankind. As the civil magistrate is invested with a portion of divine authority for the government of men, so wise legislation is a reservoir of moral regulation and principles, drawn from the springs and fountains of eternal justice. When government is thus conducted it leagues all the virtues on its side; whatever is venerable, whatever is good rallies round the standard of authority; and to support the dignity of the laws is to support virtue itself. In persecution it is directly the opposite. When innocent persons [suffer] for a resolute adherence to the dictates of conscience, the sentiments of moral approbation are necessarily disjoined from the operation of the laws.

* * * * * * * * * *

The fear of civil punishment is a motive which the wisdom of mankind has superadded to the other motives which operate to restrain men from criminal conduct. The contempt and hatred of our fellow-creatures and the dread of punishment from an invisible Judge are not always found in fact to be of sufficient force to control the unruly passions of bad men. In addition to this, men have contrived so to organize society that the disturbers of other men's peace and the invaders of their rights shall have to dread an adequate punishment from the arm of a public person who represents the community. As

* Lib. x. Epis. 97.—Ed

the fears with which human laws inspire offenders are superadded motives, they presuppose the existence of an original one. They are a superstructure which can only stand on the foundation of those distinctions of right and wrong which the simplest dictates of the understanding recognise. To disjoin the fear of human [laws] from its natural associates, the forfeiture of public esteem and the dread of Divine wrath, is a solecism of the most glaring nature.

Again, the terror of punishment is designed to operate on the community at large, not on a small number of people of a peculiar manner of thinking. But the great body of a people are affected only by what is palpable; they are unable to comprehend subtle and refined reasoning. It is only what is plain and evident that is tangible by their gross conceptions. Admitting, therefore, that the criminality of persisting to follow the dictates of conscience in matters of religion were capable of demonstration, it would remain a very improper object of punishment, because the evidence of its criminality could never be generally understood. The guilt of the sufferer would always be considered as very equivocal, and the sentiments of the community [divided] between the condemnation of the persecuted party and the government. From this will naturally follow two parties in the state, influenced with the most vehement mutual resentment and antipathy, and all the combustible materials already collected are liable to be kindled by the sparks of religious contention. Have not religious persecutions been almost invariably the harbinger of civil wars, alarming commotions, and awful calamities? Persecution in matters of religion raises up the very hydra it is meant to destroy. The only plausible ground on which it can be defended is the danger to the state accruing from a diversity of opinion on matters of the first importance, and the necessity, in order to secure public tranquillity, to establish uniformity of opinion But when persecutions are adopted, the lawfulness of those very measures becomes a subject of contention as interesting as the dissensions it is designed to terminate.

The question of the claim to liberty of conscience is surely a question of this kind.

* * * * * * * * * *

* * * * * * * * * *

SHORT STATEMENT

OF THE

REASONS

FOR

CHRISTIAN IN OPPOSITION TO PARTY COMMUNION.

[PUBLISHED IN 1826.]

PREFACE.

After having discussed so largely in some former publications the question of strict communion, that is, the prevailing practice in the Baptist denomination of confining their fellowship to members of their own community, it was not my intention to trouble the public with the subject any further, not having the least ambition for the last word in controversy. But it has been suggested to me that it would not be difficult to condense the substance of the argument within a smaller compass, so as to render it accessible to such as have neither the leisure nor the inclination to peruse a large performance. It has been my endeavour to cut off every thing superfluous, and without doing injury to the merits of the cause, to present the reasoning which sustains it in a concise and popular form: how far I have succeeded must be left to the judgment of the reader.

I would only remark here, that all I have seen and heard concurs to convince me that the practice of strict communion rests almost entirely on *authority*, and that were the influence of a few great names withdrawn it would sink under its own weight. Among those of recent date none has been more regarded than that of the late venerable Fuller; and as he left a manuscript on this subject to be published after his death, he is considered as having deposed his dying testimony in its favour. That he felt some predilection to a practice to which he had been so long accustomed, and whose propriety was very rarely questioned in his early days, is freely admitted; but that he all along felt some hesitation on the subject, and that his mind was not completely made up, I am induced to believe from several circumstances. First, from the fact of his proposing himself to commune at Cambridge with the full knowledge of there being Pedobaptists present. Secondly, from a conversation which passed many years ago between him and the writer of these lines. In reply to his observation, that we act precisely on the same principle with our Pedobaptist brethren, since they also insist on baptism as an essential prerequisite to communion, it was remarked that this was a mere *argumentum ad hominem*, it might serve to silence the clamours of those Pedobaptists who while they adhered to that principle charged us with bigotry; but that still it did not touch the merits of the question, since a previous inquiry occurs, whether any thing more is requisite to communion on scriptural grounds than a vital union with Christ; his answer was, *When mixed communion is placed on that footing, I never yet ventured to attack it.* Hence I am compelled to consider his posthumous tract rather as a trial of what might be adduced on that side of the controversy with a view to provoke further inquiry, than the result of deliberate and settled conviction. Be this as it may, great as his merits were, he was but a man, and as such liable to err even on subjects of much greater importance. All I wish is, that without regard to human names or authorities, the matter in debate may be entirely determined by an unprejudiced appeal to reason and Scripture.

The prevalence of this disposition to bow to authority and to receive opinions upon trust is strikingly illustrated by the following anecdote. A highly respected friend of mine, on asking one of his deacons, a man of primitive piety and integrity, what objections he had to mixed communion, he replied with great simplicity that he had two—in the first place, Mr. Fuller did not approve of it; and in the next, the Scripture declares that "he who pulls down a hedge a serpent shall bite him." The good man very properly placed that reason first which carried the greatest weight with it.

In short, there is a certain false refinement and subtlety in the argument for strict communion which would never occur to a plain man who was left solely to the guidance of Scripture. In common with almost every other error, it derived its origin from the public teachers of religion, and with a change of sentiment in them it will gradually disappear; nor will it be long ere our churches will be surprised that they suffered themselves to be betrayed by specious but hollow sophistry into a practice so repulsive and so impolitic.

Amicus Plato, amicus Socrates, sed magis amica veritas.

OCTOBER 7 1826.

A SHORT STATEMENT.

It is admitted by all denominations of Christians, with the exception of one, that the sacrament of the Lord's Supper is of perpetual obligation, and that it was designed by its Founder for one of the principal indications and expressions of that fraternal affection which ought to distinguish his followers. Though the communion of saints is of larger extent, comprehending all those sentiments and actions by which Christians are especially united, the joint participation of this right is universally acknowledged to constitute an important branch of that communion. So important a part has it been considered, that it has usurped the name of the whole; and when any dispute arises respecting the terms of communion, it is generally understood to relate to the terms of admission to the Lord's table.

Whether all real Christians are entitled to share in this privilege, whether it forms a part of that spiritual provision which belongs to the whole family of the faithful, or whether it is the exclusive patrimony of a sect, who (on the ground of their supposed imperfection) are authorized to repel the rest, is the question which it is my purpose in the following pages briefly and calmly to discuss.

The first conclusion to which we should naturally arrive would probably favour the more liberal system; we should be ready to suppose that he who is accepted of Christ ought also to be accepted of his brethren, and that he whose right to the thing signified was not questioned possessed an undoubted right to the outward sign. There are some truths which are so self-evident that a formal attempt to prove them has the appearance of trifling, where the premises and the conclusion so nearly coincide that it is not easy to point out the intermediate links that at once separate and connect them. Whether the assertion that all sincere Christians are entitled to a place at the Lord's table is of that description will more clearly appear as we advance; but I must be permitted to say, that a feeling of the kind just mentioned has occasioned the greatest difficulty I have experienced in this discussion.

It is well known that a diversity of sentiment has long subsisted in this country in relation to the proper subjects of baptism, together with the mode of administering that rite. While the great body of the Christian world administer baptism to infants, and adopt the practice of sprinkling or pouring the sacramental water, there are some who contend that baptism should be confined to those who are capable of understanding the articles of the Christian religion, or, in other words, to adults, and that the proper mode is the immersion of the whole body. They who maintain the last of these opinions were formally designated by the appellation of *Anabaptists;* but as that term implied that they assumed a right of *repeating* baptism, when in reality their only reason for baptizing such as had been sprinkled in their infancy was, that they looked upon the baptism of infants as a mere human invention, the candour of modern times has changed the invidious appellation of Anabaptist to the more simple one of Baptist.

It is not my intention to attempt the defence of that class of Christians, though their views are entirely in accordance with my own; one consequence, however, necessarily results. We are compelled by virtue of them to look upon the great mass of our fellow-christians as *unbaptized.* On no other ground can we maintain our principles or justify our conduct. Hence it has been inferred, too hastily in my opinion, that we are bound to abstain from their communion, whatever judgment we may form of their sincerity and piety. Baptism, it is alleged, is, under all possible circumstances, an indispensable term of communion; and however highly we may esteem many of our Pedobaptist brethren, yet, as we cannot but deem them *unbaptized,* we must of necessity consider them as disqualified for an approach to the Lord's table. It is evident that this reasoning rests entirely on the assumption that baptism is invariably a necessary condition of communion—an opinion which it is not surprising the Baptists should have embraced, since it has long passed current in the Christian world, and been received by nearly all denominations of Christians. The truth is, it has never till of late become a practical question, nor could it while all parties acknowledged each other's baptism. It was only when a religious denomination arose whose principles compelled them to deny the validity of any other baptism besides that which they themselves practised, that the question respecting the relation which that ordinance bears to the Lord's Supper could have any influence on practice. But a doctrine which can have no possible influence on practice is received with little or no examination; and to this must be imputed the facility with which it has been so generally admitted that baptism must necessarily and invariably precede an admission to the Lord's table. The wide circulation, however, of this doctrine ought undoubtedly to have the effect of softening the severity of censure on that conduct (however singular it may appear) which is its necessary result: such is that of the great majority of the Baptists in confining their communion to those whom they deem baptized; wherein they act precisely on the same principle with all other Christians, who assume it for granted that baptism is an essential preliminary to the reception of the sacrament. The point on which they differ is the nature of that institution, which we place in immersion, and of which we suppose rational and accountable agents the only fit subjects; this opinion, combined with the other generally received one, that none are entitled to receive the Eucharist but such as have been baptized, leads inevitably to the practice which seems so singular and gives so much offence—the restricting of communion to our own denomination. Let it be admitted that baptism is under all circumstances a necessary condition of church-fellowship, and it is impossible for the Baptists to act otherwise. That their practice in this particular is harsh and illiberal is freely admitted, but it is the infallible consequence of the opinion generally entertained respecting communion, conjoined with their peculiar views of the baptismal rite. The recollection of this may suffice to rebut the ridicule and silence the clamour of those who loudly condemn the Baptists for a proceeding which, were they but to change their opinion on the subject of baptism, their own principles would compel them to adopt. They both concur in a common principle, from which the practice deemed so offensive is the necessary result.

Considered as an *argumentum ad hominem*, or an appeal to the avowed principles of our opponents, this reasoning may be sufficient to shield us from that severity of reproach to which we are often exposed, nor ought we to be censured for acting upon a system which is sanctioned by our accusers. Still it leaves the real merits of the question untouched; for the inquiry remains open, whether baptism *is* an indispensable prerequisite to communion; in other words, whether they stand in such a relation to each other that the involuntary neglect of the first incurs a forfeiture of the title to the last.

The chief, I might say the only, argument for the restricted plan of communion is derived from the example of the apostles and the practice of the primitive church. It is alleged, with some appearance of plausibility, that the first duty enjoined on the primitive converts to Christianity was to be baptized, that no repeal of the law has taken place since, that the apostles uniformly baptized their converts before they admitted them to the Sacrament, and that during the first and purest ages the church knew of no members who had not submitted to that rite; and that consequently in declining a union with those who, however estimable in other respects, we are obliged to consider as *unbaptized*, we are following the highest precedents, and treading in the hallowed steps of the inspired teachers of religion. Such in a few words is the sum and substance of their reasoning who are the advocates of strict communion; and as it approaches with a lofty and imposing air, and has prevailed with thousands to embrace what appears to me a most serious error, we must bespeak the reader's patience while we endeavour to sift it to the bottom, in order to expose its fallacy.

Precedent derived from the practice of inspired men is entitled to be regarded as *law* in exact proportion as the spirit of it is copied and the *principle* on which it proceeds is acted upon. If, neglectful of these, we attend to the letter only, we shall be betrayed into the most serious mistakes, since there are a thousand actions recorded of the apostles in the government of the church which it would be the height of folly and presumption to imitate. Above all things, it is necessary before we proceed to found a rule of action on precedent, carefully to investigate the circumstances under which it occurred and the reasons on which it was founded. The apostles, it is acknowledged, admitted none to the Lord's Supper but such as were previously baptized; but under what circumstances did they maintain this course? It was at a time when a mistake respecting the will of the Supreme Legislator on the subject of baptism was impossible; it was while a diversity of opinion relating to it could not possibly subsist, because inspired men were at hand, ready to remove every doubt and satisfy the mind of every honest inquirer. It was under circumstances that must have convicted him who declined compliance with that ordinance of wilful prevarication, and stubborn resistance to the delegates and representatives of Christ, who commissioned them to promulgate his laws, with an express assurance that "whoever rejected them rejected him, and whoever received them received him," and that to refuse to obey their word exposed the offender to a severer doom than was allotted to Sodom and Gomorrah.* Their instructions were too plain to be mistaken, their authority too sacred to be contemned by a professor of Christianity without being guilty of daring impiety. In such a state of things, it may be asked, How could they have acted differently from what they did? To have received into the church men who disputed their inspiration and despised their injunctions would have been to betray their trust, and to renounce their pretensions as the living depositaries of the mind of Christ: to have admitted those who, believing their inspiration, yet refused a compliance with their orders, would have let into the church the most unheard-of licentiousness, and polluted it by incorporating with its members the worst of men. Neither of these could be thought of, and no other alternative remained but to insist as a test of sincerity on a punctual compliance with what was known and acknowledged as the apostolic doctrine. "We are of God," says St. John: "he that knoweth God heareth us; he that is not of God heareth not us; hereby we know the spirit of truth and the spirit of error."† In short, the apostles refused to impart the external privileges of the church to such as impugned their authority or contemned their injunctions, which whoever persisted in the neglect of baptism at that time and in those circumstances must necessarily have done.

But in declining the communion of modern Pedobaptists, however eminent their piety, there is really nothing analogous to their method of proceeding. The resemblance fails in its most essential features. In repelling an unbaptized person from their communion, supposing such a one to have presented himself, they would have rejected the violator of a known precept; he whom we refuse is at most chargeable only with mistaking it. The former must either have neglected an acknowledged precept, and thus evinced a mind destitute of principle, or he must have set the authority of the apostles at defiance, and thus have classed with parties of the worst description. Our Pedobaptist brethren are exposed to neither of these charges: convince them that it is their duty to be baptized in the method which we approve, and they stand ready, many of them at least we cannot doubt stand ready, to perform it; convince them that it is a necessary inference from the correc‘

* Matt. x. 14, 15 † 1 John iv. 6.

interpretation of the apostolic commission, and they will without hesitation bow to that authority.

The most rigid Baptist will probably admit, that however clear and irresistible the evidence of his sentiments may appear to himself, there are those whom it fails to convince, and some of them at least illustrious examples of piety; men who would tremble at the thought of deliberately violating the least of the commands of Christ or of his apostles; men whose character and principles consequently form a striking contrast with those of the persons whom it is allowed the apostles would have repelled. But to separate ourselves from the best of men because the apostles would have withdrawn from the worst, to confound the broadest moral distinctions by awarding the same treatment to involuntary and conscientious error which they were prepared to inflict on stubborn and wilful disobedience, is certainly a very curious method of following apostolic precedent. "The letter killeth," says St. Paul, "the spirit maketh alive." Whether the contrariety of these was ever more strongly marked than by such a method of imitating the apostles, let the reader judge.

For the clearer illustration of this point let us suppose a case. A person proposes himself as a candidate for admission to a Baptist church. The minister inquires into his views of the ordinance of baptism, and respectfully asks whether he is convinced of the divine authority of the rite which was administered to him in his infancy. He confesses he is not; that on mature deliberation and inquiry he considers it as a human invention. On his thus avowing his conviction, he is urged to confess Christ before men, by a prompt compliance with what he is satisfied is a part of his revealed will: he hesitates, he refuses, alleging that it is not essential to salvation, that it is a mere external rite, and that some of the holiest of men have died in the neglect of it. Here is a parallel case to that of a person who should have declined the ordinance of baptism in primitive times; and in entire consistence with the principles which we are maintaining, we have no hesitation in affirming that the individual in question is disqualified for Christian communion. To receive him under such circumstances would be sanctioning the want of principle, and pouring contempt on the Christian precepts. Yet the conduct we have now supposed would be less criminal than to have shrunk from baptism in the apostolic age, because the evidence by which our views are supported, though sufficient for every practical purpose, is decidedly inferior to that which accompanied their first promulgation: the utmost that we can pretend is a very high probability; the primitive converts possessed an absolute certainty. Now since we are prepared to visit an inferior degree of delinquency to that which would have ensured the rejection of a candidate by the apostles with the same severity, how preposterous is it to charge us with departing from apostolical precedent! In the same circumstances, or in circumstances nearly the same, we are ready instantly to act the same part: let the circumstances be essentially varied, and our proceeding is proportionably different. The apostles refused the communion of such, and such only, as were insincere, "who held the truth in unrighteousness," avowing their conviction of one system and acting upon another: and wherever similar indications display themselves we do precisely the same. They admitted the weak and erroneous, providing their errors were not of a nature subversive of Christianity; and so do we. They tolerated men whose sentiments differed from their own, providing they did not rear the standard of revolt by a deliberate resistance to the only infallible authority; and such precisely is the course we pursue. We bear with those who mistake the dictates of inspiration in points which are not essential; but with none who wilfully contradict or neglect them. In the government of the church, as far as our means of information reach, the immediate ambassadors of Christ appear to have set us an example of much gentleness and mildness, to have exercised a tender consideration of human imperfection, and to have reserved all their severity for a contumacious rejection of their guidance and disdain of their instructions. And wherever these features appear, we humbly tread in their steps; being as little disposed as they to countenance or receive those who impugn their inspiration or censure their decisions.

They were certainly strangers to that scheme of ecclesiastical polity which proposes to divide the mystical body of Christ into two parts, one consisting of such as enjoy communion with him, the other of such as are entitled to commune with each other. In no part of their writings is the faintest vestige to be discerned of that state of things of which our opponents are enamoured, where a vast majority of sincere Christians are deemed disqualified for Christian fellowship, and while their pretensions to acceptance with God and a title to eternal life are undisputed, are yet to be kept in a state of seclusion from the visible church. Had they in any part of their epistles appeared to broach such a doctrine,—had they lavished high encomiums on the faith and piety of those with whom they refused to associate at the Lord's Supper, our astonishment at sentiments so singular and so eccentric would have been such, that scarcely any conceivable uniformity of manuscripts or of versions could have accredited the passages that contained them. That the primitive church was composed of professed believers, and none debarred from its privileges but such whose faith was essentially erroneous or their character doubtful, is a matter of fact which appears on the very surface of the inspired records, and was probably never called in question, in any age or country, until an opposite principle was avowed and acted upon by the modern Baptists, who appropriate its title and its immunities to themselves, while with strange inconsistency they proclaim their conviction that the persons whom they exclude are indisputably in possession of its interior and spiritual privileges. For this portentous separation of the internal from the outward and visible privileges of Christianity,—for confining the latter to a mere handful of such as have "obtained like precious faith with themselves," in vain will they seek for support in the example of the apostles. They repeatedly and earnestly warn us against resting in external advantages, and of the danger of substituting the outward sign for the inward and spiritual grace: but never give the slightest intimation of the possibility of possessing the first, without being entitled to the last. The assertion of such an opinion, and the practice founded upon it, the reader will at once perceive, is a departure from the precedent and example of the earliest age which it would be difficult to parallel.

In opposition, however, to all that has been urged to show the obvious disparity between the two cases, our opponents still reiterate the cry, The apostles did not tolerate the omission of baptism, and therefore we are not justified in tolerating it! But is the omission of a duty to be judged of in relation to its moral quality, without any regard to circumstances, without any consideration whether it be voluntary or involuntary, whether it proceed from perversity of will or error of judgment, from an erroneous interpretation of our Lord's precepts or a contempt of his injunctions; and supposing our Pedobaptist brethren to be sincere and conscientious, is there any resemblance between them and those whom the apostles, it is allowed, would have repelled, except in the mere circumstance of their being both unbaptized, the one because they despised the apostolic injunctions, the other because they mistake them? The former (supposing them to have existed at all) must have been men over whose conscience the word of God had no power; the latter tremble at his word, and are restrained from following our example by deference to his will. If such opposite characters are the natural objects of a contrary state of feeling, they must be equally so of a contrary treatment; nor can any thing be more preposterous than to confound them together, under the pretence of a regard to apostolic precedent. Our treatment of mankind should undoubtedly be the expression of our feelings, and regulated by our estimate of their character. Strict communion prescribes the contrary; it sets the conduct and the feelings at variance, and erects into a duty the mortification of our best and holiest propensities.

The discipline of the church, as prescribed by Christ and his apostles, is founded on principles applicable to every age and to every combination of events to which it is liable, in a world replete with change, where new forms of error, new modes of aberration from the paths of rectitude and truth, are destined to follow in rapid and unceasing succession. Among these we are compelled to enumerate the prevailing notions of the Christian world on the subject of baptism—an error which, it is obvious, could have no subsistence during the age of the apostles. Here then arises a new case, and it becomes a matter of serious inquiry how it is to be treated. It plainly cannot be decided by a reference to apostolic precedent, because nothing of this kind then existed, or could exist. The precept which enjoined the baptism of new converts might be resisted, but it could not be mistaken, and therefore no inference can be drawn from the treatment which it is admitted the apostles would have assigned to wilful disobedience, that is applicable to the case of involuntary error. The only method of arriving at a satisfactory conclusion is, to consider how they conducted themselves towards sincere though erring Christians, together with the temper they recommend us to cultivate towards such as labour under mistakes and misconceptions not inconsistent with piety. Without expecting a specific direction for the regulation of our conduct in this identical particular, which would be to suppose the error in question *not* new, it is quite sufficient if the general principle of toleration which the New Testament enjoins is found to comprehend the present instance.

If action be founded on conviction, as it undoubtedly is in all well-regulated minds, we are as much obliged to mould our sentiments into an agreement with those of the apostles as our conduct: inspired precedents of thought are as authoritative as those of action. The advocates of strict communion are clamorous in their demand that, in relation to church-fellowship, we should treat all Pedobaptists exactly in the same manner as the apostles would have treated unbaptized persons in their day. But must we not for the same reason *think* the same of them? This, however, they disclaim as much as we do: they are perfectly sensible, nor have they the hardihood to deny, that the difference is immense between a conscientious mistake of the mind of Christ on a particular subject, and a deliberate contempt or neglect of it. Who can doubt that the apostles would be the first to feel this distinction; and as they would undoubtedly, in common with all conscientious persons, regulate their conduct by their sentiments, that, could they be personally consulted, they would recommend a correspondent difference of treatment? To sum up the argument in a few words: Nothing can be more hollow and fallacious than the pretension of our opponents that they are guided by inspired precedent, for we have no precedent in the case; in other words, we have no example of the manner in which they conducted themselves towards such as fell into an error on the subject of baptism; the Scriptures make no allusion to such an error which attaches at present to many most tenacious of its authority, humbly submissive to its dictates, and deeply imbued with its spirit; to men, in a word, of the most opposite character to those who may be supposed, in consequence of setting light by the authority of inspired teachers, to have neglected baptism in the first ages.

Thus much may suffice for apostolic precedent. There is still one more view of the subject to which the attention of the reader is requested for a moment. It remains to be considered whether there is any *peculiar connexion* between the two ordinances of baptism and the Lord's Supper, either in the nature of things or by divine appointment, so as to render it improper to administer the one without the other. That there is no *natural* connexion is obvious. They were instituted at different times and for different purposes; baptism is a mode of professing our faith in the blessed Trinity, the Lord's Supper as a commemoration of the dying love of the Redeemer: the former is the act of an individual, the latter of a society. The words which contain our warrant for the celebration of the Eucharist convey no allusion to baptism whatever: those which prescribe baptism carry no anticipative reference to the Eucharist. And as it is demonstrable that John's baptism was a separate institution from that which was enacted after our Lord's resurrection, the Lord's Supper is evidently *anterior* to baptism, and the original communicants consisted entirely of such as had not received that ordinance. To all appearance, the rites in question rest on independent grounds. But perhaps there is a *special* connexion between the two, arising from *divine appointment.* If this be the case, it will be easy to point it out. Rarely, if ever, are they mentioned together, and on no occasion is it asserted, or insinuated, that the validity of the sacrament depends on the previous observation of the baptismal ceremony. That there was such a connexion between circumcision and the passover we learn from the explicit declaration of Moses, who asserts that "no uncircumcised person shall eat thereof." Let a similar prohibition be produced in the present instance, and the controversy is at an end.

The late excellent Mr. Fuller, in a posthumous pamphlet on this subject, laboured hard to prove an *instituted* connexion between the two ordinances; but his conclusion from the premises is so feeble and precarious, that we strongly suspect his own mind was not fully made up on the subject. His reasoning is certainly very little adapted to satisfy an impartial inquirer. The whole performance appears more like an experiment of what might be advanced in favour of a prevailing hypothesis, than the result of deep and deliberate conviction.

On this point our opponents are at variance with each other; Mr. Kinghorn roundly asserts that baptism has no more connexion with the Lord's Supper than with *every other part* of Christianity. Thus what Mr. Fuller attempts to demonstrate as the main pillar of his cause, Mr. Kinghorn abandons without scruple. What a fortunate position is that to which men may arrive who proceed in the most opposite directions—a sort of mental antipodes, which you will reach with equal certainty whether you advance by the east or by the west. From the title of Mr. Kinghorn's book, which is, "Baptism a Term of Communion," we should be led to expect that it was his principal object to trace some *specific* relation which these rites bear to each other. No such thing: he denies there is any such relation: baptism, he declares, is no otherwise connected with the Lord's Supper than it is with every other part of Christianity. But on his hypothesis it is essential to the Eucharist, and consequently it is essential to every part of Christianity; so that the omission of it, from whatever cause, is such an error in the first concoction, that it vitiates every branch of religion, disqualifies for all its duties, and incurs the forfeiture of all its privileges. This is the statement of a man who makes loud professions of attachment to our Pedobaptist brethren; nor can he escape from this strange dilemma but by retracing his steps, and taking his stand with Mr. Fuller on a supposed *instituted* relation between the two ordinances. Meanwhile, it is instructive to observe in what inextricable labyrinths the acutest minds are entangled which desert the high road of common sense in pursuit of fanciful theories.

Having cleared the way, by showing that Scripture precedent, properly interpreted, affords no countenance or support to strict communion, the remaining task is very easy. For nothing can be more evident than that the whole genius of Christianity is favourable to the most cordial and affectionate treatment of our fellow-christians. To love them fervently, to bear with their imperfections, and cast the mantle of forgiveness over their infirmities is to fulfil the law of Christ. A schism in his mystical body is deprecated as the greatest evil, and whatever tends to promote it is subjected to the severest reprobation. "Now I beseech you, by the name of the Lord Jesus," is the language of St. Paul, "that ye all speak the same thing, and that there be no divisions among you; but that ye be perfectly joined together in the same mind and in the same judgment. For it has been declared unto me, by them who are of the house of Chloe, that there are contentions among you. Now this I say, that every one of you saith, I am of Paul, and I of Apollos, and I of Cephas, and I of Christ. Is Christ divided? was Paul crucified for you? or were ye baptized in the name of Paul?" In applying these and innumerable other passages of similar import to the point under discussion, two questions occur. First, Are our Pedobaptist brethren a part of the mystical body of Christ? or, in other words, Do they form a portion of that church which he has purchased by his precious blood? If they are not, they are not in a state of salvation, since none can be in that state who are not vitally united to Christ. The Bible acknowledges but two classes into which the whole human race is distributed, the church and the world; there is no intermediate condition; whoever is not of the first necessarily belongs to the last. But the advocates for strict communion are loud in their professions of esteem for pious Pedobaptists, nor is there any thing they would more resent than a doubt of their sincerity in that particular. The persons whom they exclude from their communion are then, by their own confession, a part of the flock of Christ, a portion of his mystical body, and of that church which he has bought with his blood.

The next question is, Whether a formal separation from them on the account of their imputed error amounts to what the Scripture styles *schism?* Supposing one part of the church at Corinth had formally severed themselves from the other, and established a separate communion, allowing those whom they had forsaken, at the same time, the title of sincere Christians, would this have been considered as a *schism?* That it would is demonstrable from the language of St. Paul, who accuses the Corinthians of having *schisms** among them, though they never dreamed of forming a distinct and separate communion. If they are charged with schism on account of that spirit of contention and that alienation of their affections from each other which merely tended to an open rupture, how much more would they have incurred that censure had they actually proceeded to that extremity? *Schism*, in its primitive and literal sense, signifies the breaking of a substance into two or more parts, and when figuratively applied to a body of men it denotes the division of it into parties; and though it may be applied to such a state of contention as consists with the

* The original word rendered divisions is σχισματα, *schisms*

preservation of external union, it is most eminently applicable to a society whose bond of union is dissolved, and where one part rejects the other from its fellowship. If there is any meaning in terms, this is schism in its highest sense. The great apostle of the gentiles illustrates the union of the faithful by that which subsists between the members of the natural body. "Now ye are the body of Christ, and members in particular." He shows, in a beautiful and impressive manner, that the several members have each his distinct function, and are pervaded by a common sympathy, with the expressive design "that there be no schism in the body." But when one part of the Christian church avowedly excludes another from their communion, when they refuse to unite in the most distinguishing branch of social worship, and hold themselves in a state of seclusion, they virtually say to the party thus repelled, "We have no need of thee;" they cut themselves off from the body, and are guilty of a schism so open and conspicuous that none can fail to perceive it. How is it possible for them to evade the conclusion to which this reasoning conducts us, unless they are prepared to deny the claim of the Pedobaptists to be regarded as the members of Christ, or place them in some intermediate station between the world and the church? But the language of the New Testament, which uniformly identifies the objects of the Divine favour with the members of Christ's church, is directly opposed to such a fiction. "He loved the *church*, and gave himself for it, that he might sanctify and cleanse it, by the washing of water through the Word, that he might present it to himself a glorious church, not having spot, or wrinkle, or any such thing."

It deserves the serious consideration of our opponents, that they are *contending* for that schism in the body of Christ against which he so fervently prayed, so anxiously guarded, and which his apostles represent as its greatest calamity and reproach. "The glory," said our Lord, "which thou hast given me, I have given them, that they may be one, even as we are one; I in them, and thou in me, that they may be made perfect in one; that the world may know that thou hast sent me, and hast loved them as thou hast loved me." Here it cannot be doubted that our Pedobaptist brethren are comprehended in this prayer because our Lord declares it was preferred, not merely for the disciples then existing, but for those also who should hereafter believe through their word, adding, "that they *all* may be one, as thou, Father, art in me, and I in thee, that they also may be one in us, that the world may believe that thou hast sent me." In these words we find him praying for a visible union among his disciples—such a union as the world might easily perceive; and this he entreats in behalf of them all, that they *all* may be one. The advocates of strict communion plead for a visible *disunion;* nor will it avail them to reply that they cultivate a fraternal affection towards Christians of other denominations, while they insist on such a visible separation as must make it apparent to the world that they are *not* one. Internal sentiments of esteem are cognizable only by the Searcher of hearts; external indications are all that the world has to judge by; and so far are they from exhibiting these, that they value themselves in maintaining such a position towards their fellow-christians as confounds them, in a very important point, with infidels and heathens. If a rent and division in the body is pregnant with so much scandal and offence as the Scriptures represent it, if the spirit of love and concord is the distinguishing badge of the Christian profession, it is surprising it has never occurred to them, that by insisting on such a separation as was unheard of in the primitive times, every approach to which is denounced in Scripture as a most serious evil, they are acting in direct opposition to the genius of the gospel and the solemn injunctions of its inspired teachers. What degree of criminality may attach to such a procedure it is not for us to determine; but we have no hesitation in affirming, that it is most abhorrent from the intention of the Head of the church, and miserably compensated by that more correct view of the ordinance of baptism which is alleged in its support. "Charity is the end of the commandment," "the fulfilling of the law;" and since the religion of Christ is not ceremonial, but vital, and consists less in correct opinions and ritual observances than in those graces of the Spirit which are the "hidden man of the heart," it deserves serious consideration whether so palpable a violation of the unity of the church is not more offensive in the eyes of Him who "tries the hearts and the reins," than an involuntary mistake of a ceremonial precept.

Here we must be allowed once more to recur to the vain boast of a scrupulous adherence to the example of the apostles (the futility of which has, I trust, been sufficiently demonstrated), and request our opponents to reflect for a moment on their essential deviation in this particular. Say, did the apostles refuse the communion of good men? Did they set the example of dividing them into two classes, a qualified and a disqualified class; and while they acknowledged the latter were objects of the Divine favour equally with themselves, enjoin on their converts the duty of disowning them at the Lord's table? Are any traces to be discovered in the New Testament of a society of *Purists*, who, under the pretence of superior illumination on one subject, kept themselves aloof from the Christian world, excluding from their communion myriads of those whom they believed to be heirs of salvation? Did they narrow their views of church-fellowship, as Mr. Kinghorn avows is the case of the modern Baptists, to the purpose of holding up to view *one neglected truth?* On this plan, as many separate communions will be witnessed as there are varieties of religious taste and predilection, while each fancies it perceives some neglected duty or some truth not rendered sufficiently prominent, till almost every inquiry will give birth to some solitary and antisocial sect. The direct tendency of such a principle is not merely to annihilate the unity of the church, but to contract the heart, to narrow the understanding, and, in the room of "holding forth the word of life," to invest every petty speculation and minute opinion with the dignity of a fundamental truth.

The revival or propagation of some one particular truth being the avowed object of their union, the members of such a society will almost inevitably attach to it an undue importance; and as their attention will be chiefly directed towards that in which they differ from others, and in which they are conceived to excel, it will be a miracle if they escape a censorious, conceited, disputatious spirit. While their constitution is founded not so much on a separation from the world as from the church, they will be almost irresistibly tempted to transfer to the latter a large portion of the associations and feelings of which the former is the proper object.

How refreshing is it to turn from these rigid and repulsive principles to the contemplation of the generous maxims of the New Testament! "Him that is weak in the faith," says St. Paul, "receive ye, not to doubtful disputations;"* and after illustrating his meaning by adducing examples of various diversities of sentiment among his converts, he proceeds to inculcate the most perfect mutual toleration. It is observable that the differences of opinion which he specifies related to the obligation of certain positive institutes, to which, though abrogated by the new dispensation, part of the church adhered, while its more enlightened members understood and embraced the liberty with which Christ had made them free. "We that are strong ought to bear the infirmities of the weak, and not to please ourselves." A moment's attention to the connexion will convince the reader that the term *weak* in both these passages denotes persons whose conceptions are erroneous; for the inspired writer is not adverting to the different degrees of conviction with which the same truths are embraced, but to a palpable difference of judgment. Thus far the case here decided is precisely similar to that under present discussion: our difference from the Pedobaptists turns on the nature and obligation of a positive institute. The error of which St. Paul enjoined the toleration consisted in adhering to certain ceremonies which had been abrogated; the error with which we are concerned consists in mistaking a ceremony which is still in force. Neither of the ancient nor of the modern error is it pretended that they are fundamental, or that they endanger the salvation of those who hold them. Thus far they stand on the same footing, and the presumption is that they ought to be treated in the same manner. Before we come to this conclusion, however, it behooves us to examine the *principle* on which the apostle enjoins toleration, and if this is applicable in its full extent to the case of our Pedobaptist brethren, no room is left for doubt. The *principle* plainly is, that the error in question was not of such magnitude as to preclude him who maintained it from the favour of God. "Let not him who eateth despise him who eateth not; and let not him who eateth not judge him who eateth; *for God hath received him.* Who art thou that judgest another man's servant? To his own master he standeth or falleth. Yea, he shall be holden up; *for God is able to make him stand.*" In the same manner, in the next chapter of the same epistle, after reminding the strong that it is their duty to bear the infirmities of the weak, he adds, "Wherefore, receive ye one another, as Christ also hath received us, to the glory of the Father." If such is the reason assigned for mutual toleration, and it is acknowledged to be a sufficient one,

* Rom. xiv. 1.

which none can deny without impeaching the inspiration of the writer, it is as conclusive respecting the obligation of tolerating every error which is consistent with a state of salvation as if that error had been mentioned by name; and as few, if any, are to be met with who doubt the piety of many Pedobaptists, it not only justifies their reception, but renders it an indispensable duty. Nothing can be more futile than the attempt to turn aside the edge of this reasoning by remarking that there is no mention of baptism, and that this is not the subject of which St. Paul is treating, as though the Bible contained no general principles, no maxims of universal application, but that precise directions must be found for every possible emergence that in the lapse of ages may occur. Were it constructed upon this plan, the Bible must be infinitely more voluminous than the statutes at large. It is composed on one widely different; it gives general rules of action, broad principles, leaving them to be applied under the guidance of sound discretion; and wherever it has decided a doubtful question, accompanied with an express statement of the principle on which the decision is founded, such explanation has all the force of an apostolic canon, by which we are bound to regulate our conduct in all the variety of cases to which it applies. Hence we have only one alternative, either to deny that those who differ from us on the subject of baptism are accepted of God, or to receive them into fellowship on exactly the *same ground* and on the *same principle* that Paul enjoined the toleration of sincere Christians.

Before I dismiss this part of the subject, on which the patience of the reader has been severely tasked, I must beg leave to notice a striking inconsistence in the advocates of strict communion. Nothing is more certain than that the communion of saints is by no means confined to one particular occasion, or limited to one transaction, such as that of assembling around the Lord's table; it extends to all the modes by which believers recognise each other as the members of a common head. Every expression of fraternal regard, every participation in the enjoyments of social worship, every instance of the unity of the Spirit exerted in prayer and supplication or in acts of Christian sympathy and friendship, as truly belongs to the communion of saints as the celebration of the Eucharist. In truth, if we are strangers to communion with our fellow-christians on other occasions, it is impossible for us to enjoy it there; for the mind is not a piece of mechanism which can be set a-going at pleasure, whose movements are obedient to the call of time and place. Nothing short of an habitual sympathy of spirit, springing from the cultivation of benevolent feeling and the interchange of kind offices, will secure that reciprocal delight, that social pleasure, which is the soul of Christian communion. Its richest fruits are frequently reserved for private conference, like that in which the two disciples were engaged in their way to Emmaus, when their hearts burned within them, while the Lord opened to them the Scriptures. When they take sweet counsel together as they go to the house of God in company, when they bear each other's burthens, weep with those that weep, and rejoice with them that rejoice; say, have

Christians no mutual fellowship? Is it not surprising that, losing sight of such obvious facts, our opponents always reason on the subject of communion as though it related merely to the sacrament? In every other particular they act just as we do.

However our opponents may deviate from Scripture, let them at least be consistent with themselves, and either follow out their own principles to their just consequence by withholding from the members of other denominations every token of fraternal regard, or freely admit them to the Lord's table. As the case stands at present, their mode of proceeding is utterly untenable. In a variety of instances they indulge themselves in those acts of communion with Pedobaptists which are peculiar to Christians: they frequently make them their mouth in addressing the Deity; they exchange pulpits; and even engage their assistance in exercises intended as a preparation for the Eucharist; and after lighting the flame of devotion at their torch, they most preposterously turn round to inform them that they are not worthy to participate. It would be difficult to convince a stranger to our practice that it were possible to be guilty of such an absurdity. Is the observance of an external rite, let me ask, a more solemn part of religion than addressing the Majesty of heaven and of earth? And shall we depute *him* to present our prayers at His footstool who would defile a sacrament by his presence? Suppose them to relax from their rigour, and to admit pious Pedobaptists to their fellowship, to what would it amount? To nothing more than a public acknowledgment of their union to Christ and their interest in his benefits; and as they fully acknowledge both, why scruple to do it at the table of their common Lord. Why select an ordinance designed for the commemoration of the dying love of the Redeemer as the signal for displaying the banners of party; and by reviving the remembrance of differences elsewhere consigned to oblivion, give the utmost publicity to dissensions which are the reproach of the church and the triumph of the world?

The only colour invented to disguise this glaring inconsistency is so pure a logomachy, that it is difficult to speak of it with becoming gravity. They remind us, forsooth, that the expressions of Christian affection in praying and preaching for each other are not church acts, as though there were some magic in the word *church* that could change the nature of truth, or the obligations of duty. If it is our duty to recognise those as fellow-christians who are really such, what is there in the idea of a church that should render it improper there? If the church is "the pillar and ground of truth," it is the proper place for the fullest disclosure of its secrets; and if Christians are under an obligation to love each other with a pure heart, fervently, its organization can never have been designed to contract the heart, by confining the movements and expressions of charity within narrower limits. The duty of churches originates in that of the individuals of which they consist, so that when we have ascertained the sentiments and principles which ought to actuate the Christian in his private capacity, we possess the standard to which the practice of churches should be uniformly adjusted.

Nor is it in this particular only that the persons whose opinions we are controverting are betrayed into lamentable inconsistency. Their concessions on another branch of the subject lay them open to the same imputation. They acknowledge that many Pedobaptists stand high in the favour of God; enjoy intimate communion with the Redeemer; and would, on their removal hence, be instantaneously admitted to glory. Now, it seems the suggestion of common sense that the greater includes the less, that they who have a title to the most sublime privileges of Christianity, the favour of God, the fellowship of Christ, and the hope of glory, must be unquestionably entitled to that ordinance whose sole design is to prepare us for the perfect fruition of these blessings. To suppose it possible to have an interest in the great redemption without being allowed to commemorate it, that he may possess the substance who is denied the shadow, and though qualified for the worship of heaven, be justly debarred from earthly ordinances, is such an anomaly as cannot fail to draw reprobation on the system of which it is the necessary consequence. Men will, ere long, tremble at the thought of being more strict than Christ, more fastidious in the selection of the members of the church militant than he is in choosing the members of the church triumphant.

Hitherto our attention has been occupied in stating the arguments in favour of mixed communion, and replying to the objections to that practice. It is but justice to the subject and to the reader, before we close the discussion, to touch on another topic.

In every inquiry relating to Christian duty, our first concern should undoubtedly be to ascertain the will of the Supreme Legislator; but when this has been done to our satisfaction, we may be allowed to examine the practical tendency of different systems, the effect of which will be to confirm our preference of that course of action which we have found most consonant with the oracles of truth. We are far from resting the merits of our cause on the basis of expedience; we are aware that whoever attempts to set the useful in opposition to the true is misled by false appearances, and that it behooves us, on all occasions, fearless of consequences, to yield to the force of evidence. But having, in the preceding pages, proved (we would hope to the satisfaction of the reader) that the practice of strict communion has no support from Scripture or reason, it cannot be deemed improper briefly to inquire into its tendency.

The first effect necessarily resulting from it is a powerful prejudice against the party which adopts it. When all other denominations find themselves lying under an interdict, and treated as though they were heathens or publicans, they must be more than men not to resent it; or if they regard it with a considerable degree of apathy, it can only be ascribed to that contempt which impotent violence is so apt to inspire. We are incompetent judges of the light in which our conduct appears to those against whom it is directed, but the more frequently we place ourselves in their situation the less will be our surprise at the indications of alienation and disgust which they may evince. The very appellation of Baptist, together with the tenets by which it is designated, become associated with the idea of bigotry; nor will it permit the mind which entertains that prejudice to give an impartial attention to the evidence by which our sentiments are supported. With mingled surprise and indignation they behold us making pretensions which no other denomination of Protestants assumes, placing ourselves in an attitude of hostility towards the whole Christian world, and virtually claiming to be the only church of Christ upon earth. Fortified as it is by its claims to antiquity and universality, and combining in its exterior whatever is adapted to dazzle the imagination and captivate the senses, there is yet nothing in the Church of Rome that has excited more indignation and disgust than this very pretension. What then must be the sensation produced, when, in the absence of all these advantages, a sect comparatively small and insignificant erects itself on a solitary eminence, from whence it repels the approach of all other Christians! The power of prejudice to arrest the progress of inquiry is indeed to be lamented; nothing could be more desirable than that every opinion should, in the first instance, be judged of by its intrinsic evidence, without regard to the conduct of the persons who embrace it; but the strength and independence of mind requisite to such an effort is rather to be admired than expected. There are few who enter on the investigation of theological questions in that elevated state; secret antipathies or predilections will be sure to instil their venom, and obscure the perception of truth and the suggestions of reason.

By the stern rejection of the members of all other denominations until they have embraced our distinguishing tenets, what do we propose to effect—to intimidate or to convince? We can do neither. To intimidate is impossible, while there are others far more numerous than ourselves ready to receive them with open arms. The hope of producing conviction by such an expedient is equally groundless and chimerical, since conviction is the result of evidence, and no light whatever can be pretended to be conveyed by interdicting their communion, unless it be that it manifests our intolerance. We propose to extirpate an error, and we plant a prejudice; and instead of attempting to soften and conciliate the minds of our opponents, we inflict a stigma. Professing serious concern that the ordinance of baptism, as it was practised in the first ages, is fallen into neglect, we attempt to revive an unpopular rite, by a mode of procedure which, without the remotest tendency towards the removal of error or the elucidation of truth, answers no other purpose than to make *ourselves* unpopular.

By this preposterous conduct, we do all in our power to place our Pedobaptist brethren beyond the reach of conviction. Since it is unreasonable to expect, however attractive the ministry, that a pious Pedobaptist will statedly attend where he must despair of ever becoming a member, and of enjoying the privileges to which every serious person is supposed to aspire; he attaches himself, as a necessary consequence, to a connexion in which there is no such impediment, but where he is certain of hearing nothing but what will foster his prejudices and confirm his error. Thus he is excluded from the only

P 2

connexion where the arguments for adult baptism are stated, and is exposed to the constant operation of an opposite species of instruction. The practice which we are reprobating is nearly equivalent to an inscription over the door, Let none but Baptists enter within these walls—an admirable expedient, truly, for diffusing the Baptist sentiments; about as rational as to send a man from London to Constantinople to study the evidences of Christianity!

Mr. Kinghorn is delighted with this separation of the Baptists from other denominations in the offices of devotion, avowing it as his opinion that no Pedobaptist can without great impropriety statedly attend the ministry of one of our denomination. If we may judge from what he has written on this subject, he appears less anxious to promote and extend the peculiar tenets of the Baptists, than to preserve inviolate their sacred seclusion and solitude. His sentiments on this subject will probably remind the poetical reader of Gray's beautiful description of the bird of night, which

> ———— "does to the moon complain
> Of such as, wandering near her secret bowers,
> Molest her ancient, solitary reign."

Whatever his intention may be, it must be obvious that by the policy he recommends, of keeping the Baptists and Pedobaptists entirely separated from each other, even as hearers of the word, he is strengthening the barriers of party, building up a middle wall of partition, and by cutting off the channels of communication and the means of conviction, resigning both to the entire and unmitigated operation of their respective systems. Is it possible to imagine any thing more calculated to stifle inquiry, to render the public mind stationary, and to perpetuate our divisions to the end of the world? From him who was really solicitous to extend the triumphs of truth we should expect nothing would be more abhorrent than such a system; he surely would leave nothing unattempted to break down the rampart of prejudice; and by making the nearest approaches to his opponents consistent with truth, avail himself of all the advantages which a generous confidence seldom fails to bestow, for insinuating his sentiments and promoting his views.

Of the tendency of mixed communion to promote a more candid inquiry into our principles, it is scarcely possible to doubt; whether it would have the effect of rapidly extending the Baptist denomination *as such* is less certain. For were that practice universally to prevail, the mixture of Baptists and Pedobaptists in Christian societies would probably ere long be such, that the appellation of Baptist might be found not so properly applicable to churches as to individuals, while some more comprehensive term might possibly be employed to discriminate the views of collective bodies. But what then? Are we contending for names, or for things? If the effect of a more liberal system shall be found to increase the number of those who return to the primitive practice of baptism, and thus follow the Lamb whithersoever he goeth, he must be possessed of a deplorable imbecility and narrowness of mind who will lament the disappearance of a name, especially when it is remembered that whenever just views on this subject shall become universal, the name by which we are at present distinguished will necessarily cease. An honest solicitude for the restoration of a divine ordinance to its primitive simplicity and purity is not merely innocent, but meritorious ; but if the ultimate consequence of such an improvement should be to merge the appellation of a party in that which is derived from the divine Founder of our religion, it is an event which none but a bigot will regret.

It were well, however, if the evil resulting from the practice of strict communion were confined to its effect on other denominations. If I am not much mistaken, it exerts a pernicious influence on our own. Were it consistent with propriety, it would be easy to adduce exceptions; individuals have come within the narrow range of my own observation whose temperament has been so happy, that they have completely surmounted the natural tendency of their principles, combining the greatest candour towards Pedobaptists with a conscientious refusal of their communion. Such instances however must, in the nature of things, be rare. Generally speaking, the adoption of a narrow and contracted theory will issue in a narrow and contracted mind. It is too much to expect that a habit of treating all other Christians as aliens from the fold of Christ, and unworthy of a participation of the privileges of his church, can be generally unaccompanied with an asperity of temper, a proneness to doubt the sincerity, to censure the motives, and depreciate the virtues of those whom they are accustomed to treat with so much rigour. Conceiving themselves to be a highly privileged class, as the only legitimate members of his church, they are almost inevitably exposed to think more highly of themselves than they ought to think; and founding their separation, not on that which distinguishes the followers of Christ from the world, but on a point in which Christians dissent from each other, they are naturally tempted to attach superlative importance to the grounds of difference.

The history of the present controversy affords a melancholy confirmation of these remarks; for the few who have ventured to appear on the liberal side of the question have, for the most part, been assailed by ungenerous insinuations and odious personalities. Their claim to be considered as Baptists is very reluctantly conceded, and the part they have taken has been imputed to the love of popularity, or to some still more unworthy motive. Some churches, in their zeal for strict communion, have even lost sight of their own principles, and substituted the doctrine opposed in these pages as a term of admission, instead of the ordinance of baptism. Others have refused the privilege of occasional communion to such as have been known to sit down with Pedobaptists at the Lord's table.

Leaving, however, to those to whom it may be more grateful the unwelcome office of exposing the infirmities of their brethren, let me close this subject by one more remark. In addition to all the other reasons for retracing our steps, we may with great propriety allege the spirit of the times, the genius of the age, distinguished as it is, beyond all former example, by the union of Christians in the promotion of a common cause, and their merging their minor differences in the cultivation of great principles and the pursuit of great objects. Instead of confining themselves, each to the defence of his own citadel, they are sallying forth in all directions, in order to make a powerful and combined attack on the kingdom of darkness. The church of Christ, no longer the scene of intestine warfare among the several denominations into which it is cantoned and divided, presents the image of a great empire, composed of distant but not hostile provinces, prepared to send forth its combatants, at the command of its invisible sovereign, to invade the dominions of Satan and subdue the nations of the earth. The weapons of its warfare have already made themselves felt in the East and in the West; and wherever its banner is unfurled, it gathers around it, without distinction of name or sect, "the called, the chosen the faithful," who, at the heart-thrilling voice of Him whose "vesture is dipped in blood," and who goes forth "conquering and to conquer," rush to the field, unmindful of every distinction but that of his friends and foes, and too eager for the combat to ask any other question than "Who is on the Lord's side? Who?" And is it possible, after mingling thus their counsels, their efforts, their prayers, and standing side by side in the thickest of the conflict, in coming up "to the help of the Lord, to the help of the Lord against the mighty," for them to turn their backs on each other, and refuse to unite at that table which is covered with the memorials of his love and the fruits of his victory? No. As we hope when the warfare of time is accomplished, and these mortal tabernacles in which it is performed shall be dissolved, to celebrate a never-ending feast with Abraham, and Isaac, and Jacob, and the whole army of the faithful of every age, from every clime, and from every tongue, let us begin by feasting together here, to present a specimen of that harmony and love which are at once the element and the earnest of eternal felicity.

ARTICLES

PUBLISHED IN

THE ECLECTIC REVIEW.

REVIEW

OF

FOSTER'S ESSAYS.

Essays, in a Series of Letters, on the following Subjects:—On a Man's writing Memoirs of Himself; On Decision of Character; On the Application of the Epithet Romantic; On some of the Causes by which Evangelical Religion has been rendered less acceptable to Persons of cultivated Taste. By JOHN FOSTER. 2 vols. 12mo. 1805. 1 vol. 8vo. pp. 458. Seventh Edition, 1823.

THE authors who have written on human nature may be properly distinguished into two classes, the metaphysical and the popular. The former contemplate man in the abstract; and, neglecting the different shades of character and peculiarities of temper by which mankind are diversified, confine their attention to those fundamental principles which pervade the whole species. In attempting to explore the secrets of mental organization, they assume nothing more for a basis than a mere susceptibility of impression, whence they labour to deduce the multiplied powers of the human mind. The light in which they choose to consider man in their researches is not that of a being possessed already of the exercise of reason and agitated by various sentiments and passions, but simply as capable of acquiring them; and their object is, by an accurate investigation of the laws which regulate the connexion of the mind with the external universe, to discover in what manner they are actually acquired. They endeavour to trace back every mental appearance to its source. Considering the powers and principles of the mind as a complicated piece of machinery, they attempt to discover the *primum mobile*, or, in other words, that primary law, that ultimate fact which is sufficiently comprehensive to account for every other movement. This attention to the internal operations of the mind, with a view to analyze its principles, is one of the distinctions of modern times. Among the ancients scarcely any thing of this sort was known. Comprehensive theories and subtile disquisitions are not unfrequent in their writings; but they are chiefly employed for the illustration of different modes of virtue and the establishment of different ideas of the supreme good. Their most abstracted speculations had almost always a practical tendency. The schoolmen, indeed, were deeply immersed in metaphysical speculations. They fatigued their readers in the pursuit of endless abstractions and distinctions; but the design, even of these writers, seems rather to have been accurately to arrange and define the objects of thought than to explore the mental faculties themselves. The nature of particular and universal ideas, time, space, infinity, together with the mode of existence to be ascribed to the Supreme Being, chiefly engaged the attention of the mightiest minds in the middle ages. Acute in the highest degree, and endued with a wonderful patience of thinking, they yet, by a mistaken direction of their powers, wasted themselves in endless logomachies, and displayed more of a teasing subtlety than of philosophical depth. They chose rather to strike into the dark and intricate by-paths of metaphysical science than to pursue a career of useful discovery: and as their disquisitions were neither adorned by taste nor reared on a basis of extensive knowledge, they gradually fell into neglect when juster views in philosophy made their appearance. Still they will remain a mighty monument of the utmost which the mind of man can accomplish in the field of abstraction. If the metaphysician does not find in the schoolmen the materials of his work, he will perceive the study of their writings to be of excellent benefit in sharpening his tools. They will aid his acuteness, though they may fail to enlarge his knowledge.

When the inductive and experimental philosophy recommended by Bacon had, in the hands of Boyle and Newton, led to such brilliant discoveries in the investigation of matter, an attempt was soon made to transfer the same method of proceeding to the mind. Hobbes, a man justly infamous for his impiety, but of extraordinary penetration, first set the example; which was not long after followed by Locke, who was more indebted to his predecessor than he had the candour to acknowledge. His celebrated Essay has been generally considered as the established code of metaphysics. The opinions and discoveries of this great man have since been enriched by large accessions, and, on some points corrected and amended by the labours of Berkeley, Hume, Reid, and a multitude of other writers. Still there seems to be a principle of mortality inherent in metaphysical science, which sooner or later impairs the reputation of its most distinguished adepts. It is a circumstance worthy of remark, that there has never been a reputation of this kind which has continued with undiminished lustre through the revolutions of a century. The fame of Locke is visibly on the decline; the speculations of Malebranche are scarcely heard of in France; and Kant, the greatest metaphysical name on the continent. sways a doubtful sceptre amid a host of opponents. It is not our intention to inquire at large into the reason of the transitory fame acquired by this class of writers. Whether it be that the science itself rests on a precarious foundation; that its discoveries can never be brought to a decisive test; that it is too remote from the business of life to be generally interesting; that it does not compensate by its use for its defects in the fascinations of pleasure; and that it is not, like the intricacies of law, interwoven with the institutions of society: the fact itself is unquestionable. He who aspires to a reputation that shall survive the vicissitudes of opinion and of time, must think of some other character than that of a metaphysician.

Grand and imposing in its appearance, it seems to lay claim to universal empire, and to supply the measures and the criteria of all other knowledge; but it resembles in its progress the conquests of a Sesostris and a Bacchus, who overran kingdoms and provinces with ease, but made no permanent settlements, and soon left no trace of their achievements.

The case is very different with the popular writers, who, without attempting to form a theory or to trace their first elements, the vast assemblage of passions and principles which enter into the composition of man, are satisfied with describing him as he is. These writers exhibit characters, paint manners, and display human nature in those natural and affecting lights under which it will always appear to the eye of an acute and feeling observer. Without staying to inquire why it is that men think, feel, reason, remember,—are attracted by some objects or repelled by others,—they take them as they are, and delineate the infinitely various modifications and appearances assumed by our essential nature. From the general mass of human passions and manners they detach such portions as they suppose will admit of the most beautiful illustrations, or afford the most instructive lessons. Next to a habit of self-reflection, accompanied with an attentive survey of real life, writers of this kind are the best guides in the acquisition of that most important branch of knowledge, an acquaintance with mankind. As they profess to consider human nature under some particular aspect, their views are necessarily more limited than those of metaphysical writers; but if they are less extensive, they are more certain; if they occupy less ground, they cultivate it better. In the language of Bacon, "they come home to men's business and bosom." As they aim at the delineation of living nature, they can never deviate far from truth and reality without becoming ridiculous; while for the fidelity of their representations they appeal to the common sense of mankind, the dictates of which they do little more than imbody and adorn. The system of Locke or of Hartley, it is possible to conceive, may be exploded by the prevalence of a different theory; but it is absurd to suppose that the remarks on life and manners contained in the writings of Addison or of Johnson can ever be discredited by a future moralist. In the formation of a theory, more especially in matters so subtile and complicated as those which relate to the mind, the sources of error are various. When a chain of reasoning consists of many links, a failure of connexion in any part will produce a mass of error in the result, proportioned to the length to which it is extended. In a complicated combination, if the enumeration of particulars in the outset is not complete, the mistake is progressive and incurable. In the ideal philosophy of Locke, for example, if the sources of sensation are not sufficiently explored, or if there be, as some of the profoundest thinkers have suspected, other sources of ideas than those of sensation, the greater part of his system falls to the ground. The popular writers of whom we have been speaking are not exposed to such dangers. It is possible, indeed, that many particular views may be erroneous; but as their attention is continually turned to living nature, provided they be possessed of competent talents, their general delineations cannot fail of being distinguished by fidelity and truth. While a few speculative men amuse themselves with discussing the comparative merits of different metaphysical systems, these are the writers whose sentiments, conveyed through innumerable channels, form the spirit of the age; nor is it to be doubted that the Spectator and the Rambler have imparted a stronger impulse to the public mind than all the metaphysical systems in the world. On this account we are highly gratified when we meet with a writer who, to a vein of profound and original thought, together with just views of religion and of morals, joins the talent of recommending his ideas by the graces of imagination and the powers of eloquence. Such a writer we have the happiness of reviewing at present. Mr. Foster's name is probably new to most of our readers; but if we may judge from the production before us, he cannot long be concealed from the notice and applause of the literary world. In an age of mediocrity, when the writing of books has become almost a mechanical art, and a familiar acquaintance with the best models has diffused taste and diminished genius, it is impossible to peruse an author who displays so great original powers without a degree of surprise. We are ready to inquire by what peculiar felicity he was enabled to desert the trammels of custom, to break the spell by which others feel themselves bound, and to maintain a career so perfectly uncontrolled and independent. A cast of thought original and sublime, an unlimited command of imagery, a style varied, vigorous, and bold, are some of the distinguishing features of these very singular essays. We add with peculiar satisfaction, that they breathe the spirit of piety and benevolence, and bear the most evident indications of a heart deeply attached to scriptural truths. Though Mr. F. has thought fit to give to his work the title of "Essays, in a Series of *Letters*," the reader must not expect any thing in the epistolary style. They were written, the author informs us, in letters to a friend, but with a view to publication; and in their distinct development of a subject and fulness of illustration, they resemble regular dissertations rather than familiar epistles. We could have wished, indeed, that he had suppressed the title of Letters, as it may excite in the reader an expectation of colloquial ease and grace, which will not be gratified in the perusal. A little attention to this circumstance, though it might have impaired the regularity of their method, would have rendered them more fascinating. The subjects appear to us well chosen, sufficiently uncommon to afford scope for original remarks, and important enough to call forth the exertions of the strongest powers. They are the following: 1. On a Man's writing Memoirs of himself; 2. On Decision of Character; 3. On the Application of the Epithet Romantic; 4. On some of the Causes by which Evangelical Religion has been rendered less acceptable to Persons of cultivated Taste.

We shall endeavour to give our readers an idea of the general design of each of these essays; and to enable them, by a few extracts, to judge of the manner in which that design is executed

In the first essay, the author expatiates at large on the influence of external events in the formation of character. This influence he traces to four sources:—instruction, companionship, reading, and attention to the state and manners of mankind.

Among the many objects calculated to form the character and impress the heart, Mr. F. enumerates natural scenery; at the same time deploring that want of fancy and sensibility which often renders it productive of so little effect. The passage in which he adverts to this subject is so beautiful, that we cannot prevail on ourselves to withhold it from the reader. He will see at once that the writer has viewed nature with the eye of a poet, and has deeply imbibed the delicious enchantment which he so eloquently describes.

"It might be supposed that the scenes of nature, an amazing assemblage of phenomena, if their effect were not lost through familiarity, would have a powerful influence on all opening minds, and transfuse into the internal economy of ideas and sentiment something of a character and a colour correspondent to the beauty, vicissitude, and grandeur which continually press on the senses. On minds of genius they often have this effect; and Beattie's *Minstrel* may be as just as it is a fascinating description of such a spirit. But on the greatest number this influence operates feebly; you will not see the process in children, nor the result in mature persons. The charms of nature are objects only of sight and hearing, not of sensibility and imagination; and even the sight and hearing do not receive impressions sufficiently distinct or forcible for clear recollection; it is not, therefore, strange that these impressions seldom go so much deeper than the senses as to awaken pensiveness or enthusiasm, and fill the mind with an interior permanent scenery of beautiful images at its own command. This defect of fancy and sensibility is unfortunate amid a creation infinitely rich with grand and beautiful objects, which, imparting something more than images to a mind adapted and habituated to converse with nature, inspire an exquisite sentiment that seems like the emanation of a spirit residing in them. It is unfortunate, I have thought within these few minutes, while looking out on one of the most enchanting nights of the most interesting season of the year, and hearing the voices of a company of persons, to whom I can perceive that this soft and solemn shade over the earth, the calm sky, the beautiful stripes of cloud, the stars, and waning moon just risen, are things not in the least more interesting than the walls, ceiling, and candlelight of a room."—Vol. I. pp. 26, 27. Pp. 22, 23, *Seventh Edition.*

Towards the close of the essay, in tracing the steps by which some have arrived at the last stage of daring impiety, the denial of a God, the author evinces, in a masterly manner, the presumption of the atheist, and places the extreme absurdity of pretending to demonstrate the non-existence of a Deity in a light in which we do not remember to have seen it exhibited. Speaking of a pretended heroism attached to atheistic impiety, he adds:

"But, indeed, it is heroism no longer, if he *knows* that there is no God. The wonder then turns on the great process by which a man could grow to the immense intelligence that can know that there is no God. What ages and what lights are requisite for THIS attainment! This intelligence involves the very attributes of divinity, while a God is denied. For, unless this man is omnipresent, unless he is at this moment in every place in the universe, he cannot know but there may be in some place manifestations of a Deity by which even *he* would be overpowered. If he does not know absolutely every agent in the universe, the one that he does not know may be God. If he is not himself the chief agent in the universe, and does not know what is so, that which is so may be God. If he is not in absolute possession of all the propositions that constitute universal truth, the one which he wants may be that there is a God. If he cannot with certainty assign the cause of all that exists, that cause may be a God. If he does not know every thing that has been done in the immeasurable ages that are past, some things may have been done by a God. Thus, unless he knows all things, that is, precludes another Deity, by being one himself, he cannot know that the Being whose existence he rejects does not exist. But he must *know* that he does not exist, else he deserves equal contempt and compassion for the temerity with which he firmly avows his rejection, and acts accordingly." —Vol. I. pp. 60–62. Pp. 48, 49, *Seventh Edition.*

The next essay, *On Decision of Character*, appears to us superioi to the former. The subject is pursued with greater regularity, the conceptions are more profound, and the style is more chaste and classical. After placing in strong contrast the features of a decisive and of an irresolute character, he proceeds to analyze the elements of which the former is composed. Among these, he assigns the first place to a firm confidence in our own judgment; which, he justly observes, notwithstanding the general disposition of mankind to overrate their powers, is no common attainment. With those who are most disposed to think highly of their own abilities, it is common, when they arrive at the moment of action, to distrust their judgment; and, as the author beautifully expresses it, "their mind seems all at once placed in a misty vacuity, where it reaches round on all sides, and finds nothing to lay hold of." The next ingredient essential to decision of character is a state of cogent feeling, an intense ardour of mind, precluding indifference and delay.

In addition to these qualities, courage is required, without which, it is obvious that resolutions the most maturely formed, are liable to vanish at the first breath of opposition. In the remaining part of the essay, Mr. F. illustrates the influence of several circumstances of an external nature, which tend to form or to augment the quality of which he has been treating. The principal of these are *opposition*, *desertion*, and *success*. It would prolong this article too much to attempt to follow the author in these particulars: suffice it to remark, that under each of them will be found many just and important observations. He concludes with briefly recommending a discipline conducive to the attainment of a decisive character. He particularly insists on the propriety of inuring the mind to a habit of reasoning; and that not in a superficial and desultory manner, but by steadily following the train till we reach a legitimate conclusion.

We cannot dismiss this part of the work without presenting our readers with an extract from the character of Howard, whose virtues have been emblazoned by the gorgeous eloquence of Burke; but we are mistaken if they have ever been painted in a more masterly manner than in the following portrait:—

"In this distinction (*decision*) no man ever exceeded, for instance, or ever will exceed, the late illustrious Howard. The energy of his determination was so great, that if, instead of being habitual, it had been shown only for a short time on particular occasions, it would have appeared a vehement impetuosity; but by being unintermitted it had an equability of manner, which scarcely appeared to exceed the tone of a calm constancy, it was so totally the reverse of any thing like turbulence or agitation. It was the calmness of an intensity, kept uniform by the nature of the human mind forbidding it to be more, and by the character of the individual forbidding it to be less. The habitual passion of his mind was a measure of feeling almost equal to the temporary extremes and paroxysms of common minds: as a great river in its customary state is equal to a small or moderate one when swollen to a torrent. The moment of finishing his plans in deliberation, and commencing them in action, was the same. I wonder what must have been the amount of that bribe, in emolument or pleasure, that would have detained him a week inactive after their final adjustment. The law which carries water down a declivity was not more unconquerable and invariable than the determination of his feelings towards the main object. The importance of this object held his faculties in a state of excitement which was too rigid to be affected by lighter interests, and on which, therefore, the beauties of nature and of art had no power. He had no leisure feeling which he could spare, to be diverted among the innumerable varieties of the extensive scene which he traversed; all his subordinate feelings lost their separate existence and operation, by falling into the grand one. There have not been wanting trivial minds to mark this as a fault in his character But the mere men of taste ought to be silent respecting such a man as Howard; he is above their sphere of judgment. The invisible spirits who fulfil their commission of philanthropy among mortals do not care about pictures, statues, and sumptuous buildings; and no more did he, when the time in which he must have inspected and admired them would have been taken from the work to which he had consecrated his life.* The curiosity which he might feel was reduced to wait till the hour should arrive when its gratification should be presented by conscience, which kept a scrupulous charge of all his time, as the most sacred duty of that hour. If he was still at every hour, when it came, fated to feel the at ractions of the fine arts but the second claim, they might be sure of their revenge; for no other man

* Mr. Howard, however, was not destitute of taste for the fine arts. His house at Cardington was better filled with paintings and drawings than any other, on a small scale, that we ever saw —Rev.

will ever visit Rome under such a despotic consciousness of duty, as to refuse himself time for surveying the magnificence of its ruins. Such a sin against taste is very far beyond the reach of common saintship to commit. It implied an inconceivable severity of conviction that he had *one thing to do;* and that he who would do some great thing in this short life must apply himself to the work with such a concentration of his forces, as, to idle spectators, who live only to amuse themselves, looks like insanity. His attention was so strongly and tenaciously fixed on his object, that, even at the greatest distance, as the Egyptian Pyramids to travellers, it appeared to him with a luminous distinctness as if it were nigh, and beguiled the toilsome length of labour and enterprise by which he was to reach it. It was so conspicuous before him, that not a step deviated from the direction, and every movement and every day was an approximation. As his method referred every thing he did and thought to the end, and as his exertion did not relax for a moment, he made the trial, so seldom made—what is the utmost effect which may be granted to the last possible efforts of a human agent; and, therefore, what he did not accomplish, he might conclude to be placed beyond the sphere of mortal activity, and calmly leave to the immediate disposal of Providence."—Pp. 156–160. Pp. 125–128, *Seventh Edition.*

We have one remark to make before we conclude our review of this essay. We are a little apprehensive that the glowing colours in which the imagination of Mr. F. has painted an unyielding constancy of mind, may tend to seduce some of his readers into an intemperate admiration of that quality, without duly distinguishing the object to which it is directed, and the motives by which it is sustained. We give our author full credit for the purity of his principles; we are firmly persuaded that he is not to be classed among the impious idolaters of mental energy. But we could wish that he had more fully admonished his readers to regard resolution of character not as a virtue so much as the means of virtue—a mere instrument, that owes its value entirely to the purpose to which it is employed; and that wherever nature has conferred it, an additional obligation is imposed of purifying the principles and regulating the heart. It might at first view be thought impossible, as Mr. F. intimates, that men should be found who are as resolute in the prosecution of criminal enterprises as they could be supposed to be in the pursuit of the most virtuous objects. It is surely a melancholy proof of something wrong in the constitution of human nature, that a quality so important as that of energetic decision is so little under the regulation of principle; that constancy is so much more frequently to be seen in what is wrong than in what is right; and, in fine, that the *world* can boast so many more heroes than the *church.*

In the third essay, *On the Application of the Epithet Romantic*, Mr. Foster takes occasion to expose the eagerness with which terms of censure are adopted by men who, instead of calmly weighing the merits of an undertaking or a character, think it sufficient to express their antipathy by some opprobrious appellation. The epithet *romantic* holds a distinguished place in the vocabulary of contempt. If a scheme of action which it requires much benevolence to conceive and much vigour to execute be proposed, by many it will be thought completely exploded when they have branded it with the appellation of *romantic.* Thus selfishness and indolence, arraying themselves in the garb of wisdom, assume the pride of superiority when they ought to feel the humiliation of guilt. To imitate the highest examples, to do good in ways not usual to the same rank of life, to make great exertions and sacrifices in the cause of religion and with a view to eternal happiness, to determine without delay to reduce to practice whatever we applaud in theory, are modes of conduct which the world will generally condemn as romantic, but which this author shows to be founded on the highest reason. In unfolding the true idea of the *romantic*, as applicable to a train of sentiments or course of conduct, he ascribes whatever may be justly so denominated to the predominance of the imagination over the other powers. He points out the symptoms of this disease as apparent—in the expectation of a peculiar destiny, while the fancy paints to itself scenes of unexampled felicity,—in overlooking the relation which subsists between ends and means,—in counting upon casualties instead of contemplating the stated order of events,—and in hoping to realize the most momentous projects without any means at all, or by means totally inadequate to the effect. Some of the illustrations which the author introduces on this part of his subject are peculiarly happy. We are delighted to find him treating with poignant ridicule those superficial pretenders who, without disavowing any dependence on divine agency, hope to reform the world and to bring back a paradisiacal state by the mere force of moral instruction. For the prospect of the general prevalence of virtue and happiness we are indebted to revelation. We have no reason to suppose the minds of our modern infidels sufficiently elevated to have thought of the cessation of wars and the universal diffusion of peace and love, but for the information which they have obtained from the Scriptures. From these they derive the doctrine of a Millennium; and they have received it as they have done every thing else, only to corrupt it: for, exploding all the means by which the Scriptures have taught us to expect the completion of this event, they rely merely on the resources of reason and philosophy. They impiously deck themselves with the spoils of revelation, and take occasion from the hopes and prospects which she alone supplies, to deride her assistance and to idolize the powers of human nature. That Being who planted Christianity by miraculous interposition, and by the effusion of his Spirit produced such effects in the hearts of millions as afford a specimen and a pledge of an entire renovation, has also assured us that violence and injustice shall cease, and that *none shall hurt or destroy in all his holy mountain, because the earth shall be full of the knowledge of God.* But it seems revelation is to have no concern in this work; philosophy is to effect every thing; and we are to look to the Political Justice of Godwin and the Moral Code of Volney for that which Christians were so weak as to expect at the hand of Deity.

The conclusion which our author draws from the insufficiency of mere human agency to effect that great renovation in the character and condition of men which revelation teaches us to expect, is most just and consolatory. We should have been happy to transcribe the passage; but lest we should exceed our limits, we refer our readers to vol. II. pp. 87, 88. Pp. 244–247, *Seventh Edition.*

The last essay in these volumes attempts to assign *some of the causes that have rendered evangelical religion less acceptable to persons of cultivated taste.* This essay is the most elaborate. Aware of the delicacy and difficulty of his subject, the author seems to have summoned all the powers of his mind, to enable him to grasp it in all its extent, and to present it in all its force and beauty. This essay is itself sufficient, in our opinion, to procure the author a brilliant and lasting reputation.

It is proper to remind our readers, that in tracing the causes which have tended to produce in men of taste an aversion to evangelical religion, Mr. F. avowedly confines himself to those which are of a *subordinate* class, while he fully admits the *primary cause* to be that *inherent corruption* of nature which renders men strongly indisposed to any communication from heaven. We could, however, have wished that he had insisted on this more largely. The Scriptures ascribe the rejection of the gospel to one general principle: *the natural man receiveth not the things of God, neither can he know them, because they are spiritually discerned.* The peculiar doctrines of Christianity are distinguished by a spirit irreconcilably at variance with that of the world. The deep repentance it enjoins strikes at the pride and levity of the human heart. The mystery of an incarnate and crucified Saviour must necessarily confound the reason and shock the prejudices of a mind which will admit nothing that it cannot perfectly reduce to the principles of philosophy. The whole tenor of the life of Christ, the objects he pursued, and the profound humiliation he exhibited, must convict of madness and folly the favourite pursuits of mankind. The virtues usually practised in society, and the models of excellence most admired there, are so remote from that holiness which is enjoined in the New Testament, that it is impossible for a taste which is formed on the one to perceive the charms of the other. The happiness which it proposes in a union with God and a participation of the image of Christ, is so far from being congenial to the inclinations of worldly men, that it can scarcely be mentioned without exciting their ridicule and scorn. General speculations on the Deity have much to amuse the mind and to gratify that appetite for the wonderful which thoughtful and speculative men are delighted to indulge. Religion, viewed in this light, appears more in the form of an exercise to the understanding than a law to the heart. Here the soul expatiates at large, without feeling itself controlled or alarmed. But when evangelical truths are presented, they bring God so near, if we may be allowed the expression, and speak with so commanding a voice to the conscience, that they leave no alternative but that of submissive acquiescence or proud revolt. As men of taste are for the most part men of the world, not at all distinguished from others by a greater familiarity with religious ideas, these observations are applicable to them in their utmost extent.

Though we thought it right to suggest these hints, we wish not to be understood to convey any censure on Mr. F. for confining his attention principally to other topics. In discussing more fully and profoundly some of the subordinate causes which have come in aid of the primary one, to render men of cultivated taste averse to evangelical piety, we think he has rendered an important service to the public.

The first cause he assigns is that of its being the religion of many weak and uncultivated minds; in consequence of which it becomes inseparably associated in the conceptions of many with the intellectual poverty of its disciples, so as to wear a mean and degraded aspect. We regret that we cannot follow the author in his illustration of this topic. We must be content with observing, that he has exposed the weakness of this prejudice in a most masterly and triumphant manner.

The second cause which the author assigns as having had, in his opinion, a considerable influence in prejudicing elegant and cultivated minds against evangelical piety, is the peculiarity of language adopted in the discourses and books of its teachers, the want of a more classical form of diction, and the profusion of words and phrases which are of a technical and systematical cast.

We are inclined to think, with Mr. F., that the cause of religion has suffered considerably from the circumstance here mentioned. The superabundance of phrases appropriated by some pious authors to the subject of religion, and never applied to any other purpose, has not only the effect of disgusting persons of taste, but of obscuring religion itself. As they are seldom defined, and never exchanged for equivalent words, they pass current without being understood. They are not the vehicle, they are the substitute of thought. Among a certain description of Christians, they become by degrees to be regarded with a mystic awe, insomuch that if a writer expressed the very same ideas in different phrases he would be condemned as a heretic. To quit the magical circle of words, in which many Christians suffer themselves to be confined, excites as great a clamour as the boldest innovation in sentiment. Controversies which have been agitated with much warmth might often have been amicably adjusted, or even finally decided, could the respective partisans have been prevailed on to lay aside their predilection for phrases, and honestly resolve to examine their real import. In defiance of the dictates of candour and good sense, these have been obstinately retained, and have usually been the refuge of ignorance, the apple of discord, and the watchwords of religious hostility. In some instances the evil which we lament has sprung from a more amiable cause. The force and solemnity of devotional feelings are such, that they seem to consecrate every thing with which they have been connected; and as the bulk of pious people have received their religious impressions from teachers more distinguished for their simplicity and zeal than for comprehension of mind and copiousness of language, they learn to annex an idea of sanctity to that set of phrases with which they have been most familiar. These become the current language of religion, to which subsequent writers conform, partly perhaps from indolence, and partly from the fear of offending their brethren.

To these causes we may add the contentious and sectarian spirit of modern times, which has taught the different parties of Christians to look on one another with an unnatural horror, to apprehend contamination from the very phrases employed by each other, and to invent, each for itself, a dialect as narrow and exclusive as their whimsical singularities. But while we concur in the main with Mr. F. on this subject, we are disposed to think that he has carried his representations too far, both with respect to the magnitude of the abuse itself, and the probable advantages which would ensue on its removal. The repugnance of the human mind in its unenlightened state to the peculiarities of the Christian doctrine is such, that we have little hope of its yielding to the voice of the charmer, charm he never so wisely. Till it is touched and humbled by grace, we are apprehensive that it will retain its aversion, and not suffer itself to be cheated into an approbation of the gospel by any artifice of words. Exhibit evangelical religion in what colours you will, the worldly-minded and the careless will shrink from the obtrusion of unwelcome ideas. Cowper has become, in spite of his religion, a popular poet, but his success has not been such as to make religion popular; nor have the gigantic genius and fame of Milton shielded from the ridicule and contempt of his admirers that system of religion which he beheld with awful adoration.

In treating subjects properly theological, we apprehend great caution should be used not to deviate wantonly and unnecessarily from the phraseology of Scripture. The apostle tells us, that in preaching the gospel he did not use the enticing words of man's wisdom, but such words as the Holy Ghost taught him. We do not, indeed, contend that in the choice of *every* particular word or phrase he was immediately inspired; but we think it reasonable to believe that the unction which was on his heart, and the perfect illumination that he possessed, led him to employ such terms in the statement of the mysteries of Christianity as were better adapted than any other to convey their real import, which we are the more inclined to conclude, from observing the sameness of phraseology which pervades the writings of the apostles when they are treating on the same subject. As the truths which the revelation of the New Testament unfolds are perfectly original and transcendently important, it might naturally be expected that the communication of them would give birth to an original cast of phraseology, or, in other words, a steady adherence to certain terms, in order to render the ideas which they conveyed fixed, precise, and unchangeable.

In teaching the principles of every science, it is found necessary to select or invent terms which, though originally of a more lax signification are afterward restricted and confined *to one peculiar modification of thought*, and constitute the technical language of that science. Such terms are always capable of being defined (for mere words convey nothing to the mind); but to substitute a definition in their place would be tedious circumlocution, and to exchange the term itself for a different one would frequently lead to dangerous mistakes.

In the original elementary parts of a language there are, in truth, few or no synonymes; for what should prompt men, in the early period of literature, to invent a word that neither conveyed any new idea, nor enabled them to present an old one with more force and precision? In the progress of refinement, indeed, regard to copiousness and harmony has enriched language with many exotics, which are merely those words in a foreign language that perfectly correspond to terms in our own; as *felicity* for *happiness*, *celestial* for *heavenly*, and a multitude of others. Since, then, the nature of language is such that no two terms are exactly of the same force and import (except in the case last mentioned), we cannot but apprehend that dangerous consequences would result from a studied attempt to vary from the standard phraseology where the statement of doctrines is concerned, and that by changing the terms the ideas themselves might be changed or mutilated. In teaching a religion designed for the use and benefit of all mankind, it is certainly desirable that the technical words, the words employed in a peculiar and appropriate sense, should be few: but to fix and perpetuate the ideas, and to preserve *the faith once delivered to the saints* from the caprices of fancy and the dangers of innovation, it seems necessary that there should be some. We are inclined to think, that in inculcating Christian morality, and in appeals and addresses to the heart, a much greater latitude may be safely indulged than in the statement of *peculiar doctrines;* and that a more bold and varied diction, with a wider range of illustration and allusion than is usually employed, would often be attended with the happiest effect. Mr. Foster has given, in many parts of these volumes, beautiful specimens of what we intend.

With respect to the copious use of Scripture language, which Mr. F. condemns (in our opinion with too much severity) as giving an uncouth and barbarous air to theological books, we prefer a middle course; without applauding the excess to which it is carried by many pious writers, on the one hand, or wishing it to be kept so entirely apart as Mr. F. contends, on the other. To say nothing of the inimitable beauties of the Bible, considered in a literary view, which are universally acknowledged, it is the book which every devout man is accustomed to consult as the oracle of God; it is the companion of his best moments, and the vehicle of his strongest consolations. Intimately associated in his mind with every thing dear and valuable, its diction more powerfully excites devotional feelings than any other; and when temperately and soberly used, imparts an unction to a religious discourse which nothing else can supply. Besides, is there not room to apprehend that a studied avoidance of the Scripture phraseology, and a care to express all that it is supposed to contain in the forms of classical diction, might ultimately lead to a neglect of the Scriptures themselves, and a habit of substituting flashy and superficial declamation, in the room of the saving truths of the gospel? Such an apprehension is but too much verified by the most celebrated sermons of the French; and still more by some modern compositions in our own language, which usurp that title. For devotional impression, we conceive that a very considerable tincture of the language of Scripture, or at least such a colouring as shall discover an intimate acquaintance with those inimitable models, will generally succeed best.

It is impossible to establish a universal rule, since different methods are equally adapted to different purposes; and therefore we are willing to allow, with Mr. F., that where the fashionable and the gay are addressed, and the prejudices arising from a false refinement are to be conciliated, whatever in the diction might repel by an appearance of singularity should be carefully shunned. Accordingly, we equally admire, in *The Rise and Progress of Religion*, by Dr. Doddridge, and in *The Rural Philosophy* of Mr. Bates, the dexterity with which these excellent writers have suited their composition to their respective classes of readers. On the whole, let it once for all be remembered, that men of taste form a very small part of the community, of no greater consequence in the eyes of their Creator than others; that the end of all religious discourse is the salvation of souls; and that to a mind which justly estimates the weight of eternal things, it will appear a greater honour to have converted a sinner from the error of his way, than to have wielded the thunder of a Demosthenes, or to have kindled the flame of a Cicero.

We hasten to close this article, by making a few observations on the last cause which our author has assigned for the general distaste that persons of polite and elegant attainments usually discover towards evangelical religion. This is, the neglect and contempt with which it has been almost constantly treated by our fine writers; of whose delinquency, in this respect, the author takes a wide and extensive survey, exposing their criminality with a force of eloquence that has perhaps never before been exerted on this subject. Though his attention is chiefly directed to the influence of modern literature, yet, as the writings of the ancients, and especially of the poets, have had a powerful operation in forming the taste and sentiments of succeeding generations, he has extended his notice to these, and has made some most striking animadversions on the ancient authors of the epopœia, and particularly on Homer.

We must do justice to his intrepidity in venturing to attack the idol of all classical scholars; nor can he have failed to foresee the manner in which it will be attempted to be repelled. They will remind him, that the lawfulness of defensive war has seldom been called in question; that the one in which Homer's heroes were engaged was not only just, but meritorious, being undertaken to avenge a most signal affront and injury; that no subject could be more suited to the epic muse, either on account of its magnitude or the deep interest it excited; that having chosen it, the poet is to be commended for throwing into it all the fire of which it was susceptible; that to cherish in the breasts of youth a gallant and warlike spirit is the surest defence of nations; and that this spirit, under proper regulations, constitutes that θυμοειδής which Plato extols so highly in his republic, as the basis of a manly, heroic character. This, and much more than this, will be said: but when our Grecians have spent all their arrows, it will still remain an incontestable fact, that an enthusiastic admiration of the Iliad of Homer is but a bad preparation for relishing the beauties of the New Testament. What then is to be done? Shall we abandon the classics, and devote ourselves solely to the perusal of modern writers, where the maxims inculcated and the principles taught are little, if at all, more in unison with those of Christianity?—a fact which Mr. F. acknowledges and deplores. While things continue as they are, we are apprehensive, therefore, that we should gain nothing by neglecting the unrivalled productions of genius left us by the ancients, but a deterioration of taste, without any improvement in religion. The evil is not to be corrected by any partial innovation of this kind. Until a more Christian spirit pervades the world, we are inclined to think that the study of the classics is, on the whole, advantageous to public morals, by inspiring an elegance of sentiment and an elevation of soul which we should in vain seek for elsewhere.

The total inattention of the great majority of our fine writers to all the distinguishing features of the religion they profess, affords a most melancholy reflection. It has no doubt excited the notice of many, and has been deeply lamented; but it has never been placed in a light so serious and affecting as in the volumes before us. In the observations which our author makes on the Essay on Man, we are delighted and surprised to find at once so much philosophical truth and poetical beauty. His critique on the writings of Addison and Johnson evinces deep penetration; and as respects the former, is uncommonly impressive and important.

We take our leave of this work with sincere reluctance. For the length to which we have extended our review, the subject must be our apology. It has fared with us as with a traveller who passes through an enchanting country, where he meets with so many beautiful views and so many striking objects which he is loath to quit, that he loiters till the shades of the evening insensibly fall upon him. We are far, however, from recommending these volumes as faultless. Mr. F.'s work is rather an example of the power of genius than a specimen of finished composition: it lies open in many points to the censure of those minor critics, who, by the observation of a few technical rules, may easily avoid its faults without reaching one of its beauties. The author has paid too little attention to the construction of his sentences. They are for the most part too long, sometimes involved in perplexity, and often loaded with redundances. They have too much of the looseness of an harangue and too little of the compact elegance of regular composition. An occasional obscurity pervades some parts of the work. The mind of the writer seems at times to struggle with conceptions too mighty for his grasp, and to present confused masses, rather than distinct delineations of thought. This, however, is to be imputed to the originality, not the weakness of his powers. The scale on which he thinks is so vast, and the excursions of his imagination are so extended, that they frequently carry him into the most unbeaten track, and among objects where a ray of light glances in an angle only, without diffusing itself over the whole. On ordinary topics his conceptions are luminous in the highest degree. He places the idea which he wishes to present in such a flood of light, that it is not merely visible itself, but it seems to illumine all around it. He paints metaphysics, and has the happy art of arraying what in other hands would appear cold and comfortless abstractions, in the warmest colours of fancy. Without the least affectation of frivolous ornaments, without quitting his argument in pursuit of imagery, his imagination becomes the perfect handmaid of his reason, ready at every moment to spread her canvass and present her pencil. But what pleases us most, and affords us the highest satisfaction, is to find such talents enlisted on the side of true Christianity; nor can we help indulging a benevolent triumph at the accession of powers to the cause of evangelical piety, which its most distinguished opponents would be proud to possess

REVIEW

OF

CUSTANCE ON THE CONSTITUTION.

A concise View of the Constitution of England. By George Custance. *Dedicated by permission to William Wilberforce, Esq. M. P. for the County of York.* 12mo. pp. 474. Price 6*s*. bds. Kidderminster · Gower. London: Longman & Co. Hatchard. 1808

It were surely to be wished that every man had a competent acquaintance with the laws and constitution of the country to which he belongs. Patriotism is a blind and irrational impulse, unless it is founded on a knowledge of the blessings we are called to secure, and the privileges we propose to defend. In a tyrannical state it is natural for the ruling power to cherish political ignorance, which can alone reconcile men to the tame surrender of their natural rights. The diffusion of light and knowledge is very unfavourable to ill-founded pretensions of every sort, but to none more than the encroachments of arbitrary power and lawless violence. The more we explore the recesses of a dungeon the less likely are we to be reconciled to take up our residence in it. But the venerable fabric of the British constitution, our hereditary mansion, whether it be tried by the criterion of convenience or of beauty of ancient prescription or of practical utility, will bear the most rigid examination; and the more it is contemplated, will be the more admired.

The Romans were so conscious of the importance of imparting to the rising generation an early knowledge of their laws and constitution, that the contents of the twelve tables were committed to memory, and formed one of the first elements of public instruction. They were sensible that what lays hold of the mind at so early a period is not only likely to be long remembered, but is almost sure to command veneration and respect. We are not aware that similar attempts have been made to render the British youth acquainted with the principles of our admirable constitution, not inferior surely to that of the Roman republic; a defect in the system of education which the circumstances of the present crisis loudly call upon us to supply. When our existence as an independent nation is threatened, when unexampled sacrifices must be made, and perhaps the utmost efforts of patience and of persevering courage exerted for our preservation, an attachment to that constitution which is the basis of all our prosperity cannot be too zealously promoted, or too deeply felt. It is a just and enlightened estimate of the invaluable blessings that constitution secures, which alone can make us sustain our present burdens without repining, as well as prepare us for greater privations and severer struggles. For this reason we cannot but look upon the performance before us as a most seasonable publication. One cause of the attention of youth being so little directed to our national laws and constitution, in schools, is probably the want of suitable books. We have an abundance of learned and able writers on these subjects, but few, if any, that are quite adapted to the purpose we are now speaking of. Millar's is a very profound and original work; but it supposes a great deal of previous knowledge, without which it can be scarcely understood, and is in every view better adapted to aid the researches of an antiquary or the speculations of a philosopher than to answer the end of an elementary treatise. De Lolme's performance may be deemed more suitable; yet, able and ingenious as it is, it labours under some essential deficiencies, considered in the light of an elementary work. There is in it a spirit of refined speculation, an eagerness to detect and display latent, unthought-of excellences in the frame of government, which is very remote from the simplicity requisite in the lessons of youth. Of Blackstone's Commentaries it would be presumptuous in us to attempt an eulogium, after Sir William Jones has pronounced it to be the most *beautiful outline* that was ever given of any science. Nothing can exceed the luminous arrangement, the vast comprehension, and, we may venture to add from the best authorities, the legal accuracy of this wonderful performance, which in style and composition is distinguished by an unaffected grace, a majestic simplicity, which can only be eclipsed by the splendour of its higher qualities. Admirable, however, as these commentaries are, it is obvious that they are much too voluminous and elaborate to answer the purpose of an introduction to the study of the English constitution. We do, therefore, most sincerely congratulate the public on the appearance of a work which we can safely recommend as well fitted to supply a chasm in our system of public instruction. The book before us is, in every view, well adapted for the instruction of youth: the clear and accurate information it conveys upon a most important subject, and the truly Christian tincture of its maxims and principles, are well calculated to enlarge the understanding and improve the heart. We beg leave particularly to recommend it to the attention of schools, in which we conceive a general acquaintance with the laws and constitution of the country might be cultivated with much advantage, as forming a proper preparation for the active scenes of life. Legal provisions for the security of the best temporal interests of mankind are the result of so much collective wisdom and experience, and are so continually conversant with human affairs, that we know no study more adapted to invigorate the understanding, and at the same time to give a practical turn to its speculations. The close cohesion of its parts tends to make the mind severely argumentative, while its continual relation to the state of society and its su cessive revolutions fences it on the side of metaphysical abstraction and useless theories. What we look upon (for the reasons already mentioned) to be a most useful and interesting study at all times, we would earnestly recommend as an indispensable duty at the present crisis.

Of the merits of the work before us the public may form some judgment, when we inform them that it contains whatever is most interesting to the general reader in Blackstone, together with much useful information derived from Professor Christian, De Lolme, and various other eminent authors. Some will be ready to accuse the writer of having carried his partiality towards whatever is established too far; nor dare we say the charge is entirely unfounded. We are not disposed, however, to be severe upon him on this account. We wish to see the minds of our youth preoccupied with a strong bias in favour of our national institutions. We would wish to see them animated by a warm and generous enthusiasm, and to defer the business of detecting faults and exposing imperfections to a future period. Let us only be allowed to remark, that this policy should be temperately employed; lest the mind should suffer a revulsion, and pass, perhaps rather abruptly, from implicit admiration to the contrary extreme; lest, indignant at having been misled, it substitute general censure for undistinguishing applause.

We wish our author had, in common with Blackstone, expressed his disapprobation of the severity of the criminal code. The multiplicity of capital punishments we shall always consider as a reproach to the English nation; though, numerous as they are, they bear no proportion to what they would be, were the law permitted to take its course. The offences deemed capital by the common law are few; the sanguinary complexion of the criminal law, as it now stands, has arisen from the injudicious tampering of the legislature. To us it appears evident, that the *certainty* of punishment will restrain offenders more than its severity; and that when men are tempted to transgress, they do not weigh the emolument they had in view against the penalty awarded by law, but simply the probability of detection and punishment against that of impunity. Let the punishments be moderate, and this will be the most effectual means of rendering them certain. While nothing can exceed the trial by jury, and the dignified impartiality with which justice is administered, we are compelled to look upon the criminal code with very different emotions, and earnestly to wish it were carefully revised, and made more humane, simple, and precise.

As little can we concur with the author before us in the defence he sets up of the donation of pensions and sinecures, where there are no pretensions of personal merit or honourable services. Standing quite aloof from party politics, we must affirm, that to whatever extent such a practice exists, exactly in the same proportion is it a source of public calamity and disgrace. To look at it, as our author does, only in a pecuniary view, is to neglect the principal consideration. It is not merely or chiefly as a waste of public money that the granting of sinecures and pensions to the undeserving ought to be condemned; the venality and corruption it indicates and produces is its worst feature, and an infallible symptom of a declining state. With these exceptions, we have accompanied the author with almost uninterrupted pleasure, and have been highly gratified with the good sense, the extensive information, and the unaffected piety he displays throughout the work. Though a firm and steady churchman himself, he manifests a truly Christian spirit towards the Protestant dissenters; and so far from looking with an evil eye on the large toleration they enjoy, that he contemplates with evident satisfaction the laws on which that toleration is founded.

Of the style of this work it is but justice to say, that, without aspiring to any high degree of ornament, it is pure, perspicuous, and correct, well suited to the subject on which it is employed.

As a fair specimen of Mr. C's manner of thinking, we beg leave to lay before our readers the following just and appropriate remarks on *duelling*:—

"Deliberate duelling falls under the head of *express malice;* and the law of England has justly fixed the crime and punishment of murder upon both the principal and accessaries of this most unchristian practice. Nothing more is necessary with us to check this daring violation of all law, than the same firmness and integrity in the trial of duellists which so eminently distinguish an English jury on all other occasions.

"Perhaps it will be asked, What are *men of honour* to do, if they must not appeal to the pistol and the sword? The answer is obvious: if one *gentleman* has offended another, he cannot give a more indisputable proof of genuine courage, than by making a frank acknowledgment of his fault, and asking forgiveness of the injured party. On the other hand, if he have received an affront, he ought freely to forgive, as he hopes to be forgiven of God. And if either of the parties aggravate the matter by sending a challenge to fight, the other must not be a partaker of sin, if he would obey God rather than man.

"Still it will be said, that a *military* or *naval* man, at least, must not decline a challenge, if he would maintain the character of a man of courage. But is it not insulting the loyalty and good sense of the brave defenders of our laws, to imagine that they of all men must violate them to preserve their honour; since the king has expressly forbidden any military man to send a challenge to fight a duel, upon pain of being cashiered, if an officer; and of suffering corporal punishment, if a non-commissioned officer, or private soldier? Nor ought any officer or soldier to upbraid another for refusing a challenge, whom his majesty positively declares *he* considers as having only acted in obedience to his royal orders; and fully acquits of any disgrace that may be attached to his conduct.* Besides, what necessary connexion is there between the foolhardiness of one who risks the eternal perdition of his neighbour and of himself in an unlawful combat, and the

"* See Articles of War, sec 7."

patriotic bravery of him who, when *duty* calls, boldly engages the enemy of his king and country? None will dispute the courage of the excellent Colonel Gardiner, who was slain at the battle of Preston Pans, in the rebellion in 1745. Yet he once refused a challenge, with this dignified remark: 'I fear sinning, though I do not fear fighting.'* The fact is, that fighting a duel is so far from being a proof of a man's possessing *true* courage, that it is an infallible mark of his *cowardice*. For he is influenced by 'the fear of man,' whose praise he loveth more than the praise of God."

* "See Doddridge's Life of Colonel Gardiner, an interesting piece of biography, worthy the perusal of every officer in the army and navy."

REVIEW

OF

ZEAL WITHOUT INNOVATION.

PREFACE TO THE SECOND EDITION.

It was the opinion of some sincere friends of religion, that a republication of the following strictures might have its use in certain quarters, where the literary journal in which they first appeared may possibly not have extended. The writer of these remarks has nothing in view but the promotion of Christian charity, the vindication of calumniated innocence, and the counteraction of those insidious arts by which designing men are seeking to advance their personal interest, or those of a party, at the expense of truth and justice. How far the author here animadverted upon falls under this description, must be left to the decision of an impartial public. If it be thought that more commendation ought to have been given in the following strictures to those parts of the work which are confessedly unexceptionable, the writer must be allowed to remark, that the effect of what is good in the performance is entirely defeated by the large infusion of what is of an opposite quality. In appreciating the merits of a writer, the general tendency of his work should be principally regarded, without suffering the edge of censure to be abated by such a mixture of truth as only serves to give a safer and wider circulation to misrepresentation and falsehood.

It has been deemed a capital omission in the following critique, that no notice is taken of the author's illiberal treatment of the puritans. This omission arose partly from a wish to avoid prolixity, and partly from an apprehension it would lead to a discussion not perfectly relevant to the matter in hand. It would be no difficult matter to construct such a defence of the puritans as would leave this or any other author very little to reply; but to do justice to the subject would require a deduction of facts, and a series of arguments, quite inconsistent with the limits to which we are confined. To oppose assertion to assertion, and invective to invective, could answer no end but the reviving animosities which we should be happy to see for ever extinguished. The controversy between the puritans and their opponents turns entirely on these two questions:—Has any religious society, assuming the name of a church, a right to establish new terms of communion, distinct from those enjoyed by Christ and his apostles? Admitting they have such a right, ought these terms to consist in things which the imposers acknowledge to be indifferent, and the party on whom they are enjoined look upon as sinful? Is not this a palpable violation of the apostolical injunction, "Him that is weak in the faith receive ye, but not to doubtful disputations?" We are persuaded we speak the sentiments of some of the best men in the Church of England, when we assert that the basis of communion was made narrower at the Reformation than is consistent with the dictates of Christian charity or sound policy, and that the puritans were treated with a severity altogether unjustifiable. The author of Zeal without Innovation declares himself "dissatisfied with the trite remark that there were faults on both sides, when the guilt of aggression rests so clearly on the heads of the nonconformists." To infer their guilt as aggressors because they were the first to complain, is begging the question at issue. Before we are entitled to criminate them on this head, it is requisite to inquire into the *justice* of their complaints. They who first discover a truth, are naturally the first to impugn the opposite error. They who find themselves aggrieved are necessarily the first to complain. So that to attach culpability to the party which betrays the first symptoms of dissatisfaction, without further inquiry, is to confer on speculative error, and on practical tyranny, a claim to unalterable perpetuity—a doctrine well suited to the mean and slavish maxims inculcated by this writer. The learned Warburton was as little satisfied as himself with the trite remark of there being faults on both sides, but for an opposite reason. "It would be hard," he affirms, "to say who are most to blame; those who oppose established authority for things indifferent, or that authority which rigidly insists on them, and will abate nothing for the sake of tender, misinformed consciences: I say it would be hard to solve this, had not the apostle done it for us, where he says, 'We that are strong ought to bear the infirmities of the weak, *and not to please ourselves.*' 'I myself,' says he, 'do so, and all for the gospel's sake.' This is the man who tells us he had fought a good fight and overcome. And we may believe him; for in this contention, he is always the conqueror who submits."

When the question is fairly put, whether a tender conscience, admitting it to be erroneous, shall be forced, or the imposition of things confessedly indifferent be dropped, it can surely require but little sagacity to return a decisive answer. The arguments which induced Locke to give his suffrage in favour of the nonconformists, the reasons which prevailed on Baxter and on Howe to quit stations of usefulness in the church, and doom themselves to an unprofitable inactivity, will not easily be deemed light or frivolous. The English nation has produced no men more exempt from the suspicion of weakness or caprice than these.

Desirous of composing rather than inflaming the dissensions which unhappily subsist among Christians, we decline entering further on this topic, heartily praying, with the apostle, that "grace may be with *all* them that love our Lord Jesus Christ in sincerity."

REVIEW.

Zeal without Innovation: or, the Present State of Religion and Morals considered, with a View to the Dispositions and Measures required for its Improvement. To which is subjoined an Address to young Clergymen, intended to guard them against some prevalent Errors. 1808.

There are some works which require to be viewed only in a literary light. No important principles are discussed, nor any momentous interests at stake. When this is the case, nothing more is necessary than for a reviewer to exhibit the author's plan, and to give an impartial judgment on the ability with which it is executed. If the merit of the performance be very conspicuous, it is the less necessary to multiply words in order to show it; and if it have little or none, it need not be conducted to the land of forgetfulness with the pomp of criticism. For this reason the utility of periodical criticism may, in a literary view, be fairly questioned; as it seems like an attempt to anticipate the decision of the public, and prematurely to adjust those pretensions which, if left to itself, it will be sure to adjust in time with the most perfect impartiality. A reviewer may give a momentary popularity to what deserves to be forgotten, but he can neither withhold nor bestow a lasting fame. Cowper, we will venture to say, is not the less admired because the Critical Review, with its usual good taste and discernment, could discover in him no traces of poetic genius.

There are other works, which owe their importance more to the subjects on which they treat, and their tendency to inflame the prejudices and strike in with the humour of the public, than to any extraordinary ability. Their infection renders them formidable. They are calculated to increase the violence of an epidemic disease. The matter of contagion ought not to be slighted on account of the meanness of the vehicle by which it is transmitted. We are sorry to be under the necessity of classing the performance before us with works of that nature; but our conviction of its deserving that character must be our apology for bestowing a degree of attention upon it to which it is not otherwise entitled. The author's professed design is to present a view of the state of religion and morals, and to suggest such remedies as are best adapted to correct the disorder under which they languish. A more noble and important undertaking cannot be conceived. We have only to lament that in the pursuit of it he betrays so many mean partialities and ungenerous prejudices as utterly disqualify him from doing justice to the subject. While we would wish to give him credit for *some* portion of good intention, we are firmly convinced that had *his eye been single, his whole body had been* more *full of light.* In an attempt to trace the causes of degeneracy in religion and morals, and to point out the proper correctives, nothing is more requisite than a large and catholic spirit, totally emancipated from the shackles of party, joined with extensive knowledge and a discriminating judgment. . In the first of these qualities the author is lamentably deficient. He looks at every thing so entirely through the medium of party, that though he cannot be said to be absolutely blind, he is quite incapable of seeing afar off. His remarks are often shrewd,—such as indicate a mind awake and attentive to the scenes which have passed before him. He is sometimes acute, never comprehensive; accurate in details, with little capacity for tracing the consequences and unfolding the energy of general principles. While the title of the work leads us to expect his attention would be entirely directed to the best means of promoting the moral improvement of mankind, the watchful reader will perceive there are *subordinate objects* which he is at least equally solicitous to advance. There is a complication in his views, *a wheel within a wheel,* quite incompatible with simplicity of mind and perfect purity of intention. There appears too much reason to regard him as an artful, bigoted partisan, acting under the disguise of a philanthropist and a reformer. Severe as this censure may seem, we are persuaded our readers will acknowledge its justice when they are apprized of the leading statements and positions contained in this singular work.

The author sets out with descanting on the state of religion in this country, which he represents as very deplorable: in proof of this, he adduces, among other facts, the violation of the Christian Sabbath and the prevailing neglect of public worship. As these symptoms of degeneracy are not found in an equal degree among dissenters and Methodists, he is led by the course of his subject to notice the state of religion among them, where he acknowledges there is no room to complain of a deficiency of zeal. He does not affect to deny that their teachers exhibit the great truths of Christianity with energy and effect, and that much good has resulted from their labours. We should naturally suppose a pious man would here find ground for satisfaction, and that, however he might regret the mixture of error with useful efforts, he would rejoice to perceive that real and important good was done anywhere. It is but justice to him to let him convey his feelings on this subject in his own words.

"From the sad state of things represented in the preceding section, many turn with pleasure to what is passing among our separatists, whose places of worship generally exhibit a very different scene to our parish churches. Here there appears to be some life and effect. The officiating minister has not half-empty pews to harangue, but a crowded auditory 'hanging on his lips.' Whether, however, in what is now before us we shall find no cause of uneasiness, when all its circumstances are considered, admits of great doubt.

"It cannot be denied, that with all the fanaticism charged on separatists (and it is to be feared with great truth in some instances), many a profligate has been reclaimed, and much good in other ways has been done among the lower orders by the labours of their ministers. From these circumstances, and the known ignorance and dissoluteness of the times, many, without the least degree of adverse intention to our established church, have in the simplicity of their hearts concurred in forwarding the endeavours of the separatists. And hence it is that in all the more populous parts of the country, we see that multitude of dissenting chapels, which of late years has increased and is still increasing.

"To some good men, free from all prejudice against the Church of England, it is matter of no regret that the number of separatists increases, provided there be with this circumstance an increasing regard to Christianity. With such persons all consideration of forms and modes of worship is sunk in the greater importance of genuine faith and piety. But it enters not in the thoughts of such persons that 'tares may spring up with the wheat,' and that what at present has a good effect may operate to the production of something hereafter of a very different nature. Now such we conceive to be the nature of the case before us. We have reason to apprehend ill consequences from increasing separatism, with whatever zeal for important truths, and with whatever success in propagating them it be at present accompanied.

"And first, it may be observed that it goes to the annihilation of the established church as a national institution. The bulk of every newly-raised congregation of separatists is composed of persons educated within the pale of the Church of England. Of these many are heads of families, or likely to become so. By commencing dissenters, they and their posterity, however multiplied, are broken off from the national church. These detachments from the establishment, going on as they have done of late years, must consequently increase the number of those who prefer a differently constituted church; and these may in time amount to such a majority as to render it again a question with those in power, whether the Church of England shall any longer have the support of the state."—Pp. 14–17.

That the increase of dissenters, *in itself considered*, cannot be a pleasing circumstance to a conscientious churchman is certain; and if this is all the author means to say, he talks very idly. The true question evidently is, whether the good accruing from the labours of dissenters is a proper subject of congratulation, *although* it may be attended with this incidental consequence, an increased separation from the established church. In a word, is the promotion of genuine Christianity, or the advancement of an external communion, the object primarily to be pursued? Whatever excellence may be ascribed to our national establishment by its warmest admirers, still it is a human institution—an institution to which the first ages of the church were strangers, to which Christianity was in no degree indebted for its original success, and the merit of which must be brought to the test of utility. It is in the order of means. As an expedient devised by the wisdom of our ancestors for promoting true religion, it is entitled to support just as far as it accomplishes its end. This end, however, is found in some instances to be accomplished by means which are of a different description. A fire which threatens immediate destruction is happily extinguished before it has had time to extend its ravages; but it is extinguished by persons who have volunteered their services, without waiting for the engineers who act under the direction of the police. Here is *zeal*, but unfortunately accompanied with *innovation*, at which our author is greatly chagrined. How closely has he copied the example of St. Paul, who rejoiced that Christ was preached, though from envy and contention! With him the promulgation of Divine truth was an object so much at heart, that he was glad to see it accomplished even from the most criminal motives and by the most unworthy instruments. With our author, the dissemination of the same truth, by some of the best of men, and from the purest motives, is matter of lamentation and regret. It requires little attention to perceive he has been taught in a different school from the apostle, and studied under a different master.

The eternal interests of mankind are either mere chimeras, or they are matters of infinite importance; compared with which, the success of any party, the increase of any external communion whatever, is mere dust in the balance; and for this plain reason, that the promotion of these interests is the very end of Christianity itself. However divided good men may have been with respect to the propriety of legislative interference in the affairs of religion, the arguments by which they have supported their respective opinions have been uniformly drawn from the supposed tendency of such interference, or the contrary, to advance the moral improvement of mankind; and, supposing this to be ascertained, the superior merit of the system to which that tendency belongs was considered as decided. Viewed in this light, the problem is extensive, affording scope for much investigation; while the authority of religion remains unimpaired, and the disputants on each side are left at liberty to indulge the most enlarged sentiments of candour towards each other. Such were the principles on which Hooker and the ablest of his successors rested their defence of the established church. The high church party, of which Mr. Daubeny may be looked upon as the present leader, have taken different grounds. Their system is neither more nor less than popery, faintly disguised, and adapted to the meridian of England. The writer before us, without avowing the sentiments of Daubeny, displays nearly the same intolerance and bigotry, under this peculiar disadvantage, that his views want the cohesion of system, his bigotry the support of principle. This formal separation of the interests of the church from those of true religion must inevitably produce the most deplorable consequences. Will the serious and conscientious part of the public be led to form a favourable opinion of a religious community, by hearing it avowed by her champions that men had better be suffered eternally to perish than to find salvation out of her pale? Will they not naturally ask what those *higher ends* can be, in comparison of which the eternal welfare of a large portion of our fellow-creatures is deemed a trifle. Could such a spirit be supposed generally prevalent in the clergy of the established church, it would at once lose all that is sacred in their eyes, and be looked upon as a mere combination to gain possession of power and emolument under pretence of religion. We are mistaken if much mischief has not already accrued from the indulgence of this spirit. It has envenomed the ill qualities naturally generated by the domination of a party. It has produced serious injury to the church, by imboldening men to appear in her defence who bring nothing into the controversy but overweening pride, ceremonial hypocrisy, and priestly insolence. Haughty, contemptuous airs, a visible disdain of the scruples of tender consciences, and frequently of piety itself, except under one garb and fashion, have been too generally assumed by her champions. These features have given inexpressible disgust to pious and candid minds; hurt, as they well may be, to see a religious community, however numerous or respectable, continually vaunting itself, laying exclusive claims to purity and orthodoxy, and seeming to consider it as a piece of condescension to suffer any other denomination to subsist. They cannot dismiss it from their minds that humility is a virtue proper to a church as well as to an individual, and that ecclesiastical pride may happen to be as offensive to Heaven as pride of any other kind. In the Church of Rome these qualities have been ever conspicuous; but finding nothing of this sort, in an equal degree, in any other Protestant communion, and recollecting that "the lofty looks of men shall be humbled, and the haughtiness of men be made low," one naturally feels some apprehension that they may not pass unpunished, though they are found in the precincts of a cathedral.

Our author derives no satisfaction from the acknowledged success of dissenters in "turning sinners from the error of their way," from an apprehension that their success may eventually prove injurious to the establishment. He pretends to foresee, from this cause, a continual transfer of hearers from the church to the conventicle. We beg leave to ask the writer, how such a consequence can ensue, but from the superior zeal and piety of sectaries? To suppose that with only an *equal* share of these qualities they will be able to make successful inroads on the church, is to abandon the defence of the hierarchy altogether; since this is acknowledging a radical defect in the system, which operates as a dead weight on its exertions, and disqualifies it for maintaining its ground against rivals; that, in short, instead of being the most efficacious mode of exhibiting and impressing revealed truth, it is intrinsically weak and ineffectual. For that system must surely be acknowledged to be so which is incapable of interesting the people, and which, by rendering public worship less attractive, produces a general preference of a different mode. To suppose this to be the case is to suppose something essentially wrong, which should be immediately examined and corrected. On this supposition the men are acquitted, the system is arraigned. As this, however, is far from being the opinion of the author, the conclusion turns with irresistible force, that a permanent increase of dissenters can *only* arise from their superior piety and zeal. Now, these are really, in our opinion, qualities too valuable to be dispensed with, whatever interests they may obstruct. Regretting, deeply as we may, in common with our author, that they should have formed an alliance so unfortunate, we must still think it better, not only for their possessors, but for the world at large, for them to be found even here than to have no existence at all; and it is upon this point we are at issue with this *conscientious* reformer. For our parts, we are really so old-fashioned and puritanical, that we had rather behold men awakened and converted among dissenters and Methodists, than see them sleep the sleep of death in the arms of an establishment.

But our author, it seems, is filled with pious alarm for the cause of *orthodoxy*, from the increasing separation from the church. "By the sound doctrine its instituted forms express, it will," he tells us, "as long as it stands, be a witness to the truth, in periods the most barren of ministerial qualification; a rallying point to all truly Christian pastors; and *an accredited voucher for the purity of their instruction.*"—P. 17. How much were the primitive Christians to be pitied, who were unhappily destitute of any such "voucher;" and had nothing to secure the permanence of truth but the promised presence of Christ, the illumination of the Spirit, and the light of the Scriptures—poor substitutes, undoubtedly, for the solid basis of creeds and formularies! We should readily concur with the author in his views of the security derived from the subscription of articles, if we could forget a few stubborn facts, which we beg leave humbly to recall to his recollection. Is it not a fact, that the nature and extent of the assent and consent signified by subscription have been the subject of a very thorny controversy, in which more ill faith and chicane have been displayed than were ever known out of the school of the Jesuits; and that the issue of this controversy has been to establish very generally the doctrine of Paley, that none are excluded by it but Quakers, Papists, and Baptists? Is it not a fact, that the press is teeming every week with publications of the most acrimonious description, written by professed churchmen against persons who have incurred this acrimony merely by their attachment to these articles? Is it not a fact, that the doctrines they exhibit are so scorned and detested in this country, that whoever seriously maintains them is stigmatized with the name of "Methodist?" and that that part of the clergy who preach them are, *for that reason alone*, more insulted and despised by their brethren than even the dissenters themselves? It is with peculiar effrontery that this author insists on subscription to articles as a sufficient security for the purity of religious instruction, when it is the professed object of his work to recall his contemporaries to that purity. If he means that the "voucher" he speaks of answers its purpose because *it is* credited, he is plainly laughing at the simplicity of the people: if he means to assert it is *entitled* to credit, we must request him to reflect how he can vindicate himself from the charge of "speaking lies in hypocrisy."

A long course of experience has clearly demonstrated the inefficacy of creeds and confessions to perpetuate religious belief. Of this the only faithful depository is, not that which is "written with ink," but on the "fleshly tables of the heart." The spirit of error is too subtile and volatile to be held by such chains. Whoever is acquainted with ecclesiastical history must know, that public creeds and confessions have occasioned more controversies than they have composed; and that when they ceased to be the subject of dispute they have become antiquated and obsolete. A vast majority of the dissenters of the present day hold precisely the same religious tenets which the puritans did two centuries ago, because it is the instruction they have uniformly received from their pastors; and for the same reason the articles of the national church are almost effaced from the minds of its members, because they have long been neglected or denied by the majority of those who occupy its pulpits. We have never heard of the church of Geneva altering its confession, but we know that Voltaire boasted there was not in his time a Calvinist in the city; nor have we heard of any proposed amendment in the creed of the Scotch, yet it is certain the doctrines of that creed are preached by a rapidly decreasing minority of the Scottish clergy. From these and similar facts we may fairly conclude, that the doctrines of the church, with or without subscription, are sure to perpetuate themselves where they are faithfully preached; but that the mere circumstance of their being subscribed will neither secure their being preached nor believed.

"Separatism," says the author, "has no *fixed or perpetual character*: what it is at present we may by attentive observation be able to pronounce; but no human foresight can ascertain what it will be hereafter. Though now, in its numerous chapels, the soundest doctrine should be heard, we have no security that they will not become the schools of heresy. Here, if the licentious teacher get a footing, he moulds the whole system of ministration to his views; not a prayer, not a psalm, not a formulary of any kind but in this case will become the vehicle of error."—Pp. 17, 18.

How far, in creatures so liable to mistake, a fixed and perpetual character is an enviable attribute, we shall not stay to inquire; with what right it is claimed on this occasion it is not very difficult to determine. The Thirty-nine Articles will unquestionably always remain the same; that is, they will always be the Thirty-nine Articles: but it is not quite so certain that they are universally believed; much less that they will always continue to be so; and least of all, that after having ceased to be believed, they will receive the sanction of every successive legislature. For our parts, such is our simplicity, that when we read of a fixed and perpetual character, our attention is always wandering to men, to some mode of thinking or feeling to which such perpetuity belongs; instead of resting in the useful contemplation of pen, ink, and paper. With every disposition, however, to do the author justice, we have some fear for the success of his argument; suspecting the dissenters will be ready to reply, "Our pastors cordially embrace the doctrine contained in your articles; and as this cannot be affirmed of the majority of yours, the question of perpetuity is reduced to this amusing theorem,—In which of two given situations will a doctrine last the longest—where it is believed without being subscribed, or where it is subscribed without being believed?"

"Every addition separatism makes to its supporters alters the proportion existing in this country between the monarchical and the democratic spirit; either of which preponderating to a considerable degree, might be productive of the most serious consequences. For it is certain, that as our church-establishment is favourable to monarchy, so is the constitution of our dissenting congregations to democracy. The latter principle is cherished in all communities, where the power resides not in one, or a few, but is shared, in certain proportions, among all the members; which is the case in most of the religious societies under consideration. Let it be remembered, then, that if religion increase in this way, there is that increasing with it which is not religion; there is something springing up which is of a different nature, and which will be sure to stand, whether that better thing with which it may grow do or not."—P. 20.

The equal justice it is our duty to maintain obliges us to notice another aspersion which the author casts upon dissenters.

In this statement the author has exhibited his usual inattention to facts. That the people had, in the first ages, a large share in ecclesiastical proceedings, and that their officers were chosen by themselves, is incontrovertibly evident, as well from Scripture as from the authentic monuments of antiquity. The Epistles of St. Cyprian, to go no further, are as full in proof of this point as if they had been written on purpose to establish it. The transfer of power, first from the people to their ministers, and afterward from them to the Bishop of Rome, was a gradual work, not fully accomplished till many centuries had elapsed from the Christian era. Until the conversion of Constantine, the Christian church was an *imperium in imperio*, a spiritual republic. subsisting in the midst of the Roman empire, on which it was completely independent; and its most momentous affairs were directed by popular suffrage. Nor did it, in this state, either excite the jealousy or endanger the repose of the civil magistrate; since the distinction between the concerns of this world and those of another, so ably illustrated by Locke, taught the Christians of that time to render to Cæsar the things which are Cæsar's, and to God the things that are God's. Instructed to yield obedience to princes for conscience' sake, they were not the less orderly or submissive because they declined their interference in the suppression of error, or the punishment of ecclesiastical delinquency. If there be that inseparable connexion between political disaffection and the exercise of popular rights in religion which this writer contends, the primitive Christians must have been in a deplorable state: since it would have been impossible for them to quiet the just apprehensions of government without placing a heathen emperor at the head of the church. What must we think of the knowledge of a writer who was ignorant of these facts; of the candour which suppressed them; or of the humanity which finds an occasion of aspersing his fellow-christians in what escaped the malignity of heathen persecutors!

The dissenters will not fail to remind the writer that the British is a mixed, not an absolute monarchy; that the habit of considering the people as nothing is as repugnant to its spirit as that of making them every thing; and that to vest the whole power in the hands of one person, without check or control, is more suited to the genius of the Turkish than the British government. And to this retort, it must be confessed, the conduct of the high church party, who have seldom scrupled to promulgate maxims utterly subversive of liberty, would lend a very colourable support. The whole topic, however, is invidious, absurd, and merely calculated to mislead; since the constitution of the Christian church is fixed by the will of its Founder, the dictates of which we are not at liberty to accommodate or bend to the views o human policy. The dispute respecting ecclesiastical government must like every other on religion, be determined, if it ever be determined at all, by an appeal to Scripture, illustrated perhaps occasionally by the approved usages of the earliest antiquity. To connect political consequences with it, and to make it the instrument of exciting popular odium, is the indication of a bad cause and of a worse heart. After the specimens our readers have already had of the author's spirit, they will not be surprised to find he is not quite satisfied with the Toleration Act, which he complains has been perverted from its purpose of affording relief to tender consciences to that of *making* dissenters. We are not acute enough to comprehend this distinction. We have always supposed that it was the intention of the legislature by that act to enable Protestant dissenters to worship where they pleased, after giving proper notice to the magistrate: how their availing themselves of this liberty can be construed into an abuse of the act we are at a loss to conceive. This writer would tolerate dissenters, but not allow them to propagate their sentiments; that is, he would permit them that liberty of thinking which none can restrain, but not of speaking and acting, which are alone subject to the operation of law.

It is quite of a piece with the narrow prejudices of such a man to complain of it as an intolerable hardship, that a minister of the establishment is sometimes in danger, through the undistinguishing spirit of hospitality, of being invited to sit down with religionists of different descriptions; and he avows his manly resolution of going without his dinner rather than expose himself to such an indignity. It is certainly a most lamentable thing to reflect, that a regular clergyman may possibly lose *caste* by mixing at the hospitable board with some of those who will be invited to the marriage-supper of the Lamb. When Burke was informed that Mr. Godwin held gratitude to be a crime, he replied, "I will take care not to be accessory to his committing that crime." We hope the lovers of hospitality will take the hint, and never insult the author of "Zeal without Innovation" by exposing him to the touch of the ceremonially unclean.

Although we have already trespassed on the patience of our readers, we cannot dismiss this part of the subject without craving their indulgence a little longer. We are much concerned to witness the spirit of intolerance that pervades many recent publications. If the uniform course of experience can prove any thing, it is that the extension of any particular frame of church government will of itself contribute little to the interests of vital Christianity. Suppose every inhabitant of the kingdom were to return to the bosom of the establishment to-morrow, what real accession would be gained to the kingdom of Christ? Is there any magic in the change of a name which can convert careless, profane, irreligious dissenters into devout and pious churchmen? The virtuous part of them do honour to the Christian profession in the situation they occupy at present; and for the vicious, they could only infect and disgrace the community with which they proposed to associate. What means this incessant struggle to raise one party on the ruins of another? this assumption of infallibility, and the clamorous demand for the interposition of the legislature, which we so often witness? If the writers to whom we allude will honestly tell us they are apprehensive of their "craft" being in danger, we will give them credit for sincerity; but to attempt to cover their bigotry under the mask of piety is too gross a deception. Were the measures adopted for which these men are so violent, they would scarcely prove more injurious to religion than to the interests of the established church; to which the accession of numbers would be no compensation for the loss of that activity and spirit which are kept alive by the neighbourhood of rival sects. She would suffer rapid encroachments from infidelity; and the indolence and secularity too incident to opulent establishments would hasten her downfall. Amid the increasing degeneracy of the clergy, which must be the inevitable effect of destroying the necessity of vigilance and exertion, the people that now crowd the conventicle would not repair to the church: they would be scattered and dissipated, like water no longer confined within its banks. In a very short time, we have not the smallest doubt, the attendance at church would be much less than it is now. A religion which, by leaving no choice, can produce no attachment,—a religion invested with the stern rigour of law, and associated in the public mind and in public practice with prisons, and pillories, and gibbets,—would be a noble match, to be sure, for the subtle spirit of impiety, and the enormous and increasing corruption of the times. It is amusing to reflect what ample elbow-room the worthy rector would possess; how freely he might expatiate in his wide domain; and how much the effect of his denunciations against schism would be heightened by echoing through so large a void

> "Hic vasto rex Æolus antro
> Luctantes ventos tempestatesque sonoras
> Imperio premit."

The Gallican church no doubt looked upon it as a signal triumph when she prevailed on Louis the Fourteenth to repeal the edict of Nantes, and to suppress the Protestant religion. But what was the consequence? Where shall we look, after this period, for her Fenelons and her Pascals—where for the distinguished monuments of piety and learning which were the glory of her better days? As for piety, she perceived she had no occasion for it when there was no lustre of Christian holiness surrounding her; nor for learning, when she had no longer any opponents to confute or any controversies to maintain. She felt herself at liberty to become as ignorant, as secular, as irreligious as she pleased; and, amid the silence and darkness she had created around her, she drew the curtains and retired to rest. The accession of numbers she gained by suppressing her opponents was like the small extension of length a body acquires by death: the feeble remains of life were extinguished, and she lay a putrid corpse, a public nuisance, filling the air with pestilential exhalations. Such, there is every reason to believe, would be the effect of similar measures in England. That union among Christians which it is so desirable to recover must, we are persuaded, be the result of something more heavenly and divine than legal restraints or angry controversies. Unless an angel were to descend for that purpose, the spirit of division is a disease which will never be healed by troubling the waters. We must expect the cure from the increasing prevalence of religion, and from a copious communication of the Spirit to produce that event. A more extensive diffusion of piety among all sects and parties will be the best and only preparation for a cordial union. Christians will then be disposed to appreciate their differences more equitably; to turn their chief attention to points on which they agree; and, in consequence of loving each other more, to make every concession consistent with a good conscience. Instead of wishing to vanquish others, every one will be desirous of being vanquished by the truth. An awful fear of God and an exclusive desire of discovering his mind will hold a torch before them in their inquiries, which will strangely illuminate the path in which they are to tread. In the room of being repelled by mutual antipathy, they will be insensibly drawn nearer to each other by the ties of mutual attachment. A larger measure of the spirit of Christ would prevent them from converting every incidental variation into an impassable boundary; or from condemning the most innocent and laudable usages for fear of symbolizing with another class of Christians—an odious spirit, with which the writer under consideration is strongly impregnated. The general prevalence of piety in different communities would inspire that mutual respect, that heartfelt homage for the virtues conspicuous in the character of their respective members which would urge us to ask with astonishment and regret, Why cannot we be one? What is it that obstructs our union? Instead of maintaining the barrier which separates us from each other, and employing ourselves in fortifying the frontiers of hostile communities, we should be anxiously devising the means of narrowing the grounds of dispute, by drawing the attention of all parties to those fundamental and catholic principles in which they concur.

To this we may add, that a more perfect subjection to the authority of the great Head of the church would restrain men from inventing new terms of communion, from lording it over conscience, or from exacting a scrupulous compliance with things which the word of God has left indifferent. That sense of imperfection we ought ever to cherish would incline us to be looking up for superior light, and make us think it not improbable, that in the long night which has befallen us, we have all more or less mistaken our way, and have much to learn and much to correct. The very idea of identifying a particular party with the church would be exploded; the foolish clamour about schism hushed; and no one, however mean and inconsiderable, be expected to surrender his conscience to the claims of ecclesiastical dominion. The New Testament is surely not so obscure a book that were its contents to fall into the hands of a hundred serious, impartial men, it would produce such opposite conclusions as must necessarily issue in their forming two or more separate communions. It is remarkable, indeed, that the chief points about which real Christians are divided are points on which that volume is silent—mere human fabrications, which the presumption of men has attached to the Christian system. A larger communication of the Spirit of truth would insensibly lead Christians into a similar train of thinking; and being more under the guidance of that infallible Teacher, they would gradually tend to the same point, and settle in the same conclusions. Without such an influence as this, the coalescing into one communion would probably be productive of much mischief: it certainly would do no sort of good, since it would be the mere result of intolerance and pride acting upon indolence and fear.

During the present disjointed state of things, then, nothing remains but for every one to whom the care of any part of the church of Christ is intrusted, to exert himself to the utmost in the promotion of vital religion, in cementing the friendship of the good, and repressing with a firm and steady hand the heats and eruptions of party spirit. He will find sufficient employment for his time and his talents in inculcating the great truths of the gospel, and endeavouring to "form Christ" in his hearers, without blowing the flames of contention, or widening that breach which is already the disgrace and calamity of the Christian name. Were our efforts uniformly to take this direction, there would be an *identity* in the impression made by religious instruction; the distortion of party features would gradually disappear; and Christians would everywhere approach towards that ideal beauty spoken of by painters, which is combined of the finest lines and traits conspicuous in individual forms. Since they have all drunk into the same spirit, it is manifest nothing is wanting but a larger portion of that spirit to lay the foundation of a solid, cordial union. It is to the immoderate attachment to secular interest, the love of power, and the want of reverence for truth, not to the obscurities of revelation, we must impute the unhappy contentions among Christians—maladies which nothing can correct but deep and genuine piety. The true *schismatic* is not so properly the person who declines a compliance with what he judges to be wrong, though he may be mistaken in that judgment, as the man who, like the author before us, sedulously employs every artifice to alienate the affections of good men from each other.

Having animadverted on the illiberality of this writer towards persons of different persuasions, we now proceed to notice his representations of the state of religion, together with his treatment of that description of the clergy with whom he has been accustomed to associate.

The cause of religion he represents as in a very declining state.

"Some persons now living," he says, "can remember the time when absence from church was far from being so common as it is now become. Then, the more considerable heads of families were generally seen in the house of God, with their servants as well as children. This visible acknowledgment of the importance of religion had a good effect on families of inferior condition: the presence of the merchant and his household brought the tradesman and his family; and the example of the latter induced his journeymen and out-door servants to come to church. But this is not a description of modern habits. In many pews, once regularly filled by the entire household to which they belonged, it is now common to see only a small portion of the family, and often not an individual. Two or three of the younger branches, from the female side of the house, occasionally attend, with perhaps the mother, but without the father and the sons: the father, wearied with business, wants a little relaxation; and to the young men, not suspecting their want of instruction, a rural excursion offers something interesting, while the tranquil service of a church is too tame an occupation for their unexhausted spirits. Nor among the few who attend public worship are they always the same individuals that we see in the house of God. So that it does not appear to be from steady principle, and still less from the influence of parental authority, that some of the family are occasionally there. The children are left to themselves; they may go to church if they choose to do so; they incur no displeasure from the father, they excite no grief in his bosom if they stay away. There is no disreputation attaching to absence. It falls rather upon the contrary conduct; any uniform attendance on divine worship being frequently considered a mark of imbecility or demureness.

"To account for the thinness of our parochial congregations, some allege that there is not a sufficient quantity of naturally attractive circumstances in the ordinary service of the church. But it is observable, that where our liturgy is used in its *grandest* form, the attendance is as far from being numerous as it is elsewhere. It might be expected, and especially in an age in which a taste for *music* so generally prevails, that in a metropolis containing near a million of inhabitants, there might be more persons drawn by the grandeur of cathedral worship to the place where it is performed, than could well be accommodated in one church. The cathedral of London, however, presents no such scene. With a numerous attendance of ministers, the finest specimens of church-music, and these performed with that effect which professional qualification gives to such compositions, the seats of St. Paul's cathedral are seldom half-filled." Pp. 2–4.

Though we acknowledge the truth of his statement in a great measure, we are far from drawing from it the inference he wishes to impress. Whenever places of worship are thinly attended, at least in the established church, we have uniformly found it to proceed from a cause very distinct from the general decay of piety: it results from the absence of that sort of instruction which naturally engages the attention and fixes the heart. In one view, we are fully aware a great alteration has taken place: an attachment to the mere forms of religion has much subsided; the superstitious reverence formerly paid to consecrated places and a pompous ceremonial has waxed old; so that nothing will now command a full attendance at places set apart for Divine worship, but the preaching of the gospel, or of something, at least, that may be mistaken for it. Instead of concurring with the author in considering this as evincing the low state of Christianity among us, we are disposed to look upon it in a contrary light, being fully convinced that a readiness to acquiesce in the mere forms and ceremonies of religion, to the neglect of that truth which sanctifies the church, is one of the most dangerous errors to which men can be exposed. There is something in the constitution of human nature so abhorrent from the absence of all religion, that we are inclined to believe more are ruined by embracing some counterfeit instead of the true, than by the rejection of true and false altogether. We are not sorry, therefore, to learn that the music at St. Paul's is not found a sufficient substitute for "the joyful sound," nor a numerous show of ministers accepted by the people in the room of "Christ crucified set forth before them." Let the truths which concern men's eternal salvation be faithfully taught in that noble edifice, and the complaint of slender attendance will soon cease. In the mean time, of that part of the citizens who might be expected to frequent the cathedral, some are too gay and fashionable not to prefer the music of the theatre and the opera; and some are serious Christians, whose hunger for the bread of life will not be satisfied or diverted by the symphonies of an organ, or the splendour of canonical dresses.

He who is resolved to see nothing but what grows in his own enclosure, may report that "all is barren," though the fields around him bloomed like the garden of Eden; and such is the strength of this writer's prejudices, that it is morally impossible for him to give a just representation of facts. In forming his estimate of the state of religion, he is resolved to look only where he knows nothing is to be seen; and absurdly complains of the want of a crop where he is conscious the soil has never been cultivated. Effects must be looked for from their natural causes: men do not gather grapes of thorns, nor figs of thistles; nor are the fruits of Christianity to be expected in the absence of the gospel. Notwithstanding this writer's gloomy prognostications, we have no doubt of the kingdom of Christ making sensible advances; and in support of this opinion, we adduce the wider extension of religious truth, the multitude of places where the gospel is preached in its purity, the general disposition to attend it, the establishment of Sunday-schools, the circulation, with happy effect, of innumerable tracts, the translation of the Scriptures into foreign languages, and their more extensive communication to all nations, the formation of missionary societies, the growing unanimity among Christians, and the prodigious increase of faithful ministers in the established church. We presume these facts may be allowed a degree of weight sufficient to overbalance the thin attendance at St. Paul's. It is not a little surprising that a writer who professes to exhibit a correc' idea of the religious state of the nation, should pay no attention to these circumstances, or content himself with alluding to them in terms expressive of chagrin and vexation. Regarding the extensive institutions and the diffusive benefits which the efforts of serious Christians in different connexions have produced, as a contraband article, not entitled to be mentioned in the estimate of our moral wealth, he represents us as generally sunk in spiritual sloth and poverty. We should not learn from this writer that attempts were making for the universal propagation of Christianity; that translations of the Scriptures were going on in different languages; or that a zeal for the conversion of pagans had occasioned a powerful reaction at home, by producing efforts hitherto unexampled towards carrying the gospel into the darkest corners of the kingdom. We should never suspect from reading his work, that any material alteration had taken place within the last fifty years, or that new life had been infused into the professing world beyond what we might conjecture, perhaps, from certain indirect references and dark insinuations. Without noticing these facts, he calls upon us to join in pathetic lamentations over the prostrate state of religion, upon no better ground than the neglect of places of worship where the gospel is *not* preached, and where there is little to attract attention besides the privilege of hearing *fine music* and seeing *fine ministers* for nothing. It is a consolation to us to be convinced that the state of things is much otherwise than he represents; that more persons are brought acquainted with the glad tidings of the gospel, and more minds penetrated with the concerns of eternity, than at any period since the Reformation.

Thus far we dispute the justice of this author's statement, and are disposed to question the truth of the inference he has drawn from some insulated facts. But this is not the only fault we have to find with this part of his work. He has not only, in our opinion, been betrayed into erroneous conclusions, but has utterly failed in catching the distinguishing features in the aspect of the times; so that his picture bears no sort of resemblance to the original. He has painted nothing; he has only given an account of a particular distortion or two; so that a foreigner would no more be able, by reading his work, to form an idea of the state of religion in England, than of a countenance he had never seen by being told its chin was too long, or its nostrils were too wide. It must be evident to every one that the most striking characteristic of the present times is the violent, the outrageous opposition that is made to religion by multitudes, and the general disposition in the members of the community to take a decided part. To this circumstance the writer has never adverted. It is impossible to suppose it could escape his attention: we must therefore impute his silence to the well-weighed dictates of prudence, which admonished him of the possibility of betraying himself into inconveniences by such a discussion: nor need we be surprised, notwithstanding his boasted magnanimity, at his yielding to these suggestions; since his magnanimity is of that sort which makes a man very ready to insult his brethren, but very careful not to disgust his superiors. As we are happily exempt from these scruples, we shall endeavour, in as few words as possible, to put the reader in possession of our ideas on this subject.

The leading truths of revelation were all along retained in the Church of Rome, but buried under such a mass of absurd opinions and superstitious observances, that they drew but little attention, and exerted a very inconsiderable influence in the practical application of the system. At the Reformation, they were effectually extricated and disengaged from errors with which they had been mingled, were presented in a blaze of light, and formed the basis of our national creed. As it was by pushing them to their legitimate consequences that the Reformers were enabled to achieve the conquest of popery, they were for a while retained in their purity, and every deviation from them denounced as menacing a revolt to the enemy. The Articles of the church were a real transcript of the principles the Reformers were most solicitous to inculcate; and being supported by the mighty impulse which produced the Reformation, while that remained fresh and unbroken they constituted the real faith of the people. Afterward they underwent an eclipse in the Protestant Church of England, as they had done in the Church of Rome, though from causes somewhat different. The low arminianism and intolerant bigotry of Laud paved the way for a change, which was not a little aided and advanced by the unbounded licentiousness and profligacy which overspread the kingdom after the Restoration: for it must be remembered that there is an intimate connexion between the perception and relish of truth and a right disposition of mind; that they have a reciprocal influence on each other; and that the mystery of faith can only be placed with safety in a pure conscience. When lewdness, profaneness, and indecency reigned without control, and were practised without a blush, nothing, we may be certain, could be more repugnant to the prevailing taste than the unadulterated word of God. There arose also, at this time, a set of divines who, partly in compliance with the popular humour, partly to keep at a distance from the puritans, and partly to gain the infidels who then began to make their appearance, introduced a new sort of preaching, in which the doctrines of the Reformation, as they are usually styled, were supplanted by copious and elaborate disquisitions on points of morality. Their fame and ability imboldened their successors to improve upon their pattern, by consigning the Articles of the church to a still more perfect oblivion, by losing sight still more entirely of the peculiarities of the gospel, guarding more anxiously against every sentiment or expression that could agitate or alarm, and by shortening the length, and adding as much as possible to the dryness, of their moral lucubrations. From that time, the idea commonly entertained in England of a perfect sermon was that of a discourse upon some moral topic, clear, correct, and argumentative, in the delivery of which the preacher must be free from all suspicion of being moved himself, or of intending to produce emotions in his hearers; in a word, as remote as possible from such a method of reasoning on righteousness, temperance, and judgment as should make a Felix tremble. This idea was very successfully realized, this singular model of pulpit eloquence carried to the utmost perfection; so that, while the bar, the parliament, and the theatre frequently agitated and inflamed their respective auditories, the church was the only place where the most feverish sensibility was sure of being laid to rest. This inimitable apathy in the mode of imparting religious instruction, combined with the utter neglect of whatever is most touching or alarming in the discoveries of the gospel, produced their natural effect of extinguishing devotion in the established church, and of leaving it to be possessed by the dissenters; of whom it was considered as the distinguishing badge, and from that circumstance derived an additional degree of unpopularity. From these causes the people gradually became utterly alienated from the Articles of the church, eternal concerns dropped out of the mind, and what remained of religion was confined to an attention to a few forms and ceremonies. If any exception can be made to the justice of these observations, it respects the doctrines of the Trinity and the atonement, which were often defended with ability, though in a dry and scholastic manner, and the discussion of which served to mark the return of the principal festivals of the church; while other points not less important,—such as the corruption of human nature, the necessity of the new birth, and justification by faith,—were either abandoned to oblivion, or held up to ridicule and contempt. The consequence was, that the creed established by law had no sort of influence in forming the sentiments of the people; the pulpit completely vanquished the desk; piety and puritanism were confounded in one common reproach; an almost pagan darkness in the concerns of salvation prevailed; and the English became the most irreligious people upon earth.

Such was the situation of things when Whitfield and Wesley made their appearance; who, whatever feelings the severest criticism can discover in their character, will be hailed by posterity as the second reformers of England. Nothing was farther from the views of these excellent men than to innovate in the established religion of their country; their sole aim was to recall the people to the good old way, and to imprint the doctrine of the Articles and Homilies on the spirits of men. But this doctrine had been confined so long to a dead letter, and so completely obliterated from the mind by contrary instruction, that the attempt to revive it met with all the opposition which innovation is sure to encounter, in addition to what naturally results from the nature of the doctrine itself, which has to contend with the whole force of human corruption. The revival of the old appeared like the introduction of a new religion; and the hostility it excited was less sanguinary, but scarcely less virulent, than that which signalized the first publication of Christianity. The gospel of Christ, or that system of truth which was laid as the foundation of the Reformation, has since made rapid advances; and in every step of its progress has sustained the most furious assault. Great Britain exhibits the singular spectacle of two parties contending, not whether Christianity shall be received or rejected, but whether it shall be allowed to retain any thing spiritual: not whether the Articles and Homilies shall be repealed, but whether they shall be laid as the basis of public instruction. Infidelity being too much discredited by the atrocities in France to hope for public countenance, the enemies of religion, instead of attacking the outworks of Christianity, are obliged to content themselves with vilifying and misrepresenting its distinguishing doctrines. They are willing to retain the Christian religion, providing it continue inefficient; and are wont to boast of their attachment to the established church, when it is manifest there is little in it they admire, except its splendour and its emoluments. The clerical order, we are sorry to say, first set the example; and, since evangelical principles have been more widely diffused, have generally appeared in the foremost ranks of opposition. This is nothing more than might be naturally looked for. With all the respect we feel for the clergy on account of their learning and talents, it is impossible not to know that many of them are mere men of the world, who have consequently the same objections to the gospel as others, together with some peculiar to themselves. As the very attempt of reviving doctrines which have been obliterated through their neglect, implies a tacit censure of their measures, so, wherever that attempt succeeds, it diminishes the weight of their ecclesiastical character. Deserted by the people, and eclipsed in the public esteem by many much their inferiors in literary attainments, they feel indignant: and if, as we will suppose, they sometimes suspect their being neglected has arisen from their inattention to important truths and indispensable duties, this increases their uneasiness, which, if it fails to reform, will inevitably exasperate them still more against those who are the innocent occasions of it. It is but fair to acknowledge, that in conducting the controversy, they have generally kept within decent bounds, have often reasoned where others have railed, and have usually abstained from topics hackneyed by infidels and scoffers. But they cannot be vindicated from the charge of having, by a formal opposition to the gospel, inflamed the irreligious prejudices of the age, obstructed the work they were appointed to promote, and imboldened others, who had none of their scruples or restraints, to outrage piety itself. The dragon has cast from his mouth such a flood of heresy and mischief, that Egypt, in the worst of her plagues, was not covered with more loathsome abominations. Creatures which we did not suspect to have existed have come forth from their retreats, some soaring into the regions of impiety on vigorous pinions, others crawling on the earth with a slow and sluggish motion, only to be tracked through the filthy slime of their impurities. We have seen writers of every order, from the Polyphemuses of the north to the contemptible dwarfs of the Critical Review; men of every party, infidels, churchmen, and dissenters —a motley crew, who have not one thing in common, except their antipathy to religion,—join hands and heart on this occasion: a deadly taint of impiety has blended them in one mass; as things the most discordant, while they are *living* substances, will do perfectly well to putrefy together.

We are not at all alarmed at this extensive combination; we doubt not of its producing the most happy effects. It has arisen from the alarm the great enemy has felt at the extension of the gospel; and by drawing the attention of the world more powerfully to it, will ultimately aid the cause it is intended to subvert. The public will not long be at a loss to determine where the truth lies, when they see in one party a visible fear of God, a constant appeal to his oracles, a solicitude to promote the salvation of mankind; in the other, an indecent levity, an unbridled insolence, an unblushing falsehood, a hard unfeeling pride, a readiness to adopt any principles and assume any mask that will answer their purpose, together with a manifest aim to render the Scriptures of no authority and religion of no effect.

Having so often alluded to the "evangelical clergy," we shall close this division of our remarks with exhibiting a slight outline of the doctrine by which the clergy of this class are distinguished. The term *evangelical* was first given them simply on account of their preaching the gospel, or, in other words, their exhibiting with clearness and precision the peculiar truths of Christianity. In every system there are some principles which serve to identify it, and in which its distinguishing essence consists. In the system of Christianity, the rules of moral duty are not entitled to be considered in this light, partly because they are not peculiar to it, and partly because they are retained by professed infidels, who avow without scruple their admiration of the morality of the gospel. We must look then elsewhere, for the distinguishing character of Christianity. It must be sought for in its doctrines, and (as its professed design is to conduct men to eternal happiness) in those doctrines which relate to the way of salvation, or the method of a sinner's reconciliation with God. There are some, we are aware, who would reduce the whole faith of a Christian to a belief of the messiahship of Christ, without reflecting, that until we have fixed some specific ideas to the term Messiah, the proposition which affirms him to be such contains no information. The most discordant apprehensions are entertained by persons who equally profess that belief; some affirming him to be a mere man, others a being of the angelic order, and a third party essentially partaker of the divine nature. The first of these look upon his sufferings as merely exemplary; the last, as propitiatory and vicarious. It must be evident, then, from these views being at the utmost distance from each other, that the proposition that Christ is the Messiah conveys little information, while the import of its principal term is left vague and undetermined. The Socinian and Trinitarian, notwithstanding their verbal agreement, having a different object of worship, and a different ground of confidence, must be allowed to be of different religions. It requires but a very cursory perusal of the Articles of the established church to determine to which of these systems *they* lend *their* support; or to perceive that the deity of Christ, the doctrine of atonement for sin, the guilt and apostacy of man, and the necessity of the agency of the Spirit to restore the divine image, are asserted by them in terms the most clear and unequivocal. This question stands quite independent of the Calvinistic controversy. Are the clergy, styled evangelical, to be blamed for preaching *these* doctrines? Before this can be allowed, the Articles must be cancelled by the same authority by which they were established; or it must be shown how it consists with integrity to gain an introduction to the church, by signifying an unfeigned assent and consent to certain articles of religion, with the intention of immediately banishing them from notice. The clamour against the clergy in question cannot, without an utter contempt of decency, be excited by the mere fact of their being known to hold and inculcate these doctrines; but by the manner of their teaching them, or the exclusive attention they are supposed to pay them, to the neglect of other parts of the system. The measure of zeal they display for them, they conceive to be justified, as well by a view of the actual state of human nature, as by the express declaration of the inspired oracles. Conceiving, with the compilers of the Articles, that the state of man is that of a fallen and apostate creature, they justly conclude that a mere code of morals is inadequate to his relief; that, having lost the favour of God by his transgression, he requires, not merely to be instructed in the rules of duty, but in the method of regaining the happiness he has forfeited; that the pardon of sin, or some compensation to divine justice for the injury he has done to the majesty of the supreme Lawgiver, are the objects which ought in the first place to occupy his attention. An acquaintance with the rules of duty may be sufficient to teach an innocent creature how to secure the felicity he possesses, but can afford no relief to a guilty conscience, nor instruct the sinner how to recover the happiness he has lost. Let it be remembered, that Christianity is essentially a restorative dispensation; it bears a continual respect to a state from which man is fallen, and is a provision for repairing that ruin which the introduction of moral evil has brought upon him. Exposed to the displeasure of God and the curse of his law, he stands in need of a Redeemer; disordered in his powers, and criminally averse to his duty, he equally needs a Sanctifier. As adapted to such a situation, much of the New Testament is employed in displaying the character and unfolding the offices of both, with a view of engaging him to embrace that scheme of mercy which the Divine benignity has thought fit to exhibit in the gospel. The intention of St. John in composing the evangelical history coincides with the entire purpose and scope of revelation: "These things are written," said he, "that ye may believe that Jesus is the Christ, and that, believing, ye might have life through his name." Whoever considers, that upon every hypothesis except the socinian, Christianity is a provision of mercy for an apostate and sinful world, through a Divine Mediator, will acknowledge that something more is included in the idea of preaching the gospel than the inculcation of moral duties; and that he who confines his attention to these exchanges the character of a Christian pastor for that of a fashionable declaimer, or a philosophical moralist. If we turn our eyes to the ministry of the apostles, we perceive it to have consisted in "testifying repentance toward God, and faith toward our Lord Jesus Christ:" repentance, which is natural religion modified by the circumstances of a fallen creature, including a return to the path of duty; and faith, which is a practical compliance with the Christian dispensation, by receiving the Saviour as the way, the truth, and the life. Faith and repentance being the primary duties enjoined under the gospel, and the production of these the professed end of the inspired writers, we need not wonder that those who are ambitious to tread in their steps insist much, in the course of their ministry, on the topics which supply the principal motives to these duties;—the evil of sin, the extent of human corruption, together with the dignity, power, and grace of the Redeemer. Remembering that the object of repentance is God, they do not, in treating of sin, satisfy themselves with displaying its mischievous effects in society: they expatiate on its contrariety to the Divine nature; they speak of it chiefly as an affront offered to the authority of the Supreme Ruler; and represent no repentance as genuine which springs not from godly sorrow, or a concern for having displeased God. In this part of their office they make use of the moral law, which requires the devotion of the whole heart and unfailing obedience, as the sword of the Spirit, to pierce the conscience, and to convince men that "by the deeds of it no flesh living can be justified, but that every mouth must be stopped, and the whole world become guilty before God." The uniform course of experience serves to convince them, that till a deep impression of this truth be made on the heart, the character of the Saviour, and the promise of pardon through his blood, will produce no gratitude, and excite no interest. In inculcating faith in Christ, they cannot satisfy themselves with merely exhibiting the evidences of Christianity: a mere assent to which, upon historical grounds, undeniably fails, in innumerable instances, of producing those effects which are uniformly ascribed to that principle in the New Testament; neither overcoming the world, nor purifying the heart, nor inducing newness of life. They are of opinion that the external evidences of the Christian religion are chiefly of importance on account of their tendency to fix the attention on Christ, the principal object exhibited in that dispensation; and the faith on which the Scriptures lay so much stress, and connect with such ineffable benefits, they conceive essentially to involve a personal reliance on Christ for salvation, accompanied with a cordial submission to his authority. Attempting to produce this Scriptural faith, in a dependence upon the Divine blessing (without which the best means will be unsuccessful), they dwell much on the dignity of his character as the Son of God, the admirable constitution of his person as "Immanuel, God with us," the efficacy of his atonement, and the gracious tenor of his invitations, together with the agency of that Spirit which is intrusted to him as the Mediator, to be imparted to the members of his mystical body. In their view, to preach the gospel is to preach Christ; they perceive the New Testament to be full of him: and while they imbibe that spirit with which it is replete, they feel a sacred ambition to diffuse "the savour of his name in every place."

Let it not be inferred from hence, that they are inattentive to the interests of practical religion, or that their ministry is merely occupied in explaining and enforcing a doctrinal system. None lay more stress on the duties of a holy life, or urge with more constancy the necessity of their hearers showing their faith by their works; and they are incessantly affirming, with St. James, that the former without the latter is dead, being alone. Though, in common with the inspired writers, they ascribe their transition from a state of death to a state of justification solely to faith in Christ previous to good works actually performed, yet they equally insist upon a performance of those works as the evidence of justifying faith ; and, supposing life to be spared, as the indispensable condition of final happiness. The law, not altered in its requirements (for what was once duty they conceive to be duty still), but attempered in its sanctions to the circumstances of a fallen creature, they exhibit as the perpetual standard of rectitude, as the sceptre of majesty by which the Saviour rules his disciples. They conceive it to demand the same things, though not with the same rigour, under the gospel dispensation as before. The matter of duty they look upon as unalterable, and the only difference to be this ; that whereas under the covenant of works the condition of life was sinless obedience, under the new covenant an obedience sincere and affectionate, though imperfect, is accepted for the sake of the Redeemer. At the same time they do not cease to maintain, that the faith which they hold to be justifying comprehends in it the seminal principle of every virtue ; that if genuine it will not fail to be fruitful ; and that a Christian has it in his power to show his faith "*by his works*," and by no other means. Under a full conviction of the fallen state of man, together with his moral incapacity to do what is pleasing to God, they copiously insist on the agency of the Spirit, and affectionately urge their hearers to implore his gracious assistance. From *no class* of men will you hear more solemn warnings against sin, more earnest calls to repentance, or more full and distinct delineations of the duties resulting from every relation in life, accompanied with a peculiar advantage of drawing from the mysteries of the gospel the strongest motives to strengthen the abhorrence of the one, and enforce the practice of the other. In their hands, morality loses nothing but the pagan air with which it is too often invested. The morality which they enjoin is of heavenly origin, the pure emanation of truth and love, sprinkled with atoning blood, and baptized into an element of Christian sanctity. That they are not indifferent to the interests of virtue is sufficiently apparent, from the warm approbation they uniformly express of the excellent work of Mr. Wilberforce, which is not more conspicuous for the orthodoxy of its tenets than for the purity and energy of its moral instruction. If we look at the effects produced from the ministry of these men, they are such as might be expected to result from a faithful exhibition of the truth of God. Wherever they labour, careless sinners are awakened, profligate transgressors are reclaimed, the mere form of religion is succeeded by the power, and fruits of genuine piety appear in the holy and exemplary lives of their adherents. A visible reformation in society at large, and in many instances unequivocal proofs of solid conversion, attest the purity of their doctrines and the utility of their labours ; effects which we challenge their enemies to produce where a different sort of teaching prevails.

The controversy between them and their opponents, to say the truth, turns on a point of the greatest magnitude: the question at issue respects the choice of a supreme end, and whether we will take "the Lord to be our God." Their opponents are for confining religion to an acknowledgment of the being of a God and the truth of the Christian revelation, accompanied with some external rites of devotion, while the world is allowed the exclusive dominion of the heart; *they* are for carrying into effect the apostolic mission by summoning men to repentance, and engaging them to an entire surrender of themselves to the service of God, through a Mediator. In the system of human life, their opponents assign to devotion a very narrow and limited agency: *they* contend for its having the supreme control. The former expect nothing from religion but the restraint of outward enormities by the fear of future punishment; in the views of the latter it is productive of positive excellence, a perennial spring of peace, purity, and joy. Instead of regarding it as a matter of occasional reference, they consider it as a principle of constant operation. While their opponents always overlook, and frequently deny, the specific difference between the church and the world, in *their* views the Christian is a pilgrim and stranger in the earth, one whose heart is in heaven, and who is supremely engaged in the pursuit of eternal realities. Their fiercest opposers, it is true, give to Jesus Christ the title of the Saviour of the world: but it requires very little attention to perceive that their hope of future happiness is placed on the supposed preponderancy of the virtues over the vices, and the claims which they then conceive to result on the *justice* of God; while the opposite party consider themselves as mere pensioners on *mercy*, flee for refuge to the Cross, and ascribe their hopes of salvation entirely to the grace of the Redeemer.

For our parts, supposing the being and perfections of God once ascertained, we can conceive of no point at which we can be invited to stop, short of that serious piety and habitual devotion which the evangelical clergy enforce. To live without religion, to be devoid of habitual devotion, is natural and necessary in him who disbelieves the existence of its object; but upon what principles he can justify his conduct who professes to believe in a Deity without aiming to please him in all things, without placing his happiness in his favour, we are utterly at a loss to comprehend.

We cannot dismiss this part of the subject without remarking the exemplary moderation of the clergy of this class on those intricate points which unhappily divide the Christian church; the questions, we mean, that relate to predestination and free-will, on which, equally remote from pelagian heresy and antinomian licentiousness, they freely tolerate and indulge a diversity of opinion, embracing Calvinists and Arminians with little distinction, provided the Calvinism of the former be practical and moderate, and the Arminianism of the latter evangelical and devout. The greater part of them lean, we believe, to the doctrine of general redemption, and love to represent the gospel as bearing a friendly aspect towards the eternal happiness of all to whom it is addressed; but they are much less anxious to establish a polemical accuracy than to "win souls to Christ."

The opposition they encounter from various quarters will not surprise those who reflect that they are not of the world, that the world loves only its own, and naturally feels a dislike to such as testify that its works are evil. The Christianity of the greater part of the community is merely nominal; and it necessarily follows, that wherever the truths of religion are faithfully exhibited and practically exemplified they will be sure to meet with the same friends and the same enemies as at their first promulgation; they will be still exposed to assault from the prejudices of unrenewed minds, they will be upheld by the same almighty Power, and will continue to insinuate themselves into the hearts of the simple and sincere with the same irresistible force.

We hope our readers will excuse the length to which we have extended our delineation of the principles of the clergy styled "evangelical," reflecting how grossly they have been misrepresented, and that, until the subject is placed fairly and fully in view, it is impossible to form an equitable judgment of the treatment they have met with from the writer under consideration.

The first charge he adduces against the evangelical clergy is that of enthusiasm. Enthusiasm, according to Mr. Locke, is that state of mind which disposes a person to give a stronger assent to a religious proposition than the evidence will justify. According to the more common and popular notion, it implies a pretence to supernatural communications, on which is founded a belief in certain doctrines, and the performance of certain actions, which the Scriptures have not authorized or revealed—a dangerous delusion, as it tends to disannul the standard of religion, and, by the extravagances and follies it produces, to bring piety into disgrace. We hold enthusiasm in as much abhorrence as our author does; but we ask, what is the proportion of the evangelical clergy who are guilty of it? and for *every* individual among them to whom it attaches, we will engage to produce *ten* among their opponents who are deficient in the essential branches of *morality*. Yet we should esteem it extreme illiberality in a writer to brand the clergy in general with immorality. There may be some few among the many hundreds whom the author has undertaken to describe who are real enthusiasts; but where is the candour or justice of mingling this feature in the delineation of the body? We appeal to the religious public, whether they are not, on the contrary, eminently conspicuous for their close adherence "to the law and to the testimony," and for their care to enjoin nothing on their hearers without direct warrant from the Bible? If every one is to be charged with enthusiasm whose piety is of a more fervid complexion than the accuser is disposed to sympathize with, or can readily account for, we must indeed despair of convincing this writer of the futility of his allegation. They have the *zeal* which, to him who makes what is most prevalent in the church his model, must look like *innovation.*

He frequently insinuates that there is a disposition in them to symbolize with the dissenters, though he had allowed, at the very outset of his work, that they most strictly conform to the prescribed ritual, have no scruples against canonical obedience, and are most firmly attached to the ecclesiastical constitution. Speaking of the established church, he says,

"They (the evangelical clergy) approve, they admire the church in which they serve. They rejoice in being ministers of such a church Instead of being indifferent to its continuance, their devoutest wish is that it may stand firm on its basis. They consider it as the greatest of blessings to their country. They observe, with no little anxiety, separatism gaining ground upon it. And this, not from an invidious principle, but because hereby an alienation, *in perpetuity*, is produced in many minds, from a constitution which they consider as best providing for the universal conveyance and permanent publication of Christian truth. Its continuance they likewise consider as the surest pledge of religious liberty to all who wish for that blessing. And in this view they pity the shortsightedness of those religious persons who forward any measures which make against the stability of the national church. They view them as men undermining the strongest bulwark of *their own* security and comfort, and conceive that Protestant sects, of every name, however they might prefer their own modes of religion, would devoutly pray for the support and prosperity of the Church of England as it now stands: '*Sua si bona norint.*' In short, the ecclesiastical establishment of this country is in their views what 'the ark of God' was in the estimation of the pious Israelite; and 'their hearts tremble' more for that than for any thing else, the stability of which may seem to be endangered in these eventful times. They would consider its fall as one of the heaviest judgments that could befall the nation."—Pp. 128, 129.

Any such approach to the dissenters as is inconsistent with their professional engagements is incompatible with the truth of this testimony. But let us go on to notice another imputation.

"I am constantly," says the author, "ready to admit that there is a great deal of truth in what is often alleged by their opponents; namely, that under their preaching there has arisen an unfavourable opinion of the body of the clergy. To excite a hatred of what is evil is undoubtedly one purpose of Christian instruction. But while the preacher is attempting this, he must take care that he do not call forth the malignant passions. This he is almost sure to do if he point out a certain set of men as persons to whom his reprehensions particularly apply. The hearers, too generally apt to forget themselves, are drawn still further from the consideration of their own faults, when they can find a defined class of men on whom they can fasten the guilt of any alleged error; on them they will discharge their gall, and mistake their rancour for *righteousness*."—Pp. 154, 155, *Second Edition.*

Two questions arise on this point: first, how far an unfavourable opinion of the body of the clergy is just; and, secondly, what sort of influence the evangelical party have had in producing it. "The clergy, as a body," the author complains, "are considered by them and their adherents as men who do not preach the gospel." If we understand him, he means to assert that the clergy, as a body, *do* preach the gospel; for we cannot suspect him of being so ridiculous as to complain of their being considered in their just and true light. Here we have the very singular spectacle of gospel ministers exclaiming with bitterness against some of their brethren for preaching the doctrines of the new birth, justification by faith, the internal operations of the Spirit, and whatever else characterized the faith of the Reformers, which we have the satisfaction of learning, from this most liberal writer, are no parts of the gospel. Or, if he demur in assenting to such a proposition, it is incumbent on him to explain what are the *doctrines distinct* from those we have mentioned, the inculcation of which has excited the opposition of the clergy. We, in our great simplicity, supposed that the ministers styled evangelical had been opposed for insisting on points intimately related to the gospel; but we are now taught, from high authority, that the controversy is entirely of another kind, and relates to subjects with respect to which the preachers of the gospel may indifferently arrange themselves on either side. We are under great obligations to our author for clearing up this perplexing affair, and so satisfactorily showing both parties they were fighting in the dark. Poor George Whitfield! how much to be pitied, who exhausted himself with incredible labours, and endured a storm of persecution, in communicating religious instruction to people who were already furnished with more than ten thousand preachers of the gospel! To be serious, however, on a subject which, if there be one in the world, demands seriousness,—it is an incontrovertible fact, that the doctrines of the Reformation are no longer heard in the greater part of the established pulpits, and that there has been a general departure from the truths of the gospel, which are exhibited in the ministry of a small though increasing minority of the clergy. The author *knows* this to be a fact, although he has the meanness to express himself in a manner that would imply his being of a contrary opinion. We wish him all the consolation he can derive from this trait of godly simplicity, as well as from his reflection on the effect which his flattery is likely to produce, in awakening the vigilance and improving the character of his newly-discovered race of gospel ministers. With respect to the degree in which an unfavourable opinion of the clergy is to be ascribed to the representations of the evangelical party, we have to remark, that they possess too much attachment to their order to delight in depreciating it; and that they are under no temptation to attempt it with a view to secure the preference of their hearers; who, supposing them to have derived benefit from their labours, will be sufficiently aware of the difference between light and darkness, between famine and plenty. Were they to insinuate, with this author, that all their clerical brethren are actually engaged in the same cause, and are promoting the same object with themselves, they would at once be charged with a violation of truth, and be considered as insulting the common sense of the public.

The author is extremely offended at Dr. Haweis, on account of the following passage in his History of the Church of Christ. "Different itinerant societies have been established in order to send instruction to the poor, in the villages where the gospel is not preached. Probably not less than five hundred places of divine worship have been opened within the last three years." Dr. Haweis, in making this representation, undoubtedly conceived himself to be stating a simple fact, without suspecting any lover of the gospel would call it in question. The author's comment upon it is curious enough. "It would be scarcely credible," he says, "were not the time and place marked with sufficient precision, that a clergyman beneficed in the Church of England was describing, in the foregoing passage, something which had lately been taking place in this country!" It is surely very credible that there are five hundred places in England where the gospel is not preached; the incredible part of the business, then, consists in a "beneficed clergyman" daring to assert it, who, according to the author, is a sort of personage who is bound never to utter a truth that will offend the delicate ears of the clergy, especially on so trivial an occasion as that of describing the state of religion in England. What a magnanimity of spirit, and how far is this author from the suspicion of being a man-pleaser!

After acknowledging that the ministers he is characterizing have been *unjustly* charged with infringing on canonical regularity, he adds,

"Would it were as easy to defend them *universally*,* against those who accuse them of vanity, of courting popularity, of effrontery, of coarseness, of the want of that affectionate spirit which should breathe through all the ministrations of a Christian teacher, of their commonly appearing before a congregation with an objurgatory aspect, as if their minds were always brooding over some matter of accusation against their charge, instead of their feeling towards them as a father does towards his children."—P. 157.

The reader has in this passage a tolerable specimen of the "vanity" and "effrontery" of this writer, as well as of that "objurgatory aspect" he has thought fit to assume towards his brethren, not without strong suspicion of assuming it from a desire to "court popularity." It would be a mere waste of words to attempt to reply to such an accusation, which merits attention on no other account than its exhibiting a true picture of his mind.

"As for the matter," he proceeds to observe, "of which the sermons delivered by some of them are composed, it is contemptible in the extreme. Though truths of great importance are brought forward, yet, as if those who delivered them were born to ruin the cause in which they are engaged, they are presented to the auditory associated with such meanness, imbecility, or absurdity, as to afford a complete triumph to those who are adverse to their propagation. We are disgusted by the violation of all the rules which the common sense of mankind teaches them to expect the observance of on the occasion. It is true, indeed, that something is heard about Christ, about faith and repentance, about sin and grace; but in vain we look for argument, or persuasion, or suavity, or reverential demeanour; qualities which ought

* The word *universally*, marked in italics, was inserted *after* the first edition.

never to be absent, where it is of the utmost importance that the judgment be convinced, and the affections gained."—P. 158.

Unfair and illiberal in the extreme as this representation is, it contains an important concession,—that the lowest preachers among them have the wisdom to make a right selection of topics, and to bring forward truths of great importance; a circumstance sufficient of itself to give them an infinite superiority over the "apes of Epictetus."* A great diversity of talents must be expected to be found among them; but it has not been our lot to hear of any whose labours a good man would think it right to treat with indiscriminate contempt. As they are called, for the most part, to address the middle and lower classes of society, their language is plain and simple; speaking in the presence of God, their address is solemn; and as becomes "the ambassadors of Christ," their appeals to the conscience are close and cogent. Few, if any, among them aspire to the praise of consummate orators—a character which we despair of ever seeing associated in high perfection with that of a Christian teacher. The minister of the gospel is called to declare the testimony of God, which is always weakened by a profuse employment of the ornaments of secular eloquence. Those exquisite paintings and nice touches of art in which the sermons of the French preachers excel so much, excite a kind of attention, and produce a species of pleasure, not in perfect accordance with devotional feeling. The imagination is too much excited and employed, not to interfere with the more awful functions of conscience; the hearer is absorbed in admiration; and the exercise which ought to be an instrument of conviction, becomes a feast of taste. In the hand of a Massillon, the subject of death itself is blended with so many associations of the most delicate kind, and calls up so many sentiments of natural tenderness, as to become a source of theatrical amusement, rather than of religious sensibility. Without being insensible to the charms of eloquence, it is our decided opinion that a sermon of Mr. Gisborne's is more calculated to "convert a sinner from the error of his way," than one of Massillon's. It is a strong objection to a studied attempt at oratory in the pulpit, that it usually induces a neglect of the peculiar doctrines of Christian verity, where the preacher feels himself restrained, and is under the necessity of explaining texts, of obviating objections, and elucidating difficulties, which limits the excursions of imagination, and confines it within narrow bounds. He is therefore eager to escape from these fetters; and, instead of "*reasoning out of the Scriptures*," expatiates in the flowery fields of declamation. It would be strange, however, if the evangelical clergy did not excel their contemporaries in the art of preaching, to which they devote so much more of their attention. While others are accustomed to describe it under the very appropriate phrase of "doing duty," it is their business and their delight. They engage in it under many advantages. Possessed of the same education with their brethren, they usually speak to crowded auditories; the truths they deliver command attention

* Horsley.

and they are accustomed to ascend the pulpit under an awful sense of the weight and importance of their charge. Under such circumstances, it is next to impossible for them not to become powerful and impressive. Were it not indelicate to mention names, we could easily confirm our observations by numerous living examples. Suffice it to say, that perhaps no denomination of Christians ever produced so many excellent preachers; and that it is entirely owing to them that the ordinance of preaching has not fallen, in the established church, into utter contempt.

With respect to the remarks the author makes on the "hypochondriacal cast of preaching heard among them," of their "holding their hearers by details of conflicts and experiences," and of their "*prosings* on the hidings of God's face,"* we need not detain our readers. To good men it will be matter of serious regret to find a writer from whom different things were to be expected treat the concerns of the spiritual warfare in so light and ludicrous a manner; while the irreligious will heartily join in the laugh. It should be remembered that he is performing quarantine, purging himself from the suspicions of *Methodism*, and that nothing can answer this purpose so well as a spice of profaneness.

After expressing his contempt of the evangelical clergy as *preachers*, he proceeds to characterize them in the following manner as *writers*:—

"Here," says he, "I can with great truth affirm, that many included in that description of clergymen now under consideration are sorely grieved by much of what comes out as the produce of authorship on their side. And well they may be; to see, as is frequently the case, the blessed truths of the gospel degraded, by being associated with newspaper bombast, with impudence, with invective, with dotage, with drivelling cant, with buffoonery, and scurrility! Who can read these despicable publications without thinking contemptuously of all who abet them? But let not every one in whom an occasional coincidence of opinion may be recognised be included in this number. For it is a certain truth, that the writings of avowed infidels are not more offensive to several of the clergy in question than are some of the publications here alluded to. Let them not, therefore, be judged of by that which they condemn; by productions which they consider as an abuse of the liberty of the press, and a disgrace to the cause which their authors profess to serve."—P. 179.

Whoever remembers that the most learned interpreter of prophecy now living ranks with the evangelical clergy, whoever recalls to his recollection the names of Scott, Robinson, Gisborne, and a multitude of others of the same description, will not easily be induced to form a contemptuous opinion of their literary talents, or to suspect them of being a whit behind the rest of the clergy in mental cultivation or intellectual vigour. In a subsequent edition the author has explained his meaning, by restricting the censure to all who have ranged themselves *on the side* of the clergy under consideration. But as far as

* In the second edition, the author has changed the term "*prosings*" into "*discoursings*."

the most explicit avowal of the same tenets can indicate any thing have not each of the respectable persons before mentioned ranged themselves on their side? Or if he will insist upon limiting the phrase to such as have defended them in controversy, what will he say of Overton, whose work, for a luminous statement of facts, an accurate arrangement of multifarious articles, and a close deduction of proofs, would do honour to the first polemic of the age? In affecting a contempt of this most able writer, he has contradicted himself, having, in another part of this work, borne a reluctant testimony to his talents. He closes his animadversions on the clergy usually styled evangelical with the following important concessions:—

"We are ready to own, though there have been a few instances to the contrary, that the moral conduct of the men in question is consistent with their calling; and that, though the faults above detailed are found among them, yet, as a body, they are more than free from immoralities."—P. 162.

The men to whom their accusers ascribe an assemblage of virtues so rare and so important, must unquestionably be "the excellent of the earth," and deserve a very different treatment from what they have received at his hands.

Before we put a final period to this article, we must beg the reader's patience to a few remarks on the general tendency of the work under examination.

For the freedom of censure the author has assumed he cannot plead the privilege of reproof. He has violated every law by which it is regulated. In administering reproof, we are not wont to call in a third party, least of all the party to whom the persons reproved are directly opposed. Besides, if reproof is intended to have any effect, it must be accompanied with the indications of a friendly mind; since none ever succeeded in reclaiming the person he did not appear to love. The spirit this writer displays towards the objects of his censure is decidedly hostile; no expressions of esteem, no attempt to conciliate; all is rudeness, asperity, and contempt. He tells us in his preface, "It is difficult to find an apology for disrespectful language under any circumstances: if it can be at all excused, it is when he who utters lets us know from whence it comes; but he who dares to use it, and yet dares not to put his name to the abuse, gives us reason to conclude that his cowardice is equal to his insolence."—(Pref. p. iv.) In violation of his own canon, he seems to have assumed a disguise for the very purpose of giving an unbridled indulgence to the insolence he condemns.

If we consider him in the light of a public censor, he will appear to have equally neglected the proprieties of that character. He who undertakes that office ought, in all reason, to direct his chief attention to vice and impiety; which, as the common foes of human nature, give every one the privilege of attack. Though his subject naturally led him to it, we find little or nothing of the kind. In his eagerness to expose the aberrations of goodness, the most deadly sins and the most destructive errors are scarcely noticed. In surveying the state of morals, the eccentricities of a pious zeal, a hairbreadth deviation from ecclesiastical etiquette, a momentary feeling of tenderness towards dissenters, are the things which excite his indignation; while the secularity, the indolence, the ambition, and dissipation too prevalent in the church almost escape his observation. We do not mean to assert that it is always improper to animadvert on the errors and mistakes of good men; we are convinced of the contrary. But whenever it is attempted, it ought to be accompanied with such expressions of tenderness and esteem, as shall mark our sense of their superiority to persons of an opposite description. In the moral delineations with which the New Testament abounds, when the imperfections of Christians are faithfully reprehended, we are never tempted to lose sight of the infinite disparity between the friends and the enemies of the gospel. Our reverence for good men is not impaired by contemplating their infirmities: while those who are strangers to vital religion, with whatever amiable qualities they may be invested, appear objects of pity. The impression made by the present performance is just the reverse. The character of the unquestionably good is placed in so invidious a light on the one hand, and the bad qualities of their opponents so artfully disguised and extenuated on the other, that the reader feels himself at a loss which to prefer. Its obvious tendency is to obliterate every mark and characteristic by which genuine religion is ascertained.

The writer of this work cannot have intended the reformation of the party on which he has animadverted; for, independently of his having by the rudeness of his attack forfeited every claim to their esteem, he has so conducted it, that there is not one in fifty guilty of the faults he has laid to their charge. Instead of being induced to alter their conduct, they can only feel for him those sentiments which unfounded calumny is apt to inspire. The very persons to whom his censures apply will be more likely to feel their resentment rise at the bitterness and rancour which accompany them, than to profit by his admonitions.

As we are fully convinced that the controversy agitated between the evangelical party and their opponents involves the essential interests of the gospel, and whatever renders Christianity worth contending for, we cannot but look with jealousy on the person who offers himself as an umpire; especially when we perceive a leaning towards the party which we consider in the wrong. This partiality may be traced almost through every page of the present work. Were we to look only to speculative points, we might be tempted to think otherwise It is not, however, in the cool, argumentative parts of a work that the bias of an author is so much to be perceived, as in the declamatory parts, when he gives a freer scope to his feelings. It is in the choice of the epithets applied to the respective parties, in the expression of contemptuous or respectful feeling, in the solicitude apparent to please the one, combined with his carelessness of offending the other, that he betrays the state of his heart. Judged by this criterion, this author must be pronounced an *enemy* to the evangelical party. We hope this unnatural alienation from the servants of Christ will not prove contagious, or it will soon completely overthrow that reformation which the established church has experienced within the last fifty years.

When Samson was brought into the house of Dagon to make sport for the Philistines, it was by the Philistines themselves: had it been done by an Israelite, it would have betrayed a blindness much more deplorable than that of Samson. Great as were the irregularities and disorders which deformed the church at Corinth, and severely as they were reprehended, it is easy to conceive, but impossible to express, the indignation Paul would have felt, had a Christian held up those disorders to the view and the derision of the heathen world. It is well known that the conduct of Luther, of Carlostadt, and of many other reformers, furnished matter of merited censure, and even of plausible invective; but he who had employed himself in emblazoning and magnifying their faults would have been deemed a foe to the Reformation. Aware that it will be replied to this, the cases are different, and neither the truth of Christianity nor the doctrines of the Reformation are involved in the issue of the present controversy; we answer without hesitation, that the controversy now on foot *does* involve nearly all that renders it important for Christianity to be true, and most precisely the doctrines of the Reformation, to which the papists are not more inimical (in some points they are less so) than the opponents of the evangelical clergy. It is the old enmity to the gospel, under a new form; an enmity as deadly and inveterate as that which animated the breast of Porphyry or of Julian.

The impression of character on the public mind is closely connected with that of principles; so that, in the mixed questions more especially which regard religion and morals, it is vain to expect men will condescend to be instructed by those whom they are taught to despise. Let it be generally supposed that the patrons of orthodox piety are weak, ignorant, and enthusiastic, despicable as a body, with the exception of a few individuals; after being inured to such representations from their enemies, let the public be told this by one who was formerly their friend and associate,—and is it possible to conceive a circumstance more calculated to obstruct the efficacy of their principles? Will the prejudices of an irreligious world against the gospel be mitigated by being inspired with contempt for its abetters? Will it be won to the love of piety by being schooled in the scorn and derision of its most serious professors?

We can readily suppose, that, stung with the reproaches cast upon his party, he is weary of bearing the Cross: if this be the case, let him at once renounce his principles, and not attempt, by mean concessions and a temporizing policy, to form an impracticable coalition between the world and the church. We apprehend the ground he has taken is untenable, and that he will be likely to please neither party. By the friends of the gospel he will be in danger of being shunned as an "accuser of the brethren;" while his new associates regard him with the contempt due to a sycophant.

It must give the enlightened friends of religion concern, to witness a spirit gaining ground among us, which, to speak of it in the most favourable terms, is calculated to sow the seeds of discord. The vivid attention to moral discrimination, the vigilance which seizes on what is deemed reprehensible, is unhappily turned to the supposed failings of good men, much to the satisfaction, no doubt, of an ungodly world. The practice of caricaturing the most illustrious men has grown fashionable among us. With grief and indignation we lately witnessed an attempt of this kind on the character of Mr. Whitfield, made, if our information be correct, by the present author; in which every shade of imperfection which tradition can supply, or ingenuity surmise, is industriously brought forward for the purpose of sinking him in public estimation. Did it accomplish the object intended by it? It certainly did not. While the prejudice entertained against Whitfield by the enemies of religion was already too violent to admit of increase, its friends were perfectly astonished at the littleness of soul, and the callousness to every kind feeling, which could delight in mangling such a character. It was his misfortune to mingle freely with different denominations, to preach in unconsecrated places, and convert souls at uncanonical hours: whether he acted right or wrong in these particulars, it is not our province to inquire. That he approved him self to his own conscience, there is not the least room to doubt. Admitting his conduct, in the instances alluded to, to have been inconsistent with his clerical engagements, let it be temperately censured; but let it not efface from our recollection the patient self-denial, the inextinguishable ardour, the incredible labours, and the unexampled success of that extraordinary man. The most zealous votaries of the church need be under no apprehension of her being often disgraced by producing such a man as Mr. Whitfield. *Nil admirari* is an excellent maxim when applied, as Horace intended it, to the goods of fortune: when extended to a character, nothing can be more injurious. A sensibility to the impression of great virtues bordering on enthusiasm, accompanied with a generous oblivion of the little imperfections with which they are joined, is one of the surest prognostics of excellence.

> "Verum, ubi plura nitent—non ego paucis
> Offendar maculis, quas aut incuria fudit,
> Aut humana parum cavit natura—"

The modern restorers of the piety of the Church of England were eminent for their godly simplicity and fidelity. Sincerely attached, as it became them, to the establishment of which they were ministers, their spirit was too enlarged, too ardent, too disinterested to suffer them to become the tools of a party, or to confound the interests of Christianity with those of any external communion. From their being looked upon as innovators, as well as from the paucity of their numbers, they were called to endure a much severer trial than falls to the lot of their successors. They bore the burden and heat of the day: they laboured, and others have entered into their labours. We feel, with respect to the greater part of those who succeed them, a confidence that they will continue to tread in their steps. But we cannot dissemble our concern at perceiving a set of men rising up among them, ambitious of new-modelling the party, who, if they have too much virtue openly to renounce their principles, yet have too little firmness to endure the consequences; timid, temporizing spirits, who would refine into insipidity, polish into weakness, and, under we know not what pretences of regularity, moderation, and a care not to offend, rob it utterly of that energy of character to which it owes its success. If they learn, from this and other writers of a similar description, to insult their brethren, fawn upon their enemies, and abuse their defenders, they will soon be frittered to pieces; they will become, "like other men," feeble, enervated, and shorn of their strength. We would adjure them to be on their guard against the machinations of this new sect. We cannot suspect them of the meanness of submitting to be drilled by their enemies, whom they are invited to approach in the attitude of culprits, beseeching them (in our author's phrase) to "inquire whether there may not be some found among them of unexceptionable character!" We trust they will treat such a suggestion with ineffable contempt.

After the taste our readers have had of this writer's spirit, they will not be surprised at his entire disapprobation of Mr. Overton's work. The discordance of sentiment must be great between him who wishes to betray, and him whose aim is to defend. Mr. Overton, in behalf of his brethren, boldly appeals from their accusers to the public. This writer crouches to those very accusers, approaches them in a supplicating tone, and, as the price of peace, offers the heads of his brethren in a charger. Overton, by a copious detail of facts, and by a series of irrefragable arguments, establishes their innocence: this writer assents to their condemnation, entreating only that execution may be respited till an inquiry is made into the degrees of delinquency. The author of "The True Churchman ascertained" clothes himself with the light of truth: the author of "Zeal without Innovation" hides himself in the thickest gloom of equivocation.

Before we close this article, we must entreat our reader's patience while we make one observation relating to the permanence of the ecclesiastical establishment. It is possible the dignitaries of the church may be at a loss to decide whether the services of the evangelical class shall be accepted or rejected; but we are persuaded the people will feel no difficulty in determining whether or not to continue their attendance at the places from whence they are banished. Teachers of the opposite description have already lost their hold on the public mind; and they will lose it more and more. Should the secession from the established church become so general as that its services are no longer the objects of popular suffrage, it will be deprived of its firmest support. For the author of the Alliance acknowledges that the compact between church and state, which he allows to be a virtual rather than a formal one, rests mainly upon the circumstance of the established religion being that of the majority, without which it becomes incapable of rendering those services to the state for the sake of which its privileges and emoluments were conferred. Nothing but an extreme infatuation can accelerate such an event. But if pious and orthodox men be prevented from entering into the church, or compelled to retire from it, the people will retire with them; and the apprehension of the church being in danger, which has so often been the watchword of party, will become, for once, well founded.

REVIEW

OF

GISBORNE'S SERMONS.

Sermons, principally designed to illustrate and to enforce Christian Morality. By the Rev. T. GISBORNE, A. M. 8vo. pp. 430. 1809.

WE have read these sermons with so much satisfaction, that, were it in our power to aid their circulation by any testimony of our approbation, we should be almost at a loss for terms sufficiently strong and emphatic. Though the excellent author is possessed already of a large share of the public esteem, we are persuaded these discourses will make a great accession to his celebrity. Less distinguished by any predominant quality than by an assemblage of the chief excellences in pulpit composition, they turn on subjects not very commonly handled, and discuss them with a copiousness, delicacy, and force which evince the powers of a master. They are almost entirely upon moral subjects, yet equally remote from the superficiality and dryness with which these subjects are too often treated. The morality of Mr. Gisborne is arrayed in all the majesty of truth and all the beauties of holiness. In perusing these sermons, the reader is continually reminded of real life, and beholds human nature under its most unsophisticated aspect, without ever being tempted to suppose himself in the schools of pagan philosophy. We cannot better explain the professed scope and object of the author than by copying a few sentences from his preface.

"Of late years it has been loudly asserted, that among clergymen who have showed themselves very earnest in doctrinal points, adequate regard has not been evinced to moral instruction. The charge has perhaps been urged with the greatest vehemence by persons who have employed little trouble in examining into its truth. In many cases it has been groundless, in many exaggerated. In some instances there has been reason, I fear, for a degree of complaint; and in more, a colourable pretext for the imputation. I believe that some preachers, shocked on beholding examples, real or supposed, of congregations starving on mere morality, substituted for the bread of life, eager to lay broad and deep the foundations of the gospel, and ultimately apprehensive lest their own hearers should suspect them of reverting towards *legality*, have not given to morals, as fruits of faith, the station and the amplitude to which they have a scriptural claim. Anxious lest others should mistake, or lest they should themselves be deemed to mistake, the branch for the root; not satisfied with proclaiming to the branch, as they were bound habitually to proclaim, *Thou bearest not the root, but the root thee*, they have shrunk from the needful office of tracing the ramifications. They have not left morality out of their discourses, but they have kept it too much in the background. They have noticed it shortly, generally, incidentally; in a manner which, while perhaps they were eminent as private patterns of moral duties, might not sufficiently guard an unwary hearer against a reduced estimate of practical holiness, nor exempt themselves from the suspicion of undervaluing moral obedience."—Pref. pp. vii. viii.

To the truth of these remarks we cordially assent, as they point to a defect in the ministration of some excellent men, which the judicious part of the public have long lamented, and which Mr. Gisborne, in his present work, has taught his contemporaries how to remedy. Extremes naturally lead to each other. The peculiar doctrines of the gospel had been so long neglected by the most celebrated preachers, and the pernicious consequences of that neglect, in wearing out every trace of genuine religion, had been so deeply felt, that it is not to be wondered at if the first attempts to correct the evil were accompanied with a tendency to the contrary extreme. In many situations, those who attempted to revive doctrines which had long been considered as obsolete, found themselves much in the same circumstances as missionaries, having intelligence to impart before unknown, and exposed to all the contempt and obloquy which assailed the first preachers of Christianity. While they were engaged in such an undertaking, it is not at all surprising that they confined their attention almost entirely to the doctrines peculiar to the Christian religion, with less care to inculcate and display the moral precepts which it includes in common with other systems than their intrinsic importance demanded. They were too much occupied in removing the rubbish and laying the foundations, to permit them to carry their superstructure very high. They insisted, in general terms, on the performance of moral duties; urged the necessity of that holiness without which "none shall see the Lord;" and, by a forcible application of truth to the conscience, produced in many instances the most surprising as well as the most happy effects. But still, in consequence of limiting their ministry too much to the first elements of the gospel, and dwelling chiefly on topics calculated to alarm the careless and console the faithful, a wrong taste began to prevail among their hearers—a disrelish of moral discussions, a propensity to contemplate Christianity under one aspect alone,—that of a system of relief for the guilty, instead of a continual discipline of the heart. Those wished for stimulants and cordials whose situation required alteratives and correctives. Preachers and hearers have a reciprocal influence on each other; and the fear of being reproached as "*legal*," deterred some good men from insisting so much on moral and practical subjects as their own good sense would have dictated. By this means the malady became more inveterate, till the inherent corruption of human nature converted the doctrine of the gospel, in a greater or less degree, into the leaven of antinomianism. An error which at first appeared trivial at length proved serious; and thus it came to pass that the fabric of sacred truth was almost universally reared in such a manner as to deviate sensibly from the primitive model.

When we look at Christianity in the New Testament, we see a set of discoveries, promises, and precepts, adapted to influence the whole character: it presents an object of incessant solicitude, in the pursuit of which new efforts are to be exerted and new victories accomplished, in a continued course of well-doing, till we reach the heavenly mansions. There is scarce a spring in the human frame and constitution it is not calculated to touch, nor any portion of human agency which is exempted from its control. Its resources are inexhaustible; and the considerations by which it challenges attention embrace whatever is most awful or alluring in the whole range of possible existence. Instead of being allowed to repose on his past attainments, or to flatter himself with the hope of success without the exercise of diligence and watchfulness, the Christian is commanded to work out his salvation with fear and trembling. In the *actual* exhibition of religion the solicitude of serious minds has been made to turn too much on a particular crisis, which has been presented in a manner so insulated that nothing in the order of means seemed instrumental to its production. In short, things have been represented in such a manner as was too apt to produce despondency before conversion, and presumption after it.

It must be allowed, the judicious management of practical subjects is more difficult than the discussion of doctrinal points, which may also account in part for the prevalence of the evil we are now speaking of. In treating a point of doctrine, the habit of belief almost supersedes the necessity of proof: the mind of the hearer is usually preoccupied in favour of the conclusions to be established; nor is much address or ingenuity necessary to conduct him in a path in which he has long been accustomed to tread. The materials are prepared to the preacher's hands; a set of texts, with their received interpretations, stand ready for his use; the compass of thought which is required is very limited; and this little circle has been beaten so often that an ordinary understanding moves through it with mechanical facility. To discuss a doctrinal position to the satisfaction of a common audience requires the smallest possible exertion of intellect. The tritest arguments are in fact the best: the most powerful considerations to enforce assent are rendered by that very quality the most conspicuous, as the sun announces himself by his superior splendour. In delineating the duties of life the task is very different. To render these topics interesting, it is necessary to look abroad, to contemplate the principles of human nature, and the diversified modes of human feeling and action. The preacher has not to do with a few rigid and unbending propositions: he is to contemplate and portray a real state of things—a state which is continually changing its aspect while it preserves its essential character, and the particulars of which mock the powers of enumeration. If he does not think with great originality, he must at least think for himself: he must use his own eyes, though he may report nothing but what has been observed before. As there lies an appeal on these occasions to the unbiassed good sense and observation of unlettered minds, the deficiencies of an injudicious instructer are sure to be detected. His principles will fail of interesting for want of exemplification, or his details will be devoid of dignity, and his delineations of human life disgust by their deviation from nature and from truth.

In points of casuistry, difficulties will occur which can only be solved and disentangled by nice discrimination, combined with extensive knowledge. The general precepts, for example, of justice and humanity may be faithfully inculcated and earnestly insisted on without affording a ray of useful direction to a doubting conscience. While all men acknowledge the indispensable obligation of these precepts, it is not always easy to discover what is the precise line of action they enforce. In the application of general rules to particular cases of conduct, many relations must be surveyed, opposing claims must be reconciled and adjusted, and the comparative value of different species of virtue established upon just and solid principles.

These difficulties have been evaded, rather than overcome, by the greater part of moralizing preachers; who have contented themselves with retailing extracts from the works of their celebrated predecessors, or with throwing together a few loose and undigested thoughts on a moral duty, without order and arrangement, or the smallest effort to impress its obligation upon the conscience, or to deduce it from its proper sources. To the total want of unction, to the cold, pagan, anti christian cast of these compositions, joined to their extreme super ficiality, must be ascribed in a great measure the disgust which many serious minds have contracted against the introduction of moral topics into the pulpit. Our readers will not suspect we mean to apply this censure indiscriminately, or that we are insensible to the extraordinary merits of a Barrow or of a Tillotson, who have cultivated Christian morals with so universal an applause of the English public. We admire, as much as it is possible for our readers to admire, the rich invention, the masculine sense, the exuberantly copious, yet precise and energetic diction, which distinguish the first of these writers, who, by a rare felicity of genius, united in himself the most distinguishing qualities of the mathematician and of the orator. We are astonished at perceiving in the same person and in the same composition the close logic of Aristotle combined with the amplifying powers of Plato. The candour, the good sense, the natural arrangement, the unpremeditated graces of Tillotson, if they excite less admiration, give us almost equal pleasure. It is indeed the peculiar boast of the English nation to have produced a set of divines who, being equally acquainted with classical antiquity and inspired writ, and capable of joining, to the deepest results of unassisted reason, the advantages of a superior illumination, have delivered down to posterity a body of moral instruction more pure, copious, and exact than subsists among any other people; and had they appealed more frequently to the peculiar principles of the gospel, had they infused a more evangelical spirit into their discourses, instead of representing Christianity too much as a mere code of morals, they would have left us nothing to wish or to regret. Their decision of moral questions was for the most part unquestionably just; but they contemplated moral duties too much apart, neglecting to blend them sufficiently with the motives and principles of pure revelation, after the manner of the inspired writers; and, supposing them to believe, they forgot to inculcate the fundamental truth—that "*by the deeds of the law no flesh living shall be justified.*" Those internal dispositions whence right conduct can alone flow were too little insisted on; the agency of the Spirit was not sufficiently honoured or acknowledged; and the subordination of the duties of the second to those of the first table not enough kept in view. The virtues they recommended and enforced were too often considered as the native growth of the human heart, instead of being represented as "*fruits of the Spirit.*" Jesus Christ was not laid as the foundation of morality; and a very sparing use was made of the motives to its practice deduced from his promises, his example, and his sacrifice. Add to this, that the labours of these great men were employed almost entirely in illustrating and enforcing the obligation of particular duties, while the doctrine of the Cross engaged little of their attention, except so far as it was impugned by the objections of infidels or mutilated by the sophistry of papists. From the perusal of their writings the impression naturally results, that a belief of the evidences of revealed religion, joined to a correct deportment in social life, is adequate to all the demands of Christianity. For these reasons, much as we admire, we cannot recommend them in an unqualified manner, nor consider them as safe guides in religion.

By these remarks we intend no offence to any class of Christians. That the celebrated authors we have mentioned, with others of a similar stamp, have refined the style and improved the taste of the English pulpit, while they have poured a copious stream of knowledge on the public mind, we are as ready to acknowledge as their warmest admirers; but we will not disguise our conviction, that for the just delineation of the "truth as it is in Jesus," we must look to the Baxters, the Howes, and the Ushers of an earlier period. He who wishes to catch the flame of devotion by listening to the words "which are spirit and are life," will have recourse to the writings of the latter, notwithstanding their intricacy of method and prolixity of style.

It is with peculiar satisfaction we call the attention of our readers to a work which unites in a considerable degree the excellences of each class of divines alluded to, without their defects. The discourses are on the following subjects: Our Lord Jesus Christ the Foundation of Morality; on the Evils resulting from false Principles of Morality; on the Changes produced by the Coming of Christ in the Situation of Men as to the Divine Law; Justification not attainable by Acts of Morality; on Living after the Flesh or after the Spirit; the Love of God an Inducement to strict Morality; on Brotherly Love; on the Love of

Money; on the Sacrifice of Worldly Interest to Duty; on Christian Bounty; on Discontent; on Worldly Anxiety; on Christian Obedience to Civil Rulers; Christian Patriotism illustrated by the Character of Nehemiah; on quiet Diligence in our Proper Concerns; on Partiality; on Suspicion; on doing Evil to produce Good; on the Superiority of Moral Conduct required of Christians. The reader will perceive it was not the author's design to make a systematic arrangement of Christian duties, and that there are many vices and virtues not comprehended within the plan of his present work. In the discussion of the subjects which he has selected, he has evinced much observation of human life, a deep insight into the true principles of morals, and an intimate acquaintance with the genius of the Christian religion. He has erected his edifice upon a solid basis; in the choice of his materials he has carefully excluded the wood, hay, and stubble, and admitted no ornaments but such as are fitted to grace the temple of God.

The intelligent reader will discover in these discourses the advantage resulting from studying morality as a science. It will yield him great satisfaction to find the writer ascending on all occasions to first principles, forming his decision on comprehensive views, separating what is specious from what is solid, and enforcing morality by no motives which are suspicious or equivocal. He will not see vanity or ambition pressed into the service of virtue, or any approach to the adoption of that dangerous policy which proposes to expel one vice by encouraging another. He will meet with no flattering encomiums on the purity and dignity of our nature, none of those appeals to the innate goodness of the human heart, which are either utterly ineffectual, or, if they restrain from open profligacy, diffuse at the same time the more subtle poison of pride and self-righteousness. Mr. Gisborne never confounds the functions of morality with the offices of the Saviour, nor ascribes to human virtue, polluted and imperfect at best, any part of those transcendent effects which the New Testament teaches us to impute to the mediation of Christ. He considers the whole compass of moral duties as branches of religion, as prescribed by the will of God, and no farther acceptable to him than as they proceed from religious motives.

The disposition in mankind to seek justification by the works of the law has been so much flattered and encouraged by the light in which moral duties have been usually placed, that Mr. Gisborne has shown his judgment by counteracting this error at the outset. We recommend to the serious attention of our readers, with this view, the fourth sermon, on Justification not attainable by Acts of Morality. We have never seen a publication in which that important argument is set in a more clear and convincing light.

Though Mr. Gisborne for a series of years has distinguished himself as the able opponent of the doctrine of expediency, yet on no occasion has he exerted more ability in this cause than in his present work. We recommend it to the thinking part of the public to forget for a moment that they are reading a sermon, and conceive themselves attending to the arguments of a sober and enlightened philosopher To purify the sources of morals, and to detect the principles of a theory which enables us to err by system and be depraved by rule, is to do good of the highest sort; as he who diminishes the mass of human calamity by striking one from the list of diseases, is a greater benefactor to mankind than the physician who performs the greatest number of cures. It is in this light we look upon the labours of the present author; to whom we are more indebted than to any other individual for discrediting a doctrine which threatens to annihilate religion, to loosen the foundation of morals, and to debase the character of the nation. We recommend to universal perusal the admirable discourse, on the Evils resulting from false Principles of Morality.

The two discourses which propose to illustrate the Character of Nehemiah contain the most valuable instruction, adapted in particular to the use of those who occupy the higher ranks, or who possess stations of commanding influence and authority. They evince just and enlarged views of the duties attached to elevated situations, and breathe the purest spirit of Christian benevolence. The sermon on the Love of Money displays, perhaps, most of the powers of the orator, and demonstrates in how masterly a manner the author is capable, when he pleases, of enforcing "the terrors of the Lord." It contains some awful passages, in which, by a kind of repeated asseveration of the same truth, and the happy reiteration of the same words, an effect is produced resembling that of repeated claps of thunder. We shall present our readers with the following specimen.

"Fourthly. Meditate on the final condition to which the lover of money is hastening. The *covetous*, the man who is under the dominion of the love of money, 'shall not inherit the kingdom of God.' In the present life he has a foretaste of the fruits of his sin. He is restless, anxious, dissatisfied: at one time harassed by uncertainty as to the probable result of his projects; at another, soured by the failure of them; at another, disappointed in the midst of success, by discerning, too late, that the same exertions employed in some other line of advantage would have been more productive. But suppose him to have been, through life, as free from the effects of these sources of vexation as the most favourable picture could represent him, 'he shall not inherit the kingdom of God.' He may not have been a miser; but he was a lover of money. He may not have been an extortioner; but he was a lover of money. He may not have been fraudulent; but he was a lover of money. 'He shall not inherit the kingdom of God.' He has had his day and his object. He has sought, and he may have accumulated, earthly possessions. By their instrumentality he may have gratified many other appetites and desires. But he did not seek first the kingdom of God; therefore he shall not obtain it. He 'loved the world;' therefore he 'shall perish with the world.' He has wilfully bartered his soul for money. In vain is he now aghast at his former madness. In vain does he now detest the idol which he worshipped. The gate of salvation is closed against him. He inherits the bitterness of unavailing remorse, the horrors of eternal death."—Pp. 145, 146.

If we were called to specify the discourse in the present volume that appeared to us the most ingenious and original, we should be inclined to point to the eighteenth, on Suspicion

Having expressed our warm approbation of this performance, justice compels us to notice what appear to us its principal blemishes: which, however, are so overbalanced by the merit of the whole, that we should scarcely deem them worthy of remark, were it not requisite to vindicate our claim to impartiality. Against the sentiments or the arrangement of these discourses we have nothing to object: the former are almost invariably just and important, often striking and original; the latter is natural and easy, preserving the *spirit* of method even where it may seem to neglect the form; equally remote from the looseness of an harangue and the ostentation of logical exactness. With the style of this work we cannot say that we are quite so much satisfied. Perspicuous, dignified, and correct, it yet wants something more of amenity, variety, and ease. Instead of that flexibility which bends to accommodate itself to the different conceptions which occur, it preserves a sort of uniform stateliness. The art of transposition, carried, in our opinion to excess, together with the preference of learned to plain Saxon words, give it an air of Latinity, which must necessarily render it less intelligible and acceptable to unlettered minds. It is indeed but fair to remark, that the discourses appear to have been chiefly designed for the use of the higher classes. But while we allow this apology its just weight, we are still of opinion that the composition might have assumed a more easy and natural air, without losing any thing of its force or beauty. Addresses from the pulpit should, in our apprehension, always make some approach to the character of plain and popular.

Another blemish which strikes us in this work, is the frequent use of interrogations, introduced, not only in the warm and impassioned parts, where they are graceful, but in the midst of argumentative discussion. We have been struck with the prevalence of this practice in the more recent works of clergymen, beyond those of any other order of men. With Demosthenes we know interrogation was a very favourite figure; but we recollect, at the same time, it was chiefly confined to the more vehement parts of his speeches, in which, like the eruptions of a furnace, he broke out upon and consumed his opponents. In him it was the natural expression of triumphant indignation: after he had subdued and laid them prostrate by the force of his arguments, by his abrupt and terrible interrogations he trampled them in the mire. In calm and dispassionate discussion, the frequent use of questions appears to us unnatural; it discomposes the attention by a sort of starting and irregular motion, and is a violation of dignity, by affecting to be lively where it is sufficient praise to be cogent and convincing. In a word, when, instead of being used to give additional vehemence to a discourse, they are interspersed in a series of arguments, as an expedient for enlivening the attention and varying the style, they have an air of undignified flippancy. We should scarcely have noticed these little circumstances in an inferior work; but we could not satisfy ourselves to let them pass without observation in an author who, to merits of a more substantial nature, joins so many and such just pretensions to the character of a fine writer.

REVIEW

OF

GREGORY'S LETTERS.

Letters to a Friend on the Evidences, Doctrines, and Duties of the Christian Religion. By Olinthus Gregory, LL.D., *of the Royal Military Academy, Woolwich.* 1812.

As this is a work of no ordinary merit, and written upon a subject which all must confess to be of the last importance, we shall endeavour, after being indulged with a few preliminary remarks, to give a pretty copious analysis of its contents ; not doubting the greater part of our readers will be solicitous to avail themselves of the rich entertainment and instruction which its perusal will unquestionably afford. The first volume is employed in the discussion of a subject which has engaged the powers of the wisest of men through a series of ages ; and minds of every size, and of every diversity of acquisition, having contributed their quota towards its elucidation, the accumulation of materials is such, that it has become more necessary, perhaps more difficult, to arrange than to invent. In the conduct of so extensive an argument, the talents of the writer will chiefly appear in giving the due degree of relief and prominence to the different branches of the subject,—in determining what should be placed in a strong and brilliant light, and what should be more slightly sketched,—and disposing the whole in such a manner as shall give it the most impressive effect. If there is little room for the display of invention, other powers are requisite, not less rare or less useful ; a nice and discriminating judgment, a true logical taste, and a talent of extensive combination. An ordinary thinker feels himself lost in so wide a field ; is incapable of classifying the objects it presents ; and wastes his attention on such as are trite and common, instead of directing it to those which are great and interesting. If there are subjects which it is difficult to discuss for want of data to proceed upon,—and, while they allure by their appearance of abstract grandeur, are soon found to lose themselves in fruitless logomachies and unmeaning subtleties, such as the greater part of the discussions on time, space, and necessary existence,—there are others whose difficulty springs from an opposite cause, from the immense variety of distinct topics and considerations involved in their discussion, of which the divine origination of Christianity is a striking specimen; which it has become difficult to treat as it ought to be treated, merely in consequence of the variety and superabundance of its proofs.

On this account we suspect that this great cause has been not a little injured by the injudicious conduct of a certain class of preachers and writers, who, in just despair of being able to handle a single topic of religion to advantage, for want of having paid a devout attention to the Scriptures, fly like harpies to the evidences of Christianity, on which they are certain of meeting with something prepared to their hands which they can tear, and soil, and mangle at their pleasure.

Diripiuntque dapes, contactuque omnia fœdant.

The famine, also, with which their prototypes in Virgil threatened the followers of Æneas, is not more dismal than that which prevails among their hearers. The folly we are adverting to did not escape the observation nor the ridicule of Swift, who remarked in his days that the practice of mooting on every occasion the question of the origin of Christianity was much more likely to unsettle the faith of the simple than to counteract the progress of infidelity. It is dangerous to familiarize every promiscuous audience to look upon religion as a thing which yet remains to be proved, to acquaint them with every sophism and cavil which a perverse and petulant ingenuity has found out, unaccompanied, as is too often the case, with a satisfactory answer; thus leaving the poison to operate, without the antidote, in minds which ought to be strongly imbued with the principles and awed by the sanctions of the gospel. It is degrading to the dignity of a revelation established through a succession of ages by indubitable proofs, to be adverting every moment to the hypothesis of its being an imposture, and to be inviting every insolent sophist to wrangle with us about the title, when we should be cultivating the possession. The practice we are now censuring is productive of another inconvenience. The argument of the truth of Christianity being an argument of accumulation, or, in other words, of that nature that the force of it results less from any separate consideration than from an almost infinite variety of circumstances, conspiring towards one point and terminating in one conclusion; this concentration of evidence is broken to pieces when an attempt is made to present it in superficial descants; than which nothing can be conceived better calculated to make what is great appear little, and what is ponderous, light. The trite observation that a cause is injured by the adoption of feeble arguments, rests on a basis not often considered perhaps by those who most readily assent to its truth. We never think of estimating the powers of the imagination on a given subject by the actual performance of the poet; but if he disappoint us, we immediately ascribe his failure to the poverty of his genius, without accusing his subject or his art. The regions of fiction we naturally conceive to be boundless; but when an attempt is made to convince us of the truth of a proposition respecting a matter of fact or a branch of morals, we take it for granted that he who proposes it has made himself perfectly master of his argument; and that, as no consideration has been neglected that would favour his opinion, we shall not err in taking our impression of the cause from the defence of its advocate. If that cause happen to be such as involves the dearest interests of mankind, we need not remark how much injury it is capable of sustaining from this quarter.

Let us not be supposed by these remarks to comprehend within our censure the writer who, amid the multifarious proofs of revelation, selects a single topic with a view to its more elaborate discussion, provided it be of such a nature that it will support an independent train of thought; such, for example, as Paley has pursued in his Horæ Paulinæ, to which a peculiar value ought to be attached as a clear addition to the body of Christian evidences. All we mean to assert is, that it is incomparably better to be silent on the evidences of Christianity than to be perpetually adverting to them in a slight and superficial manner; and that a question so awful and momentous as that relating to the origin of the Christian religion ought not to be debased into a trivial commonplace. Let it be formally discussed, at proper intervals, by such men, and such only, as are capable of bringing to it the time, talents, and information requisite to place it in a commanding attitude. That the author of the present performance is possessed of these qualifications to a very great degree will sufficiently appear from the analysis we propose to give of the work, and the specimens we shall occasionally exhibit of its execution.

It is ushered in by a modest and dignified dedication to Colonel Mudge, lieutenant-governor of that royal military institution of which the author is so distinguished an ornament. The whole is cast into the form of Letters to a Friend; and the first volume, we are given to understand, formed the subject of an actual correspondence. As much of the epistolary style is preserved as is consistent with the nature of a serious and protracted argument, without ill-judged attempts at refreshing the attention of the reader by strokes of gayety and humour. The mind of the writer appears to have been too deeply impressed with his theme to admit of such excursions, the absence of which will not, we are persuaded, be felt or regretted.

Before he proceeds to state the direct proofs of the divinity of the Christian religion, he shows, in a very striking manner, the absurdities which must of necessity be embraced by those who deny all pretences to revelation; enumerating, in the form of a creed, the various strange and untenable positions which form the subject of skeptical belief. In this part of the work, that disease in the intellectual temperament of infidels is placed in a stronger and juster light than we remember to have seen it, which may not improperly be denominated the credulity of unbelievers. This representation forms the contents of the first letter.

The necessity of revelation is still more indisputably evinced by an appeal to facts, and a survey of the opinions which prevailed among the most enlightened heathens respecting God, moral duty, and a future state. Under each of these heads, our author has selected with great judgment, numerous instances of the flagrant and pernicious errors entertained by the most celebrated pagan legislators, poets, and philosophers, sufficient to demonstrate, beyond all contradiction, the inability of unassisted reason, in its most improved and perfect state, to conduct man to virtue and happiness, and the necessity, thence resulting, of superior aid. Much diligence of research and much felicity of arrangement are displayed in the management of this complicated topic, where the reader will find exhibited, in a condensed form, the most material facts adduced in Leland's voluminous work on this subject. All along he holds the balance with a firm and steady hand, without betraying a disposition either to depreciate the value of those discoveries and improvements to which reason really attained, or charging the picture of its aberrations and defects with deeper shades than justly belong to it. The most eminent among the pagans themselves, it ought to be remembered, who, having no other resource, were best acquainted with its weakness and its power, never dreamed of denying the necessity of revelation: this they asserted in the most explicit terms, and on some occasions seem to have expected and anticipated the communication of such a benefit. We make no apology for citing, from the present work, the following remarkable passage out of Plato, tending both to confirm the fact of a revelation being anticipated, and to evince, supposing nothing supernatural in the case, the divine sagacity of that great author. He says, "This just person (the inspired teacher of whom he had been speaking) must be poor, and void of all qualifications but those of virtue alone; that a wicked world would not bear his instructions and reproofs; and therefore, within three or four years after he began to preach, he should be persecuted, imprisoned, scourged, and at last be put to death."* In whatever light we consider it, this must be allowed to be a most remarkable passage, whether we regard it as merely the conjecture of a highly enlightened mind, or as the fruit of prophetic suggestion: nor are we aware of any absurdity in supposing that the prolific Spirit scattered on certain occasions some seeds of truth amid that mass of corruption and darkness which oppressed the pagan world. The opinion we have ventured to advance is asserted in the most positive terms in several parts of Justin Martyr's Second Apology. Without pursuing this inquiry further, we shall content ourselves with remarking, that, as the sufficiency of mere reason as the guide to truth never entered into the conception of pagans, so it could never have arisen at all but in consequence of confounding its results with the dictates of revelation, which, since its publication, has never ceased to modify the speculations and aid the inquiries of those who are least disposed to bow to its authority. On all questions of morality and religion, the streams of thought have flowed through channels enriched with a celestial ore, whence they have derived the tincture to which they are indebted for their rarest and most salutary qualities.

Before we dismiss the subject we would just observe, that the inefficacy of unassisted reason in religious concerns appears undeniably in

* De Republica, Lib. ii.

two points: the doubtful manner in which the wisest pagans were accustomed to express themselves respecting a future state, the existence of which Warburton is confident none of the philosophers believed; and their proud reliance on their own virtue, which was such as left no room for repentance. Of a future state Socrates, in the near prospect of death, is represented by Plato as expressing a hope, accompanied with the greatest uncertainty; and, with respect to the second point, the lofty confidence in their own virtue, which we have imputed to them, the language of Cicero, in one of his familiar letters, is awfully decisive: "Nec enim dum ero, angor ulla re, cum *omni caream culpa;* et si non ero, sensu omni carebo."—"While I exist, I shall be troubled at nothing, since I have no fault whatever; and if I shall not exist, I shall be devoid of all feeling."* So true is it that life and immortality were brought to light by the Saviour; and that until he appeared, the greatest of men were equally unacquainted with their present condition and their future prospects.

The next letter, which is the fourth in the series, is on mysteries in religion. Aware that, while the prejudice against whatever is mysterious subsists, the saving truths of the gospel can find no entrance, the author has taken great, and, as far as the force of argument can operate, successful pains to point out the weakness of the foundations on which that prejudice rests. He has shown, by a large induction of particulars in natural religion, natural philosophy, and in pure and mixed mathematics, that with respect to each of these sciences, we arrive, by infallible steps, to conclusions of which we can form no clear, determinate conceptions; and that the higher parts of mathematics especially, the science which glories in its superior light and demonstration, teem with mysteries as incomprehensible to the full as those which demand our assent in revelation. His skill as a mathematician, for which he has long been distinguished, serves him on this occasion to excellent purpose, by enabling him to illustrate his subject by well-selected examples from his favourite science; and by that means to prove, in the most satisfactory manner, that the mysterious parts of Christianity are exactly analogous to the difficulties inseparable from other branches of knowledge, not excepting those which make the justest pretensions to demonstration. We run no hazard in affirming, that rarely, if ever, have superior philosophical attainments been turned to a better account, or a richer offering brought from the fields of science into the temple of God. Some of his illustrations, being drawn from the sublimer speculations of mathematics, must necessarily be unintelligible to ordinary readers: but many of them are plain and popular; and he has succeeded in making the principle on which he reasons throughout perfectly plain and perspicuous, which is this—that we are able, in a multitude of instances, to ascertain the *relations* of things, while we know little or nothing of the *nature* of the things themselves. If the distinction itself is not entirely new, the force of argument with which it is supported, and the extent to which its illustration is carried, are such as evince much original thinking. We should seriously

* Vol. I. p. 51

recommend this part of the work to the perusal of the barrister, if he were capable of understanding it; and to all, without exception, who have been perverted by the shallow and ambiguous sophism, first broached, we believe, by Dr. Foster, that where mystery begins religion ends; when the fact is, that religion and mystery both begin and end together, a portion of what is inscrutable to our faculties being intimately and inseparably blended with its most vital and operative truths. A religion without its mysteries is a temple without its God.

Having thus marked out the ground, removed the rubbish, and made room for the foundation, our author proceeds, with the skill of a master, to erect a firm and noble structure, conducting the argument for the truth of Christianity through all its stages, and commencing his labours in this part of his subject with establishing the genuineness and authenticity of the sacred volume. As he manifestly aims at utility, not at display, we are glad to find he has availed himself of the profound and original reasoning of Hartley, which he has fortified all along with ingenious reflections of his own, and crowned by an appeal to the principal testimonies of Christian and pagan antiquity. The letter devoted to this subject is long, but not more so than the occasion demanded, and is replete with varied and extensive information. To the whole he has annexed a very accurate and particular account of the researches and discoveries of Dr. Buchanan, made during his visit to the Syrian churches in India; nor are we aware that there is a single consideration of moment, tending to confirm the genuineness and integrity of the Scriptures in their present state, which, in the course of our author's extended investigation, has escaped his notice. By some he will be blamed for placing the proofs of the authenticity of the sacred records before the argument from prophecy and miracles; but we think he is right in adopting such an arrangement; since the reasoning on this part not only stands independent of the sequel, but greatly abridges his subsequent labour, by enabling him to appeal on every occasion to the testimony of Scripture, not indeed as inspired, but as an authentic document, that point having been previously established; while it is in perfect unison with that solicitude he everywhere evinces to imbue the mind of his readers with a serious and devotional spirit. Here is a book of a singular character and of high antiquity, from which Christians profess to derive the whole of their information on religion; and it comes down to us under such circumstances that every thing relating to it is capable of being investigated apart from the consideration of prophecies and miracles, except its claim to inspiration. Why, then, should not the pretensions of this book be examined at the very outset, as far as they are susceptible of an independent examination; since the proof of its being genuine and authentic will extend its consequences so far into the subsequent matter of discussion, as well as exert a great and salutary influence on the mind of the inquirer?

The next letter is devoted to the subject of prophecy; in which, after noticing a few of the more remarkable predictions relating to the revolutions of power and empire, he descends to a more particular investigation of the prophecies relating to the Messiah, which he arranges under three heads: such as respect the time and place of his appearance; his character, doctrine, rejection, and final triumph; and the exact correspondence between his contemptuous treatment and sufferings, and the representations of the ancient oracles. Under the last he embraces the opportunity of rescuing the proof from the fifty-third chapter of Isaiah from the cavils of the Jews, as well as from the insinuation of certain infidels that the prophecy was written after the event; which he triumphantly refutes by an appeal to a remarkable passage in the books of Origen against Celsus. In confirming the inference from prophecy, we again meet with a judicious application of the author's mathematical skill, by which he demonstrates, from the doctrine of chances, the almost infinite improbability of the occurrence of even a small number of contingent events predicted of any one individual; and the absolute impossibility, consequently, of accounting for the accomplishment of such numerous predictions as were accomplished in the person of the Messiah, without ascribing it to the power and wisdom of the Deity.

From the consideration of prophecy, he proceeds to the evidence of miracles, and the credibility of human testimony. He begins with stating, in few and simple terms, but with much precision, the just idea of a miracle, which, he remarks, has oftener been obscured than elucidated by definition; while the sentiments entertained by good men upon the subject have been almost uniformly correct when they have not been entangled or heated by controversy. This branch of the evidences of revelation is certainly very little indebted to the introduction of subtle refinements. In resting the evidence of the Jewish and Christian revelations on the ground of miracles, the author restricts his proposition to *uncontrolled miracles;* on the propriety of which, different judgments will probably be formed by his readers. We believe him to be right: since, admitting the limitation to be unnecessary, it is but an extreme of caution, a leaning to the safe side; for who will deny that it is much easier to prove it to be inconsistent with the wisdom and goodness of the Deity, to permit an *uncontrolled* miracle to be performed in support of error, than to demonstrate, from a metaphysical consideration of the powers and capacities of spiritual agents of a high order, their incapacity of accomplishing what, to our apprehensions, must appear supernatural? The writer of this at least must confess for himself he could never find any satisfaction in such speculations, not even in those of Farmer, ingenious as they are; which always appeared to him to be like advancing to an object by a circuitous and intricate path, rather than taking the nearest road. But to return to the present performance. After exhibiting the most approved answers to the flimsy sophistry of Hume, intended to evince the incredibility of miracles,—and corroborating them by a copious illustration of the four criteria of miraculous facts suggested by Leslie, in his admirable work entitled A Short Method with the Deists,—he reduces the only suppositions which can be formed respecting the miracles recorded in the New Testament to the four following, which we shall give in the words of the author:—

"Either, first, the recorded accounts of those miracles were absolute fictions, wickedly invented by some who had a wish to impose upon mankind.

"Or, secondly, Jesus did not work any true miracles; but the senses of the people were, in some way or other, deluded, so that they believed he really did perform miracles, when in fact he did not.

"Or, thirdly, that the spectators were not in any way deluded, but knew very well he wrought no miracles; yet were all (both enemies and friends, the Jews themselves not excepted, though they daily 'sought occasion against him') united in a close confederacy, to persuade the world he wrought the most surprising things. So that, while some actively circulated reports of those amazing occurrences, the rest kept their counsel, never offering to unmask the fraud, but managing the matter with so much dexterity and cunning, and such an exact harmony and correspondence, that the story of Jesus Christ's performing miracles should become current, should obtain almost universal credit, *and not a single person be able to disprove it.*

"Or, fourthly, that he did actually perform those astonishing works; and that the accounts given of them by the Christian writers in the New Testament are authentic and correct.

"He that does not adopt the last of these conclusions will find it a matter of very small consequence which of the other three he chooses; for that the stories cannot be *fictions* is evident from the reasonings of Leslie, already adduced; and it will be seen further, from a moment's consideration, that the denial of the miracles of Jesus Christ, *in any way*, leads necessarily to the admission of a series of real miracles of another kind."

He closes this part of his disquisition with an elaborate confutation of the notion too generally admitted by the advocates of revelation, that the evidence of miraculous facts necessarily grows weaker in proportion to the distance of the time at which they were performed; and in no part does the vigour of his understanding appear to more advantage than in his reasonings on this point, where, among many excellent, we meet with the following profound remark:—

"It is only," he observes, "with regard to the facts recorded in the Bible, that men ever talk of the daily diminution of credibility. Who complains of a decay of evidence in relation to the actions of Alexander, Hannibal, Pompey, or Cæsar? How many fewer of the events recorded by Plutarch, or Polybius, or Livy, are believed now (on account of a diminution of evidence) than were believed by Mr. Addison, or Lord Clarendon, or Geoffrey Chaucer? We never hear persons wishing they had lived ages earlier, that they might have had better proofs that Cyrus was the conqueror of Babylon, that Darius was beaten in several battles by Alexander, that Titus destroyed Jerusalem, that Hannibal was entirely routed by Scipio, or Pompey by Julius Cæsar; though we sometimes find men of ardent and enterprising minds exclaiming, 'O that I had lived and been present when such splendid events occurred, how lively an interest should I have taken in such scenes, how much concern in their termination!' And, indeed, it is the frequent hearing of such exclamations that causes men *to confound weight of evidence with warmth or depth of feeling; and to lose sight of the essential difference between real evidence, or the true basis of belief in history, and the sensible impression or influence which such history may make upon the mind.*"

We have only to remark, before we dismiss this subject, that, whereas the evidence of facts which occurred at a distant period is usually placed under the head of *successive* evidence, this distinction, as applicable to the miracles of the gospel, must either be rejected altogether, or admitted with a caution against being misled by the ambiguous use of words. The evidence, in this case, is not to be confounded for a moment with that of a report transmitted through successive ages to the present time, since the record which contains the miraculous facts carries us back to the apostolic age; so that, admitting its antiquity to be what it pretends, of which there is the most satisfactory evidence, the only link in the succession is that which separates the performers or spectators of the miracles from their narrators, who in the case before us, however, are frequently the same persons.

In order to give that conspicuous place which is due to the greatest and most momentous of these miracles, as well as to do justice to the independent train of proofs by which it is supported, Dr. G. has assigned a separate letter to the Resurrection of Christ, in which he has placed this great fact in the clearest light; and, to remove every shadow of hesitation arising from the minute variations in the account given of it by the evangelists, has taken the pains to digest from their separate narratives a distinct statement of the whole transaction, which, as far as we have had time to examine it, appears very satisfactory.

To this succeeds an ample illustration of the argument for the truth of Christianity, drawn from its early and extensive propagation; where the fact is placed beyond all contradiction, by numerous and decisive testimonies, adduced from the ancient apologists and pagan writers. The dates of the ten successive persecutions are accurately assigned; and the most striking circumstances attending the last, in particular, are distinctly and forcibly exhibited. This forms the subject of the ninth letter, which closes with some admirable observations on the intrinsic excellence of the religion of Jesus, tending to show that it corresponds to all the characters, and fulfils all the indications, which a revelation from heaven might be expected to possess.

The remaining letters which compose this volume are employed in proving the inspiration of the Scriptures, and answering various miscellaneous objections and cavils advanced against the Bible. Although we have already adduced some specimens of the author's style and composition, and shall have occasion to produce more in the course of our strictures on the second volume, yet we cannot deny ourselves the pleasure of laying before our readers the following highly beautiful and eloquent passage. Speaking of the analogy between the difficulties offered in the sciences and the mysteries of religion, he observes,—

"Philosophers, notwithstanding all these difficulties, recommend the cultivation and diffusion of the sciences, because of their tendency to sharpen the intellectual faculties of man, and meliorate his condition in society. With how much greater reason and earnestness, then, should Christians recommend the dissemination and adoption of 'pure and undefiled religion,' considering its direct tendency to enlarge the understanding, and yet fill it with the contemplation of Deity; to purify and harmonize the passions, to refine the moral sense, to qualify and strengthen for every function in life; to sustain under the pressure of affliction, to afford consolation in sickness, and enable us to triumph in death!

"What other science can even make a pretension to dethrone oppression, to abolish slavery, to exclude war, to extirpate fraud, to banish violence, to revive the withered blossoms of paradise? Such are the pretensions and blessings of genuine Christianity; and wherever genuine Christianity prevails, they are experienced. Thus it accomplishes its promises on earth, where alone it has enemies; it will, therefore, accomplish them in heaven, where its friends reign. Here, indeed, its advocate must be reduced to silence; for how shall he display the meaning of its *celestial* promises! How describe dignity so vast, or picture glory so brilliant! How shall language delineate what mind cannot imagine! And where is that mind, among puny and ephemeral creatures, that can penetrate the thick obscure; that can describe the light of perfect knowledge, that can feel the glow of perfect love, that can breathe the air of perfect happiness?"—Vol. I. pp. 75, 76.

We proceed to notice the most important positions and reasonings contained in the second volume, which the author has devoted to a display of the doctrines and duties of Christianity. We are aware that many will suspect him of a partial and bigoted attachment to his own opinions, in consequence of the anxiety he manifests to communicate and support those views of Christianity which in his estimation form its most striking peculiarity. It is plain our author considers the evidences of Christianity as entirely subservient to its doctrines; and that he is consequently far from supposing, with some modern divines, that he has accomplished his work by proving that Christianity is a true and a genuine revelation from God. He judges it necessary to spend some time and some labour in considering *what it is* that is true, *what it is* that is revealed. Were we not familiar with the fact, we should not be a little surprised at the prevalence of a contrary persuasion: we should probably think it strange that such an anxiety should be evinced to rest the truth of Christianity on the firmest possible basis, along with such a profound indifference to every attempt to investigate its import. Some wonderful charm, it seems, is contained in a bare avowal that Christianity is a revelation from God, apart from any distinct perceptions of its truths, or any solemn advertence to its genuine scope and tendency. Embalmed and preserved like some Egyptian monarch, in the form of a venerable and antiquated document, it is to be carefully kept, and always approached with respect, but never allowed to take its place among the living, nor supposed to be useful to mankind according to any known law of operation. The most magnificent appellations are applied to it: it is the light of the world, the true riches, the treasure hid in the field, and the pearl of great price. All these, and a thousand other encomiums, are lavished on the Scriptures by men who at the same time feel no scruple in insinuating that this boasted communication from heaven contains no truths beyond the limits of reason, and that what the bulk of Christians in our ages have deemed such are the distempered visions of enthusiasm, if they are not in some instances to be ascribed to the erroneous conceptions entertained by the apostles of the religion they were appointed to propagate. It is the *possession* of a revelation, not the *use*, which these men are accustomed to contemplate and to value. As the miser conceives himself rich by the treasure which he never employs, so the persons to whom we allude suppose themselves enlightened by a book from which they profess to derive no information, and saved by a religion which is allowed to engage little or none of their attention. This is one of the most distinguished features in the character of those who, with exemplary modesty, style themselves *rational* Christians. In this spirit, a distinguished prelate of the present age* has published a collection of tracts for the benefit of the junior clergy, in which not a single treatise is admitted which professes to exhibit a view of Christian doctrine; and has introduced it with a preface, ingeniously calculated, under pretence of decrying dogmas, to bring all such inquiries into contempt. It certainly is not difficult to perceive whence this manner of thinking proceeds, nor whither it tends. It proceeds from a rooted aversion to the genuine truths of revelation; and had it not received a timely check, would have terminated in the general prevalence of skepticism. It presents a neutral ground, on which professed Christians and infidels may meet, and proceed to assail with their joint force the substantial truth of our religion. There is nothing in such views of Christianity to appal the infidel; nothing to mortify the pride, nothing to check or control the exorbitances of that "carnal mind" which is "enmity against God." In stripping the religion of Christ of all that is spiritual, it renders it weak and inefficacious as an instrument of renovating the mind; and, by fostering its pride and sparing its corruption, prepares it for shaking off the restraints of religion altogether. It gives us, however, unfeigned satisfaction to perceive, that the evil we so much deprecate appears to have met with a fatal check; and that the present times are distinguished by two things, which we cannot but consider as most favourable prognostics,—an increased attention to the peculiar doctrines of Christianity, and a growing unanimity with respect to the modes in which those doctrines are entertained. There is less disposition on the one hand to receive for Christianity a system of pagan ethics, and on the other to confound points of doubtful speculation with its fundamental doctrines. The religious zeal of the present day is more open and catholic than in

* Bishop Watson

former times, partaking less of the acrimony of party, and more of the inspiration of truth and charity. The line of demarkation between sound doctrines and heresy is better ascertained than it has ever been before; and the Christian world are equally averse to whatever approaches to Socinian impiety, and to the mooting of interminable questions.

In the statements of the peculiar doctrines of Christianity, there are two extremes to be avoided. The one is, that of pusillanimously shrinking from their bold originality, and attempting to recommend them to the acceptance of proud and worldly-minded men by the artifices of palliation and disguise; of which, in our opinion, the Bishop of Lincoln has given an egregious specimen in his late work.* The other extreme is that of stating them in a metaphysical form, mixing doubtful deductions with plain assertions, and thereby encumbering them with needless subtleties and refinements. We should neither be ashamed of the dictates of the Spirit, nor "add to his words, lest we be reproved." They will always appear with the most advantage, and carry the most conviction, when they are exhibited in their native simplicity, without being mixed with heterogeneous matter, or with positions of doubtful authority. In our apprehension, the true way of contemplating the peculiar doctrines of Christianity is to consider them as *facts* believed on the authority of the Supreme Being, not to be proved by reason; since their truth does not result from any perceptible relations in our ideas, but they owe their existence entirely to the will and counsel of the Almighty Potentate. On this account, we never consider it safe to rest their truth on a philosophical basis, nor imagine it is possible to add to their evidence by an elaborate train of reasoning. Let the fair grammatical import of Scripture language be investigated; and whatever propositions are, by an easy and natural interpretation, deducible from thence, let them be received as the dictates of infinite Wisdom, whatever aspect they bear, or whatever difficulties they present. Repugnant to reason they never can be, because they spring from the Author of it; but superior to reason, whose limits they will infinitely surpass, we must expect to find them, since they are a communication of such matters of fact, respecting the spiritual and eternal world, as need not have been communicated, if the knowledge of them could have been acquired from any other quarter. The facts with which we have become acquainted in the natural world would appear stupendous, were they communicated merely on the evidence of testimony; they fail to astonish us, chiefly because they have been arrived at step by step, by means of their analogy to some preceding one. We have climbed the eminence by a slow progression, and our prospect has insensibly widened as we advanced, instead of being transported thither instantaneously by a superior power. Revelation conducts us to the truth at once, without previous training, without any intellectual process preceding, without condescending to afford other proof than what results from the veracity and wisdom of the

* Entitled "A Refutation of Calvinism"

Creator: and when we consider that this truth respects much sublimer relations and concerns than those which subsist in the material world, —that it regards the ways and counsels of God respecting man's eternal destiny,—is it surprising it should embrace what greatly surpassed our previous conjectures, and even transcends our perfect comprehension? To a serious and upright mind, however, its discoveries are no sooner made than they become supremely acceptable: the interposition of the Deity in the great moral drama is seen to be absolutely necessary; since none but infinite wisdom could clear up the intricacies, nor any power short of omnipotence relieve the distress it produced. These very truths, which some ridicule as mysteries, and others despise as dogmas, are, to the enlightened, "sweeter than honey or the honeycomb;" apart from which, whatever else is contained in the Bible would be perfectly tasteless and insipid. Though he receives every communication from God with devout and grateful emotions, he feels no hesitation in confessing, that it is in these parts of revelation he especially exults and triumphs; it is these which, in his estimation, entitle it to the appellation of "*marvellous light.*"

If it is no small gratification to find so perfect a concurrence in these sentiments on the part of our author, to find them stated and illustrated in so able a manner as they are throughout this work is a still greater. The first letter in this volume is devoted to a general view of the Christian doctrines, designed to obviate certain prejudices, and to prepare the mind for that serious inquiry into their nature and import which cannot fail, under the blessing of God, of conducting it to the most satisfactory conclusions.

Our author never loses sight of the gospel as a *restorative dispensation:* this is its primary and most essential feature; and the most dangerous and numerous aberrations from it may be traced to the neglect of considering it in this light. It is not a proscription of a rule of life to the innocent, but the annunciation of a stupendous method of relief for the sinner. Overlooking all petty varieties and subordinate distinctions, it places the whole human race on one level abases them all in the dust before the Infinite Majesty; and offers, indiscriminately, a provision of sanctification to the polluted, and of pardon to the guilty. These are the glad tidings; this is the jubilee of the whole earth, proclaimed in the songs of angels, celebrated in the praises of the church, alike in her militant and her triumphant state—whether toiling in the vale of mortality, or rejoicing before the throne.

The second letter in the series which composes this volume is on the Depravity of Human Nature, where the reader will find the evidence of that melancholy but fundamental truth exhibited with much conciseness, perspicuity, and force. The third is employed in stating the arguments for the atonement of Christ, under the four divisions of typical, prophetical, historical, and declaratory proofs; and the whole is closed by a very luminous and satisfactory answer to the most specious objections against that momentous truth. In adverting to the objection to a vicarious sacrifice, founded on the notion of its being unjust that the innocent should be appointed to suffer in the room of the guilty, we meet with the following admirable passage of Archbishop Tillotson, remarkable for that perfect good sense, simplicity, and perspicuity which distinguish the writings of that excellent prelate.

"'If the matter,' says he, 'were searched to the bottom, all this perverse contention about our Saviour's suffering for our benefit, but not in our stead, will signify just nothing. For if Christ died for our benefit, so as, some way or other, *by virtue of his death and sufferings*, to save us from the wrath of God, and to procure our escape from eternal death; this, for aught I know, is all that anybody means by his dying in our stead. For he that dies with an intention to do that benefit for another, or to *save him from death*, doth certainly, to all intents and purposes, die in his place and stead. And if they will grant this to be their meaning, the controversy is at an end, and both sides are agreed in the thing, and do only differ in the phrase and manner of expression; which is to seek a quarrel, and an occasion of difference, when there is no real ground for it—a thing which ought to be very far from reasonable and peaceable minds. For many of the Socinians say, that our Saviour's voluntary death and sufferings procured his exaltation at the right-hand of God, and power and authority to forgive sins, and to give eternal life to as many as he pleased: so that they grant that his obedience and sufferings, in the meritorious consequence of them, redound to our benefit and advantage as much as we pretend to say they do; only they are loath, in express terms, to acknowledge that Christ died in our stead; and this for no other reason that I can imagine but *because they have denied it so often and so long*.'"—Vol. II. p. 64.

We have only to say, on this part of the subject, that we heartily commiserate the state of that man's mind, who, whatever Socinian prejudices he may have felt against the most glorious of all doctrines, that of the atonement, does not feel them shaken at least, if not removed, by the arguments adduced in this letter.

The next is devoted to the defence of the Divinity of Jesus Christ, which our author evinces in a masterly manner, from the predictions of the ancient prophets, compared with their application in the New Testament; from the conduct, the miracles, and the discourses of our Lord; from the declarations of his apostles; and from the concurrent testimony of the early Christian writers and martyrs, before the council of Nice. Under the last head the reader will meet with a copious induction of passages attesting this grand doctrine, selected with much judgment, and applied with great force. The author all along contends for the divinity of Christ as a *fundamental* tenet; and, of course, will forfeit all pretensions to candour with *rational* Christians, on whose approbation, indeed, he appears to set very little value.

In the next letter, which is on Conversion, he has treated of the nature and necessity of that new birth on which our Lord insisted so strenuously in his discourse with Nicodemus, in a manner which will be as offensive to mere nominal Christians as it will be instructive and satisfactory to serious and humble inquirers after truth. He shows, from well-known and indubitable facts, the reality of such a change;

and evinces its indispensable necessity from the express declarations of Scripture, the corruption of human nature, the exalted character of the Deity, and the nature of that pure and perfect felicity to which good men aspire after death. In illustrating this subject, he has made a happy use of Bishop Burnet's Narrative of the Conversion of the Earl of Rochester,—has carefully guarded his readers against the pernicious error of confounding regeneration with baptism,—and has closed the discussion with solving certain difficulties arising out of the subject, which have often perplexed serious minds.

As every effect naturally invites us to contemplate the cause, he passes from conversion to the consideration of Divine influence, which is the subject of the succeeding letter: and were we to give our opinion of the comparative merit of the different parts of this volume, we should be inclined to assign the palm to the disquisition on this confessedly mysterious subject. In no part, certainly, is the vigour of the author's very powerful understanding more eminently exerted; in none are the prejudices founded on a pretended philosophy more triumphantly dispelled. He has shown, in the most satisfactory manner, that the belief of an immediate divine influence on the mind, not only accords with the sentiments of the wisest men in pagan times, but that it is rendered highly reasonable by the close analogy it bears to the best-established laws of the material world. Though there are many admirable passages in this portion of the work, which it would gratify us to lay before our readers, we must content ourselves with the following.

"No person can look into the world with the eye of a philosopher, and not soon ascertain that the grand theatre of phenomena which lies before him is naturally subdivided into two great classes of scenery: the one exhibiting constrained, the other voluntary motion; the former characteristic of matter, the latter as clearly indicating something perfectly distinct from matter, and possessing totally opposite qualities. 'Pulverize matter,' says Saurin, 'give it all the different forms of which it is susceptible, elevate it to its highest degree of attainment, make it vast and immense, moderate or small, luminous or obscure, opaque or transparent, there will never result any thing but *figures;* and never will you be able, by all these combinations or divisions, to produce one single sentiment, one single thought.' The reason is obvious: a substance compounded of innumerable parts, which every one acknowledges matter to be, cannot be the subject of an individual consciousness; the seat of which *must* be a simple and undivided substance; as the great Dr. Clarke has long ago irrefragably shown. Intellect and volition are quite of a different nature from corporeal figure or motion, and must reside in, or emanate from, a different kind of being, a kind which, to distinguish it from matter, is called spirit, or mind. Of these, the one is necessarily inert, the other essentially active. The one is characterized by want of animation, life, and even motion, except as it is urged by something *ab extra;* the other is living, energetic, self-moving, and possessed of power to move other things. We often fancy, it is true, that matter moves matter; but this, strictly speaking, is not correct. When one wheel, or lever, in a system of machinery, communicates motion to matter, it can, at most, only communicate what it has received; and if you trace the connexion of the mechanism, you will at length arrive at a first mover, which first mover is, in fact, *spiritual.* If, for example, it be an animal, it is evidently the spiritual part of that animal from whence the motion originally springs. If, otherwise, it be the descent of a weight, or the fall of water, or the force of a current of air, or the expansive power of steam, the action must be ultimately referred to what are styled powers of nature, that is, to gravitation or elasticity; and these, it is now well known, cannot be explained by any allusion to material principles, but to the indesinent operation of the Great Spirit in whom we live, and move, and have our being—the finger of God touching and urging the various subordinate springs, which, in their turn, move the several parts of the universe. Thus God acts in all places, in all times, and upon all persons. The whole material world, were it not for his Spirit, would be inanimate and inactive: all motion is derived either from his energy or from a spirit which he animates; and it is next to *certain,* that the only primary action is that of spirit, and the most direct and immediate that of spirit upon spirit." —P. 154.

We doubt not the intelligent reader will be of opinion, that the author has gone to the very bottom of this subject, and will feel himself highly gratified in seeing it placed in so clear and convincing a light; the more so, as he has taken care to guard against its most obvious abuse, by showing that the influence for which he contends is not to be expected independent of means,—among which he considers prayer, and a conscientious regard to known duty as the principal. We earnestly recommend this part of the performance to such of our readers as have, upon too light grounds, imbibed philosophical prejudices against the doctrine contended for; a doctrine which lies at the foundation of all spiritual religion, though treated by many with an excess of insolence and scorn, which can hardly be accounted for without adverting to the injudicious conduct of its advocates.

The important doctrine of Justification by Faith forms the subject of the next letter in the series. Here, after confirming the position he means to defend by the authority of the Homilies, he proceeds to a more particular discussion of the subject, under three heads of inquiry: What is meant by justification?—what by faith?—and what is the genuine import of "justification by faith?" Under each of these the reader will meet with much instruction, arising from a very luminous statement of truth, accompanied with happy illustrations. The charge against the doctrine pleaded for, of its tending to licentiousness, is very successfully combated and refuted.

The exhibition of the leading *doctrines* of Christianity is completed in the three following letters,—on Providence, the Resurrection, and the Eternal Existence of Man after Death. We perused with much satisfaction the author's masterly defence of a particular providence, the denial of which is, to all practical purposes, equivalent to the denial of a providence altogether. Trust in God is the act of an individual, as all the exercises of piety must necessarily be; so that if the providence of God embraces not the concerns of individuals, no rational foundation can be conceived for expecting protection from danger, or relief under distress, in answer to prayer. The denial of a particular providence is, it must be confessed, the best possible expedient for keeping God at a distance—and on that account so vehemently insisted on by certain periodical writers, the poison of whose impiety, prepared, it is generally understood, by *hallowed* hands, and distributed through the nation in a popular and seducing vehicle, has met with a powerful antidote and rebuke from Dr. Gregory, who, himself a layman, will be honoured as the champion of that religion which a clergyman has insulted and betrayed.* How is it that the conductors of the publication alluded to allot to this clerical associate the province of libelling religion? Is it that its alliance with nominal sanctity gives rank impiety a new zest, at the same time that its total dereliction of principle more perfectly incorporates the specific design of the article with the general character of the work?

In treating of the Resurrection of the Dead, the author has happily availed himself of the striking analogies which the system of nature presents, as if designed on purpose, as Tertullian more than insinuates, to excite the expectation of such an event. Among others highly deserving attention, we shall present our readers with the following, in the words of Dr. Gregory:—

"Nearly allied to these are the examples of peculiar transformations undergone by various insects, and the state of rest and insensibility which precede those transformations: such as the chrysalis or aurelia state of butterflies, moths, and silkworms. The myrmeleon formicaleo, of whose larva, and its extraordinary history, Reaumur and Roësel have given accurate descriptions, continues in its insensible or chrysalis state about four weeks. The libellula, or dragon-fly, continues still longer in its state of inaction. Naturalists tell us that the worm repairs to the margin of its pond, in quest of a convenient place of abode during its insensible state. It attaches itself to a plant, or piece of dry wood, and the skin, which gradually becomes parched and brittle, at last splits opposite to the upper part of the thorax: through this aperture the insect, now become winged, quickly pushes its way; and, being thus extricated from confinement, begins to expand its wings, to flutter, and finally to launch into the air with that gracefulness and ease which are peculiar to this majestic tribe. Now, who that saw for the first time the little pendant coffin in which the insect lay entombed, and was ignorant of the transformation of which we are now speaking, would ever predict that in a few weeks, perhaps in a few days or hours, it would become one of the most elegant and active of *winged* insects? And who that contemplates with the mind of a philosopher this curious transformation, and knows that two years before the insect mounts into air, even while it is living in water, it has the rudiments of wings, can deny that the body of a dead man may

* See the Article on Methodism, in the Edinburgh Review

at some future period be again invested with vigour and activity, and soar to regions for which some latent organization may have peculiarly fitted it?"—P. 225.

In descanting on the change that will be effected by the resurrection, when we shall be invested with a glorified body, the language of the author rises to a high pitch of elevation, and exhibits a scene which surpasses the brightest visions of poetry; while the exactness of the delineation in its most essential lineaments is attested by the "true sayings of God." The science with which the mind of the author is so richly imbued enables him to mingle a refined spirit of philosophy with the colours of imagination, which, without diminishing their brightness, compels the assent of the understanding, while it captivates the heart.

In the letter on the Eternal Existence after Death, the author strenuously opposes the sleep of the soul, and urges formidable, and, we apprehend, irrefragable arguments for interpreting the passages of Scripture which speak of the everlasting misery of the impenitent, in their obvious and literal sense: nor have we met with a discussion of this awful subject so calculated to carry conviction to a philosophical mind, provided it be disposed to bow to the authority of revelation. His confutation of the reasoning of his opponents, founded on the supposed ambiguity of the terms employed to denote an eternal duration, is particularly masterly.

On the third branch of his subject, which relates to the Duties of Christianity, he is comparatively brief,—not, it is evident, from his undervaluing their importance, but partly, we conceive, on account of the length of his former discussions, and partly because in this part there is little room for controversy. He has contented himself with arranging the duties of Christianity under three heads—those which relate to God, to our fellow-creatures, and to ourselves; and with illustrating and enforcing them by a direct appeal to the language of Scripture.

Having endeavoured to put our readers in possession of the general plan and design of this work, we shall close this article with a few general observations on it.

Dr. Gregory, throughout, denominates the abetters of the simple humanity of Christ, Socinians, instead of employing their favourite appellation of Unitarians. We rejoice that he has done so, and hope his example will be generally followed. To accede to the appellation of Unitarians is to yield up the very point in debate; for, ask them what they mean by Unitarian, and they will feel no scruple in replying that it denotes a believer in one God, in opposition to a tritheist. That this is not asserted at random is evident, as well from many other facts, as from the following very remarkable one,—that when a noted academic was some years since expelled from the university of Cambridge, amid various points which he insisted on in his defence, one was this, that it was quite absurd to censure him for avowing Unitarian principles, since he never heard but of one person who publicly declared himself *not a Unitarian.* Now what did he mean by this singular assertion?

Did he mean to say that he never heard of more than one person who publicly affirmed his belief in a *plurality of persons* in the Godhead? This is impossible. What could he mean, then, but that he never knew but of one person who affirmed himself *not to be a believer in one God?*—which is neither more nor less than to identify the term Unitarian with a believer in one God, and the term Trinitarian with a believer in three. Let the intelligent public judge whether it is not high time to withhold from these men an appellation which assumes the question at issue, and which cannot be bestowed without being converted into an occasion of insult and triumph over their opponents. There was a time when the learning and moderation of Lardner, and the fame and science of Priestley, combined to throw a transitory splendour over their system, and to procure from the Christian world a forbearance and complaisance to which they were ill entitled. That time is past. Such *rational* Christians as they are should have discernment to perceive that it is not with them as in months past, when the candle of their leader shone around them: it becomes them to bow their spirit to the humbled state of their fortunes. They should learn at last to know themselves. The world is perfectly aware, whether they perceive it or not, that Socinianism is now a headless trunk, bleeding at every vein, and exhibiting no other symptom of life but its frightful convulsions.

But why should they be offended at being styled Socinians, when it is undeniable that they agree with Socinus in his fundamental position (the simple humanity of Christ), which is all the agreement that subsists between the followers of Calvin or Arminius and those eminent persons? The Calvinists are far from concurring in every particular with Calvin,—the Arminians with Arminius; yet neither of them have violently disclaimed these appellations, or considered them as terms of reproach. Why are the Socinians only offended at being denominated after Socinus? Is it because they differ in the nature of Christ's person from that celebrated heresiarch? This they will not pretend. But they differ from him in many respects! In what respects? Is it in those respects in which his sentiments gave most offence to the Christian world? Is it that they have receded from him in that direction which brings them nearer to the generally received doctrine of the church? Just the reverse. In the esteem of all but themselves they have descended many degrees lower in the scale of error, have plunged many fathoms deeper in the gulf of impiety; yet, with an assurance of which they have furnished the only example, they affect to consider themselves injured by being styled Socinians, when they know in their own consciences that they differ from Socinus only in pushing the degradation of the Saviour to a much greater length—and that in the views of the Christian world their religious delinquencies differ from his only as treason differs from sedition, or sacrilege from theft. The appellation of Socinian, as applied to them, is a term of forbearance, calculated, if they would suffer it, not to expose, but to hide a part of their shame. Let them assume any denomination they please, provided it be such as will fairly represent their sentiments. Let them be styled antiscripturalists, humanitarians, semideists, Priestleians, or Socinians.

But let them not be designated by a term which is merely coveted by them for the purpose of chicane and imposture.

Our readers will perceive that the system which Dr. Gregory strenuously abets is orthodoxy; but it is moderate and catholic; it is the orthodoxy of the first three centuries; it is that system which, communicated by Christ and his apostles, pervaded the church long before the confusion of modern sects arose, or even the distinction between Protestants and Catholics was heard of: it is the orthodoxy which has nourished the root of piety in every age, warmed the breasts of saints and martyrs, and will continue to subsist in the church till the heavens and the earth are no more.

We congratulate the public on the accession of Dr. G. to such a cause; and sincerely rejoice, that amid his multifarious scientific pursuits he has found time and inclination to meditate so deeply, and to exhibit so successfully, "the truth as it is in Jesus." We hope his example will stimulate other men of science and genius to pursue so noble a career. We will venture to assure them that upon a dying bed, it will occasion no regret to reflect upon their having enrolled their names with such illustrious laymen as Boyle, Newton, and Locke in the defence of Christianity.

In a beautiful passage of Euripides, Medea is introduced, expressing her surprise that amid such a multitude of inventions and inquiries, the art of persuasion, the mistress of human volition, should alone have been neglected. This neglect cannot be imputed to Dr. Gregory. He has united with extraordinary attainments in the severer sciences, the art of recommending his sentiments with the most impressive effect; and though he is above a solicitude respecting the minuter graces of finished composition, he exhibits in an eminent degree the most important ingredients of good writing. He is correct and luminous, and often rises to the tone of the most impassioned feeling. His language is eminently easy, flowing, and idiomatic. The abstractions of science have not in him exerted the influence often imputed to them, of chilling the heart, and impairing the vigour of the imagination. While he reasons with the comprehension and depth which distinguish the philosopher, he feels with ardour, and paints with force. He is often inspired and transported with his theme. In the midst of pursuits which are not always found to have a propitious effect on the religious character of their votaries, he has found the means of preserving his devotion in its warmth, his faith in its purity, and his sensibility in its infantine freshness and vigour.

We must conclude with earnestly recommending this work to the attentive perusal of young persons whose minds have been cultivated by science and letters; and must be permitted to add, that we are acquainted with no book, in the circle of English literature, which is equally calculated to give persons of that description just views of the evidence, the nature, and the importance of revealed religion.

REVIEW

OF

BELSHAM'S MEMOIRS OF LINDSEY.

Memoirs of the late Rev. Theophilus Lindsey, A. M., including a brief Analysis of his Works; together with Anecdotes and Letters of eminent Persons, his Friends and Correspondents: also, a general View of the Progress of the Unitarian Doctrine in England and America. By THOMAS BELSHAM, *Minister of the Chapel in Essex-street.* 8vo. Pp. xxiv. 544. 1812.

As the Life of Mr. Lindsey is evidently adopted as a vehicle for the propagation of Socinian sentiments, we shall be excused for being more copious in our remarks upon it than the biography of a man of such extreme mediocrity of talents could otherwise possibly justify. If a zealous attachment to any system of opinions can be supposed to be aided by its association with personal reputation, we cannot wonder at finding Mr. Lindsey's fondness for socinianism so ardent and so persevering, inasmuch as the annals of religion scarcely furnish an instance of a celebrity acquired so entirely by the adoption of a particular creed. Luther and Calvin would have risen to distinction, in all probability, if the Reformation had never been heard of; while the existence of such a man as Mr. Lindsey would not have been known beyond the precincts of his parish, had he not, under a peculiar combination of circumstances, embraced the tenets of Socinus.

His reputation is altogether accidental and factitious. Though the leading events of his life, with one exception, are marked by no striking peculiarities, yet, by the help of a great deal of adventitious matter, Mr. B. has contrived to make it the groundwork of a bulky and not unentertaining volume—disfigured, however, throughout by that languid and inelegant verbosity which characterizes all his compositions. It must be confessed Mr. Belsham has taken care in this work to exhibit himself as no ascetic, no religious enthusiast, but quite a man of the world; not by a lively delineation of its manners and foibles, still less by a development of the principles by which mankind are actuated, but by such a profusion of compliments bestowed on men of rank and title, and so perfect a prostration before secular grandeur, as has never been paralleled we suspect, in a Christian divine. At the "pomp and circumstance" of human life, this philosopher appears awed and planet-struck, and utterly incapable of exercising that small portion of discrimination with which nature has endowed him. Every nobleman or statesman he has occasion to introduce is uniformly ushered in with a splendid retinue of gorgeous epithets, in which there are as little taste and variety as if they had been copied verbatim from the rolls at the herald's office. Orators of pre-eminent powers, together with virtuous and enlightened noblemen, meet us at every turn; and we are not a little surprised at finding so much of the decoration and splendour of this mortal scene in so close contact with the historical details of unitarianism. We have long remarked the eagerness of Socinians to emblazon their system by associations with learning, rank, and fashion; but on no other occasion have we seen this humour carried so far as in hese Memoirs.

The leading events of Mr. Lindsey's life are the following. He was born June 20, 1723, at Middlewich in Cheshire, where his father was a mercer in respectable circumstances, but was afterward reduced by misfortunes. His mother, whose maiden name was Spencer, was distantly related to the Marlborough family; and previously to her marriage lived twenty years in the family of Frances, Countess of Huntingdon,—a circumstance which led to considerable intimacy, that continued for some years, with the celebrated Selina, Countess of Huntingdon, who married the son of that lady. Under the patronage of Lady Betty and Lady Ann Hastings, Mr. Lindsey was educated, first at a school in the neighbourhood of Middlewich, whence he was removed, and placed under the care of the Rev. Mr. Barnard, master of the free grammar-school in that town, who is represented as a gentleman of distinguished learning and piety. His vacations were usually spent at the mansion of his noble patronesses, in the vicinity of Leeds, during the life of Lady Betty Hastings; and, after her decease, at Ashby Place, near Ashby de la Zouch, in Leicestershire, where Lady Ann then fixed her residence. In the eighteenth year of his age, May 21, 1741, he was admitted a student at St. John's, Cambridge, where he acquitted himself with credit in his academical exercises, and behaved with such exemplary propriety as to attract the attention of Dr. Reynolds, Bishop of Lincoln, who thought fit to intrust him with the care of his grandson, a youth of fifteen. He was elected fellow of St. John's College in April, 1747. Having been ordained by Bishop Gibson, he was, at the recommendation of Lady Ann Hastings, presented to a chapel in Spital Square by Sir George Wheeler. In a short time after his settlement in London, the Duke of Somerset received him into his house in the capacity of domestic chaplain. He continued, after the decease of that nobleman, to reside some time with the duchess-dowager, better known by the title of Countess of Hertford; and at her request he accompanied her grandson, the present Duke of Northumberland, then about nine years of age and in a delicate state of health, to the Continent, where he continued two years, at the expiration of which time he brought back his noble pupil, improved both in his health and learning. From this distinguished personage he continued to receive attentions and favours as long as he lived. Immediately after his return from the Continent, he was presented by the Earl of Northumberland to the valuable rectory of Kirkby Whiske, in the north riding of Yorkshire; at first, under condition to resign it when the person for whom it was intended should come of age; but this young man dying a short time afterward, it was given to Mr. Lindsey unconditionally, in the usual form. In this very retired situation Mr. Lindsey continued about three years; and, during his residence in Yorkshire, he became acquainted with the celebrated Archdeacon Blackburne, at Richmond,—a circumstance which led to important consequences, and to which he was indebted, under Providence, for the most important blessing of his life.

In the year 1756, at the request of the Huntingdon family, he resigned the living of Kirkby Whiske for the living of Piddletown, in Dorsetshire, which was in the gift of the Earl of Huntingdon. In this place he lived seven years; and in 1760 married Miss Elsworth, the step-daughter of Archdeacon Blackburne,—a lady whose principles were congenial with his own, and who is represented as possessed of a superior understanding and of exalted virtue. It was during his residence in that situation that he first began to entertain scruples concerning the lawfulness of Trinitarian worship, and of his continuing to officiate in the established church. It appears he had, from his early youth, disapproved of some things in the Thirty-nine Articles. Some years afterward, these doubts were matured into a full conviction that the divinity of Christ was an erroneous tenet, and that the Father was the sole object of worship; in consequence of which, while in Dorset shire, he took some previous steps with a view to quitting his preferment in the church. In the year 1762, upon the appointment of the late Duke of Northumberland to be lord-lieutenant of Ireland, he was strongly urged to accept the place of chaplain to his grace; which, from the preference he gave to a retired situation, he declined. An opportunity occurring the year following of exchanging his living for that of Catterick in Yorkshire, he made the exchange, for the sake of enjoying the society of Archdeacon Blackburne and his family, who lived in that neighbourhood. On this occasion, Mr. Belsham justly remarks, "It may appear singular that Mr. Lindsey could submit to that renewed subscription which was requisite in order to his induction to a new living.

"And the case," he adds, "appears the more extraordinary, as many clergymen who, in consequence of a revolution in their opinions, had become dissatisfied with the Articles, would never, for the sake of obtaining the most valuable preferment, subscribe them again, though while they were permitted to remain unmolested, they did not perceive it to be their duty to retire from the church."—P. 17.

The extreme want of candour and sincerity evinced by such conduct is very unsatisfactorily apologized for by Mr. Lindsey, and is very gently reproved by Mr. Belsham. The principal plea alleged by Mr L. in defence of himself is, that as he continued to officiate in the forms of the liturgy, his renewed subscription gave him little concern, since he considered himself every time he used the liturgy as virtually repeating his subscription. At length, he brought himself, he says, to consider the Trinitarian forms in the liturgy, and the invocations at the entrance of the litany, as

"A threefold representation of the one God, the Father, governing all things by himself and by his Son and Spirit; and as a threefold way of addressing him as a Creator, and original benevolent cause of all things, as Redeemer of mankind by his Son, and their Sanctifier by his Holy Spirit."—P. 23.

How far he was influenced by mercenary considerations in retaining his station under such circumstances it is impossible to say; but that he was guilty of much collusion and impious prevarication in this affair cannot be reasonably doubted. Nor is there any species of simulation or dissimulation in religion which might not be justified on pretences equally plausible: and when we recollect that Mr. L. persisted in that conduct for a series of years, we shall find it difficult to conceive of him as that prodigy of virtue which Mr. Belsham represents him. "He must be a severe moralist," says Mr. B., "whom such a concession does not satisfy." And what is this concession that is to stop every mouth, and to convert censure into praise? We will give it in Mr. L.'s own words—it is this:

"Not," says he, "that I now justify myself therein; yea, rather I condemn myself. But as I have humble hope of the Divine forgiveness, let not men be too rigid in their censures."—P. 24.

It is impossible to conceive a confession of conduct extremely criminal in terms of lighter reprehension; but, agreeably to the theory of Mr. B., the merit of repentance so much exceeds the moral turpitude of transgression, that the faintest indications of it transport him with admiration. For our parts, were we not aware of the tendency of Socinianism to produce a most attenuated conception of the evil of sin, we should have expected to find such insincerity and impiety deplored in the strongest language of penitential sorrow. As we wish, however, to do ample justice to the real virtues of Mr. L., we feel a pleasure in quoting the following account of the manner in which he conducted himself while he was rector of Catterick.

"No sooner was he settled," says his biographer, "in his new situation, than he applied himself with great assiduity, in his extensive and populous parish, to perform the duties of a parochial minister. He regularly officiated twice on the Sunday in his parish church, and in the interval between the services he catechised young people. He visited the sick, he relieved the poor, he established and supported charity schools for the children, he spent considerable sums of money in feeding the hungry, in clothing the naked, in providing medicines for the diseased, and in purchasing and distributing books for the instruction of the ignorant. In his domestic arrangements, the greatest economy was observed, that he and his excellent lady might have the greater surplus to expend in liberality and charity; for it was a rule with him to lay up nothing from the income of his living."—P. 26.

This is unquestionably a pleasing picture of the character of an exemplary Christian pastor. It does not appear that any considerable success attended his labours. On this head he contents himself with expressing a faint hope that some of the seed he had sowed might not be lost.

In this situation he continued ten years, till a dangerous fit of sickness roused his conscience, and rendered his continuance in the discharge of his ecclesiastical functions insupportable. We are far from wishing to depreciate the value of that sacrifice which Mr. Lindsey tardily and reluctantly made to the claims of conscience; but we cannot conceal our surprise, that a measure to which he was forced in order to quell the apprehensions he most justly entertained of the displeasure of the Almighty, after a system of prevarication persisted in for upwards of ten years, should be extolled in terms which can only be applied with propriety to instances of heroic virtue. To prefer the surrender of certain worldly advantages to a perseverance in conduct highly criminal evinces a mind not utterly insensible to the force of moral obligation, and nothing more. Our admiration must be reserved for a higher species of excellence; for an adherence to the side of delicacy and honour, where many plausibilities might be urged to the contrary; or a resolute pursuit of the path of virtue, when it is obstructed by the last extremities of evil. Mr. Lindsey renounced, it is true, a respectable and lucrative situation in the church, rather than continue any longer in the practice of what he considered as idolatry. But he was unencumbered with a family; he possessed some personal property; and enjoyed the friendship of several great and noble personages, whc were never likely to suffer him to sink into absolute poverty. He merely descended to the level where many of the best, and some of the greatest, of men have chosen to place themselves, and where his friend Dr. Priestley, whose talents would have commanded any preferment in the church, chose, from an attachment to the same principles, to remain for life. We approve his resignation of his living; but we confess we are more disposed to wonder that he could reconcile himself to continue in his situation so long, than that he should feel himself compelled to quit it at last.

This event took place in the year 1773; after which he came to London, and a plan was set on foot for opening a chapel for him in the metropolis, where, retaining the use of a liturgy modified agreeably to his views, he might promulgate the tenets of Socinus. Many persons, Mr. B. informs us, both of the establishment and among the dissenters, aided the undertaking, among whom are particularly enumerated Dr. Priestley and Dr. Price, Samuel Shore, Esq., of Norton Hall, in Yorkshire, and Robert Newton, Esq. of Norton House, in the same village.

These gentlemen, in conjunction with others, entered into a subscription, to indemnify him for the necessary expenses incurred in procuring and fitting up his chapel. The place fixed upon for this grand experiment was a room in Essex House, Essex-street, which, having before been used as an auction-room, was capable, at a moderate expense, of being turned into a convenient place of worship. Here Mr. L. introduced his improved liturgy, formed very much upon the plan of Dr. Clarke's, but with such variations as corresponded to the difference of his views from those of that celebrated divine. From this period, the life of Mr. L. proceeds in a very equable and uniform course, with little worthy of remark besides the various publications to which the system he had adopted gave birth: and over the congregation formed in Essex-street he continued to preside till his seventieth year, when he thought fit to retire from a public station: after which he lived sixteen years, when he was attacked with a disease which was judged to be a pressure of the brain, and expired in the eighty-sixth year of his age. Such are the outlines of a narrative which Mr. Belsham has contrived to extend to upwards of five hundred octavo pages. It is by no means our intention to follow the biographer through his boundless excursions, or to criticise every remark which appears to us justly obnoxious to censure. We shall content ourselves with selecting a few passages, and making a few observations, which may serve to illustrate the genius and progress of Socinianism, the promotion of which evidently appears to be the sole object of the writer of these Memoirs.

The secession of Mr. Lindsey from the established church produced much less impression than might have been expected; nor does it appear that his example was followed by one individual among the clergy, until Mr. Disney, his brother-in-law, after the lapse of some years, adopted the same measure, and afterward became his colleague in the ministry. The establishment of a Socinian chapel with a reformed liturgy in the metropolis is narrated by our biographer with the utmost pomp, as forming a distinguished epoch in the annals of religion; and, undoubtedly, great hopes were entertained of its producing a memorable revolution among the Episcopalians: but these expectations were frustrated. The attendance, composed chiefly of persons of opulence (among whom the Duke of Grafton made the principal figure), was at no time very numerous; and no similar society was formed from among the members of the established church in any part of the United Kingdom. The utmost that the efforts of Lindsey, Priestley, and others effected was to convert the teachers of Arianism among the dissenters into Socinians, who exerted themselves with tolerable success to disseminate their principles in their respective congregations: so that the boasted triumphs of Socinianism consisted in sinking that section of the dissenting body who had already departed from the faith a few degrees lower in the gulf of error. From these very Memoirs under consideration we derive the most convincing evidence that the tenets of Socinus, with respect to the nation at large, have lost ground, and that the people of England are much less favourably disposed to them than formerly. They also present us a very full and particular account of the association of a part of the clergy at the Feathers Tavern, to procure relief in the matter of subscription; for which purpose, agreeably to a resolution of the general body, on the 6th of February, 1772, a petition was presented to the House of Commons. The number of the petitioners amounted to nearly two hundred and fifty, among whom the names of the celebrated Archdeacon Blackburne, and Law, bishop of Carlisle, were the most distinguished. Of the state of the public mind in the metropolis we have a striking picture in a letter from John Lee, afterward solicitor-general, a zealous friend of the discontented clergy. "It will surprise you who live in the country," says he, "and consequently have not been informed of the discoveries of the metropolis, that the Christian religion is not thought to be an object worthy of the least regard; and that it is not only the most prudent, but the most virtuous and benevolent thing in the world, to divert men's minds from such frivolous subjects with all the dexterity that can be. This is no exaggeration, I assure you; on the contrary, it seems to be the opinion (and their conduct will show it) of nine-tenths of both houses of parliament!" Allowing for some slight exaggeration arising from the chagrin and vexation of the writer, it is still impossible not to perceive, if any credit is due to his statement, that the parliament were not in a disposition to feel any conscientious objections to the repeal of the Articles, and that if they opposed such a measure, that opposition originated simply from the fear of innovation, common to politicians. The manner in which the debate was conducted when the affair came actually under the consideration of the House confirms this conclusion.

There was not one member who expressed his belief in the Articles: it was treated entirely as a political question, without once adverting to its intrinsic merits as involving a religious controversy; and Mr. Hans Stanley opposed the bringing up of the petition, as it tended to disturb the peace of the country, which, in his opinion, ought to be the subject of a fortieth Article, which would be well worth all the thirty-nine.* With such levity and contempt was the national creed treated at that time. Will the sturdiest champion of Socinianism affirm that a similar discussion in the House of Commons, or in the upper House, would be conducted in a similar manner at present? or that there would not be one member who would contend for the continuance of the Articles on the ground of their intrinsic excellence and verity? The fact is, that through the secularity and irreligion of the clergy, evangelical truth was nearly effaced from the minds of the members of the establishment in the higher ranks, and that an indolent acquiescence in established formularies had succeeded to the ardour with which the great principles of religion were embraced at the Reformation. Such was the state of the public mind, that in a contest between orthodoxy and heresy, the former proved triumphant merely because it was already established, and had the plea of antiquity and prescription in its favour. Since that period, vital religion has revived in the national church; the flame of controversy has been widely spread; the inconsistency of Socinianism with the Scriptures, together with its genuine tendency and character, has been fully developed; it has lost the attraction of novelty; it has revolted the minds of men by its impiety; and, having been weighed in the balance, has been found wanting. If among the clergy there still subsists a small remnant who are attached to those unscriptural tenets, they are content

* See pages 54, 55, of these Memoirs.

with being connived at, and nothing could now urge them to the imprudence of presenting their claims for legal security to the legislature. We hear nothing of an intention to renew the scenes which took place at the Feathers Tavern in 1772.

We consider this as a decisive proof that Socinianism has lost ground in the nation, notwithstanding its prevalence in societies of a certain description among the dissenters. Those who never formally renounced the orthodox doctrine have, in consequence of recent discussions, become more than ever attached to it: while that class of dissenters who were already moving in an heretical direction, have reposed in Socinianism as their natural centre of gravity. From several other circumstances recorded in these Memoirs, the same inference may be drawn with respect to the discredit under which this system lies at present, compared with the countenance and indulgence with which it was received thirty or forty years back. While Mr. Lindsey was deliberating on the propriety of quitting his living, it was suggested to him by Dr. Priestley, that he might continue to officiate, by making such alterations in the public offices of devotion as correspond to his peculiar views. "Nor was there any ground to suspect," says Mr. B., "that he would have met with any molestation from his superiors." Mr. Chambers, who held the living of Oundle, in Northamptonshire, Mr. Disney, for many years, and others, did so without being called to account for their conduct. We should be sorry to express ourselves with an improper degree of confidence; but we may venture to express a firm persuasion, that such a silent repeal of the doctrine of the church by the mere authority of a parochial minister would not now be permitted to pass unnoticed or uncensured in any part of the kingdom. The dignitaries of the church are alive to the importance of the distinguishing truths of Christianity, and would show themselves prompt and eager, as appears from recent instances, to discourage the open disavowal of them. We have no hesitation in asserting that the hope of rendering the tenets of the Polish heresiarch popular and prevalent throughout this nation was at no period so completely extinguished as at the present; and from a certain air of despondency which the memorialist of Lindsey betrays amid all his gasconades, we are convinced he is of the same opinion. The disposition on all occasions to vaunt of their success, and to predict with great confidence the speedy triumph of their principles, is a peculiar feature in the character of modern Socinians; and the absurd and exaggerated statements of matters of fact into which this propensity betrays them, are truly ludicrous. All other sorts of enthusiasts of whom we have either heard or read are in this respect cold and phlegmatic compared with them. In various extracts from the letters of Mr. Lindsey's correspondents, and of others, representations are made of numerous and rapid conversions to Socinianism, which Mr. B., from a regard to truth and decency, finds it necessary to correct and apologize for as the effusion of well-intended but intemperate zeal. The boast of success is almost invariably the precursor of a statement on the part of Mr. B., in which it is either repealed or qualified; and it is but doing him justice to say, that his judgment and experience have exempted him from those illusions and deceptions of which his party have become the easy dupes. We had been confidently informed, for instance, that almost all the people of Boston, in the province of Massachusetts, were becoming Socinians, and that the ministers, with the exception of one or two, had already declared themselves; when it appears, from the unimpeachable authority of Mr. Wells, himself a Socinian, and an inhabitant of that city, that there is but one professedly Unitarian chapel throughout New-England: and so little sanguine is he with respect to the spread of that doctrine, that he strongly deprecates its discussion, from a conviction that it will issue in producing among the body of the people a more confirmed attachment to orthodoxy.* It is also worthy of remark, that these extravagant boasts of success are not accompanied with the slightest advertence to the moral or spiritual effects which the Socinian doctrine produces on the character: this is a consideration which rarely, if ever, enters into the mind of its most zealous abetters, who appear to be perfectly satisfied if they can but accomplish a change of sentiment, however inefficacious to all practical purposes. Their converts are merely proselyted to an opinion, without pretending to be converted to God; and if they are not as much injured by the change as the proselytes made by the Pharisees of old, it must be ascribed to causes totally distinct from the superior excellence of the tenets they have embraced. They have been taught to discard the worship of Christ, and to abjure all dependence upon him as a Saviour—an admirable preparation, it must be confessed, for a devout and holy life. Let the abetters of those doctrines produce, if they can, a single instance of a person who, in consequence of embracing them, was reclaimed from a vicious to a virtuous life, from a neglect of serious piety to an exemplary discharge of its obligations and duties; and their success, to whatever extent it has been realized, would suggest an argument in their favour deserving some attention. But who is ignorant that among the endless fluctuations of fashions and opinions recorded in the annals of religion, the most absurd and pernicious systems have flourished for a while; and that Arianism, for instance. which these men profess to abhor almost as much as orthodoxy, prevailed to such a degree for years as to threaten to become the prevalent religion of Christendom!† Socinianism can boast but few converts compared with infidelity; in England, at least, they have gone hand in hand, and their progress has been simultaneous, derived from the same causes and productive of the same effects. Shall we therefore affirm that infidelity is to be rejected with less confidence because it possesses in reality that to which Socinianism only pretends? When we reflect on the inert and torpid character of Socinianism, it is surprising any serious expectation should be entertained of its final triumph. From innumerable passages in these Memoirs it appears that the far greater part of those who have embraced it in the established

* See his letter in the Appendix of the Memoirs.

† See the second book of Sulpicius Severus, chap. 35. "Tum hæresis Arii prorupit *totumque orbem* invecto errore turbaverat."

church have been content to retain their situation; and it is certain that of the two hundred and fifty who joined in the petition for relief in the matter of subscription, Mr. Lindsey was the only person who made any sacrifice of emolument to principle. We find both Mr. Lindsey and Mr. Belsham incessantly reproaching Unitarians with timidity in declining the avowal of their sentiments, and the former remarking with just indignation that amid the multitudes that concurred in his views, there was but one member of the established church that afforded him any pecuniary aid towards defraying the necessary expenses attendant on the opening of his chapel. The avowal of Socinianism among dissenters has rarely been followed by worldly privations; and in the Church of England, where such consequences must have ensued, it has not been made. Except in the instances of Lindsey, Jebb, and a very few others, the converts to Socinianism have stooped to the meanest prevarication and the most sacrilegious hypocrisy rather than sacrifice their worldly emolument and honours. Compare this with the conduct of the puritans in the reign of Charles the Second, who, though the points at issue were comparatively trifling and insignificant, chose to the number of two thousand to encounter every species of obloquy and distress rather than do violence to their conscience, and learn the difference between the heroism inspired by Christian principle and the base and pusillanimous spirit of heresy. What an infatuation to expect that a system which inspires its votaries with no better sentiments and feelings than are evinced by these decisive facts will ever become the prevailing belief,—a system which, while it militates against every page of revelation, is betrayed by the selfish timidity of its followers! The system of Socinus is a cold negation: the whole secret of it consists in thinking meanly of Christ; and what tendency such a mode of thinking can have to inspire elevation or ardour it is not easy to comprehend. If it is calculated to relieve the conscience of a weight which the principles of orthodoxy render it difficult to shake off, without complying with the conditions of the gospel, infidelity answers the same purpose still better, and possesses a still higher degree of simplicity,—meaning by that term what Socinians generally mean—the total absence of mystery.

Great part of these Memoirs are occupied in giving a copious analysis of Mr. L.'s publications, which, possessing no intrinsic merit, nor having excited more than a temporary interest, it would be trifling with the patience of our readers to suppose they could derive either entertainment or instruction from seeing them abridged. Of Mr. Lindsey, considered as a writer, it is sufficient to observe, that the measure of intellect he displays is the most ordinary, and that he was not possessed of the power, in its lowest degree, of either inventing what was rare or embellishing what was common. He was perspicuous, because he contented himself on all occasions with the most commonplace thoughts; he was simple, because he aspired to nothing more than to convey his meaning in intelligible terms, without the least conception of force, elegance, or harmony. Though his writings are replete with professions of unbounded liberality and candour, it is evident from his treatment of Mr. Robinson, of Cambridge, that he was indulgent only towards those who approached nearer to infidelity than himself. Nothing can be conceived more splenetic and acrimonious than his examination of that ingenious author's Plea for the Divinity of Christ, who, in return for compliments and condescensions which, however unworthy of the cause he was defending, were sufficient to soften a Cerberus, met with nothing but rudeness and insolence. It was truly amusing to see the imbecility of a Lindsey assuming the airs of a Warburton. Throughout the whole of that publication he affects to consider Mr. Robinson as a mere superficial declaimer, although his friend Archdeacon Blackburne, Mr. B. informs us, always spoke of the Plea as a most able and unanswerable performance. So much for the modesty of this heretical confessor!

But it is time to leave Mr. L. to that oblivion which is the infallible destiny of him and of his works, and to proceed to make a few remarks on the narrative and the miscellaneous strictures of his biographer. In the first place, we congratulate him on his abatement of that tone of arrogance which so strikingly characterized his former publications. Not that we ever expect him to exhibit himself in the light of an amiable or unassuming writer, which would be for the Ethiopian to change his skin; but it is with pleasure we remark less insolence and dogmatism than he has displayed on other occasions. He writes like a person who is conscious he is supporting a sinking cause; an air of despondency may be detected amid his efforts to appear gay and cheerful. He knows perfectly well that he is celebrating the obsequies, not the triumph, of Socinianism: and from the little advantage it has derived from its former efforts, his vanity will not prevent him from suspecting that he is giving dust to dust, and ashes to ashes.

In this as in all his former publications, he evinces a total ignorance of human nature, together with that propensity to overrate the practical effect of metaphysical theories which almost invariably attaches to metaphysicians of an inferior order. He who invents a metaphysical system which possesses the least claims to public regard must have paid a profound attention to the actual constitution of human nature. He must have explored the most delicate and intricate processes of the mind, and kept a vigilant eye on the various phenomena which it presents. He is necessarily *above* his theory, having been conducted to it by an independent effort of thought. He has not adjusted his observations to his hypothesis, but his hypothesis to his observations. The humble disciple, the implicit admirer proceeds too often in a directly opposite manner. All he knows of the mental constitution in its more intricate movements he derives from the system prepared to his hand, which he adopts with all its crudities, and confidently employs as the key which is to unlock all the recesses of nature. Having been accustomed to contemplate the human mind with a constant view to the technical arrangements to which he has devoted himself, he estimates the practical importance of metaphysical theories by what has passed in his own mind. We are fully convinced that the bulk of mankind are very little influenced by metaphysical theories: and that even in minds which are more prone to speculation, metaphysical dogmas are seldom so firmly embraced, or so deeply realized, as to be productive of important practical effects. The advocate of necessity and the champion of liberty will, in the same state of moral proficiency, act precisely the same part in similar circumstances. Mr. Belsham, however, in the plenitude of his enthusiasm for the doctrine of philosophical necessity, ascribes without hesitation the ruin of multitudes of young persons to their embracing the opposite tenet. It is truly surprising that he who was so quick-sighted as to perceive the tendency of the notion of liberty to promote immoral conduct, should entertain no suspicion of a similar tendency in the doctrine of God's being the author of sin, which Mr. B. repeatedly asserts.

"The true solution of the first difficulty," says Mr. B., "whether God be the author of sin, appears to be this: that God is, strictly speaking, the author of evil; but that, in the first place, he never ordains or permits evil but with a view to the production of a greater good, which could not have existed without it. And, secondly, that though God is the author of evil both natural and moral, he is not the approver of evil; he does not delight in it for its own sake; it must be the object of his aversion, and what he would never permit or endure, if the good he intends could have been accomplished without it. With respect to the justice of punishment, the best and only philosophical solution of it is, that under the divine government all punishment is remedial. Moral evil is the disease, punishment is the process of cure, of greater or less intensity, and of longer or shorter duration, in proportion to the malignity and inveteracy of the malady, but ultimately of sovereign efficacy, under the divine government, to operate a perfect cure; so that those whose vices have been the means of proving, purifying, and exalting the virtues of others, shall in the end share with them in their virtue and their triumph, and the *impartial justice* and infinite benevolence of the Divine Being will be made known, adored, and celebrated through the whole created universe."—Pp. 323, 324.

The malignant tendency of such representations as the foregoing is so obvious, that it is quite unnecessary to point it out to our readers. How vain are all precautions against sin, if in all cases it is produced by the omnipotent power of the Deity! and what motive can remain for avoiding it, if it is certain of being ultimately crowned with happiness and glory! The distinction between producing it and approving of it for its own sake, with which the doctrine is attempted to be palliated, is perfectly futile; for this is ascribing no more to the Deity than must, in justice, be ascribed to the most profligate of mankind, who never commit sin for its own sake, but purely with a view to certain advantages with which it is connected: and the difference between the two cases arises, not from any distinction in the moral character of the proceeding, but simply from the superior comprehension of view with which the conduct of the Deity is accompanied. As the perpetration of vice is, upon this system, a calamity, not a crime, it is but fitting and necessary it should receive a compensation; and for this

Mr. B. has provided, by representing the ultimate happiness of such as have been the means of purifying the virtue of others by their vices, as the effect of the impartial justice of the Deity. Persons of this description are, it seems, a species of benefactors; and it is but right they should, in due time, be rewarded. They are the scavengers of the universe; and, having done a great deal of necessary though dirty work, they are entitled to commiseration at present, and to proportionable compensation in another state of being. How admirably are these views adapted to promote a horror of sin! What tenderness of conscience, fear of offending, deep humility, and penitence may we expect to find in Mr. Belsham and in his admirers! Doubtless, their eyes are a fountain of tears, which, like Jeremiah, they are incessantly pouring out for those vices and impieties which are the sure and certain pledges of endless felicity!

To expect Mr. B. to write a bulky volume without intermingling a large portion of infidelity would be to expect grapes of thorns, and figs of thistles. In the work under consideration, he fully maintains the consistency of his character. He more than insinuates his disbelief of a great, if not the greater, part of the Mosaic history. Mr. Lindsey having expressed himself in terms of just reprehension with respect to the conduct of those who reject the books of Moses, Mr. B. takes upon him to censure the severity of his friend.

"But surely, if the venerable writer," says he, "had reconsidered the case with his usual calmness and impartiality, he would have seen that a person may be a very firm believer in the divine mission and doctrine of Christ, and be well satisfied with the general evidence of the divine legation of Moses, while he at the same time may entertain very serious doubts whether the books commonly attributed to Moses were really written throughout by him, and whether either the narrative or the institute exist at present exactly in the form in which he delivered them."—P. 408.

But, supposing the narrative to be in certain points false, the institution misrepresented and disguised, and the books which we term the Pentateuch the production of some unknown author,—who does not see the impossibility of separating the truth from the falsehood, and of attaching, on any consistent principles, to any part of it the credit due to a divine communication? The spirit of infidelity evinced in these passages is little different from that which pervades the pages of Bolingbroke and Voltaire. But such is the genuine progress of Socinianism: it begins with denying some of the clearest propositions in the New Testament, in order to which its claims to inspiration must be weakened or annulled; whence it proceeds to dispute the authority of the Old, till the whole Bible be virtually set aside as the umpire of controversy. Among the other sublime discoveries to which Mr. B. has been led by a critical investigation of the writings of the New Testament, one is, that the Lord Jesus Christ possesses no authority whatever; or, to use a term of his own invention, no *external* authority. Speaking of the Duke of Grafton, he says—

"In a paper dated January 1, 1792, the duke expresses a belief that the exaltation of Christ to dominion and authority was the consequence of his submission to those sufferings which 'were so efficacious, perhaps so necessary, to his own glory, and to the future happiness of mankind.' His mind seems at this time to have been perplexed with some obscure notion of the unscriptural doctrines of meritorious sufferings, and of the external authority of Jesus Christ; which, however, he regards as a mystery, which 'it will probably never be given to man in the present state' to understand, and which therefore 'must consequently be ranked among those articles the belief of which cannot be necessary to salvation.'"—P. 327.

Though the apostles have affirmed the exaltation of the Saviour to the government of the universe in every variety of form which language can supply,—though he himself declared that all power was given to him in heaven and in earth,—his possession of external authority is unblushingly asserted to be an unscriptural tenet. We challenge Mr. B. to invent terms more strongly expressive of the highest dominion and authority than those which the inspired writers have employed in describing the exaltation of the Saviour. We can regard this assertion of Mr. Belsham's in no other light than as a specimen of that theological audacity which forms the principal feature in that gentleman's character, and which happily can have no other effect than to inspire a complete abhorrence of the system which renders such a procedure necessary. We cheerfully accept, however, the concession implied in these daring positions, that the doctrine of the meritorious sufferings of Christ is inseparably connected with his exaltation; and as the latter cannot, without the utmost indecency, be denied, the former follows of course. We can annex no other meaning to the epithet *external*, as applied to *authority*, than what might be more clearly expressed by the term *personal;* or, in other words, Mr. B.'s intention is to assert that our Lord possesses no authority whatever apart from the credit due to his mission and to his doctrine, and that the Christian church is in no other sense governed by Christ, than the Jews might be affirmed to be governed by Moses after his decease. It must be obvious, however, to every one, that this is not to explain, but boldly and unequivocally to contradict, the writings of the apostles on this important subject.

We shall close these strictures on Mr. Belsham by quoting one passage more, which illustrates at once his insufferable arrogance and his servile deference to authority.

"What childish simplicity and ignorance," says he, "does it betray in some to feign or to feel alarmed at the tendency of those doctrines which are avowed by such men as Lindsey, Priestley, Hartley, and Jebb; and which are represented by them as lying at the foundation of all right views of the divine government, of all rational piety and virtuous practice, and of all rational and substantial consolation! And yet such persons feel no alarm at the vulgar notion of philosophical liberty, or the power of acting differently in circumstances precisely similar; a notion the fond persuasion of which encourages men to venture into circumstances of moral danger, and to which thousands of the young and inexperienced especially are daily falling victims." —P. 394.

The arrogance, folly, and absurdity of this passage are scarcely to be paralleled, even in the writings of its inimitable author. The most celebrated metaphysicians and reasoners, in every age and in every country—Malebranche, Cudworth, Clarke, Butler, Chillingworth, Reid, and innumerable others, who have avowed the strongest apprehensions of the immoral tendency of the doctrine of fatalism, or, as it has been styled, of philosophical necessity, are consigned by a writer who has not capacity sufficient to appreciate their powers, much less to rival their productions, to the reproach of childish simplicity and ignorance; and this for no other reason than their presuming to differ in opinion from Lindsey, Priestley, Hartley, and Jebb! What is this but to enjoin implicit faith? and why might not a Roman Catholic, with equal propriety, accuse of childish simplicity and ignorance those who should suspect the pernicious tendency of sentiments held by Pascal, Fenelon, and Bossuet? We must be permitted to remind Mr. B. that we hold his pretensions to a liberal and independent turn of thought extremely cheap; that, possessing nothing original even in his opinions, to say nothing of his genius, his most vigorous efforts have terminated in his becoming a mere train-bearer, in a very insignificant procession.

Having already detained our readers longer on this article than we ought, we should now put a period to our remarks, but that there is one particular connected with the history of Mr. Lindsey which we conceive has been too often set in such a light as is calculated to produce erroneous impressions. We refer to the resignation of his living in deference to his religious scruples. He is on this account everywhere designated by Mr. Belsham by the title of "the venerable confessor;" and what is more to be wondered at, the late excellent Job Orton, in a letter to his friend the late Rev. Mr. Palmer, of Hackney, speaks of him in the following terms:

"'Were I to publish an account of silenced and ejected ministers, I should be strongly tempted to insert Mr. Lindsey in the list he mentions in his Apology with so much veneration. He certainly deserves as much respect and honour as any of them for the part he has acted. Perhaps few of them exceeded him in learning and piety. I venerate him as I would any of your confessors. As to his particular sentiments, they are nothing to me. An honest pious man, who makes such a sacrifice to truth and conscience as he has done, is a glorious character, and deserves the respect, esteem, and veneration of every true Christian.'"

We have no scruple in asserting that this unqualified encomium is repugnant to reason, to Scripture, and to the sentiments of the best and purest ages of the Christian church. To pass over the absurdity of denominating Mr. L. a silenced and ejected minister, merely on account of his voluntary withdrawment from a community whose distinguishing tenets he had abandoned, we are far from conceiving that the merit attached to his conduct on this occasion was of such an order as to entitle him for a moment to rank with confessors and martyrs. To the praise of manly integrity for quitting a situation he could no longer conscientiously retain, we are ready to acknowledge Mr. L. fully entitled. We are cordially disposed to admire integrity wherever we perceive it; and we admire it the more in the present instance, because such examples of it among beneficed ecclesiastics have been rare. But we cannot permit ourselves to place sacrifices to error on the same footing as sacrifices to truth, without annihilating their distinction. If revealed truth possess any thing of sanctity and importance, the profession of it must be more meritorious than the profession of its opposite; and, by consequence, sacrifices made to that profession must be more estimable. He who suffers in the cause of truth is entitled to admiration; he who suffers in the defence of error and delusion to our commiseration: which are unquestionably very different sentiments. If truth is calculated to elevate and sanctify the character, he who cheerfully sacrifices his worldly emolument to its pursuit must be supposed to have participated in no common degree of its salutary operation. He who suffers equal privations in the propagation of error evinces, it is confessed, his possession of moral honesty; but unless persuasion could convert error into truth, it is impossible it should impart to error the effects of truth. Previous to the profession of any tenets whatever, there lies an obligation on all to whom the light of the gospel extends, to believe the truth. We are bound to confess Christ before men, only because we are bound to believe on him. But if, instead of believing on him, we deny him in his essential characters, which is the case with Socinians, the sincerity of that denial will indeed rescue us from the guilt of prevarication, but not from that of unbelief. It is possible, at least, since some sort of faith in Christ is positively asserted to be essential to salvation, that the tenets of the Socinians may be such as to exclude that faith: that it does exclude it no orthodox man can consistently deny; and how absurd it were to suppose a man should be entitled to the reward of a Christian confessor merely for denying, *bona fide*, the doctrine which is essential to salvation! The sincerity which accompanies his profession entitles him to the reward of a confessor: the error of the doctrine which he professes exposes him at the same time to the sentence of condemnation as an unbeliever! If we lose sight of Socinianism for a moment, and suppose an unbeliever in Christianity, *in toto*, to suffer for the voluntary and sincere promulgation of his tenets, we would ask Mr. Orton in what rank he would be inclined to place his infidel confessor. Is *he* entitled to rank with *any* of the confessors? If he is, our Saviour's terms of salvation are essentially altered; and though he pronounces an anathema on him who shall deny him before men, the sturdy and unshaken denial of him in the face of worldly discouragement would answer, it seems, as well as a similar confession Men are left at their liberty in this respect; and they are equally secure of eternal happiness, whether they deny or whether they confess the Saviour, providing they do it firmly and sincerely. If these consequences appear shocking, and he be forced to assert the negative, then it is admitted that the truth of the doctrine confessed enters essentially into the inquiry, whether he who suffers for his opinions is to be, *ipso facto*, classed with Christian confessors. Let it be remembered that we are not denying that he who hazards his worldly interest rather than conceal or dissemble his tenets, how false or dangerous soever they may be, is an honest man, and, *quoad hoc*, acts a virtuous part,—but that he is entitled to the same kind of approbation with the champion of truth. That the view we have taken of the subject is consonant to the Scriptures will not be doubted by those who recollect that St. John rests his attachment to Gaius and to the elect Lady, on the truth which dwelt in them; that he professed no Christian attachment but for the truth's sake; and that he forbade Christians to exercise hospitality, or to show the least indication of friendship, to those who taught any other doctrine than that which he and his fellow-apostles had taught. The source of the confusion and absurdity which necessarily attach to the opinions of Mr. Orton and others, here expressed on this subject, consists in their confounding together moral sincerity and Christian piety. We are perfectly willing to admit that the latter cannot subsist without the former; but we are equally certain that the former is by no means so comprehensive as necessarily to include the latter. We should have imagined it unnecessary to enter into an elaborate defence of so plain a position as this, that it is one thing to be what the world styles an honest man, and another to be a Christian—a distinction, obvious as it is sufficient to solve the whole mystery, and to account for the conduct of Mr. L., without adopting the unmeaning jargon of his biographer, who styles him, in innumerable places, the *venerable confessor.* How repugnant the language we have been endeavouring to expose is to that which was held in the purest and best ages of the church, must be obvious to all who are competently acquainted with ecclesiastical history. The Marcionites, we are informed by Eusebius, boasted of their having furnished a multitude of martyrs; but they were not the less on that account considered as deniers of Christ. Hence, when orthodox Christians happened occasionally to meet at the places of martyrdom with Montanists and Manichæans, they refused to hold the least communion with them, lest they should be supposed to consent to their errors.* In a word, the *nature* of the doctrine professed must be taken into consideration before we can determine that profession to be a Christian profession; nor is martyrdom entitled to the high veneration justly bestowed on acts of heroic piety, on any other ground than its being, what the term imports, an *attestation of the truth.* It is the saint which makes the martyr, not the martyr the saint.

* Euseb. lib. 5, c. 14.

REVIEW

OF

BIRT ON POPERY.

A Summary of the Principles and History of Popery, in Five Lectures, on the Pretensions and Abuses of the Church of Rome. By JOHN BIRT. 8vo. pp. 176. 1823.

AT a time when popery is making rapid strides, and Protestants in general have lost the zeal which once animated them, we consider the publication we have just announced as peculiarly seasonable. What may be the ultimate effect of the efforts made by the adherents of the Church of Rome to propagate its tenets, aided by the apathy of the opposite party, it is not for us to conjecture. Certain it is, there never was a period when the members of the papal community were so active and enterprising, or Protestants so torpid and indifferent. Innumerable symptoms appear of a prevailing disposition to contemplate the doctrines of popery with less disgust, and to witness their progress with less alarm, than has ever been known since the Reformation. All the zeal and activity are on one side; and while every absurdity is retained, and every pretension defended, which formerly drew upon popery the indignation and abhorrence of all enlightened Christians, we should be ready to conclude from the altered state of public feeling, that a system once so obnoxious had undergone some momentous revolution. We seem on this occasion to have interpreted in its most literal sense the injunction of "hoping all things and believing all things." We persist in maintaining that the adherents to popery are materially changed, in contradiction to their express disavowal; and while they make a boast of the infallibility of their creed, and the unalterable nature of their religion, we persist in the belief of its having experienced we know not what melioration and improvement. In most instances, when men are deceived, it is the effect of art and contrivance on the part of those who delude them: in this, the deception originates with ourselves; and instead of bearing *false* witness against our neighbour, such is the excess of our candour, that we refuse to credit the unfavourable testimony which he bears of himself.

There is, in the mean time, nothing reciprocal in this strange method of proceeding: we pipe to them, but they will not dance. Our con cessions, instead of softening and mollifying, seem to have no othe. effect upon them than to elate their pride and augment their arrogance

An equal change in the state of feeling towards an object which has itself undergone no alteration whatever, and where the party by which it is displayed profess to adhere to their ancient tenets, it would be difficult to specify. To inquire into the causes of this singular phenomenon would lead to discussion foreign to our present purpose. Let it suffice to remark, that it may partly be ascribed to the length of time which has elapsed since we have had actual experience of the enormous cruelties of the papal system, and to the fancied security we possess against their recurrence;—partly to the agitation of a great political question, which seems to have had the effect of identifying the cause of popery with that of Protestant dissenters. The impression of the past has in a manner spent itself; and in many its place is occupied by an eagerness to grasp at present advantages, and to lay hold of every expedient for shaking off the restraints which a narrow and timid policy has imposed. The influence of these circumstances has been much aided by that indifference to religious truth which too often shelters itself under the mask of candour: and to such an extent has this humour been carried, that distinguished leaders in parliament have not scrupled to represent the controversy between the papists and the Protestants as turning on obscure and unintelligible points of doctrine, scarcely worth the attention of enlightened minds; while a beneficed clergyman of some distinction has treated the whole subject as of no more importance than the idle disputes agitated by the schoolmen. It was but a few years since that a celebrated nobleman, in the House of Peers, vehemently condemned the oath of abjuration for applying the term *superstitious* to the doctrine of transubstantiation. In exactly the same spirit the appellation of papist is exchanged for Catholic,—a concession which the adherents of the Church of Rome well know how to improve, as amounting to little short of a formal surrender of the point at issue. For if the papists are really entitled to the name of *Catholics*, Protestants of every denomination are involved in the guilt of schism.

This revolution in the feelings of a great portion of the public has probably been not a little promoted by another cause. The present times are eminently distinguished by the efforts employed for the extension of vital religion: each denomination of Christians has taken its station, and contributed its part towards the diffusion of evangelical sentiments. The consequence has been, that the professors of serious piety are multiplied, and form at present a very conspicuous branch of the community. The space which they occupy in the minds of the public is not merely proportioned to their numerical importance, still less to their rank in society: it is in a great measure derived from the publicity of their proceedings, and the numerous associations for the promotion of pious and benevolent objects which they have originated and supported. By these means, their discriminating doctrines, essential to vital piety, have become better known, and more fully discussed than heretofore. However beneficial as to its general effects such a state of things may have been, one consequence which might be expected has been the result. The opposition of the enemies of religion has become more virulent, their hatred more heated and inflamed, and they have turned with no small complacency to the contemplation of a system which forms a striking contrast to the object of their detestation. Popery, in the ordinary state of its profession, combines the "form of godliness" with a total denial of its power. A heap of unmeaning ceremonies, adapted to fascinate the imagination and engage the senses,—implicit faith in human authority, combined with an utter neglect of Divine teaching,—ignorance the most profound, joined to dogmatism the most presumptuous,—a vigilant exclusion of biblical knowledge, together with a total extinction of free inquiry,—present the spectacle of religion lying in state, surrounded with the silent pomp of death. The very absurdities of such a religion render it less unacceptable to men whose decided hostility to truth inclines them to view with complacency whatever obscures its beauty or impedes its operation. Of all the corruptions of Christianity which have prevailed to any considerable extent, popery presents the most numerous points of contrast to the simple doctrines of the gospel; and just in proportion as it gains ground the religion of Christ must decline.

On these accounts, though we are far from supposing that popery, were it triumphant, would allow toleration to any denomination of Protestants, we have the utmost confidence that the professors of evangelical piety would be its first victims. The party most opposed to them look to papists as their natural ally, on whose assistance, in the suppression of what they are pleased to denominate fanaticism and enthusiasm, they may always depend: they may, therefore, without presumption, promise themselves the distinction conferred on Ulysses,—that of being last devoured.

Whether popery will ever be permitted, in the inscrutable counsels of Heaven, again to darken and overspread the land, is an inquiry in which it is foreign from our province to engage. It is certain that the members of the Romish community are at this moment on the tip-toe of expectation, indulging the most sanguine hopes, suggested by the temper of the times, of soon recovering all that they have lost, and of seeing the pretended rights of their church restored in their full splendour. If any thing can realize such an expectation, it is undoubtedly the torpor and indifference of Protestants, combined with the incredible zeal and activity of papists; and universal observation shows what these are capable of effecting,—how often they compensate the disadvantages arising from paucity of number, as well as almost every kind of inequality.

From a settled persuasion that popery still is what it always was—a detestable system of impiety, cruelty, and imposture, fabricated by the father of lies—we feel thankful at witnessing any judicious attempt to expose its enormities and retard its progress. The Lectures published some years since by Mr. Fletcher are well adapted for this purpose, and entitle their excellent author to the esteem and gratitude of the public. The Protestant, a series of periodical papers, composed by Mr. M'Gavin, of Glasgow, contains the fullest delineation of the popish system, and the most powerful confutation of its principles, in a popular style, of any work we have seen. Whoever wishes to see popery drawn to the life, in its hideous wickedness and deformity, will find abundant satisfaction in the pages of that writer.

The author before us has been studious of conciseness, and has contented himself with exhibiting a brief, but a very correct and impressive, outline of that copious subject. As these lectures were delivered at Manchester, it is probable the author's attention was more immediately directed to it by witnessing the alarming progress which the tenets of the Romish church are making in that quarter. There is nothing in them, however, of a local nature, or which is calculated to limit their usefulness to any particular part of the kingdom. They are adapted for universal perusal, and entitled to an extensive circulation.

The first lecture is on the claim of the Church of Rome to the appellation of *Catholic*, the futility and absurdity of which the author has exposed in a concise but highly satisfactory manner. On this part of the argument, he very acutely remarks, that "no church which is not coeval with Christianity itself ought to pretend to be the universal Christian church.

"The contrary sentiment is evidently unreasonable and absurd; for it supposes that something which has already a distinct and complete existence may be a part of something else which is not to come into being until a future period; or, which is equivalent to this, that what is entirely the creation of to-day may include that which was created yesterday. This would be in opposition to all analogy; and, therefore, if the Church of Rome had not an earlier commencement than all other Christian churches—if the origin of that church be not coincident and simultaneous with the first moment of Christianity—then the pretension of the Church of Rome to be the 'catholic church' is altogether vain. Now it is clear from the Acts of the Apostles, that many Christian churches flourished in the East before the gospel was even preached at Rome. It was enjoined on the apostles that their ministry should begin at Jerusalem; and in that city the first Christian church was actually constituted. Until the persecution which arose about the stoning of Stephen, Christ was not preached beyond the borders of Palestine, and even then, with a scrupulous discrimination, 'to the Jews only.' In fact, churches were formed in Jerusalem and Judea, at Damascus and Antioch, and the gospel was sent even into Ethiopia, before there is any evidence of its being known at Rome."—Pp. 10, 11.

The second lecture is an historical exposition of the principal events which led to the elevation of the Church of Rome to supremacy: in tracing these much acumen is evinced, as well as an intimate acquaintance with ecclesiastical history.

The third lecture consists of a masterly delineation of the genius and characteristics of the papal ascendency. In this part of the work, the judicious author enters deeply into the interior spirit of popery. After setting in a striking light the seeming impossibilities it had to encounter ere it could accomplish its object, he enumerates the expedients employed for this purpose under the following heads. The votaries of the papal see succeeded, 1. By enslaving the mental faculties to human authority; 2. By giving to superstition the semblance and sanction of religion; 3. By administering the affairs of their government on the corruptest principles of worldly policy. Each of these topics is illustrated with great judgment, and a copious induction of facts. On the last of these heads we beg leave to present to our readers the following extract, as a specimen of the style and spirit of this writer.

"'My kingdom is *not* of this world,' saith our Lord; 'My kingdom *is* of this world,' is truly the sentiment of the pope; and here lies the difference. The only consistent view of this church is that of a political establishment, employing, indeed, religious terms and denominations, but only as the pretext and colour of an inordinate pursuit of secular and temporal objects. Read its history as that of a Christian church; you stumble at every step, and every period shocks you with the grossest incongruities: read the same history as one of the kingdoms of this world; all is natural and easy, and the various proceedings and events are just what you are prepared to expect. The papal supremacy was conceded by an earthly monarch; all its interests have varied with the fluctuations of human affairs; and when the princes of this world shall withdraw their support, it will fall, and 'great will be the fall thereof.' The bishops of Rome have ever pursued, under the guise of religion, some earthly advantage; and thus Pope Leo the Tenth exclaimed most appropriately, 'O, how profitable has this fable of Jesus been unto us!'

"The first object of these subtle politicians was to provide a revenue, ample and permanent. Kings and nations were accordingly laid under tribute; and to the utmost extent of papal influence, the treasures of Christendom flowed into the exchequer of Rome. On every hand, art, fraud, and intimidation were equally and successfully employed in transferring the wealth of the world to the coffers of the church.

"This was effected partly by regular ecclesiastical taxes, but principally by selling every thing the Church of Rome had to bestow, and by perpetually inventing new articles of bargain and sale. Hence the multiplying of sacraments; hence the sale of pardons, indulgences, benefices, dignities, and of prayers for the living and the dead. Every thing was prostituted; and under the pretence of being the 'bride, the Lamb's wife,' this church became the 'mother of harlots.' In the same spirit the death-beds of the rich were besieged, that they might bequeath their property to the clergy; and the consciences of opulent criminals were appeased, in return for liberal donations to ecclesiastical funds. Thus an amount of riches almost incredible accrued to the papal treasury."—Pp. 94–96.

The fourth lecture is occupied by giving a rapid sketch of the most interesting events in the past history of the Romish community. We have seldom, if ever, seen so large a body of facts exhibited with perfect perspicuity within so small a compass: the author's complete mastery of the subject appears from the ease with which he has condensed an immense mass of historical matter, without the least indication of disorder or confusion.

The last of these lectures presents an animated and instructive view of the prospects which are opening on the Christian church, and the probable issue of the causes and events which are in present operation.

The notice we have taken of this publication will, we trust, induce our readers to avail themselves of the instruction and the pleasure which an attentive perusal cannot fail to bestow. It is distinguished for precision and comprehension of thought, energy of diction, and the most enlarged and enlightened principles of civil and religious freedom; nor should we find it easy to name a publication which contains within the same compass so much information on the subject which it professes to treat. A little redundance of ornament, and excess in the employment of figurative language, are excrescences very pardonable in a young writer, and which more mature years and experience may be safely left to correct. On the whole, we cannot dismiss the work before us without sincerely congratulating the author on that happy combination of philosophical discrimination with Christian piety which it throughout displays.

MISCELLANEOUS PIECES,

COLLECTED FROM

DIFFERENT SOURCES.

CHARACTER OF CLEANDER.

[*Written in* 1786.]

"NEC ASPERA TERRENT."

WHOEVER contemplates the various calamities that fill the world, and the still more numerous avenues by which we are exposed to distress, will be affected with a sense of the misery of man. In this survey, we need not search for remote and distant evils; we need not crowd our imagination with the horrors of war, the progress of armies, or the desolation of states. In the most familiar walks of life we meet with scenes at which humanity must bleed: scenes of distress lie open on every side: every quarter is filled with the groans of the dying, and lamentations for the dead. In the mass of mankind we can scarcely select an individual in whose bosom there does not rankle unpublished griefs; and, could we look into the hearts of the most tranquil, we should often find them a prey to unpitied regrets, torn with anxiety, and bleeding with disappointments.

Retiring from this melancholy spectacle, without looking any further, we might be ready to consider the world as a great nursery of disease, a vast receptacle of miseries, filled with beings whom Providence has endowed with sensibility to suffer, rather than capacities to enjoy; but to him who views the moral influence of afflictions, the evils they are intended to correct, and the benefits they impart, they will appear in a very different light; he will consider them as at once the punishments of vice, and the cure of it. Sorrow is, indeed, the offspring of guilt, but the parent of wisdom. Stern in her aspect, and severe in her deportment, she is, however, sent on a message of mercy. She is destined to follow in the footsteps of intemperance, to break her enchantments, to expose her delusions, and to deliver from thraldom such as are entangled in her snares, or are sleeping in her arms. Whoever surveys the course of his past life, with a view to remark the false steps he has taken in it, will find that as they have been preceded by indiscretion, they have been recalled by distress. To every object our attachment is proportioned to the pleasures we have received or expect to receive from it, and the passion will continue to be cherished as long as the recollection of it calls up ideas of pleasure rather than of pain. Now, every vicious pursuit is founded on indulgence, and disguised by inclination. To the licentious and abandoned, therefore, there is no prospect of the termination of their vices, till, by actual experience of the miseries they inflict, they convey to the mind more sentiments of aversion than of love.

From the moment that the enchantment is dispelled, the false colours stripped off, they will be regarded as specious deformities and real dangers. Multitudes who could never be persuaded by the calls of interest, or the voice of conviction, to restrain the license of their passions, and abandon their criminal pursuits, have been reclaimed by the lash of adversity. The decay of health, the desertion of friends, and the neglect of the world have not unfrequently softened those hardier spirits to whom the charms of virtue have been displayed in vain.

Nor is sorrow less effectual in the correction of foibles than in the extinction of vice. Cleander, in other respects a man of virtue and honour, had, from his infancy, accustomed himself to the unbounded indulgence of his tongue. Upon all occasions he trod on the very brink of decorum, a total stranger to the delicacies of friendship, which generously hides the faults it cannot correct. His ridicule was turned on the imperfections of his friends and his enemies, with indiscriminate severity. The splendour of distinguished virtue, which sets at a distance the reproaches of the world, and almost sanctifies the blemishes of an illustrious character, exempted no foibles from the scourge of Cleander; but rather quickened his acuteness to remark and his asperity to expose them, as it furnished a display of his penetration in discovering imperfections where there appeared to the world nothing but unmingled excellence. It was, indeed, his delight to remark the shades of a brilliant character, and to portray with exactness the secret gradations of excellence by which it fell short of perfection. Yet in Cleander this conduct by no means sprang from envy of superior worth, or the malignant desire of degrading every one to his own level. He possessed the magnanimity of a virtuous mind, and disdained to lessen his own inferiority by any other means than that of honest emulation. It had its basis in a taste for ridicule and the pride of wit. His deportment could not fail to issue in perplexity and distress. His enemies considered him as a kind of beast of prey, a savage of the desert, whom they were authorized to wound by every weapon of offence, some by open defamation, and some by poisoned arrows in the dark. His friends began to look upon him with alienation and distrust, esteeming their character too sacred to be suspended, for the sport of an individual, on the breezy point of levity and wit.

His appearance was a signal for general complaint; and he could scarcely enter into company hoping to enjoy the unmingled pleasures of social converse, but he had innumerable jealousies to allay, and misunderstandings to set right. He was everywhere received with marks of disgust; met with resentment for which he could not account; and was obliquely insulted for careless strokes of satire, of which he retained no recollection. Wherever he turned himself, he found his path was strewed with thorns; and that even they who admired his wit secretly vilified his character, and shrunk from his acquaintance. His peace began to bleed on every side; his reputation was tarnished; his fairest prospects blasted; and Cleander, at length awakened from his delusions, was convinced, when it was too late, of a lesson he had often been taught in vain, that the attachments of friendship and the tranquillity of life are too valuable to be sacrificed to a blaze of momentary admiration.

A consideration of the benefit of afflictions should teach us to bear them patiently when they fall to our lot; and to be thankful to Heaven for having planted such barriers around us, to restrain the exuberance of our follies and our crimes.

Let these sacred fences be removed; exempt the ambitious from disappointment, and the guilty from remorse; let luxury go unattended with disease, and indiscretion lead into no embarrassments or distresses; our vices would range without control, and the impetuosity of our passions have no bounds; every family would be filled with strife, every nation with carnage, and a deluge of calamities would break in upon us which would produce more misery in a year than is inflicted by th hand of Providence in a lapse of ages.

A REVERY.

[*Written in* 1786.]

"Aux peupliers qui bornent mon séjour,
J'avois juré de suspendre ma lyre;
De respirer, d'être heureux sans délire,
D'oser sur tout, être heureux sans l'amour
J'avois juré; mais je l'ai vu sourire,
Et sur son aile il emporte aujourd'hui
Tous les sermens que j'ai faits contre lui."
Dorat.

ENGLISHED THUS:

"On the tall poplars which surround my cot,
And mark the bound'ries of my humble lot,
Where I so oft of Cupid's power have sang
I fiercely swore my unstrung lyre to hang:
To breathe in peace—to taste the quiet joy
Of calm contentment, which can never cloy:
But, more than all, to banish from my heart
Tormenting love, and its too pleasing smart:
Thus did I swear—but listening Cupid smiled,
And, while with his enchantments he beguiled,
He wafted on his pinions far away
My fruitless oaths, rebellious to his sway."
Ineptus.

AFTER reading some passages in the fourth book of Virgil, in which he paints the distress of Dido upon her being deserted by Æneas, I could not help revolving in my mind, with a good deal of uneasiness, the miseries of love. My reflections threw me into a REVERY, which presented to my mind an imaginary train of circumstances, which I shall now relate, hoping they may tend to cherish that virtuous sensibility which is the ornament of our nature. My fancy naturally carried me into the times of heathenish superstition, which I hope will be my apology for mentioning gods and goddesses. I imagined that the power of Love had occasioned general discontent, and that the different orders of men had entered into an agreement to petition Jupiter for her removal.

I thought that at the head of these complainers stood the men of learning and science; they lamented with vehemence the inroads of love, and that it often betrayed them from the paths of knowledge into perplexity and intrigue. They alleged that it extinguished in the bosom of the young all thirst after laudable improvement, and planted in its stead frivolous and tormenting desires. That the pursuit of truth called for a tranquil and serene state of mind; while love was constantly attended with tumult and alarm. Whatever turn she takes, said they, she will ever be an enemy to labour; her smiles are too gay, and her disappointments too melancholy, for any serious application. They were grieved to see that so trifling a passion should occupy so much time and attention, and that man, who was formed to contemplate the heavens and the earth, should spend half his life in gaining the good graces of the weaker and more inconsiderable part of his species. I thought I perceived that this turn for love and gallantry gave particular offence to the whole tribe of astronomers and profound philosophers. They saw, with indignation, that many of our youth were more anxious to explain a look than to solve a problem, and that they would often be playing with a fan when they should be handling a quadrant. It infatuates every one, said they, who is so unhappy as to be touched with it. He is often more attentive to every change of countenance in a celebrated beauty than to the phases of the moon; and is more anxious to be acquainted with all her manœuvres than with the motion of the whole planetary system. One in particular affirmed, upon his knowledge, that he had been acquainted with students in anatomy who looked with more curiosity into the countenance of a young beauty than upon the dissection of a bullock's eye. Some, who pretend to see much farther than the vulgar, considered every thing relating to love as capricious and visionary. Since we are all formed of the same materials, it seemed to them very unreasonable that a little difference in form and colour should raise such violent commotions. Beauty, they said, was but a superficial covering, and every thing at the bottom was alike. Upon this principle, they looked upon it as the height of philosophy to view with indifference what has always given mankind the greatest pleasure. This humour they carried so far, that they lamented they could not strip nature herself of her delusions, as they termed them, by taking off those agreeable colourings of light and shade which lie upon objects around us, and give them all their richness and beauty. They would have been glad to have turned the creation into a colourless and dreary waste, that they might have wandered up and down, and taken a closer survey of it.

The next class of petitioners, I observed, were the men of business. They set out with remarking that they did not join in the complaints that were made against love upon their own account; for though they had been weak enough, in the younger part of their lives, to fall under its influence, it was many years since they had felt the slightest impression of it. They had in view the welfare of their children, and this being neither more nor less than their affluence, they were led to consider love chiefly in the light of an expensive passion. Its little tendernesses and endearments appeared to them inexpressibly ridiculous, and they wondered how anybody could be foolish enough to spend hours in tattling to women, without thinking to gain a farthing by it. They gave a long list of young men, who had been frugal and industrious, till they were enticed by love to prefer pleasure to profit. They declared that when we take an account of balls and treats, and trinkets of various kinds, with the loss of time inseparably attendant upon them, it was at the peril of a fortune to attempt the heart of a beloved object. I was a good deal amused with the manner in which they treated of love; they considered it as they would any other commodity, setting a price upon every part of it. They reckoned a sigh at a shilling, and if it chance to be observed by the person for whom it is intended, it was well even if half a guinea cleared the expense of it. A side glance was rated at half as much as a full view; they portioned out all the parts of a beautiful person, and made a valuation of each of them. The same scale was applied to their very attitudes; for the sight of a beautiful woman dancing was accounted a matter of enormous expense; and if she chanced to smile with any degree of complacency upon any one, it was well if he was not ruined; under these impressions, they considered love as the certain forerunner of poverty.

There was one complaint raised against this passion which I thought had something in it more plausible than any I have yet mentioned; it turned upon the ease with which it makes its approaches upon us, and the impossibility of guarding against its first advances. We have been able, said they, by art to manage the elements, so as in general to prevent any dangerous overflowings of them. We brave the storm in ships, and dive into the sea in bells; but the ingenuity of man has hit upon no contrivance to save us from the influcnce of love. Could we call it in to amuse a leisure hour, or to relieve the languor of a few tedious moments, and then dismiss it again, it might be esteemed a blessing in a life so barren of enjoyment. But it is an influence that is shed all around us, and pours itself upon us from every corner. It often lies hid between the keys of a harpsichord, and is shaken out with a few touches of the fingers. It flounces in an apron, and is trailed along with a petticoat. No circumspection can preserve us from it; for it will often steal upon us when we are least upon our guard. It hides itself in a lock, and waves in ringlets of the hair. It will enter by an eye, an ear, a hand, or a foot. A glance and a gaze are sometimes equally fatal.

I was next presented with a scene which I thought as interesting and solemn as can enter into the imagination of man. This was no other than a view of the whole train of disappointed lovers. At the sight of them my heart insensibly melted into the most tender compassion. There was an extreme dejection, mingled with a piercing wildness, in their looks, that was very affecting. Cheerfulness and serenity, I could easily perceive, they had long been strangers to. Their countenances were overspread with a gloom which appeared to be of long standing, and to be collected there from dark and dismal imaginations. There was at the same time all that kind of animation in their features which betokens troubled thoughts. Their air and manner was altogether singular, and such as marks a spirit at once eager and irresolute. Their step was irregular, and they ever and anon started and looked around them, as though they were alarmed by some secret terror. I was somewhat surprised, in looking through the whole assembly, not to see any one that wept. When they were arrived at the place where they had determined to present their united petitions, I was particularly attentive to observe every thing that passed. Though I listened, I could not learn any thing distinctly. After an interval of profound silence, a murmur only of broken sighs and piercing exclamations was heard through the assembly. I should have mentioned that some of them fell off before they had got to the place of rendezvous. They halted for some time, and continued in a melancholy suspense, whether they should turn back or go forward. They knew not which to prefer, the tranquillity of indifference or the tender distresses of love; at length they inclined to the latter, not having resolution even to wish for the extinction of a passion which mingled itself with the very elements of their existence. "Why," said they, "should we banish from our minds the image of all that is pleasing and delightful, and which if we could once forget, there would be nothing left in the world worth remembering?" The agitation and anxiety felt upon this occasion, could I lay it fully open to the reader, would form a much more interesting picture than the deliberations of Cæsar, whether he should pass the Rubicon.

I imagined there were several other distinct bodies of men who complained to the heavenly powers of the tyranny of love, but the particulars having in a great measure faded from my memory, the reader must excuse my passing them over in silence. I must not, however, forget to observe, that the number and unanimity of those who presented their petitions on the occasion were such, that they might fairly be considered as representing the sentiments of far the greater part of mankind.

Perhaps Providence never chastises the folly of men more justly than by granting the indulgence of their requests. Upon this occasion I observed their wishes were accomplished, and they were relieved from a tyranny of which they had so heavily complained. Upon an appointed day the goddess of love took her flight to the higher regions, from which she had descended; her influence was at once withdrawn, and all her enchantments were broken up. I thought nothing could equal the joy that was expressed upon this occasion. The air rung with acclamations, and every man was in haste to congratulate his neighbour on their deliverance from a thraldom which had sunk the spirit and degraded the dignity of the human race. They seemed all to be lightened of a load, and to break forth with fresh vivacity and spirit. Every one imagined he was entering upon quite a new career, and that the world was laid fresh open before him.

I could not help feeling an inward delight in seeing my fellow-creatures made at once so happy. At the same time I was anxious to know what would follow upon this new revolution, and particularly whether it would answer the high expectations that were formed from it. Upon my looking around I was a witness to appearances which filled me with melancholy and regret. A total change had taken place in the whole train of human affairs, and I observed to my sorrow the change was everywhere for the worse. It was melancholy now to enter into company; for instead of conversation enlivened by vivacity and wit, there was nothing heard of but a drowsy humming, to the last degree tiresome and insipid. In the social intercourse of men the heart had no place; pleasure and the desire of pleasing were equally unknown.

Those whom I had an opportunity of observing I thought very much resembled the loungers and coxcombs of our day, who, without any view of receiving pleasure, mingle in a crowd and engage in conversation, not to enjoy time, but to kill it. I now sought in vain for those friendly meetings at which I had often been present, where every one, desirous of adding something to the pleasure of the whole, drew forth the fairest ideas of his mind, and by the display of tender sentiments melted the heart and soothed the imagination. With what regret did I recollect those conversation parties in which my heart was wont to be full, and to pour itself forth as we talked ourselves alternately into sadness and into joy!

I had an opportunity of correcting a mistake into which I had fallen, in imagining that love reached only to courtship and marriage; I saw that it insensibly mingles with our most trifling actions, refining our thoughts and polishing our manners when we are least aware of it. The men had now entirely thrown aside that tenderness and gallantry which are the great ornaments of human nature, and are so peculiarly needful to temper and soften the rudeness of masculine strength. Men and women were now placed quite upon a level, so that the harmonious softness of the female voice was drowned in turbulence and noise. The ear was filled, but the heart was left empty. Politeness was exchanged for a tame civility, wit for merriment, and serenity for dulness. I began to think more highly than ever of the fair sex, and regarded them in a new light, as a beautiful mirror lying in the fancy of a lover for him to dress his thoughts by. People were everywhere falling a prey to dejection, and complaining of the faintness of human enjoyments, as might well be expected when the influence of love was withdrawn from them, which, by inspiring romantic hopes and romantic fears, keeps the mind always in motion, and makes it run clear and bright. You may be sure nothing could make a more ridiculous appearance than courtship, at a time when women retained their vanity after they had lost their charms. Such is the force of habit that you might often see a pretty creature twirling her fan and playing off her little enchanting airs before her lover, who perhaps sat all that time perfectly insensible, fingering his buttons or picking his teeth. Vanity, I perceived, was a kind of instinct in women, that made them employ the whole artillery of their charms when they knew they could do no execution. Indeed, their airs appeared so ridiculous now in the eyes of the men that they had often much ado to refrain from laughter. The coquettes particularly, in their flutterings to and fro, made as odd a figure as fish which should be frozen around in the very act of swimming. Out of respect to the ladies, however, I would compare them to the Grecian chiefs, who, according to the representation of the poets, carried with them so lively an impression of their former employments, that they would be marshalling their troops and brandishing their swords even in the shades below. However, the fair sex were soon relieved from this sort of ridicule. They no longer took any pains to smooth their brow, to soften their features into a smile, or to light up the beam of brightness in their eye. Careless of offending where they knew they could not please, they became negligent in their persons and vulgar in their air. I cannot express the regret I felt upon beholding the fairest and most beautiful part of the creation thus thrown into shade.

I thought I perceived that the fine arts began to languish, the paintings that made their appearance at the time were neither boldly sketched nor so brightly coloured as those I was wont to survey; they were chiefly confined to still-life. I observed, however, that the extinction of love affected poetry still more than painting. It no longer regaled the mind with descriptions of beauty, or softened it with tender distress. Its enchantment was entirely dissolved,—that enchantment that will carry us from world to world without moving from our seat, will raise a visionary creation around us, will make us to rejoice when there is nothing to rejoice in, and tremble when there is nothing to alarm us. These interesting situations, which awaken the attention and enchain the mind in solemn suspense till it breaks forth into agony or rapture, now no longer existed in nature, and were no longer described by the poet; he wrote rather from memory than feeling, for the breath of inspiration had ceased.

Upon this occasion I was not at all surprised at the decline of eloquence. I have often thought love the nurse of sensibility, and that, if it were not cherished by this passion, it would grow cold, and give way to a selfish indifference. My conjecture was now abundantly confirmed; for though I saw many discourses composed at this time that were well-argued, elegant, and correct, they all wanted those essential touches that give language its power of persuading.

One thing a good deal surprised me, and that was to observe that even the profound parts of learning were less attended to than ever. I was well aware that few apply themselves closely to study but with the hope of sometimes displaying their acquisitions to the public; and I had imagined fame was a sufficient recompense for any toil human nature could sustain; but I was surprised to find that, in all great and noble undertakings, the desire of appearing respectable in the eyes of a beloved object was of more consequence than the general admiration of mankind.

These I thought were not the only melancholy consequences that flowed from the departure of love. It may be sufficient, however, to observe in general that human nature was becalmed, and all its finest emotions frozen into a torpid insensibility. The situation of mankind was truly pitiable. Strangers to the delicate pleasures of the heart, every thing around them looked cheerless and barren. Calamity left them nothing to hope, and prosperity gave them nothing to enjoy.

I observed that they were now as desirous of bringing back the agency of love as they had been before to exclude it. At length I imagined that Jupiter was touched with compassion at their unhappy situation, and appointed a day in which Love was to revisit the abodes of men. An immense number of people, of all orders and ranks, and of every age and condition, assembled themselves, as you may suppose, to behold the descent of the goddess, and to hail her approach. The heavens, I thought, glowed as she descended, and so many beautiful streaks of light glanced along the surface of the sky, that they divided it into separate tracts, brightened up every cloud within it, and turned the whole into an aerial landscape. The birds at the same time leaping among the branches, and warbling their sprightliest notes filled the air with a confused melody of sounds that was inexpressibly delightful. Every thing looked brighter than before, every thing smelled sweeter, and seemed to offer up fresh incense to the goddess. The face of nature was changed, and the creation seemed to grow new again. My heart glowed with delight. I rejoiced in the renovation of nature, and was revived through my inmost powers. There thrilled through me a delightful sensation of freshness and novelty, similar to what a happy spirit may be supposed to feel when he first enters a new state of existence, and opens his eyes on immortality.

I thought I had but a very confused idea of the person of the goddess herself; for her raiment was so full of light and lustre that I could scarcely take a steady view of her. I observed, however, that her complexion was rather too glowing, and the motions of her eye too piercing and fiery for perfect feminine beauty. Her beauty, I thought, was too raised, and had too much glory in it to be entirely attractive. I was very much astonished to observe that whoever she glanced her eye upon immediately fell under the influence of the passion over which she presided. It was a very singular sight to see a whole assembly, one after another, falling into love; and I was much entertained in observing the change it occasioned in the looks of each of them, according to their different temper and constitution; some appeared wild and piercing, others dejected and melancholy. The features of several glowed with admiration, while others looked down with a timid and bashful respect. A trait of affectation was plainly to be discerned in all of them, as might well be expected from a passion the very first effect of which is to make one lose the possession of one's self. Several ladies in particular, seemingly careless and gay, were whispering to those who stood next them, and assuming airs of particular vivacity, while you might easily see their countenance was checkered with anxiety lest they should chance not to please those upon whom they had fixed their affections. The greater part of the fair sex, however, I observed, smiled with an ineffable sweetness, nor could any thing appear more lovely than their features, upon which there was imprinted a tender reserve, mingled with modest complacency and desire. I imagined that after the goddess had thoroughly surveyed the assembly, and they had seated themselves into some degree of composure, she thus addressed them:—

"Ye children of men, ye abound in the gifts of Providence, and many are the favours Heaven has bestowed upon you. The earth teems with bounty, pouring forth the necessaries of life and the refinements of luxury. The sea refreshes you with its breeze and carries you to distant shores upon its bosom; it links nation to nation in the bonds of mutual advantage, and transfers to every climate the blessings of all. To the sun you are indebted for the splendour of the day, and the grateful return of season; it is he who guides you as you wander through the trackless wilderness of space, lights up the beauties of nature around you, and makes her break forth into fruitfulness and joy. But know that these, though delightful, are not the pleasures of the heart. They will not heal the wounds of fortune; they will not enchant solitude, or suspend the feeling of pain. Know that I only am mistress of the soul. To me it belongs to impart agony and rapture. Hope and despair, terror and delight, walk in my train. My power extends over time itself, as well as over all sublunary beings. It can turn ages into moments, and moments into ages. Lament not the dispensations of Providence, among which the bestowment of my influence is one. He who feels it may not be happy; but he who is a stranger to it must be miserable."

AN

ESSAY ON POETRY AND PHILOSOPHY

[*Written in* 1787.]

It has been observed that it seldom falls to the share of one man to be both a philosopher and a poet. These two characters, in their full extent, may be said to divide between them the whole empire of genius; for all the productions of the human mind fall naturally under two heads—works of imagination, and works of reason. There are indeed several kinds of composition which, to be perfect, must partake of both. In our most celebrated historians, for instance, we meet with a just mixture of the penetration that distinguishes the philosopher and the ardour of the poet; still their departments are very wide of each other, and a small degree of attention will be sufficient to show why it is so extremely difficult to unite in any high degree the excellence of each. The end of the poet is to give delight to his reader, which he attempts by addressing his fancy and moving his sensibility; the philosopher purposes merely to instruct, and therefore thinks it enough if he presents his thoughts in that order which will render them the most perspicuous, and seems best adapted to gain the attention. Their views demand, therefore, a very different procedure. All that passes under the eye of the poet he surveys in one particular view; every form and image under which he presents it to the fancy are descriptive of its effects. He delights to paint every object in motion, that he may raise a similar agitation in the bosom of the reader. But the calm, deliberate thinker, on the contrary, makes it his chief endeavour to seek out the remoter causes and principles which give birth to these appearances.

It is the highest exertion of a philosopher to strip off the false colours that serve to disguise, to remove every particular which fancy or folly have combined, and present to view the simple and naked truth. But the poet, who addresses the imagination and the heart, neglects no circumstance, however fanciful, which may serve to attach his descriptions more closely to the human mind. In describing the awful appearances of nature, he gladly avails himself of those magic terrors with which ignorance and superstition have surrounded them; for though the light of reason dispels these shades, they answer the highest purpose of the poet, in awakening the passions. It is the delight of poetry to combine and associate; of philosophy to separate and distinguish. The one resembles a skilful anatomist, who lays open every thing that occurs, and examines the smallest particulars of its make; the other a judicious painter, who conceals what would offend the eye, and embellishes every subject he undertakes to represent: the same object, therefore, which has engaged the investigating powers of the philosopher, takes a very different appearance from the forming hand of the poet, who adds every grace of colouring, and artfully hides the nakedness of the inward structure under all the agreeable foldings of elegance and beauty. In philosophical discussions, the end of which is to explain, every part ought to be unfolded with the most lucid perspicuity. But works of imagination never exert a more powerful influence than when the author has contrived to throw over them a shade of darkness and doubt. The reason of this is obvious: the evils we but imperfectly discern seem to bid defiance to caution; they affect the mind with a fearful anxiety, and by presenting no limits the imagination easily conceives them boundless. These species of composition differ still further with respect to the situation of mind requisite to produce them. Poetry is the offspring of a mind heated to an uncommon degree; it is a kind of spirit thrown off in the effervescence of the agitated feeling. But the utmost calmness and composure is essential to philosophical inquiry: novelty, surprise, and astonishment kindle in the bosom the fire of poetry; while philosophy is reared up by cool and long-continued efforts. There is one circumstance relating to this kind of composition too material to be omitted. In every nation it has been found that poetry is of much earlier date than any other production of the human mind. As in the individual, the imagination and passions are more vigorous in youth, which in mature age subside, and give way to thought and reflection.

Something similar to this seems to characterize that genius which distinguishes the different periods of society. The most admired poems have been the offspring of uncultivated ages. Pure poetry consists of the descriptions of nature and the display of the passions; to each of which a rude state of society is better adapted than one more polished. They who live in that early period in which art has not alleviated the calamities of life are forced to feel their dependence upon nature. Her appearances are ever open to their view, and therefore strongly imprinted on their fancy. They shrink at the approach of a storm, and mark with anxious attention every variation of the sky. The change of seasons, cloud or sunshine, serenity and tempest, are to them real sources of sorrow and of joy; and we need not, therefore, wonder they should describe with energy what they feel with so much force. But it is one chief advantage of civilization, that by enabling us in some measure to control nature, we become less subject to its influence. It opens many new sources of enjoyment. In this situation the gay and the cheerful can always mingle in company, while the diffusion of knowledge opens to the studious a new world, over which the whirlwind and the blast can exert no influence. The face of nature gradually retires from view, and those who attempt to describe it often content themselves with copying from books, whereby their descriptions want the freshness and glow of original observation: like the image of an object reflected through various mediums, each of which varies somewhat of its form, and lessens its splendour. The poetry of uncivilized nations has, therefore, often excelled the productions of a more refined people in elevation and pathos. Accustomed to survey nature only in her general form and grander movements, their descriptions cannot fail of carrying with them an air of greatness and sublimity. They paint scenes which every one has felt, and which therefore need only to be presented to awaken a similar feeling again. For a while they delight us with the vastness of their conceptions; but the want of various embellishments, and the frequent recurrence of the same images, soon fatigues the attention, and their poetry may be compared to the world of waters, which fills us with amazement, but upon which we gaze for a moment, and then turn away our eyes. It is the advantage of enlightened nations that their superior knowledge enables them to supply greater variety, and to render poetry more copious. They allure with an agreeable succession of images. They do not weary with uniformity, or overpower us with the continuance of any one exertion; but by perpetually shifting the scene they keep us in a constant hurry of delight.

> "The poet's eye, in a fine phrensy rolling,
> Doth glance from heaven to earth, from earth to heaven,
> And, as imagination bodies forth
> The forms of things unknown, the poet's pen
> Turns them to shapes, and gives to airy nothing
> A local habitation and a name."
>
> *Shakspeare's Midsummer Night's Dream.*

cannot help observing that poetical genius seems capable of much greater variety than talents for philosophizing. The power of thinking and reasoning is a simple energy, which exerts itself in all men nearly in the same manner; indeed, the chief varieties that have been observed in it may be traced to two—a capacity of abstract and mathematical reasoning, and a talent for collecting facts and making observations; these qualities of mind, blended in various proportions, will for the most part account for any peculiarities attending men's modes of thinking. But the ingredients that constitute a poet are far more various and complicated. A poet is in a high degree under the influence of the imagination and passions, principles of mind very various and extensive. Whatever is complicated is capable of much greater variety, and will be extremely more diversified in its form, than that which is more simple. In this case every ingredient is a source of variety; and by being mingled in the composition in a greater or less degree, may give an original cast to the whole.

To explain the particular causes which vary the direction of the fancy in different men would perhaps be no easy task. We are led, it may be at first through accident, to the survey of one class of objects; this calls up a particular train of thinking, which we afterward freely indulge; it easily finds access to the mind upon all occasions; the slightest accident serves to suggest it. It is nursed by habit, and reared up with attention, till it gradually swells to a torrent, which bears away every obstacle, and awakens in the mind the consciousness of peculiar powers. Such sensations eagerly impel to a particular purpose, and are sufficient to give to composition a distinct and determinate character.

Poetical genius is likewise much under the influence of the passions. The pleased and the splenetic, the serious and the gay, survey nature with very different eyes. That elevation of fancy which, with a melancholy turn, will produce scenes of gloomy grandeur and awful solemnity, will lead another, of a cheerful complexion, to delight, by presenting images of splendour and gayety, and by inspiring gladness and joy. To these and other similar causes may be traced that boundless variety which diversifies the works of imagination, and which is so great, that I have thought the perusal of fine authors is like traversing the different regions of the earth; some glow with a pleasant and refreshing warmth, while others kindle with a fierce and fiery heat; in one we meet with scenes of elegance and art, all is correct and regular, and a thousand beautiful objects spread their colours to the eye, and regale the senses; in another we behold nature in an unadorned majestic simplicity, scouring the plain with the tempest, sitting upon a rock, or walking upon the wings of the wind. Here we meet with a Sterne, who fans us with the softest delicacies; and there with a Rousseau, who hurries us along in whirlwind and tempest. Hence that delightful succession of emotions which are felt in the bosom of sensibility. We feel the empire of genius, we imbibe the impression, and the mind resembles an enchanted mansion which, at the touch of some superior hand, at one time brightens into beauty, and at another darkens into horror. Even where the talents of men approach most nearly, an attentive eye will ever remark some small shades of difference, sufficient to distinguish them. Perhaps few authors have been distinguished by more similar features of character than Homer and Milton. That vastness of thought which fills the imagination, and that sensibility of spirit which renders every circumstance interesting, are the qualities of both: but Milton is the most sublime, and Homer the most picturesque. Homer lived in an early age, before knowledge was much advanced; he would derive little from any acquired abilities, and therefore may be styled the poet of nature. To this source perhaps we may trace the principal difference between Homer and Milton. The Grecian poet was left to the movements of his own mind, and to the full influence of that variety of passions which are common to all: his conceptions are therefore distinguished by their simplicity and force. In Milton, who was skilled in almost every department of science, learning seems sometimes to have shaded the splendour of genius.

No epic poet excites emotions so fervid as Homer, or possesses so much fire; but in point of sublimity he cannot be compared to Milton. I rather think the Greek poet has been thought to excel in this quality more than he really does, for want of a proper conception of its effects. When the perusal of an author raises us above our usual tone of mind, we immediately ascribe those sensations to the sublime, without considering whether they light on the imagination or the feelings; whether they elevate the fancy or only fire the passions.

The sublime has for its object the imagination only, and its influence is not so much to occasion any fervour of feeling, as the calmness of fixed astonishment. If we consider the sublime as thus distinguished from every other quality, Milton will appear to possess it in an unrivalled degree; and here indeed lies the secret of his power. The perusal of Homer inspires us with an ardent sensibility; Milton with the stillness of surprise. The one fills and delights the mind with the confluence of various emotions; the other amazes with the vastness of his ideas. The movements of Milton's mind are steady and progressive: he carries the fancy through successive stages of elevation, and gradually increases the heat by adding fuel to the fire.

The flights of Homer are more sudden and transitory. Milton, whose mind was enlightened by science, appears the most comprehensive; he shows more acuteness in his reflections, and more sublimity of thought. Homer, who lived more with men, and had perhaps a deeper tincture of the human passions, is by far the most vehement and picturesque. To the view of Milton the wide scenes of the universe seem to have been thrown open, which he regards with a cool and comprehensive survey, little agitated, and superior to those emotions which affect inferior mortals. Homer, when he rises the highest, goes not beyond the bounds of human nature; he still connects his descriptions with human passions, and though his ideas have less sublimity, they have more fire. The appetite for greatness—that appetite which always grasps at more than it can contain—is never so fully satisfied as in the perusal of "Paradise Lost." In following Milton we grow familiar with new worlds, we traverse the immensities of space, wandering in amazement, and finding no bounds. Homer confines the mind to a narrower circle, but that circle he brings nearer to the eye; he fills it with a quicker succession of objects, and makes it the scene of more interesting action.

FRAGMENT ON POPERY.

[*Written about* 1824. *Not published before.*]

WHEN two parties, each formidable for their numbers and the weight of their influence and property, are animated by an equal degree of zeal, it is natural to anticipate the final success of that which possesses the most inherent strength. But if one be torpid and inactive, and the other eager and enterprising,—if one reposes on its arms, while the other is incessantly on the alert,—such a difference in their spirit is sufficient to annihilate the greatest disparity of force, and to incline the balance to the side on which superior vigour is exerted. This, if I am not greatly mistaken, is pretty nearly the case at present between the Protestants and the papists, as far, at least, as respects their situation in these kingdoms. The papists appear to be stimulated by zeal and elevated by hope; the Protestants content themselves with being silent spectators of their progress, while many of them seem secretly to rejoice at their success. New popish chapels are rising on every side, in situations skilfully selected, with a view to attract the public attention. The consecration is announced with ostentatious publicity, and numerously attended by the most elegant and fashionable part of a Protestant population, by men of opulence, merchants, and magistrates, who are seen on no other occasions beyond the precincts of the established [church.]

Judging from the practice of a multitude in the higher classes, we are necessitated to infer, that if the popish doctrine is not true it is innocent and harmless; and if not entitled to an exclusive preference, it is only inferior to that particular form of the Protestant worship which they have adopted; and that, while they decline submission to its claims, it possesses a majesty which entitles it to their occasional homage and veneration. The honest fervour of indignation with which its pretensions were repelled and its impiety resented has disappeared: popery is now viewed by the greater part of the people with careless indifference or secret complacency.

But popery, it is alleged, is changed; its venom is exhaled; and, however erroneous in a speculative view, it is no longer fraught with the mischief and the danger which rendered it so formidable to our ancestors. *An infallible religion changed* is nearly a contradiction in terms. A religion which is founded on the assumption of a supernatural exemption from error on the part of its adherents, may be confuted by argument, suppressed by force, or relinquished from conviction; but it is impossible to conceive of its susceptibility of change. If it undergoes any alteration, it can only [be] in consequence of its professors renouncing some one or more of the doctrines which formerly characterized it. But those doctrines are neither more nor less than the recorded decisions of the church, of a church affirmed by all Catholics to be infallible. The supposed infallibility of the church is the corner-stone of the whole system of popery, the centre of union amid all the animosities and disputes which may subsist on minor subjects; and the proper definition of a Catholic is one who professes to maintain the absolute infallibility of a certain community styling itself the church. For a person to dissent from a single decision of the church is to confess himself not a Catholic; because it is to affirm, not only that the church may err, but that it actually has erred, and is therefore not infallible. An infallibility extending to some points of religious belief and not to others is a ridiculous chimera, which, could it be reduced to an object of conception, would subvert every rational ground of confidence: for what assurance can we have that a community which has erred once will not fall into the same predicament again? Positive qualities may be conceived to subsist under [all] possible degrees of magnitude; they are susceptible, to an unlimited extent, of *more* or *less:* but infallibility is a negative idea, which admits of no degrees. Detect the smallest error in the individual, or the community, which makes this pretension, and you as effectually destroy it as by the discovery of a million. If a Catholic, then, professes to have changed his opinions on any subject on which the authority of the church has been interposed, so as to dissent from its decisions, he has relinquished Catholicism, and renounced the only principle which distinguished him.

The supposed dominion over the consciences of men assumed by the Roman pontiff, is sanctioned by the decision of general councils, and incorporated with their most solemn and public acts, and must consequently be allowed to constitute one of the fundamental tenets of the papal system; and though that usurpation, considered in itself, would be a mere annunciation of a doctrine which might be rejected with impunity, the interference of the civil magistrate to enforce the papal claims was countenanced and demanded by the same authority. Beyond the narrow precincts of their temporal domain the bishops of Rome were incapable of personally carrying their persecuting edicts into force; but princes and magistrates were diligently instructed that it was their indispensable duty to suppress and punish the heretics against whom the church had denounced its anathemas. Ecclesiastics, affecting a peculiar horror of blood, declined the office of executioners, which they devolved on the temporal authorities in each state; but it is equally certain, that in the violences which [civil magistrates] committed in the suppression of heresy and the support of the authority of the church, they acted not merely agreeably to her wishes, but in obedience to her dictates. If there was any difference in this respect between the ecclesiastical and temporal powers, it was that princes could with great difficulty, on many occasions, be induced to keep [pace] with the prompt and unrelenting fury of their spiritual directors. The grand lesson in which they [were] indoctrinated, with infinitely more care than any other, was the implicit obedience which they vowed to the pontiff and the church in the enactment and execution of penal laws against the abetters of heretical opinions,—an epithet bestowed upon all opinions not in accordance with the tenets of the papal community. When John Huss, the Bohemian reformer, was arrested, cast into prison, and publicly burnt alive at Cônstance, in spite of a "safe-conduct" given him by the Emperor Sigismund, merely because he refused to belie his conscience by abjuring his pretended heresy, all was executed under the eyes and by the express authority of the council, who solemnly decreed that the safe-conduct of the emperor ought to be considered as no impediment to the exercise of ecclesiastical jurisdiction; but, notwithstanding this, that it was perfectly competent for the ecclesiastical judge to take cognizance of his errors, and to *punish* them agreeable to the dictates of justice, although he presented himself before them in dependence upon that protection, but for which he would have declined appearing. Nor were they satisfied with this impious decision [alone.] Because murmurs were heard, on account of the violation of a legal protection, they had the audacity to add, that since the said John Huss had, by impugning the orthodox faith, forfeited every privilege, and since no promise or faith was binding, either by human or divine right, in prejudice of the Catholic faith, the said emperor had done as became his royal majesty in violating his "safe-conduct;" and that whoever, of any rank or sex, dares to impugn the justice of the holy council, or of his majesty, in relation to their proceedings with John Huss, shall be punished, without hope of pardon, as a favourer of heretical pravity, and guilty of the crime of high-treason.*

* Though I have nearly translated the language of the holy council, as given by L'Enfant in his History of the Council of Constance, the reader will probably not be displeased to see the original.

"Præsens sancta synodus ex quovis salvo-conductu per imperatorem, reges, et alios seculi principes hæreticis vel de hæresi diffamatis, putantes eosdem sic à suis erroribus revocare, quocunque vinculo se adstrinxerint, concesso, nullum fidei catholicæ vel jurisdictioni ecclesiasticæ præjudicium generari, vel impedimentum præstari posse seu debere, declarat; quominus salvo dicto conductu nonobstante, liceat judici competenti ecclesiastico de ejusmodi personarum erroribus inquirere, et aliàs contra eas debite procedere, easdemque punire, quantum justitia suadebit, si suos pertinaciter recusaverint revocare errores, etiamsi de salvo-conductu confisi ad locum venerint judicii, alias non venturi.

"Quo statuto, sive ordinatione lecto, idem statutum fuit approbatum per dictos dominos, episcopos nomine quatuor nationum, ac Reverendissimum Patrem Dominum Cardinalem Vivariensem, nomine Collegii Cardinalium, per verbum, *Placet*.

"DE SALVO-CONDUCTU HUSSONIS.

"Sacrosancta, &c. Quia nonnulli nimis intelligentes aut sinistræ intentionis, vel forsan solentes sapere plus quàm oportet, nedum regiæ majestati, sed etiam sacro, ut fertur, concilio, linguis maledictis detrahunt publicè et occulte dicentes, vel innuentes, quod salvus-conductus per invictissimum principem Dominum Sigismundum Romanorum et Ungariæ, &c., Regem quondam Johanni Hus, heresiarchæ damnatæ memoriæ datus, fuit contra justitiam aut honestatem indebitè violatus: cumtamen dictus Johannes Hus fidem orthodoxam pertinaciter impugnans se ab omni conductu et privilegio reddiderit alienum; nec aliqua sibi fides aut promissio, de jure naturali, divino, vel humano, fuerit in præjudicium Catholicæ fidei observanda: idcirco dicta sancta synodus præsentium tenore declarat: dictum invictissimum principem circa prædictum quondam Johannem Hus, nonobstante memorato salvo-conductu, ex juris debito fecisse quod licuit, et quod decuit regiam majestatem: statuens et ordinans omnibus et singulis Christi fidelibus, cujuscunque dignitatis, gradus, præ-

Here, then, we have the decision of a general council, that a dissent from the Catholic faith, persisted in, exposes the offender to the forfeiture of all his rights, not excepting such as he may claim from express solemn stipulations. If there ever was an assembly fairly entitled to the epithet of œcumenical, or universal, it was certainly the Council of Constance; composed of delegates from every kingdom and country of Europe; held in the presence of an emperor, and many other sovereign princes; called by the order of a pope, and signalized by the absolute deposition of two pontiffs, a forced abdication of a third, and the creation of a fourth; which extinguished a schism of forty years, and reunited the obedience of Christendom under one head. If the boasted infallibility of the church is to be found anywhere, it is undoubtedly in the acts and decrees of such an assembly.

Nor is it easy to conceive of any thing more absurd than the supposition that it was guided by inspiration in respect to some of its decisions, and not of others. Such a partial and capricious inspiration would completely frustrate the purpose for which it was introduced, and expose us to all the perplexity and uncertainty which it was designed to prevent; since, on this supposition, nothing short of another inspiration could enable us to distinguish and select the suggestions of the first.

I am aware, that when Catholics are pressed with the consequences resulting from the pretended infallibility of general councils, summoned by the authority of the pope, they take refuge in the subtile and slippery distinction between the doctrines which are, and those which are not, points of faith. Thus, in the present instance, to serve a turn, they will probably assert, or insinuate, that although the most cruel intolerance has obtained the sanction and support of general councils, their *proper* infallibility is not impaired, because the principle which authorizes persecution is not a *point of faith.*

Without entering into the mazes of a frivolous and unintelligible dispute about words, it is sufficient to remark, that the supernatural and infallible guidance of a church which leaves it to stumble on the threshold of morality, to confound the essential distinctions of right and wrong, to recommend the violation of the most solemn compacts, and the murder of men against whom not a shadow of criminality is alleged, except a dissent from its dogmas, is nothing worth; but must ever ensure the ridicule and abhorrence of those who judge the tree by its fruits, and who will not be easily persuaded that the eternal fountain of love and purity inhabits the breast which "breathes out cruelty and slaughter." If persecution for conscience' sake is contrary to the principles of justice and the genius of Christianity, then I say, this holy and infallible church was so abandoned of God as to be permitted to legitimate the foulest crimes,—to substitute murders for sacrifice, and

eminentiæ, conditionis, status, aut sexus existant, quod nullus deinceps sacro concilio aut regiæ majestati de gestis circa prædictum quondam Johannem Hus detrahat sive quomodolibet obloquatur. Qui verò contrarium fecerit, tamquam fautor hereticæ pravitatis et reus criminis læsæ majestatis irremissibiliter puniatur."—*L'Enfant's History of the Council of Constance*, vol. ii. p. 491, English edit. 1730.

to betray a total ignorance of the precepts and spirit of the religion which she professed to support; and whether the Holy Ghost condescended at the same moment to illuminate one hemisphere of minds so hardened, and hearts so darkened, may be safely left to the judgment of common sense.*

It would give us unfeigned pleasure to find that the Catholics have in good earnest renounced the intolerant principles of their predecessors; but when we look around for some proof of this, we see nothing that is satisfactory. In the midst of much courtesy, much urbanity and address, we meet with nothing that partakes of the nature of solid concession;—no steps retraced, no errors revoked, no protest opposed to the persecuting maxims of former times. Whatever breathes an air of liberality issues from the unofficial communications of private individuals. We anxiously wish for some important concessions at the fountain-head,—some exposition of the Catholic faith from the supreme pontiff, or his accredited agents, calculated to satisfy us that intolerance is at last expunged from the papal creed. We wish, but we wish in vain. On the contrary, we perceive in the restoration of the Jesuits,—in the total suppression (as far as his [the pope's] influence extends) of Bible societies,—in his opposition to the toleration established in Belgium.—in the exclusion of the Protestant religion from Spain and Portugal, at the very moment they were indebted for their existence to the arms of Protestants,—decisive evidence of a determination to maintain the ancient system with inflexible rigour. We are at a loss to discover a single concession in favour of the claims of conscience, proceeding from an authority which Catholics are bound to respect. The renunciation of the rights of the pope to interfere in temporal matters, and the inviolable obligation of oaths taken to heretics, will be considered perhaps, by some, as important concessions; but they are far from settling the question. What security have we that the persecuting maxims of popery are revoked, or that the consciences of its adherents are not still instructed in the indispensable duty of demanding the interference of the magistrate in the suppression and punishment of heresy?

The fundamental principle of the Catholic system is the supposed infallibility of the Church of Rome. Until this point is determined, it is to little purpose to engage in particular controversies, or attempt to expose the erroneousness of her doctrines, or the idolatry of her worship. These are merely a superstructure erected without foundation. As it is the design of the following pages to furnish a popular antidote to the seductions of her priests and advocates, it becomes indispensably necessary to examine the pleas by which her pretension to infallibility is attempted to be supported. This is the more requisite, because there is reason to fear that multitudes of Protestants are in a great measure ignorant of the *true grounds* of popery; and that while they

* Shortly after the execution of Huss, a letter written to the council, in the name of the Holy Ghost, was found at the gates of some of the churches at Constance, to this effect: "The Holy Spirit to the Council of Constance, greeting. Take care of your own affairs as well as you can For our part we cannot be with you; for we are busy about other affairs: farewell."—Ed.

strongly reprobate in detail its errors and absurdities, having little or no acquaintance with the principle which forms the keystone of the whole system, they are easily liable to be baffled and confounded when they encounter a subtle disputant. It will be in vain for you to urge, in debating with a Catholic, the absurdity of transubstantiation, or the idolatry of the mass. You begin the controversy at the wrong end; and, though you accumulate ever so large a pile of invincible argument, or Scriptural proof, you make no progress. He will [seldom, if ever,] descend to meet you on that ground; he professes to prostrate both his reason and his faith before the majesty of the church. In the mysteries of faith the dictates of reason are fallacious, the interpretation of the Scriptures is precarious and uncertain, and no basis of a divine and supernatural faith can be laid, but in submission to an authorized infallible guide,—which guide is the Roman Catholic Church! You will be reminded of the innumerable sects and schisms, convulsions and disorders, which have sprung from the exercise of a pretended free inquiry; whence he will infer the necessity of some visible standard of appeal, some acknowledged infallible judge: and the promise of the Spirit to the apostles to lead them into all truth,—together with the pre-eminence of Peter above his colleagues, to whom, as an immoveable rock and foundation of the church, "the keys of the kingdom of heaven" were exclusively assigned,—will be triumphantly urged to support the claims of the bishop of Rome, his legitimate representative and successor. Thus, by a mixture of specious probabilities, with the assumption of innumerable facts, a web of sophistry will be weaved sufficient often to entangle the "unlearned and unstable." That it is nothing more, however, than unfounded and presumptuous sophistry, a little attention will enable us to perceive.

That the church is infallible is not a self-evident proposition; it is not one of those truths which are acknowledged the moment they are announced, like the assertion that two and two are four. It must therefore be *proved:* nor can it be proved by her own assertion; because it is just as easy for any other community to declare itself infallible as for the Church of Rome. To allow her a prerogative so extraordinary merely because she claims it would legitimate the boldest imposture. As little can it be proved by any appeal to the principles of reason: the possession of infallibility by an individual, or by a number of individuals, is a matter of fact whose truth must be evinced in the same manner as other facts. Hence it necessarily follows, that the pretensions to infallibility assumed by the Catholic church must solely rest on the testimony of Scripture. For this purpose it is alleged that St. Peter was constituted the prince of the apostles, the foundation on which the church was to be built; that to him were primarily and chiefly given the keys of the kingdom of heaven; that as Jesus Christ prayed for him that his faith should not fail, he possessed a guarantee for the truth of his doctrines and the infallibility of his decisions; and that, having established his episcopal throne at Rome, he transmitted his immunities and prerogatives unimpaired to his successors in that see.

Such, for substance, is the argument deduced from Scripture in support of this extraordinary pretension. To this are added other considerations of the nature of probabilities, in favour of this assumed infallibility: such as the pretended necessity of some living standard of appeal, some visible judge of controversies, together with the error, confusion, and uncertainty to which it is asserted the church must be for ever abandoned, in the absence of some such living oracle. If Christians are left to interpret the Scriptures for themselves without an infallible guidance, their interpretations will necessarily vary in proportion to the different degrees of their capacity or attention. Their interpretation can at best be but probable; and a probable conclusion can never be admitted as the ground of a divine faith. It will not be at all necessary to discuss accurately at large the arguments founded on the passages of Scripture before adduced. Suffice it to observe, that the links which compose the chain of the argument are numerous, and that it would not be easy to prove any one of them to the satisfaction of an unprejudiced inquirer. In that argument it is assumed for granted that St. Peter was invested with a supremacy over the rest of the apostles; that the keys were *exclusively* given to him; that his faith was more indefectible than that of his brethren; that he exercised the episcopal office at Rome; and that he devolved his peculiar power and prerogatives on his successors in that sacred office. Every one of these arbitrary assumptions is destitute of a shadow of truth, either from Scripture or antiquity. That Peter was *ever* at Rome we have no evidence but vague and uncertain tradition; that he exercised the episcopal functions there is still more uncertain, or rather extremely improbable, as it is neither insinuated in Scripture nor very consistent with his higher character and functions. But supposing both these points were conceded, what evidence have we of that devolution of his power and prerogatives on his successors on which the authority assumed by the bishop of Rome entirely rests? From the language of Scripture and the [testimony] of antiquity, there is much more reason for affirming that James the Less was bishop of the Church of Jerusalem, than that Peter sustained that office at Rome; and by a parity of reason, his successors must be supposed to have inherited his powers and his infallibility; and the rather, since the church at Jerusalem was the mother of all other churches, planted, not by one, but by all the apostles, often dignified by their united presence,—a church on which the redundance of spiritual gifts was first poured, and consecrated by the blood of the first martyr. If, in opposition to this, we are reminded that the succeeding bishops of Jerusalem derived from St. James the rights attached to the episcopal function, but not his personal prerogatives and immunities as an apostle,—this very distinction applies precisely to the successors of St. Peter.

This may suffice to show the extreme frivolity and levity of the proofs adduced from Scripture in support of the claim of papal or Catholic infallibility. But, admitting the arguments derived from this quarter were much more cogent than they are, it is evident that they are entirely deduced from the interpretation of certain passages of

Scripture, and consequently depend on the correctness of that interpretation. Is this interpretation, I would ask, to be taken for granted, or is it to be proved and sustained by the principles of sound criticism? Are we to take the mere affirmation of the Church of Rome on this subject, and at once admit that the inference she deduces from these passages is just because she asserts it to be so? This is impossible, because this would [be to] acknowledge her infallibility, which is the very point to be proved. We are inquiring after the *proofs* of her infallibility: she refers us for satisfaction to the passages of Scripture before adduced. Her supposed infallibility can afford no sort of security for her correct interpretation of these passages, because her object in urging these passages is to prove her infallibility. To say that she has put a right construction on these texts because she is infallible, and at the same time attempt to prove her infallibility by that construction, would be an insult to common sense. Her right to be acknowledged as the infallible guide and director of our faith, must either be blindly submitted to without proof or inquiry, or it must be left to be determined by the private judgment of every individual; and if the votaries of the Church of Rome are not willing to confess they admit the validity of her claims without any reasons whatever, they must have exercised the right of free inquiry as well as Protestants, not indeed in respect to particular controversies, but in relation to this great controversy. What is the standard of truth, and who is the judge of controversy? The Church of Rome boldly affirms, that if individuals are left to judge for themselves, such is the obscurity of Scripture, that no certainty could be obtained, no conclusion deduced, in which the conscience may safely rest. Yet, with egregious inconsistency, she refers us to that very Scripture in proof of the justice of her claims. Here I would ask, can we without an infallible guide attain the real meaning of the texts which she quotes in her favour? If not, it is impossible for them to prove her infallibility. If we can, then it follows that there are some parts of Scripture whose meaning may be certainly ascertained without her infallible guidance. And what then becomes of her complaint of the hopeless obscurity of Scripture, which is affirmed to render her aid so indispensable? And what must we think of her outcries against the supposed arrogance of pretending to the exercise of free inquiry, and of judging of the Scriptures for ourselves, when, without such an exercise and such a power of judging, it is found impossible to obtain the least proof or presumption of her boasted infallibility?

Some parts of Scripture, then, the Church of Rome herself must allow, are capable of being understood without her aid. Those declarations of Scripture on which she rests her claim to implicit submission and obedience, she *must* allow to be sufficiently plain and intelligible, to bind the conscience of every member of her community who is prepared to assign a reason for his being a Catholic: and as an entire agreement with the dogmas of the church is all the faith which she requires in order to the salvation of her members, she must acknowledge, as well as ourselves, that the Scriptures contain a rule of faith sufficient for the purpose of salvation; the only difference is, that in our opinion the Scripture clearly unfolds a system of saving truth, while in [that of the Roman Catholics] they are obscure in every point, except in the few passages which direct us to the church, the only authentic and immediate source of saving knowledge.

We ascribe some efficacy to the word of God itself; while they contend that the principal or only benefit it affords consists in conducting us to the church. The Scriptures themselves indeed affirm, that they are "able to make us wise unto salvation," and by them we must be judged at the last day." The church asserts, on the contrary, that they are covered with an impenetrable obscurity, [not to be removed] without her interference, and that we shall be judged at the last day, not by our submission *to the Scriptures*, but our obedience *to her*. In her system the principal use of the Scriptures was to give birth to the church, whose place she now occupies, whose prerogatives she assumes as the sole directory of conscience, and the living oracle of God. Her treatment of the Scripture almost reminds us of the fabulous history of Jupiter, who ascended to supreme [power] by the mutilation and banishment of his father.

The portentous doctrine of infallibility, as it is employed in the Catholic church, stamps an entirely new character on the Christian religion, substitutes a new object of faith and dependence, deifies what is human, hides and cancels what is divine, and transfers our allegiance from God to mortals.

But to return to the argument. On all systems, the preference of one religion to another must either be founded on caprice, custom, or some other principle equally unworthy of determining the choice of a reasonable being, or upon examination. If the Catholics wish to convert us to their persuasion, they must assign their reasons for affirming that there is in existence an infallible community, styling itself the church; that that community is their church, in preference to the Greek church, the Armenian, or the Nestorian. Here they must admit the exercise of private judgment in examining these reasons; unless they have the effrontery to assert that their bare affirmation supersedes the necessity of any further proof: and, admitting the Scriptures to be the word of God, which is the easiest task for ordinary Christians—to learn from them what is necessary for salvation, or to judge of the claims of the church to supremacy and infallibility? For the former, if you believe the Scriptures themselves, nothing more is requisite than a candid and honest mind; for the latter, a deep acquaintance with history and antiquity, and, particularly, a clear comprehension of the meaning of a portion of Scripture by no means the most plain and perspicuous. Involved as those passages are which are urged from the New Testament in support of the papal claims, in language highly figurative and metaphorical, is it easier for a plain unlettered Christian to judge of the precise meaning of the term "keys," and "the kingdom of heaven opening and shutting," than to learn the import of that declaration, "Believe on the Lord Jesus Christ, and thou shalt be saved?" There is so much room for variation in the interpretation of the passages [on which the papists lay such great stress,] that it would not be easy to find two commentators, in any community, whose expositions perfectly coincide; with respect to the latter, he that runs may read. St. John distinctly informs us with what purpose he wrote his gospel, in the following words: "And many other signs truly did Jesus in the presence of his disciples, which are not written in this book; but these are written that ye might believe that Jesus is the Christ, and that, believing, ye might have life through his name." Is there sufficient evidence in what St. John wrote to convince us that Jesus is the Christ; and is it within the power of ordinary men to judge of this evidence? If this question be answered in the affirmative, then what occasion is there for the interposition of an infallible interpreter, since he who is convinced by this record that Jesus is the Christ is already in a state of salvation? If it be replied in the negative, that the writing of St. John is not sufficient to prove to an impartial reader that Jesus is the Christ, it must be confessed, however reluctantly, that the beloved apostle was a most impertinent and fallacious writer, in representing his performance as a fit instrument for the accomplishment of an object to which it is not adequate.

* * * * * * * * * *

THE CHARACTER OF THE REV. R. HALL,

OF ARNSBY.

[*Written in* 1791.*]

THE distinguished talents of our deceased friend will long live in the remembrance of all who knew him. His advantages of education were extremely small; but possessing from his infancy a contemplative cast of mind, and a habit of patient thinking, he laid in a large stock of useful knowledge. In the character of a minister of the gospel, there have been but few more generally esteemed. Attentive only to the improvement of his hearers, he forgot himself, and appeared entirely absorbed in his subject. Though he was unacquainted with the graces of oratory and the embellishments of language, scarcely any man spoke with a more striking and visible effect. From nature he derived a large share of sensibility; and as he excelled at the same time in taking a profound and comprehensive view of a subject, the understanding and affections of his hearers were equally interested in his discourses, which generally flowed in a stream of argument and pathos. From a natural diffidence of temper, heightened by a consciousness of his want of education, he often ascended the pulpit with tremor; but as soon as this subsided, he generally led his hearers, step by step, into a large field of serious and manly thinking, kindled as he advanced, and expatiated with increasing energy and conviction till the subject was exhausted. His eminent piety lent a peculiar unction to the sentiments he delivered, led him to seize the most interesting views of every subject, and turned topics, which in the hands of others would have furnished barren speculation only, into materials for devotion and prayer. He appeared to the greatest advantage upon subjects where the faculties of most men fail them; for the natural element of his mind was greatness. At times he seemed to labour with conceptions too big for his utterance; and if an obscurity ever pervaded his discourses, it must be traced to this source—the disproportion of his language to the vastness of his conceptions. He had great force without ornament, and grandeur without correctness. His ministry, in the hands of God, was effectual to the conversion of great numbers; and in this particular he was distinguished in a manner not very

* This sketch was published anonymously, at the end of Dr. Ryland's funeral sermon for Mr Hall, of Arnsby.—ED.

common; for the last years of his life were the most successful. But it was not only in the pulpit that he shone; in his private sphere of action as a Christian, his virtues were not less distinguished than his talents as a minister. Deep devotion and unaffected humility entered far into this part of his character. Few men have passed through greater vicissitudes of life than the deceased, and perhaps in each of them no man preserved with a more inviolable consistency the character of a Christian. He was very early introduced into the schools of affliction, and the greater part of his subsequent life was distinguished by an uncommon succession of trials and distresses. On his first entrance into the ministry his fortitude was exercised in a scene of persecution and reproaches, which lasted for many years. His worldly prospects at the same time were gloomy and precarious in a high degree: he had a very numerous family, and an income extremely limited.—He united great susceptibility of heart with firmness of mind; and, endowed with these dispositions, he met reproaches with gentleness, sustained adversity with fortitude, and pains and sorrows of various kinds with exemplary patience. In the habitual frame of his spirit he "walked with God." The consolations that supported him through life awaited him at death; for so tranquil were his last moments, so completely was he reconciled to the prospect of both worlds, that he declared, a little time before he expired, he *would not give a straw to live or die.* From his first acquaintance with religion to the close of life, he was never known to express the least hesitation respecting his state, but enjoyed an uninterrupted assurance of a happy immortality. His conversation breathed so much of heaven, was so tinctured with the very spirit of religion, that none could enjoy it without an opportunity of being made better. It was evident to all who knew him, that his religion was not a transient impression, but a permanent principle; that it blended itself with all his feelings and his actions; and that it raised his thoughts, his views, and his passions towards heaven.

In the first years of his ministry he encountered, as has been already remarked, much persecution and reproach; but at length his exemplary conduct dissipated these prejudices, and gained him so completely the esteem of all classes of mankind, that it may be doubted whether he had an enemy in the world: certainly he had none but those whom his piety made such. He was distinguished as a lover of peace, and was as anxious to heal breaches as he was cautious to avoid them. With some, his extreme solicitude for the propagation of evangelical sentiments might seem like bigotry: but those who knew him best were well convinced that this was no part of his character, and that he regarded sentiments in no other light, nor cherished them in any higher degree, than as he conceived them favourable to the interests of holiness and virtue.

His brethren in the ministry will long and deeply lament him; for to them his talents and dispositions peculiarly endeared him. How many private circles hath he cheered and enlightened by his presence! In how many public solemnities hath he lifted up an ensign to the people, invited them to the standard of the Cross, and warmed and exalted their affections, while "his doctrine dropped as rain, and his speech distilled as the dew!" Great abilities are often allied to pride, but the character of the deceased was an illustrious exception to this rule. His talents and virtues were in some measure concealed from the world, and almost entirely from himself, by a veil of the most unaffected modesty. He was never so happy as when he was permitted to sit in the shade, though the high opinion entertained of his abilities seldom allowed him that indulgence. It would be difficult to conceive a human mind more completely purged from the leaven of pride or of envy than was that of our deceased friend. In this particular his magnanimity was so great that he seemed on all occasions desirous of sinking the recollection of himself in the reputation and applause of his contemporaries. To cultivate the seeds of reflection and improvement in the minds of his inferiors,—to behold the growing talents and virtues of his brethren,—to draw merit from its obscurity, and give confidence to timid worth,—formed some of the highest satisfactions of his life.

His temper was grave and contemplative, yet few men took greater delight in Christian society; and on these occasions he seldom failed to mix with serious converse a vein of pleasantry and humour, in which he greatly excelled. From his integrity and knowledge, it may be inferred he was eminently skilled for imparting advice; yet so carefully did he shun every inclination to dictate, that he scarcely ever gave it unsolicited. His sentiments, when required, he imparted with tenderness and freedom; but he never made advice a disguise for arrogance, or an engine of rule, nor ever presumed to think himself affronted if his counsels were not followed. In his whole deportment, prudence and humility were conspicuous; a prudence, however, that was candid and manly, as far removed from *art* as his humility was from meanness. He had failings, no doubt, (for who is free?) but they were scarcely ever suffered to influence his conduct, or to throw even a transient shade over the splendour of his character. Upon the whole, if a strong and penetrating genius, simplicity of manners, integrity of heart, fidelity in friendship—and all these virtues consecrated by piety the most ardent and sincere on the high altar of devotion —have any claim to respect, the memory of the deceased will long be cherished with tears of admiration and sorrow by those who knew him.

FUNERAL ORATION

Delivered at the Interment of the Rev. HABAKKUK CRABB, *of Royston, in Hertfordshire, on the 1st of January,* 1795.*

AMONG the many appearances which man presents to the view of a contemplative mind, death is one of the most extraordinary. Whatever be the station he has filled, and however he has conducted himself in it,—whether he has adorned it by virtue or degraded it by vice,—whether he has passed obscurely through the world, or filled it with the fame of his actions,—he soon disappears, and the "place which once knew him knows him no more." Over all the sons of Adam death hath reigned. The worthy and beneficent are embalmed by the tears of tender but transient regret. The chasm their departure has occasioned in society is filled up by their successors, who tread the same circle of life and death, and thus perpetuate the established order of the universe.

But though the grave terminates the business of life, it does not terminate the inquiries of the living. Whether the whole of existence is comprised within the present life, or whether it be merely a passage into an unseen state, is a question which has engaged the attention of men in every age; nor would it be possible (were it ever so proper) to detail within the limits of this address the various reasonings and conjectures to which it has given occasion. When we contemplate death under its sensible appearances—the destruction of the external organs, and the corruption of the whole mass—we are tempted to regard it as the extinction of being, and to suppose its effects upon the human race are the same as upon the inferior orders of creatures. Whatever has been the object of the senses in both, is reduced to putrefaction and dust. But when again we recollect in how many important respects we are distinguished above the brutes, we cannot help indulging higher expectations, and looking for a nobler destiny. Our superior comprehension of mind qualifies us for a longer duration of being. While the brute is capable of enjoying little more than the present moment, the remembrance of what is past, and the anticipation of what is to come, enable us to multiply our resources, and to diffuse our existence, if I may so speak, over a larger surface. To compare one state of being with another, to learn wisdom from experience, and to regulate our future expectations by what has already occurred, are employments congenial

* This first appeared in the Introduction to a volume of Mr. Crabb's posthumous Sermons, published in 1795.—ED

with the human mind. But it is evident that a creature possessed of such faculties will be capable of continually making new acquisitions of knowledge, and of advancing nearer and nearer to perfection.

Among all the tribes of creatures with which we are acquainted, man is the only one that appears to have any dread of annihilation, or the remotest conception of another state. How shall we account for the universal prevalence of these sentiments, in spite of all the sensible appearances of death, unless they are either the vestige of some early revelation or the incorrupted dictate of nature? How is it that we are the only beings that extend their anxieties beyond the grave; that we are so reluctant to quit the present scene; and that, when we are at length compelled to depart, we grasp at the very shadow of immortality, and console ourselves with the hope of surviving in the regrets of our friends and the reputation of our actions?

Though there seems to be much plausibility in these topics, it must be confessed the best arguments for a future state are derived from the moral part of our nature; or, in other words, from our capability of good and ill desert. For since it is plain that God has made us moral agents, and placed us under a law, we may be assured he has not made us so in vain, but that he will call us to an account for our actions; and, as there is no exact distribution of rewards and punishments in this life, we are entitled to expect another suited to the respective characters of men and the moral attributes of the Deity. If, after all, we consider actual opinions on this head, we shall find the wisest among the heathen were far from attaining any certainty. When they gave scope to their feelings and their hopes, they sometimes painted the elysian abodes of the virtuous in the warmest colouring of eloquence; in their cooler moments they subsided into skepticism; so that, on the whole, the idea of a future state seems to have operated not so much as a fixed principle as a vague presentiment.

Revelation can alone boast of having "brought life and immortality to light." The religion of Jesus Christ places the reality of a future state at the foundation of its truths. It is there so constantly reverted to, so often repeated, and so solemnly enforced, that it has never been by any class of Christians disputed or denied. Nor is the reality only of a future state revealed in Christianity: as far as is consistent with the present limitation of our faculties, it affords us the justest views of its nature; which it makes to consist, not in sensual gratifications or festive bowers—the visions of a Mahometan paradise,—but in enjoyments the most suited to the rational and immortal mind; a union with God, the knowledge of his perfections, and the eternal fruition of his love. The information which Christianity imparts on these subjects is not conveyed in dark and symbolical expressions, or in a chain of philosophical reasoning; but in a manner the most perspicuous and popular. With what majestic simplicity does our Lord assure us of the resurrection of the just!—"I am the resurrection and the life. He that believeth in me, though he were dead, yet shall he live, and whosoever liveth and believeth in me shall never die." "This is the will of him that sent me, that every one which believeth on the Son may have everlasting life, and I will raise him up at the last day." When many of the disciples of our Lord went back, and walked no more with him, being offended with the sublime mysteries of his doctrine, he took occasion to ask his twelve apostles, "Will ye also go away?" To which Peter, in the name of them all, made this reply, "Lord, to whom shall we go? Thou hast the words of eternal life." In this short answer we behold the distinguished lustre of Christianity. It explains at once the ground of a rational attachment to it, and will be sufficient to justify its profession from the reproach of folly, however mysterious its doctrines, however arduous its duties, and however painful or costly its sacrifices.

There are two purposes connected with the present solemnity to which the doctrine of immortality ought to be applied. The first regards the regulation of life; the second, the inspiring us with fortitude in the contemplation of our own deaths, and those of our relatives and friends. If we consider ourselves as candidates for an eternal state of happiness, it becomes us to regard life, with all its vicissitudes, as a probationary state, and to look upon every thing that is not directly or indirectly conducive to our eternal welfare as foreign to our purpose, and undeserving our pursuit. Heavenly-mindedness is, in this view, as much the dictate of reason as of Scripture. It is nothing more than the placing our affections where we expect our felicity; the wisdom of preferring the end to the means —that which is permanent to that which is transitory. Let the men of the world, who disbelieve the declarations of the gospel respecting eternal realities, lead a life, if they please, of dissipation and vice; but for a professor of religion to confine his affections to the earth is equally impious and absurd. Distracted between his inordinate attachment to the present, and his apprehension of a future world, his religion, if it will bear that name, must be a constant source of disquietude. He has neither the calmness of insensibility, nor the triumph of faith. His prevailing regard to the interests of the present life renders it impossible for him to set his affections on a better state; while the carnal and reluctant glances he is compelled to take of that state are sufficient to imbitter his enjoyments and disturb his repose.

The misery which persons of this description suffer from an inward conflict between principle and practice, is the chief reason that has induced superficial observers to represent Christianity as a gloomy, melancholy system. There is no other foundation for this charge than that its claims are grand and extensive; that it disdains a compromise with the corrupt attachments of the heart; and that they who will not allow it the dominion of their affections will find it the troubler of their thoughts.

Whoever lives under the habitual influence of those tempers which qualify us for heaven, derives from his view of the eternal world the purest serenity and delight. In the midst of the severest disappointments of human life, secret consolations spring up in his mind, which sometimes swell into rapture, disarm the world of its terrors, and afford him a prelibation of unutterable bliss. In vain will ye look elsewhere for true magnanimity and moral grandeur. It is religion alone which both animates and softens the heart, cherishes sensibility, instils fortitude, and enables us to triumph without extravagance, and to suffer without dejection.

If the Scripture doctrine of immortality is entitled to so much weight in the regulation of LIFE, its influence is not less sovereign in dispelling the terrors of DEATH, and consoling us under the loss of our dearest friends and relatives. "I would not have you be ignorant, brethren, concerning them which are asleep, that ye sorrow not as others who have no hope; for, if we believe that Jesus died and rose again, even so them also which sleep in Jesus will God bring with him. For the Lord himself shall descend from heaven with a shout, with the voice of the archangel, and the trump of God. Then we which are alive and remain shall be caught up together with them in the clouds, to meet the Lord in the air; so shall we be ever with the Lord. Wherefore comfort one another with these words." And who can fail being penetrated with the divine consolation they afford? If ever Christianity appears in its power, it is when it erects its trophies on the TOMB; when it takes up its votaries where the world leaves them, and fills the breast with immortal hope in dying moments.

Nor are the words I have quoted adapted to support the mind of a Christian in the view of his *own* dissolution only; they administer the firmest support amid the breaches which death is continually making in the church of Christ. A degree of sorrow, on such occasions, nature compels us to feel, and religion does not condemn. At the decease of Lazarus, while his sisters were lamenting his loss, "Jesus wept." But the sorrow which a Christian feels in such situations is mingled with hope. By the light of faith, he traces his deceased friends into an eternal world. Instead of considering them as lost or extinct, he beholds them still under the eye of Divine Providence. The period of their trial is closed: they have entered into rest, where, sheltered from the storms of life and the dangers of temptation, their happiness is for ever fixed and unalterable. Their separation is neither final nor complete. The pious living and the pious dead are still one family, under one Head; and, when he "who is their life shall appear, they shall appear together with him in glory." The friendships which have had virtue and religion for their basis will survive all human ties, outlive the habitable globe, and form, in all probability, a principal part of the happiness of the blessed.

It is not unusual, I am aware, on occasions like these to pass high encomiums on the character of the deceased; a mode of proceeding the less requisite in the present instance, as the character of Mr. Crabb was too well established, and held in too high esteem, to have any thing to hope from praise, or to fear from censure. His mild and gentle spirit rendered it nearly impossible for him to have any enemies. The innocence and sanctity of his behaviour, the sensibility of his heart, the fidelity with which he discharged the duties of life, and the equanimity with which he bore its rebukes and sufferings, will leave a lasting impression on the minds of all his friends and acquaintance. You of this church and congregation have lost a friend, an instructer, a pastor; one who was anxious, on every occasion, to promote your spiritual and eternal welfare; who knew how to rejoice with them that rejoice, and weep with them that weep. You, my friends, will long remember, I trust, the affectionate exhortations he addressed to you, and make it appear on the day of solemn account that he has not laboured in vain, nor spent his strength for naught. His relation to you as your pastor has ceased; but its effects and consequences will never cease; they will reach into eternity, and "become the savour of life unto life, or of death unto death." If the duties of the ministerial character appeared so weighty in the eyes of an apostle that he was ready to sink under it, and exclaimed, "Who is sufficient for these things?" you will recollect it was its connexion with the eternal interests of his hearers which rendered his situation so arduous, and his responsibility so awful.

You have now before you one more example of the uncertainty of life. Your deceased friend and pastor was cut off in the midst of his days. His sun, instead of performing the usual circuit, set in its meridian. He, no doubt, often endeavoured, during his continuance among you, to convince you of the vanity of the world, and the insufficiency of all its enjoyments to render you happy; but Providence determined he should do more; that he should instruct you from the tomb on these topics, and bring them home to your senses.

Another year is passed away, and you have entered upon a new portion of time.* The division of time into distinct periods, besides its utility in business and in science, is favourable to moral reflection. On the entrance upon a new year, a contemplative mind will be naturally employed in estimating its acquisitions, comparing its improvements, retracing past occurrences, and revolving future prospects. The giddy and thoughtless feel their attention for a moment fixed, and, suspecting all is not right, form some indistinct resolution of repentance and amendment, which they are determined to execute as soon as some present scheme shall be finished, some prevailing passion gratified, or some expected change in their situation shall take place. The present moment seems always attended with insuperable difficulties; but they still flatter themselves with the hope of some more auspicious period, when their minds will be disengaged, their passions composed, and religion assert its power. Thus year rolls on after year, the self-delusion is repeated, and while they are planning new schemes of life they sink into the grave.

If a hardened contempt of religion has slain its thousands, a feeble and irresolute spirit has slain its ten thousands. Are there none in this assembly who, it is to be feared, are convinced of the importance of religion, and are yet unwilling to pay an immediate attention to it, flattering themselves they shall have ample opportunities of satisfying all its demands?

Vain, presumptuous man! hast thou penetrated the counsels of the

* This Oration was delivered on New-year's Day.

Almighty, or been permitted to read thy destiny, that while thou beholdest the ravages of death all around thee,—the multitudes which fall at thy right hand and at thy left, the young and the old, the feeble and the strong, hurried into eternity,—thou shouldst suppose thyself alone firm and immoveable amid this flux and succession of being? Wouldst thou wish to surmount the fear of death? Acquaint thyself with him who is the resurrection and the life; with that Saviour who is its author, its revealer, and its pattern. "Take his yoke upon you, and learn of him." Attend to his instructions, and yield yourself up to his guidance. You will then be able to converse familiarly with death. You will feel no terror in the prospect of future judgment, but will wait for its approach, and be able to stand before the Son of God at his coming. "Finally, let us who are of the light and of the day be sober, putting on the breastplate of faith and love, and for a helmet the hope of salvation." Instead of murmuring at such afflictive dispensations as separate us from those we esteem and love, let us employ them as inducements to set our affections on a better world, where we shall shortly join them; remembering, that whatever ties of affection are broken by death are taken from the enjoyments of time to enrich the prospect of eternity.

SKETCH

OF THE

CHARACTER OF MRS. M. CARRYER.

[*Written in* 1812.]

It is not my intention to attempt a laboured eulogium on our departed sister, but justice compels me briefly to notice some of the distinguishing traits of her character. I regret that, partly owing to the natural reserve of the deceased, and partly owing to my own unsocial humour, my acquaintance with her was so limited. I knew enough of her, however, to convince me that she was a person of no ordinary worth; and, from the testimony of all who were favoured with her intimacy, I am fully persuaded her piety was of the most solid kind, not evaporating in talk, nor obtruding itself in an ostentatious profession, but operating in a constant and exemplary discharge of every private and social duty. She was a pattern of diligence, as well in her attention to domestic engagements as in the constancy with which she applied herself to the means of grace, in the closet and in the sanctuary. As a wife, a mother, and a member of a Christian church, her behaviour was such that it is impossible to say which character she adorned most. Averse from every kind of display, her religion was of a retired nature; planted by the rivers of water, and fed by a secret spring, its leaf never withered, and it brought forth its fruit in its season. Her faith was such as purified the heart, and manifested itself in a series of wise and holy actions. Her hope was an anchor of the soul, sure and steadfast, entering into that within the veil. In the former part of her experience, she was sometimes considerably agitated by doubts and fears; but during the progress of the malady which terminated her dissolution, her painful apprehensions gradually subsided, and although she sowed in tears, she reaped in joy. Her dying testimony to the excellence of religion, and to the power and grace of the Redeemer, was most affecting; and will, it is humbly hoped, leave a lasting impression on survivors. She often expressed her gratitude to Providence for directing her choice to a companion in life, from whose example, and from whose prayers, she derived important assistance in her walk with God; so that the change of situation, which to many females becomes a temptation and a snare, became to her a great means of spiritual improvement. The virtues which adorn a single state she exhibited, not only unimpaired, but with increasing lustre, in her conjugal capacity. The essential benefit she derived from her obedience to the Scriptural injunction to "marry in the Lord," conveys an impressive admonition to the youth of both sexes. Let such as attach any importance to the cultivation of piety, and whose first solicitude it is to be prepared for eternity, avoid taking to their bosoms a domestic enemy, with whom it will be requisite to live in a state either of perpetual counteraction or of sinful compliance; and from whom, without the interposition of Divine grace, they must anticipate an eternal separation. Our dear departed sister made a wise choice, and determined to select as a companion for life one with whom she could indulge a confident hope of sharing a blessed eternity.

Her rapid advancement in every Christian grace was manifest to every one except to herself: for she often expressed the deep sense she entertained of her manifest imperfections, while others beheld nothing in her but what was "pure, lovely, and of good report." As she was clothed with humility, so she was eminently sober-minded, at the utmost distance from indulging in the levities, follies, and vain competitions of the age. She was chaste, a keeper at home, a lover of her husband, a lover of her children, and one who guided her house with discretion. Kindness to the indigent entered deeply into her character; she delighted "to do good to all men, especially to such as are of the household of faith." She was perfectly superior to the vanity of dress; her attire was suited to her station, neither mean nor splendid, but such as became a woman professing godliness. Her conviction of the nothingness of the world was profound, and she longed, would her modesty have permitted, to admonish her young friends from her dying bed to be on their guard against its fascinations and its snares. To her relations she often exclaimed, almost with her dying breath, "The world! the world!" intending to warn them of what she conceived to form their chief danger.

On the whole, among the numerous losses which this church has recently sustained I know of none more entitled to lasting lamentation than the present; nor has there been a member removed during the period of my ministry whose life has been more exemplary, or whose memory will be more precious.

THE CHARACTER

OF THE LATE

REV. THOMAS ROBINSON,

VICAR OF ST. MARY'S, LEICESTER;

As exhibited in a Speech delivered at the Annual Meeting of the Leicester Auxiliary Bible Society, April, 1813.

It is with a melancholy satisfaction I rise to express my entire approbation of the sentiments contained in the resolution just read.

It would, in my opinion, have been unnatural to usher our annual report into the world without noticing that solemn and affecting dispensation which has deprived this society, this town, and this county of its principal ornament. We are weakened this day by the falling of a pious and a great man in Israel. In the formation of this society our incomparable friend had a principal share; and through every stage he gave it an unremitted attention, and watched over its interests with a parental solicitude. The idea of instituting an auxiliary society in Leicester was no sooner suggested to him than it engaged his most cordial good wishes; he lent to its support the vigour of his masculine understanding, the energies of his capacious heart; and to him, beyond any other individual, it is indebted for the patronage and the maturity it has attained. He was indeed the father of this institution.—But of what institution formed for the promotion of the temporal and spiritual welfare of mankind in this place was he not the father? We can look nowhere throughout this large and populous town without perceiving the vestiges of his unwearied solicitude for the advancement of the happiness of his fellow-creatures. He has inscribed his history in the numerous charitable and religious foundations which owe their existence or their prosperity to his influence. Our jails, our hospitals, our schools, our churches, are replete with monuments of his worth, and with the effects of his energetic benevolence.

It is recorded of the great Hannibal, that when an infant his father conducted him to an altar, and made him vow eternal hostility to the Roman republic. Our venerable friend, when he first entered Leicester, appears with an ardour not less intense to have devoted himself to its interests. From the moment he entered the place he appears to have relinquished all selfish pursuits, all idea of private gratification, and to have formed that system of conduct from which he never departed, which had the most immediate tendency to meliorate the state of its inhabitants. He became altogether a public character; he meditated, he wrote, he preached, he breathed, only for the public. Rarely, if ever, was there a mind more perfectly purified from every tincture of selfishness or vanity. He made the most extensive sacrifices of his time and of his repose, with a spontaneity and alacrity which implied an almost total oblivion of his existence as an individual. Endowed with a capacity for high attainments in science, and distinguished at the university by the honours assigned to superior merit, he generously declined the pursuit of literary eminence for the sole purpose of doing good. It is but few who are capable of adequately appreciating the magnitude of such a sacrifice. Dr. Paley was certainly one of those few: and I had it from the lips of our venerable friend, that in addicting himself to the duties of a parish-priest he had, in the opinion of that great man, chosen the better part; a choice which it is evident Heaven singularly sanctioned and approved. In fixing his system of life he had unquestionably a view to a future account, and formed his determination on the assured persuasion of his appearing before the judgment-seat of Christ, where the salvation of one soul will cause a more glorious distinction than the greatest literary attainments; where all greatness of a merely intellectual nature will disappear, and nothing endure the scrutiny but active and disinterested virtue.

In the mean time, how narrow the bounds of his influence, how confined the ascendency of his character, had he been only the solitary student instead of being the zealous and exemplary pastor and the active citizen! On the former supposition, he had inscribed his memorial in books; on the present, he inscribed it on hearts; and instead of his being an object of the admiration of the few, he was the man of the people.

In separate parts of his character it were not impossible to find some who equalled, and others who excelled him; but in that rare combination of qualities which fitted him for such extensive usefulness he stands unrivalled. As a pastor and public instructer it may be possible to meet with some who have attained the same eminence; as a public man he may have been equalled; but where shall we look in modern times for such an example of the union of the highest endowments as a pastor and preacher, with the qualifications adapted to the functions of civil life? It is this rare union which appears to me to give the character of our venerable friend its decided pre-eminence. It is not necessary to recall to your recollection the talents of Mr. Robinson as a public instructer; you have most, if not all of you, witnessed his pulpit exertions on that spot where he was accustomed to retain a listening throng hanging upon his lips, awed, penetrated, delighted, and instructed by his manly, unaffected eloquence. Who ever heard him without feeling a persuasion that it was the man of God who addressed him; or without being struck with the perspicuity of his statements, the solidity of his thoughts, and the rich unction of his spirit? It was the harp of David which, struck by his powerful hands, sent forth more than mortal sounds, and produced an impression far more deep and permanent than the thunder of Demosthenes or the splendid coruscations of Cicero.

The hearers of Mr. Robinson were too much occupied by the subjects he presented to their attention to waste a thought on the speaker; this occupied a second place in the order of their reflections; but when it did occur, it assumed the character, not of superficial admiration, but of profound attachment. Their feelings towards him were not those of persons gratified, but benefited; and they listened to his instructions, not as a source of amusement, but as a spring of living water. There never was a settled pastor, probably, who had formed a juster conception of the true end of preaching, who pursued it more steadily, or attained it to a greater extent. He preached immortal truth with a most extraordinary simplicity, perspicuity, and energy, in a style adapted to all capacities, equally removed from vulgarity and from affected refinement: and the tribute paid to his exertions consisted not in loud applauses; it was of a higher order; it consisted of penitential sighs, holy resolutions, of a determination of the whole soul for God, and such impressions on the spirits of men as will form the line of separation between the happy and the miserable to all eternity.

In a word, by "the manifestation of the truth he commended himself to every man's conscience in the sight of God;" and the success which followed was such as might be expected from such efforts. Through the protracted period of his labours many thousands, who have finished their course with joy, derived from his ministry, there is reason to believe, the principle of a new life.

His residence in Leicester forms an epoch in the religious history of this county. From that time must be dated, and to his agency under Providence must be ascribed, a decided improvement in the moral and religious state of this town and its vicinity; an increase of religious light; together with the general diffusion of a taste and relish for the pure word of God. It is only once in an age that an individual is permitted to confer such benefits on the place of his residence as this ancient and respectable borough derived from the labours of Mr. Robinson; and the change which Baxter accomplished at Kidderminster *he* effected at Leicester. It was the boast of Augustus, that he found the city of Rome composed of brick, and left it marble. Mr. Robinson might say, without arrogance, that he had been the instrument of effecting a far more beneficial and momentous change. He came to this place while it was sunk in vice and irreligion; he left it eminently distinguished by sobriety of manners and the practice of warm, serious, and enlightened piety. He added not aqueducts and palaces, nor did he increase the splendour of its public edifices: but he embellished it with undecaying ornaments; he renovated the minds of the people, and turned a large portion of them "from darkness to light, and from the power of Satan to God." He embellished it with living stones, and replenished it with numerous temples of the Holy Ghost. He extended its intercourse with heaven, and prepared a numerous class of its inhabitants for the enjoyment of celestial bliss. Of the number of those who will devoutly acknowledge him as their spiritual father at the day of final audit, that day only can determine

Nor was his usefulness confined to the permanent inhabitants of this place; it was extended to the asylum of the sick, and to the cell of the criminal: the former found in him a physician to the soul, and returned to their homes, not only with recruited health, but with renovated minds; and the latter were, in many instances, by penitence and prayer, prepared for their awful destiny. Of him it may be said, to an extent seldom equalled by a mere mortal, "He went about doing good." "When the eye saw him, it gave witness of him; when the ear heard him, it blessed him; for he helped the poor and the fatherless, and delivered them that were ready to perish." In addition to his numerous avocations, he undertook the weekly instruction of an excellent and extensive school, which was formed in his own parish under his auspices, to which he imparted the elements of religious knowledge with a tenderness and assiduity which will never be forgotten.

There was scarcely a charitable institution set on foot, or a scheme of benevolence devised, of which he did not form the principal spring. He was truly the centre about which every thing of public utility revolved: while his wisdom guided, his spirit animated, and his character impressed itself on all useful undertakings.

Though he came to this place a stranger, without any of the means of acquiring adventitious distinction, it is not to be wondered at that a man endued with such moral and intellectual qualities should gradually acquire distinguished ascendency. Obstructions and difficulties, indeed, he encountered at the outset of his career; but they gradually gave way to the energy of his character, and at length formed a vantage-ground, on which he stood more pre-eminent. By slow degrees, by a continual series of virtuous exertions, and a patient and unremitted perseverance in well-doing, he acquired a degree of influence over all classes of society which has been the lot of few individuals. Whatever was the subject of dispute, the eminence of Mr. Robinson's services was never called in question; and however discordant the sentiments and feelings of the public on other topics, they perfectly coalesced in the homage due to his worth. To the veneration in which he was so generally held may be ascribed the principal part of that freedom from party animosities, of that concord and harmony, which have for a long period so happily distinguished this town. The deference due to his opinion on all occasions of difficulty, the unbought tribute of esteem and affection claimed by his worth, we delighted to pay. We felt gratified on finding such a rock on which we could repose our confidence, such a great example of what is most dignified in human nature, on which we could fix our eyes. By a reflex act, the virtuous part of the community felt better pleased with themselves, in proportion as they became susceptible of love and admiration towards an object so fitted, on every principle of reason and religion, to command them.

Though I have had the honour of a personal acquaintance with Mr. Robinson for upwards of thirty years, it is comparatively but of late that I had an opportunity of contemplating him more nearly. While placed at a distance, I admired him as one of the remote luminaries which adorn the hemisphere; I certainly perceived him to be a star of the first magnitude: but no sooner was I stationed upon the spot, than I became sensible of the lustre of his beams, felt the force of his attraction, and recognised in him the sun and centre of the system. His merit was not of that kind which attracts most admiration at a distance. It was so genuine and solid, that it grew in estimation the more closely it was inspected. It is possible some men may have extended their influence to a wider circle, and moved in a more extended sphere. But where influence is diffused beyond a certain limit, it becomes attenuated in proportion to its diffusion; it operates with an energy less intense. Mr. Robinson completely filled as large a sphere of personal agency as is, perhaps, possible to an individual. He left no part of it unoccupied, no interstices unsupplied, and spread himself through it with an energy in which there was nothing irregular, nothing defective, nothing redundant.

Our deceased friend was eminently distinguished by a steady uniformity of conduct. While he appeared to multiply himself by the extent and diversity of his exertions, the principles upon which they were conducted, the objects they were destined to promote, were invariably the same. He was not active at intervals, and at other times torpid and inert; he did not appear the public man at one time, and at another absorbed in selfish pursuits: his efforts to do good in season and out of season were constant, and his course knew no other variety than that of the shining light, which shineth more and more unto the perfect day. His goodness, founded on principle and corroborated by habit, operated with the steadiness of a law of nature, the beneficial results of which can never be sufficiently appreciated till they are suspended. They who contemplated Mr. Robinson at the distance of forty years, viewed him with the same emotions which he excited at a more advanced age, moderated, however, and chastised by the apprehension that it was possible some unexpected temptation might occur to divert him from his career. We have seen it completed, we have witnessed his perseverance and his conquest, and have seen his virtues and his fame placed under the safeguard and seal of death and immortality.

Though he had reached that period of life which constitutes old age, it was a *cruda viridisque senectus*. His age had impaired little or nothing of his vigour: its chief effect was that of imparting additional dignity to his countenance, and weight to his character. He fell like a noble tree, after two or three strokes, with all his sap and verdure, with extended boughs and rich foliage, while thousands were reposing under his shadow and partaking of his fruits. Seldom has death gained a richer spoil than in the extinction of the earthly existence of this admirable man.

Having expatiated so largely on the eminent benefits accruing to mankind from the services of our departed friend, let me request your attention for a few moments longer, while I endeavour to portray more distinctly the leading features of his character. The predominant property of his mind, intellectually considered, appeared to me to be a strong and masculine understanding, copious in its resources, versatile in its operations, and eminently prompt in its decisions. He saw with a rapid glance the different bearings of a subject, and the proper measures to be adopted in the most intricate concerns. He possessed good sense in an exquisite degree, rarely, if ever, misled by the illusions of imagination, either in himself or others. To this was united a warmth and vivacity of temperament which made business his delight, action his element; accompanied with a resolution in his pursuits not to be relaxed by fatigue, nor damped by discouragements, nor retarded by difficulties. To resolve and to execute, or at least to make a vigorous attempt, were with him the same thing. He joined in an eminent degree the *fortiter in re* with the *suaviter in modo;* none more inflexible in his purposes, none more conciliating in his manners. Without losing a particle of his dignity, without meanness, artifice, or flattery, he knew how to adapt himself to all sorts of society, and was equally acceptable in the character of the saint, the sage, and the cheerful, engaging companion. By his amenity of manners and benignity of mind he smoothed the asperity of contradiction, and left to the machine of public business the least possible friction.

It is almost unnecessary to state, that he laid the foundation of public confidence in his integrity, which was such that it was not only never sacrificed, but, as far as my information extends, never suspected. They who might differ from him the most on some subjects, of a religious or political nature, never called in question the honesty of his intentions. To this he joined, as a necessary instrument of success in active life, an uncommon share of prudence: by which I mean, not that timid policy which creeps along the shore, without venturing to commit itself to the ocean,—which shuns danger, without aspiring to conquest; his prudence was of a more generous and enlarged sort,—the result, not so much of calculation at the moment, as of well-regulated passions and established principles. He loved mankind too well to betray, or to speak evil of any. Vanity never made him loquacious, nor pride capricious. Having purified his mind, under the influence of religion, from vanity, pride, and resentment, the chief temptations to imprudence were precluded. His ardent mind left him no leisure for trifling, nor the great object he so steadily pursued the least disposition to mingle with the details of scandal, or the privacies of domestic life.

The foundation of all these virtues was laid in Christian piety. It was this which formed the basis of his character, and directed and regulated his pursuits. His piety was warm, manly, enlightened; at an equal distance from the moroseness of bigotry, the weakness of superstition, and the intemperate sallies of enthusiasm. His character is a practical illustration of the efficacy of the Bible, of which he was an humble and diligent student, whence he deduced his principles, and formed his maxims. Religion with him was not an occasional feeling, but an habitual element; not a sudden or transient impulse, but a permanent principle, a second nature, producing purity of intention, elevation of mind, and an uninterrupted series of useful exertions. Had he been spared to attend this anniversary, he would undoubtedly have delighted us by an impressive exhibition of the excellences of revealed truth. Providence has adopted another mode of instruction; and now invites us to learn from his life and from his death the lessons we are no longer permitted to hear from his lips. He, being dead, yet speaketh;—he speaks in his writings, he speaks from his tomb, and points to that volume which it is the object of this assembly to circulate, as the source of all his virtues, and of all his greatness. After exhibiting, for our imitation, the lives of the holy men recorded in Scripture,—men of whom the world was not worthy,—it has pleased God to present to our attention his own, formed on the same model, and replete with the same spirit. The reader of the "Scripture Characters" will be powerfully impelled to copy their example, by the reflection that there are few of their excellences which their biographer did not attain; that they were shown in his life with no less advantage than in his writings; and that, in his most popular work, he did nothing more than inculcate by his pen what he was incessantly enforcing by his practice.

The loss which the church of Christ has sustained by the extinction of such a luminary is great; the loss to this populous town and neighbourhood irreparable. Ages may revolve ere a similar calamity occurs. The shepherd is torn from his flock, the spiritual father from his children; the sage counsellor, the patron of the poor and the destitute, and the great example of the power of religion, whose very countenance could not be beheld without tender veneration, is no more. The name of Robinson will long combine with the mention of this place a train of solemn emotions, and the stranger will indulge a pious curiosity in inspecting the spot where he dwelt, and the church where he exercised his ministry.

We knew the precarious tenure by which we possessed him in common with all other blessings; we knew he was mortal; but notwithstanding we received repeated warnings by a succession of attacks, few had sufficient fortitude steadily to realize the approaching event. When the intelligence was circulated through the town, "Mr. Robinson is dead!—Mr. Robinson is dead!" it was a thunderclap: it produced a sensation of dismay and astonishment, as though we scarcely believed to be possible what we knew to be certain; and such an air of desolation and sorrow was impressed upon the countenance of the inhabitants, that a *stranger* must have perceived they had sustained no ordinary calamity. It was such as no event could have produced but the removal of a saint and a prophet. Whoever wishes to learn how much piety dignifies a character, how much sainted worth, in its power over the heart, preponderates over every other species of eminence, let him turn to this scene, and compare the tears of a populous neighbourhood with the unmeaning decorations of funereal grandeur. None *spoke* of his virtues, none was *eloquent* in his praise; every heart was *oppressed* with a sense of its loss.

I cannot close this address without remarking that the possession of such a man as Mr. Robinson incurs a proportionable weight of responsibility, and that the time is approaching when it will be inquired what improvement we have derived from the exercise of such talents and the exhibition of such an example.

It is incumbent on his hearers especially to reflect that he who watched for souls is gone to give an account, not only of the principles on which *he* conducted, but of the reception *they* gave to his embassy, and that against the impenitent and unbelieving he is compelled to be "a swift witness before God." His warning voice, his pathetic appeals and expostulations, will be heard no more; but his record is on high, and the ministry he so long exercised among us will infallibly be a savour of life unto life, or of death unto death. His life was not so properly employed as consumed in the incessant labour to bring sinners to repentance; and awful will be the doom of those who persist in rejecting the overtures of mercy, the word of reconciliation dispensed with such admirable zeal, ability, and address.

To the pastoral cares, studies, and instructions of this most eminent servant of God, death has put a final termination; but the enjoyment of such a ministry, and even the opportunity of witnessing such an example, will form a conspicuous feature in our probation, and be replete with consequences which stretch into eternity.

Permit me to indulge one more reflection: the life and ministry of this great man of God affords a demonstration of the futility of the clamour which is raised against the doctrine of salvation by grace through faith, as though it tended to relax the obligations to virtue and to annul the commands of God. Who ever insisted on this doctrine more constantly, or urged its importance more earnestly, than he? and where, among its opponents, shall we discover indications of similar usefulness? Through a period of more than forty years he employed himself in beating down the arrogance of a self-justifying spirit, in evincing the impossibility of being accepted on the footing of our own works, and in directing men of every description to seek for pardon in the blood of the Cross. If there were any one topic on which he delighted to dwell more than others, this was unquestionably the topic.

To his manly and unsophisticated understanding it was evident to a demonstration that repentance must be grafted on humility, and that there was no room to apprehend his hearers would be tempted to contemn the authority, in consequence of being abased before the majesty of God. He was also perfectly convinced that the blood of Christ, sprinkled by faith, was the only effectual balm for afflicted consciences. On these principles he conducted his ministry for near half a century, and we may challenge his enemies (if there be any remaining) to deny that its fruits were most salutary. If the apostolic doctrine which affirms that we are justified by faith without the deeds of the law, possess the tendency to licentiousness which its opponents ascribe to it, that tendency could not have failed to operate under a course of instruction so long continued, and of which the tenet in question formed so distinguishing a feature. "By their fruits ye shall know them: men do not gather grapes of thorns, nor figs of thistles."

To conclude: The fittest improvement we can make of the melancholy event we are now deploring will be a serious attention to the exhortation of St. Paul addressed to primitive Christians on the loss of eminent pastors:—"Remember them which have had the rule over you; and considering the end of their conversation, imitate their faith."

FRAGMENT.

CHARACTER OF THE REV. JOHN SUTCLIFF.

[*Written in* 1814. *Not published before.*]

A SWEET humility formed a very distinguishing feature in his character. Who ever witnessed in our deceased brother those airs of arrogance or that fondness for display which are frequently found in persons of very inferior talents and acquirements to those which he possessed? In truth, his aversion to ostentation might alone be said to be carried to excess, since it prevented him in his public ministry from availing himself of [those] ample stores of knowledge by which he could often have delighted and instructed his hearers. He had far more learning than the mere hearer of his discourses would have conjectured; for he seemed almost as anxious to conceal as some are to display.

Nor was it in this particular alone that his humility was apparent. It diffused itself over the whole of his character and deportment, and gave it a certain beauty which [no] artifice could successfully imitate. His humility was not displayed in depreciating his performances, nor in speaking of himself in degrading terms: it appeared rather in forgetting himself, and in a natural readiness to give others the superiority. It accompanied him so incessantly, that he might truly be said to "be clothed with humility."

As his disposition little inclined him to ecstasy and rapture, so his piety shone with a mild and steady lustre, perfectly free from the false fire of enthusiasm, and equally from a lukewarm formality. There were few men in whom it appeared more natural, or more manifestly as a principle interwoven with the inmost texture of his mind. His great modesty seldom permitted him to advert to his own experience either in public discourse or in more private conversation; but a savour of experimental piety pervaded his whole character.

The mild and placid cheerfulness which marked his countenance and deportment would lead us to suppose that he habitually walked in the Divine light, and the evidences of his interest in the Divine favour were rarely, if ever, impaired or eclipsed. He was one of the few men whose cheerfulness appeared to be increased by age; verifying, in this particular, the description given of "the path of the just, that is as the shining light, which shineth more and more unto the perfect day." His life was truly exemplary, being filled up with an uninterrupted series of useful, benevolent, and pious actions, proceeding from their principles, and distinguished by an eminent decorum of time and place. He was a pattern to believers, "in faith, in purity, and in conversation." Though rather the opposite to loquacious, he had a high relish for the pleasures of Christian society, in which it is difficult to say whether he imparted or received most pleasure. "The law of kindness was on his tongue;" and so attentive was he on every occasion to the feelings of those with whom he conversed, that his company was both inoffensive and delightful.

Through a long series of years his attendance at the association and at ministers' meetings was so constant and punctual that his occasional absence was severely felt, and that meeting seemed essentially defective which was not graced with his presence. His appearance among us was hailed as a certain presage of harmony and love. Multitudes can witness the deep and pungent regret experienced at the last annual association at the melancholy tidings of that fatal illness which prevented his attendance.

Few men took a deeper interest than our deceased brother in the general state of the church and the propagation of the gospel abroad. The future glory of the kingdom of Christ and the best means of promoting it were his favourite topics, and usurped a large part of his thoughts and his prayers; nor was he ever more in his element than when he was exerting his powers in devising plans for its extension. The Baptist mission in India is under incalculable obligations to his sagacity and prudence.

MEMOIR

OF

THE REV. THOMAS TOLLER,

[*Written in* 1821.]

THE subject of the following Memoir was born at South Petherton, a populous village in Somersetshire, A. D. 1756. His parents were John and Mary Toller, whose maiden name was Northcote. His father was an attorney of eminence, two of whose sons were educated for that profession. Of the early years of Thomas, the subject of the following narrative, I have little information, further than that both his parents were eminently pious, and that he always considered himself indebted, under God, for his first religious impressions to the tender solicitude of his mother for the promotion of his eternal welfare. Whether those impressions issued at that period in genuine conversion is not known: nor are we possessed of any authentic information of the circumstances connected with that event. The extreme diffidence and modesty which distinguished Mr. Toller probably prevented his relating to his nearest friends the early exercises of his mind on religious subjects: the consequence is, that in this instance, as in many others, we are left to infer the reality of the change from its effects. The light and insinuations of the Divine Spirit so often accompany the conduct of a strictly religious education, that some of the most eminent Christians have acknowledged themselves at a loss to assign the precise era of their conversion; but whether this was the case with our excellent friend it is impossible to say.

At the early age of fifteen, his parents sent him to the academy at Daventry in Northamptonshire, over which Dr. Ashworth, the worthy successor of the celebrated Dr. Doddridge, presided: his assistant in the academy was the Rev. Mr. Robins, who afterward occupied the same station with distinguished ability. Of both his tutors he was wont to speak in terms of high respect: of Mr. Robins he was often heard to say, that he considered him as the wisest and the best man he ever knew. Among many other mental endowments, he was remarkable for delicacy of taste and elegance of diction; and, perhaps, my reader will excuse my observing, that the first perception of these qualities which the writer of these lines remembers to have possessed, arose from hearing him preach at Northampton on a public occasion. It is to be lamented that he has left none of those productions behind him, which a correct and beautiful imagination, imbodied in language of the most classic purity, rendered so impressive and delightful. The qualities of his heart corresponded to those of his genius; and though long before his death his bodily infirmities obliged him to relinquish a commanding station and retire into obscurity, he retained to the last such an ascendency over the minds of his former pupils, and such an interest in their affections, as nothing but worth of the highest order can command.

To return from this digression. At the time of Mr. Toller's admission into the Daventry academy, the literary reputation of that seminary was higher than that of any among the dissenters; but partly owing to a laxness in the terms of admission, and partly to the admixture of lay and divinity students, combined with the mode in which theology was taught, erroneous principles prevailed much; and the majority of such as were educated there became more distinguished for their learning than for the fervour of their piety, or the purity of their doctrine. The celebrated Priestley speaks of the state of the academy, while he resided there, with great complacency: nothing, he assures us, could be more favourable to the progress of free inquiry; since both the tutors and students were about equally divided between the orthodox and Arian systems. The arguments by which every possible modification of error is attempted to be supported were carefully marshalled in hostile array against the principles generally embraced; while the theological professor prided himself on the steady impartiality with which he held the balance between the contending systems, seldom or never interposing his own opinion, and still less betraying the slightest emotion of antipathy to error, or predilection to truth. Thus a spirit of indifference to all religious principles was generated in the first instance, which naturally paved the way for the prompt reception of doctrines indulgent to the corruption and flattering to the pride of a depraved and fallen nature.

To affirm that Mr. Toller derived no injury from being exposed at so tender an age to this vortex of unsanctified speculation and debate, would be affirming too much, since it probably gave rise to a certain general manner of stating the peculiar doctrines of the gospel which attached chiefly to the earlier part of his ministry; though it is equally certain that his mind, even when he left the academy, was so far imbued with the grand peculiarities of the gospel that he never allowed himself to lose sight of the doctrine of the Cross as the only basis of human hope.

Of the conduct of his academical studies nothing memorable is recorded. From a very accomplished man, who I believe was his fellow-student, I have merely heard that he had no relish for the mathematics, a circumstance which has been often recorded in the biography of men of indisputable intellectual pre-eminence.

After a residence at Daventry of four years, he was appointed to supply a destitute congregation at Kettering, where he preached for the first time October 1, 1775; and his services proved so acceptable, that, after repeated visits, he was invited to take up his permanent residence with them, with which he complied in June of the ensuing year, and was ordained pastor May 28, 1778. On his first coming to Kettering, the church was in a divided and unsettled state. His immediate predecessor was a gentleman of the name of Fuller, who, at the end of two years, in consequence of much dissension in the church, resigned the pastoral charge. Mr. Fuller was preceded by the Rev. Mr. Boyce, who sustained the pastoral office for a long series of years with the highest reputation and success, and whose death was deplored as an irreparable calamity, leaving it very improbable that a successor could be speedily found capable of uniting the suffrages of a people whose confidence and esteem he had so long exclusively enjoyed. Such is the imperfection of the present state, that the possession of a more than ordinary portion of felicity is the usual forerunner of a correspondent degree of privation and distress; and the removal of a pastor who has long been the object of veneration generally places a church in a critical situation, exposed to feuds and dissensions, arising out of the necessity of a new choice. That of Mr. Toller, notwithstanding his extreme youth, was nearly unanimous. When he first supplied the congregation, nothing was more remote from his expectation than being invited to a permanent residence: his highest ambition was to be tolerated as a transient supply; and when, to his no small surprise, they made choice of him as their stated minister, he entered on that office with that heartfelt conviction of its importance, and unfeigned distrust of his own sufficiency, which are the surest omen of success. He commenced his career with fear and trembling; and instead of being elated by the preference shown him by a large and respectable society, he trembled, and was ready to sink under the weight of his responsibility.

Few men probably have been more indebted for the formation of their character to the fervent piety of their audience. Such was the state of his mind at that period, that had he been connected with a people of an opposite character, his subsequent history would have exhibited, in all probability, features very dissimilar from those which eventually belonged to it. If, in a lengthened ministerial course, the people are usually formed by their pastor, in the first stage it is the reverse; it is the people who form the minister. Mr. Toller often expressed his gratitude for that merciful providence which united him at so early a period with a people adapted to invigorate his piety, and confirm his attachment to the vital, fundamental truths of Christianity. The reciprocal influence of a minister and a congregation on each other is so incessant and so powerful, that I would earnestly dissuade an inexperienced youth from connecting himself with a people whose doctrine is erroneous, or whose piety is doubtful, lest he should be tempted to consult his ease by choosing to yield to a current he would find it difficult to resist. To root up error, and reclaim a people from inveterate habits of vice and irreligion, is unquestionably a splendid achievement; but it requires a hardihood of character and decision of principle not often found in young persons.

Little variety must be looked for in the subsequent sketch of Mr. Toller's life. As he travelled little, and seldom mingled in the scenes of public business,—as his habits were domestic and his disposition retired,—years glided away, without presenting an occurrence of sufficient magnitude to entitle it to a permanent record. Through a long series of years, he persevered in the exemplary discharge of his spiritual functions, among a people who, in proportion as his talents unfolded themselves, regarded him with increasing love and veneration, as well on account of his ministerial qualifications, as his amiable, prudent, and consistent deportment. He was the centre of union to a large and an extensive circle of ministers and of people, who, however they might differ in other particulars, unanimously concurred in their admiration of his talents, and their esteem of his virtues. He was surrounded by friends who vied with each other in demonstrations of respect, and by an audience who looked forward to each succeeding Sabbath as to a mental feast, and who hung upon his lips with an attention which might have tempted a stranger to suppose they were hearing him for the first time or the last. From the commencement of his residence at Kettering, the attachment of his people went on still increasing, till it arrived at a point beyond which it would have been idolatry. This extraordinary attachment must be ascribed partly to the impression produced by his public services, and partly to the gentleness and amenity of his private manners. It may be possible to find other preachers equally impressive, and other men equally amiable; but such a combination of the qualities calculated to give the ascendant to a public speaker with those which inspire the tenderness of private friendship, is of rare occurrence. The leisure which the retired and tranquil tenor of his life secured he employed in the perusal of the best authors in our language, which, by continually adding to his mental stores, imparted to his ministry an ample and endless variety. Although he almost invariably preached from notes composed in short-hand, his immediate preparations for the pulpit, there is reason to believe, were neither long nor laborious. His discourses were not the painful productions of a barren mind, straining itself to meet the exigences of the moment; but, gathered from a rich and cultivated soil, they were a mere scantling of the abundance which was left behind. He considered every new accession to the stock of his ideas, every effort of reflection, as a preparation for the pulpit; and looked upon those who are necessitated to afford a portion of periodical instruction every week without having accumulated mental stores, as in much the same situation with the Israelites who were doomed to produce their tale of bricks without straw. Preachers of this description may indeed amass a heap of glittering and misplaced ornaments, or beat the air with the flourishes of a tumid, unmeaning rhetoric; but the deficiency of real matter, of solid information, cannot fail eventually to consign them to contempt. Whether Mr. Toller was ever a severe student, or ever was engaged in a regular and systematic pursuit of the different branches of literature or of science, I cannot ascertain; but that he was much devoted to reading is matter of notoriety. By the incessant accumulation of fresh materials, he became "a scribe well instructed in the mysteries of the kingdom of God," and, "like a wise householder," was enabled "to bring out of his treasure things new and old." The settlement of Mr. Fuller, the venerable secretary of the Baptist Mission, in the same place, by giving scope to a virtuous emulation, was probably equally beneficial to both parties. From the absence of competition, and the abundance of leisure attending a country retirement, the mental faculties are in danger of slumbering; the rust of sloth too often blunts their edge, and impairs their brightness; which nothing could be more fitted to counteract than the presence of such a man as Mr. Fuller, distinguished for constitutional ardour and industry.

In the year 1793 he entered into the married state with Miss Elizabeth Gale, the eldest daughter of Mr. William Gale, who then resided at Cranford, in the neighbourhood of Kettering. By this lady he had two children,—John, who died in his infancy, and Thomas, who still survives him, and under the most pleasing auspices succeeds his father in the pastoral office. During the short period of this union he appears to have enjoyed the highest degree of connubial felicity; but not long after the birth of her second child Mrs. Toller betrayed symptoms of consumption, and after languishing a considerable time under the attack of that incurable malady, through the whole of which her ardent attachment to her husband and profound submission to the will of God were most conspicuous, she expired on the 15th of September, 1796.

It was about this period of his life that my acquaintance with him commenced. I had known him previously, and occasionally heard him; but it was at a season when I was not qualified to form a correct estimate of his talents. At the time referred to we were engaged to preach a double lecture at Thrapstone, nine miles from Kettering; and never shall I forget the pleasure and surprise with which I listened to an expository discourse from 1 Peter ii. 1–3. The richness, the unction, the simple majesty which pervaded his address produced a sensation which I never felt before: it gave me a new view of the Christian ministry. But the effect, powerful as it was, was not to be compared with that which I experienced a few days after, on hearing him at the half-yearly association at Bedford. The text which he selected was peculiarly solemn and impressive: his discourse was founded on 2 Peter i. 12–15,—"Yea, I think it meet as long as I am in this tabernacle to stir you up by putting you in remembrance; knowing that shortly I must put off this my tabernacle, even as our Lord Jesus Christ hath showed me," &c. The effect of this discourse on the audience was such as I have never witnessed before or since. It was undoubtedly very much aided by the peculiar circumstances of the speaker, who was judged to be far advanced in a decline, and who seemed to speak under a strong impression of its being the last time he should address his brethren on such an occasion. The aspect of the preacher, pale, emaciated, standing apparently on the verge of eternity, the simplicity and majesty of his sentiments, the sepulchral solemnity of a voice which seemed to issue from the shades, combined with the intrinsic dignity of the subject, perfectly quelled the audience with tenderness and terror, and produced such a scene of audible weeping as was perhaps never surpassed. All other emotions were absorbed in devotional feeling: it seemed to us as though we were permitted for a short space to look into eternity, and every sublunary object vanished before "the powers of the world to come." Yet there was no considerable exertion, no vehemence displayed by the speaker. no splendid imagery, no magnificent description: it was the simple domination of truth, of truth indeed of infinite moment, borne in upon the heart by a mind intensely alive to its reality and grandeur Criticism was disarmed; the hearer felt himself elevated to a region which it could not penetrate; all was powerless submission to the master-spirit of the scene. It will be always considered by those who witnessed it as affording as high a specimen as can be easily conceived of the power of a preacher over his audience, the habitual or even frequent recurrence of which would create an epoch in the religious history of the world.

During this interview he was invited by the writer of these lines to pay a visit to his friends at Cambridge: with that invitation he shortly after complied. His health had long been much impaired, and serious apprehensions had been entertained, by others as well as by himself, of his being far advanced in a decline. By his excursion to Cambridge, however, in the course of which he met with the most flattering attentions from all quarters, his spirits were revived, his health improved, and from that time the symptoms of disease gradually subsided. During his visit he afforded the people of Cambridge and its vicinity several opportunities of hearing him; and on no occasion was he heard without admiration and delight: for, though no single discourse was equally impressive with that which was delivered at Bedford, he sustained to the full the high reputation he had acquired; nor will the numerous and respectable congregations he addressed ever cease to consider this as one of the most favoured seasons of their lives. From that time his celebrity as a preacher was diffused through a much wider circle than before: he began universally to be esteemed one of the most distinguished ministers of the age,—a character which he maintained with undiminished lustre to the end of his life.

He continued a widower till the year 1803, when he took for his second wife Elizabeth, the eldest daughter of Mr. William Wilkinson, of Northampton, by whom he had five children, Richard, William, Joseph, Henry, and George, all of whom, together with their mother, survive him. To what degree this union contributed to the happiness of the latter stages of his life the delicacy due to a most amiable woman, whose humility renders her as averse to receive praises as she is careful to deserve them, forbids me to say. Suffice it to observe, that notwithstanding the disparity of years, there never was a connexion which more completely realized the highest anticipations of the friends of both parties.

In the year 1799 the congregation assembling in Carter-lane, London, under the pastoral care of the excellent Mr. Taylor, wanting a supply for one part of the day, applied to Mr. Toller, and offered him for one service on.y a salary considerably beyond what he then enjoyed. To this invitation he gave a decided negative. In the eginning of the following year the congregation at Clapham gave him a similar invitation, which he also declined. The two congregations then united their invitations, offering a large salary on condition of his undertaking a single service at each place. This joint application he refused. The people of Kettering, hearing of these repeated attempts to remove him, became justly alarmed: a few of them waited upon him, informing him of the uneasiness they felt at the repeated attempts which had been made and were still making to effect a separation. They assured him of his entire possession of the hearts of his people, and that though their situation did not permit their making such proposals as the other parties, they would do all in their power, and most gladly rectify any circumstances which gave him uneasiness. His reply was, that if he found his services still acceptable, no pecuniary advantages should ever tempt him to relinquish his charge. At the same time he intimated, that as the two congregations still persisted in their application, he wished his people publicly to express their sentiments on the subject, that he might be armed with conclusive reasons for declining invitations so earnestly and repeatedly urged. This gave occasion to three separate addresses—from the young people, from the members of the Benevolent Society, and from the congregation at large; each expressive of the high esteem they entertained for his character, their sense of the benefit derived from his ministry, and their extreme reluctance to resign advantages which they so highly prized. To these addresses a most affectionate and appropriate reply was made by their pastor, in which he assured them of his unalterable attachment, together with his final determination to accede to their wishes; and thus ended the last attempt to remove Mr. Toller from his station.

The reader will naturally be surprised to find that on this occasion no address was presented by the church. As this omission cannot with a shadow of probability be ascribed to indifference on their part, it must be imputed to the church not occupying that rank in the esteem of the auditory to which it is justly entitled. In every Christian congregation the church ought to be regarded as the principal object, to which the auditory are but an appendage, and for a union with which it should be their highest ambition to become qualified. Congregations are the creatures of circumstances; churches the institution of God: and if we adhere to the maxims and examples of Scripture, and of primitive antiquity, in all religious proceedings their judgment will first be consulted, and their official character recognised. But here we meet with a trans action of great moment, in which three classes of persons, to which no function is assigned in the New Testament, act a conspicuous part, while the church is wholly overlooked. My reason for animadverting on this procedure is, that in the economy of modern dissenters a growing tendency may be perceived to merge the church in the congregation, and to commit the management of the most weighty matters to a body of subscribers in preference to the members; an innovation. should it generally prevail, productive of incalculable evils. Many of those who compose the auditors, in distinction from the church, may possess genuine piety; but while they persist in declining to make a public profession of Christ, it is scarcely possible for them to give proof of it: the greater part, it is no breach of candour to suppose, are men of the world; and surely it requires little penetration to perceive the danger which religion must sustain by transferring the management of its concerns from persons decidedly religious to those whose pretensions to interfere are founded solely on pecuniary considerations. The presumptuous intermeddling of worldly, unsanctified spirits with ecclesiastical concerns has been the source of almost every error in doctrine, and enormity in practice, that has deformed the profession of Christianity from the time of Constantine to the present day; nor is dissent of much importance, except as far as it affords an antidote to this evil. The system which confounds the distinction between the church and the congregation has long since been carried to perfection in the Presbyterian denomination; and we all know what preceded and what has followed that innovation,—the decay of piety, the destruction of discipline, a most melancholy departure, in a word, both in principle and in practice, from genuine Christianity.

No event contributed more to make Mr. Toller extensively known beyond the limits of the dissenting connexion than the active part which he took in promoting the objects of the Bible Society. Strongly impressed with the truth of our Lord's declaration, that "the kingdom of God cometh not with observation," and constitutionally averse to every thing noisy and ostentatious, it was rarely that he could be prevailed upon to engage in those popular religious societies, the existence of which may be said to constitute an era in the history of religion. Of societies even formed for the propagation of Christianity in foreign parts he was more disposed to admire the zeal that animated the exertions than to anticipate the success, having formed an opinion that the final triumph of the gospel over paganism was destined to be effected by the renewal of those miraculous gifts which attended its first promulgation.

But the Bible Society, by the simplicity of its object, and the comprehensive catholicism of its constitution, so consonant to the unbounded liberality of his views, commanded his unqualified approbation; and having been chosen one of the secretaries for the Northern Auxiliary Branch, in the county of Northampton, from its first formation, he directed the entire force of his mind to it; attending regularly, as long as his health would permit, the various meetings held in the vicinity. The sensation produced by his speech at the first meeting at Northampton, where his grace the Duke of Grafton presided, will never be forgotten. Departing from the usual practice on such occasions, he addressed a considerable part of it to the noble chairman, contrasting his then situation with that which he occupied in the House of Lords; a task which, difficult as it was, he performed with a dignity, pathos, and decorum that astonished and delighted the audience. Its effect on the duke himself was to draw tears from his eyes, and induce him to double his original donation. In strokes of sudden pathos and unpolished grandeur Mr. Toller was almost unequalled; and as his whole soul was engaged in promoting the Bible Society, on no occasion were his peculiar powers displayed to more advantage.

It has been already remarked, that missionary efforts excited at their commencement but little of his attention; not because he was indifferent to their object, but from a settled conviction that the conversion of the heathen was not to be effected by ordinary means, but by miraculous interposition. Whether he entirely relinquished that expectation I am not prepared to say; it is certain his views underwent some modification upon that subject. The astonishing progress of the Bible Society in circulating the Scriptures throughout the world,—the unparalleled exertions of Dr. Carey and of others in translating them into the principal languages of the East, and of the success of the London Missionary Society in Africa and the South Sea, where whole tribes and nations have been led by a simultaneous impulse to abandon their idols, and to worship the one living and true God, opened a new prospect, and convinced him that the general emancipation of the pagan world from the power of darkness might be accomplished without that supernatural agency which he formerly deemed indispensable. A pertinacious adherence to one mode of thinking, in spite of superior evidence, was no part of his character; and though not very apt to change his opinion on subjects on which he had long exercised his mind, his firmness was untinctured with obstinacy.

During the greater portion of his life he was occasionally liable to great depression of spirits; but about seven years previous to its close, in consequence of a sudden interruption of the profuse perspiration which had constantly attended his public exercises, and which was thrown back upon the system, he sunk into such a state of despondency as disqualified him, for some time, for the discharge of his ministerial functions. His mind, during this season, was harassed with the most distressing apprehensions of a future state, and possessed with such a view of his pollution in the sight of a holy God, that he was tempted to suppose all his past experience in religion was delusive. Of his state of mind during this melancholy period, I know not whether he has left any written account; but I recollect, when adverting to it in familiar conversation, he described it as a year of almost incessant weeping and prayer. Though none who were acquainted with him will entertain a doubt of the sincerity of his piety previous to that afflictive visitation, as little can it be doubted that it was a source of great spiritual improvement, that he "did business in the mighty waters," and that he was brought to a more profound knowledge of himself, and a more deep and humble reliance on the power and grace of the Redeemer, than he had before experienced. From that time his discourses were more thoroughly imbued with the peculiarities of the gospel, his doctrinal views more clear and precise, and his whole conversation and deportment such as announced a rapid advance in spirituality. That generality in his statements of revealed truth which was the consequence of his education at Daventry, and which almost invariably characterized the pupils of that seminary, totally disappeared, and he attained "to all the riches of the full assurance of the mystery of God the Father and of Christ." Though he survived that affliction several years, it probably shortened his life, by giving that concussion to his nervous system from which he never perfectly recovered; and from that time the circulation of his blood appears to have been less regular, and the depression of his spirits more frequent than before.

In the year 1813, the friends of Mr. Toller determined to carry into effect an idea which had before been suggested, that of raising a sum of money to be presented as a testimony of their esteem, as well as with a view to lay the basis of a permanent provision for his family As soon as he had intelligence of the design, he, in a letter to a gentleman who had taken an active part in the affair, communicated very freely his sentiments on the occasion, in which, without positively declining it, he suggested some objections to the measure, intimating his fear that, by occasioning a diversity of sentiment on its propriety, it might destroy that harmony and cordiality of feeling which had so long prevailed in his connexions. It breathes such a spirit of tenderness, humility, and modesty, that I cannot doubt the reader will be gratified by its insertion.* It is almost unnecessary to add, that the apprehensions and scruples which arose from his extreme delicacy were overruled, and a sum amounting to nearly a thousand pounds was contributed, with a promptitude and alacrity which did equal honour to those who conferred and to him who received the favour. When it is recollected that he had repeatedly resisted the most earnest solicitations to remove to a superior situation, and was charged with the care of a numerous and increasing family, the whole transaction cannot fail to impress the reader with admiration of the liberality in which the donation originated, and of the delicate reluctance with which it was accepted. The desire of wealth never took possession of his mind. Contented and thankful for that decent competence which he was at no time suffered to want, he was frugal without being parsimonious, and generous without profusion.

The system of his life was eminently uniform and tranquil, distinguished by few of the events and vicissitudes which are adapted in the recital to amuse or to agitate the reader. In the summer months he frequently rose at a very early hour, and was often met in his solitary walks in the neighbouring woods, by peasants who were "going forth to their work and to their labour till the evening." In these silent and retired scenes he took great delight; and from his observation of the beauties of nature, and the operations of husbandry, he frequently derived those images and illustrations which furnished a rich repast for his audience. Possessed of great sensibility, and a rich and lively imagination, he was accustomed more than almost any

* See p. 409.

other man to clothe the abstractions of religion in the garb of sensible images, to illustrate his conceptions by frequent allusions to the most striking scenes in nature and in life. What is said of our Lord may almost be affirmed of him, that he taught the people in parables, and without a parable he spake not unto them. Truth compels me to confess that he sometimes carried this peculiarity to excess; but along with this concession it is but justice to observe, that the habit of appealing to the imagination was not only admirably adapted to a numerous class of subjects, but greatly contributed to that power of delectation which so eminently distinguished his ministry. His discourses were never vapid, tedious, or uninteresting. A certain intensity of devotional feeling, a deep and solemn pathos, accompanied with tones expressive of the greatest sensibility, sustained the attention of the audience in full vigour.

It was his custom, during the greater part of his ministry, to devote the morning service to exposition, in the course of which he went very much at large through the life of Moses and of Christ, each of which occupied him several years. A great part of both Testaments was thus brought before the minds of his hearers. He was strongly impressed with a conviction of the advantages resulting from that mode of instruction, by its affording a more ample variety of topics, imparting a more profound and extensive acquaintance with the Scriptures, and enabling the teacher of religion to introduce many practical remarks, many minute points and details, which, however useful in the conduct of life, would with difficulty find a place in a regular discourse. It is evident from the writings of the fathers, that this was the primitive mode of preaching, handed down to the Christian Church from the Jewish synagogue; and wherever a people are more desirous of acquiring real knowledge than of a momentary excitement, it will be decidedly preferred. Unhappily, the taste of most hearers is the reverse: they are a sort of spiritual epicures, who prefer a poignant and stimulating to a simple and nourishing diet, and would infinitely rather have their passions awakened than their conscience directed, or their understanding enlarged.

For this reason, expositions will generally be preferred by the intelligent part of an audience, and sermons by a promiscuous multitude. The peculiar talents of Mr. Toller qualified him, above most men, for combining the advantages of both methods, by infusing that degree of pathos and animation into his expository lectures which rendered them little less affecting than his sermons. Though he possessed, there is reason to believe, a competent knowledge of the Scriptures in their original tongues, from condescension to his audience, and his extreme abhorrence of whatever savours of pedantry, he was yet sparing of critical remarks, and availed himself less of the advantages of a liberal education and of incessant reading, for exact interpretations of the sacred volume, than he might with unexceptionable propriety have done. His expositions were practical and popular, not critical or elaborate. In order to preserve a unity of design, and to perpetuate an identity of impression, it was his usual practice to select some portion of the paragraph which he had been expounding in the former part of the day as the basis of the afternoon discourse.

It would be great injustice to the memory of my invaluable friend, while speaking of his ministerial qualifications, not to mention his striking superiority in the discharge of the devotional part of his public functions, his almost unrivalled eminence in prayer. His addresses to the Supreme Being united every excellence of which they are susceptible: they were copious without being redundant, fervent without extravagance, elevated without the least appearance of turgidity or pomp. He poured out his whole soul in an easy, unaffected flow of devotional sentiment; adoration seemed to be his natural element; and, as he appeared to lose all consciousness of any other presence but that of the Deity, he seldom failed to raise his audience to the same elevation, to make them realize the feelings of Jacob, when he exclaimed, "How awful is this place!" If this encomium admits of any abatement, it must be on the ground of their length, which was not unfrequently equal to that of his sermons. Nor was he less admirable in family devotion: many a time have I been surprised at the promptitude, ease, and grace with which he would advert to the peculiar circumstances of the family, or of its principal members, with an allusion sometimes to minute incidents, without once impairing the solemnity, or detracting from the dignity, which ought ever to accompany a religious exercise. His petitions in behalf of each individual were stamped with something exclusively proper to his situation or character, so that while he was concurring in an act of social worship, he felt, ere he was aware, as if he were left alone with God.

In his public discourses he was apt to limit himself too much for time, either to do full justice to his subject, or to prolong the impression until it had completely incorporated itself with the mind of the hearer: the curtain was let fall at the moment the scene was most interesting, and the current of emotion suddenly checked and interrupted when it was just rising to its height. The mind is so constituted, that in order to produce a permanent effect, a train of thought, however interesting, must occupy the attention for a considerable space: the soul kindles by degrees, and must pass through successive gradations of feeling before it reaches the utmost elevation of sublime and pathetic emotion. Hence it is that the most powerful speakers, in every age, have had recourse to a frequent repetition of the same arguments and topics, quite useless on any other account than its tendency to prolong the impression, and to render it by that means more durable and intense. Had Mr. Toller paid more attention to this principle of our constitution, I will not say he would have been a more interesting and delightful preacher,—for it is not easy to conceive how his sermons could have been much more impressive than they frequently were, during their delivery,—but their power over the audience would probably have been more lasting and more salutary. The defect which we have taken the liberty of noticing may perhaps be ascribed to the habit of writing his sermons, a practice more favourable to accuracy of language and condensation of thought than to copiousness and expansion.

But it is time to return to our narrative, which a few words will despatch. During several of the last years of his life, our excellent friend exhibited symptoms of a tendency to apoplexy; and in the year 1819, as he was going to his study, he was seized with a fit, which appeared instantly to deprive him of all sensation, to the inexpressible alarm of his family. But before medical aid could be procured, his bodily strength and the possession of his mental powers were restored, and in two hours he displayed no indications of the awful event, except a degree of lassitude, and a slight contortion in the muscles about the mouth, both of which shortly disappeared. This circumstance, it is remarked by one of his friends, afforded a melancholy confirmation of their fears. They had long apprehended the seeds of apoplexy were lurking in his constitution, so that they looked upon this visitation as a voice from God, preparing them, by no doubtful warning, for the speedy dissolution of a connexion which had long been the source of so much improvement and delight.

The circumstances attending the last scene of his life, I cannot give better than in the words of a respectable friend from whom I received the account. "He had," says the writer of the following narrative, "for many years supposed it probable he should be subject to apoplexy or palsy. His fears fixed on the latter: and to his nearest friends he has often said, in allusion to these apprehensions, 'I do not fear, on the whole, to die; nor do I fear, I hope, to suffer, if I may but have the needful support from God; but if I am doomed to a long scene of suffering, and to become a burden to myself and friends, I do fear that faith and patience may fail, and that I may at last dishonour the cause I have preached, and the Master whom I serve and love.' The attack which has been mentioned removed the fear of palsy almost entirely: he was convinced the disorder was apoplexy; and the consequent conviction that such probably would be his end,—that, without pain or long affliction, he should, when his great Master had done with his services, be thus kindly dismissed,—had an immediate and an exhilarating effect upon his mind. After this, he had frequent seizures of the same kind, which lasted for a very short time, seldom more than five minutes in the whole; but they left evident traces on his bodily frame, though they had no other effect upon his mind than to confirm his hope of immediate dismission 'when his work was done.' Near the close of the year 1820, one of these attacks left him so weak and shattered in constitution as to convince him he should never be able to resume his full pastoral duties again; and he, in a very affectionate manner communicated this conviction to his people. They immediately sought an assistant, and most naturally turned their attention to the son of their beloved pastor, who had been preaching at Wem, in Shropshire, for some time, but at that moment was visiting his father; to whom he had hurried in dreadful doubt, from the account that he had received, whether he should see his face any more. From this attack he gradually recovered, and continued for some weeks to gain strength.

On Sunday the 25th of February, he preached in the morning with all his usual animation, from Isa. lxiii. 7–13, and remarked, at the close of the discourse, what encouragement this passage affords the widow and the fatherless to put their trust in God, finishing his last public discourse with these words :—

'To thee our infant race we leave ;
Them may their fathers' God receive,
That ages yet unborn may raise
Successive hymns of humble praise.'

He spent the evening surrounded by his family, and conversing with his children in a strain of cheerful piety ; and after a night of sound repose, arose as well as usual the next morning. About noon leaving the parlour, he was found a few minutes after in an apoplectic fit, or a seizure resembling apoplexy. Several medical men repaired to the spot, but life was extinct."

His remains were interred in the burying-ground belonging to the meeting-house, on Thursday the 8th of March. On that occasion the Rev. Mr. Horsey, of Northampton, engaged in prayer ; the Rev. Mr. Edwards, of the same place, delivered the funeral oration ; and the writer of these lines endeavoured to improve the providence by a suitable discourse. A considerable number of the clergy in the vicinity, and nearly all the dissenting ministers of the county, attended the procession, which was rendered deeply affecting by the tears of a vast assembly, consisting of all the respectable inhabitants of the town, who felt on this occasion that they had lost a father and a friend.

Having already glanced at the most distinguishing features in the character of Mr. Toller, an elaborate delineation of it will neither be necessary nor expected.

It is remarkable, that though he invariably delivered his sermons from notes, to which he strictly adhered, his style of composition was eminently colloquial; it had all the careless ease, negligence, and occasional inaccuracy which might be looked for in an extemporaneous address. He appears never to have turned his attention to composition as an art ; and the force and beauty with which he sometimes expressed himself was the spontaneous effect of a vivid imagination, accompanying the truest sensibility. His most affecting illustrations (and the power of illustrating a subject was his distinguishing faculty) were drawn from the most familiar scenes of life ; and, after he became a father, not unfrequently from the incidents which attach to that relation. An example of this (supplied by the friend whose words have been already quoted) will afford the reader some idea of the manner in which he availed himself of images drawn from the domestic circle. His text was Isaiah xxvii. 5 :—"Let him take hold of my strength, that he may make peace with me ; and he shall make peace with me."—"I think," said he, "I can convey the meaning of this passage so that every one may understand it, by what took place in my own family within these few days. One of my little children had committed a fault for which I thought it my duty to chastise him. I called him to me, explained to him the evil of what he had done, and told him how grieved I was that I must punish him for it. He heard me in silence, and then rushed into my arms, and burst into tears. I could sooner have cut off my arm than have then struck him for his fault: he had taken hold of my strength, and he had made peace with me."

He possessed great originality, not so much, however, in the stamina of his thoughts, as in the cast of his imagination. He seldom reminded you of any other speaker to whom he bore the slightest resemblance; his excellences and his defects rendered it equally evident that he had formed himself on no preceding model,—that he yielded without restraint to the native bias of his character and genius. The effect of imitation would, undoubtedly, have been the acquisition of more elegance and correctness, probably at the expense of higher qualities —of that noble simplicity and careless grandeur which were the distinguishing features of his eloquence. In the power of awakening pathetic emotions he far excelled any speaker it has been my lot to hear. Often have I seen a whole congregation melted under him like wax before the sun: my own feelings, on more than one occasion, have approached to an overpowering agitation. The effect was produced apparently with perfect ease. No elaborate preparation, no peculiar vehemence or intensity of tones, no artful accumulation of pathetic images led the way: the mind was captivated and subdued, it scarcely knew how. Though it will not be imagined that this triumph of popular eloquence could be habitual, much less constant, it may be safely affirmed that a large proportion of Mr. Toller's discourses afforded some indication of these powers.

Of the personal character of the subject of these memoirs it may be observed, in general, that it was marked by none of the eccentricities which are supposed to be the appendages of genius, and that it consisted of a combination of amiable and pleasing, rather than of striking qualities. Candour, in all the modes of its operation, was a conspicuous feature. As his affection was extended to all, without exception, who "love our Lord Jesus Christ in sincerity," so he was particularly ingenious in putting the best construction on unfavourable appearances, in extenuating what he could not justify, and in discovering reasons for hoping well of those whom the honest but untempered zeal of many good men would prompt them to condemn. It was his delight to narrow the grounds of debate among sincere Christians, to multiply the points of contact, and to detect the indications of spiritual consanguinity and of common origin, amid the discrepances which arise from real diversity of sentiment in some instances, and a diversity of language in more. Whether this benevolent solicitude to comprehend within the pale of salvation as many as possible may not sometimes have led him to extenuate the danger of speculative error too much, may be fairly questioned. Since the charity which the Scriptures so earnestly inculcate consists in a real solicitude for the welfare of others, not in thinking well of their state, he cannot be justly accused of a violation of its dictates who contends that those doctrines are essential to salvation on which his own hopes of it are exclusively founded.

There is another branch of candour which was eminently exemplified in the subject of the preceding Memoir. His tenderness in whatever concerned individual reputation was remarkable. He felt as much solicitude about the character of the absent as the feelings of the present: the wanton depreciation of their intellect or their virtue gave him visible pain, and where he could not speak favourably of either he was silent. Having no passion for display, he was never tempted to sacrifice his friend to his jest; his gayest sallies never inflicted a pang nor occasioned a blush. His humour was a gentle and lambent flame, which cheered and exhilarated, but never scorched. Hence few men possessed more friends or fewer enemies: it may be doubted whether, among the numerous lists of the former, he lost the esteem of one. The friends of his youth who did not descend into the grave before him were the delight and solace of his age; and in proportion as their ranks were thinned, he wisely consulted his happiness by cultivating the affection of a succeeding generation, by which he escaped that solitude and desertion which is the lot of those who shut their hearts against new attachments, neglect the good within their reach in a hopeless attempt to grasp a phantom, and perversely refuse to attach a value to any other pleasures than those which have withered under the blast of death.

It was not his practice to devote much of his time to ministerial visits. In justification of this part of his conduct he was accustomed to quote the apostolic injunction: "Is any sick among you? let him *call* for the elders of the church," &c. He possessed, or fancied he possessed, little talent for the ordinary topics of religious conversation; and his extreme aversion to the ostentation of spirituality rendered him somewhat reluctant to engage in those recitals of Christian experience in which many professors so much delight. There adhered to his natural disposition a delicacy and reserve which rendered it impossible for him to disclose, except in the most confidential intercourse, the secret movements and aspirations of his heart towards the Best of beings.

He possessed, notwithstanding this, a high relish for the pleasures of society. An inexhaustible fund of anecdote, which he was wont to relate with a dry and comic humour, rendered him in his livelier moments a most fascinating companion. A great versatility of features combined with much power of imitation to give a peculiar poignance to the different incidents of his story. His imitations, however, were *specific*, not individual, seldom if ever descending to personal mimicry—an illiberal art, more befitting the buffoon than the Christian or the gentleman. Mr. Toller's indulgence of these sallies was occasional, not habitual; they formed at times the seasoning of his conversation, not the staple commodity; and never were they carried so far as to impair the dignity of his character or the reverence inspired by his virtues. They were invariably such as a virgin might listen to without a blush, and a saint without a sigh.

Mr. Toller was much of a practical philosopher. Deeply convinced of the vanity and imperfection of the present state, which he considered less as a scene of enjoyment than as a perpetual conflict with unavoidable evils, he was always disposed to make the best of passing events: to yield where resistance was unavailing, to beguile the sorrows which he could not remove, and by setting the good against the evil, to blunt the arrows of adversity and disarm disappointment of its sting. Possessing a genuine but not a sickly sensibility, he [showed it rather] in enduring the vicissitudes of life with equanimity, than in any excessive delicacy or refinement of feeling.

"Speak evil of no man," is an injunction of which he never lost sight; and without assuming the severity of reproof, he well knew how, by an expressive silence, to mark his aversion to scandal. He showed a constant solicitude to give no offence to Jew or gentile, or the household of God. Hence the efficacy of his ministry was never obstructed or impaired by the personal prejudice of his hearers, who regarded him, not only with the deference due to a zealous and enlightened teacher, but with the affection of a friend. He was an ardent lover of peace. On no occasion did he offend by haughtiness, negligence, the indulgence of a capricious humour, or the sallies of intemperate anger. It has been asserted by some that knew him in early life, that his original disposition was hasty and irritable. If this was the case, he affords a striking example of the conquest of religion and philosophy over the early tendencies of nature, since few men were equally distinguished by an unaffected sweetness and serenity of temper.

During every period of my acquaintance with him, he exhibited the most decided indications of piety; but in the latter stages of his life this part of his character shone with distinguished lustre: devotion appeared to be his habitual element. Seldom has religion presented more of the lovely and attractive than in the character of Mr. Toller: if it did not inflame him with the zeal which distinguished more active and enterprising spirits, it melted him into love, clothed him with humility, and decked him, in an eminent degree, with the "ornaments of a meek and quiet spirit."

It has rarely been the privilege of one town, and that not of considerable extent, to possess at the same time, and for so long a period, two such eminent men as Mr. Toller and Mr. Fuller. Their merits as Christian ministers were so equal, and yet so different, that the exercise of their religious functions in the same place was as little adapted to produce jealousy as if they had moved in distant spheres. The predominant feature in the intellectual character of Mr. Fuller was the power of discrimination, by which he detected the minutest shades of difference among objects which most minds would confound: Mr. Toller excelled in exhibiting the common sense of mankind in a new and impressive form. Mr. Fuller never appeared to so much advantage as when occupied in detecting sophistry, repelling objections, and ascertaining with a microscopic accuracy the exact boundaries of truth and error: Mr. Toller attached his attention chiefly to those parts of Christianity which come most into contact with the imagination and the feelings, over which he exerted a sovereign ascendency. Mr. Fuller convinced by his arguments; Mr. Toller subdued by his pathos. The former made his hearers feel the grasp of his intellect; the latter the contagion of his sensibility. Mr. Fuller's discourses identified themselves, after they were heard, with trains of thought; Mr. Toller's with trains of emotion. The illustrations employed by Mr. Fuller (for he also excelled in illustration) were generally made to subserve the clearer comprehension of his subject; those of Mr. Toller consisted chiefly of appeals to the imagination and the heart. Mr. Fuller's ministry was peculiarly adapted to detect hypocrites, to expose fallacious pretensions to religion, and to separate the precious from the vile; he sat as "the refiner's fire and the fuller's soap:" Mr. Toller was most in his element when exhibiting the consolations of Christ, dispelling the fears of death, and painting the prospects of eternity. Both were original: but the originality of Mr. Fuller appeared chiefly in his doctrinal statements; that of Mr. Toller in his practical remarks. The former was unquestionably most conversant with speculative truth; the latter perhaps possessed the deeper insight into the human heart.

Nor were the characters of these eminent men, within the limits of that moral excellence which was the attribute of both, less diversified than their mental endowments. Mr. Fuller was chiefly distinguished by the qualities which command veneration; Mr. Toller by those which excite love. Laborious, zealous, intrepid, Mr. Fuller passed through a thousand obstacles in the pursuit of objects of public interest and utility; Mr. Toller loved to repose, delighting and delighted, in the shade of domestic privacy. The one lived for the world; the other for the promotion of the good of his congregation, his family, and friends. An intense zeal for the advancement of the kingdom of Christ, sustained by industry that never tired, a resolution not to be shaken, and integrity incapable of being warped, conjoined to a certain austerity of manner, were the leading characteristics of Mr. Fuller: gentleness, humility, and modesty, those of Mr. Toller. The secretary of the Baptist Mission attached, in my opinion, too much importance to a speculative accuracy of sentiment; while the subject of this Memoir leaned to the contrary extreme. Mr. Fuller was too prone to infer the character of men from their creed; Mr. Toller to lose sight of their creed in their character. Between persons so dissimilar, it was next to impossible a very close and confidential intimacy should subsist: a sincere admiration of each other's talents, and esteem for the virtues which equally adorned them both, secured without interruption, for more than thirty years, those habits of kind and respectful intercourse which had the happiest effect in promoting the harmony of their connexions and the credit of religion.

Much as Mr. Fuller was lamented by the religious public in general, and especially in his own denomination, I have reason to believe there was not a single individual out of the circle of his immediate relatives who was more deeply affected by his death than Mr. Toller. From that moment he felt himself nearer to eternity; he accepted the event as a most impressive warning of his own dissolution; and while a thousand solemn and affecting recollections accompanied the retrospect of a connexion which had so long and so happily subsisted, one of his favourite occupations was to revive a mental intercourse by the frequent perusal of the sermons of his deceased friend. It is thus that the friendship of high and sanctified spirits loses nothing by death but its alloy: failings disappear, and the virtues of those whose "faces we shall behold no more" appear greater and more sacred when beheld through the shades of the sepulchre. Their spirits are now united before the Throne; and if any event in this sublunary scene may be supposed to engage the attention of the subject of this Memoir, in his present mysterious elevation, it is probably the desire that the child of his prayers who now succeeds him in his office may surpass his example, and be the honoured instrument of turning more sinners to righteousness, and of conducting more sons to glory, than himself.

MR. TOLLER'S LETTER,

Referred to in page 399.

My Dear Sir,

It would be idle in me to affect ignorance of the business which has principally occasioned your visit to Kettering just now; and though it may seem indelicate to interfere during the discussion of that business, yet I cannot with an easy mind suffer the intended meeting to take place on Monday, without offering a few observations on what may be called, in parliamentary language, "the previous question."

Considering the proposed measure as originating with you and some other friends, I can view it in no other light than as a noble instance of the most unquestionably disinterested friendship and affection; and let the result be what it may, I shall retain a deep and lasting sense of it as such: but at the same time I cannot but feel a painful apprehension, that what you mean for nothing but good should be the incidental occasion of real harm: that is, the probable means of disturbing the harmony and peace which at present exist in my congregation.

There are some among us whose inclination would prompt them to support any measure for the benefit of me or my family, but whose general circumstances are, like my own, comfortable and competent; indeed, just sufficient to fill up the annual supply, with a little besides to assist the poor and needy, but who could not advance any thing like a round sum, which would tell on an occasion like this. Some such, I am afraid, would be grieved to contribute nothing; and yet more than a trifle would be a real inconvenience. There are others in superior circumstances, and by no means backward to do good in the abstract; but who, from education, economical habits, and other causes, have never been accustomed to do so on a large scale; and who, from an apprehension of there being no direct and immediate necessity in the case, would be hurt and perhaps disgusted at the suggestion that a handsome sum was expected from them. Now, any instance of this sort would grate more upon my mind than the friendship of others would gratify it; nor could I prevail upon myself to receive a single shilling from a reluctant hand if I knew it, or as the result of solicitation and admonition: and if any thing of the kind goes forward in a way satisfactory to me, it must be on a ground which is hardly attainable perhaps in any similar case, namely, that every subscriber be, in the fullest sense, a volunteer; for I can most truly say, that I had a thousand times rather matters should rest as they are, than that the plan should advance a single step at the risk of exciting sensations or producing effects similar to those alluded to above: and therefore, on this ground, if it shall appear to you and other friends prudent to adjourn the further consideration of the business to a future day, be assured that such a resolution will not give me the slightest pain.

I have now told you all my heart, and shall leave the event with Providence and your discretion,—only repeating, that I shall never cease to admire the principles by which you and others have been actuated, and shall retain a lasting sense of obligation for the kindness of your intention.

I am, with best wishes and prayers,

Yours most affectionately,

THOS. N. TOLLER.

P.S.—You are at full liberty to show this letter to whomsoever you think proper: **indeed**, with that view I write it.

PREFACE TO THE MEMOIRS

OF THE

REV. JOSEPH FREESTON.

[*Written in* 1821.]

Of all the species of literary composition, perhaps biography is the most delightful. The attention concentrated on one individual gives a unity to the materials of which it is composed, which is wanting in general history. The train of incidents through which it conducts the reader suggests to his imagination a multitude of analogies and comparisons; and, while he is following the course of events which mark the life of him who is the subject of the narrative, he is insensibly compelled to take a retrospect of his own. In no other species of writing are we permitted to scrutinize the character so exactly, or to form so just and accurate an estimate of the excellences and defects, the lights and shades, the blemishes and beauties, of an individual mind.

The progress of a human being in his passage through time to eternity only requires to be exhibited with fidelity in order to become an interesting object to a contemplative mind; whatever may have been the moral or intellectual qualities of the individual, and however degraded by vice, or exalted by piety and virtue. Conquests achieved or objects attained,—conscience cowering under the tyranny of the passions, or asserting her dignity by subjecting them to her sway,—are equally instructive,—providing the reader is informed by what steps virtuous or vicious habits were superinduced, by what stratagems temptation prevailed, or by what efforts and expedients it was repelled. The moral warfare which every rational and accountable creature has to sustain, pregnant with consequences which reach to eternity, possesses an intrinsic and essential importance, totally independent of the magnitude of the events, or the publicity and splendour of the scenes to which it is attached. The moral history of a beggar, which faithfully revealed the interior movements of his mind, and laid open the secret causes which contributed to form and determine his character, might enlarge and enlighten the views of a philosopher. Whatever tends to render our acquaintance with any portion of our species more accurate and profound is an accession to the most valuable part of our knowledge; and. though to know ourselves has ever been deemed of the most consequence, it may be doubtful whether the power of self-examination is ever exerted with so much vigour as when it is called into action by the exhibition of individual character. The improvement derived from narrative in this view will be proportional to the degree in which the objects described and the incidents related bear a resemblance to those with which the reader is conversant; and for this reason the biography of private persons, though less dazzling, is more instructive to the majority of readers than that of such as are distinguished by the elevation of their rank and the splendour of their achievements. Few require to be taught the arts by which the favour of princes is conciliated, or the machinations of rival candidates for power defeated; few need to be warned against the errors and mistakes which have produced the loss of battles or the failure of negotiations. Events of this order may fill the imagination, and diffuse their dignity and pathos over the page of history, but they afford little useful instruction to the bulk of mankind. But when a character selected from the ordinary ranks of life is faithfully and minutely delineated, no effort is requisite to enable us to place ourselves in the same situation: we accompany the subject of the narrative with an interest undiminished by distance, unimpaired by dissimilarity of circumstances; and from the efforts by which he surmounted difficulties and vanquished temptations we derive the most useful practical lessons.

He who desires to strengthen his virtue and purify his principles will always prefer the solid to the specious; will be more disposed to contemplate an example of the unostentatious piety and goodness which all men may obtain, than of those extraordinary achievements to which few can aspire: nor is it the mark of a superior, but rather of a vulgar and superficial taste, to consider nothing as great or excellent but that which glitters with titles or is elevated by rank.

The biography of such as have been eminent for piety has ever been a favourite species of reading with those who possess a devotional spirit. "As face answers to face in a glass, so does the heart of man to man." To trace the steps by which a piety feeble in its rudiments has attained to maturity,—to observe the holy arts by which devout habits were strengthened and temptations defeated,—to discern the power of truth in purifying and transforming the minds of such as have attained to high degrees of sanctity,—is equally delightful and edifying. To the real Christian experimental religion opens a new world, replete with objects, emotions, and prospects of which none but those who are taught of God can form any just or adequate conception; and the joys and sorrows, the elevations and depressions, the dangers and escapes, incident to the spiritual warfare, produce in congenial breasts a lively sympathy.

Publications of this nature have accordingly met for the most part with a welcome reception, and have become one of the most popular and powerful instruments of piety. The religious public have long learned to form a just estimate of the Diary of Mr. Williams, of Kidderminster, an industrious and opulent manufacturer, who demonstrated the possibility of combining a prudent attention to commercial pursuits with a splendid exhibition of the Christian graces. The masculine sense, the fervent piety, the active benevolence of that most excellent man, will long contribute to enlighten and to animate Christians in a private rank, and to shed a lustre on the religious profession. A more perfect example perhaps was never exhibited to the imitation of active tradesmen. A devotion fervent but rational, zeal tempered by the exactest discretion, and a benevolence invariably regulated by the dictates of prudence and justice,—a transparent candour without weakness, and a wisdom without art,—combine to form a living picture of exalted yet attainable excellence.

The Life and Diary of David Brainerd, missionary to the American Indians, exhibits a perfect pattern of the qualities which should distinguish the instructer of rude and barbarous tribes; the most invincible patience and self-denial, the profoundest humility, exquisite prudence, indefatigable industry, and such a devotedness to God, or rather, such an absorption of the whole soul in zeal for the Divine glory and the salvation of men, as is scarcely to be paralleled since the age of the apostles. Such was the intense ardour of his mind, that it seems to have diffused the spirit of a martyr over the most common incidents of his life. His constitutional melancholy, though it must be regarded as a physical imperfection, imparts an additional interest and pathos to the narrative; since we more easily sympathize with the emotions of sorrow than of joy. There is a monotony in his feelings, it must be acknowledged, and consequently a frequent repetition of the same ideas, which will disgust a fastidious or superficial reader; but it is the monotony of sublimity.

The Life of Fletcher, of Madeley, affords in some respects a parallel, in others a contrast, to that of Brainerd: and it is curious to observe how the influence of natural temperament varies the exhibition of the same principles. With a considerable difference in their religious views, the same zeal, the same spirituality of mind, the same contempt of the world, is conspicuous in the character of each. But the lively imagination, the sanguine complexion of Fletcher permits him to triumph and exult in the consolatory truths and prospects of religion. He is a seraph who burns with the ardours of divine love; and spurning the fetters of mortality, he almost habitually seems to have anticipated the rapture of the beatific vision. Brainerd, oppressed with a constitutional melancholy, is chiefly occupied with the thoughts of his pollutions and defects in the eyes of Infinite Purity. His is a mourning and conflicting piety, imbued with the spirit of self-abasement, breathing itself forth in "groanings which cannot be uttered;" always dissatisfied with itself, always toiling in pursuit of a purity and perfection unattainable by mortals. The mind of Fletcher was habitually brightened with gratitude and joy for what he had attained; Brainerd was actuated with a restless solicitude for further acquisitions. If Fletcher soared to all the heights, it may be affirmed with equal truth that Brainerd sounded all the depths of Christian piety; and while the former was regaling himself with fruit from the tree of life, the latter, on the waves of an impetuous sea, was "doing business in the mighty waters."

Both equally delighted and accustomed to lose themse ves in the contemplation of the Deity, they seemed to have surveyed that Infinite Object under different aspects; and while Fletcher was absorbed in the contemplation of infinite benignity and love, Brainerd shrunk into nothing in the presence of immaculate purity and holiness.

The different situations in which they were placed had probably considerable effect in producing or heightening their respective peculiarities. Fletcher exercised his ministry in the calm of domestic life, surrounded with the beauties of nature; Brainerd pursued his mission in a remote and howling wilderness, where, in the midst of uncultivated savages, he was exposed to intolerable hardships and fatigues.

The religious public have lately been favoured with a rich accession to the recorded monuments of exalted piety, in the Life and Religious Experience of the lamented Henry Martyn. It is delightful to behold, in the history of that extraordinary man, talents which attracted the admiration of one of the most celebrated seats of learning consecrated to the honour of the Cross; an enterprising genius, in the ardour of youth, relinquishing the pursuit of science and of fame, in order to travel in the steps of a Brainerd and a Schwartz. Crowned with the highest honours a university could bestow, we see him quit the luxurious shades of academic bowers, for a tempestuous ocean and a burning clime,—for a life of peril and fatigue, from which he could expect no other reward than the heroic pleasure of communicating to perishing millions the word of eternal life. He appears to have formed his religious character chiefly on the model of Brainerd: and as he equalled him in his patience, fortitude, humility, and love, so he strictly resembled him in his end. Both nearly at the same age fell victims to a series of intolerable privations and fatigues, voluntarily incurred in the course of their exertions for the propagation of the faith of Jesus. And though their death was not a violent one, the sacrifices they made and the sufferings they endured entitle them to the honours and rewards of a protracted martyrdom. Their memory will be cherished by the veneration of all succeeding ages; and he who reads their lives will be ready to exclaim, "*Here* is the faith and patience of the saints."

If the biography of men such as these fails to produce all the benefit we might expect, some will be ready to impute it to that hopeless superiority of character which seems to place them almost above the reach of imitation. The justice of the inference, however, may be fairly questioned, since he who proposes for his imitation a model approaching to perfection, though he may not equal, will, probably, in the fervour of his exertions to copy it, take a higher flight than if he had contented himself with the contemplation of an inferior standard. He who forms his taste on the inimitable productions of a Raphael will reach nearer to perfection than he could arrive by the study of an inferior artist: and, for the purpose of restoring man to the image of his Maker, the wisdom of God has thought fit to exhibit a faultless model in the character of the incarnate Redeemer.

Before I dismiss the reader to the perusal of the following narrative, it may not be improper to apprize him of what he is to expect. If he hopes to be amused by the recital of striking occurrences and eventful passages, he will find himself disappointed. The following is not the history of a man bustling on the busy stage of life, and exposed to great vicissitudes of good or evil fortune: it is the simple unpretending narrative of a dissenting minister, who passed his days in the retirement of the country, in tranquil meditation, in the exercise of unosten tatious piety, and an assiduous attention to the spiritual improvement of his flock. Though he did not enjoy the benefit of a liberal education, my revered friend was possessed of an active inquisitive mind, which prompted him to devote much of his time to reading, and enabled him to acquire a large fund of general, but especially of theological knowledge. Few men, in similar circumstances, have availed themselves to an equal extent of the information which the best books in our language, on moral and religious subjects, supply. Reading with him was not merely a habit, but a passion. His curiosity was not limited within the circle of his profession: he was delighted with works on general literature, and purchased and perused some of the valuable elementary treatises on science. But as devotion was his peculiar element, it is not to be wondered at that theology in its various branches was his favourite study. Though he was far from neglecting the antiquities and the criticism of theology, as far as they are accessible to a mere English scholar, he placed his principal delight in the perusal of works immediately devoted to the inculcation of doctrinal and experimental religion: and in this pursuit his attention was forcibly drawn to the writings of the puritan divines, who, with all their imperfections of style and method, are unquestionably the safest of all uninspired guides. The masculine sense, the profound learning, the rich and unequalled unction of these fathers of the modern church, exerted a powerful influence on his mind, and greatly contributed to form and mature his character.

Of the great Mr. Howe, who shines in the firmament with a preeminent and unrivalled lustre, he always spoke in terms of just admiration, assigning him that preference among the nonconformist divines which it is surprising any one should dispute. The reader of the succeeding narrative will perceive, that for many years it was his constant practice to devote a considerable portion of each day to the perusal of the best practical writers; to which, under God, he was undoubtedly indebted for that habitual spirituality of mind which so remarkably distinguished him, and in which very few whom I have had the happiness of knowing appeared to equal, none to surpass him. His sense of the Divine presence, his relish for devout meditation and intercourse, his advertence to the great realities of a future life, seemed scarcely ever to forsake him; and the least that can be affirmed is, that "he walked with God."

Though he exercised his ministry, through the whole of his life, among the General Baptists, his sentiments approached nearer to hose of Mr. Baxter than to the system of Arminius, nor would his statements of Christian doctrine have given the slightest offence to a congregation of moderate Calvinists. But to polemical theology he was not attached; his religion was entirely of a practical and experimental character: nor did he attach the smallest importance to correct views of Christian doctrine, any further than as they tended to influence the heart. To Socinianism, in all its modifications, he entertained a most hearty and decided aversion, and few circumstances gave him more poignant uneasiness than to see some of the most conspicuous members of his church embrace and patronise that destructive heresy. In the latter years of his life he devoted a considerable portion of his time to composition; and his tract on Socinianism, his Directions and Encouragements for Travellers to Sion, his Advice to a young Minister, with other publications of a similar tendency,—the result of long experience, of much well-digested reading, and of patient thought,—will perpetuate and enrol his name among the most useful practical writers of the present day. Fond as he was of retirement, he retained a keen relish for the pleasures of society, for which he was eminently fitted by the gentleness of his manners, the amenity of his temper, and the variety of his knowledge. His conversation expressed and inspired serenity and cheerfulness rather than mirth; and he possessed, to a very extraordinary degree, the happy art of mingling a seasoning of piety with his hours of the greatest relaxation. The natural temperament of my revered friend inclined in some degree, I have been informed, to the irascible; but who ever beheld him betrayed for a moment into language or deportment incompatible with the meekness of the gospel? His exquisite sensibility is abundantly conspicuous in the following narrative, nor could it escape the observation of any person who enjoyed much of his intimacy; but it was so directed and refined, by a higher principle, as to become one of the most attractive qualities in his character.

The extreme depression of the manufacture in the place of his residence was a source of much uneasiness, both by the intense sympathy he felt for the sufferers, and the degree in which it affected his personal resources. It is painful to reflect, that a man "of whom the world was not worthy," perhaps never received from his people more than a moiety of the means of his subsistence; and that, after sinking the greater part of his scanty property, he must often have been involved in irretrievable difficulties, but for the casual liberality of friends whom his superior merit had attached. That, in a situation so full of embarrassment and perplexity, he retained a curiosity so eager, a passion for study and inquiry so unabated, as to induce him to spend a large sum of money in the purchase of books, is a decisive proof of his possessing a mind of no ordinary vigour. But I check myself. It was not my intention to write an encomium on the excellent person who is the subject of the following Memoir, but merely to introduce it to the reader's attention by a few prefatory remarks; and having already trespassed too long on his patience, I must be permitted to close, by expressing my earnest prayer that the effect of its perusal on as many as read it may be to assimilate their minds, in some degree at least, to the character of its excellent and lamented author.

EXTRACT

FROM MR. HALL'S ROUGH NOTES

OF THE

FUNERAL SERMON FOR DR. RYLAND.

Early in life he formed an intimacy with a set of writers who, however they may push some theoretical views to excess, are eminent for their elevated ideas of the moral character of the Deity, and for the zeal with which they contend for its influence on doctrinal and practical religion. Firm champions of disinterested love, they set themselves, with the greatest ardour, to expose those religious affections which are founded on mere selfishness, and which are excited merely by the conviction their possessors entertain of their having been the object of the Divine predilection, without any perception of the excellence and moral beauty of the Divine nature. They laid as the foundation of all vital religion a perception of moral beauty, a complacency in the Deity on account of his own intrinsic excellence, which, they contend, is a separate principle from mere gratitude for benefits expected or received, however it may enlarge and extend it. The originality displayed by these writers, at the head of whom the celebrated Edwards is placed by universal consent,—the acumen of their logic, and the fervour of their piety,—seized powerfully on the mind of Dr. Ryland in his early years, and gave a decisive turn to his subsequent studies and pursuits. From that time to the close of his life, the relation which Christianity bears to the display of the Divine character was ever present to his thoughts: he delighted in whatever tended to deepen and enlarge his conceptions of that ineffable original; he delighted especially to contemplate him under the character in which John presents him, when he affirms that "God is love,"—as a being possessing an infinite propensity to impart his "fulness," by diffusing the greatest possible sum of happiness throughout his vast dominions. These lofty musings were, with him, not the object of speculation only, or the discriminating features of a creed. He formed the interior of his character upon them; they were his mental aliment, and intimately incorporated with his thoughts. Nor can it be doubted that, in a mind so prepared by divine grace as was his, they exercised a most [beneficial] influence, and produced a luxuriant crop of Christian virtues. He appeared to be penetrated with a perpetual sense of the Divine presence ; not as a source of terror or dismay, but of habitual peace, confidence, and joy. " He endured as seeing him that is invisible." His love to the Great Supreme was equally exempt from slavish timidity and presumptuous familiarity. It was an awful love, such as, in a very inferior degree, the beatific vision must be supposed to inspire, trembling with ecstasy, while prostrate with awe.

[*Compare the above with* pp. 220, *and* 215, Vol. I.]

AN ADDRESS,

CIRCULATED AT THE FORMATION OF THE LEICESTER AUXILIARY BIBLE SOCIETY, FEBRUARY 19, 1810.

We feel peculiar satisfaction in announcing to the public the formation of an Auxiliary Bible Society at Leicester, the object of which is, to co-operate with the parent society in London in giving as extensive a circulation as possible to the Holy Scriptures. Notwithstanding the diversity of sentiment which unhappily prevails among Christians, we may fairly presume on the concurrence of all parties and denominations in promoting a design so disinterested as that of diffusing the light of revelation. In the prosecution of this design our party is the world; the only distinction we contemplate is between the disciples of revelation and the unhappy victims of superstition and idolatry; and as we propose to circulate the Bible without notes or comments, truth only can be a gainer by the measure. To those who confine their views to this country, the want of Bibles may not appear very urgent; but, without insisting on the many thousands even *here* who are destitute of them, it is certain that in pagan, Mahometan, and popish countries they are extremely rare, and their number totally inadequate, not merely to supply the immense population in those parts, but even the increasing demand which a variety of circumstances have combined to produce. To supply this demand, to whatever extent it may be carried, is the aim of the society in London with which this is designed to co-operate. Their ambition, as far as it may please God to smile upon their efforts, is, by imparting the Holy Scriptures, to open the fountain of revelation to all nations. It was natural and necessary for the first movement in so great an enterprise to commence at the heart of the empire; nor is it less so, that, having commenced there, it should propagate itself through the larger vessels and arteries to the remotest extremities of the body. We have the pleasure of perceiving that the example of the metropolis has already been followed in several of our principal towns and cities; and there is room to hope that similar institutions will, ere long, be formed in every part of the kingdom. Nor has the emulation excited been confined to this nation and its dependencies; societies of the same description have been formed at Philadelphia, at Berlin, and at Basle, each of which derives support and assistance from the original one established in the metropolis of Great Britain. While so general an alacrity has been evinced on this occasion, it had ill become the character of the town of Leicester to stand neuter, highly distinguished as it is for its great and ancient respectability, as well as for the extent of its establishments, and exertions in the cause of religion and charity. We have the pleasure of reflecting that the meeting so obligingly called by the mayor was numerously and respectably attended, that the utmost harmony prevailed in its proceedings, and that there appeared throughout an utter oblivion of party distinctions, with an emulation in each individual to promote to the utmost the purposes for which we were convened.

In whatever light we consider the British and Foreign Bible Society, it appears to us replete with utility. Its formation will, we trust, constitute a new era in the history of religion, which may be styled the era of unanimity. It affords a rallying point for the piety of the age, an unsuspicious medium of communication between the good of all parties and nations, a centre of union and co-operation in the advancement of a common cause, which cannot fail to allay the heats and smooth the asperities of discordant sentiment. By giving the most effectual aid to means already set on foot for the conversion of pagan nations, it also promises to accelerate the period when truth shall become victorious in the earth. When the pure light of revelation once shines amid the darkness of polytheism, we may venture to hope that the latter will be gradually expelled, that the contrast of truth and error, of sacred mysteries and preposterous fictions, they respectively display, will be deeply and extensively felt. What the Bible Society proposes, let it be remembered, is not to circulate such a number of copies of the New Testament in foreign parts as shall merely suffice to gratify the curiosity of the learned, to adorn a museum, or to enrich a library; but to lay them open, if possible, to all classes of society in every nation. What incalculable benefits may be expected to result from the completion of such a plan! Wherever the Scriptures are generally read, the standard of morals is raised, the public mind is expanded, a spirit of inquiry excited, and the sphere of intellectual vision inconceivably enlarged. While they contribute most essentially to the improvement of reason, by presenting to its contemplation the noblest objects, they aid its weakness and supply its deficiencies by information beyond its reach. If "to know the only true God, and Jesus Christ whom he has sent," be, as our Saviour assures us, "eternal life," to adopt effectual measures for imparting that knowledge must be allowed to be the most genuine exercise of benevolence. It is to be lamented that Protestant nations have been too long inattentive to this object: we rejoice to find that they are now convinced of their error; and that, touched with commiseration for the unhappy condition of mankind, they are anxious to impart those riches which may be shared without being diminished, and communicated without being lost to the possessor. Such is the felicity of religion,—such the unbounded liberality of its principles. Though we should be sorry to administer fuel to national vanity, we cannot conceal the satisfaction it gives us to reflect, that while the fairest portion of the globe has fallen a prey to that guilty and restless ambition which, by the inscrutable wisdom of Providence, is permitted for a time to take peace from the earth, this favoured country is employed in spreading the triumphs of truth, multiplying the means of instruction, and opening sources of consolation to an afflicted world. In these eventful times, so pregnant with difficulty and danger, we consider this as affording a most favourable omen of the ultimate intentions of Providence respecting this nation.

Having briefly explained our object and motives, we beg leave to recommend the Leicester Auxiliary Bible Society to the patronage of an enlightened public, not doubting they will feel the propriety of lending their support to an institution which, besides the circulation of the Scriptures abroad, promises to provide for our domestic wants, by enabling the poorest person to possess himself of that invaluable treasure.

A SPEECH,

DELIVERED AT THE SECOND ANNIVERSARY MEETING OF THE LEICESTER AUXILIARY BIBLE SOCIETY, APRIL 13, 1812.

Permit me to say that I heartily concur in the sentiments so forcibly expressed by the respectable speakers who have preceded me. The more I reflect upon the constitution, operation, and genius of the Bible Society, the more is my conviction confirmed of its excellence and utility. It is matter of surprise to me, that an institution so admirable, and so beneficial, should meet with the least opposition from the professors of our common Christianity, when the propriety of making the Scriptures as extensively known as possible might be supposed to pass among Protestants for an incontrovertible maxim. To imagine such a measure can be carried into effect without being productive of much good, and still more to augur mischievous consequences as the probable result, approaches so near to an impeachment of the perfection and sufficiency of the divine oracles, that to my poor judgment it appears difficult, if not impossible, to distinguish them. For my part, I am at an utter loss to conceive of a revelation from heaven *that must not be trusted alone;* of a rule of life and manners which in the same breath is declared to be perfect, and yet so obscure and incompetent that its tendency to mislead shall be greater than its tendency to conduct in the right path; of a fountain of truth (and the only original fountain as our opponents themselves allow) more calculated, when left to its silent operation, to send forth bitter waters than sweet. If these must appear to a candid and impartial mind untenable and contradictory propositions, then must the chief objections of our opponents fall to the ground, and their prognostics of danger, from the operations of the Bible Society, be pronounced chimerical and unfounded. Whoever weighs the arguments of our opponents must be convinced that they all turn upon the following supposition—that the Scriptures are so ambiguous and obscure, that when left to themselves they are more likely to generate error than truth, to foment division than to produce unanimity and agreement. If this implies no reflection on the excellence of the Bible, and the wisdom of its Divine Author, what, I will ask, can imply such a reflection? And if this be not admitted, how is it possible for a moment to entertain a scruple respecting the propriety of giving them the most extensive circulation?

To dread the indiscriminate perusal of the Scriptures, and, under pretence of tender consideration for the weakness of the common people, prohibit their circulation, has always been regarded as one of the most detestable features of popery. From the very dawn of the Reformation it has been stigmatized by Protestants of every description, as constituting a principal branch of the mystery of iniquity. But wherein does the maxim of our opponents differ from that of the papists on this subject? If any difference can be perceived, it is certainly not in the *nature* but in the *extension* of the principle. The papists contend that the common people are not to be intrusted with the Bible *at all;* while our opponents assert that they are not to be trusted with it *alone.* The former instruct their votaries to shut their ears against the voice of God altogether; the latter insist that it is dangerous to hear it except in immediate conjunction with their own interpretation. Surely this must be considered as strange language in a Protestant country, and most offensive to Protestant ears.

What is the reason that the Scriptures may not be trusted alone? "Why," say our opponents, "they are liable to be misinterpreted, and wrested to countenance the respective opinions and practices of different sects and parties." Be it so: we admit this to be possible; but what remedy can be devised to obviate this evil? Is their use to be entirely proscribed? "No," say our opponents, "but they must be invariably accompanied by another book, which may be considered in the light of an authorized commentary." But we would ask again, are we to judge of this commentary; or are we to receive it simply on the ground of authority, and upon the principle of implicit faith; or is any exercise of private judgment permitted to us? If it be replied that it is not, this is neither more nor less than open and barefaced popery. If the judgment is to be exerted at all, and every thing is not to be taken upon trust, their commentary must be judged of by some criterion, and what can that be but the Scriptures? The Scriptures must then, after all, be appealed to, before it is possible to determine on the correctness of the commentary; and thus we are led back to the precise point from which we set out, that is, the examination of the Scriptures. According to the views of our opponents, we are either to admit the principle of implicit faith to its utmost extent, which is open and avowed popery; or we are first to interpret the Scriptures by the commentary, and then judge of the commentary by the Scriptures. This is the circle out of which it is impossible for our opponents to escape, and they may be lashed round it to all eternity! Let it once be admitted that the sacred volume is the only standard of truth, and the only infallible directory in practice, and it will necessarily follow that all other modes of instruction must be tried by it; and consequently, that every idea of giving it a corrective, or a companion, call it which you please, must be futile and absurd. I am persuaded I am speaking the sentiments, on this occasion, of every individual present at this meeting, and not abetting the views of any particular party. I trust none in the present assembly will do me the injustice of supposing that any reflection is intended upon the liturgy: though a Protestant dissenter, I am by no means insensible to its merits. I believe that the evangelical purity of its sentiments, the chastised fervour of its devotion and the majestic simplicity of its language, have combined to place it in the very first rank of uninspired compositions. The maxim we wish to establish, as amply sufficient to overrule the objections of ou· opponents, is simply that which in the hands of the immortal Chillingworth was found capable of demolishing the whole fabric of popery. "The Bible," said he, "the Bible alone, is the religion of Protestants."

The conduct of those who have distinguished themselves by their opposition to the Bible Society is also inconsistent in another point. While they deprecate the operations of the Bible Society in circulating the Bible alone in this country, they applaud this very identical measure in its application to foreign parts. This appears to me a very extraordinary conduct. Their proceeding can only be justified on the admission, that notwithstanding the possible perversion of the Scripture to ill purposes, it is calculated, when left to itself, to do good on the whole. In this instance, it is conceded that its use more than counterbalances the possible inconveniences arising from its abuse; a clear surplus of good is contemplated as the probable result, for, without such an expectation, how can the measure in question be entitled to commendation for a moment? I would ask, then, what principle of reasoning is that which will justify an opposition to the scheme of action which, it is admitted, is likely on the whole to do good, although it may possibly be accompanied with a portion of evil allowedly inferior. Are not all the calculations of prudence founded on a comparison of advantages and disadvantages? Have not all the plans of benevolence which have ever been devised proceeded on a necessary compromise with contingent evils, where, if it can be demonstrated that these bear no proportion to the good likely to result, every requisition is satisfied, and every reasonable suffrage secured? Are we to sit still, and attempt nothing for the improvement of our species, until we are mathematically certain that nothing can possibly spring from our efforts but pure, unmingled, defecated good; and this in a world abounding with imperfections of all sorts, where evil is so widely diffused as to insinuate itself into every mode of action, and every element of enjoyment? If this is not pretended, why should it be deemed necessary for the operations of the Bible Society to furnish an exception; or that it should be perfectly free from that portion of inconvenience and evil which cleaves to all the works of men? When our enemies object to the distribution of the Scriptures alone in this country, and at the same time applaud the same measures with respect to foreign parts, they surely forget that the same objections apply, and with equal force, to the latter as to the former proceeding. The obscurity of which they complain, which exposes them to the danger of being misinterpreted, their liability to be wrested to countenance error, heresy, and schism, are properties which, I presume, we shall not be very ready to ascribe to them. But, admitting them to possess these qualities, will they lose them by being conveyed to distan countries? Is their tendency to be pronounced pernicious or salutary according to the degrees of latitude and longitude? Are there not a variety of sects and parties on the Continent, as well as in Great Britain, to whose views the perversion of them may be rendered subservient? Is the information they afford in this country doubtful and obscure, and does it become at once clear and decisive when it is communicated in foreign parts? As our opponents seem to suppose they possess a valetudinarian habit, and require a very delicate management in this country, perhaps they imagine their constitution may be improved by a sea-voyage, and change of air!

Let it be carefully remembered, that the topics insisted upon by the objectors to the Bible Society are precisely those on which the papists have been wont to insist in their controversy with Protestants,—the obscurity of the Scriptures, the danger of misinterpretation, and the facility with which they may be wrested to the support of heresy and schism. It is surely little to the credit of our opponents, that they have no other weapons to attack us with but what have been undeniably forged in the camp of the Philistines. It would, unquestionably, be an ill omen to this country, if pleas drawn from the supposed insufficiency of Scripture should be again received, and become popular, which have been the principal means, in former ages, of involving the world in the darkness of superstition and idolatry. The perversion of the Bible can proceed only from the corruption of its readers:—now, what is the remedy for this corruption but the Scriptures themselves? Have they who oppose our proceeding discovered, in the plenitude of their wisdom, any better corrective of the ill propensities of the heart, the attachment to vice, a conceit of superior understanding, and the love of change, which are the prolific sources of error, than those lively oracles which God himself has declared are able to make us wise unto salvation? "The heavens and the earth," it is true, "declare the glory of God, and the firmament showeth his handiwork." This effect, however, they must be understood to produce only in minds rightly disposed; for, in point of fact, they have been the innocent means of enticing millions to idolatry, while they never, as far as we know, reclaimed a single individual from that impiety. Hence the Psalmist, after celebrating these works of the Most High, directs our attention to a superior source of illumination, adding, "The law of the Lord is perfect, converting the soul." St. Paul congratulates Timothy upon his having known, from a child, the Holy Scriptures, which were able to make him, with faith in Christ, wise unto salvation. "All Scripture is given by inspiration of God, and is profitable for doctrine, for correction, for reproof, for instruction in righteousness; that the man of God may be perfect, thoroughly furnished unto every good word and work." When I reflect on these passages, and others of the same import, I feel no difficulty in acceding to the declaration of Lord Francis Osborne, that a child might answer the ablest of our opponents, provided that child were a Christian.

It is asserted that we have no reason to expect the conversion of foreign nations in consequence of the sole perusal of the sacred volume and in support of this opinion our adversaries urge a passage in the Epistle of St. Paul to the Romans:—"How shall they call on him on whom they have not believed; and how shall they believe on him of whom they have not heard; and how shall they hear without a preacher?" This inference appears to me to be founded upon an entire misconstruction of the passage: the apostle means to distinguish between the situation of those who are necessarily unacquainted with the character of the Saviour, and that of the persons to whom this information was conveyed; without intending to determine, or at least to lay any stress on, the precise mode of communication by which they obtained it. This is the more manifest from the extension of meaning in which the term *preach* is used by the same writer:—"For Moses," saith the same St. Paul, "hath in every city them that *preach* him, being *read* in the synagogue every Sabbath-day." But such is the want of candour on the part of our adversaries, and such the unworthy artifices by which they pervert the language of Scripture from the simplicity and majesty of its meaning.

It might be naturally concluded, from this species of objection to the Bible Society, that our opponents were distinguished by a more than ordinary portion of zeal for the propagation of Christianity in foreign parts, by the aid of missionaries: I sincerely wish the result of an attention to facts were such as would justify this inference. The friends of the Bible Society, it is well known, are the warmest supporters of foreign missions; and the holy flame by which they are animated expands in all directions, stimulating them at once to the most active exertions in the distribution of the Scriptures at home, and for the support of the ministry of the gospel in pagan countries. When we compare with their conduct the coldness and indifference of our adversaries to this object, we are compelled to perceive that the invidious preference they give to one mode of doing good is not so much to be ascribed to their peculiar attachment to it, as to a desire of depreciating and depressing the importance of another.

Permit me to close these observations (for the length of which I ought already to apologize to the respectable audience I am addressing) with briefly noticing some of the indirect, though important, advantages likely to result from the establishment and progress of the Bible Society. The direct benefit we contemplate as the fruit of this institution will undoubtedly be reaped by that innumerable multitude, among all nations, who by means of it will be furnished with an opportunity of perusing the sacred volume; but there are other collateral advantages of the most important kind which have already been experienced in part, and may be expected to accrue still more hereafter, from the admirable society of which this is an auxiliary branch. Among these we cannot pass over its tendency to promote a good understanding among Christians of different denominations. It pretends not, indeed, to cast any light on the questions which have unhappily divided the Christian world; but as far as the objects of it are concerned, it consigns them to oblivion;—it presents a common ground of co-operation, and a centre of union, without a sacrifice of principle, or the surrender of the smallest atom of the respective opinions and practices by which we are distinguished. Who but the Author and Giver of all concord could have put into the hearts of the children of men a design so beneficial and godlike, so adapted to allay the heats and animosities which have so often disturbed the peace of society, and disfigured our common Christianity? It is like the "precious ointment upon the head, that ran down upon the beard, even Aaron's beard, that went down to the skirts of his garments." It is, indeed, a most sacred perfume; and while it is so abundantly poured out in the view of all nations, I cannot but imagine I see it ascending in clouds of incense to heaven, grateful to God, to his saints, and to the holy angels, consecrating this happy soil, and drawing down upon it a copious shower of benedictions and blessings. How much unanimity strengthens, and discord enfeebles, the sinews of empire, is too obvious to need to be insisted on; nor was there ever a period in the history of Great Britain when the former was more to be desired or the latter more to be deprecated. The Bible Society is a solemn and public recognition, calculated beyond any event that has yet transpired to confound infidelity, and to expel from the nation the last relics of that detestable impiety, to shut up every crevice of the infernal pit, and disperse every atom of the pestilential stream. The sophistry of infidels had been successfully confuted by a succession of able writers; they have retired, baffled, from the field, their arrows spent, their ammunition exhausted; and nothing remained but to signalize the victory by a public monument, and to imbody the national sentiment by erecting a public trophy out of the spoils of the enemy. This idea the Bible Society has nobly realized, by taking pledges from the statesmen, the senators, the nobles of the land, of their devoted attachment to the Word of God: they have publicly lifted up their voice, and declared, in the face of all Europe, that the Bible is the religion of Great Britain. What lustre does this shed upon our country! It appears the grand seminary of Christian principle: perhaps there is no single moment, night or day, in which some voice does not rise up to heaven in its behalf: and prayer is the grand key that unlocks the celestial treasury.

It is not too much to hope that the attachment to the gospel avowed by those who have co-operated in the measures of this society, will be followed by an increased attention on their part to explore its contents, to imbibe its spirit, and to regulate their lives by its precepts; and that thus the interests of vital Christianity may keep pace with the more extensive promulgation of revealed truth. Let our activity in the cause be followed up by an increased spirit of attachment and investigation; let us earnestly desire to taste that bread of life which it is the property of this society to communicate: then shall we be a happy because a holy people, and this will throw around us a greater splendour than Roman or Grecian genius could bestow. Should the sentiments of that divine book take possession of the heart, and mould the character of the inhabitants of this country, it would secure to the nation a higher protection than all its military and naval preparations; and even the rocks with which our isle is girt would in comparison be a feeble rampart against the assaults of our enemy. With perfect composure we leave the decision of this great controversy—and a greater never engaged the attention of mankind—to the arbitration of the Supreme Judge, without the smallest apprehension that we shall be called to an account—in that day when the earth and the works thereof shall be burnt up, and the elements shall melt with fervent heat—for having unrolled too widely that volume which discloses to the eye of faith the realities and prospects of eternity. Nor will it be deemed presumption if I affirm, that in a dying hour, when the interests and passions which now agitate us shall shrink to their due dimensions, it will afford us more satisfaction in the retrospect to have been the friends than the enemies of the Bible Society

A SPEECH,

DELIVERED AT

THE GUILDHALL, LEICESTER,

Tuesday, July 15, 1817.

AT THE SEVENTH ANNIVERSARY OF THE AUXILIARY BIBLE SOCIETY.

It has been usual on these occasions to eulogize the Bible Society, I will not say beyond its merits, for they are more than equal to the powers of the most exalted panegyric; but the frequency of these encomiums must be my apology for saying but little on that topic at present. The stores of rhetoric appear to me to be exhausted; while every department of nature and of art has been summoned and made to contribute its share to the illustration of the divine simplicity of its principle, the sanctity of its object, and the extent and grandeur of its operations Never was there an institution which at once went so far forward in the distribution of its benefits, and exerted such a reflex energy on its members and patrons, producing a generous enthusiasm, which kindles at every step, and is raised to a more intense degree by every fresh achievement.

I consider this society as a new moral power, which, combining the energies of Christendom in one great effort, promises to change the face of the universe; while, in imitation of Him in whose cause it is enlisted, it travels in the greatness of its strength, "mighty to save." It possesses every characteristic of the work of God, in which the simplest means are made to produce the greatest effects; where there is the utmost economy in the contrivance, and the greatest splendour and magnificence in the design. The imbecility of man appears in the littleness of his ends, which he accomplishes, for the most part, by complicated and laborious operations. Omnipotence, on the contrary, places opulence in the end, and parsimony in the means. While our pride is mortified by perceiving how little we can effect by the greatest efforts, the Almighty touches a secret spring known only to himself, and impresses a single motion, which propagates itself in circles continually extending, till it reaches the extremity of the universe, and diffuses order and happiness through regions most remote from its origin, and most unconscious of its cause.

Of so similar a character is the Bible Society, and so analogous to the movements of Divine power, that it appears to me it would be impious not to acknowledge the agency of the Spirit in its first conception, as much as the superintendence of Providence in its support. To fix upon a course of action which gives scope to every virtuous energy, while it stands perfectly aloof from the spirit of party,—which draws towards itself the best propensities of our common nature, and unites the pious of every nation and profession in one harmonious family,—is not the work of a mortal; it bespeaks the finger of God. Its direct benefits are too obvious to escape the most careless observation; but the indirect influence it exerts in harmonizing the spirits and conciliating the affections of such as had long been alienated from each other, is so remarkable as to make it doubtful whether its instruments or its objects,—whether those who share or those who dispense its munificence,—are the greatest gainers.

The utility of this admirable institution, however, has been called in question, its constitution censured, and its operations arraigned. To give the Bible to all classes and descriptions, without note or comment, is represented by some as a dangerous experiment, adapted to perplex and mislead uncultivated minds. Excellent as the Scriptures are allowed to be, some preparation, it is asserted, is necessary ere they are communicated in their full extent, and that the best use that can be immediately made of them is to compose and distribute such selections and abridgments as seem best calculated for popular instruction.

That some portions of the sacred volume are of more universal interest than others,—that the New Testament, for example, has a more immediate relation to our prospects and to our duties than the Old,—is freely conceded: just as one star differs from another star in glory, though they are all placed in the same firmament, and are the work of the same hand. But to this restrictive system, this jealous policy, which would exclude a part of the word of God from universal inspection and perusal, we feel insuperable objections; nor are we disposed to ascribe to any description of men whatever that control over Divine communications which such a measure implies. We are persuaded that no man possesses a right to curtail the gifts of God, or to deal out with a sparing hand what was intended for universal patrimony. If the manner in which revelation was imparted be such as makes it manifest that it was originally designed for the benefit of all, we are at a loss to conceive how any man can have a right, by his interference, to render it inaccessible.

The question itself, whether it was designed to be communicated to mankind at large without distinction, or to a particular class, with a discretionary power of communicating it at such times and in such proportions as they might deem fit, can only be determined by itself. If it bear decisive indications of its being intended for private custody,—if it be found to affirm or even to insinuate that it is not meant for universal circulation,—we must submit to hold it at the discretion of its legitimate guardians, and to accept with becoming gratitude such portions as they are pleased to bestow. From the word of God there can be no appeal: it must decide its own character, and determine its own pretensions. Thus much we must be allowed to assume: that if it was originally given to mankind indiscriminately, no power upon earth is entitled to restrict it; because, on the supposition which we are now making, since every man's original right in it was equal, that right can be cancelled by no authority but that which bestowed it. If it was at first promulgated under the character of a universal standard of faith and practice, we are bound to recognise it in that character; and every attempt to alter it, to convert into private what was originally public property, or to make a monopoly of a universal grant, is an act of extreme presumption and impiety. It is to assume a superiority over revelation itself.

Let us see then how the matter stands. Let us ascend to its original, and examine in what shape it was first communicated.

Though we are accustomed to speak of the Bible as *one* book, it is in truth a collection of many, composed at different periods and by different writers, as holy men of God were moved by the Holy Ghost.

To speak first of the Old Testament. The Old Testament was distributed by the Jews into three parts:—the Pentateuch; the earlier and later Prophets, including some historical compositions; and the Hagiographs, or Holy Writings, consisting chiefly of the Book of Job, the Proverbs, and the Psalms.

With respect to the Pentateuch, it is a matter of notoriety that it was delivered with the utmost publicity, and was neither more nor less than the public and municipal law of the Jewish commonwealth, which every king, on his ascending the throne, was commanded to copy with his own hand, as the perpetual rule of his government; and every head of a family to teach and inculcate on his children, when he sat in his house, and when he walked by the way. It was first proclaimed from the top of Mount Sinai, with ineffable splendour, in the hearing of the whole nation, prefaced with the remarkable words, "Hear, O Israel." There is surely no pretence for representing it as a deposite committed to a particular class, when an accurate acquaintance with it was requisite in order to regulate the private as well as public life of every Israelite. Though, in process of time, its interpretation gave birth to a particular profession, whose followers are styled scribes in the New Testament, nothing was further from their thoughts than the assumption of a right to withhold it from public perusal: their employment was, partly by an accurate transcription to preserve the purity of the copies, and partly to elucidate its obscurities.

If we descend to the Prophets, we shall find them addressing their instructions, and announcing their predictions, in the most public manner, to all descriptions of persons—to princes, to nobles, to the populace, in crowded assemblies, in places of the most public resort. Such was the manner in which Jeremiah prophesied:—"I am full," saith he, "of the fury of the Lord; I am weary with holding in; I will pour it out upon the children abroad, and upon the assembly of young men together." (Jer. vi. 11.) When strong political reasons seemed to dictate a different proceeding, when he was violently importuned by his sovereign to conceal his predictions, lest he should weaken the hands of the people and encourage their enemies, he remained inflexible, and continued to divulge the suggestions of inspiration with the same publicity as before. Yet it is the prophetic part of Scripture which is the most obscure, and most liable to be perverted to the purposes of popular delusion.

Of the Hagiographs little need be said. As they consist chiefly of maxims of civil prudence, sentiments of devotion, and sublime descriptions of the Deity and his works, it is probable none will contend for their restricted circulation.

Let us take a rapid glance at the New Testament. Here the Gospels will claim our first attention: and with respect to these, if we are to credit the earliest ecclesiastical writers, they are a mere abstract of the preaching of the respective apostles and evangelists whose names they bear. We are informed, that when they were about to leave certain countries, where they had been employed for a considerable time in disseminating the gospel, the inhabitants of those districts were anxious to possess a permanent record of the principal facts in which they had been instructed, that by reading them at their leisure they might in the absence of their teachers impress them on their memory. The Gospels of Mark and Luke are affirmed, by the earliest historians, to have been composed from the preaching of St. Peter and St. Paul, and not to have been published until they had received the entire approbation of those apostles. This part of Scripture, then, supplies no pretence or apology for the practice of restricted distribution.

The Epistles next come in order: and these, as is evident from their inscriptions, were addressed to whole assemblies of the faithful; in which rich and poor, learned and unlearned, Jew and gentile, were incorporated on terms of religious equality. They were also read publicly every Lord's-day; in the devotional exercises of which the recitation of the Scriptures, after the manner of the ancient synagogue, occupied a conspicuous place. We find St. Paul strongly adjuring one of the societies to which he wrote to take care that his epistle was read to "all the holy brethren."

There is one extraordinary book, of a character totally distinct from the rest, which closes the canon of inspiration. The book to which I refer, you are aware, is the Revelation of St. John;—a composition distinguished, above all others, by a profusion of obscure, figurative diction; delineating, by a sort of hieroglyphics, the principal revolutions destined to befall the Christian church, from the earliest times till the consummation of all things. This portion of Scripture is a fertile mine of erroneous, extravagant conjecture, and supplies, by its injudicious interpretation, more gratification to a heated imagination to a taste for the marvellous and incredible, than the whole of the New Testament besides; insomuch, that few have been found capable of preserving a perfect sobriety and composure in the midst of its stupendous scenery, where the curtain rises and falls so often, where new creations so rapidly succeed each other, accompanied by myriads of the angelic order, and the sound of trumpets, and of voices, and thunderings, and lightnings. Yet it is sufficiently remarkable, that this is the only book to the perusal of which an express benediction is attached: "Blessed is he that readeth, and they that hear the words of this prophecy." Its integrity is also guarded and secured by a fearful measure denounced against such as shall presume to alter it in the minutest tittle, by adding to or taking away from its words. The Holy Spirit, foreseeing, what actually ensued, that the peculiar features of this prophecy would excite the prejudices of some, and in others its obscurity induce neglect, judged it necessary to employ a special precaution against its falling into contempt or oblivion.

Thus it appears, from a rapid induction of particulars, that the Bible is a common property, over which there is no human control; that, as "all Scripture is given by inspiration of God," so it is all "profitable for doctrine, for reproof, for correction, for instruction in righteousness, that the man of God may be perfect, thoroughly furnished for every good word and work."

In addition to what has been said, it is also proper to remark, that translations of the sacred book were early made, for the benefit of the unlearned, in the vernacular language of the countries into which Christianity had spread; that various versions in the Latin were published in the West, and the Syriac in the East, either during the lives of the apostles or in the period immediately succeeding: nor was it ever made a question during the first centuries, whether the inspired writings should be laid open to universal inspection. The Christian fathers were well known to have inculcated their perusal on all sorts of men; nor are the most celebrated of them, St. Austin and St. Chrysostom, ever more eloquent than when engaged in unfolding their excellence, and expatiating on their utility, to persons of every description.

It was not till "the man of sin" had placed himself in the temple of God, and exalted himself "above all that is called God, and that is worshipped," that a different policy prevailed, and the people were told that they must be content to derive their religious information only through the medium of priests.

Is it possible to conceive a greater insult? If we should resent the attempt to disturb an ancient possession, and to remove the landmarks which bound and ascertain the inheritance of our fathers, what ought we to feel when a scheme is set on foot to deprive us of the record of our salvation, of the charter of our immortality? Who are they who pretend a right to sit in judgment on the contents of revelation,—to determine what is proper to be communicated and what withheld, as though they were sifting the chaff from the wheat? Is it come to this, that the medicine of life is to be dealt out with a sparing and cautious hand, and mixed with foreign ingredients, like arsenic or hemlock, which are only safe when administered in a diluted form, and in small quantities? What is it which has lifted these pretenders to such an envied superiority over their fellow-creatures, while the whole species, sick and infirm, are consigned to the skill of the same great Physician, and are either in a state of spiritual death, or under one and the same process of cure?

Apprehensive as I am of exhausting your patience, there are yet two considerations to which I would direct your attention, sufficient to demonstrate the importance of not relinquishing that right with which God and nature have invested you.

First, The great mass of mankind have no possible motives to tempt them to pervert the dictates of inspiration. The Bible is safest in the custody of those who have no temptation to abuse it, by forcing upon it a language foreign from its original intention. Such is the precise situation of the great body of the people. Their concern in religion is of the purest and most unsuspicious nature, since the only advantage which it is conceivable they can derive from it is assistance towards holy living and dying. If it fail to put them in possession of a share in the common salvation, there is no subordinate end to be answered, no private emolument attainable by its means to compensate for their loss. If it be ineffectual to enlighten and to save them, there is no other benefit which they can flatter themselves with the hope of deriving from it. You in this assembly who sustain no clerical character possess this advantage, at least, over the ministers of religion, that you have no temptations to make a gain of godliness. Your religion either promotes your eternal welfare, or it is nothing to you. How far this is from being the case with the Romish hierarchy, through all its ranks and gradations, from his holiness to the meanest ecclesiastic, few of you need to be informed. The loftiest pretensions to universal empire, the prostration of Christendom at their feet, a plenary power of absolution, of opening the gates of purgatory and of paradise;—this gigantic dominion, extending to the living and the dead, founds itself entirely on a perverted interpretation of the Scriptures: and were they laid open to the people in their true intent and meaning, the whole fabric would melt and disappear like a cloud. When we remember this, we cease to be surprised at the extreme animosity which his holiness has evinced to the free circulation of the Scriptures. Their circulation is the sure presage of his destruction; and the roar of his bull (if I may be allowed a pun on so serious a subject) is but the instinctive cry of a beast which feels itself goaded to madness by the operations of the Bible Society. To commit the custody of the Bible to men who have so deep and vital an interest in its suppression, would be to commit the lamb to the care of the wolf. No, my countrymen! the situation of his holiness possesses nothing in common with ours; and our feelings accord to our situations. He calls for darkness (and well he may), to prevent the detection of his errors; we, for light, to conduct us in the pursuit of truth. He courts the shade, to conceal his enormities; we ask for illumination, to enable us to perform our duties. The book which we are employed in circulating sufficiently solves the problem:—"He that doeth evil hateth the light, neither cometh to the light, lest his deeds should be reproved: he that doeth truth cometh to the light, that his deeds may be made manifest that they are wrought in God." When the Romish church found she had deviated too far from the religion of the New Testament to render a reconciliation practicable, she proceeded to take away the key of knowledge, by opposing every possible obstacle to its progress; and having availed herself of the ignorance of the age and the apathy of the people to establish her claims to infallibility, she became a standard to herself. Thus she rendered detection impossible: nor did she ever feel herself safe till the stage was completely darkened, till every chink and crevice was closed through which a ray could penetrate. Thus was the reign of superstition established: but were we to attempt a recital of a thousandth part of the fearful impieties she was guilty of, and the bloody tragedies she acted in the dark,—her impostures, oppressions, cruelties, and murders,—we should detain you till midnight, and leave the tale half-told. Suffice it to observe, that this mystery of iniquity was founded on a prevailing ignorance of the Scriptures, and was completed by reducing them to a monopoly.

Secondly, The next remark to which I would request your attention is, that heresies have seldom or never taken their rise from the mass of the people. Look at the history, trace the origin of the principal corruptions of Christianity which have prevailed at different periods, and you will uniformly find that they commenced in the higher classes, among men of leisure and speculation; that they were the product of perverted ingenuity and of unsanctified talent. Adapted to subserve the purposes of avarice and ambition, they were the invention of spiritual wickedness in high places. The commonalty, tenacious of the habits of thinking and acting to which they have been trained, are slow in adopting novelties, and the last to be misled by the illusions of hypothesis, or the false refinements of theory. The progress of opinion is from the higher to the lower orders; and it is as unnatural for it to begin at the bottom as for water to ascend from the valleys to the hills. The doctrine of transubstantiation is too much at war with common sense to have originated with the common people, any more than the doctrines of purgatory, auricular confession, the worship of the host, or the infallibility of the pope; all of which were gradually obtruded on the laity by the artifices of a designing priesthood, whose interest and ambition they promoted. Far from running into these absurdities of their own accord, the people, harassed, confounded, and dismayed, were hunted into the toils by men who made merchandise of souls. Let but the great body of the people be enlightened by the word of God, let them comprehend its truths, and imbibe its maxims, and they will form the firmest bulwarks against the encroachments of popery, as well as every other erroneous and delusive system. It is in a virtuous and an enlightened population, and especially in a yeomanry and peasantry informed and actuated by the true spirit of religion, we look for the security and preservation of its best interests. It was among them that Christianity commenced its earliest triumphs; among them the Reformation begun by Luther found its first and fastest friends: and as it was in this department of society our holy religion first penetrated, should the time arrive for its disappearance in other quarters, it is here that it will find its last and safe retreat.

An ingenious allusion was made, in your report, to Catholic emancipation—a subject on which the public mind is much divided. To agitate the question of the expediency of that measure on the present occasion would be highly improper; but I may be permitted to remark, that however our sentiments may vary on the subject of emancipation, considered in a political light, we are unanimous in desiring to bestow that moral emancipation which is of infinitely greater value, and which will best ensure the wise improvement of the liberty Catholics possess, as well as of the power they aspire to. We are most solicitous to emancipate them from that intolerable yoke of superstition and priestcraft, under which reason is crippled and made dwarfish, conscience is oppressed, and religion expires. We are perfectly convinced, that nothing will so essentially contribute to raise our fellow-subjects in Ireland to their just intellectual and moral elevation, as the wide and unimpeded circulation of the sacred Scriptures.

Let us then proceed with unabated ardour in this glorious career. Let us endeavour to give as wide an extension as possible to the waters of life. Let them flow freely, in opposition to the narrow and mischievous policy which would confine them in artificial pools and reservoirs, where they become stagnant and putrid. Let us join our prayers with our efforts, that the word of God may have "free course and be glorified," whatever opposing force it may sweep away in its progress: and should his holiness the pope, while he is buffeting with the waves, and attempting to arrest the current, be thrown down, and his triple crown totter and tumble from his head, instead of feeling the smallest concern, let us rejoice and exult in the sure presage it will afford of the speedy arrival of that long-looked-for moment, when at the decree of the Eternal, at the oath of the archangel, Babylon the Great shall sink like lead in the mighty waters.

FRAGMENT.

SPEECH

DELIVERED AT A MEETING OF THE LEICESTER AUXILIARY BIBLE SOCIETY.

[*Not published before.*]

If the Scriptures are in reality what they profess to be, we can be at no loss to perceive the obligation we are under to make them as extensively known as possible. On this subject we must allow them to speak for themselves; they assert their claim to be received as an immediate revelation from God, an inspired guide in the conduct of life and in the pursuit of immortality, "a light shining in a dark place" to direct us in the paths of salvation. They affirm themselves to be the voice of God addressing his creatures on a subject of the last importance. Whether their claim to this character is valid or not, is a question to be discussed with infidels, not among Christians, and is therefore to be put out of view in discussing the merits of this society. It is a Christian institution, set on foot by professed Christians in a Christian land. It is strange, that among men professing Christianity a doubt should arise for a moment on the propriety of circulating as widely as possible the records of our common faith, the charter of the common salvation.

But we are not agreed among ourselves on various articles of belief, on the diverse modes of discipline and of worship. True; nor do we profess such agreement: but that the Scriptures are the standard to which we must all appeal, that they contain the infallible rule of the faith and practice of Christians, we are agreed; and what possible objection, then, can a diversity of opinions on other subjects create to the universal distribution of the oracles of God? Are your peculiar views, we would ask the objector, sanctioned, in your apprehension, by these oracles?—then, instead of acting a hostile part, we are your allies;—for we are circulating the very book on which your views are founded; we are diffusing that light, [and] that only, by which you profess to have been conducted to the conclusions at which you have arrived. What greater advantage could you wish for the propagation of your doctrines, than that mankind should have free and [universal] access to the sources of your own conviction? It must be assumed for granted that in consequence of faithfully consulting its dictates you have been guided aright. Why anticipate, in regard to others, an opposite result? why suppose it will bewilder them in the paths of error and heresy, when your own experience attests it has led you into those of rectitude and truth? Is it agreeable to reason to expect that the same tree shall bring forth good fruit and evil fruit; or that the same fountain will send forth sweet water and bitter?

In the midst of that unhappy diversity of sentiment which divides professing Christians, what can be conceived more unexceptionably proper than the circulation of that book, in the belief of whose inspiration we all concur, and may therefore act in perfect concert and harmony without the smallest sacrifice of principle? If our professions are sincere, we are in such a course of proceeding, at once promoting our respective views, our discriminating tenets, and exhibiting an edifying example of unanimity and concord, combining in one and the same effort the interests of charity and of truth.

We are aware that destructive errors may be, and have been, deduced from an erroneous interpretation of the Bible; there is nothing so absurd and extravagant in the defence of which it has not been quoted; but as this is far from implying any reflection on that sacred book, so it has uniformly arisen from partial and defective views of its contents, where single passages have been violently torn from their connexion, and made to speak a language most remote from the scope and design of the writer. The proper antidote to this evil is [a] diligent and serious perusal of the whole; which will seldom fail, to all practical purposes, to ascertain that which is ambiguous, to elucidate what is obscure, and explain what is figurative and metaphorical. From a full conviction that a *comprehensive* view of the Scriptures is the most effectual corrective of the mistakes into which we may be betrayed by the cursory perusal of detached portions, it is the invariable plan of this society [to] distribute the whole of the Scriptures: nor can we sufficiently admire the inconsistency of those who, deprecating the danger of this, propose a partial distribution of the sacred volume, when it is obvious that the most alarming deviations from truth have arisen from this very cause, an exclusive attention to particular parts, without adverting to the relations they bear to the whole, and the reciprocal light which one portion of Revelation derives from the other. If "all Scripture is given by inspiration of God, and is profitable for doctrine, for reproof, for correction, for instruction in righteousness," we are at a loss to conceive how any part can have an opposite tendency, or how the withholding a portion of the instruction it affords can be productive of more illumination than giving it in all its extent. "The foolishness of God is wiser than man," and the conduct of his providence in putting his revelation into our hands, without the smallest limitation or restriction, affords a presumption, or rather a proof, of its tendency to good, and good only; [while of the contrary] it is difficult to conceive the possibility without contradicting the decisions of infinite Wisdom. If a part only would have been more beneficial than the whole, only a part would have been given; or if the benefit to be derived from the whole is restricted to some privileged class or order, without extending to mankind at large, we should undoubtedly have been furnished with some intimation of this, some mark or criterion by which to distinguish those favoured individuals who are allowed access to the whole counsel of God. We certainly are at a loss to discern in the adversaries of this institution that transcendent piety, that lofty superiority to worldly passions, or that resplendent exhibition of the Christian character which might induce a suspicion of their being, in some peculiar manner, the confidential depositaries of the Divine secrets. Whatever pretensions of this sort they may really possess, we can only lament that extreme modesty and reserve which has so effectually concealed [them] from the public view.

Gentlemen, on casting a survey over the different orders into which society is distributed, I am at an utter loss to fix on any description of persons who are likely to be injured by the most extensive perusal of the word of God. The poor, we may be certain, will sustain no injury from their attention to a book which, while [it] inculcates, under the most awful sanctions, the practice of honesty, industry, frugality, subordination to lawful authority, contentment, and resignation to the allotments of Providence, elevates them to the hope of "an inheritance incorruptible, undefiled, and that fadeth not away;" a book, which at once secures the observation of the duties which attach to an inferior condition, and almost annihilates its evils, by opening their prospects into a state where all the inequalities of fortune will vanish, and the obscurest and most neglected piety shall be crowned with eternal glory. "The poor man rejoices that he is exalted;" and while he views himself as the member of Christ, and the heir of a blessed immortality, he can look with undissembled pity on the frivolous distinctions, the fruitless agitations, and the fugitive enjoyments of the most eminent and the most prosperous of those who have their portion in this world. The poor man will sustain no injury by exchanging the vexations of envy for the quiet of a good conscience, and fruitless repinings for the consolations of religious hope. The less is his portion in this life, the more ardently will he cherish and embrace the promise of a better, while the hope of that better exerts a reciprocal influence, in prompting him to discharge the duties, and reconciling him to the evils, which are inseparable from the present. The Bible is the treasure of the poor, the solace of the sick, and the support of the dying; and while other books may amuse and instruct in a leisure hour, it is the peculiar triumph of that book to create light in the midst of darkness, to alleviate the sorrow which admits of no other alleviation, to direct a beam of hope to the heart which no [other] topic of consolation can reach; while guilt, despair, and death vanish at the touch of its holy inspiration. There is something in the spirit and diction of the Bible which is found peculiarly adapted to arrest the attention of the plainest and most uncultivated minds. The simple structure of its sentences, combined with a lofty spirit of poetry,—its familiar allusions to the scenes of nature, and the transactions of common life,—the delightful intermixture of narration with the doctrinal and preceptive parts,—and the profusion of miraculous facts, which convert it into a sort of enchanted ground,—its constant advertence to the Deity, whose perfections it renders almost visible and palpable,—unite in bestowing upon it an interest which attaches to no other performance, and which, after assiduous and repeated perusal, invests it with much of the charm of novelty: like the great orb of day, at which we are wont to gaze with unabated astonishment from infancy to old age. What other book besides the Bible could be heard in public assemblies from year to year, with an attention that never tires, and an interest that never cloys? With few exceptions, let a portion of the sacred volume be recited in a mixed multitude, and though it has been heard a thousand times, a universal stillness ensues, every eye is fixed, and every ear is awake and attentive. Select, if you can, any other composition, and let it be rendered equally familiar to the mind, and see whether it will produce this effect.

The importance of attaching a distinct sanction to the rules of moral conduct is immediately obvious; and whatever eloquence may be employed in painting the beauty of virtue, and the odious deformity of vice, will have little influence in the moment of temptation, and in the conflicts of passion, upon the most cultivated minds, and on those of an inferior description none at all. These topics appeal to feelings which are feeble and evanescent, while the passions to which they are opposed are violent and intense. Nothing short of a "Thus saith the Lord," accompanied and enforced with the prospect of eternal happiness or misery, will be sufficient to secure the practice of what is right, when vice and crime are recommended by the allurements of pleasure, or the promise of immediate advantage. But it is the word of God only to which the sanction of his authority is attached, and which incessantly reminds us that the lessons which it teaches are not merely the dictates of reason, but the voice of God. In human instructions, however excellent, there must of necessity be a separation; the instruction is [in] one place, the sanction in another; in the Scriptures, and in the Scriptures alone, they are combined and incorporated. Here, it is not a man addressing his exhortations to a fellow-creature; it is the Father of our spirits, the Judge of the universe, speaking from heaven, and grappling with the conscience of the moral and accountable being which he has formed. Let this persuasion be really and deeply felt, and the word of the Lord is "quick and powerful, sharper than a two-edged sword." There is no room for evasion, no pretext for [inattention,] and no possibility of escape, except [by] immediate compliance and submission.

ADDRESS

IN BEHALF OF THE

BAPTIST ACADEMICAL INSTITUTION

AT STEPNEY.

[*Written in* 1811 *or* 1812.]

In calling the attention of the public to a new seminary, intended to be established near London, for the education of candidates for the Christian ministry, we are desirous of presenting a short account of the motives by which we are actuated, and the objects we have in view.

We beg leave to premise, that nothing is further from our intention than to interfere with the respectable seminaries already subsisting, from which the church of Christ has derived essential benefit. We congratulate the public on their institution, rejoice in their prosperity, and feel a cordial concurrence with the views of their generous patrons and supporters. We are persuaded, however, that the ground is not yet so fully occupied as to leave no room for a further extension of the means of instruction to students in theology; and that, among the churches of the Baptist denomination at least, a difficulty is frequently experienced in procuring young men possessed of those qualifications which the state of society renders desirable. Having been supplied, by the noble munificence of a worthy individual, with a house and premises at Stepney well fitted for an academy, we are desirous of realizing the liberal intentions of the donor, by carrying into execution the plan of public utility he has meditated.

At this period, no apology can be necessary for attempting to assist young men designed for the ministry in the acquisition of such branches of knowledge as may qualify them more completely for the successful discharge of that sacred function; since, whatever prejudices unfavourable to learning may have formerly prevailed in serious minds, they appear to have subsided, and Christians in general admit the propriety of enlisting literature in the service of religion. From the recent multiplication of theological seminaries among Protestant dissenters, such an inference may be fairly deduced. While we assert the absolute sufficiency of the Scriptures for every saving purpose, it is impossible to deny the usefulness of the knowledge derived from books, in unfolding many of its obscurities, explaining many of its allusions, and producing more fully to the view the inestimable treasure it contains. The primary truths of revelation, it is acknowledged, offer themselves at first view in the sacred volume; but there are latent riches and gems of inestimable value, which can be brought to light only by a deeper and more laborious research. There are numberless exquisite harmonies and retired beauties in the scheme of revelation, which are rarely discovered without the union of great industry with cultivated talent. A collection of writings, composed on various occasions, and at remote intervals of time, including detached portions of history the most ancient, and of poetry awfully sublime, but often obscure,—a book containing continual allusions to manners unknown in this part of the world, and to institutions which have long ceased to exist,—must demand all the aid that ingenuity and learning can bring towards its elucidation.

The light of revelation, it should be remembered, is not opposite to the light of reason; the former presupposes the latter; they are both emanations from the same source; and the discoveries of the Bible, however supernatural, are addressed to the understanding, the only medium of information, whether human or divine. Revealed religion is not a cloud which overshadows reason; it is a superior illumination designed to perfect its exercise and supply its deficiencies. Since truth is always consistent with itself, it can never suffer from the most enlarged exertion of the intellectual powers, provided those powers be regulated by a spirit of dutiful submission to the oracles of God. The evidences of Christianity challenge the most rigid examination; the more accurate and extensive the inquiry, the more convincing will they appear. Unexpected coincidences between inspired history and the most undisputed remains of antiquity will present themselves, and striking analogies be perceived between the course of Providence and the supreme economy of grace. The gradual development of the plan of revelation, together with the dependence of its several parts on each other, and the perfect consistency of the whole, will employ and reward the deepest investigation. In proof of the assistance religion may derive from learning, rightly directed, we appeal to the writings of an Usher, a Newton, and a Bryant; to the ancient apologists of Christianity, who by means of it unmasked the deformities of polytheism; to the Reformers, whom it taught to remove the sacred volume from the dust and obscurity of cloisters, and exhibit it in the dialects of Europe, and to the victorious impugners of infidelity in modern times. Such are the spoils which sanctified learning has won from superstition and impiety, the common enemies of God and man. Nor must we forget to notice, among the most precious fruits of cultivated reason, *that* consciousness of its own deficiencies, and sense of its own weakness, which prompts it to bow to the authority of revelation, and depose its honours at the cross; since its incapacity to solve the most important questions, and to satisfy the most distressing doubts, will be felt with the truest conviction, and attested with the best grace, by such as have made the largest essay of its powers.

An unconverted ministry we look upon as the greatest calamity that can befall the church; nor would we be supposed to insinuate by the preceding observations that education can ever be a proper substitute for native talent, much less for real piety: all we mean to assert is, that the union of both will much enlarge the capacity of doing good. Without descending to particulars, we must be allowed to remark, for example, that the art of arranging ideas in their proper order, and of investigating the nature of different sorts of evidence, as well as an acquaintance with the fundamental rules of composition and rhetoric, are of essential service to a public speaker.

The existing state of society supplies additional reasons for extending the advantages of academical education. If former periods have given birth to more renowned scholars, none ever produced so many men of reading and reflection as the present; never was there a time when books were so multiplied, knowledge so diffused,—and when, consequently, the exercise of cultivated talents in all departments was in such demand. When the general level of mental improvement is so much raised, it becomes necessary for the teachers of religion to possess their full share of these advantages, if they would secure from neglect the exercise of a function the most important to the interests of mankind. If in the days of inspiration there were schools of the prophets, and miraculous infusions of wisdom did not supersede human means of instruction, much less are they to be neglected in the present times, when no such communications are expected. To this we must add, that perverted literature is one of the most powerful weapons in the hands of the enemies of divine truth, who leave no effort untried to recommend their cause by the lustre of superior acquisitions, and to form in the public mind the dangerous association between irreligion and talents, weakness and piety.

In insisting so strongly on the advantages of a regular education, we mean no disrespect to those excellent persons who have exercised their ministry, much to the benefit of the church, without those advantages; many of whom are men of vigorous minds, who have surmounted great obstacles in the pursuit of knowledge; and others by their piety and good sense well fitted for the stations which they occupy. We trust that such ministers will always be highly esteemed in our churches: there are situations, it is probable, which they are better qualified to fill than persons of a higher education. To the improvement of the higher classes, however, it will scarcely be denied, men of the latter character are best suited; and as their salvation is not in itself less important than that of the lower orders, so their superior weight in society attaches to their character and conduct peculiar consideration. It is also manifest, from the examples of a Brainerd, an Elliot, and a Schwartz, that where piety in a candidate for the ministry is once secured, a course of academical studies is no impediment to the growth and development of qualities the most conducive to success,—deep humility, eminent spirituality, unshaken perseverance, and patient self-denial.

With respect to the principles we wish to see prevail in our future seminary, it may be sufficient to observe, they are in general the principles of the Reformation; and were we to descend to a more minute specification we should add, they are the principles which distinguish the body of Christians denominated Particular or Calvinistic Baptists. While we feel a cordial esteem for all who love the Lord Jesus Christ in sincerity,—disclaiming all pretensions to that vaunted liberality which masks an indifference to revealed truth, we feel no hesitation in declaring, that nothing would give us more concern than to see the seminary we have in contemplation become the organ of infidel or heretical pravity.

We conceive some advantages may accrue from fixing the proposed seminary in the vicinity of the metropolis. It may be hoped that its pecuniary resources will be benefited by being placed in the centre of commercial opulence; that a residence of a few years near the capital of a great empire may give an expansion to the youthful mind; and that the means which it affords of obtaining the assistance of teachers in various departments of science, nowhere else to be found, may improve the taste and direct the exertions of the students.

We conclude with recommending our undertaking to the patronage of the public and to the blessing of God, and with expressing our hope, that through the influence of the Divine Spirit, in a copious effusion on the future patrons, tutors, and students of this seminary, however small in its beginning, it will become respectable for learning and piety, be a nursery of faithful and able ministers, and a blessing to the church of Christ.

LETTER

TO THE COMMITTEE OF

THE BAPTIST MISSIONARY SOCIETY.

To the Committee of the Baptist Missionary Society, convened in London on the 15th instant.

Bristol, March 12, 1827.

GENTLEMEN,

IT is with much diffidence that I presume to address you on the present occasion, nor am I certain whether I am perfectly in order in so doing; but conceiving this to be a crisis in the mission, and not being able to be present at the meeting, I could not satisfy myself without communicating the result of my reflections on the important business which has called you together.

Dr. Marshman, it seems, as the representative of the brethren at Serampore, has instituted a demand of one-sixth of all the money collected or subscribed towards the society, to be paid annually in aid of the missionary operations going on there. It must strike every one as strange that this demand should almost immediately follow a preceding one which was acceded to, which he then professed to consider as perfectly satisfactory, and as putting a final termination to all dispute or discussion on the subject of pecuniary claims—that notwithstanding this, he should now bring forward a fresh requisition of one-sixth of the same amount, accompanied, as I am informed, by an intimation that it is possible this may not be his ultimatum. This proceeding has all the appearance of a tentative process, designed to ascertain how far our anxiety to avoid a breach will prompt us to submit to his encroachments. What security have we against future requisitions if we yield to the present? What reason to suppose our ready compliance in this instance will not encourage him to embrace an early opportunity of making further demands? It has all the appearance of the commencement of a series of unfounded pretensions and endless exactions.

That a set of men, in the character of missionaries, after disclaiming the authority of the society which sent them out, and asserting an entire independence—after claiming an absolute control (whether rightfully or not) over a large property which that society had always considered as its own, should demand an annual payment from those from whom they had severed themselves, and thus attempt to make their constituents their tributaries, is a proceeding scarcely paralleled in the history of human affairs.

I am utterly at a loss to understand on what principles the Serampore brethren, in the position in which they have placed themselves, have any claim whatever on the funds of the society whose authority they have renounced, after appropriating to themselves the management of an extensive revenue, in the disposal of which they will not brook the smallest interference or control. Without reverting to former grounds of controversy, it will surely be admitted that the independence we have, for the sake of peace, conceded to them is reciprocal—that our right to it is not less than theirs—and that we are consequently at liberty to dispose of our income in the way which we conceive most conducive to the purposes of our institution.

It may be very proper, under certain circumstances, for us to aid the brethren at Serampore by occasional donations, regulated by the state of our funds, and the attention necessary to other objects; but this is essentially different from absolutely engaging to pay an annual sum, which would, in my humble opinion, be equally inconsistent with the interests and the honour of this society. As our brethren of Serampore have chiefly exerted themselves in translations, and are confessedly in possession of great pecuniary resources, there seems no imperious necessity for regularly diverting those funds to their aid which are unequal to the demand which Bengal alone would create, were our mission (a most desirable event) concentrated within that province. Calcutta, to say nothing of other stations, cries aloud for more labourers, but cries in vain.

It has been said that we are indebted for our success to the celebrity attached to the names of Carey, Marshman, and Ward; and that but for the unbounded confidence of the religious public in these men, our funds would never have been realized. Supposing this to be the case, to take advantage of such a circumstance in order to bring the society into subjection, would not be to make a very generous use of their influence. But I believe it is a mistake; it is my firm conviction that the Baptist mission, like other kindred institutions, rests on the basis of its own merits, and that it will not fail to secure the confidence of the public, in proportion to the purity of its motives, the wisdom of its counsels, and the utility of its objects. If it cannot sustain the ordeal of public opinion on these principles, let it sink, rather than owe its support to the illusion of a name.

To contemplate the possibility of being compelled to an open rupture with our brethren of Serampore is unquestionably painful; it is their knowledge alone of our extreme reluctance to hazard that consequence which imboldens them to advance these exorbitant claims. If we can avoid it by a consistent and dignified mode of procedure, let it be avoided; but if peace can only be purchased by an ignominious surrender of our rights as a society,—by a tame submission to unreasonable demands,—and by subjecting it to a sort of feudal dependence, in all time to come, on persons we know not whom, whose characters we cannot ascertain, and whose actions we cannot control,—the pur chase is, in my humble opinion, too dear. The treatment of the Serampore brethren has not been such that we need shrink from its most ample exposure to the public; nor have we any other censure to fear on that head, except it be for lavishing upon them a too overweening confidence. We have no such secrets to conceal, that it should cost us a large annual payment to secure their suppression.

Of the three brethren with whom we were lately in treaty, one is already gone into eternity, and the remaining two are advancing to that period of life which ought to make us pause ere we enter into engagements which will give to persons of whom we know little or nothing a permanent right of interference with our funds.

The crisis is most solemn; and a hasty compliance with the present requisition may, when it is too late, make matter for bitter and unavailing repentance. That you may be indulged on this, and on every other occasion, with "the wisdom which is from above," is the sincere prayer of, Gentlemen,

Your obedient humble servant,

ROBERT HALL.

PREFACE

TO

HALL'S HELP TO ZION'S TRAVELLERS

[*Written in* 1814.]

An aversion to religious controversy may arise from one of two causes, in their nature the most opposite,—a contempt of religion itself, or a high degree of devotional feeling. They who consider the objects of religion as visionary and uncertain, or who, rejecting revelation, feel their inability to find a place where they may fix their footing, will naturally feel an emotion of contempt for theological contests, similar to that which we should experience towards men who were fighting for possessions in the air.

There are not a few who would engage with the utmost seriousness and ardour in a dispute on the nature and effects of paper currency, who would be ashamed of being suspected of directing their attention for a moment to the most weighty question in theology. Attentive to all the aspects and combinations of the material and of the political world, they are accustomed to regard religion as a sort of Utopia, a land of shadow and of fiction, where, wrapt in pleasing vision, credulity reposes on the lap of imposture. Persons of this sort are so completely overcome by the enchantments of the present state, so entirely devoted to the wisdom which St. James denominates earthly and sensual, that they are incapable of being impressed with a conviction of the possibility of a higher order of objects, or a more elevated and refined condition of being, than that with which they are conversant; and though they may possess a subtle and penetrating genius, they are not less disqualified for religious inquiries than an idiot or an infant. "They mind earthly things."

How far the indisposition to religious controversy which prevails at present may be justly ascribed to the Sadducean temper, I shall not pretend to determine. It is certain, however, that in some this indisposition proceeds from a better cause. While the former class of persons think religion not worth disputing about, there are others who conceive it to be a subject too sacred for dispute. They wish to confine it to silent meditation, to sweeten solitude, to inspire devotion, to guide the practice and purify the heart, and never to appear in public but in the character of the authentic interpreter of the will of Heaven They conceive it degraded when it is brought forward to combat on the arena. We are fully convinced that a disputatious humour is unfavourable to piety, and that controversies in religion have often been unnecessarily multiplied and extended; but how they can be dispensed with altogether we are at a loss to discover, until some other method is discovered of confuting error than sound and solid argument. As we no longer live in times (God be thanked!) when coercion can be employed, or when any individual or any body of men is invested with that authority which could silence disputes by an oracular decision, there appears no possibility of maintaining the interests of truth, without having recourse to temperate and candid controversy. Perhaps the sober use of this weapon may not be without its advantages even at the present season. Prone as we are to extremes, may there not be some reason to apprehend we have passed from that propensity to magnify every difference subsisting among Christians to a neglect of just discrimination; to a habit of contemplating the Christian system as one in which there is little or nothing that remains to be explored? Let us cultivate the most cordial esteem for all that love the Lord Jesus Christ in sincerity. Let us anxiously guard against that asperity and contempt which have too often mingled with theological debates; but let us aim at the same time to acquire and retain the most accurate conceptions of religious truth. Every improvement in the knowledge of Christ and the mysteries of his gospel will abundantly compensate for the labour and attention necessary to its attainment.

However unhappily controversies have too often been conducted, the assistance they have afforded in the discovery of truth is not light or inconsiderable. Not to mention the Reformation, which was principally effected by controversy, how many truths have by this means been set in a clearer view! and while the unhappy passions it has awakened have subsided, the light struck out in the collision has been retained and perpetuated.

As the physical powers are scarcely ever exerted to their utmost extent but in the ardour of combat, so intellectual acumen has been displayed to the most advantage and to the most effect in the contests of argument. The mind of a controversialist, warmed and agitated, is turned to all quarters, and leaves none of its resources unemployed in the invention of arguments, tries every weapon, and explores the hidden recesses of a subject with an intense vigilance, and an ardour which it is next to impossible in a calmer state of mind to command. Disingenuous arts are often resorted to, personalities are mingled, and much irritative matter is introduced; but it is the business of the attentive observer to separate these from the question at issue, and to form an impartial judgment of the whole. In a word, it may be truly affirmed that the evils of controversy are transient, the good it produces is permanent.

These observations I beg leave to submit to the reader as an apology for the republication of a treatise which is professedly controversial. Coinciding with the venerable author in the general aim and drift of the following sheets, I am far from pledging myself to the approbation and support of every position contained in them; nor would I be understood to attach all the importance to some of the points of discussion which they appear in his estimation to have possessed.

If there be any impression in the following treatise which implies that the questions at issue between the Calvinists and Arminians are of the nature of *fundamentals* (of which, however, I am not aware), I beg leave, as far as they are concerned, to express my explicit dissent; being fully satisfied that upon either system the foundations of human hope remain unshaken, and that there is nothing in the contrariety of views entertained on these subjects which ought to obstruct the most cordial affection and harmony among Christians.

Having no pecuniary interest in this work, I may perhaps be allowed with more freedom to communicate my opinion of its merit. I am much mistaken if the candid reader will not perceive in the author an impartial love of truth, together with a degree of ingenuity and acuteness in its illustration and defence not always to be met with in theological discussions.

The sentiments of my honoured father were decidedly Calvinistic. His object, however, in the following treatise was not so much to recommend that system in general as to disengage it from certain excrescences, which he considered as weakening its evidence and impairing its beauty. On reviewing his religious tenets during the latter years of his life, and impartially comparing them with the Scriptures, he was led to discard some opinions which he had formerly embraced, and which he afterward came to consider as having a pernicious tendency.

From the moral impotence which the oracles of truth ascribe to man in his fallen state, a certain class of divines were induced to divide moral and religious duties into two classes, natural and spiritual; comprehending under the latter those which require spiritual or supernatural assistance to their performance, and under the former those which demand no such assistance. Agreeable to this distinction, they conceived it to be the duty of all men to abstain from the outward acts of sin, to read the Scriptures, to frequent the worship of God, and to attend with serious assiduity to the means of grace; but they supposed that repentance, faith in Christ, and the exercise of genuine internal devotion were obligatory only to the regenerate. Hence their ministry consisted almost entirely of an exhibition of the peculiar mysteries of the gospel, with few or no addresses to the unconverted. They conceived themselves not warranted to urge them to repent and believe the gospel,—those being the spiritual duties, from whose obligation they were released by the inability contracted by the fall.

These conclusions were evidently founded upon two assumptions: first, that the impotence which the Scriptures ascribe to the unregenerate is free from blame, so as to excuse them from all the duties to which it extends. In opposition to this, the author of the following treatise has proved, in a very satisfactory manner, that the inability under which the unconverted labour is altogether of a moral nature, consisting of the corruption of the will, or an aversion to things of a spiritual and divine nature that is in itself criminal; and that, so far from affording an excuse for what would otherwise be a duty, it stamps with its own character all its issues and productions.

In considering the moral character of an action, we are naturally led to inquire into its motive; and according as that is criminal, laudable, or indifferent, to characterize the action whence it proceeds The motive, however, appears no otherwise entitled to commendation than as it indicates the disposition of the agent; so that, in analyzing the elements of moral character, we can ascend no higher than to the consideration of the disposition, or the state of the will and of the affections, as constituting the essence of that portion of virtue or of vice which we respectively ascribe to it. To proceed further will only involve us in a circle; since to whatever we might trace the disposition in question, should we be induced, for example, to ascribe it to the free exercise of the will, that exercise would fall under the same predicament, and be considered either as virtuous or vicious, according to the disposition whence it proceeds. When the Scriptures have placed the inability of mankind to yield holy and acceptable obedience in an evil disposition, or in blindness or hardness of heart, they have conducted us to the ultimate point on this subject, and have established the doctrine of human criminality upon a basis which cannot be shaken or disturbed without confounding the first principles of moral dis crimination. Though this is manifest, this impotence is entirely of a moral nature, totally distinct from the want of natural faculties. It is equally evident, that to whatever extent it exists, while it actually subsists, it is as effectual an impediment to the performance of holy actions as any physical privation whatever: and on that account, and on that alone, may without absurdity be styled an *inability*. This important distinction was not wholly unknown to our earlier divines, though they neglected to avail themselves of it as fully as they ought: it is clearly stated by the great Mr. Howe, in his Blessedness of the Righteous, as well as adverted to by Mr. Baxter in several of his practical works. But the earliest regular treatise on this subject it has been my lot to meet with was the production of Mr. Truman, an eminent nonconformist divine. In his Dissertation on Moral Impotence, as he styles it, he has anticipated the most important arguments of succeeding writers, and has evinced throughout a most masterly acquaintance with his subject. This work is mentioned in terms of high respect by Nelson, in his Life of Bishop Bull, who remarks that his thoughts were original, and that he had hit upon a method of defending Calvinism, against the objections of Bull and others, peculiar to himself. His claim to perfect originality, however, was not so well-founded as Nelson supposed. Since his time the subject has been fully discussed by the celebrated Jonathan Edwards, in his Treatise on the Will, and the distinction defended with all the depth and precision peculiar to that amazing genius.

Another principle assumed as a basis by the high Calvinists is, that the same things cannot be the duty of man and the gift of God; or, in other words, that what is matter of promise can on no occasion be the matter of obligation. The Scriptures frequently affirm faith and repentance to be the gift of God; hence it is concluded that they cannot be obligatory on the unregenerate,—a conclusion diametrically opposed to innumerable passages in the Old and New Testaments, which insist in the most peremptory style on true conversion and a lively faith as the most essential duties, which other passages are equally express in exhibiting as matter of promise. "A new heart will I give them," says the Lord, by Ezekiel, "and a new spirit will I put within them, and I will take away the heart of stone, and give them a heart of flesh." The same prophet cries, "Make yourselves a new heart; for why will ye die, ye house of Israel?"—in exact accordance with the language of St. James, "Cleanse your hands, ye sinners, and purify your hearts, ye double-minded." The burthen of our Saviour's ministry, as well as that of his forerunner, was, "Repent, for the kingdom of God is at hand;" while St. Peter, who perfectly knew the genius of Christianity, affirms that Christ is "exalted, to give repentance and the remission of sins." "Circumcise your hearts," said Moses, "and be no longer stiff-necked." The same Moses had been previously commissioned to declare, "The Lord thy God will circumcise thy heart, and the heart of thy seed." Now the circumcision of the heart, we are taught by St. Paul, in his Epistle to the Romans, to regard as the distinguishing feature of the truly regenerate—of him "who is a Jew inwardly, whose praise is not of man, but of God." Whoever impartially weighs the import of these scriptures must be convinced that the same things are in fact matter of command and the subject of promise, and must consequently be prepared to acquiesce in the decision of Infinite Wisdom on this subject, however much he may be at a loss to explain or account for it. The consistency of the promises and of the commands in question arises from the matter of each being of a moral nature. If we will allow ourselves to reflect, we shall perceive that the will, and the will only, is the proper object of command, and that an agent is no otherwise accountable, or susceptible of moral government, than as he is the subject of voluntary powers: we shall also perceive that the disordered state of the will, or the radical indisposition of an agent to comply with legitimate commands, which is the same thing, by no means exempts him from their obligation, nor tends in the least degree to render the addressing such commands to him absurd or improper. That they will not be complied with while that disordered state subsists is true: but legitimate commands, enforced by proper sanctions, are among the strongest motives; that is, they tend in their own nature to incline the will, and therefore they cannot be withheld without virtually relinquishing the claim of authority and dominion. This may suffice to evince the propriety of issuing commands, notwithstanding the known and radical indisposition to comply; or, which comes to the same thing, whatever be the *state of the will.*

With respect to the other side of the supposed contradiction, what can be plainer than that the will, as well as every other faculty of the mind, is under Divine control, and that God can, with infinite ease, in what instances and in what manner he please, so change and modify it as to induce a prompt and cheerful compliance with his requisition? What should prevent Him, at whose disposal are the hearts of the mightiest of men, "to make his people willing in the day of his power?"

It is instructive as well as amusing to trace the coincidence which is often found between systems which appear at first view at the utmost variance from each other. The grosser Arminians and Pelagians contend, that it is the duty of all men to repent and believe, because all possess an inherent power of so doing without special and Divine assistance. The high Calvinists, on the contrary, deny that men in a state of unregeneracy are under an obligation to perform those duties, because they are not possessed of the requisite ability. Thus both concur in making moral ability the measure of obligation; a position which, when the terms are accurately defined and cleared of their ambiguity, conducts us to this very extraordinary conclusion, that men are obliged to just as much of duty as they are inclined to. On these and other points connected with them the reader, if we are not mistaken, will find much solid instruction in the following treatise, accompanied with such a constant attention to the great end of theological discussion—the promotion of practical piety—as can scarcely fail of affording high satisfaction to serious minds. To this treatise, and to another on a similar subject by my excellent and judicious friend Mr. Fuller, the dissenters in general, and the Baptists in particular, are under great obligation for emancipating them from the fetters of prejudice, and giving free scope to the publication of the gospel. By these means a considerable revolution has been effected in the sentiments of the denomination to which I have the honour to belong: the excrescences of Calvinism have been cut off;—the points of defence have been diminished in number and better fortified;—truth has shone forth with brighter lustre;—and the ministry of the gospel has been rendered more simple, more practical, and more efficacious.

In reply to such as may object to the metaphysical subtlety which pervades some parts of the following treatise, I would avail myself of the distinction admirably illustrated by the author of the Light of Nature Pursued.* He observes, that although metaphysical reason rarely, if ever, conduces to the discovery of truth, it is of great advantage in the detection of sophistry; and that the mist and confusion in which moral subjects have been involved, by crude and undigested metaphysics, can only be exploded by the temperate use of that which is true and genuine: so that the chief praise of metaphysics is the cure of its own ills, the repair of the mischief which itself has wrought. The reader will observe that the author employs metaphysics, not to rear the fabric of truth, which can only be effected by a profound deference to inspiration, but to demolish a rotten superstructure which conceals its beauty. For the want of elegance or polish, discernible in the following sheets, it will be sufficient apology to inform the reader, that the author, destitute of the advantages of early education, had no other

* Abraham Tucker.

resources to depend upon, in his religious inquiries, than what were derived from the vigour of his understanding, and his unbiassed integrity of heart. Had he enjoyed the benefit of literary culture, he would have undoubtedly written in a style and manner more adapted to gain the attention of the superior classes: whether his reasoning would have been more cogent, or his method of handling his subject better fitted for the instruction of plain serious Christians, for whose benefit he principally laboured, is more questionable.

Gratitude and veneration compel me to add, that with all the imperfections of the work, and the disadvantages under which the author of it laboured, I shall ever esteem it one of the greatest favours an indulgent Providence has bestowed upon me, to have possessed such a father, whom, in all the essential features of character, it will be my humble ambition to imitate, though conscious it must ever be

—— 'Haud passibus æquis."

ROBERT HALL.

PREFACE TO JANEWAY'S LIFE.

[*Written in* 1816.]

At the request of a highly esteemed friend, I feel no hesitation in recommending the remarkable narrative now republished, to the serious attention of the reader. It exhibits a life eminently formed on the example of Christ, and a death-bed scene of extraordinary elevation and triumph. It is next to impossible to contemplate either, as they are exhibited in the following memorial, without feeling an increasing conviction of the reality and dignity of true religion. I am aware that some will object to the strain of devout ecstasy which characterizes the sentiments and language of Mr. Janeway in his dying moments; but I am persuaded they will meet with nothing, however ecstatic and elevated, but what corresponds to the dictates of Scripture and the analogy of the faith. He who recollects that the Scriptures speak of a "peace which passeth all understanding, and a joy unspeakable and full of glory," will not be offended at the lively expressions of those contained in this narrative: he will be more disposed to lament the low state of his own religious feeling than to suspect the propriety of sentiments the most rational and scriptural, merely because they rise to a pitch that he has never reached. The sacred oracles afford no countenance to the supposition that devotional feelings are to be condemned as visionary and enthusiastic, merely on account of their intenseness and elevation; provided they be of a right kind, and spring from legitimate sources, they never teach us to suspect they can be carried too far. David "danced before the Lord with all his might;" and when he was reproached for degrading himself in the eyes of the people by indulging these transports, he replied, If this be to be vile, "I will yet make myself more vile." That the objects which interest the heart in religion are infinitely more durable and important than all others will not be disputed: and why should it be deemed irrational to be affected by them in a degree somewhat suitable to their value, especially in the near prospect of their full and perfect possession? Why should it be deemed strange or irrational for a dying saint, who has spent his life in the pursuit of immortal good, to feel an unspeakable ecstasy at finding he has just touched the goal, finished his course, and in a few moments is to be crowned with life everlasting? While he dwells on the inconceivably glorious prospect before him, and feels himself lost in wonder and gratitude, and almost oppressed with a sense of his unutterable obligations to the love of his Creator and Redeemer, nothing can be more natural and proper than his sentiments and conduct. While the Scriptures retain their rank as the only rule of faith and practice,—while there are those who feel the power of true religion,—such death-bed scenes as Mr. Janeway's will be contemplated with veneration and delight. It affords no inconsiderable confirmation of the truth of Christianity that the most celebrated sages of pagan antiquity, whose last moments have been exhibited with inimitable propriety and beauty, present nothing equal nor similar; nothing of that singular combination of humility and elevation, that self-renouncing greatness, in which the creature appears annihilated, and God all in all. I am much mistaken if the serious reader will not find in the closing scenes of Mr. Janeway's life the most perfect form of Christianity: he will find it, not, as it is too often, clouded with doubts and oppressed with sorrows; he will behold it ascend the mount, transfigured, glorified, and encircled with the beams of celestial majesty.

Let me be permitted, however, to observe, that the experience of Mr. Janeway in his last moments, while it developes the native tendency of Christianity, is not to be considered as a standard to ordinary Christians. He affords a great example of what is attainable in religion, and not of what is indispensably necessary to salvation. Thousands die in the Lord who are not indulged with the privilege of dying in triumph. His extraordinary diligence in the whole of his Christian career, his tenderness of conscience, his constant vigilance, his vehement hunger and thirst after righteousness, met with a signal reward, intended, probably, not more for his own personal advantage, than as a persuasive to others to walk in his steps. As he was incessantly solicitous to improve his graces, purify his principles, and perfect holiness in the fear of the Lord, no wonder he was favoured with an abundant entrance into the joy of his Lord. "He which soweth sparingly shall reap sparingly; and he which soweth bountifully shall reap also bountifully"

ROBERT HALL.

RECOMMENDATORY PREFACE

TO A

VOLUME OF HYMNS,

Composed by the late Rev. B. Beddome, M. A

[*Written in* 1818.]

FAR be it from me to indulge the presumptuous idea of adding to the merited reputation of Mr. Beddome by my feeble suffrage. But having had the pleasure of a personal acquaintance with that eminent man, and cherishing a high esteem for his memory, I am induced to comply the more cheerfully with the wishes of the editor, by prefixing a few words to the present publication. Mr. Beddome was on many accounts an extraordinary person. His mind was cast in an original mould; his conceptions on every subject were eminently his own; and where the stamina of his thoughts were the same as other men's (as must often be the case with the most original thinkers), a peculiarity marked the mode of their exhibition. Favoured with the advantages of a learned education, he continued to the last to cultivate an acquaintance with the best writers of antiquity, to which he was much indebted for the chaste, terse, and nervous diction, which distinguished his compositions both in prose and verse. Though he spent the principal part of a long life in a village retirement, he was eminent for his colloquial powers, in which he displayed the urbanity of the gentleman and the erudition of the scholar, combined with a more copious vein of attic salt than any person it has been my lot to know. As a preacher, he was universally admired for the piety and unction of his sentiments, the felicity of his arrangement, and the purity, force, and simplicity of his language, all of which were recommended by a delivery perfectly natural and graceful. His printed discourses, taken from the manuscripts which he left behind him at his decease, are fair specimens of his usual performances in the pulpit. They are eminent for the qualities already mentioned; and their merits, which the modesty of the author concealed from himself, have been justly appreciated by the religious public. As a religious poet, his excellence has long been known and acknowledged in dissenting congregations, in consequence of several admirable compositions inserted in some popular compilations. The variety of the subjects treated of, the poetical beauty and elevation of some, the simple pathos of others, and the piety and justness of thought which pervade all the compositions in the succeeding volume, will, we trust, be deemed a valuable accession to the treasures of sacred poetry, equally adapted to the closet and to the sanctuary. The man of taste will be gratified with the beautiful and original turns of thought which many of them exhibit; while the experimental Christian will often perceive the most secret movements of his soul strikingly delineated, and sentiments portrayed which will find their echo in every heart. Considerable pains have been taken to arrange the hymns in such a manner as is best adapted to selection, from a persuasion, which we trust the event will justify, that they will be found the properest supplement to Dr. Watts that has yet appeared.

A PREFACE

TO

ANTINOMIANISM UNMASKED,

BY THE REV. SAMUEL CHASE.

[*Written in* 1819.]

It is with considerable reluctance that I have complied with the request of the highly esteemed author of the following work, by prefixing a short preface; not from the slightest hesitation respecting the excellence of the work itself, but from an aversion to the seeming arrogance of pretending to recommend what might rest so securely on its own merits. The reader, if I am not greatly mistaken, will find in this treatise a train of close and cogent reasoning from the oracles of God sufficient to overturn from their foundation the principles which compose the antinomian heresy; which, he will be at no loss to perceive, are as much opposed to the *grace* as to the authority of the great Head of the church.

The fundamental tenet of the system to which this treatise is opposed consists in the denial of the *obligation* of believers to obey the precepts of Christ, in supposing that their interest in the merits of the Redeemer releases them from all subjection to his authority; and as it is acknowledged on all hands that he is the sole Lord of the Christian dispensation, the immediate consequence is, that as far as *they* are concerned, the moral government of the Deity is annihilated—that they have ceased to be accountable creatures. But this involves the total subversion of religion: for what idea can we form of a religion in which all the obligations of piety and morality are done away; in which nothing is binding or imperative on the conscience? We may conceive of a religious code under all the possible gradations of laxness or severity—of its demanding more or less, or of its enforcing its injunctions by penalties more or less formidable;—but to form a conception of a system deserving the name of religion, which prescribes no duties whatever, and is enforced by no sanctions, seems an impossibility. On this account it appears to me improper to speak of antinomianism as a *religious* error; religion, whether true or false, has nothing to do with it: it is rather to be considered as an attempt to substitute a system of subtle and specious impiety in the room of Christianity. In their own estimation, its disciples are a privileged class, who dwell in a secluded region of unshaken security and lawless liberty, while the rest of the Christian world are the vassals of legal bondage, toiling in darkness and in chains. Hence, whatever diversity of character they may display in other respects, a haughty and bitter disdain of every other class of professors is a universal feature. Contempt or hatred of the most devout and enlightened Christians out of their own pale seems one of the most essential elements of their being; nor were the ancient Pharisees ever more notorious for "trusting in themselves that they were righteous, and despising others."

Of the force of legitimate argument they seem to have little or no perception, having contracted an inveterate and pernicious habit of shutting their eyes against the plainest and most pointed declarations of the word of God. The only attempt they make to support their miserable system is to adduce a number of detached and insulated passages of Scripture, forcibly torn from their context, and interpreted with more regard to their sound than to their meaning, as ascertained by the laws of sober criticism. Could they be prevailed upon to engage in serious dispassionate controversy, some hope might be indulged of reclaiming them; their errors would admit of an easy confutation: but the misfortune is, they seem to feel themselves as much released from the restraints of reason as of moral obligation; and the intoxication of spiritual pride has incomparably more influence in forming their persuasions than the light of evidence.

As far as they are concerned, my expectation of benefit from the following treatise is far from being sanguine. To others, however, who may be in danger of falling a prey to their seduction, it may prove an important preservative; to the young and inexperienced it will hold out a faithful warning, by unmasking the deformity, and revealing the danger of that pretended doctrine of grace which is employed to annul the obligation of obedience. They will learn from this treatise, that the authority of Christ as Legislator is perfectly compatible with his office as the Redeemer of his people; that the renewal of the soul in true holiness forms a principal part of the salvation he came to bestow; that the privileges of the evangelical dispensation are inseparably combined with its duties; and that every hope of eternal life is necessarily presumptuous and unfounded, which is not connected with "keeping the commandments of God." They will perceive the beautiful analogy subsisting between the Mosaic and Christian dispensations; and that the redemption wrought out upon the cross is just as subservient to the spiritual dominion of Christ over his people, as was the deliverance of the Israelites from Egypt to the erection of a theocracy in the Holy Land: in a word, they will plainly see that the regal authority of Christ over his church belongs to the very essence of the evangelical economy, considered as an annunciation of the *kingdom* or *reign* of God.

To trace the progress of antinomianism, and investigate the steps by which it has gradually attained its fearful ascendency, though an interesting inquiry would lead me far beyond the limits of this preface. Suffice it to suggest a few circumstances which appear to me to have contributed not a little to that result. When religious parties have been long formed, a certain technical phraseology, invented to designate more exactly the peculiarities of the respective systems, naturally grows up. What custom has sanctioned in process of time becomes law; and the slightest deviation from the consecrated diction comes to be viewed with suspicion and alarm. Now the technical language appropriated to the expression of the Calvinistic system in its nicer shades, however justifiable in itself, has, by its perpetual recurrence, narrowed the vocabulary of religion, and rendered obsolete many modes of expression which the sacred writers indulge without scruple. The latitude with which they express themselves on various subjects has been gradually relinquished; a scrupulous and systematic cast of diction has succeeded to the manly freedom and noble negligence they were accustomed to display; and many expressions, employed without hesitation in Scripture, are rarely found, except in the direct form of quotation, in the mouth of a modern Calvinist.

In addition to this, nothing is more usual than for the zealous abetters of a system, with the best intentions, to magnify the importance of its peculiar tenets by hyperbolical exaggerations, calculated to identify them with the fundamental articles of faith. Thus, the Calvinistic doctrines have often been denominated by divines of deservedly high reputation, *the doctrines of grace;* implying, not merely their truth, but that they constitute the very essence and marrow of the gospel. Hence persons of little reflection have been tempted to conclude that the zealous inculcation of these comprehends nearly the whole system of revealed truth, or as much of it, at least, as is of vital importance; and that no danger whatever can result from giving them the greatest possible prominence. But the transition from a partial exhibition of truth to the adoption of positive error is a most natural one: and he who commences with consigning certain important doctrines to oblivion will generally end in perverting or denying them. The authority of the laws of Christ, his proper dominion over his people, and the absolute necessity of evangelical obedience in order to eternal life, though perfectly consistent in my apprehension with Calvinism, form no part of it, considered as a separate system. In the systematic mode of instruction they are consequently omitted, or so slightly and sparingly adverted to, that they are gradually lost sight of; and when they are presented to the attention, being supported by no habitual mental associations, they wear the features of a strange and exotic character. They are repelled with disgust and suspicion, not because they are perceived to be at variance with the dictates of inspiration (their agreement with which may be immediately obvious), but simply because they deviate from the trains of thought which the hearer is accustomed to pursue with complacency. It is purely an affair of taste; it is neither the opposition of reason nor of conscience which is concerned, but the mere operation of antipathy.

The paucity of practical instruction,—the practice of dwelling almost exclusively in the exercise of the ministry on doctrinal and experimental topics, with a sparing inculcation of the precepts of Christ and the duties of morality,—is abundantly sufficient, without the slightest admixture of error, to produce the effect of which we are speaking: nor is it to be doubted that even holy and exemplary men have by these means paved the way for antinomianism. When they have found it necessary to advert to points of morality, and to urge them on Scriptural motives, the difference between these and their usual strain of instruction has produced a sort of mental revulsion. Conscious, meanwhile, that they have taught nothing but the pure and uncorrupted word of God,—have inculcated no doctrine but what appears to be sustained by the fair interpretation of the word,—they are astonished at perceiving the eager impetuosity with which a part of their hearers run into antinomian excesses: when a thorough investigation might convince them, that though they have inculcated truth, it has not been altogether "as it is in Jesus;" that many awakening and alarming considerations familiar to the Scriptures have been neglected, much of their pungent and practical appeal to the conscience suppressed, and a profusion of cordials and stimulants administered, where cathartics were required.

In the New Testament, the absolute subserviency of doctrinal statements to the formation of the principles and habits of practical piety is never lost sight of; we are continually reminded that obedience is the end of all knowledge, and of all religious impressions. But the tendency, it is to be feared, of much popular and orthodox instruction is, to bestow on the belief of certain doctrines, combined with strong religious emotion, the importance of an ultimate object, to the neglect of that great principle that "circumcision is nothing, and uncircumcision nothing, but the keeping of the commandments of God." While it is but candid to suppose that some are beguiled through the "good words and fair speeches" by which the apostles of antinomianism recommend themselves to the unlearned and unstable, it can scarcely be doubted that they are chiefly indebted for their success to the aversion which many feel to Christianity as a *practical* system. Divest it of its precepts and its sanctions,—represent it as a mere charter of privileges,—a provision for investing a certain class with a title to eternal life, independent of every moral discrimination,—and it will be eagerly embraced: but it will not be the religion of the New Testament; it will not be the religion of him who closed his Sermon on the Mount by reminding his hearers that he who "heareth his sayings, and doeth them not, shall be likened to a man who built his house upon the sand, and the storm came, and the rains descended, and the winds blew, and beat on that house, and it fell, because it was founded upon the sand."

The most effectual antidote to the leaven of antinomianism will probably be found in the frequent and earnest inculcation of the practical precepts of the gospel; in an accurate delineation of the Christian temper; in a specific and minute exposition of the personal, social, and relative duties, enforced at one time by the endearing, at another by the alarming motives which revelation abundantly suggests. To overlook the distinguishing doctrines of the gospel, under the pretence of advancing the interests of morality, is one extreme; to inculcate those doctrines without habitually adverting to their purifying and transforming influence, is another, not less dangerous. If the former involves the folly of attempting to rear a structure without a foundation, the latter leaves it naked and useless.

A large infusion of practical instruction may be expected to operate as an alterative in the moral constitution. Without displacing a single article from the established creed—without modifying or changing the minutest particle of speculative belief,—it will generate a habit of contemplating religion in its true character, as a system of moral government, as a wise and gracious provision for re-establishing the dominion of God in the heart of an apostate creature. Though there must unquestionably be a perfect agreement between all revealed truths, because truth is ever consistent with itself, yet they are not all adapted to produce the same immediate impression. They contribute to the same ultimate object, "the perfecting the man of God," by opposite tendencies; and while some are immediately adapted to inspire confidence and joy, others are fitted to produce vigilance and fear; like different species of diet, which may, in their turn, be equally conducive to health, though their action on the system be dissimilar. Hence it is of great importance, not merely that the doctrine that is taught be sound and scriptural, but that the proportion maintained amid the various articles of religious instruction coincide as far as possible with the inspired model; that each doctrine occupy its proper place in the scale; that the whole counsel of God be unfolded, and no one part of revealed truth be presented with a frequency and prominence which shall cast the others into shade. The progress of antinomianism, if I am not greatly mistaken, may be ascribed, in a great measure, to the neglect of these precautions,—to an intemperate and almost exclusive inculcation of doctrinal points.

Even when the necessity of an exemplary conduct is enforced upon Christians, an attentive and intelligent hearer will frequently perceive a manifest difference between the motives by which it is urged, and those which are presented by the inspired writers. The latter are not afraid of reminding every description of professors, without exception, that "if they live after the flesh they shall die;" and that they will then only "be partakers of Christ, if they hold fast the beginning of their confidence, and rejoicing of their hope, firm unto the end;" while too many content themselves with insisting on considerations which, whatever weight they may possess on a devout and tender spirit, it is the first effect of sinful indulgence to impair. Of this nature is the menace of spiritual desertion, darkness, absence of religious consolation, and other spiritual evils, which will always be found to be less alarming just in proportion to the degree of religious declension. To combat the moral distempers to which the professors of religion are liable by such antidotes as these, is appealing to a certain refinement of feeling, which the disease has extinguished or diminished, instead of alarming them with the prospect of death. It was not by sentimental addresses, nor by an appeal to the delicacies and sensibilities of a soul diseased, that the apostles proposed to alarm the fears or revive the vigilance of disorderly walkers: they drew aside the veil of eternity; they presented the thought, in all its terror, of the coming of Christ, "as a thief in the night." I would not be understood to insinuate that the more refined topics of appeal may not occasionally be resorted to with great propriety; all I would be supposed to regret is, the exclusive employment of a class of considerations, of one order of motives, derived from religious sensibility, to the neglect of those which are founded on eternal prospects and interests. As it is seldom safe for an accountable creature to lose sight of these in his most elevated moments; so least of all can they be dispensed with in the season of successful temptation. It is then especially, if I am not greatly mistaken, whatever may have been our past profession or attainments, that we need to be reminded of the awful certainty of future retribution, to recall to our remembrance that "whatsoever a man soweth, that shall he also reap." If, in the scheme of doctrine we have embraced, we suspect there is something incompatible with the use of such admonitions, we may be assured, either that the doctrine itself is false, or that our inference from it is erroneous, since no speculative tenets in religion can be so indubitably certain as the universality of the moral government of God.

Before I close this preface, I must be permitted to add, that the prevailing practice of representing the promises of the gospel as *unconditional*, or, at least of carefully avoiding the obvious phraseology which the contrary supposition would suggest, appears to me directly to pave the way to antinomianism. The idea of *meritorious* conditions is, indeed, utterly incompatible with the gospel, considered as a system of grace. But if there be no conditions of salvation whatever, how it is possible to confute the pretensions or confound the confidence of the most licentious professor, I am at an utter loss to discover. It will be in vain to allege the entire absence of internal holiness, together with all the fruits of the Spirit, as defeating his hope of eternal life; since, upon the supposition we are combating, the answer is ready, that the enjoyment of future felicity is suspended on no conditions. The absurdity of this notion is not less palpable than its presumption. All promises must either be made to individuals by name, or indefinitely to persons of a specific character. A moment's attention will be sufficient to satisfy us that the promise of pardon in the New Testament is of the latter description; in no one instance is it addressed to the individual by name, but to the penitent, the believing, the obedient, or to some similar specification of character. Before any person, therefore, can justly appropriate the promise to himself, he must ascertain his possession of that character; or, which is precisely the same thing, he must perceive that he comes within the prescribed condition. When it is affirmed that "except we repent we shall perish," is it not manifest that he only is entitled to claim exemption from that doom who is conscious of the feelings of a penitent? For the same reason, if he only who believes shall be saved, our assurance of salvation, as far as it depends upon evidence, must be exactly proportioned to the certainty we feel of our actual believing. To abandon these principles is to involve ourselves in an inextricable labyrinth, to lie open to the grossest delusions, to build conclusions of infinite moment on phantoms light as air. He who flatters himself with the hope of salvation, without perceiving in himself a specific difference of character from "the world that lieth in wickedness," either founds his persuasion absolutely on nothing, or on an immediate revelation,—on a preternatural discovery of a matter of fact on which the Scriptures are totally silent. This absurd notion of unconditional promises, by severing the assurance of salvation from all the fruits of the Spirit, from every trace and feature of a renovated nature and a regenerate state, opens the widest possible door to licentiousness.

As far as it is sustained by the least shadow of reasoning, it may be traced to the practice of confounding the secret purposes of the Supreme Being with his revealed promises. That in the breast of the Deity an eternal purpose has been formed respecting the salvation of a certain portion of the human race, is a doctrine which it appears to me is clearly revealed. But this secret purpose is so far from being incompatible with the necessary conditions of salvation, that they form a part of it; their existence is an inseparable link in the execution of the divine decree: for the same wisdom which has appointed the end has also infallibly determined the means by which it shall be accomplished; and as the personal direction of the decree remains a secret until it is developed in the event, it cannot possibly, considered in itself, lay a foundation for confidence. That a certain number of the human race are ordained to eternal life may be inferred from many passages of Scripture; but if any person infers from these general premises that he is of that number, he advances a proposition without the slightest colour of evidence. An assurance of salvation can, consequently, in no instance, be deduced from the doctrine of absolute decrees, until they manifest themselves in their actual effects; that is, in that renewal of the heart which the Bible affirms to be essential to future felicity.

But I am detaining the reader too long from the pleasure and advantage he may promise himself from the perusal of the following treatise, where he will meet with no illiberal insinuations, no personal invective,—the too frequent seasoning of controversy, and the ordinary gratification of vulgar minds,—but a series of calm and dispassionate reasonings out of the Scriptures. That they may produce all the beneficial results which the excellent author has so much at heart, is the fervent prayer of the writer of these lines.

ROBERT HALL.

Leicester, July 2, 1819

A LETTER

TO

THE REV. W. BENNETT,

Author of an Essay on the Gospel Constitution.

January 18, 1810.

DEAR SIR,

I OUGHT sooner to have acknowledged to you the great pleasure I derived from the performance you were so kind as to give me at Northampton. I have read it with as much attention as I am able; and though the subject is involved in so much difficulty, I admired the perspicuity with which it was treated, so as to be within the limits of an ordinary capacity. There is a precision and comprehension in the choice of terms, and a luminous track of thought pervading the whole, which, according to my apprehension, has scarcely been equalled, and never exceeded, in the discussion of such points. I do think you have steered a happy medium, between the rigidity of Calvinism and the laxness of Arminianism, and have succeeded in the solution of the grand difficulty—the consistency between general offers and invitations, and the speciality of divine grace. This interesting question is handled with masterly ability. I am particularly delighted with your explicit statement and vindication of the established connexion between the use of instituted means and the attainment of divine blessings, and the consequent hypothetical possibility of the salvation of all men where the gospel comes. On this point the representations of Calvinists have long appeared to me very defective; and that, fettered by their system, they have by no means gone so far in encouraging and urging sinners to the use of prayer, reading the Scriptures, self-examination, &c., as the Scriptures justify. They have contented themselves too much with enjoining and inculcating the duty of faith, which, however important and indispensable, is not, I apprehend, usually imparted till men have been earnestly led to seek and strive. Here the Arminians, such of them as are evangelical, have had greatly the advantage of the Calvinists in pleading with sinners. Your great principle of the design of religion, in every dispensation of it, being intended as the pursuit of the plan of divine government for exercising the moral powers and faculties of creatures, is grand and noble, and gives conti nuity and harmony to the whole scheme. I lent your book to Mr. B— who is much pleased with it, and only wishes you had expressed yourself more fully in favour of the general extent of Christ's death. I think you have asserted it by implication, though I wish you had asserted it unequivocally, because I am fully persuaded it is a doctrine of Scripture, and that it forms the only consistent basis of unlimited invitations. I think the most enlightened Calvinists are too reserved on this head; and that their refusal to declare, with the concurrent testimony of Scripture, that Christ died for all men, tends to confirm the prejudices of Methodists, and others, against election and special grace. With this small exception, if it be an exception, your work appears to me to be entitled to the highest approbation and applause; and I cannot but hope it will have an important effect in bringing good men nearer together; than which I know nothing more desirable. Wishing you much success in every labour of your hands,

I remain, dear Sir,

With high esteem,

Your affectionate brother,

Robert Hall

AN EXTRACT

FROM

DR. JOHNSON'S PREFACE TO COWPER'S CORRESPONDENCE.

"I ACCOUNT myself particularly fortunate in being favoured with the opinion of confessedly one of the best judges of composition that this country has to boast—the Rev. Robert Hall, of Leicester. In a letter addressed to me, on the 19th of August of the present year, 1823, he writes thus :—

"'It is quite unnecessary to say that I perused the letters with great admiration and delight. I have always considered the letters of Mr. Cowper as the finest specimen of the epistolary style in our language ; and these appear to me of a superior description to the former, possessing as much beauty with more piety and pathos. To an air of inimitable ease and carelessness, they unite a higher degree of correctness, such as could result only from the clearest intellect, combined with the most finished taste. I have scarcely found a single word which is capable of being exchanged for a better.

"'Literary errors I can discern none. The selection of words and the structure of the periods are inimitable; they present as striking a contrast as can well be conceived to the turgid verbosity which passes at present for fine writing, and which bears a great resemblance to the degeneracy which marks the style of Ammianus Marcellinus, as compared to that of Cicero or of Livy. A perpetual effort and struggle is made to supply the place of vigour, garish and dazzling colours are substituted for chaste ornament, and the hideous distortions of weakness for native strength. In my humble opinion, the study of Cowper's prose may, on this account, be as useful in forming the taste of young people as his poetry.

"'That the letters will afford great delight to all persons of true taste, and that you will confer a most acceptable present on the reading world by publishing them, will not admit of a doubt.'"

THE

SPIRITUAL CONDITION AND PROSPECTS

OF

THE JEWS

[*Written in* 1826.]

Few perhaps are to be found who have made religion the object of their serious attention, who have not bestowed some thought on the spiritual condition and prospects of the Jews,—a people on many accounts the most remarkable of any that have appeared on the stage of time. Intermingled with all nations, but uniting with none,—distinguished by their attachment to one portion of revelation, and their aversion to another,—equally removed from the errors of polytheism, and the belief of Christianity, they occupy a station peculiar to themselves: "they dwell alone, and are not reckoned among the people." In this state of seclusion, it seems generally taken for granted that they are not only the frown of Providence, but that they are universally under the Divine malediction, exposed to the doom of the impenitent and unbelieving. Their disbelief of the gospel is supposed, without any exception, to render them liable to the penalties of eternal death. I have sometimes been tempted to doubt of this; and the design of my addressing you on the present occasion is briefly to state the grounds on which my doubts are founded, not with a view to provoke controversy, but solely to elicit the inquiry of superior minds.

1. An essential difference exists between the Jews and other unbelievers, in a particular of great moment; which is, that they are already in the possession of the oracles of God, and, in these, of all that is absolutely necessary to salvation. That the Old Testament is sufficient to conduct men to eternal life is evident, from the testimony it bears of itself, as well as from the acknowledged scope and design of a revelation; for it would be a reflection on infinite Wisdom to suppose it capable of communicating a revelation which necessarily failed in its principal object, that of "making men wise unto salvation." Nor is it less certain that some of the eminent saints and favourites of the Most High flourished under the Jewish dispensation. The doctrines taught by Moses and the prophets, it must be confessed, are in themselves an adequate instrument of sanctification, so that, if he who conscientiously avails himself of it falls short of eternal life, it must

be ascribed to the intervention of a subsequent and more perfect revelation.

2. As a subsequent dispensation, however, has been given, enforced by the penalty of eternal death, it may be thought this is sufficient at once to determine the future condition of those who reject it, and consequently to preclude the unconverted part of the Jews from all hope of salvation. It is agreed that the deliberate rejection of the gospel involves a sentence of condemnation: but that only can be said to be *rejected* which is adequately proposed. By the ancient Jews, Christianity was rejected. Our Lord "came to his own, and his own received him not." They heard his discourses; they witnessed his miracles, or at least had the same evidence of them as they had of other matters of public notoriety; they beheld the spotless innocence of his life, and the perfect correspondence of the leading events of his history to the predictions of their prophets; nor was there any prejudice existing against Christianity, but what was of recent growth, the pure effect of carnality, impenitence, and hardness of heart. They knew enough of the Christian religion to discern its sanctifying tendency, and to hate it on that account: their rejection of it betrayed an enmity to the true character of God, and therefore incurred all the guilt included in that solemn assertion of our Lord, "But now they have both seen and hated both me and my Father." Their opposition to Christ was not the resistance made to the encroachments of a foreign dominion; it was domestic rebellion. The evidence of Christianity was presented in all its force and splendour; it came into actual contact with the mind, and on that very account produced a feeling of hostility to its spirit and its claims, which would not have been felt towards an object more remote.

3. But the position in which Christianity stands towards modern Jews is very different. Their knowledge of it must be derived almost entirely from the New Testament, and the causes which may in many instances be supposed to divert their attention from it, are very dissimilar to those which originated the incredulity of their ancestors. The prohibition of the New Testament is a primary element in Jewish education. The absolute sufficiency of the writings of Moses and the prophets, and the impropriety of presuming to add to these lively oracles, and to abrogate an everlasting law, are among the first principles instilled into the infant mind. They are taught to repose with the utmost confidence on a religion which even Christians confess to be of divine origin; while the system which has superseded it is comparatively of recent origin, and little accredited by its efficacy in correcting the vices and forming the manners of its followers. They are told, indeed, that Christianity is the sequel and completion of the ancient religion,—that it substantiates its types and accomplishes its prophecies; but they are told so by those whom they have few inducements to regard. Respect for paternal authority, veneration for an illustrious ancestry, deference to age and rank, combine with the fear of innovation, and an attachment, though too exclusive, to Moses and the prophets, to keep them ignorant of the

New Testament, and consequently estranged from the principal means of conviction. But the principles which we have alluded to are usually the strongest in the most virtuous and susceptible minds; nor is it difficult to conceive what an effectual bar they may prove to the perusal of the Christian records, apart from those criminal prejudices which occasioned the rejection of Christianity by their ancestors. The disbelief of Christianity on the part of such as have been trained on Christian principles can seldom, if ever, be imputed to ignorance—convictions must be stifled, and the force of evidence evaded; but the unbelief of modern Jews is the natural consequence of their want of acquaintance with an inspired record.

The portion of revelation which the Jew possesses already contains whatever is absolutely necessary to be known in order to obtain eternal life. Jews and Christians, at variance about every thing else, unite their suffrages in its favour, affirming unanimously that it was for upwards of two thousand years the authentic revelation of the will of Heaven. A Jew, therefore, cannot doubt of its competence to make him wise unto salvation. On the other hand, he is taught, from a quarter which God and nature enjoin him to revere, to look upon the New Testament as an imposture. In this instance, it is but candid to suppose that the records of our religion are neglected, not always from the love of vice, or the predominance of worldly interests, but from a conscientious fear of innovation and dread of impiety. He is necessarily ignorant of a book which never engaged his attention; and that it failed to engage it is the effect of an exclusive, and, in that respect only, an erroneous attachment to an inspiration of an earlier date.

4. Supposing him, from these and similar causes, to remain all his life unacquainted with the Christian system, and consequently uninfluenced by its doctrines, have we any authority for asserting that he cannot possibly be the subject of divine grace, possessed as he is of an instrument of sanctification, which the Holy Ghost, for ages, condescended to employ? A new revelation can make no alteration in the intrinsic nature of that which precedes it; and if the Old Testament ever was sufficient to make men wise unto salvation, why should we doubt of its being still competent for that purpose? Had it been the only companion of one that was shipwrecked on a desert island, shall we hesitate to believe that its serious perusal might be instrumental to his salvation? Here indeed the absence of other means of instruction would be the unavoidable consequence of providential arrangements, which cannot with equal propriety be affirmed in the case of our Jew. But though his ignorance of the New Testament cannot be said to be the necessary consequence of the circumstances attending his birth and education, the obstacles which they may be supposed to present are very powerful, and not at all necessarily complicated with deep moral pravity. The utmost tenderness of conscience, the greatest solicitude for salvation, could not be supposed to prevent a youth strictly educated in the principles of Judaism from contracting prejudices against Christianity, the natural operation of which would be to indispose him to the perusal of its inspired records. The agency of

the Spirit is of a moral, not a physical nature; nor is it his manner to interfere with the action of natural causes.

5. Admitting, however, that as much criminality attaches to the prejudice which keeps a conscientious Jew ignorant of the New Testament as the most zealous will contend for, it appears to be of the same order with that which operates in other instances, without our suspecting for a moment that it is incompatible with salvation. What shall we say of the prejudice which prompted such men as Pascal and Fenelon to reject the Protestant doctrine with which they were far better acquainted than a modern Jew can be supposed to be with the Christian Scriptures? The opportunities which they enjoyed for satisfying themselves of the truth of the reformed religion were at least equal to those which a Jew possesses for becoming an enlightened convert to the Christian faith; and the circumstances, whatever they were, that indisposed those illustrious men to the impartial examination of the Lutheran or Calvinistic tenets, were neither more numerous nor more powerful than those which produce a similar indisposition in Jews to investigate the evidence of our holy religion. Nor ought it to be forgotten that it is impossible to continue in the papal communion without committing idolatry, a sin against which the most fearful maledictions of Scripture are pointed. Notwithstanding this, however, all candid Protestants acknowledge the possibility of salvation within the Romish pale.

With all their prejudices and imperfections, it is contended that they maintained a body of saving truth, which, under the agency of the divine Spirit, was, it is charitably hoped, rendered effectual to their sanctification. But this is precisely the mode of reasoning we adopt in relation to a pious Jew. He also possesses a system of saving truth. He possesses, in the law and the prophets, what our Lord himself has affirmed to contain sufficient motives to repentance, together with that expectation of a future Messiah, and of the spiritual benefits he is appointed to confer, by which saints under the ancient economy were justified. Let it be carefully kept in mind that it is the bare possibility that a Jew, without becoming a convert to Christianity, may obtain salvation, for which we contend; or, in other words, that we are not warranted to conclude that the Holy Spirit, on no occasion whatever, deigns to employ the ancient oracles for saving purposes. Of the extreme danger to which the great majority both of Jews and papists are exposed, and of the strict propriety of speaking of them in the mass as in a state of alienation from God, we entertain no doubt; while we would indulge a hope, for similar reasons in both cases, that there will be found among both some with the "mark of God on their foreheads." The denunciations of divine vengeance on the patrons and supporters of the Roman hierarchy in the Apocalypse are as awful as words can express, and conceived in very general terms: "The smoke of their torment ascendeth," says John, "for ever and ever; and they have no rest day or night who worship the beast and his image, and whosoever receiveth the mark of his name," yet, notwithstanding these fearful menaces, we venture a charitable opinion of many who have been entangled in the errors of the papacy. We presume to hope that the merciful God will distinguish between the impious inventor of a system, and those who, without imbibing its spirit, have in different degrees been duped by its sophistry. And why should not a similar judgment be formed respecting a serious and conscientious Jew?

6. The question before us is, properly speaking, a question *de jure* rather than *de facto*: it does not so properly relate to the fact whether there are any Jews in a state of salvation who are not converts to Christianity, as to the possibility of the thing. We know so little of the real character of modern Jews, insulated as they are from general society, that it is difficult to speak with any degree of positivity on that subject. A general and superficial view of that people would tempt us to form the most melancholy conclusion. But I have been informed by a learned Jew, extensively acquainted with his own nation, that there are to be found among them men of a very different stamp from what is generally prevalent. He solemnly assured me that he knew one Jew in particular, a foreigner, who was accustomed to spend the night preceding their great fast in the synagogue, prostrate in tears and supplications; and, on my asking what he was praying for, he replied, with some quickness, "For the pardon of his sins and the sins of his people, and for the speedy arrival of the promised Messiah;" he declared, at the same time, that this was not a solitary instance. Admitting this representation to be correct (and there is nothing in it which exceeds the bounds of credibility), I should feel little hesitation in believing that "He who delighteth in mercy" would not despise the prayer of such a penitent, because he wanted that explicit knowledge of Christ which was for ages withheld from the Jewish church. Prevented from attending to the evidences of Christianity, by the influence of prejudices which it was extremely difficult for him to surmount, and at all events not more criminal than those which kep Fenelon within the trammels of popery, what should induce us tc form such an opposite judgment, in two cases, as to place the latter in the list of eminent saints, while we consign the former to destruction? Dark as popery is, we must allow that the respective degrees of illumination enjoyed in the two cases were very unequal, but the fainter of the two we must either confess is in itself saving, or give up the patriarchs and prophets for lost.

Perhaps it is unnecessary to remind your readers, that while I plead for the possibility of a Jew's obtaining salvation without that clear and explicit knowledge of Christ which Christians possess, I am far from supposing two distinct methods of salvation: whoever are justified, whether under the Jewish or Christian economies, are alike justified by faith in the Messiah. But I am at a loss to perceive why that more vague and imperfect knowledge of his character supplied by Moses and the prophets, which formerly availed for that purpose, should necessarily be ineffectual now.

7. These views are, in my humble opinion, considerably confirmed by the tenor of the prophetic writings, which seem on various occasions to recognise a relation as all along subsisting between the Su-

preme Being and the Jews previously to the period of their accession to the Christian church. It appears to me evident from ancient prophecy, that the scene of the future conversion of the Jews is their own land, where it is probable, from Zechariah, that a supernatural interposition of the Messiah will take place in their favour, that he will suddenly reveal himself to them as a nation, and thus effect the accomplishment of the remarkable prediction recorded in the twelfth and thirteenth chapters of that prophecy. Before their final deliverance, however, we read of a severe purgation which they are destined to undergo, during which two parts shall be cut off, and a third only left, and that the third part is to be brought through the fire, and to be refined as silver is refined, and to be tried as gold is tried. "They shall call on my name, and I will hear them; I will say, It is my people, and they shall say, The Lord is my God." To the same purpose the prophet Ezekiel, where predicting, as I conceive, the final restoration of the Jews to their own land, tells us that previously to that event the Lord "will plead with them in the wilderness of the people, as he pleaded with their fathers in the wilderness of Egypt; that he will bring them into the bond of the covenant, purge out from them the rebels and those that transgress, so that they shall not enter into the land of Israel:" and he adds, "Ye shall know that I am the Lord."

The latter chapters of Ezekiel, describing the erection of a certain temple, are involved in so much obscurity, that it seems difficult to arrive at any determinate conclusion respecting the import of that mysterious prophecy. It is certain that the attempt to spiritualize it produces little besides perplexity and confusion; nor have we any example in Scripture of an allegory so perfectly dark and enigmatic as it must be confessed to be on that supposition. The third chapter of Hosea seems to present us with a just and striking picture of the present condition of the Jews; they have remained "many days without a king, and without a prince, and without a sacrifice, and without an image, and without an ephod, and without a teraphim." Separated alike from Christians and from heathens, they still retain their conjugal relation to the Lord; they are under his frown, but not severed from his covenant, and occupy a peculiar and intermediate station between the members of the Christian church and the worshippers of idols.

The preceding remarks, let it be remembered, are designed to apply, not to the great mass of the Jewish people, who appear to be in a state of deep alienation from God, but solely to such among them (if such there be) as are conscientious disciples of Moses and the prophets, and who, though they are destitute of the superior illumination of the gospel, faithfully improve the light which they enjoy.

The chief practical use to be derived from the hypothesis which I have ventured to suggest is, to inspire us with an increased tenderness and respect for the seed of Abraham, as containing, notwithstanding its occupying a distinct fold, a portion of the true church of God. If we can be induced to hope that he has still a people among them, we shall be ready to look upon them with something like fraternal affection, and to embrace every opportunity of reprobating and removing the cruel privations and restrictions imposed by Christian nations, who, absurdly imagining that they do an acceptable service to God by their persecution and depression, are in reality treasuring up wrath by aggravating the affliction of those whom he has smitten. It is surprising that any man can read the ancient prophecies with attention without perceiving that he surveys the treatment of his ancient people with a jealous eye; and that while he signalizes his displeasure against them by the course of his providence, he will enter into a severe reckoning with those who shall be found "to help on the affliction." A large arrear of guilt has been contracted by the nations of Christendom on this account; and in this age of liberality, when such mighty efforts are made to procure the removal of political disabilities on the score of religion, it is surely high time their attention was turned to the relief of the oppressed and persecuted children of Abraham. Their political emancipation and restoration to the equal rights of citizenship might be reasonably expected to soften their prejudices, and dispose them to a more favourable hearing of the Christian cause; nor could any thing be more becoming the character and pretensions of the Jewish Society than to take the lead in that noble enterprise. As the basis of all social virtue is laid in justice, so by none should its obligations be deemed more sacred than by those who make loud professions of Christian zeal and exalted charity.

Having thus freely stated my present opinions upon a subject which I think has not often been discussed, simply with a view to excite inquiry, I have no intention to enter into controversy by defending them, but shall cheerfully leave them to the consideration of your readers.

THE

SUBSTANCE OF A CHARGE,

DELIVERED AT THE ORDINATION OF THE REV. J. K. HALL, AT KETTERING, NOVEMBER 8, 1815.

[*From the Notes of the Rev. S. Hillyard, of Bedford.*]

I SHALL not select any particular passage of Scripture, as it is not my intention to confine myself to any one subject, but to communicate such miscellaneous hints of advice as may be suitable to the present occasion.

If, however, I refer to one passage more than another, it will be the exhortation of Paul to Timothy:—"Preach the word; be instant in season, out of season; reprove, rebuke, exhort, with all long-suffering and doctrine."

The solemn transactions of this day will not be done with when the service is closed; they will undergo a review at the tribunal of the great Judge, in whose name we are now assembled. Nothing in this state is final: every thing in time is connected with eternity. The church of Christ here, who have chosen you for their pastor, and you, my brother, who have accepted this office, will have your determinations, your motives, and your ends adjudged by "Him who seeth not as man seeth," and will meet with a reward according to their sincerity and purity.

You now stand as a watchman situated on an eminence; if you see danger you must "blow the trumpet," and warn the people, that "he that taketh warning may deliver his soul;" and "if any man take not warning, his blood shall be upon his own head;" if the people be not warned, they may be taken away in their iniquity; but "their blood," saith the Lord, "will I require at the watchman's hands."

You are a steward of the manifold mysteries of God, to bring out of the treasury "things new and old, that every one may have a portion." "Moreover, it is required of a steward that he be found faithful."

The principal duty of this office consists in your engagement to preach the gospel:—"Preach the word."

You will recollect that your work is not to dispense the principles inculcated by any human authority or supported by any human society

Though the treasure of the gospel be communicated to "earthen vessels," its origin is celestial.

There is then little scope for the exercise of invention or the flights of imagination in the discharge of this duty: these faculties are employed to find out new principles or to discover new associations; but their exercise here will only tend to mix truth with error, to "darken counsel by words without knowledge," and to impair that system of truth which God hath furnished and communicated to man. You are not required to make new discoveries; you need only to inquire and ascertain what is revealed in the word of God: find out what is "the mind of the Spirit," and submit yourself to his instructions. The best method of doing this, in connexion with reading and meditation, is to pray for spiritual illumination, like David, when he said, "Open thou mine eyes, that I may behold wonderful things out of thy law." There are many wonderful things in the law; but we need the Spirit to give us *understanding*, and still more to cause us to feel the influence of truth in our own hearts, and to communicate it to the hearts of others.

There are three things to which you must attend in preaching; the matter, the mode, and the motives: the matter must be pure, the mode "with all gravity," the motives such as are presented in the word of God, and furnished by your office and your particular station in the church.

In preaching the word, incorruptness or purity in your matter is of the first importance: in order to this, adhere to the dictates of the holy Scriptures. I mean not by this that you should confine yourself to the words, but to the sentiments: the sentiments may be lost where the words are retained; but the sentiments may be retained and communicated in different expressions.

Preach the word purely and fully; mix nothing with it that does not belong to it, or may not evidently be inferred from its language.

State every doctrine and opinion as near to the mind of the Spirit as you can ascertain.

The doctrines of the word you will bring forth in their full import, without concealing them, or endeavouring to melt them down and mould them so as to suit the prejudiced and indolent depravity of the human heart.

The gospel is not suited, and cannot be made to suit, the corrupt dispositions and inclinations of the carnal "mind;" but the faithful preaching of it is calculated to oppose and to overcome those evil prejudices so far as to excite men to attend to the doctrines it contains and the blessings it proposes. It is your duty, not to bring down the gospel into a conformity with them, but to change them into a conformity with the gospel.

Read the Scriptures frequently, with close attention and fervent prayer. Endeavour to collect as much knowledge relative to revealed truth as you can possibly acquire. Out of the Scriptures you may continually draw new treasures; and if you are "a scribe well instructed in the mysteries of the kingdom," you will not find it difficult to present a variety of interesting matter from hence that shall not only be profitable but delightful to your hearers.

There are two opposite extremes to be avoided in *the manner* of your preaching the word: the one, a manner vague and indistinct; the other, a manner too narrow, subtle, and systematical.

Some have preached the gospel rather by implication than by plain direct statements: they have treated it as if there were something in its doctrines that would not bear the exhibition. Such men have made moral instructions the main points of their ministry; the doctrines of the atonement, regeneration, the divinity of the Saviour, and the riches of his grace, if they have not been entirely suppressed, have not occupied that prominent situation which their importance demands for them; and their hearers have consequently been altogether unacquainted with them, or, having but slight hold of them, these things have gradually slidden out of their minds, and left them prepared for heretical instructers. Be not ashamed of the gospel; though it may contradict many of the fashionable and favourite notions of mankind, and though you may find mysteries connected with the subjects of it which you cannot comprehend, yet, as we know but little of the world, and of ourselves less, we must receive with simplicity what God has taught. He must "be true, though every man be a liar."—You have taken upon you the solemn charge of "feeding the flock of God," you must keep back no part of what he has provided for them; let it be your concern that at the end of your ministry you may be able to speak as St. Paul,—"I kept back nothing that was profitable to you: I take you to record this day that I am pure from the blood of all men; for I have not shunned to declare unto you all the counse of God."

Opposed to the vague and indistinct manner of preaching is the narrow and systematical method, according to which, doctrines, sometimes not the most important, have been made the themes of remark and discussion to the neglect of every other subject.

The gospel is not revealed in a systematic form; it is not confined to any particular set of doctrines; nor does it ever advance *any* doctrine as *merely* a subject of speculation.

Be upon your guard against confining your administrations; point out the practical consequences of the doctrines you preach, without which they will not produce that good which they are calculated to yield as they are revealed in the Scriptures. It is of great importance to observe the proportion which truths bear to each other, that we may not dwell upon subjects of comparatively small moment, to the neglect of others that are really weighty. We should not give too much of our attention to any favourite topics, however important: the effect of such a course will be to leave a wrong impression on the minds of the hearers. It will be likely to produce a disproportionate regard to some doctrines, ordinances, and moral duties, which is a similar deformity in the new man to the disproportionate enlargement of any particular member in the human body; and it may be that such regard to any doctrine, out of its connexion with other revealed truths, will only serve to exhibit it as a subject of speculation, and not of vital and practical utility.

An excellent man was so impressed with the doctrine of the divinity of Christ, that he made it the constant topic of his ministry; every sermon he preached was crowded with proofs, or answers to objections, relating to this important topic; and the result was, that most of his hearers became Arians and Socinians! This effect was not such as he expected, or as might be thought of at the time by others; but the consequence was natural. Such discussions produced, first, a dry speculative attention to the subject, then a fiery and contentious spirit in discussion; in this state the spirit of the doctrine was lost, and the people sunk into such a frame of mind as is suited to the reception of these or any other heresies that might be sophistically presented to them. A serious, spiritual state of mind is that which you must be concerned to promote in your hearers as the best preservative against error; and in order to this you must proclaim both the doctrinal truth and the practical exhortations of religion.

There has been long laid down a rule which is often repeated, is most excellent, and worthy of constant recollection: it is, that we must "preach the doctrines practically, and preach practice doctrinally." Preach the doctrines so as to show their influence on our practice, and recommend religious and virtuous conduct by evangelical motives. This happy combination will form a complete course of religious instruction. It is impossible to say which of these two, doctrinal or practical preaching, is most necessary; or which extreme is most dangerous—to preach doctrine without practice, or practice without doctrine. Read, then, the Scriptures of the New Testament, in order to observe how these are blended together by our Lord and his inspired apostles. You will observe *there* that the enforcement of duties by evangelical motives is the very end of the gospel; and all preaching is good and estimable only as it secures the same end by the same motives.

Be not afraid of devoting whole sermons to particular parts of moral conduct and religious duties. It is impossible to give right views of them unless you dissect characters and describe particular virtues and vices. The "fruits of the flesh" and the "fruits of the Spirit" must be distinctly pointed out. To preach against sin in general, without descending to particulars, may lead many to complain of the evil of their hearts, while at the same time they are awfully inattentive to the evil of their conduct.

You are aware that to inculcate the necessity of regeneration is a large part of your work, and must not on any account be neglected; but it must not be so taught as to lead men to suppose that if they are once regenerated they may be careless and indifferent, for then they are sure of heaven. If you do not often preach in an alarming, urgent manner, to guard them against sin and to animate them to holiness, you will be chargeable with neglect. You must warn the righteous man that he turn not from his righteousness, as well as assure the wicked man that he will perish if he persevere in his wickedness. If serious admonitions are neglected, the preaching of regeneration itself may be very hurtful, by leading numbers to suppose, that having passed the ordeal, nothing now remains but for them to wait their entrance into heaven, for which they will think they are already prepared. There is a sort of evangelical ministry which produces no effect but to awaken to a sudden apprehension of danger, and then to consign, by means of opiates, to the delusive and destructive stupidity of spiritual death.

When no pains are taken to warn the awakened of the necessity of deep repentance, of living faith, of persevering obedience, of unceasing vigilance, and of renewed conflicts, even unto the end, they are in danger of fancying they are "rich, and increased in goods, and have need of nothing," though they are "miserable, and poor, and blind, and naked."

Remind them, that when they enter on a Christian profession they only put on the armour; admonish them of the obligations they are under to be holy and active: they have entered as soldiers of the Cross, they have taken the military oath; but to take that is not to perform the duty of a soldier; the display of bravery is to be made in the day of conflict, in their watching, standing, striving, and putting to flight the enemies of their salvation.

Exhort them, therefore, incessantly that they "walk worthy of their high calling;" that they walk "as becometh the gospel of Christ;" that they "draw not back unto perdition;" that they be faithful unto death, that they may obtain "the crown of life."

I will now proceed to notice briefly those parts of your work which are not immediately connected with preaching the word: "Be instant in season, out of season," said the apostle. While engaged in ministering the word, you are instant in season; but you should also attend to your duties out of season, when it is not a time for preaching.

Remember, *this* people is *your charge*. When they are absent from you, bear them in your mind; let them have an interest in your prayers when you have retired to your closet: though they are your charge, you cannot be always speaking to them; but they must be engraved on your heart, as the high-priest bore the names of the tribes of Israel, and the good shepherd is acquainted with all his sheep.

The excellent Booth has said, "He that does not pray oftener for his people than with them, neglects an important part of his duty." It will endear them to you, and draw out your affections to them, if you pray much for them, and it will secure, through the Divine blessing, your usefulness among them. You are, as an intercessor, to "stand in the breach;" and whatever difficulty or danger may oppose, you must be, like another Moses, between God and the people.

Not only is secret prayer for them a great duty, but an habitual remembrance and affectionate respect for them must be cultivated when you are not, as well as when you are, ministering to them the word of life.

"Watch for them as one that must give an account:" take every favourable opportunity of speaking to them on the great concerns of eternity and the weighty subjects of revealed truth. If you see any of them departing into sin, remember it is said, "Thou shalt not hate thy brother, but shalt reprove him." A neglect of reproof in such circumstances would have all the bad consequences of hatred; for thus he would be left to lie under the greatest evil from which you might deliver him. No fear of giving offence should prevent you from reproving, with meekness and faithfulness, the most opulent or even the most valued friends of the society, if it be needful. If their misconduct does not require to be brought before the church, yet do not neglect to speak to them in private, and administer what counsel or reproof the circumstances may demand.

Your people will look to you, as a minister, for consolation when they are in distress, when overwhelmed with personal, domestic, or other relative calamities: manifest towards them the tenderest sympathy, a disposition "to weep with them that weep, as well as to rejoice with them that rejoice."

It will be especially your duty to attend to those who are beginning to seek and inquire after salvation. No part of your office is more delicate than the giving instruction to awakened consciences, who desire rest, but know not where or how to obtain it. The impressions they have received are in danger of wearing off; sometimes they seem pressing forward, sometimes they seem drawing backward; sometimes they are the pupils of conscience, at others the pupils of appetite and custom.

Such will require attention; and not to take opportunities of advising and directing would be to neglect a duty in which you ought to abound. It is not for me to instruct you *how* you should do this; but be not afraid to inculcate repentance. Teach them to expect salvation, not *for* their works, but *in* a course of attention to all the dictates of the Divine will respecting faith and obedience. Cherish in them tenderness of conscience, guard them against "easily besetting sins," and, at the same time, warn them not to stop at outward information, but to seek after an inward change, and the application of the blood of Jesus. Admonish them not to consider themselves as having already attained, or being already perfect; not to mistake what is preparatory for what is final, or to rest short of that connexion with Christ and conformity to him which is the pledge and commencement of life eternal.

Here we need Divine assistance: it is best to learn these things in answer to prayer, and by habitual practice. As nothing but much practice and an exact knowledge of the anatomy of the human frame will make a skilful physician, so nothing but a knowledge of the human heart and the efficacy of the gospel in healing the diseases of the soul, can teach us to bring men health and cure.

It will be useful to "exhort with much long-suffering, from house to house:" much is to be accomplished by those who have a talent for interesting and familiar religious conversation; a talent which all should cultivate. Some ministers, by an exhibition of "the mind of Christ," and a recommendation of the truth, in private, have advanced religion even more than by their public ministry: as an auxiliary, every one will find it beneficial, and it is impossible to overvalue it.

See that your social visits are conducted in the spirit of the gospel. Guard against levity. Whatever is innocent mirth, if it be allowed, should only hold a subordinate place; and the dignity of the minister should always appear.

Do not seek to cultivate the good opinion and favour merely of those who are rich, or even of those who are endowed with intellectual treasures; nor seek the gratifications of the table, nor the indulgence of sensual appetites. Despise not the meanest of the flock; look not on them with eyes of the flesh, but with eyes of the Spirit. You will then perceive the distinctions of wealth, or education, or intellect are but little, compared with the state of *all* as responsible and immortal beings. The points of difference in men are nothing, compared with the common capacity for knowing and enjoying God. They are to be regarded principally as vessels capable of experiencing the wrath, or receiving the mercy of the Almighty.

Look upon them now as you will look upon them on a dying bed: you will not think of them *then* as rich or poor, as learned or unlearned; but as sanctified or unsanctified, as "sheep or goats," as the righteous or the wicked, as persons with whom you are to rejoice for ever, or whose final ruin you must witness at the last day. Let nothing render you negligent of the improvement and comfort of any one. Remember who hath said, "Whoso shall offend one of these little ones, which believe in me, it were better for him that a millstone were hanged about his neck, and that he were cast into the depth of the sea." There is not *one* whose soul is not precious in the estimation of the Lord, not one for whom he has not shed his blood, not one for whom he would not have been ready to shed his blood, had no other soul existed. Let the dignity of human nature, viewed in this light, arm you against being imposed upon by any adventitious circumstance.

In order that you may attend to these duties aright, cultivate a devotional spirit. The more you have of the mind of Christ, the more you walk in holiness and humility, the more "will your profiting appear." Watch against spiritual as well as intellectual pride. Prostrate yourself in deep abasement before God. Remember, if you are saved, it is by an exercise of Divine mercy, by an act of grace, which is the subject of admiration among the angels of God; and nothing is more incongruous than for "such an one" to be proud of any qualities he has received. Let it be evident that you are a good man, and one that makes progress in the things of God. This will produce a great effect. There is a silent eloquence in character, by which the best sermons are most powerfully recommended. Let them, however, be delivered with all sincerity, gravity, and affection: never speak with lightness or indifference; beware of all levity of spirit and of manner; avoid all canting and hypocritical terms and phrases; consider the weight of the subject before you; never study theatrical effect; all gestures and manœuvres, and display of *self*, by which some divines obtain so great admiration, are unworthy of your subject and your office. A sound preacher of the gospel will produce, not admiration of *himself*, but of the *truth*, and adoration of that God and Saviour from whom all truths proceed; remembering that awful account which ministers and people will all have to give, when they meet before his judgment-seat.

Sincerely aim to do good, and the Lord will be with you. Mr. Baxter said he never knew a minister who was sincerely desirous of benefiting souls that was not blessed with considerable success. The more you can go out of self, and lose all recollection of your own importance,—the more you are impressed with the love of souls, the more will you be likely to manifest that truth which recommends itself "to every man's conscience in the sight of God."

Let the consciences of your hearers be the subjects of your concern. Address their understanding and affections for the purpose of getting at their consciences.

I am aware of the difficulty of your situation, in consequence of your succeeding our most invaluable and incomparable brother, Mr. Fuller. It is not possible that you should, at present, attain to that profundity of mind, those extensive views, and that pointed statement of truth which were possessed and evinced by him; but even this difficulty may be of use to you, as a stimulus to excite you to greater exertions. Should you be tempted to indolence (which I have no reason to suspect you will indulge), the recollection of serving a people who have been blessed with such a minister, the consideration of what they will expect, may serve to rouse and animate you in your work.

Another circumstance I may refer to, as a motive peculiar to your present situation; and that is, the respectable minority which have been opposed to you. This may also be overruled to your advantage, if you are more watchful over your temper and conduct (I do not say than you have been, but) than you might have been if you had been carried down the stream of universal applause; and if it excite you to conciliation and kindness towards those who oppose themselves, it may have the happiest effect on their minds, and will certainly raise and establish your character as a minister of the meek and lowly Saviour.

I need not warn you, because you have always guarded, against any thing personal in your ministry towards those who have not fixed their choice on you. You will be ready to treat them with the same kindness which you manifest to others. It is not to be wondered at (considering whom you follow, and some particular circumstances which are well known, but need not be mentioned) that there should be a part of the church who could not act with the rest in their choice; but it will be well if you can manage these circumstances for your advantage and the furtherance of the gospel.

I shall not detain you longer than to remind you whence it is that you are to derive the strength and wisdom necessary to prepare you for your work; and I cannot do this better than in the language of Paul to Timothy, "Be strong in the grace that is in Christ Jesus!" Be strong! How strangely does this exhortation sound! To tell a man that is weak to be strong would be absurd; but what would be absurd in philosophy is true and consistent with the gospel. Be strong in the grace of Christ, for his grace is communicable; and the power of Christ rests on those who seek it with a sense of their own weakness.

We are directed to seek it by prayer, and thus to be strong. Look to the Lord for all the assistance you need. Remember how dependent you are. Look to the Father and the Son: be not afraid of praying to the Son of God as Paul did; and it is often more consolatory than prayer in any other form.

You are a sinner redeemed; but you are a preacher of the word placed over this people, not to tyrannize, but to walk before them in the Lord: in hearing your voice, they should hear him; in following your footsteps, they should follow him. Your employment is that of the Son of God: it makes no appearance before the eyes of worldly men; but it will arise in a form of majesty to overshadow all created glory. Its effects will be known and felt in souls that shall enjoy Christ in his kingdom for ever, or in spirits in whom the work of death shall be finished.

Keep the commandments of Christ committed to you, without reproach. Endeavour to "present every man faultless before God." Your happiness will be diminished if one be wanting. Be concerned to "give up your account with joy, and not with grief."

Labour, that not one of those that hear you, not one that has sat down at the table, not one to whom you have "given the right hand of fellowship," should be excluded when the Lord cometh.

See to it, that you are not excluded yourself. So preach as to "save yourself, and them that hear you." It is possible for a man to bring others to Christ for salvation, and yet not be saved himself. You may preach to others, and yet be a castaway. You need grace, but do not despair. The grace of the Saviour is sufficient for you: "His strength shall be made perfect in your weakness."*

* Mr. John Keen Hall, to whom this charge was addressed, was Mr. Hall's nephew; a circumstance which, while it may serve to account for the minuteness of some of the exhortations, in my judgment, adds to their interest. Mr. J. K. Hall, who had been Mr. Fuller's colleague, survived him only fifteen years: he died in 1829.

Mr. Hillyard, to whose kindness I am indebted for the notes here published, is anxious it should be understood that his main object was to preserve *the substance* of the charge. It was seldom, indeed, that he succeeded in catching the precise language; and, towards the end, several sublime and most impressive sentences were entirely lost, from his yielding himself to the stream of feeling excited by the preacher.—Ed.

ON THE ART OF HEALING.

[*From Mr. Hall's own Notes. Not published before.*]

MATT. ix. 12.—*But when Jesus heard that, he said unto them, The whole need not a Physician, but they that are sick.*

THAT the sick need a physician* is an assertion which appeals to the dictates of common sense. Among the innumerable benefactions issuing from a wise and gracious Providence, the art of healing is not to be considered as the least. For though it is far from having reached the perfection which we naturally desire, or which may be attainable, its efficiency is such as ought to inspire the most unfeigned gratitude to the Author of every good and perfect gift. By the cure of many, and the mitigation of most of the diseases to which the human frame is incident, the total amount of ease, comfort, and refreshment which it confers is incalculable. In judicious hands it is the handmaid of nature, while it obeys her indications and assists her efforts. It never acts apart, but always in a vigilant and judicious subserviency to her fundamental laws and her salutary tendencies. It is well known that there is in all living substances a certain *vis medicatrix*, a certain effort at self-provision, an inherent and powerful tendency to recover itself from the injury it may have sustained, a principle of active resistance to the progress of disease and decay. A property of this kind seems to be inseparable from life in all its diversified modes and appearances; and nothing, surely, can afford a plainer demonstration of the benign character of the Deity.

When a bone is fractured, nothing more is necessary than to place the parts which accident has separated in their original juxtaposition, and they will very soon adhere: an exudation from the bones takes place, which forms a collar of so firm a texture that the parts often become more perfectly united than before: it is scarcely ever known that a bone is fractured twice in the same place. When the fleshy parts are separated by a wound, and a considerable chasm ensues, the self-restorative power of nature forms new flesh, produces a new set of vessels for the circulation of the blood; the interstice is filled up, and the continuity of the parts is by degrees perfectly restored. The indication of design in such a process is just as evident as in restoring communication between two places by repairing the broken arches of a bridge.

* This constituted part of a sermon that was preached for the Leicester Infirmary, from the above text, on Sunday, May 29, 1825.—ED

In constant subserviency to this mysterious law, the skilful physician explores the secret affinities subsisting between the living substance which composes the body and the material elements which surround it. By a sublime process of experiment and induction, he has ascertained, to a great extent, the relation which the corporeal frame sustains to the various objects, both natural and artificial, with which the stores of nature are fraught. He has extorted her secrets, and has summoned her powers in aid of human distress and infirmity. He has fetched from the bowels of the [earth,] from the caverns of the ocean, and from the boundless fields of air, the most powerful antidotes to disease. He has levied a contribution from all the departments and provinces of nature, and compelled them to yield their service to man, in all the varieties of physical disorder to which he is exposed; and, whether it be requisite to brace or to relax the [fibres] of the breathing frame, to retard or to accelerate its motion, to stimulate or to depress, to quicken its energies or to allay its agitations, he makes them minister to his purpose, and become the agents of his will. He has discovered the art of converting into useful ingredients substances deemed essentially noxious, and of extracting antidotes from poisons. Thus he vindicates from rash and presumptuous imputations the beneficence of nature or of its great Author, by showing that all which "he has made is very good."

A large portion of the ingenuity and industry of mankind is incessantly exerted in multiplying the pleasures of the opulent, giving a higher zest to the fruitions of luxury, and gratifying the caprices of vanity and pride; and such is the mechanism of society, that even from these the poor are fed and the indigent relieved. With the physician, however, it is far otherwise. He interposes in the moment of exigence, and obeys the call of distress. He administers the cordial to the fainting spirit, rekindles the expiring lamp of hope, and [often] decks the countenance with smiles, which death, under the ravages of disease, had marked for his victim and covered with his shade. He leaves it to others to accompany the human race in their revelry and their triumphs: while they bask on the bosom of the ocean, or spread their sails to the wind, he presents himself on the shore, and rescues the shipwrecked mariner from the waves. With a silent and invisible energy he contends with the powers of destruction, and often rescues from the grave him that [seemed] "appointed to death."

If he conducts the objects of his care sometimes through painful processes, his proceeding resembles in that respect the conduct of the gracious Author of our being, who afflicts with paternal reluctance, and smites but to heal. From the practice of an enlightened professor of the healing art nothing is more remote than the infliction of unnecessary suffering, or wanton and unfeeling experiments on the powers of human endurance. His hand never administers an uneasy sensation, but with a view to the future comfort of his patient; nor is he the author of a single privation or restraint but what is designed for his good

Considered in their leading features, its ministrations are a beautiful imitation of those of Divine Providence. Both are designed to restore what is lost, and to repair what is disordered: both have the production of ease and happiness for their ultimate object; both frequently make use of pains and privations as the means of procuring it, but neither of them [employ] an atom more of these than is deemed requisite for that purpose.

Hence it will probably be found that the medical profession has furnished more examples of active and enlightened humanity than any other walk or profession. Being daily and hourly conversant with scenes of misery, the contrary, it would seem at first, might have been expected. It might have been thought that habit would render [medical men] callous and indifferent to those varieties of suffering that so frequently offer themselves to their view. That the effect of such familiarity is to impair the force of pity, considered merely as an emotion, may be very probable. It is well it is so: for if their nerves were unstrung, and their hand to tremble at the witnessing of pain and agony, like those who were unused to such spectacles, they would be totally disabled from executing their functions. But humanity, considered as an active propensity to alleviate human distress, is improved and maintained in wholesome exercise by the benevolence of the end, notwithstanding the occasional severity of the means. The mind of a physician is continually pregnant with expedients for the mitigation of pain, the extinction of disease, and the prolongation of life; a course of thinking which cannot fail to cultivate and mature the seeds of benevolence. His success is in exact proportion to the benefits he imparts: his triumphs are signalized by the tears of gratitude, the gratulations of friendship, and the raptures of returning health.

How striking is the contrast between the art of medicine and the art of war! The last has for its object the destruction, the first the preservation of the species. The mind of the warrior teems with machinations of ruin, and anxiously revolves, among different schemes that present themselves, which shall scatter destruction to the widest extent and with the surest aim: his progress is marked by devastation and blood, by depopulated fields and smoking villages, and the laurels which he wears are bedewed with the tears of widows and orphans. The acclamations which he wins from one portion of his species are answered by the curses and execrations of another; and the delusive splendour, the proud and imposing array with which he contrives to gild the horrors of his profession are but the pomp and retinue of the king of terrors.* The art of healing proceeds with a silence and secrecy, like the great processes of nature, to scatter blessings on all within its reach; and the couch of sickness, the silent retreat of sorrow and despair, are the scene of its triumphs.

The little applause which is bestowed on physicians, compared with what is so lavishly heaped on conquerors, conveys a bitter reflection on human nature; by showing how much we suffer ourselves to be the dupes of our senses, to extol the brilliant rather than the useful: whereas, a just and impartial estimate would compel us to assign to

* The author seems here to have borrowed a little, perhaps unconsciously, from himself. See Vol. I. p. 64, &c.—Ed.

skilful practitioners of medicine the very first rank among merely human professions. For when we consider the variety of ills to which we are exposed, and how large a portion is derived from bodily infirmities, it will appear that we are more indebted to their assistance than to [that of] any other class of persons whatever.

Nor are the reflections in which we have indulged, and the train of thought we have pursued, foreign to the immediate purpose of the present discourse, which is, to invite your assistance in repairing the funds of the Leicester Infirmary,—an institution which you are aware has been productive of incalculable good. Open to the sick of all denominations, it assembles within its walls the victims of poverty and disease of every description, and provides for them the most suitable diet, skilful advice, and assiduous attentions; of each of which the greater part of its patients must necessarily have remained destitute, but for this excellent charity. If we are convinced of the utility and dignity of the medical and chirurgical arts,—if we are satisfied how much they contribute to the comfort and the preservation of life, we are prepared to appreciate the value of that charity which proposes for its object the extension of these advantages to the poor; nor is it possible to extend them so far by any other provision as by the support of a public asylum.

To administer equal medical assistance and attendance to an equal number at their own abodes, would be accompanied by an augmentation of expense which would render it insupportable. By collecting the victims of disease in our asylum, and placing them under one system of administration, not only is economy consulted by an immense saving of expense, but the improvement of science is promoted by presenting a wide field of observation on the great varieties of malady which fall under the notice of the practitioners.

By this system, also, a course of wholesome religious instruction is secured, under circumstances the most favourable to its reception.

* * * * * * * * * *

The chymical lectures, delivered by the ablest professors in our public hospitals, furnish the most important branch of medical instruction, and are adapted to benefit generations yet unborn.

* * * * * * * * * *

The erection of hospitals and infirmaries for the poor is one of the distinguishing ornaments and fruits of Christianity, unknown to the wisdom and humanity of pagan times. Compassionate consideration of the poor formed no part of the lessons of pagan philosophy; its genius was too arrogant and lofty to stoop to the children of want and obscurity. It soared in sublime speculation, wasted its strength in endless subtleties and debates; but, among the rewards to which it aspired, it never thought of "the blessedness of him that considereth the poor." You might have traversed the Roman empire, in the zenith of its power, from the Euphrates to the Atlantic, without meeting with a single charitable asylum for the sick. Monuments of pride, of ambition, of vindictive wrath, were to be found in abundance; but not one legible record of commiseration for the poor. It was reserved for the religion whose basis is humility, and whose element is devotion, to proclaim with authority, "Blessed are the merciful, for they shall obtain mercy."

There are few of us, I trust, who are prepared to regard the privations of poverty alone with indifference; much less when, combined with sickness, its victim is reduced to the last stage of helplessness. When the hands which ministered, not only to their own necessities, but to those of a numerous family, are debilitated with disease, and unnerved with sickness, the most complicated distress must necessarily ensue. Were it not for the ministration of piety, the calamity would be insupportable. In many situations, the earnings of labour are but barely sufficient for the sustenance of life on its lowest terms; no savings can be made; no superfluity be retrenched; and what must be the state of such a family when that labour is suspended by the invasion of disease? But for such asylums as these, the consequences would be too dreadful for human contemplation.

(Sickness is incident to all, and therefore a proper object of commiseration.)

* * * * * * * * * *

END OF VOL. II.

www.ingramcontent.com/pod-product-compliance
Lightning Source LLC
LaVergne TN
LVHW020922110826
845150LV00004B/738

* 9 7 8 1 4 2 5 5 5 5 0 8 5 *